PRICE

₱116-50

Peggy

1-800-338-3987

? PAPERBACK

Forensic Accounting and Fraud Examination

Second Edition

William S. Hopwood
Florida Atlantic University

Jay J. Leiner
Florida Atlantic University

George R. Young
Florida Atlantic University

McGraw-Hill Irwin

FORENSIC ACCOUNTING AND FRAUD EXAMINATION, SECOND EDITION

Published by McGraw-Hill, a business unit of The McGraw-Hill Companies, Inc., 1221 Avenue of the Americas, New York, NY 10020. Copyright © 2012 by The McGraw-Hill Companies, Inc. All rights reserved. Previous edition © 2008. No part of this publication may be reproduced or distributed in any form or by any means, or stored in a database or retrieval system, without the prior written consent of The McGraw-Hill Companies, Inc., including, but not limited to, in any network or other electronic storage or transmission, or broadcast for distance learning.

Some ancillaries, including electronic and print components, may not be available to customers outside the United States.

This book is printed on acid-free paper.

1 2 3 4 5 6 7 8 9 0 QDB /QDB 1 0 9 8 7 6 5 4 3 2 1

ISBN 978-0-07-813666-5
MHID 0-07-813666-0

Vice President & Editor-in-Chief: *Kimberly Meriwether David*
Editorial Director: *Stewart Mattson*
Publisher: *Tim Vertovec*
Executive Editor: *Richard T. Hercher, Jr.*
Editorial Coordinator: *Danielle Dalo*
Assistant Marketing Manager: *Dean Karampelas*
Project Manager: *Melissa M. Leick*
Design Coordinator: *Brenda A. Rolwes*
Cover Designer: *Studio Montage, St. Louis, Missouri*
Cover Images: *Magnifying Glass Over US Dollar Bills:* © *Comstock Images/Alamy; Man Sitting In Office: Photo used with permission from Microsoft; Financial Report:* © *Brand X Pictures*
Buyer: *Laura Fuller*
Media Project Manager: *Balaji Sundararaman*
Compositor: *Laserwords Private Limited.*
Typeface: *10/12 Times New Roman*
Printer: *Quad/Graphics*

All credits appearing on page or at the end of the book are considered to be an extension of the copyright page.

Library of Congress Cataloging-in-Publication Data

Hopwood, William S.
     Forensic accounting and fraud examination / William S. Hopwood, Jay J. Leiner, George R. Young.—2nd ed.
        p. cm.
     ISBN 978-0-07-813666-5 (alk. paper)
     1. Forensic accounting—United States. 2. Forensic accounting and fraud examination. I. Leiner, Jay J.
II. Young, George R. III. Title.
     KF8968.15.H67 2012
     363.25'6--dc22
                                                                                                 2011001151

To all the faculty and staff in the Forensic Accounting Masters Program at Florida Atlantic University.

William Hopwood

I dedicate this book to my family and friends; to my wife, Diane; my sons, Victor and Peter; and Mom and Ezio for always believing in me; to my real friends and partners, the old interdiction team (you know who you are), thanks for being there for me and pushing me that little extra step; to my coauthors, Bill and George, for supporting me and asking me to join them as a coauthor; and last, but not least, to the Broward County Sheriff's Office for giving me the opportunity to investigate cases and to Florida Atlantic University for the opportunity to educate others.

Jay Leiner

I dedicate this book to my father, George, and my mother, Wilma; my wife, Sherry, and my sons, Joshua and Angelo.

George Young

About the Authors

William S. Hopwood, PhD   *Florida Atlantic University*

William S. Hopwood is Professor of Accounting at Florida Atlantic University. He earned his master's and doctoral degrees in accounting at the University of Florida. He served as Associate Professor at the University of Illinois at Urbana-Champaign, Professor at The Florida State University, and Arthur Andersen Professor at the University of Houston. He has published many articles in *The Accounting Review, Journal of Accounting Research,* and other major accounting journals. He is also coauthor of the widely used Prentice-Hall text, *Accounting Information Systems.* He currently serves as the faculty liaison and technology coordinator for the Master of Accounting in Forensic Accounting Program at Florida Atlantic University.

Jay J. Leiner, BA, BS, MA, CFE, CFS, CHS

Florida Atlantic University

Jay J. Leiner is Adjunct Professor in the Forensic Accounting Master's Program at Florida Atlantic University. He is also in charge of the Economic Crime Unit in the Broward County Sheriff's Office and Team Leader of the Broward County Sheriff's Office Hostage Barricade Team. He has been in law enforcement for more than 25 years and has experience in testifying in both federal and state courts in many areas including money laundering, white-collar crime, and narcotics interdiction. He holds bachelor degrees in criminal justice and accounting and a master's degree in management. He is a Certified Fraud Examiner and Certified Fraud Specialist and is certified in Homeland Security. He has specialized training in electronic surveillance, financial and computer fraud, and organized crime. He is presently seeking his doctorate in business with a minor in Homeland Security.

George R. Young, PhD, CPA   *Florida Atlantic University*

George R. Young is Associate Professor at Florida Atlantic University and a Certified Public Accountant in the State of Illinois, where he practiced public accounting for nine years before entering academia. He earned a master's degree in accounting (concentration in taxation) from Southern Illinois University at Carbondale and a doctorate in accounting from the University of Texas at Arlington. Currently, he is the academic director of the Master of Accounting in Forensic Accounting Program at Florida Atlantic University and teaches tax fraud and advanced auditing in that program. He served as a member of the Technical Working Group for Education in Fraud and Forensic Accounting, an effort sponsored by a Department of Justice grant and coordinated by West Virginia University. This group was charged with recommending a model educational curriculum in fraud and forensic accounting to assist academic institutions, public and private employers, and interested students in determining the relevant knowledge, skills, and abilities needed to function as a forensic accountant. At the present time, he is a member of the Higher Education Advisory Committee of the Association of Certified Fraud Examiners. He has published articles in academic journals such as *Auditing: A Journal of Practice & Theory, Advances in Accounting Behavioral Research,* and *Research on Accounting Ethics* and in practice journals such as the *Journal of Accountancy, The CPA Journal,* and *Internal Auditor.*

Preface

WHAT'S NEW IN THE SECOND EDITION

Because of a general increase in the demand for fraud investigation services, the second edition adds five new chapters relating to fraud investigation processes. The result is that, as revised, Part II (Chapters 5–12) covers the entire fraud investigation process over the span of eight chapters. Parts III and IV (Chapters 13–18) follow up with various types of fraud applications that range from employee and vendor fraud to anti-money laundering and counterterrorism.

A major distinction of the second edition is that it follows a process-oriented approach. This means that fraud investigation is presented as an organized sequence of steps that start at some point and end at some other point. Flow diagrams are presented throughout Part II (Chapters 5–12) to graphically illustrate the sequence of steps followed in fraud investigations.

The process-oriented approach differs significantly from taxonomy-based approaches commonly followed in the literature. Taxonomy-based approaches tend to focus on classifying fraud investigation methods. Although useful, taxonomy approaches in and of themselves do not provide the most basic guidance needed by a fraud investigator, namely what to do first, second, and so on, and when to end a given phase of an investigation.

TEXT ORGANIZATION

The text seeks to provide comprehensive coverage of fraud examination and forensic accounting through a wide range of topics relevant to all types of students, regardless of their major, concentration, or level of studies. The chapters are organized into five major parts. Part I deals with topics primarily relevant to the fraud examination and forensic accounting environment. Part II introduces the theory, processes, and methods of fraud examination. Part III focuses on occupational and organizational fraud. Part IV deals with various specialized nonoccupational areas of fraud. Part V highlights forensic accounting services whose applications are typically outside the area of fraud examination.

PART I INTRODUCTION TO FORENSIC ACCOUNTING AND FRAUD EXAMINATION

This part covers various foundational areas of importance to fraud examination and forensic accounting. Chapter 1 provides a general overview. Chapter 2 focuses on the legal procedures that are frequently relevant to forensic accounting work. Both criminal and civil procedures are covered, with a special emphasis on criminal procedures because they are often ignored in the typical business law courses.

Chapters 3 and 4 provide comprehensive, self-contained units in accounting information systems and auditing. Inclusion of these chapters makes the text accessible to nonaccounting majors and even to nonbusiness majors.

PART II FRAUD EXAMINATION THEORY, PRACTICE, AND METHODS

This part discusses basic and advanced fraud examination and investigation processes. The flow of chapters in this section corresponds to the entire fraud investigation process: fraud prevention (Chapter 5), fraud detection (Chapter 6), fraud investigations and the engagement process (Chapter 7), the fraud evidence collection process (Chapter 8), physical, documentary, and observational evidence (Chapter 9), interview methods (Chapter 10), forensic science and computer forensics (Chapter 11), and fraud reports, litigation, and the recovery process (Chapter 12).

PART III OCCUPATIONAL AND ORGANIZATIONAL FRAUD

This part features specific areas of occupational and organizational fraud. Chapter 13 deals with employee and vendor fraud. Chapter 14 focuses on financial statement fraud. Chapter 15 highlights fraud and the Sarbanes-Oxley Act.

PART IV SPECIALIZED FRAUD AREAS

This part focuses on specialized areas in which frauds typically originate from specific types of individuals outside of the organization. Chapter 16 deals with tax fraud; Chapter 17 with frauds relating to bankruptcy, divorce, and identity theft; and Chapter 18 with organized crime, money anti-money laundering, and counterterrorism.

PART V OTHER FORENSIC ACCOUNTING SERVICES

This part discusses forensic accounting services not directly related to fraud. Chapter 19 deals with business valuation, and Chapter 20 focuses on dispute resolution and litigation services.

TEACHING APPROACHES AND THE SELECTION OF CHAPTERS

Chapters are written in a modular, self-contained fashion so that instructors can select chapters from each of the five major parts according to specific course requirements. Some basic teaching approaches are as follows:

Comprehensive Focus

Following this approach, an instructor can cover all, or almost all, chapters over a single school term. The auditing and accounting systems chapters could be skipped if students have completed prerequisite courses in these areas.

Fraud and Auditing Focus

Following this approach, the instructor would cover the following chapters in Part I: Chapters 1 (introduction) and 2 (legal) and Part II, Chapters 5–12 (fraud investigation processes). These chapters can then be followed by selected fraud-related applications from Part IV, Chapters 13–18 (fraud applications).

Forensic Accounting Focus

Following this approach, the instructor would cover Chapters 1–2 (introduction and legal), Chapters 5–12 (fraud investigation processes), and Chapters 19–20 (forensic accounting services).

Eclectic Focus

Because the chapters are self-contained and modular, the instructor can select any desired set of chapters to meet particular course needs. Furthermore, the chapters in Part III can be covered in almost any order.

ACKNOWLEDGMENTS

The authors would like to thank the following forensic accounting educators for their input during the development of the first and second editions of *Forensic Accounting and Fraud Examination*. The feedback from these knowledgeable instructors provided the authors valuable assistance in meeting the needs of the forensic accounting classroom.

Second Edition

Phyllis Belak, *West Chester University of Pennsylvania*
Michael J. Danaher, Jr., *Binghamton University*
Maurice Goldings, *Nova Southeastern University*
Robert Hurt, *California State Polytechnic University—Pomona*
Paula L. Irwin, *Muhlenberg College*
Chih-Chen Lee, *Northern Illinois University*
Ransom McClung, *Florida State University*
Madhuri Sarin, *West Virginia University Institute of Technology*
Michael Shapeero, *Bloomsburg University of Pennsylvania*
Robert Terrell, *University of Central Oklahoma*
Karen Forrest Turner, *University of Northern Colorado*

First Edition

David E. Booth, *Community College of Baltimore County—Essex Campus*
Nat R. Briscoe, *Northwestern State University of Louisiana*
James A. DiGabriele, *Montclair State University*
Randall E. LaSalle, *West Chester University of Pennsylvania*
Bonita Peterson-Kramer, *Montana State University—Bozeman*
Barbara Reider, *University of Montana*

Brief Table of Contents

Contents

PART TWO
FRAUD EXAMINATION THEORY, PRACTICE, AND METHODS 129

Chapter 5
Fraud Prevention and Risk Management 131

Chapter 6
Fraud Detection 167

Chapter 7
The Fraud Investigation and Engagement Processes 195

Chapter 8
The Evidence Collection Process 223

Chapter 9
Fraud Examination Evidence I: Physical, Documentary, and Observational Evidence 247

Introduction to Forensic Accounting and Fraud Examination

Chapter **One**

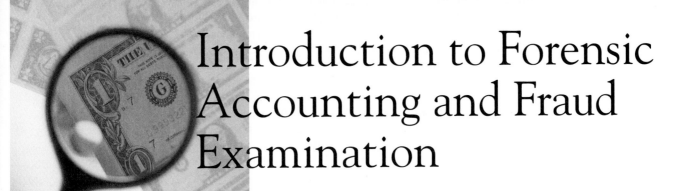

Introduction to Forensic Accounting and Fraud Examination

Adam took another gulp from the stale, bitter cup of coffee. Something about the numbers just didn't make sense. He had been staring at Aberdeen's financials for about 25 minutes and couldn't understand why revenues were just a little bit lower than expected. He added four more packets of sugar to the coffee. Maybe some important sales weren't recorded, he thought. But then he remembered that in the third quarter, he had just double checked the entire revenue system.

"No," he groaned, "There's no error. I'm being robbed again."

He reassured himself with the thought that the auditors would arrive in a couple of days. He hated paying them, but he couldn't live without them.

During the last 10 years that Adam had managed Aberdeen's four stores, the external auditors had never once failed to find some sort of problem. In fact, last year the auditors determined that 300 bicycles were missing from the inventory . . .

CHAPTER LEARNING OBJECTIVES

After reading Chapter 1, you should be able to:

- LO1: Define forensic accounting and fraud examination.
- LO2: Describe the difference between forensic accounting and auditing.
- LO3: Explain the role of forensic accountants and fraud examiners.
- LO4: Identify the knowledge and skills that forensic accountants and fraud examiners are expected to possess.
- LO5: Describe the opportunities that exist for those who choose to work as forensic accountants and fraud examiners.
- LO6: Identify the organizations that support the work of forensic accountants and fraud examiners.

FORENSIC ACCOUNTING AND FRAUD EXAMINATION

LO1 **Forensic accounting** is the application of investigative and analytical skills for the purpose of resolving financial issues in a manner that meets standards required by courts of law. Notice that forensic accounting is not limited to the use of financial investigations that result in legal prosecution; however, if this is the purpose, the investigation and analysis must meet the standards required in the court of law that has jurisdiction.

Notice, too, that the definition of forensic accounting includes no explicit reference to fraud although fraud investigations are a part of forensic accounting. **Fraud** is the result of misleading, intentional actions or inaction (including making misleading statements and omitting relevant information) to gain an advantage. Forensic accounting is broader than **fraud examination** (which focuses on fraud investigations); it also includes services (that could involve investigations) related to the purchases of businesses, valuation of divorce assets, determination of the dollar value of damages to business property, dispute resolution, and calculation of lost profits.

Separately defining the words forensic and accounting could aid your understanding of forensic accounting. The word *forensic* is an adjective that means used in (or pertaining to) courts of law. Accounting is the recording, classifying, and summarizing economic events in a logical manner for the purpose of providing financial information for decision making. When, however, these two words are combined to produce forensic accounting, the result is far greater than simply the sum of the two parts: It refers to the use of accounting and information from other sources to objectively determine facts in a manner that can support reasonable positions taken in court.

LO2 How does forensic accounting differ from traditional accounting? Traditional accounting involves using financial language to communicate results of transactions and make decisions based on that communication. Accounting can be divided into several different areas, including financial accounting, managerial accounting, information systems, tax, consulting, auditing, and forensic accounting. Each of these areas serves a distinct purpose. For example, financial accounting provides information to external users, such as investors, creditors, and government regulators, about the status of a company and the results of its operations. On the other hand, the purpose of managerial accounting is to provide relevant information to users inside the company so that the profitability of operations can be monitored and enhanced.

Of all areas of accounting just mentioned, perhaps auditing most closely resembles forensic accounting, particularly in the area of fraud examination (see Figure 1.1). Auditing can be further divided into two categories: internal and external. Internal auditing is the process by which the company's employees known as **internal auditors** verify the company's operations. Internal auditors may also be involved in collecting and evaluating information to assist in determining whether operations should be changed. Conversely,

FIGURE 1.1
Sherlock Holmes, a Forensic Accountant

external auditors are not employees of the company; they are auditors (licensed by the state in which they practice who have passed the Certified Public Accountant [CPA] examination or, if a chartered accountant [CA], have passed the Chartered Accountant examination and are licensed by the country in which they practice) hired to determine whether the company's financial statements fairly present, in all material respects, financial position, results of operations, and cash flows in accordance with specified criteria (usually generally accepted accounting principles).

The leading organization of CPAs—the American Institute of Certified Public Accountants (AICPA)—classifies forensic accounting into two categories:

1. **Investigative services** that may or may not lead to courtroom testimony.
2. **Litigation services** that recognize the role of the accountant as an expert, consultant, or other role.

The first of these services encompasses those of the fraud examiner or fraud auditor. These are services in which those knowledgeable in accounting detect, prevent, and control fraud, **defalcation,** and **misrepresentation.** The second service represents testimony of a fraud examiner as well as forensic accounting services offered to resolve valuation issues, such as those experienced in divorce cases.

THE FORENSIC ACCOUNTANT AND FRAUD EXAMINERS

LO3 **Forensic accountants** apply special skills in accounting, auditing, finance, quantitative methods, certain areas of the law, research, and investigative skills to collect, analyze, and evaluate evidential matter and to interpret and communicate findings. Finance and quantitative skills are especially important to forensic accountants who calculate damages.

As fraud examiners, forensic accountants are a mix of accountant and private investigator. In other words, the fraud examiner is a type of private investigator with a strong financial sixth sense who possesses knowledge of professional standards in accounting and law. While auditing knowledge and skills are extremely helpful to the forensic accountant, she also possesses the ability to think "out of the box." The importance of this ability cannot be

Diagnosis for HealthSouth

Ernst & Young, the financial statement auditors of HealthSouth, failed to uncover a 16-year manipulation of its net income. The SEC claimed that the large health provider had fabricated at least $1.4 billion of profits in the preceding four years. One indication was that net income had increased by nearly 500 percent while revenues grew 5 percent. How could such a well-respected CPA firm miss such financial shenanigans? Even if the external auditors had noticed the anomaly, many auditors might have accepted explanations that Health-South could have given such as "we reduced costs." That, coupled with the many other demands on the time of the auditors, could cause these types of anomalies to go unchallenged.

overemphasized; often, auditor examination of financial statements does not uncover frauds. Even when the effects of fraud are contained in the financial statements (e.g., in the form of overstated account balances), financial statement auditors are usually not the persons who detect this fraud because their work involves the examination of only a part of the accounts through the accepted practice of sampling.

So what is the difference between financial statement auditors and forensic accountants/fraud examiners who investigate fraud? Financial statement auditors (i.e., external auditors) determine whether the financial statements present fairly, in all material respects, financial position, results of operations, and cash flows of the entity being audited. They are searching for material misstatements or omissions that would affect the decisions of a reasonable user of the financial statements, whether the misstatements are the result of **errors** or fraud. However, because their focus is not specifically on fraud, which is more difficult to detect than errors (i.e., unintentional misstatements) and because they test the detail behind the financial statements by sampling, they are not likely to uncover fraud. Forensic accountants who are performing a search for fraud concentrate their efforts in areas most likely to contain the fraud and often examine the entire population rather than sample the population in targeted areas. These accountants are likely to follow leads suggested by immaterial items whereas financial statement auditors often must restrict their efforts to searching for material misstatements. In addition to these differences, the forensic accountant uses some investigative techniques that differ from those used by auditors. Also, forensic accountants who conduct fraud examinations do not give an opinion on whether fraud was committed; this is the function of the court.

Forensic accountants who practice primarily in the valuation area need knowledge and skills that enable them to determine, for example, lost profits due to business interruption and the valuation of assets for divorce cases.

Knowledge and Skills of the Forensic Accountant and Fraud Examiner

LO4 The forensic accountant or fraud examiner must have skills in many areas. Some forensic accountants, of course, specialize in certain areas such as information technology. However, all well-trained forensic accountants have at least a minimum level of knowledge and skills in the following areas.

- Auditing skills are of paramount importance to the forensic accountant because of the information-collecting and verification nature of forensic accounting. Well-trained forensic accountants must be able to collect and analyze relevant information so that the cases on which they are working will be well supported in court.

Forensic Accounting and NASCAR

Jeff Gordon, the first NASCAR race driver to own a part of a racing team, entered into divorce proceedings. W. David Ellrich, CPA, CFE, ABV, of Moore, Ellrich, and Neal, a CPA firm located in Palm Beach Gardens, Florida, was engaged to value the portion of the racing team owned by Jeff Gordon. This valuation was necessary because his wife was entitled to a share of marital assets, which were judged to include part of Gordon's interest in the racing team.

- Investigative knowledge and skills, such as surveillance tactics and interviewing and interrogation skills, assist the forensic accountant beyond the skills related to auditing and blend the financial and legal aspects of forensics.
- Criminology, particularly the study of the psychology of criminals, is important to the forensic accountant because effective investigative skills often rely on knowledge of the motives and incentives experienced by the perpetrator.
- Accounting knowledge helps the forensic accountant analyze and interpret the financial information necessary to build a case in a financial investigation, whether it is a bankruptcy setting, a money-laundering operation, or an embezzlement scheme. This includes knowledge of proper internal controls such as those related to corporate governance.
- Legal knowledge is critical to the success of the forensic accountant. Knowledge of laws and court procedures enables the forensic accountant to identify the type of evidence necessary to meet the legal standards of the jurisdiction in which the case is to be adjudicated and preserve evidence in a manner that meets the criteria of the court.
- Information technology (IT) knowledge and skills are necessary tools of the forensic accountant in a world filled with paperless crimes. At a minimum, forensic accountants must know the point at which they should contact an expert in computer hardware or software. Forensic accountants use technology skills to quarantine data, extract data through data mining, design and implement controls over data manipulation, accumulate baseline information for comparison purposes, and analyze data.
- Communication skills are required of forensic accountants so that the results of their investigation/analysis can be correctly and clearly conveyed to users of their services.

Throughout this text, you will be adding to your knowledge of these important skills—skills that can lead to opportunities in forensic accounting.

OPPORTUNITIES IN FORENSIC ACCOUNTING AND FRAUD EXAMINATION

LO5 In the past, forensic accountants who conducted fraud examinations were often called after owners suspected that fraud had been committed. Now recent major corporate scandals have prompted business owners to turn to fraud examiners for proactive fraud checkups. At times, attorneys may hire these forensic accountants to investigate the financial trail of persons suspected of engaging in criminal activity. Information provided by the forensic accountant may be the most effective way to put these persons behind bars. Bankruptcy court may also engage forensic accountants when financial information submitted to it is suspect or if there is reason to believe that employees (including managers) have taken assets.

After a 25-year career as a CPA and a CFE, Chris Poulos joined the FBI as a financial analyst who specializes in tracking down terrorists. Mr. Poulos earned undergraduate and master's degrees in accounting. His experience included working for national and regional accounting firms and 10 years of civil and criminal forensic accounting work.

Today his position as a financial analyst in the Terrorist Financing Operations Section in Washington, D.C., involves analyzing evidence to determine the sources and uses of suspected terrorists. His work for the FBI enables him to be an integral part of stopping the flow of funds to terrorist organizations.

Opportunities for qualified forensic accountants also abound in private companies, particularly after the passage of the Sarbanes-Oxley Act of 2002 (SOX). According to this act, CEOs must now certify that their financial statements are faithful representations of the financial position and results of operations of their companies and rely more heavily on internal controls to detect any misstatement that would otherwise be contained in these financials. Thus, publicly held companies are likely to see the necessity for forensic accountants as a part of a strong internal control effort to comply with governmental and market demands for accurate reporting. Beyond SOX, forensic accountants who work for private companies help prevent and detect misuse of company resources—the cost of which can be considerable. According to the Association of Certified Fraud Examiners' Report to the Nation on Occupational Fraud and Abuse, approximately 5 percent of revenues are lost each year as a result of occupational fraud and abuse; this represents $652 billion lost due to occupational fraud.

Many governmental agencies are involved in forensic activities, creating opportunities for those trained in forensic investigation. For example, the Federal Trade Commission (FTC) recently began a project to curb e-auction abuse. The widespread investigation has so far resulted in 57 cases in which civil or criminal charges have been filed, most of which involved sellers who either received payment for products they did not deliver or delivered an inferior product. The Internal Revenue Service (IRS) employs persons who use forensic skills to uncover unreported income and overstated expenses. Not surprisingly, the Governmental Accountability Office and the Federal Bureau of Investigation (FBI) employ their share of financial sleuths. Even the Bureau of Alcohol, Tobacco, and Firearms hires forensic accountants. These agencies use forensic accountants to investigate money-laundering schemes, tax evasion, identity theft, and arson.

Forensic accountants who work for the government may find themselves involved in cracking identity theft rings, tracing the financial footprints of al Qaeda at the FBI, or investigating a tax evader's drug-smuggling activities for the IRS. To say the least, it is an interesting way to spend a day!

Forensic accountants also work in the banking and insurance industries to prevent and detect fraud committed against depositors and insurance carriers.

Those who possess both IT and accounting knowledge and skills—a combination that has become one of the fastest growing areas of forensic accounting—have great career opportunities. Computer forensics, as it is now known, is an area in which competent, well-trained professionals are in high demand. Recovery of data from computers in a manner that meets the requirements of courts and the protection of confidential corporate information are two examples of the application of skills in this area.

As mentioned, forensic accountants are also involved in the determination of lost profits when businesses experience interruption including claims analysis for business insurance. In these cases, the forensic accountant may appear in court as an expert witness. Even if a case does not go to court, forensic accountants may be called on to assist in **mediation** and **arbitration.**

One of the first modern forensic accountants is Michael G. Kessler, who began his career in the early 1970s when the profession of forensic accountant was unknown. His first job out of college was that of field auditor for Associated Hospital Services of New York (later Blue Cross/Blue Shield). His job was to search for fraud and abuse committed by health care institutions and its employees against Medicare and Blue Cross/Blue Shield. He visited hospitals and health care facilities to review and compare the original documentation to the cost report submitted to insurance carriers and determine whether it properly reflected the actual revenue and expenses of the facility. After uncovering significant fraud, Associated designated him as a specialist in investigative audits.

Mr. Kessler has used his forensic experience to benefit the citizens of New York. Among the many positions he has held is director of the New York State Revenue Crimes Bureau. Today, he is the president and CEO of Kessler International, a forensic accounting and investigative consulting firm providing forensic accounting, computer forensics, risk management, and corporate investigation.

PROFESSIONAL ORGANIZATIONS

LO6 Several organizations support and promote the practice of forensic accounting and fraud examination. These include the Association of Certified Fraud Examiners, the American College of Forensic Examiners, the Association of Certified Fraud Specialists, the National Association of Certified Valuation Analysts, the National Litigation Support Services Association, the Institute of Business Appraisers, and the American Institute of Certified Public Accountants. Many of these organizations offer credentials to those who meet rigorous standards.

The Association of Certified Fraud Examiners (ACFE) was organized in 1988 to promote the detection and deterrence of fraud and white-collar crime. At last count, its membership totaled more than 31,000 members in 110 countries. It offers the Certified Fraud Examiner (CFE) credential, the most recognized fraud credential, and is one of the largest providers of continuing professional education for fraud professionals. To become a CFE, an individual must meet certain experience and education requirements and pass the CFE examination.

The Association of Certified Fraud Specialists (ACFS) is an organization that recognizes fraud as a specialty by administering the Certified Fraud Specialist (CFS) designation. The mission of the ACFS is to administer the CFS designation, provide specialized training for its members, and encourage its members to offer pro bono service to the communities in which its members reside.

There are three ways to become a CFS: (1) successfully completing a multipart examination that covers the detection, deterrence, investigation, and prosecution of white-collar crime, (2) completing the ACFS Academy core courses and taking an examination at the end of each course, or (3) being grandfathered in by means of submitting information on the experience and education of the candidate.

The National Association of Certified Valuation Analysts (NACVA) was created to advance the field of valuations and other advisory services. It supports its members by providing continuing education and offering three credentials, the certified valuation analyst (for those who are CPAs), the accredited valuation analyst (for those who are experienced in the valuation field), and the certified forensic financial analyst (for litigation consultants).

The National Litigation Support Services Association (NLSSA) is an association of CPA firms whose membership is limited to one firm in each metropolitan statistical area (MSA). It seeks to choose the leading firm in each MSA to create a network of experts.

The Institute of Business Appraisers (IBA) supports the practice of valuing closely held businesses. It provides technical information for its members and continuing professional education as well as the Certified Business Appraiser (CBA) certification. To become a CBA, the candidate must sit for a comprehensive exam on business valuation theory and practice (which may be waived under certain circumstances) and have either five years of full-time experience as a business appraiser or meet certain education standards.

The AICPA supports forensic accounting through its Business Valuation and Forensic and Litigation Services section. The section's mission is to increase awareness of the importance of business valuation and litigation support services, provide resources to its members, and create a community of persons interested in providing business valuation and forensic and litigation services.

The AICPA offers the Accredited in Business Valuation (ABV) credential. To obtain this credential, the candidate must be an AICPA member in good standing, hold a valid and unrevoked CPA certificate or license issued by a state, pass its comprehensive business valuation examination, provide evidence of 10 business valuation engagements or projects that demonstrate substantial experience and competence, and provide evidence of 75 hours of education related to business valuation.

ORGANIZATION OF THIS BOOK

This book is divided into five parts. Part I provides a basic accounting and legal background to forensic accounting. Part II provides topics relating to the theory and practice of fraud examination. Part III addresses occupational and organizational fraud. Part IV deals with specialized areas of fraud investigation. Part V focuses on forensic accounting services whose applications are typically outside the area of fraud examination.

Summary

Forensic accounting differs from other types of accounting, partly due to the work performed and partly due to the standards of law that must be met by these accountants. Whereas many accountants participate in creating or auditing financial statements, forensic accountants are more likely to be found dissecting these statements and obtaining evidence from other sources. Some forensic accountants, fraud examiners, perform investigations much like financial private investigators; others perform extensive valuation work related to financial damages experienced by businesses and the division of assets in divorce actions. Forensic accounting requires the knowledge and skills of accountants and other specialized skills that enable the forensic accountant to practice in this unique area of accounting. To aid forensic accountants, various organizations support the practice of forensic accounting, and many of these organizations offer credentials that distinguish forensic accountants from other practitioners.

Glossary

arbitration   Process of hearing and deciding a case that involves parties that have taken different positions.

defalcation   Appropriation of assets for the benefit of those who do not rightfully deserve them.

error   Unintentional misstatement or omission of information.

external auditor   Accountant who conducts an audit of the financial statements to determine whether they fairly state assets, liabilities, owners' equity, revenues, gains, expenses, losses, and cash flows in accordance with generally accepted accounting principles.

forensic accounting   Accounting specialization in which investigative and analytical skills are applied for the purpose of resolving financial issues in a manner that meets standards required by courts of law.

forensic accountant   Accountant who performs investigative and valuation services, the result of which could be used in a court of law.

fraud   Means by which a person can achieve an advantage over another by false suggestions or suppression of the truth.

fraud examination   Investigation undertaken to determine the facts of a suspected fraud.

internal auditor   Employee who verifies information produced by other employees or processes in the organization; may also work on special projects such as analyzing whether the company for which he works should make or buy a particular product.

investigative service   Function of searching for evidence that supports an objective and communicates the results of the search.

litigation service   Function of a valuation and investigation service (including testifying as an expert witness) performed to assist the court in the determination of an equitable judgment.

mediation   Act of assisting parties with differing perspectives to arrive at a compromise.

misrepresentation   Act of presenting oneself in a manner that does not agree with reality. The presentation could be the result of actions, statements, or omissions.

Review Questions

1. To what does the word *forensic* pertain?
   a. Financial audits when fraud is involved.
   b. A particular type of accounting.
   c. Matters relating to law and courts of law.
   d. Prosecutorial investigations.

2. For an act to be considered fraud, which of the following is required?
   a. Large loss.
   b. Legal entity (e.g., a corporation, partnership, or trust).
   c. Intentional harm.
   d. Intentional action or inaction.

3. Which of the following is outside the area of forensic accounting?
   a. Corporate acquisitions.
   b. Divorce.
   c. Contract disputes.
   d. None of the above.

4. Which area of accounting is most closely associated with forensic accounting?
    a. Information systems.
    b. Managerial accounting.
    c. Consulting.
    d. Auditing.

5. The Sarbanes-Oxley Act requires which of the following?
    a. Auditors to receive specialized training in the act.
    b. The CEO to certify the financial statements.
    c. Management to institute a zero tolerance policy for fraud.
    d. None of the above.

6. How do the objectives differ for forensic accountants (FAs) and external financial auditors (EFAs)?
    a. FAs are more thorough.
    b. EFAs audit a broader range of transactions.
    c. EFAs tend to concentrate their work more.
    d. FAs tend to concentrate their work more.

7. How many categories does the American Institute of Certified Accountants use to classify forensic accounting?
    a. 1.
    b. 2.
    c. 3.
    d. 4.

8. A forensic accountant who determines the amount of lost profits due to business interruption would be working in which of the following areas?
    a. Valuation.
    b. Estimation.
    c. Financial determination.
    d. Auditing.

9. Corporate scandals prompted companies to begin using which of the following?
    a. Forensic audits.
    b. Fraud-intensive audits.
    c. Proactive fraud checkups.
    d. Internal control systems.

10. Which of the following is the most recognized fraud credential?
    a. CPA.
    b. CMA.
    c. CFE.
    d. None of the above.

11. Contrast and compare the role of the following:
    a. The internal auditor.
    b. The external auditor.
    c. The external forensic accounting consultant in an external audit.

12. Mary Soto, the controller of the My Citizens Company, has gone over its inventory records many times and is concerned that one or more company employees has stolen large amounts of the company's inventory. However, she is not absolutely sure that any theft has actually taken place because large portions of the written and computer records are missing for unknown reasons. Still, rough calculations, based on total purchases and sales, show that perhaps 20 percent of the inventory is missing.

    Mary spoke to her internal auditors and demanded that they give her an explanation, but they said no explanation was possible without the missing records.

    What should Mary Soto do? Should she contact the police? Should she hire an external forensic accountant? How might a forensic accountant help in this case? Specifically, what could the forensic accountant do that Mary's internal auditors could not do?

13. Section 404 of the Sarbanes-Oxley Act requires companies to perform self-assessments of risks for business processes that affect financial reporting.

    What are some business processes that could result in risks affecting financial reporting?

14. List the various elements of fraud within the organization. Give several examples of each.

15. How important are information technology skills to the forensic accountant? Give five examples of ways that forensic accountants use information technology skills.

16. Explain the roles played by forensic accountants in areas besides those relating to fraud.

17. List and explain the most important skills required of forensic accountants.

18. What are some special considerations for forensic accountants in working with law enforcement investigations?

19. Westag Mills Company is considering a merger with a competitor. Westag's CEO has hired a forensic accounting firm to investigate the competitor. What types of investigations could the forensic accounting firm conduct? What types of external assistance might the forensic accounting firm need?

20. Whom should you call first if you suspect fraud in your company, your forensic accounting firm, or your external audit firm? Why?

The Forensic Accounting Legal Environment

CHAPTER LEARNING OBJECTIVES

After reading Chapter 2, you should be able to:

- LO1: Explain the sources of U.S. law.
- LO2: Explain the basic structure of the U.S. court systems.
- LO3: Understand the general issues relating to investigations.
- LO4: Describe arrest and pretrial procedures.
- LO5: Explain basic criminal trial procedures.
- LO6: Describe and contrast and compare various common-law financial crimes.
- LO7: Explain various major federal criminal statutes relating to financial crimes.

ROADMAP TO THE LEGAL SYSTEM

As discussed in Chapter 1, the forensic accountant constantly works in the legal environment and for this reason must have a broad, basic understanding of the legal systems in the United States. Such an understanding should encompass not only basic business law and the civil court systems but also criminal law and the criminal court systems. Of course, the forensic accountant need not have the same degree of expertise as an attorney, but a good knowledge of the legal system can help the forensic accountant to work with the various components of the legal system.

For example, assume that a company calls on you, a forensic accountant, to independently investigate a possible embezzlement. Before you even begin your investigation, several questions come to mind: What types of notes and working papers should you collect in the event that the case might end up in the hands of law enforcement? What exactly constitutes embezzlement? Can temporarily borrowing money constitute embezzlement? At what point, if any, should you contact law enforcement? Who should make the contact with law enforcement, you or the company? Which law enforcement agency should you contact? Will you be called to testify in court? Will you be permitted to refer to notes when testifying?

The current chapter does not attempt to answer all questions such as these, for laws and legal procedures can vary quite a bit from one jurisdiction to the next. Instead, the current chapter seeks to present a simple and broad roadmap of the legal system while focusing mostly on procedures. However, some attention is devoted to substantive aspects of law, especially in areas that relate to white-collar crimes.

Civil and criminal procedures are especially important to the forensic accountant because they define the logical steps that are followed in investigations and criminal and civil litigation, and forensic accountants can be called to participate in almost all of the major steps. For example, in a civil proceeding, the forensic accountant could conduct the initial investigation, assist in preparing the plaintiff's formal complaint, assist in pretrial discovery, and testify in court. Furthermore, in a criminal proceeding, the forensic accountant could also be an actual law enforcement officer who carries out the investigation, makes arrests, obtains subpoenas and warrants, makes charging decisions, participates in plea negotiations, and so on. Many of these issues are discussed in this chapter.

This chapter focuses on criminal versus civil procedures, although the two are very similar from a general perspective: In both criminal and civil cases, there can be an investigation, a plaintiff, a defendant, and a possible trial. In criminal cases, the plaintiff involves a prosecutor representing "the people" in relation to an offense that violates some law—a criminal statute. In civil cases, on the other hand, the plaintiff typically involves a private or governmental attorney representing one party in a dispute or matter involving monetary or equitable relief. Criminal cases can also be distinguished according to the players involved: the police, prosecutors, parole and probation officers, and judges in the state courts. (In federal courts, the same judges hear both civil and criminal cases.)

Given the general similarity between criminal and civil procedures, this chapter focuses more on criminal procedures because their discussion is typically lacking in most business schools. This minimizes any duplication between the subjects covered here and in other business courses. However, the focus on the criminal procedures should not be construed to mean that they are more important than civil procedures; on the contrary, in practice the opposite is often true, with the bulk of forensic accounting work being devoted to various types of civil cases. Therefore, subsequent chapters give careful attention to various types of civil cases under topics such as divorce, bankruptcy, and general litigation support.

The remainder of this chapter is divided into three main sections: Criminal and Civil Procedures, Common Law Financial Crimes, and Federal Financial Crimes: The United States Code and Acts of Congress. The Criminal and Civil Procedures section discusses in the first subsection, step by step, procedures relating to civil and criminal cases, beginning with the early investigation and ending in some type of resolution. The second subsection defines and explains various types of financial crimes, and the final subsection discusses some of the major federal statutes that pertain to financial crimes.

CIVIL AND CRIMINAL PROCEDURES

The Legal System and Jurisdiction

Civil versus Criminal Cases

As mentioned, unlike civil cases, criminal cases involve the possible violation of some criminal **statute.** Criminal cases also involve unique actors, such as police, prosecutors, and criminal courts. Finally, criminal cases involve special constitutional rights for the defendant: the right to a jury trial (except in certain cases with a penalty of less than six months in jail) and the right against self-incrimination—the defendant cannot be compelled to testify. Moreover, in criminal cases, the plaintiff's **burden of proof** is very high, so that the judge or jury must be convinced that the defendant is guilty "beyond a reasonable doubt." On the other hand, none of these constitutional rights exists in civil cases: There is no general right to a jury trial (except in certain cases) unless it is provided for by statute, and there is a much lower burden of proof: The plaintiff must convince the judge or jury by only a "preponderance of the evidence" (see Figure 2.1).

Sources of Law

LO1   Various sources of law exist in the United States. These include **constitutional law,** statutory law, case law, and administrative law. All of these sources of law can be relevant to both civil and criminal cases.

The supreme law, of course, is the U.S. Constitution. State constitutions also exist and can provide the same or additional rights as long as they do not restrict those rights granted by the U.S. Constitution.

The U.S. Constitution is a pact between the government and the people; hence, only the government or its representatives can possibly violate one's constitutional rights. Still, various federal and state laws have been enacted that have the effect of protecting individuals' constitutional rights, and civil or criminal actions can be pursued under such laws.

The **U.S. Constitution** consists of seven articles and 27 amendments. The first three articles define the three major branches of government: the executive, judicial, and

FIGURE 2.1

Civil versus Criminal Proceedings

	Civil Proceedings	Criminal Proceedings
Investigation	√	√
Formal Trial	√	√
Plaintiff	Individual, organization, or government entity	"The people"
Defendant	Individual, organization, or government entity	Individual, organization, or government entity
Burden of Proof	Preponderance of the evidence	Beyond a reasonable doubt
General Right to Jury Trial	Only if provided for by statute in most cases	Constitutional right in most cases
Legal Issues Decided	Monetary and equitable relief	Violation of criminal statutes
Players	Law enforcement, courts, attorneys, forensic accountants	Law enforcement, courts, prosecutor, defense attorneys, forensic accountants
Defendant Has a Right Not to Testify	Defendant may be compelled to testify	√

legislative. The fourth article defines the concepts of "full faith and credit" and "privileges and immunities." The *full faith and credit* concept requires that states "recognize" the public acts, records, and judicial proceedings of other states. The *privileges and immunities* concept more or less requires states to treat the citizens from other states as they do their own. For example, it would be unconstitutional for California to forbid citizens of New York from using its public beaches.

The 27 amendments bestow a wide range of rights ranging from the freedom of speech to the right of 18-year-olds to vote. However, the first 10 amendments, the Bill of Rights, have an especially important impact on civil and criminal procedures. The Fourth Amendment prevents unreasonable searches, the Fifth Amendment sets the right against double jeopardy (being tried twice for the same crime), the right against self-incrimination (testifying against oneself), and the foundation for due process (the right to be given notices of charges or claims and the opportunity to defend against them). The Sixth Amendment grants the right to a speedy trial, a jury, an attorney in criminal cases, to confront accusers, and to compel witnesses to testify. The Seventh Amendment grants the right to a jury trial in certain civil cases; the Eighth Amendment forbids excessive bail and cruel and unusual punishment; the Ninth Amendment states that the set of citizens' rights can be broader that those elaborated in the Constitution. The Tenth Amendment states that whatever authority is not vested in the federal government rests in the states.

The second source of law is **statutory,** or codified, **law.** Statutory laws are enacted by federal, state, and local legislators. The general principle of preemption applies to statutory laws: When there is a conflict between federal, state, or local statutes, the statutes of the higher authority preempt those of the lower authority. This prevents states making laws that conflict with U.S. laws. For example, New York could not pass a law that exempts its citizens from paying U.S. income taxes.

Federal statutory laws are set forth in the **United States Code.** Especially important to the forensic accountant is **Title 18 of the U.S. Code,** which sets forth a wide array of financially related crimes. Some of the Title 18 crimes are discussed later.

The third source of law is **case law,** which stems from the need for courts to interpret statutes. This need arises in part because it is impossible for legislators to conceive of and define all of the circumstances under which laws will be applied. For example, state laws have traditionally made it illegal to practice law without a license. Surprising as it may seem, such laws were once used to prosecute CPAs for preparing federal tax returns. However, courts over time interpreted state laws to say that preparing federal tax returns is not practicing law.

Only appellate courts make case law. Both the state and federal systems distinguish between trial courts and appellate courts. *Trial courts* determine facts and apply the law. *Appellate courts,* on the other hand, do not determine facts but merely review decisions of lower courts for errors in the interpretation and application of the law. Their decisions are published and widely available, and they are binding on lower courts. The decisions of trial courts are not published or binding on other courts.

The final source of law is **administrative law,** which arises from powers granted to state and federal agencies to make rules and regulations. Many such agencies operate under the executive branch of the state or federal government. Examples at the federal level include the Food and Drug Administration, the Department of Agriculture, and the Department of Justice. Other agencies are independent, such as the Federal Elections Commission and the Securities and Exchange Commission. Finally, agencies can also exist under the judicial and legislative branches of government. For example, in Florida, the state bar, which has the authority to regulate and discipline lawyers, operates under the authority of the Florida Supreme Court.

Government agencies typically exercise their powers of regulation by passing rules and regulations. At the federal level, agencies first publish their rules for public comment, and then, after a comment period and possible modifications, such rules and regulations are enacted by publishing them in the *Federal Register*. Generally speaking, regulations promulgated by a given agency are limited to enforcing statutes that the agency is granted authority to enforce.

Courts

LO2 State and federal courts operate as separate systems (see Figure 2.2). State **trial courts** tend to be specialized, with separate courts for criminal versus civil cases. Federal trial courts, on the other hand, are generalized, with the same courts hearing both civil and criminal cases.

In the federal system, the **U.S. district courts** make up the trial courts. The United States has approximately 100 federal court districts, and each district may contain multiple divisions (i.e., separate courthouses) to serve various locations within the district.

Appeals from the U.S. district courts go to one of the numbered 11 **U.S. circuit courts of appeal,** or to one of two additional courts, the United States Court of Appeals of the District of Columbia Circuit, or the United States Court of Appeals for the Federal Circuit. Each circuit court of appeals covers a particular geographical area. For example, the 9th circuit includes many western states, including California.

Appeals from circuit courts of appeals go to the **U.S. Supreme Court,** which generally reviews only cases that it agrees to review. As with all appeals courts, including the U.S. circuit courts of appeal and state appellate courts, the U.S. Supreme Court does not try facts but only reviews lower court decisions on matters of law. Hence, appeals generally take the form of legal briefs with oral arguments as permitted by the courts.

Federal courts all have limited jurisdiction. The U.S. district courts try only cases that involve criminal or civil federal law. The only exception is "diversity jurisdiction," which means that these courts have jurisdiction over civil disputes between citizens of different states for amounts more than $75,000.

State courts also tend to be structured as three-tier systems, with lower trial courts, intermediate appellate courts, and supreme courts. Matters of law relating to federal statutes or to the U.S. Constitution can be appealed from the state courts to U.S. circuit courts.

Law Enforcement

Large numbers of separate law enforcement agencies and divisions of those agencies operate within the state and federal governments. Some examples at the federal level include

FIGURE 2.2
The State and Federal Court Systems

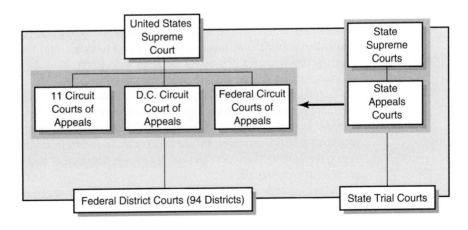

the Federal Bureau of Investigation, the Drug Enforcement Agency, the U.S. Postal Inspector, the U.S. Customs Service, and the Internal Revenue Service. Examples at the state level include city, county, and state police, as well as agencies relating to specialized areas such as the environment and child protection. In many states, much of the "heavy lifting" is done at the county level. For example, county sheriffs' offices can contain divisions that specialize in narcotics, economic crimes, insurance fraud, arson, child protection, domestic violence, and so on. When cases span multiple counties or involve large organizations, state law enforcement officers could also become involved.

District Attorney

In all criminal cases, the **district attorney,** sometimes called the **prosecutor,** is effectively the plaintiff in a criminal suit that is brought against the defendant. As such, the district attorney has the sole discretion in deciding which criminal charges to pursue and against whom.

Law enforcement officers and district attorneys normally work closely together. Both need each other to bring criminals to justice. Law enforcement officers typically provide the initial evidence; based on that evidence, the district attorney pursues the case.

Investigations and Trials

A typical criminal case begins with the initial investigation and ends with a trial verdict. Of course, in practice not all cases involve criminal charges or result in a trial. The main focus in this section is on the criminal procedures, not the investigation and prosecution. Subsequent chapters discuss in more detail techniques for investigating various financial crimes.

The exact procedures involved depend on the actual jurisdiction, but criminal procedures follow similar processes regardless of the jurisdiction. Furthermore, criminal procedures provide a reasonable "template" for civil procedures although civil cases involve no arrests, and defendants are not booked and do not need to worry about bail. Another exception is that in criminal cases, there tends to be a very large imbalance of power in favor of the plaintiff-prosecutor over the defendant. Finally, as mentioned, the burden of proof is "beyond a reasonable doubt" in criminal cases as compared to the much weaker "preponderance of the evidence" in civil cases; and in criminal cases, the defendant cannot be forced to testify whereas no such privilege exists for the defendant in civil cases.

Investigations

LO3 A forensic accountant can become involved in a financial crime investigation in many ways, such as in the capacity of in-house accountant, external auditor, or outside consultant. Regardless, the forensic accountant investigates and documents the case as needed.

If at any point before or during the investigation the forensic accountant becomes aware of probable criminal activity, he should immediately consult with management regarding the need or desirability of reporting the matter to law enforcement. The forensic accountant should also consult with his own legal council to make sure that he complies with any reporting requirements that might be applicable to the case. In some cases, a failure to report a crime could and of itself be a crime.

The forensic accountant should carefully maintain working papers that document facts only, not opinions. She should especially avoid making notes that say things such as "Jane Ladrone" stole the money or "John Ladrone" is probably innocent. Putting such opinions in **working papers** can "lock in" the accountant in regard to testimony, causing later problems if the opinion changes. The working papers, for good or bad, can greatly affect subsequent legal proceedings.

The preservation of evidence should be given high priority in any investigation. Suspect documents and computers should be quickly secured, making them safe from tampering or removal by suspects, and their **chain of custody** should be carefully recorded. For example, if the forensic accountant believes it likely that a given company computer was used to defraud the employer, it could be desirable to ask management to immediately transfer the computer to a secure location. A written record of the transfer must be kept, including the details of the transfer and the computer's serial number.

If the computer is so critical that it cannot be immediately transferred to a secure location, a bit-by-bit image copy, using special software, should be made of its hard drive. This is often done by removing the hard drive from the computer and attaching it to another computer, which makes the copy. This procedure best protects the original disk from any alteration of sensitive data. This topic is discussed in more detail in a subsequent chapter.

In some cases, the evidence trail leads directly to the guilty person. For example, an employee could be caught on videotape forging a document. In many cases, however, the evidence leads to a number of suspects, so that the investigative task then involves eliminating the innocent suspects from further consideration. This can be accomplished in part by interviewing the suspects using interviewing techniques discussed in a later chapter. Generally speaking, such interviews should focus on **fraud triangle** elements: pressure, opportunity, and rationalization (see Figure 2.3). *Pressure* usually means that the employee is under financial duress such as from credit problems, substance addiction, or gambling addiction. *Opportunity* means that the employee is in the position to commit the crime, and *rationalization* means that the employee mentally justifies the crime. Common justifications are "I was only borrowing the money" and "The company deserved what it got."

One advantage of turning the case over to law enforcement is that the authorities often have considerably stronger investigative powers. For example, in some jurisdictions, detectives can easily obtain investigative subpoenas for employees' personal banking, credit, and phone records.

The procedures for obtaining **investigative subpoenas** vary from one jurisdiction to the next. In some jurisdictions they can be issued directly by the district attorney, whereas in other jurisdictions they need to be approved by a judge or issued by a grand jury. **Grand juries** are temporary groups of citizens set up for limited periods of time to investigate specific crimes or problems. In investigating crimes, grand juries often meet secretly and have sweeping powers to compel testimony and subpoena documents.

Subpoenas are normally used when there is no immediate need to seize evidence. For example, the typical time required to obtain bank records via a subpoena can be four to six weeks. The time can be much longer if records are being sought from one state to another.

When a subpoena is not fast enough or it is necessary to seize evidence in the personal possession of a suspect, such as in a suspect's home, law enforcement authorities can obtain a **search warrant.** A judge normally issues a search warrant on the basis of an

FIGURE 2.3
The Fraud Triangle

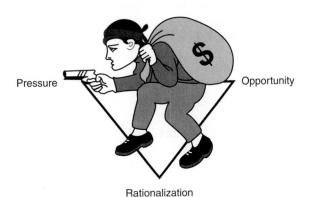

Pressure

Opportunity

Rationalization

affidavit (sworn statement) from law enforcement showing probable cause that the suspect has committed a crime. Search warrants permit authorities to immediately enter a specified location and seize documents, computers, and other objects that may be identified in the search warrant. As such, search warrants are much "stronger" than subpoenas. Search warrants can also sometimes be used to force a suspect to supply handwriting, fingerprint, DNA, or other similar types of evidence.

Although subpoenas and search warrants can be powerful tools, there is no guarantee that evidence obtained by them can be used in court. For any evidence to be admitted into court, it must be shown to be relevant, obtained legally, and not subject to certain other possible restrictions relating to the rules of evidence. For example, evidence obtained from a search warrant can be excluded from court if the judge finds the supporting affidavit to be false. Furthermore, under the **fruits of the poisonous tree** doctrine, evidence subsequently obtained because of the defective search warrant could also be excluded.

Officers can also search and seize evidence without a warrant. First, they can always search if a person gives a valid consent. Thus, an employer can usually grant permission for the search of an employee's desk. (However, the employer might not be able to legally give consent to search the employee's briefcase, U.S. mail, or automobile.) Second, an officer is permitted to "search" (and seize) items in plain sight if the officer is in a place that he is legally permitted to be at the time. Third, when making arrests, an officer is permitted to search the area immediately under the subject's control, at least within arm's reach of the suspect. Finally, an officer may be permitted to "sweep" the immediate area for other suspects, and evidence encountered during such sweeps might be subject to legal seizure.

Arrests

LO4 Authorities can generally **arrest** a suspect when there is **probable cause** that the suspect has committed a crime. Probable cause is not an exact legal standard but more or less represents what could be a reasonable basis to believe that the suspect could have committed a crime. It is a much lower standard than "beyond a reasonable doubt" and may be based on things that even seem dubious to the suspect, such as a tip from an anonymous informer.

Because probable cause is such a low standard, it does not always lead to an arrest. In many cases, the investigator might continue to gather evidence after there is probable cause but before making an arrest.

Aside from trivial cases, such as when persons are very briefly detained for questions or traffic stops, the act of arrest means taking the suspect into custody. The person may be handcuffed and transported to a booking facility. An arrest is a deprivation of the suspect's freedom and as such is not normally made without a fairly good basis. A person arrested without a proper basis could sue the law enforcement authority.

When making an arrest, the officers complete an *arrest report* that indicates the alleged crime(s), probable cause, and details surrounding the arrest. The arrest report then goes to the intake district attorney, who reviews it and follows up by filing formal charges in a criminal court.

Officers sometimes issue citations as an alternative to arrests. A **citation** requires the suspect to appear in front of a judge to answer a specific criminal charge as set forth in the citation. A copy of the citation is sent to the district attorney, who handles it in a fashion similar to an arrest report.

In some cases, an **arrest warrant** (i.e., an order from a judge to make an arrest) may be issued before the arrest is made. For example, arrest warrants are normally required when officers enter a suspect's home to make an arrest. Arrest warrants may also be used when the suspect's whereabouts are unknown or after a grand jury indictment.

Charging

In the federal system and in some state systems, only a grand jury can bring **felony charges,** that is, charges for crimes subject to a penalty of more than one year in prison. In many states, the district attorney has the sole discretion as to what charges, if any, are filed against the suspect in a criminal court.

The district attorney's discretion represents a very broad power. For example, a person accused of writing 1,000 bad checks for $10 each might face 1,000 counts of petty theft. In this case, the district attorney might decide to combine all of the petty theft charges into a single felony charge of grand theft. Alternatively, she might drop all the charges but one count of petty theft in exchange for a plea bargain. District attorneys are often elected and therefore are sensitive to the sensibilities of the community.

Many financial crimes can lead to multiple charges. For example, in an **identity theft** case, the suspect could be charged with forgery, grand theft, identity theft, postal fraud, income tax fraud, and even lying to police investigators.

All crimes contain **elements,** or specific factors, that must be present for an act to be considered a crime. For example, the typical elements in the crime of auto theft include both the act of taking the automobile and the intent to permanently deprive the owner of it. Therefore, if a suspect merely takes the car for a joyride, the crime of joyriding rather than grand theft applies because there is no intent to permanently deprive. The general element of intent can sometimes be difficult to prove in cases of financial crime. When one person shoots another person with a pistol the intent is often very obvious, but sometimes in financial fraud cases the intent is much more obscure.

As a general rule, prosecutors tend to overcharge suspects, at least initially. This happens because approximately 90 percent of all criminal cases are settled through **plea bargains,** which reduce the charges in exchange for a guilty plea or other specified act. As a result, criminal lawyers typically advise their clients to plead not guilty initially, thus putting them in the position to bargain for a plea.

Booking and Bail

After an arrest, the suspect is taken to a **booking** facility (usually a jail or police station) where the suspect is searched, fingerprinted, photographed, checked for outstanding warrants, stripped of personal items (e.g., watches, purses, wallets, and jewelry), and screened for health problems (see Figure 2.4). The searching (usually a full body search), stripping of personal possessions, and health screening are done on the theory that the suspect will be put in jail where contraband and unknown health problems cannot be permitted.

The arrest information is entered into to booking system, which creates the formal **arrest record.** Prior to this point, the arrested person usually has no arrest record for this specific crime. A person brought in for questioning and released is not arrested and thus has no arrest record.

In some districts, those issued citations are required to submit to the booking procedure within several days after the citation. Similarly, those charged by grand juries or directly indicted by a prosecutor are required to submit to the booking process; sometimes suspects are permitted to turn themselves in for booking instead of being arrested by an officer.

Suspects are not guaranteed the right to an attorney until the booking process is complete. As soon as it is complete, however, they may contact an attorney and possibly obtain bail either on their own or with the help of an attorney. Some jurisdictions have police bail that has preestablished bail schedules. The accused need only post the amount per the schedule to be immediately released pending trial. Another possibility is that the jurisdiction has duty judges who can authorize bail over the phone.

FIGURE 2.4
The Booking Process

Bail is basically a security deposit, which is forfeited if the defendant does not appear in court as required. In many cases, the defendant uses the services of a bail bond seller, who immediately posts the bail and charges a 10 percent nonrefundable fee. Many jurisdictions accept cash, personal check, or credit cards, and court-financed bail exists in some cases, although it is not generally available until the defendant appears before a judge.

For most felony charges, bail averages between $10,000 and $50,000, although it can be much higher for multiple charges, and it might not be available for some charges such as murder. The entire amount of the bail is returned at the conclusion of the criminal proceedings.

Arraignments

Defendants have the constitutional right to an **arraignment** "as quickly as possible" after an arrest. Therefore, those in custody are usually brought before a judge for an arraignment within 48 hours after arrest. There is less of a sense of urgency for those not in custody, and their arraignments might not occur until days, or even weeks later, depending on the jurisdiction.

The arraignment consists of the prosecutor providing the defendant a written copy of the charges, and the defendant entering a plea, usually one of guilty or not guilty. At the same time, the defendant can request a court-appointed attorney if she cannot afford one. Also, the judge grants, denies, increases, or lowers bail, as appropriate, and sets a tentative schedule for a preliminary hearing (if there is to be one), pretrial motions, and the trial itself. In some cases, the judge grants the defendant release on his own recognizance, meaning that no bail is required. The entire arraignment hearing could take only 5 to 10 minutes.

Discovery and Pretrial Investigation

The general exchange of information and evidence between prosecutors and defendants is called **discovery.** In the interests of promoting justice, avoiding surprises during trials, and in facilitating the more rapid settlement of cases, prosecutors are typically required to provide the defense copies of the arrest records, search warrants, witness statements, and, in general, access to all evidence in the case. However, local discovery rules vary from one jurisdiction to the next, and in federal courts, prosecutors are not required to supply the defense pretrial statements from government witnesses.

Although discovery rules tend to favor the defense, the general trend is toward requiring defendants to provide more discovery information. Already, in some jurisdictions, the defendant has substantial discovery obligations. For example, in California, the defense must give the prosecution an advance copy of its witness list, witness statements, expert reports that can be used in the trial, and any tangible evidence that the defense intends to introduce into trial. In federal courts, the defense must provide the prosecutor written notice of any planned alibi information.

Both the prosecutor and defense often find it desirable to continue their investigations in addition to conducting discovery. For example, the defense attorney might interview the prosecution witnesses if they are willing, take depositions of friendly witnesses, and have experts review the prosecution's evidence.

Discovery is also applicable to civil cases. The main difference is that the plaintiff and defendant tend to be on more equal footing. Forensic accountants can be consulted during the discovery process to help depose witnesses and evaluate evidence.

Preliminary Hearings

A **preliminary hearing** is a mini-trial like event that is sometimes held; if it is, it occurs before the trial, soon after the charges are officially filed. The main outcome of the hearing is a judge's decision either to find probable cause to bind the defendant over for trial or to completely dismiss the case. The judge can also reduce or dismiss individual charges and change the bail.

Preliminary hearings are not held in all cases, depending on the jurisdiction and how the charges are filed. In some jurisdictions, they are held in all criminal cases, and in other jurisdictions, they are held only at the request of the defense. In cases in which the charges (i.e., the indictment) was filed by a grand jury, a preliminary hearing generally does not take place because the grand jury effectively takes the place of the hearing.

Preliminary hearings operate very much like trials with witnesses and cross-examinations but with some major differences: They have only a judge, no jury, a much lower standard of proof (only probable cause versus beyond a reasonable doubt), and often hearsay evidence that cannot be used in a trial can be presented. The main goal of preliminary hearings is to dispose of weak cases so they do not go to trial.

Prosecutors almost always "win" at preliminary hearings, causing the judge to enter an order to bind the defendant over for trial. Nevertheless, the preliminary hearing can be of important strategic importance for both the prosecution and defense. For example, the defense gains an opportunity to make a "test run" of prosecution witnesses to estimate how they will perform at trials. For this reason, when permitted, prosecutors likely call only the minimal number of witnesses to establish probable cause. One way to accomplish this is by calling the arresting officer as opposed to the primary witnesses and questioning the officer about what the primary witnesses said. This brings in the witnesses' testimony (via hearsay) without subjecting them to cross-examination. On the other hand, the defense might not call any important witnesses to keep the prosecution from learning its trial strategy. Finally, in some cases, the prosecution seeks a grand jury indictment to avoid a preliminary hearing, thus completely protecting its witnesses from cross-examination by the defense.

Plea Bargains and Civil Negotiations

Prior to the trial, the defense and the prosecution are likely to engage in plea negotiations (see Figure 2.5). In many jurisdictions (e.g., in the federal court system), criminal codes provide specific rules for plea bargaining. In most cases, plea bargaining is permitted at any phase of the process after arrest until a guilty or not guilty verdict is reached and sentencing is complete.

FIGURE 2.5
Plea Bargaining

Plea bargains can involve both the charges and the sentence. For example, immediately following an arrest, a prosecutor can agree not to file certain charges in exchange for the suspect's guilty plea. Alternatively, the prosecutor can promise to recommend a reduced sentence to one or more charges in exchange for a guilty plea. Of course, the judge must always accept any sentencing recommendations, but judges are generally happy to quickly dispose of cases to unclog overcrowded court dockets.

What the prosecutor is likely to agree to in a plea bargain depends on many factors, including the defendant's history and degree of involvement in the crime(s), the specific crime(s) charged, the strength of the evidence, and even public sentiment at the time. In many cases, plea bargaining takes only a minute or two, especially with prosecutors who work with similar cases every day. For example, in an embezzlement case, the defendant may be charged with forgery, computer tampering, and grand theft. In such a case, the prosecutor could offer to drop the forgery and grand theft charges in exchange for a guilty plea on the computer-tampering charge. Furthermore, if the defendant shows remorse and has an exemplary background and the amount of the theft is not large, the prosecutor might agree to recommend only probation.

Civil negotiations are similar to plea bargains in that the plaintiff and the defendant can negotiate to settle any time during the process. The likelihood and nature of a negotiated settlement depend on the relative strength of the two cases, the possible outcomes of a trial, the effect of publicity, and the costs of litigation. Furthermore, in civil cases, negotiations are much more likely to be complex and prolonged. Formal arbitration and/or mediation (discussed in a subsequent chapter) are also more likely to become involved.

The Trial Process

LO5 The defendant has a constitutional right to a jury trial (see Figure 2.6) in criminal cases for charges that involve possible incarceration for more than six months. Being a constitutional right, it applies in all state and federal courts. A similar constitutional right also exists in federal courts for civil suits that involve monetary damages. On the other hand, no such general constitutional right exists for civil suits in state courts, although state constitutions and state laws frequently provide such a right.

Criminal defendants usually opt for a jury trial because it can offer certain advantages not available in **bench trials** (i.e., trials by judges). First, in most jurisdictions, juries typically consist of 12 persons, all of whom must vote for a guilty verdict if a conviction is to take place. This is compared to only one "vote" of guilty required by the judge in a bench

FIGURE 2.6
Typical Jury Trial Process

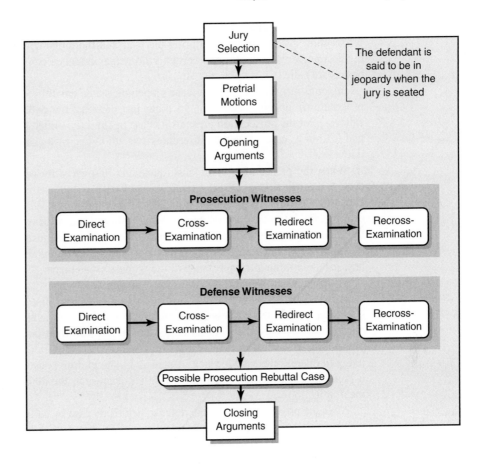

trial. Second, in many jurisdictions, the defendant has no control over which judge tries the case but routinely does have control over selecting members of the jury through the *voir dire* process. In the *voir dire* process, the attorneys or the judge asks potential jurors questions about their attitudes and backgrounds and may automatically exclude some jurors using "peremptory challenges." Additional jurors may also be excluded if an attorney can show just cause for, say, extreme bias, but judges routinely accept the word of prospective jurors who promise to set aside admitted biases.

Once the jury is seated in a jury trial, or when the first witness takes the stand in a bench trial, the criminal defendant is said to be *in jeopardy*. After that point in time, the defendant cannot be retried for the same crime if there is a verdict of not guilty or the judge dismisses the case. A second trial under these circumstances would subject the defendant to **double jeopardy,** which the U.S. Constitution does not permit. However, it does permit the same person to be tried for the same crimes separately in both state and federal courts.

After the jury is seated, the judge may hear **motions *in limine.*** In such motions, the defendant can ask the judge to exclude anticipated evidence from the trial. For example, in an embezzlement case, the defense attorney could anticipate that a prosecution police witness will mention that that the defendant was previously convicted of domestic violence. In this case, the defense attorney could make a motion *in limine* requesting that the prosecution not be permitted to mention the previous conviction.

Before the first witness is called, the prosecution makes its **opening statement,** which typically provides a roadmap to the prosecution's case. Normally, the prosecutor is granted a wide degree of latitude in the opening statement to indicate the evidence the prosecution intends to present during the trial, but the judge could disallow actual arguments against the defense, and certainly no actual evidence can be introduced until witnesses are called.

In some jurisdictions, the defense's opening statement follows immediately after the prosecution's opening statement. In other jurisdictions, the defense's opening statement follows after the prosecution presents its case in chief (i.e., after all of its witnesses testify and it rests its case). In either case, the prosecution begins its case in chief by calling its witnesses.

When the prosecution or defense questions its own witnesses, the process is called **direct examination.** Direct examination of each witness is immediately followed by **cross-examination,** or questioning, by the opposing side. The purpose of cross-examination is generally to damage the credibility of the witness, which is typically done by undermining the witness's background, highlighting inconsistencies in the witness's testimony or in statements made before the trial, demonstrating ulterior motives of the witness, or undermining the substance of the witness's statements.

In cases when a witness's testimony is damaged on cross-examination, **redirect examination** of the witness can occur: The attorney who first called the witness to the stand requestions the witness in an attempt to rehabilitate the testimony. Any additional questioning by the other side is called **recross-examination.** After the prosecution presents its last witness, it rests its case. The defense then often makes a motion for the judge to dismiss the case for lack of evidence. The motion is usually denied, but because it is made when the jury (in a jury trial) is not present, the defense has little to lose by making it.

After the prosecution rests, the defense begins its case by calling its witnesses through the same process of direct and cross-examination that applies to prosecution witnesses. However, in both criminal and civil cases, the defense has no obligation to call witnesses because the burden of proof always rests on the plaintiff. If the plaintiff presents a very strong case, sometimes called a *prima facie* case, the burden of proof shifts somewhat to the defense, which has little choice but to present a full defense case. For example, if the prosecution calls several eyewitnesses who claim they saw the crime, the defense likely calls alibi witnesses who saw the defendant far away from the crime scene at the time the crime was committed. The defense could also call experts to present evidence of the unreliability of eyewitness testimony.

After the defense rests, the prosecution normally has the opportunity to call **rebuttal witnesses** from whom the prosecution seeks to present information that will impeach the evidence presented in the defense case. The scope of the rebuttal testimony is limited to attacking evidence presented in the defense case. Rebuttal does not give the prosecution an opportunity to present any of its case a second time.

After all witnesses have testified, the prosecution and defense make their **closing arguments.** The prosecution normally presents its closing arguments first on the theory that the prosecution carries the burden of proof. This gives the defense the last word. However, some judges permit the prosecutor to present rebuttal arguments after the defense presents its closing arguments or, in cases when the prosecutor is not permitted rebuttal arguments, permits the prosecution to choose which side goes first.

The final part of the jury trial before the case goes to the jury is that the judge gives **jury instructions** on the legal principles that the jury must apply to the case. Often these instructions are complex and difficult for juries to understand because they tend to be based on the wording from previous appellate court decisions. The jury instructions are critical because they typically define the elements of the crimes (or civil wrongs) under consideration, reasonable doubt, permissible considerations in evaluating the credibility of the witnesses, and the mechanics of the deliberations.

Juries in criminal cases normally deliberate until they reach a unanimous verdict or until the judge believes they are permanently deadlocked and cannot reach a unanimous verdict. The same is true in civil cases except that jurisdictions tend to allow a verdict with dissenting votes.

In criminal cases, jury verdicts of not guilty are final and cannot be appealed. The defendant can appeal a verdict of guilty on issues of law. Typical reasons for appeal are that the trial judge improperly admitted or excluded evidence or gave faulty jury instructions.

In cases of hung juries (e.g., when juries deliberate but can't reach a unanimous verdict), the prosecution is permitted to completely retry the case. In practice, however, the prosecutor is likely to offer the defense a new, more liberal plea bargain in lieu of trying the case a second time. Furthermore, if the jury was leaning strongly against the prosecution, the prosecutor could drop the case.

Rules of Evidence

In criminal trials, the **rules of evidence** control both the content of the evidence and the manner in which it is presented. In federal and most state courts, the rules of evidence are set forth in statutory codes

Rules Relating to Evidence Content The number one rule relating to evidence is that it can be introduced only if it is shown to be relevant, meaning that the attorney must logically connect it to the questions at hand. However, not all relevant evidence is admitted. For example, judges may exclude relevant evidence that is deemed to be overly prejudicial or inflammatory to the emotions. On the other hand, nonrelevant evidence may be omitted if the opposing attorney does not object. As a general rule, it is up to the attorneys to raise objections, and judges remain silent when attorneys do not object. In many cases, attorneys deliberately do not object to the other side presenting irrelevant evidence because it can become an easy target of attack.

A second major rule of evidence, the **personal knowledge rule,** is that witnesses can testify only to things that they personally know through one or more of their own senses. For example, a security guard could testify to the fact that she saw the defendant working after hours, but the same security guard could not testify that the defendant worked at other jobs at night just because he always seemed sleepy when he came to work in the morning.

The major exception to the personal knowledge rule applies to **expert witnesses,** who are permitted to draw expert conclusions based on facts admitted into evidence. For example, a handwriting expert could testify that in her opinion, a defendant forged a given document, even though the expert did not personally witness the act of forgery.

A third major rule of evidence content excludes certain written and oral statements made out of court. One type of statement that is excluded is a **hearsay statement,** which is a witness statement that may be offered into evidence for its own truth. For example, assume that in a murder case the prosecution alleges that the defendant murdered Jane Doe on January 1, but it so happens that Jane Doe called John Doe on January 15 and said, "I'm alive." In this case, this out-of-court statement is clearly an out-of-court hearsay-type statement. Nevertheless, it is likely to be admitted not for the truth of the statement itself but for the mere fact that John Doe talked to Jane Doe on January 15, meaning that she could not have possibly died on January 1 as the prosecution alleged. In fact, in this case, the content of the out-of-court statement is totally irrelevant. Jane Doe could just have well said, "The sky is blue." The point is that a witness testified that she was alive on January 15.

There are many exceptions to the hearsay rule: dying declarations, excited utterances, defendant admissions, statements that show someone's state of mind, written government and business records, and prior inconsistent statements. Most of these exceptions are fairly self-evident, but the state-of-mind exception deserves some explanation. Any out-of-court statements that indicate a person's emotions, beliefs, or intent generally may be admitted despite the fact that they were made out of court if they are otherwise admissible. For example, the defense could impeach a prosecution eyewitness by introducing another witness who heard the eyewitness speaking angrily and jealously about the defendant one day before the alleged crime took place.

Another important rule of evidence content relates to the chain of custody, which applies to tangible evidence (exhibits) introduced into evidence. The general requirement is that before a tangible exhibit can be introduced, the attorney must show that it is what it is purported to be and that it has not been changed in any material way since the alleged crime was committed. For example, if someone used a computer to cover up an inventory theft, the computer can be admitted into evidence against a defendant if the prosecution establishes a clear chain of custody dating back from the time that the defendant used the computer. On the other hand, if many people had used the same computer between the time the defendant had used it and the trial, the judge would likely deny admitting it as evidence that the defendant had used it to cover up a theft.

Rules Relating to the Manner of Testimony   The rules relating to the manner of witness testimony prohibit the attorney from asking on direct examination **leading questions** that suggest a particular answer. On the other hand, the attorney may ask leading questions on cross-examination. Some other types of questions are completely forbidden, including those that "badger" the witnesses, questions that assume facts not in evidence, questions that misquote witnesses, and questions that ask the witness to speculate or draw improper conclusions.

Witnesses can protect themselves when forced to answer improper questions when the attorney does not object to them. One simple way for the witness to do this is by simply restating what he or another witness said earlier. For example, the prosecutor might ask a witness about the accused, "She hated her employer, didn't she, because she didn't get the raise she expected?" The witness in turn might reply, "As I said earlier, she did not get the raise she hoped for, but she was always calm about it, and I never saw any hostility from her toward the company." Other ways witnesses can avoid problems include preparing ahead of time with the attorney and bringing notes or documents to court that can be used to refresh their memory.

Scientific Evidence   Scientific evidence is not automatically admitted. For scientific evidence to be admitted as such, it must meet certain strict tests, as discussed in a later chapter. Unfortunately, the high standards for admitting scientific evidence sometimes prevent evidence that depends on new but valid scientific technologies from being admitted. For example, not all courts accepted DNA evidence when it was new.

Many jurisdictions hold mini-trials without the jury present to determine whether particular scientific evidence can be admitted. If it is admitted, its validity can still be undermined by witnesses who question it. Various types of forensic science and their usefulness in court are discussed in a later chapter.

Privileged Information   Some types of communications between individuals are **privileged** because they are not subject to discovery or required disclosure in court. The laws on what is privileged vary considerably from one jurisdiction to the next; however, some general privileges tend to apply: attorney-client, spouse-spouse, doctor-patient, psychoanalyst-patient, clergy-congregant, and accountant-client in certain tax matters.

A privilege belongs to one party, the privilege holder. Only the privilege holder can waive the privilege and give up confidentiality of the information. For example, with the attorney-client privilege, only the client can waive the privilege. Some jurisdictions permit judges to override some privileges when the public good or justice outweighs the right of the privilege holder to maintain the privilege.

The attorney-client privilege is sometimes especially important to the forensic accountant. The privilege extends not only to communications between the attorney and clients but also to communications between the attorney and investigators and others working on behalf of the attorney. Furthermore, privilege also exists for the "work product" of attorneys that is separate and beyond the attorney-client privilege. This privilege protects opinion-type material generated by attorneys in preparing cases, but it may not extend to some types of factual material. For example, clients cannot shield evidence from discovery simply by turning it over to their attorneys.

Privileges are not always what they seem. For example, a corporation is the privilege holder for communications between corporate attorneys and employees. Thus, employees of the corporation cannot individually invoke the privilege to protect themselves in criminal investigations. As result, the federal government sometimes pressures corporations to waive the privilege to make it easier to prosecute company employees. The result effectively shifts criminal liability from the companies to their employees while stripping away attorney-client privilege from some employees who can simply be doing their duties.

Finally, most privileges are subject to exceptions. For example, the attorney-client privilege does not protect communications relating to future crimes. In all cases, privileges are deemed to have been waived when people communicate in places where there is no reasonable expectation of privacy, such as in a public place where others can easily overhear. Moreover, privilege holders sometimes inadvertently waive their privileges by disclosing privileged information to others, especially to law enforcement authorities. Furthermore, once the privilege is waived a "little," it could be waived in total. For example, if a defendant tells police about some privileged doctor-patient information, the defendant could then be prevented from invoking the privilege in court.

COMMON-LAW CRIMES

LO6   Criminal statutes vary considerably from one jurisdiction to the next, but certain types of crimes exist almost universally in law. Sometimes called **common-law crimes,** they are derived from old English law. This section explains various types of common-law crimes related to financial matters as the laws tend to be applied today. These are crimes that forensic accountants are likely to encounter in one form or another.

Larceny

Larceny, which is basically theft, generally involves intentionally and permanently converting another's property to an individual's own use or possession. *Intent* is a key element, so it is impossible for a person to accidentally commit a larcenous act. Furthermore, some larceny-related statutes proscribe substantially infringing on the property rights of the owner.

Burglary

The crime of *burglary* includes unlawfully entering any building or structure with the intent of committing a crime. In general, no actual "breaking" is required. In fact, in some statutes, merely putting a hand in a window could be sufficient to support a charge of burglary (see Figure 2.7).

FIGURE 2.7
Burglary Could Include Putting One Hand in a Window

Conspiracy

When two or more people agree to commit a crime with common intent and then act on that intent, even in some small way, the crime of conspiracy arises. Criminal liability normally arises when at least one person in the conspiracy acts overtly in some way to further the conspiracy; the furthering act itself does not need to be unlawful. For example, if several people conspired to attack a given company's computer, one of the conspirators could commit the required overt act by doing something as simple as making some notes on a piece of paper relating to the company to be attacked.

Criminal liability exists even if the ultimate act of the conspiracy is impossible to carry out. For example, two individuals hatch a conspiracy to use the Internet to hack into the computers at Fort Knox and somehow steal all of the gold. In this case, criminal liability exists even if at some point the conspirators discover that the computers in Fort Knox are not connected to the Internet.

Criminal liability also exists even for a conspirator who abandons the conspiracy, although abandoning it could relieve the conspirator from criminal liability for the ultimate act. In the end, all individuals active in the conspiracy at the time the ultimate act is committed can be charged with both the conspiracy and the ultimate act.

Finally, the doctrine "the acts of one are the acts of all" applies to conspiracies. In many states, this means that conspirators can become criminally liable for crimes they do not even agree to commit, and for unanticipated crimes of other co-conspirators, as long as the crimes are committed within the scope of the conspiracy.

Embezzlement

Embezzlement occurs when a person first has lawful possession or control over someone's property and then wrongfully converts that property to the person's own use. Note that under this definition, even real property can be embezzled. Embezzlement statutes generally proscribe even the temporary unlawful conversion of property. This prevents the typical embezzler's excuse, "I was only borrowing the money."

Fraud (False Pretense)

Fraud (false pretense) involves intentional and material misrepresentation of one or more material facts with the intent of taking property from a victim. The misrepresentation must be more than mere sales hyperbole. For example, it would not be fraud for a salesperson to say that her vacuum cleaners are the best in the world, but it would be if the same salesperson sold someone a vacuum cleaner as new when she knew that it was used.

Robbery

The crime of *robbery* involves theft in the presence of the victim through force or the threat of force. Note how robbery differs from fraud and embezzlement, in which there is no force or threat of force. Also, a threat of force applicable to some future time is not robbery.

Extortion

Extortion involves the threat of future force to gain some time of benefit from the victim. The benefit does not even need to be monetary. For example, a physical threat against a person's boss demanding a promotion is extortion.

Arson

The intentional burning of or exploding a building is the crime of *arson.* Sometimes arson is committed so the actor can collect insurance or conceal another crime.

Solicitation

Solicitation involves recruiting or hiring someone to commit a crime. A person who hires or recruits someone else to commit a crime is generally guilty of both the crime of solicitation and the criminal act of the person who commits it.

Aiding and Abetting

Aiding and abetting is a crime in which one person assists another person in committing a crime. The assisting person does not need to participate in the criminal act itself, and assisting can be very broadly defined to include things such as encouraging the actor before the ultimate act is carried out. Also, most states have laws that punish accessories after the fact, that is, those who help the criminal cover up the act or provide help for the criminal in avoiding justice.

FEDERAL FINANCIAL CRIMES: THE UNITED STATES CODE AND ACTS OF CONGRESS

LO7 As previously mentioned, the United States Code (U.S.C) represents a group of statutes passed by the Congress of the United States that collectively make up statutory law for the U.S. government. The U.S.C includes 50 different numbered topics, or "titles," that deal with diverse matters that range from the elections of U.S. senators to issues of war and national defense. Each title is organized in chapters and sections, and citations of a given title, chapter, and section are written in abbreviated form. For example, the section that defines bankruptcy fraud—Title 18, Chapter 9, Section 151—may be abbreviated 18 U.S.C. §151, or very often simply 18 U.S.C 151. Citing the chapter number is not necessary because within a given title, the sections are numbered consecutively from beginning to end and do not start over at the beginning of each chapter.

Of particular interest is U.S.C Title 18, Crimes and Criminal Procedure. However, despite the fact that Title 18 is primarily devoted to criminal issues, it often includes civil remedies. Conversely, many of the U.S.C titles that predominately focus on civil matters also contain criminal penalties.

Congress often does not pass a new statute but rather passes a named act that amends one or two, or possibly many, U.S.C statutes relating to some common subject matter. For example, as discussed later, the Sarbanes-Oxley Act involved changes to Title 15 (which includes the Security and Exchange Act of 1934) and Title 18.

18 U.S.C 96: Racketeer Influenced and Corrupt Organizations Act (RICO)

The **Racketeer Influenced and Corrupt Organizations Act (RICO)** is part of the Organized Crime Control Act (OCCA) of 1970 signed by President Richard Nixon. The OCCA forbids certain organized gambling organizations, grants certain power to federal grand juries in relation to reluctant witnesses, and grants the U.S. Attorney authorization to protect witnesses, which has led to what is commonly known as the *federal witness security program.*

RICO provides criminal penalties of fines up to $25,000 and 20 years in prison. It also provides for forfeiture of properties used in covered crimes and for treble (three times actual) damages in its civil liability provisions. Individuals, corporations, and "association-in-fact enterprises" can be sued and criminally charged under the act. An association-in-fact enterprise is any group of individuals not legally organized but who operate together as an enterprise.

The act itself is very long and complicated, but in a nutshell it lists a mix of more than 30 different state and federal crimes, and violation of any two of these crimes in a related pattern over a 10-year period could lead to criminal and/or civil liability under the act.

Because RICO is a federal act, some relation to interstate commerce is required for crimes to fall under it. This is not generally an issue, however, because most cases include mail fraud, which is a crime under federal jurisdiction. The only requirement to involve mail fraud is to send a single postcard, or letter or package, through the mail in furtherance of criminal activities.

15 U.S.C 78dd: Foreign Corrupt Practices Act (FCPA) of 1977

The **Foreign Corrupt Practices Act (FCPA)** of 1977 was passed to forbid bribery payments to foreign officials for the purpose of obtaining or retaining business. Violation of the act may lead to criminal fines of up to $2,000,000 for corporations and $100,000 for individuals and a prison sentence of up to five years for individuals. Corporations are not permitted to pay the fine for company employees. The FCPA applies to all publicly traded companies in the United States.

FCPA also provides for civil enforcement actions by both the U.S. Attorney General and the Securities and Exchange Commission, with penalties ranging as high as $100,000 for individuals and $500,000 for corporations. It also contains significant accounting recordkeeping provisions that require companies to maintain a tight system of internal controls to ensure the proper recording of assets and payments. Congress reasoned that such provisions were needed to avoid deliberate misclassification of payments or misrepresentation of expenses, both of which could be used to hide illegal payments to foreign officials.

Because of the recordkeeping provisions, corporate officials can face jail time simply for having weak internal control systems. No bribery is required.

The Sarbanes-Oxley (SOX) Act of 2002

The **Sarbanes-Oxley (SOX) Act** of 2002 represents the most sweeping set of changes affecting corporate accountability and financial reporting since the Securities and Exchange Act of 1934. In total, SOX represents a large group of amendments to various sections of the U.S.C, beginning with Title 15, Section 78 (which includes the Securities and Exchange Act) and Title 18, Crimes and Criminal Procedure. For example, Title VIII, Section 802 of SOX amends 18 U.S.C 1519 (criminal penalties for altering documents) by adding the following wording at the end:

> Whoever knowingly alters, destroys, mutilates, conceals, covers up, falsifies, or makes a
> false entry in any record, document, or tangible object with the intent to impede, obstruct, or

influence the investigation or proper administration of any matter within the jurisdiction of any department or agency of the United States or any case filed under title 11, or in relation to or contemplation of any such matter or case, shall be fined under this title, imprisoned not more than 20 years, or both.

SOX is divided into 11 titles (not to be confused with U.S. Code titles), each of which deals with a separate topic. For example, SOX Title 2 relates to auditor independence, and Title 4 relates to enhanced financial disclosures.

The act was originally passed in response to a wave of major corporate scandals, including Enron and WorldCom, and to a wave of bankruptcies related to the 2001 recession. The main goal was to help restore confidence in financial statements; hence, its main focus is on making corporate officers personally responsible for their company's financial statements. It also imposes requirements that affect every single business process in the organization that feeds into the financial statements.

The details of SOX are so numerous that they are discussed separately in a subsequent chapter. Suffice it to say here that almost half of SOX is devoted to establishing the Public Accounting Company Oversight Board, which in effect is granted authority that already existed within the SEC, and that it is dominated by nonaccountants. The act also requires corporate audit boards to be dominated by individuals who have no experience in the business. These and other provisions of the act have led to its harsh criticisms by many in the business community.

Critics have complained bitterly about the increased reporting requirements mandated by Section 404 of the act. By some estimates, Section 404 first-year compliance costs for all publicly traded companies averaged $2 million, and these costs were as much as $30 million for large corporations such as GE. In effect, SOX's main effect on criminal liability is not to create new crimes but to increase penalties for crimes such as mail and wire fraud, which were increased from 5 to 20 years in prison, for example. The act does, however, establish criminal liability (10 to 20 years in prison) for corporate officers who either fail to certify or improperly certify the financial statements of their companies. The act also makes it a crime (with 5 years in prison) for an independent auditor not to maintain its working papers from an audit for 5 years.

Federal Computer Intrusions Laws

The list of U.S.C. statutes pertaining to computer crime is enormous and too large even to list here. However, some major congressional acts that specifically target computer crimes and information security follow.

- **18 U.S.C 1030: Computer Fraud and Abuse Act**   Adopted in 1984 and amended in 1986, this act was the first major federal computer crimes act. In general, it protects government computers; computers important to national security, to foreign relations, and to certain atomic energy data; computers of financial institutions; computers related to credit reports; and certain designated "protected computers" used in interstate or foreign commerce, government, and financial institutions. Specific crimes under the act include accessing a computer without authorization, trafficking in passwords, participating in electronic espionage, browsing government computers, engaging in extortion related to computers, and stealing protected computers. Penalties under this act range up to 20 years in prison. For example, the penalty is 20 years for one who "knowingly causes the transmission of a program, information, code, or command, and as a result of such conduct, intentionally causes damage without authorization, to a protected computer."

- **Electronic Communications Privacy Act of 1986**   An amendment to the Federal Wiretap Act, this act adds electronic communications.

- **U.S. Communications Assistance for Law Enforcement Act of 1994**   This act amended the Electronic Communications Privacy Act to require all communications providers to make wiretaps available to law enforcement agencies upon the presentation of a court order.

- **Economic and Protection of Proprietary Information Act of 1996**   As an amendment to industrial espionage laws, this act includes theft of electronic data.

- **Health Insurance Portability and Accountability Act of 1996**   This act sets standards for protecting health records in organizations that transmit them electronically.

- **National Information Infrastructure Protection Act of 1996**   Amending the Computer Fraud and Abuse Act, this act defines new crimes and extends protection to computers used in foreign or interstate commerce or communication.

- **The Gramm-Leach-Bliley Act of 1999**   This act provides restrictions on financial institutions' ability to provide client information to nonaffiliated third parties.

- **Cyber Security Enhancement Act (Section 225 of the Homeland Security Act of 2002)**   This act provides a safe harbor for good faith emergency disclosures by communication services to government agencies in certain emergencies. It also directs a review of the federal sentencing guidelines for a wide range of computer crimes.

- **Department of Homeland Security Cybersecurity Enhancement Acts of 2004, 2005, 2006, 2007, 2008, 2009, etc.**   Congress appears to have begun providing regular "cybersecurity enhancement" acts to keep up with issues that relate to rapidly changing technologies. Given the emphasis on antiterrorism, the trend in the new acts has been toward providing authorities more enforcement powers, broader definitions of computer crimes, and more severe penalties. A person does not need to know the details of all of the acts to know that almost any type of crime that in any way involves a computer either belonging to the government, used in foreign or interstate commerce, relating to a financial institution or securities, or involving anything resembling organized crime is likely to trigger criminal liability under a whole group of federal crimes. The list of possibilities for charging seems endless: mail fraud, theft, racketeering, computer crimes, money laundering, wire fraud, fraud against a specially protected organization, conspiracy, corrupt practices, and so on.

Many other acts of Congress not specifically directed at computer crime also make substantial criminal law in the same area. For example, the Uniting and Strengthening America by Providing Appropriate Tools Required to Intercept and Obstruct Terrorism (USA Patriot Act of 2001) contains many provisions that have no direct bearing on terrorism but have wide-ranging impact on the procedures applicable to federal investigations of computer crimes and on substantive criminal law in areas such as money laundering and computer crimes relating to extraterritorial computers. One such procedural change, for example, grants Internet service providers the right to disclose information to law enforcement authorities when there is a reasonable belief that an immediate threat exists that could lead to death or injury. The Patriot Act creates a new crime of money laundering in 18 U.S.C 1956 as a computer crime but does not define what computer-related act must be performed to justify the new charge. However, the new crime is in no way limited to terrorism cases.

Finally, many other congressional acts and U.S.C statutes relate to many types of white-collar crimes. The full list of white-collar crimes includes bribery, antitrust violations, customs fraud, racketeering, obstruction of justice, financial reporting fraud, counterfeiting, credit card fraud, bankruptcy fraud, phone and telemarketing fraud, environmental law violations, health care fraud, mail fraud, embezzlement, insurance fraud, government fraud, tax evasion, securities fraud, financial fraud, insider trading, kickbacks, public corruption, money laundering, trade secret theft, and economic espionage.

Summary

Forensic accountants routinely work in areas of law, so it is important that the forensic accountant have a basic understanding of criminal and civil procedures as well as the different types of crimes that exist. Procedures are especially important because they define the steps that are followed in many cases, from the initial problem and/or investigation until a final resolution.

Four basic sources of law exist: the U.S. Constitution, statutes, case law, and administrative law. Legislators create statutes, appellate court rulings make case law, and, for the most part, government agencies empowered to create rules and regulations to enforce statutes under their authority make administrative law.

Courts interpret the laws. In the federal system, trials are held in the district courts, and appeals are held in the circuit courts of appeal and the U.S. Supreme Court. State courts tend to follow a similar three-tier system.

In criminal cases, initial investigations are carried out by law enforcement officials, who act by collecting evidence and ruling out suspects. Evidence can be collected in many ways that can include interviews, subpoenas, and search warrants. Careful attention is paid to preserving evidence and its chain of custody. Interviews are often directed toward ruling out suspects with consideration being given not only to the physical evidence but also to the fraud triangle—pressure, opportunity, and rationalization.

When sufficient evidence exists, the usual procedure is to make an arrest or refer the matter to a grand jury, which in turn may issue an indictment and lead to a later arrest. Arrests may be made with or without arrest warrants, depending on the jurisdiction in which the arrest is made and the circumstances of the case. After being arrested, suspects become defendants and are booked at a law enforcement facility. The booking process creates a formal arrest record.

Within a business day or two after the arrest, the defendant faces an arraignment hearing in which he or she receives a copy of the charges and enters a plea, and the judge deals with issues such as setting bail, assigning a court-appointed attorney, and setting a tentative trial schedule. Then, a short time later (typically within 30 days), a mini-trial, called a *preliminary hearing,* takes place; at it, the district attorney must demonstrate probable cause to hold the defendant over for trial. Preliminary hearings are not held in all jurisdictions and in all cases, especially not in cases for which an indictment is made by a grand jury.

Before any trial takes place, discovery occurs; it involves the exchange of evidence between the prosecution and the defense. In many jurisdictions, discovery sets a much higher obligation for the prosecution to give evidence to the defense than vice versa.

Before any trial, plea bargaining (in criminal cases) or negotiations (in civil cases) can occur. In the vast majority of criminal cases, the defendant accepts reduced charges or penalties in exchange for pleading guilty.

In most criminal cases, the defendant has the right to a jury trial, and this right is usually invoked because most jury decisions must be unanimous and the defense has a say in the jury selection. Once the jury is seated, the defendant is said to be in *jeopardy,* and the trial typically begins with the opening statements from both the prosecution and the defense, with the prosecution going first. After the opening statements, the prosecution presents its case in chief by calling witnesses for direct testimony. Each witness is then cross-examined by the defense.

Evidence presented in court is subject to rules of evidence, which generally require the content of the evidence to be relevant to the charges and not overly prejudicial or inflammatory. Except for experts, witness testimony is subject to the personal knowledge rule, which limits testimony to things personally known. Attorneys cannot ask leading questions on direct examination, although such questions can be asked on cross-examination. In general, out-of-court statements are not admissible into evidence, although a number of significant exceptions to this rule exist. Finally, establishing a chain of custody is required for tangible exhibits to be admitted.

After the prosecution rests, the defense presents its case through a similar process of calling witnesses for direct testimony and cross-examination. After the defense rests, the prosecution may call rebuttal witnesses when the scope of their testimony is limited to matters covered in the defense's case. Finally, the trial usually winds down with a motion to dismiss (which is almost always denied), followed by closing arguments, instructions to the jury, jury deliberations, and, finally, a verdict.

Regarding crimes, various common-law crimes derive from Old English law and now tend to be universal across all jurisdictions. Each type of common-law crime has specific elements. For example, burglary involves the element of unlawfully entering a building or similar structure with the intent of committing some crime. The intent element is important; without it, some lesser charge, such as trespassing, could apply. Conspiracy is an especially encompassing common-law crime because individuals can be guilty of conspiracy even if the planned crime is impossible to carry out or if it is not carried out because the conspiracy is abandoned.

Regarding federal crimes, Congress passes many acts that modify various parts of the United States Code (U.S.C), which is organized according to titles, topics, and Title 18, which deals primarily with crimes. Other titles also deal with crimes.

In some cases, single acts of Congress affect many titles and sections of the U.S.C. Some of the acts discussed in the chapter include the Racketeer Influenced and Corrupt Organizations Act, the Foreign Corrupt Practices Act, the Sarbanes-Oxley Act, and various acts relating to computer intrusions. Among these acts, SOX has had the most pronounced influence on accounting since the Securities Exchange Act of 1934.

Glossary

administrative law   Source of law that stems from government agencies.

affidavit   Sworn statement often made by law enforcement officers to obtain search warrants.

arraignment   Proceeding in which a criminal defendant is brought before a judge and receives a written copy of the charges to which the defendant enters a plea of guilty or not guilty.

arrest   Procedure in which a defendant is formally detained and then booked at a law enforcement facility.

arrest record   Record created when a defendant is formally booked at a law enforcement facility.

arrest warrant   Order by a court to arrest someone.

bench trial   Trial with a judge but no jury.

booking   Procedure in which an arrest record is created and for which law enforcement takes the accused person's fingerprints and photograph.

burden of proof   Requirement in criminal trials that the prosecutor must prove the defendant guilty beyond a reasonable doubt; in civil trials, only a preponderance of the evidence is required for conviction.

case law   Source of law that results from the decisions of appellate courts.

chain of custody   Careful record that accounts for custody of evidence between the time of its collection and its presentation at trial.

citation   Alternative to an arrest procedure in which a law enforcement agent gives an accused a written document that indicates the charges.

closing argument   Final argument made by each side in a trial proceeding.

common-law crime   Type of crime, generally derived from old English law, that exists almost universally in law.

Computer Fraud and Abuse Act   First major federal computer crime act that in general protects government computers; those important to national security, to foreign relations, and to certain atomic energy data; computers of financial institutions; computers related to credit reports; and certain designated "protected computers" used in interstate or foreign commerce, government, and financial institutions.

constitutional law   One of the different sources of law in the United States, and which is derived from the U.S. Constitution.

cross-examination   In a trial, the first round of questioning of a witness by the opposing attorney.

direct examination   In a trial, the first round of questioning of a witness by the attorney calling the witness to testify.

discovery   Outside-of-trial process by which opposing sides obtain evidence or potential evidence from each other.

district attorney   Prosecutor in criminal proceedings who is said to represent "the people" in bringing a case against a defendant.

double jeopardy   Process of being tried for the same crime twice, which is not permitted under the Fifth Amendment of the U.S. Constitution, although individuals may be tried separately in state and federal courts for the same crime. Once the jury is seated in a jury trial or when the first witness takes the stand in a bench trial, the criminal defendant is said to be in jeopardy, and after that point, the defendant cannot be retried for the same crime if there is a verdict of not guilty or the judge dismisses the case.

element   Item that must be present for an individual to be found guilty.

expert witness   Individual so qualified to be permitted to give opinions in court.

felony charge   Criminal charge that could result in a prison sentence of more than one year.

Foreign Corrupt Practices Act (FCPA)   Congressional act originally designed to inhibit an organization from paying bribes to foreign governments and then covering them up in the accounting records; requires companies to maintain adequate records and internal controls.

fraud triangle   Three things generally present in most crimes: pressure, opportunity, and rationalization.

fruit of the poisonous tree   Legal doctrine that excludes from evidence anything obtained as a result of improperly obtained evidence.

grand jury   Group of citizens called to meet, generally in secret, to investigate whether criminal charges should be filed against an individual; empowered to subpoena documents and require testimony; sometimes investigates matters of general public interest. In the federal system, felony charges can be brought only via a grand jury indictment.

hearsay statement   Information overheard by a potential witness in a trial that is generally excluded from evidence with exceptions including dying declarations, excited utterances, defendant admissions, statements that show someone's state of mind, written government and business records, and prior inconsistent statements. The state-of-mind exception generally allows any type of out-of-court statement(s) that show a person's emotions, beliefs, or intent despite their being made out of court if they are otherwise admissible.

identity theft   Process in which a criminal assumes part or all of a victim's identity, generally for purposes such as stealing funds from the victim's bank account or fraudulently obtaining credit in the victim's name.

investigative subpoena   Legal request for records frequently made by law enforcement officers as part of criminal investigations; generally, the officer making the request must have probable cause that the target has committed some crime; can require the approval of a judge in some jurisdictions.

jury instruction   Formal instruction given to the jury at the end of a jury trial before the jury begins deliberations; relates to the legal principles to be applied to the case. Often these instructions are complex and difficult for juries to understand because they tend to be based on wordings from previous appellate court decisions. Instructions are critical because they typically define the elements of the crimes (or civil wrongs) under consideration, the definition of reasonable doubt, permissible considerations in evaluating the credibility of the witnesses, and the mechanics of the deliberations.

leading question   Question that suggests a particular answer; prohibited from being asked by the attorney on direct examination but not on cross-examination.

motion *in limine*   Request of the defendant to the judge to exclude from the trial anticipated evidence such as information that that the defendant was previously convicted of a crime.

opening statement   Statement presenting a roadmap of the case that the attorneys intend to present to the judge or jury.

personal knowledge rule   Rule of evidence that prevents nonexpert witnesses from testifying about matters that they did not directly observe with their own senses.

plea bargain   Agreement between the prosecution and defense that typically reduces charges in exchange for a guilty plea.

preliminary hearing   Mini-trial type of event in which a judge decides whether there is sufficient evidence to hold a formal trial against a criminal defendant.

privileged   Type of communication between individuals that is not subject to discovery or required disclosure in court; laws defining it can vary considerably from one jurisdiction to the next but include attorney-client, spouse-spouse, doctor-patient, psychoanalyst-patient, clergy-congregant, and accountant-client in certain tax matters.

probable cause   Not an exact legal standard; represents what might be a reasonable basis to believe that a suspect may have committed a crime; a much lower standard than "beyond a reasonable doubt" and that can be based on things that could seem dubious, such as an anonymous tip.

prosecutor   Attorney for the government (people) in criminal proceedings.

Racketeer Influenced and Corrupt Organizations Act (RICO)   Act that lists more than 30 different state and federal crimes for which the violation of any two in a related pattern over a 10-year period can lead to criminal and/or civil liability with criminal penalties of fines up to $25,000 and 20 years in prison; part of the Organized Crime Control Act (OCCA) of 1970.

rebuttal witness   Witness through whom the prosecution seeks to impeach the evidence presented in the defense case after the defense rests, the scope of which is limited to attacking evidence presented in the defense case.

recross-examination   Second cross-examination after a redirect examination.

redirect examination   Second direct examination after cross-examination.

rules of evidence   In criminal trials, the rules that control both the content of the evidence and the manner in which it is presented; set forth in statutory codes in the federal government and in most states.

Sarbanes-Oxley (SOX) Act A complex U.S. congressional act that added and changed many laws aimed mainly at preventing and punishing various types of financial statement fraud among public companies.

search warrant Court order that permits law enforcement authorities to search for and seize evidence.

statute Codified law that is adopted by some legistative body.

statutory law One of the different sources of law in the United States.

Title 18 of the U.S. Code Part of the United States Code devoted mostly to criminal matters.

trial court Lower court that decides facts and applies the law.

United States Code Codified source of statutory laws in the U.S. federal government.

U.S. circuit court of appeal Court in the U.S. federal court system that hears appeals over points of law from lower courts.

U.S. Constitution Supreme law in the United States.

U.S. district court Trial court in the federal court system.

U.S. Supreme Court Highest court in the United States.

working paper Document with notes that an accountant maintains as part of a client engagement.

Review Questions

1. The usual penalty in a civil case is:
   a. Monetary damages.
   b. Imprisonment.
   c. Equitable relief.
   d. Any of the above.
   e. Only *a* and *c.*
2. The burden of proof in a criminal case is:
   a. Beyond a reasonable doubt.
   b. The preponderance of the evidence.
   c. More than 50 percent of the evidence.
   d. 100 percent assurance.
   e. Probable cause.
   f. All of the above.
3. Which of the following is/are a source of law in the United States?
   a. Case law.
   b. Constitutional law.
   c. Administrative law.
   d. Statutory law.
   e. *a*, *b*, and *d* only.
   f. All of the above.
4. The first 10 amendments to the U.S. Constitution are commonly referred to as:
   a. The Privileges and Immunities clauses.
   b. The Bill of Rights.
   c. The enabling clauses.
   d. The Declaration of Independence.

5. Direct appeals of U.S. district court cases are heard by the:
   a. U.S. Supreme Court.
   b. State supreme court.
   c. U.S. district court of appeals
   d. Original trial judge.
   e. All of the above.

6. Which of the following has the discretion to bring charges against a suspect?
   a. Judge.
   b. Prosecutor.
   c. Defense attorney.
   d. Grand jury.
   e. Either *b* or *d*.
   f. None of the above.

7. Which of the following elements must be present in a criminal matter?
   a. Intent.
   b. Premeditation.
   c. Guilty act.
   d. Damages.
   e. All of the above.
   f. *a* and *c*.

8. Which of the following does *not* occur at an arraignment?
   a. Bail is set.
   b. Defendant enters a plea.
   c. Prosecutor presents the defendant a written list of the charges being brought.
   d. Pretrial motions are heard.
   e. Defendant may request a court-appointed lawyer.

9. What is name of the process by which the judge could rule out certain evidence?
   a. *Voir dire*.
   b. Motion *in limine*.
   c. Double jeopardy.
   d. Exclusionary process.
   e. *Prima facie* process.

10. Which of the following is/are an exception to the hearsay rule?
    a. Dying declaration.
    b. State of mind.
    c. Business and governmental records.
    d. Excited utterance.
    e. Prior inconsistent statements.
    f. All of the above.

11. Identify the communication(s) not privileged.
    a. Doctor-patient.
    b. Spouse-spouse.
    c. Teacher-student.

    d. Clergy-congregant.

    e. Attorney-client.

    f. All of the above.

12. The crime of intentionally and permanently converting another's property to one's own use is:

    a. Burglary.

    b. Embezzlement.

    c. Larceny.

    d. Robbery.

    e. Fraud.

    f. Extortion.

13. The crime of using the threat of force to gain some benefit from a victim is:

    a. Robbery.

    b. Extortion.

    c. Larceny.

    d. Embezzlement.

    e. Fraud.

    f. Aiding and abetting.

Please revise any false statement to make it true:

14. In a criminal investigation, the prosecutor represents the interest of the defrauded party.

15. In a criminal case, there is no constitutional right to a jury trial.

16. A state constitution may not override the U.S. Constitution.

17. A U.S. district court is considered a trial court.

18. The judge is responsible for deciding which charges are brought against a defendant in a criminal matter.

19. A search warrant or arrest warrant is always required before arresting a suspect.

20. More than one charge may be brought against a suspect in a certain situation.

21. Suspects are entitled to an attorney before being booked for a crime.

22. Discovery in a criminal trial usually favors the defense.

23. Hearsay evidence is not allowed at a preliminary hearing.

24. The defense is not required to call any witnesses on the defendant's behalf.

25. A jury verdict of not guilty in a criminal case may be appealed by the prosecution.

26. Generally, an attorney is allowed to ask leading questions of a witness.

27. Attorney-client privilege extends to the forensic accountant hired by the attorney.

28. All communication between an attorney and a client are privileged.

29. Recruiting or hiring someone to commit a crime is called *aiding and abetting*.

30. To be convicted of 18 U.S.C 96 (RICO), at least two federal or state crimes must be committed.

Discussion Questions

31. What does the term *full faith and credit* mean as indicated in the Article 4 of the U.S. Constitution?

32. Explain the concept of *double jeopardy*.

33. Explain how the concept of preemption applies when there is a conflict between local laws, state laws, and federal laws.

34. Discuss how case law evolves. In other words, once a case has been decided, what would be the process for changing the result?

35. Who is responsible for enforcing administrative laws?

36. Explain the jurisdictional limitations of the federal courts.

37. Discuss the rights, duties, and obligations of a forensic accountant hired to assist in a civil or criminal investigation.

38. What are the elements of the fraud triangle?

39. Is a search warrant always required to obtain evidence?

40. What is the fruit of the poisonous tree doctrine?

41. What is the purpose of discovery?

42. Why is hearsay allowed in a preliminary hearing?

43. What is the *voir dire* process?

44. What options does a defense attorney have to counter the testimony of a witness?

45. Discuss the importance of jury instructions.

46. Discuss the rules of evidence.

47. What element is common to the crimes of solicitation, arson, forgery, and burglary?

48. Discuss the consequences of violating the Sarbanes-Oxley Act of 2002.

49. Compare and contrast the role of the forensic accountant in the investigation of a civil matter as compared to a criminal matter. Are there any similarities in the nature of the investigations? Are the goals of the investigations the same? Is there any specific training a forensic accountant would need to conduct the different investigations?

50. Suppose the laws of a certain state require the use of either a Subchapter S corporation or a limited partnership in operating an accounting practice. What happens if the U.S. Constitution is amended prohibiting accounting firms from operating as limited partnerships? What options would an existing accounting firm have once the constitution is amended? Would the firm be required to change its method of operation?

51. Why are the legal standards different for criminal and civil matters? Separately identify the differences between these two types of matters from the perspectives of the defendant and the plaintiff/prosecutor.

52. In the investigation of a criminal or civil matter, how does the forensic accountant obtain the necessary information? Discuss the use of all investigative tools, including the subpoena, the grand jury, and the search warrant.

53. Why is bail required? Are there any mitigating factors that could decrease the amount of bail? Are there any charges for which there is no bail? What protection does a bail bond seller have?

54. Discuss the constitutional right of a defendant to have a jury trial. Are there instances when a defendant would prefer to have a trial by judge? Would the prosecutor have a preference? Discuss the benefits and detriments of both jury and judge trials from each perspective.

55. Which side has the burden of proof in a trial? Are there instances when the burden lies with the opposite party? Are there instances when the burden lies with both parties?

56. Why does the hearsay rule exist? When are exceptions to the hearsay rule allowed? Is there any consistency between the rule and exceptions; in other words, can you devise an explanation as to why allowing exceptions to the hearsay rule does not violate the rationale for it?

57. Discuss different crimes that have arisen because of the use of computers. Is the common theme of these crimes the use of a computer or the underlying act that is involved? Would any of these crimes still exist if accomplished without the use of a computer?

58. Review each of the amendments (the Bill of Rights) to the U.S. Constitution on the next page. Evaluate each amendment and explain how its provisions would affect both a prosecutor and a defense attorney.

59. Research the fraud triangle. Specifically look for its application to accountants (the AICPA Web site is www.aicpa.org). Discuss specific steps the forensic accountant could take in each area of the triangle to combat fraud.

60. Find examples of each of the following as it pertains to the role of a forensic accountant:

    Statutory law.

    Administrative law.

    Constitutional law.

    Case law.

61. You are studying for your criminal law final. To help you prepare for your exam, you created flashcards identifying different steps in the criminal process. Arrange the cards so they are in the order in which they occur in the criminal process. Attach a brief explanation of each step. The cards in alphabetical order are:

    - Appeal
    - Arraignment
    - Arrest
    - Closing argument
    - Discovery
    - Opening argument
    - Plea bargain
    - Pretrial motion
    - Search warrant

Bill of Rights

Amendment I

Congress shall make no law respecting an establishment of religion, or prohibiting the free exercise thereof; or abridging the freedom of speech, or of the press; or the right of the people peaceably to assemble, and to petition the Government for a redress of grievances.

Amendment II

A well regulated Militia, being necessary to the security of a free State, the right of the people to keep and bear Arms, shall not be infringed.

Amendment III

No Soldier shall, in time of peace be quartered in any house, without the consent of the Owner, nor in time of war, but in a manner to be prescribed by law.

Amendment IV

The right of the people to be secure in their persons, houses, papers, and effects, against unreasonable searches and seizures, shall not be violated, and no Warrants shall issue, but upon probable cause, supported by Oath or affirmation, and particularly describing the place to be searched, and the persons or things to be seized.

Amendment V

No person shall be held to answer for a capital, or otherwise infamous crime, unless on a presentment or indictment of a Grand Jury, except in cases arising in the land or naval forces, or in the Militia, when in actual service in time of War or public danger; nor shall any person be subject for the same offence to be twice put in jeopardy of life or limb; nor shall be compelled in any criminal case to be a witness against himself, nor be deprived of life, liberty, or property, without due process of law; nor shall private property be taken for public use, without just compensation.

Amendment VI

In all criminal prosecutions, the accused shall enjoy the right to a speedy and public trial, by an impartial jury of the State and district wherein the crime shall have been committed, which district shall have been previously ascertained by law, and to be informed of the nature and cause of the accusation; to be confronted with the witnesses against him; to have compulsory process for obtaining witnesses in his favor, and to have the Assistance of Counsel for his defence.

Amendment VII

In Suits at common law, where the value in controversy shall exceed twenty dollars, the right of trial by jury shall be preserved, and no fact tried by a jury, shall be otherwise re-examined in any court of the United States, than according to the rules of the common law.

Amendment VIII

Excessive bail shall not be required, nor excessive fines imposed, nor cruel and unusual punishments inflicted.

Amendment IX

The enumeration in the Constitution, of certain rights, shall not be construed to deny or disparage others retained by the people.

Amendment X

The powers not delegated to the United States by the Constitution, nor prohibited by it to the States, are reserved to the States respectively, or to the people.

Chapter **Three**

Fundamentals I: Accounting Information Systems

CHAPTER LEARNING OBJECTIVES

After reading Chapter 3, you should be able to:

- LO1: Explain the meaning of business processes.
- LO2: Identify and explain the basic transaction cycles.
- LO3: Define and explain business processes.
- LO4: Apply internal control principles to business situations.
- LO5: Define *systems development* and discuss major development issues.

BUSINESS AND INTERNAL CONTROL PROCESSES

LO1   To work effectively, all types of accountants, including forensic accountants, must be familiar with accounting information systems (AIS). Long gone are the days in which the accounting system was based on a set of "books" that could be locked in a safe. Today accountants deal with ever-more-sophisticated electronic systems that not only keep records and produce financial reports but also automatically make programmed management decisions. For example, a sales order system could automatically do all the following: take orders over the Web, check and approve customers' credit, schedule goods for shipping, electronically invoice customers, electronically collect payments, and automatically issue credits to customers' accounts. The system could, in a similar fashion, automatically handle all tasks relating to reordering inventory, receiving goods, paying vendors, and so on.

Given their sophistication and complexity, accountants typically work with AIS in pieces, focusing on one piece at a time. For example, accountants seeking to improve the overall efficiency of the AIS might focus on one high-priority component, perhaps the inventory management system. This in turn could lead to more optimal reorder levels, faster inventory turnover, reduced inventory obsolescence, fewer stock outs, and so on.

One problem, however, in optimizing an inventory system is that the tasks and activities relating to inventories can be spread across many departments. For example, despite the existence of a separate inventory department, the sales office could make the decisions regarding when to reorder inventory and how much to reorder. This leads to the conclusion that it is generally ineffective to divide the AIS into pieces along the lines of the company's organization chart. Instead, accountants generally find it more useful to divide the

AIS into various interrelated business processes. A **business process** is a set of coordinated activities and tasks that accomplish some organizational goal.

There is no one right way to divide a company's AIS into component business processes. For example, a sales order process could be defined to include everything from taking the sales order to collecting the customer's payment on account. Alternatively, it could simply be defined as only taking the order and shipping the goods.

One traditional approach is to divide the major operational activities into four **transaction cycles** (Figure 3.1): revenue, expenditures, production, and finance. The revenue cycle begins with a customer order and ends with the receipt of the customer payment. This business process is called a *cycle* because it repeats itself over and over again with each new sales order.

LO2   A similar pattern of repetition applies to the expenditure, production, and finance cycles. The typical expenditure cycle begins with a purchase requisition and ends with a payment to the vendor. The production cycle generally begins with a production requisition and ends with the finished goods being sent to the customer. Finally, the normal finance cycle begins with the collection of cash from customers and ends with the payment for the goods sold to customers. This means that the finance cycle can be viewed as a separate cycle in and of itself, or its cash receipts activity can be viewed as part of the revenue cycle, while its cash payments activity can be viewed as part of the expenditure cycle. Either view is perfectly acceptable.

FIGURE 3.1
Transaction Cycles

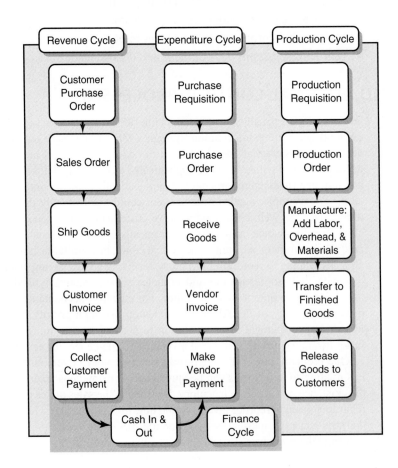

FIGURE 3.2   **SAP ERP Functional Areas**

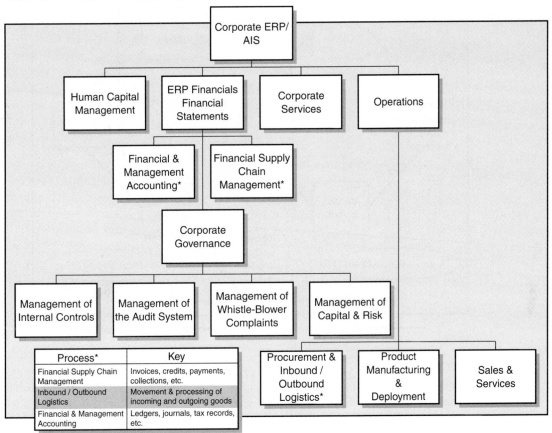

In practice, companies tend to develop their information systems in a modular fashion. For example, SAP, one of the world's largest information systems software vendors, breaks its enterprise resource planning (ERP) system into the modules shown in Figure 3.2. In this schema, the revenue, expenditure, production, and finance transaction cycles are found under Operations and ERP Financials. More specifically, the four transaction cycles are found in the four SAP modules, Financial Supply Chain Management, Procurement and Inbound/Outbound Logistics, Product Manufacturing and Deployment, and Sales and Services.

The four SAP modules collectively contain the same tasks and activities found in the four transaction cycles; however, none of the four SAP modules directly corresponds to any one of the four. This is so because the SAP modules are defined more along functional lines. For example, Financial Supply Chain Management focuses specifically on credit, collections, payments, and other financial activities. Similarly, Procurement and Inbound/Outbound Logistics focuses on the physical acquisition and movement of materials and physical goods.

See Figure 3.3 for both the transaction cycle and SAP functional views for the revenue and expenditure cycles. Note that most of the revenue and expenditure cycle activities correspond to the SAP Financial Supply Chain, and the shipping and receiving of goods corresponds to SAP's Inbound/Outbound Logistics.

Neither the SAP view nor the transaction cycle view is inherently better than the other. In fact, the SAP ERP system modules blend together to form a single integrated system,

FIGURE 3.3
Functional versus
Process Orientation

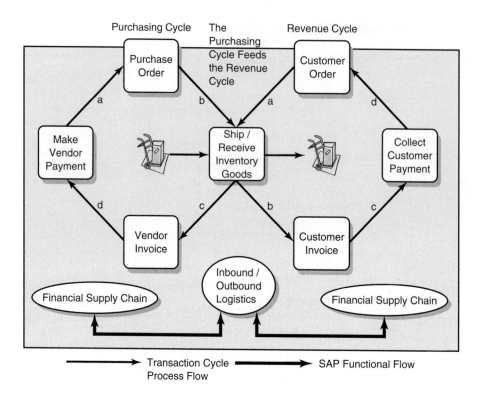

so any view of the business processes in an SAP ERP system is somewhat artificial, as it is in any system. The main reason the SAP view is presented here is because the SAP ERP system is so dominant in large businesses and because it represents one good model to help conceptualize business processes.

In practice, the view chosen to model business processes depends much on the type of work being done and the specific objectives of that work. **Audit work,** for example, concerns verifying numbers in the financial statements, so auditors are concerned with the flow of transactions through the accounts and into the financial statements, as depicted in Figure 3.4. **System engineering and development work,** on the other hand, concerns optimizing system performance, so systems engineers are concerned with more narrowly defined processes, such as the customer service process depicted in Figure 3.5. However, system engineers also are concerned with broader processes, including those corresponding to the transactions cycles.

The Internal Control Process

LO3   **Internal control** is a process effected by management, the board of directors, and other personnel that is designed to minimize risk exposures to an acceptable level given the company's objectives. **Risk exposures** include events that can adversely affect the company, such as asset losses due to theft or spoilage, accounting errors and their consequences, revenue losses, expense overruns, business interruptions, fraud and embezzlement, fines and penalties, civil liabilities, and losses of competitive advantage.

The internal control process is so important that for public companies both the Foreign Corrupt Practices Act and the Sarbanes-Oxley Act hold the chief executive officer (CEO) and the chief financial officer (CFO) criminally liable for weak internal control processes. These acts of Congress were passed in part because of a general public perception that

FIGURE 3.4 **How Transactions Flow through Accounts**

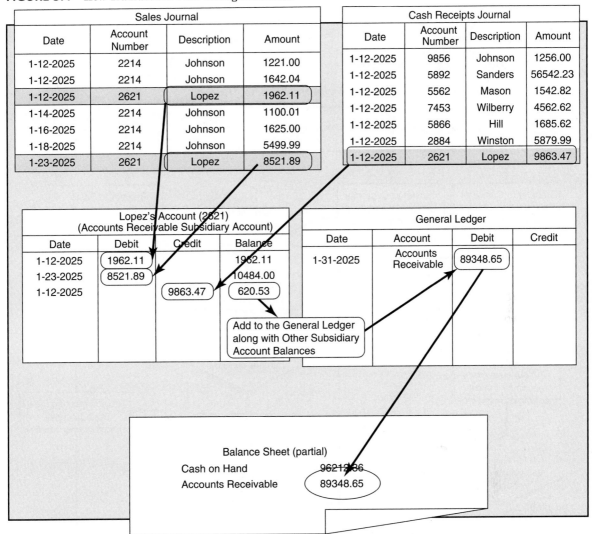

weak controls tend to lead to various types of management fraud, including bribes to foreign governments and fraudulent financial reporting. Such frauds in turn tend to lead to massive losses for creditors and shareholders.

Internal control is process oriented. It focuses on the processes by which the company is run rather than on the outcomes of the processes. For example, management's decision to launch a new product in a highly uncertain market would not normally indicate unsatisfactory internal control processes, even though it might be a bad business decision. On the other hand, such a decision could be a symptom of poor internal control if, for example, it were made in violation to the company's strategic plans, without proper internal authorizations and approvals, or without giving any thought to the risks involved. In other words, good internal control permits management to freely make decisions in accordance with the company's risk preferences, but such decisions must be made within some reasonable set of processes for making and evaluating decisions.

FIGURE 3.5   **Flowchart for a Customer Service Process**

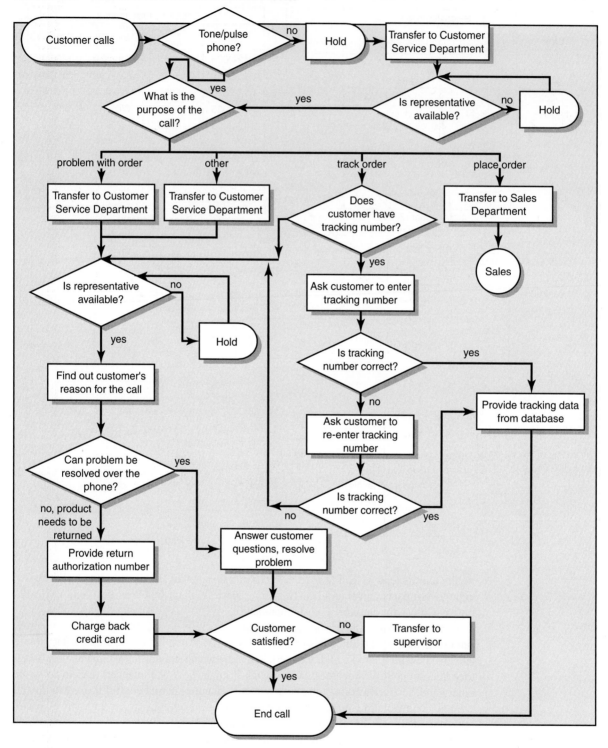

Internal controls, the specific policies and procedures that make up internal control processes, can be viewed as loss prevention tools. That is, the application of a given internal control procedure prevents losses due to risk exposures. For example, credit approval policies represent controls that prevent losses due to defaults on customer accounts. Likewise, the procedure of placing inventories behind locked doors prevents inventory thefts.

Internal controls almost never perfectly prevent all losses. For example, credit policies generally do not prevent all bad debts, nor should they because overly strict credit policies result in turning away good customers. Instead, optimal credit policies balance the costs of their implementation against the risks of the losses they prevent.

The general rule is that internal controls must provide a **reasonable assurance** (rather than a perfect assurance) that they will achieve their objectives. That is, they must reflect a balance between the benefits of reducing risk exposures versus the costs of implementing the controls. This means that internal control processes must be designed within the context of management's enterprise risk management (ERM) system. ERM involves weighing various opportunities against related risks, and managing the opportunities and risks in a way that is consistent with management's objectives and risk preferences.

When viewed within the context of ERM, management's selection of internal control processes simply represents just another business decision. Once such a decision is made and implemented, however, management must abide by the control processes it has chosen if it is to have any chance of complying with federal laws and acceptable accounting practices. Of course, management is always free to change its control processes, but even doing that must be done through reasonable, prescribed processes.

Although internal control processes leave management free to make decisions, they do impose certain constraints on those decisions. First, by law (e.g., the Sarbanes-Oxley Act) management cannot design and maintain internal control processes that are not considered to be consistent with reasonable business practices. Second, management cannot hide the risks associated with its business decisions, for the SEC requires that management report major business risks in the annual 10K report.

Components of Internal Control Processes

As discussed, the general objective of the internal control process is to reduce risk exposures to an acceptable level. **Specific objectives of internal control** include the following:

- Ensuring the integrity and reliability of the financial reports.
- Ensuring compliance with applicable laws, regulations, professional rules, and contractual obligations.
- Promoting strategic, tactical, and operational efficiency and effectiveness.

Achieving these three objectives requires a broad, encompassing view of internal control that requires not only specific policies and procedures but also a control-conscious corporate culture and the right type of leadership from the CEO, CFO, and board of directors.

The **main components of effective internal control processes** are the control environment, **risk assessment and management,** control activities, information and communication, and monitoring. Each component is discussed.

The Control Environment

The **control environment** represents the overall atmosphere in which employees operate. It consists of the following elements.

Management Philosophy and Operating Style   Management sets the tone at the top. Therefore, it is essential that the CEO and CFO not only show respect for all internal controls but also actively engage in the ongoing design and management of the internal control processes.

Ethics and the Corporate Culture   The company should have an ethics director and an ethics code of conduct as well as ongoing training programs to ensure awareness and compliance. Employees should be encouraged to recognize questionable situations and to consult the ethics director for guidance. An ethics-driven corporate culture is achieved when the employees feel that ethical behavior is in both their interests and the company's interests.

A whistle-blower system should be in place that promotes whistle-blowing and protects whistle-blowers.

Corporate cultures should be periodically audited by using interviews and questionnaires to review ethics policies and compliance with them.

Clearly Assigned Employee Responsibilities   One of the most fundamental concepts of internal control is that of employee charge and discharge. This means that employees are charged with individual responsibilities and then held accountable for their actions and performance in relation to those responsibilities. Without charge and discharge, it can be impossible or unnecessarily difficult for management to take corrective action when an internal control problem arises. For example, assume that two cashiers work out of a shared cash box so that neither one is charged with the full responsibility for the cash. In this case, it will be impossible to pinpoint individual responsibility in the event of a cash shortage, leaving no reasonable way for management to take corrective action.

The careful assignment of individual responsibilities deals with the "charge" through budgetary controls that hold employees accountable to predefined levels of revenues or costs. The discharge component is typically dealt with through report analysis.

Effective and Independent Audit Committee   The company must have an independent audit committee that is a subcommittee of the board of directors. The audit committee should hire and work with external auditors and review and respond to reports of the internal auditor and the chief corporate legal counsel. To achieve and maintain their independence, members of the audit committee should not receive any compensation from the company except for their work on the audit committee.

Effective and Independent Internal Audit Function   The internal auditor should ensure compliance with all internal control processes. This person should report directly to the board of directors (typically to the audit committee) but should *not* report to the CEO, CFO, or other members of top management.

Effective Human Resource Policies and Procedures   Proper human resources management must be exercised in the following areas: hiring, assignment of responsibilities, training, supervision, and even vacations. Appropriate background checks should be made when hiring employees, and in some cases employees who handle cash or other liquid assets should be fidelity bonded. A *fidelity bond* is a contract with an insurance company that covers any losses due to employee theft from the company. Fidelity bonding companies are especially good at performing employee background checks.

Training programs must prepare employees to be competent to efficiently and effectively carry out their duties. Inability of employees to do so creates risk exposures. For example, a salesperson who makes inaccurate product claims can subject the company to fines or lawsuits. Similarly, an improperly trained production worker might incorrectly assemble the product, which in turn could lead to losing customers because of their resulting dissatisfaction.

Adequate supervision is critical to the effective charge and discharge of employee responsibilities.

It is customary practice to require employees to take vacations. In many types of employee frauds, such as embezzlement, the cover-up is much more difficult than the fraud itself. Mandatory vacations can often expose the cover-up. For example, in one case, a bank employee was stealing money from dormant accounts. When the employee went on vacation, another employee questioned a memo that came across her desk, and that led to uncovering the ongoing scheme.

Forced job rotation is similar to mandatory vacations. It too makes cover-ups more difficult.

Risk Assessment and Management

As discussed earlier, management must design its internal control processes in light of the company's ERM system. That is, management must first identify its opportunities and objectives, then define the risks for those opportunities and objectives, and finally design the internal control processes to manage the identified risks. In other words, the company must first have good ERM practices in place before it can design effective internal control processes.

Control Activities

Control activities are the policies and procedures that help ensure that management directives are carried out. Control activities occur at all levels of the organization and encompass almost every activity. The basic accounting control activities are discussed next.

Segregation of Duties   This control activity is the foundation of all internal control processes. It is so fundamental that its absence can render all internal control processes useless. The breakdown of segregation of duties can lead to **collusion** in which the accounting function covers up or overlooks irregularities in the other functions.

Segregation of duties means the separation of the following functions: authorization, custody, and recordkeeping. Specifically, separation of duties means that no individual in the company should perform more than any one of the functions of authorization, custody, or recordkeeping.

Authorization refers to authorization for transactions, including revenue, expenditures, customer credits, account write-offs, asset retirements, security transactions, and all other types of transactions. Examples of authorization for transactions include those shown in Figure 3.6.

Custody usually refers to the direct physical custody of assets. For example, an inventory manager has custody of inventories. Sometimes, however, custody is indirect, as in the case of the treasurer who has signing authority on a company bank account. In this case, the treasurer effectively has custody of cash, even though cash is physically stored in a bank.

Recordkeeping refers to the updating and processing of the accounting records. This function is normally reserved for the accounting staff, sometimes IT staff operating under the authority of the accounting function.

FIGURE 3.6
Authorization of Transactions

Transaction	Authorizing Person	Authorizing Document
Customer sales	Salesperson	Sales order
Reorder inventory	Purchasing officer	Purchase order
Retire obsolete computer	Plant and equipment manager	Equipment removal form
Vendor payment	Treasurer's assistant	Payment voucher

The **golden rule of separation of duties** is that the accounting staff should never have even temporary control over operational resources, including cash, checks, and other assets, or the authority to authorize sales, purchases, customer credits, or other transactions. Accountants should only maintain the information system including the accounting records. See Figure 3.7 for examples of activities that would be incompatible for accountants.

The golden rule centers on the accounting function because an intact accounting record can always reveal errors and improprieties to the internal auditor. Stated differently, good accounting records keep snapshots of everything that happens, both the good and the bad, and make it possible to detect and correct problems if not prevent them. On the other hand, if the accounting system is compromised, irregularities are easily covered up. This is why it is so important that accountants remain independent from the authorization and custody functions.

Consider, for example, the proverbial bookkeeper who maintains the accounts receivable records, the company checkbook, the cash account records, and the general ledger. In this case, the bookkeeper has almost unlimited power to steal customer payments on account and cover up the losses by falsifying the accounting records. This situation can be completely avoided by taking the checkbook away from the accountant.

Adequate Documentation and Records As mentioned earlier, accounting keeps a running record of all transactions, and that record, if well kept, normally makes it possible to detect most irregularities. For this reason, the accounting system must record all financial transactions, and the record must include an **audit trail** that permits auditors to trace all account entries back to original source documents. For example, the auditor should be able to trace the write-off of Jane Doe's account balance back to a written (or computerized) authorization from the credit department. A good audit trail permits an auditor to trace any balance in any account, including the general ledger, back to their original source transactions.

Records must also be kept not only for transactions with external entities but also for transactions that occur solely within the company. Examples of such internal transactions

FIGURE 3.7
Incompatible Activities for the Accounting Function

Activities Incompatible with the Accounting Function	Proper Person to Authorize	Comment
Approve customer line of credit	Credit department within the finance function	Accountants keep the accounts receivable ledgers but do not grant credit.
Approve credit to customer's account	Credit department within the finance function	Accountants keep the accounts receivable ledgers but do not approve credits to customer accounts.
Purchase raw materials	Purchasing department	The requisition can originate in the production department, but the purchasing department has the final approval.
Pay vendor	Treasury department	The accounting staff should never have access to the cash account.

include interdepartmental transfers and services. Also, certain nontransaction records, such as records relating to internal control violations and whistle-blower complaints, must be kept.

Finally, management must maintain general documentation, including a current, well-defined organization chart, up-to-date policy and procedure manuals, written plans, and so on. The board of directors should also maintain proper records, including minutes of meetings, an up-to-date copy of the corporate charter including all amendments, adequate shareholder records, and communications with management, internal auditors, and external auditors.

Controlled Access to Assets   Access to all company assets must be granted only in accordance with management's authorization. Controlling access to assets requires adequate physical and procedural controls, including, for example, physical access controls (e.g., locked doors), computer and network access controls (e.g., passwords), close supervision, and segregation of duties.

Independent Accountability Checks and Reviews of Performance   Under the supervision of an independent internal audit function, periodic checks should be performed to verify the existence of assets and liabilities on account. The existence of assets is normally verified by performing inventory counts. Liabilities can be verified by reviewing documents and payment records and verifying details with lenders.

All employees should be periodically evaluated according to their assigned responsibilities. Records of the evaluations should be maintained in the human resources department.

Approval and Authorization   All transactions and activities should be properly authorized by management. **Authorization** grants management's permission for the initiation of a transaction. **Approval,** on the other hand, grants management's acceptance of a transaction that has already been authorized. For example, a production manager can have authorization to initiate a purchase requisition, but then the purchase requisition is likely to be subject to approval by the head of the production department and the purchasing department.

Information and Communication

Information primarily relates to the accounting system, and communication relates to the flows of information through the organization. The accounting system should be well documented, beginning with a clearly defined chart of accounts and a system of special journals and subsidiary ledgers as needed. All transactions should be processed on a consistent basis. For example, the purchase of a computer tape should be charged to IT supplies or office supplies, not to plumbing supplies.

All forms (whether paper or electronic) should be clear and simple to minimize input errors, and double checks should be in place to detect input or processing errors.

All transactions and relevant activities should be properly recorded with proper audit trails.

Monitoring

It is not enough just to have good control processes. The processes must be continually monitored and updated as needed. Internal control monitoring is part of the general corporate governance structure and involves the CEO, CFO, chief information officer (CIO), corporate legal counsel, internal auditor, and members of the audit committee. All of these individuals should periodically review reports on the functioning of the internal control process.

Both external and internal audits involve monitoring the internal control processes to assess their reliability and effectiveness. This is normally accomplished by various analytical tools that include reviews of documents, questionnaires, interviews, reviews of the accounts and transaction data, and tests of compliance.

Both internal and external auditors use internal control questionnaires, which include long lists of questions relating to specific controls within specific business processes. For example, questions relating to the handling of cash receipts could include the following:

- Do you make daily intact deposits of each day's receipts?
- Do you restrictively endorse checks "for deposit only"?
- Do you reconcile bank deposit receipts against credits to accounts receivable?

In some cases, auditors enter test transactions into the system and then monitor them for internal control compliance. Internal control compliance and auditing are discussed more thoroughly in subsequent chapters.

TRANSACTION PROCESSING CONTROLS

Transaction processing controls are those controls that are relevant to implementing good internal control processes within specific transaction cycles. General controls and application controls are the two types of transaction processing controls. **General controls** pertain to the overall environment and apply to all transactions. **Application controls,** on the other hand, apply to specific applications, processes, and transactions.

General Controls

General controls include the following:

- The general plan ꞏof organization for data processing should include segregation of duties so that data processing is segregated from other organizational functions. In general, data processing should be viewed as an accounting function; therefore, individuals in data processing should not have operating authorization and custody functions.
- General operating procedures include good documentation, training, and systems for the prevention, detection, and correction of internal control violations. In a perfect world, it would be nice to prevent all problems. When problems do inevitably occur, however, there must be procedures in place to detect and correct them.
- Hardware control policies and procedures limit exposures to hardware problems. For example, regular data backups can permit recovery if an online data storage unit fails.
- General access controls for data and hardware prevent unauthorized changes to critical data.

Application Controls

Application controls can be classified as input, processing, and output controls. These controls ensure the accuracy, integrity, and security of the processes of collecting input data, processing input data, and distributing processed data, respectively.

Accuracy means that data are free from errors. With respect to input controls, accuracy means that no errors are made in capturing transaction data. For example, input controls help ensure accuracy by preventing an employee from entering an incorrect customer account number into the system. With respect to processing controls, accuracy means that no errors are made in processing. For example, processing controls help ensure processing accuracy by double checking an employee's manual payroll calculations. With respect to output controls, accuracy means that no errors exist in reports and other outputs. For example, output controls help ensure accuracy by applying reasonableness checks to internal budget reports before they are distributed.

Integrity means that the data remain intact in that nothing is added to or removed from the transaction data as they pass through the system. With respect to input controls, integrity means that only authorized transactions are captured into the system and that no unauthorized data are added to or removed from the set of authorized transactions. For example, input controls help ensure that no authorized credit approvals are entered into the system. With respect to processing controls, integrity means that no data are added or lost during processing. For example, processing controls should help ensure that no accounts are added or deleted from accounts receivable during batch updates of the accounts receivable subsidiary ledgers. With respect to output controls, integrity means that outputs are not modified in any way before reaching their final destination. For example, output controls should help ensure that payroll checks are not modified before being distributed to employees.

Security in this context means that only authorized persons are granted access to the system. With respect to input controls (see Figure 3.8), security helps ensure that only authorized employees are permitted to enter transactions into the system. For example, input controls help ensure security by limiting access to purchase order forms to authorized employees in the purchasing department. With respect to processing controls (see Figure 3.9), security helps ensure that only authorized persons are able to effect processing. For example, processing controls help ensure security by limiting access to the inner workings of the accounting database system so that only authorized IT personnel can make changes to the data processing software. With respect to output controls (see Figure 3.10), security helps ensure that only authorized persons have access to reports and other outputs. For example, output controls help ensure that internal reports do not end up in the hands of the press. The concept of security is discussed in a much broader context in a later chapter.

Application of Internal Control Principles to the Basic Transaction Cycles

The exact application of internal control principles depends on the specific design of the information system. Controls in manual systems differ from controls in computer-based systems, and those in computer-based systems differ for batch-oriented versus real-time systems. Batch-oriented systems group transactions together and process them at one time. For example, daily sales transactions can be batched together and posted to accounts receivable every night. In real-time systems, however, sales transactions are immediately posted to accounts receivable.

Internal Control in the Revenue Cycle

The revenue cycle in Figure 3.12 shows the flow of tasks and events associated with the revenue cycle in a real-time system. The process begins with a customer sales order and ends with the receipt and recording of the customer payment. All departments have access to a common sales and accounts receivable database. Figure 3.11 summarizes various "control points" that should be applied as the sales order proceeds through the system.

Figure 3.12 and Figure 3.13 show the revenue cycle in a manual and a real-time system, respectively. The control points in the manual system are essentially the same as they are in the real-time system. The main difference in the manual system is that the control point actions rely on the receipt of documents from other departments. The documents are necessary because there is no common shared sales and accounts receivable database. For example, in the real-time system, the shipping department can look in the database to see approved sales orders. However, in the manual system, the shipping department refers instead to a paper copy of the approved sales order.

FIGURE 3.8 **Examples of Input Controls**

Input Control	Example
Approval: Permission for continued processing of an authorized transaction	A sales order is given credit approval.
Authorization: Permission for the initiation of transactions	The credit manager authorizes an account write-off.
Batch control total: Comparison of the total dollar amount of a group of transactions to the total dollar amount posted to the ledger(s)	The total for a given day's credit sales is compared to the total posted to accounts receivable for the same day.
Cancellation: Cancellation of documents so they cannot be used twice	A vendor's invoice is canceled when it is paid.
Document control count: Process of counting the number of a given type of documents to ensure that no documents have been added or lost	The number of purchase orders issued is matched with the number issued from stock.
Endorsement: Process of signing a document to limit or restrict its further processing	A check is restrictively endorsed by stamping "for deposit only" on it.
Format check: Requirement that a particular data item being entered into an electronic or paper system be in a certain format, such as alphabetic, numeric, or a 10-digit phone number	The customer's name on a sales order is checked to make sure that it contains only alphabetic characters.
Hash total: Meaningless total used to ensure that all transactions in a given batch of transactions were processed	When processing payroll the social security numbers of all employees are totaled. This total should always be the same if no employees are added or deleted. The total can be computed for each batch of payroll transactions to ensure that all employees have been processed.
Input exception report: List of transactions that contain input errors	A list of sales orders for which the customer account number is missing is checked.
Key verification: Process of entering transactions into the system twice to determine whether both entries match	At the end of the week, two separate persons enter the number of hours worked for each employee. A discrepancy report is generated for any errors.
Limit check: Check of numerical or alphabetic values to make sure they fall within a prespecified range	The number of hours worked for each employee for a week is checked to make sure it is between 0 and 50.
Reasonableness check: Comparison of the value of one data item in a given transaction to the value of another data item to determine whether the one item is reasonable	In an automobile fleet utilization log, the number of miles driven for a particular automobile is compared to the amount spent for gasoline for the same automobile in the same time period.
Serial numbering: Process of sequentially numbering documents and accounting for all numbered documents	Prenumbered restaurant guest checks are checked to ensure that everyone on the waitstaff has turned in all outstanding guest checks by the end of the shift.
Validity check: Process of checking the value for a given data item using a formula or lookup table	The account code on a purchase requisition is checked against a list of valid account numbers.

FIGURE 3.9
Examples of
Processing Controls

Processing Control	Example
Automatic error correction: Automatic correction of errors or omissions in data values	An account number is entered with unnecessary dashes. The dashes are removed during processing.
Double check: Requirement that trans-actions be processed twice and both sets of processing results compared	The computer processes payroll, and some of its calculations are double-checked by hand.
Matching: Requirement of multiple inputs for a transaction before its processing can be continued	The customer invoicing system requires a matching sales order and shipping report before generating a customer invoice.
Clearing account: Use of a special account to verify proper processing	The total cash for a given payroll is transferred to a clearing account. Paychecks are then charged against that account so that the balance is zero after payroll processing is complete.
Tickler file: Chronological "to do" list that ensures that processing is done according to schedule	Budget reports are automatically printed on the first day of every month.

FIGURE 3.10
Examples of Output
Controls

Output Control	Example
Aging: Arrangement of items according to their chronological age in the system for review and further processing	Accounts receivable are listed according to the number of days each account is overdue.
Audit: Review of system outputs and tracing numbers in reports back to the source transactions	Total sales amount in the annual income statement is verified by reviewing individual sales orders.
Reconciliation: Comparison of one number total to another total to ensure that the two totals agree	Daily receipts for customer payments are compared to the total bank deposits for the same day.

FIGURE 3.11
Internal Control
Points for the
Revenue Cycle

Event	Control Point
Customer entered into the system	Validity checks, limit checks, format and checks, etc. are applied to each data item in the transaction. Customer's credit is verified.
Goods pulled from inventory	Goods are pulled from inventory only for approved sales orders. Goods that are pulled are charged to specific customer orders.
Goods shipped	Goods are shipped only for approved customer orders. Shipping details are noted on customer orders.
Invoice sent to customer	Customers are invoiced only when the customer order record shows an approved sales order and information that the goods have been shipped.
Customer payment received and recorded	Cash receipt is handled by treasury function and applied to the customer account.

FIGURE 3.12 **Manual Sales Order Process**

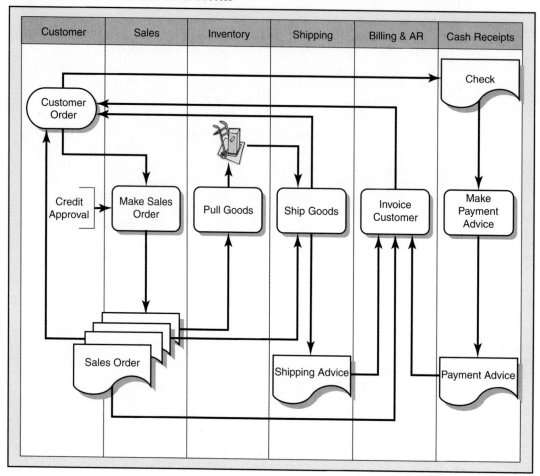

The main control requirements for the documents in the manual system are the prenumbering of documents, all of which must be accounted for, and properly routing and filing them. Except for these differences, the real-time and manual systems essentially share the same control points. In both systems, double checks and batch control totals should be used.

Internal Control in the Expenditure Cycle

Figure 3.14 and Figure 3.15 show the expenditure cycle in manual and real-time systems, respectively. The control points are listed in Figure 3.16.

Again, these same basic control points apply in a manual system except that it requires routing control over various prenumbered documents.

Internal Control in the Production Cycle

Internal control in the production cycle is somewhat similar to internal control in the purchasing cycle, although the exact control system depends on the type of production system. In a simple job-order system in which the production of each item is separately accounted for, the production process begins with a job order. Labor, overhead, and materials are then charged to the job as it progresses through the production process. Control points include

FIGURE 3.13 **Real-Time Sales Order Process (revenue cycle)**

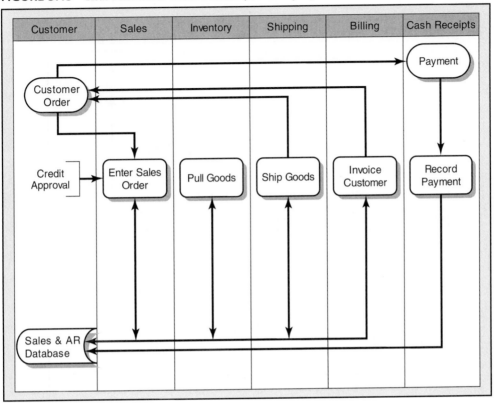

checking to ensure that the job is properly authorized; properly charged with labor, materials, and overhead; and is transferred to finished goods only after proper inspection and approval. Additional control points include measuring and responding to excess labor, waste, and spoilage.

Various reconciliations should be done in the production system. Total labor applied to jobs (plus idle time) should equal total payroll for the relevant production employees. Similar reconciliations should be applied to total materials and overhead.

Internal Control in the Operational Finance Cycle

The primary control in the purchasing side of the finance cycle is that payments be made only by an independent treasury function based on complete documentation from other departments. As discussed earlier, payments to vendors should be made based only on treasury's review and approval of a valid purchase order, a receiving report from the receiving department, and a vendor's invoice that has been reviewed and approved by accounts payable.

As with payments to vendors, employee paychecks should be made only by the treasury department and based on complete documentation. For employee paychecks, the treasury department should review employee time cards (first approved by supervisors) or contracts, wage rates, tax, and benefits rates as set by the human resources department and with the approval by the payroll department. The payroll department should make the payroll computations based on information provided by employees' supervisors and human resources, but only the treasury department should handle or process the paychecks.

FIGURE 3.14   **Manual Purchasing Process (expenditure cycle)**

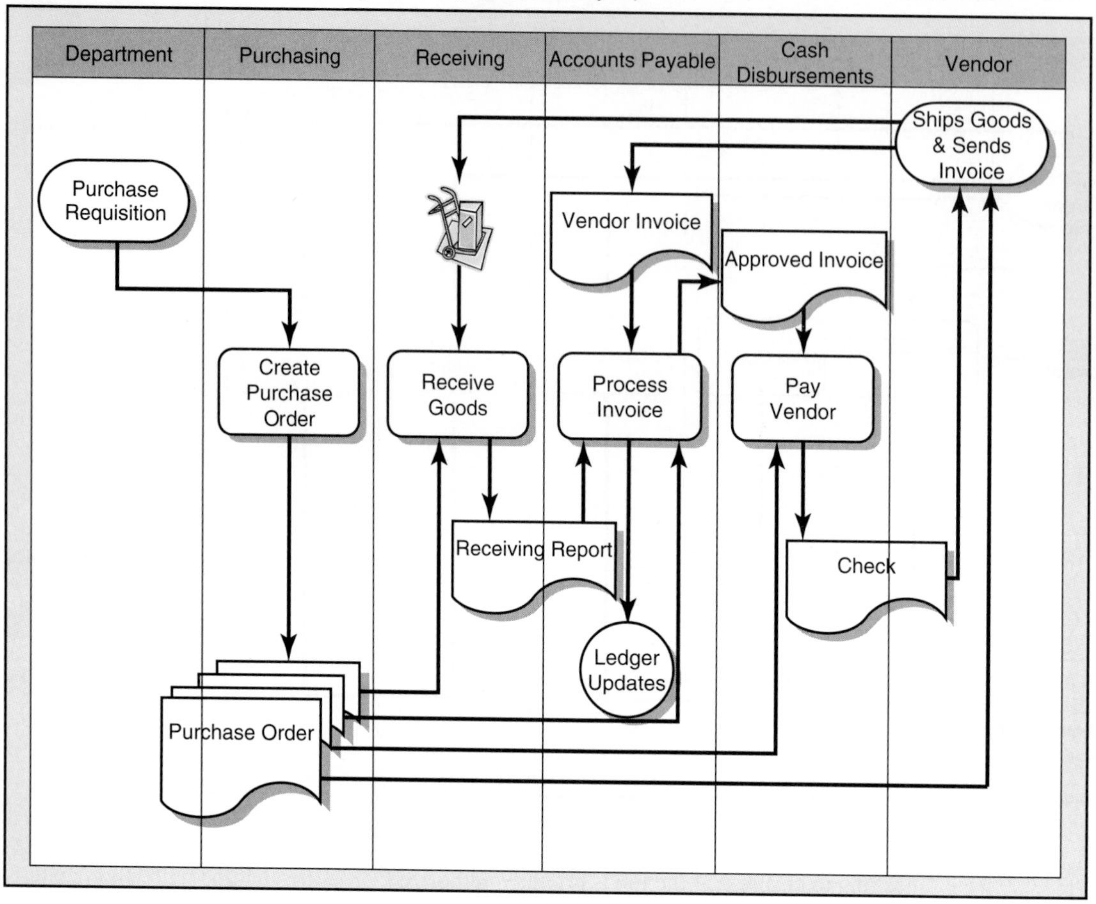

Control over the distribution of employee paychecks is necessary. Either the paychecks should be deposited directly into each employee account, or employees should be required to present identification cards before receiving their checks.

Internal Control over Cash

Cash and checks require a series of specialized controls.

Lockbox for Customer Payments on Account   Ideally, customers should send their account payments to a **lockbox service,** which collects payments, deposits them into the company's bank account, and then sends the company a remittance list. This type of service minimizes the risk of theft and embezzlement.

Customer Payments Received in the Company Mail   Cash payments should not be accepted via the mail. Checks received in the company mail should be received under the authority of the treasury function. They should be immediately endorsed restrictively ("for deposit only" to the company's account), and a remittance list should be prepared and forwarded to the accounts receivable department. The accounts receivable department should never handle checks.

Daily Deposits and Reconciliations   Each day, all collections, whether from cash sales or collections on customer accounts, should be deposited intact into a company bank account. The general accounting department should verify that for each day, the amount

FIGURE 3.15 **Real-Time Purchasing Process (expenditure cycle)**

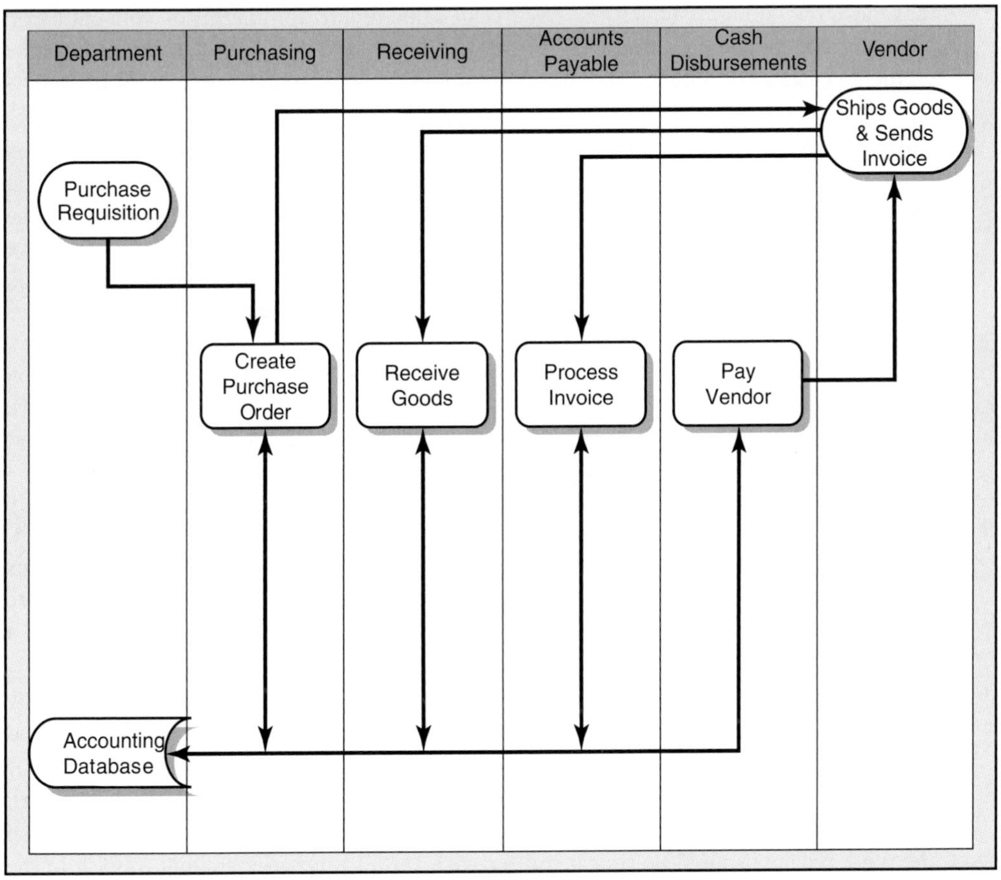

FIGURE 3.16
Control Points in a Purchasing System

Event	Control Point
Purchase requisition created	Checks (e.g., validity checks, limit checks, format checks) are applied to each data item in the transaction.
Purchase order generated	Purchasing approves the vendor and purchase terms, checks for budgetary approval, and issues prenumbered purchase order.
Receiving department accepts incoming goods	The receiving department accepts only incoming goods that relate to outstanding purchase orders. The receiving department does not have access in the system to the number of items ordered and thus must independently count the number of items in incoming shipments.
Accounts payable approves purchase	Accounts payable approves the purchase after verifying that it relates to a valid purchase order and that the goods have been received by the receiving department, and accounts receivable has a matching vendor's invoice.
Treasury department issues payment	The treasury pays the vendor based on the goods having been received in the receiving department, the purchase order being approved by accounts receivable, and having a copy of the vendor's invoice.

of the total credits to cash sales matches the amount of the bank deposit for cash sales and that these two amounts match the day's cash sales report. Similarly, for collections on customers' accounts, the amount on the deposit slip should match the total amount of the credits to customers' ledgers, and these two amounts should match the total for the remittance list.

Cash Registers   Only one employee at a time should be responsible for a cash register. Each cash register employee should begin each shift with a fixed amount of money, and at the end of the shift, the register receipts should equal the total cash in the register minus the initial fixed amount. The person responsible for each specific register should not have access to the register's special functions, such as totaling, subtotaling, transaction voiding, customer refunding, and the opening of the cash drawer without ringing up a sales transaction.

The cash register is an inherent point of weak control. This is so because the salesperson authorizes and records the transaction and then takes custody of the cash. In other words, the salesperson performs the three functions of authorization, recordkeeping, and custody, which represents a breakdown in the normal segregation of duties.

Because of the lack of segregation of duties at the cash register, companies normally apply various compensatory controls. One such control is that of the **customer audit,** which in effect converts the customers into auditors to monitor each sales transaction. This is accomplished by placing a sign at the register that offers the customer a reward if there is no sales receipt. Another compensatory control involves monitoring the cashier with a video camera and recorder.

Cash Changing Hands   Only one employee at a time should have custody of cash. Any time cash changes hands, it should be counted by the transferor and the transferee, and both employees should sign a transfer form that indicates the details of the transfer.

Imprest Account for Petty Cash   Petty cash should be managed via an **imprest fund.** A fixed amount of money should be used to fund petty cash. When it is time to replenish the fund, receipts should be exchanged for cash. At all times, the amount of cash in the fund plus the amount of the receipts in the fund should equal the fixed amount of cash placed in the fund.

Cash Payments   As previously discussed, only the treasury function should pay vendors and should do so only based on the presence of a purchase order, receiving report, and vendor invoice approved by the accounts payable department. At no time during the process should anyone but the treasury department handle the checks, and signing authority should be carefully controlled. Accounting serves as a control on the whole process by reconciling payments in the bank statement against invoices approved by the accounts payable department. This is the main way accounting can ensure that payments are made only for authorized purchases. Finally, accounting should carefully review all canceled checks to make sure the endorser matches the vendor approved for payment. Any unusual endorsements could indicate possible fraud.

Control over Inventories and Other Assets

In general, all purchases made by the company should be received in a central receiving department before being routed to their destination. The receiving department then appropriately transfers items to the property management department, which records any serial numbers and adds company property tags. This permits the property management department to conduct periodic inventories to ensure that all property is accounted for. Finally, the receiving department notifies general accounting of all items received so that accounting can approve related vendor invoices and account for the new assets.

Examples of Internal Control Problems

LO4   This section presents several simple cases to illustrate the application of internal control concepts to real situations.

Case 1: The Overly Important Accountant

Mary Gonzales serves as the accountant for Dewy, Cheetum, and Howe, a medium-size law firm. Each day she opens the mail and separates the checks from the general correspondence. She then enters the amount of each payment as a credit into the related client account. Next, she gives the checks to the secretary, who groups them together until their total exceeds $5,000. As soon as the total exceeds $5,000, she takes the batch of checks to the bank for deposit. She then sends a monthly collection report to the head partner for the law firm.

Figure 3.17 analyzes the internal control problems relating to Mary's responsibilities.

FIGURE 3.17
Internal Control Weaknesses in Cash Collections and Processing

Activity	Control Weakness	Solution
Mary opens the mail.	Mary is an accountant, so her access to cash violates the segregation of duties.	Have someone else open the mail and then send Mary a remittance list of payments for her to use for crediting client accounts.
After the checks are retrieved from the mail, they are immediately given to the secretary for deposit.	No documentation exists for the checks changing hands.	Whoever opens the mail should prepare a remittance list for the checks received. If the checks are then given to a second person, the second person should sign a copy of the remittance list acknowledging receipt of the listed checks.
The secretary holds the checks until their total exceeds $5,000.	Checks may be held overnight.	All receipts should be deposited intact each day.
The checks are deposited without a restrictive endorsement.	Without a restrictive endorsement, a check can be deposited to the wrong account.	As soon as the mail is opened, checks should be stamped "for deposit only to account number xxx."
Payments are posted to client accounts with no system of double-checking for errors.	Without double-checking the amounts posted, it is possible that errors in posting are made.	Run a batch total of each day's mail receipts. This total should be compared to the total credits of client accounts and to the bank deposit slip.
Mary sends a monthly collection report to the head partner.	There is no mention of any bank reconciliation.	A bank reconciliation that includes a comparison of the total cash deposits to the total credits to customer accounts should be performed.

Case 2: The Overworked Purchasing Manager

Bob Winston works as the purchasing manager for a retail department store. He carefully monitors all inventories and sends purchase orders to vendors whenever stock needs to be replenished. When a given order arrives at the receiving department, the manager of that department sends Bob a memo, letting him know that that all parts of the order have been received and accounted for. Bob then notifies accounts payable to pay the vendor.

Figure 3.18 analyzes the internal controls relating to the tasks surrounding Bob's responsibilities.

FIGURE 3.18 **Internal Control Weaknesses in Purchasing**

Activity	Control Weakness	Solution
Bob monitors inventories and decides when to order.	Managing the inventories and handling purchasing functions are inconsistent with the best segregation of duties. The purchasing department is supposed to independently review purchasing requests made by other departments.	An inventory manager outside the purchasing department should decide when to order.
Bob prepares the purchase order.	There is no purchase requisition.	Purchase orders should be prepared based only on approved purchase requisitions that originate outside the purchasing department.
The purchase order is sent to the vendor.	There is no indication that the purchase order is prenumbered.	All major documents should be prenumbered.
The receiving department receives the order.	There is no indication that the receiving department does blind counts for incoming shipments.	The receiving department should perform "blind counts" of all incoming shipments. This means, for example, that the receiving department has a copy of the purchase order with the quantities not included. This forces the receiving department to count the items in all incoming shipments.
The receiving department sends Bob a memo indicating that the order was received.	No copy of the receiving report is sent to the accounts payable department.	The receiving department should send a receiving report to accounts payable.
Bob notifies accounts payable to pay the vendor's invoice.	Bob is in effect authorizing the payment to the vendor.	The vendor payment should be made only by an independent treasury function based on an approved invoice from the accounts payable department, a copy of the purchase order, and a vendor's invoice.
Miscellaneous	There is no accounting for possible missing purchase order documents.	All critical documents should be prenumbered and accounted for.

SYSTEMS DEVELOPMENT

LO5   Systems development, also called the *systems life cycle,* involves the total process involving the analysis, design, and implementation of AIS. In the **classical approach to systems development,** the systems developer works with company employees to identify needs and priorities. The developer then produces a custom, original "blueprint" for the desired systems design. The design is in turn implemented through hardware, software, and other resources.

The classical approach is expensive because it requires the complete design of every aspect of the system. It is much like an architect creating a customized set of plans for a new building. Every design aspect of the entire building must be carefully considered and planned.

A second reason that the classical approach to systems development is so expensive is that it calls for custom development of all software and databases. In other words, off-the-shelf software is generally not used. This results in high costs not only for software development but also for the development of custom training manuals and procedures.

A second approach is the **turnkey approach to systems development.** Turnkey systems are akin to prefabricated houses; they come ready for use. The company purchases an entire turnkey system that includes software, documentation, training materials, and vendor support. No design or programming work is required.

Turnkey systems are obviously much less expensive than systems implemented via the classical approach. However, they require that the company make its business processes conform to the software rather than the other way around. This is not a problem for many small businesses, especially those such as attorneys, doctors, and small retailers whose operations are standardized.

Many turnkey systems permit some customization, such as naming accounts, adding some custom data items, and defining reports. Before selecting a turnkey system, the company must thoroughly evaluate the system in light of current and future needs. Many businesses grow and change, and it is important to make sure that the turnkey system can adapt as needed. For example, a clothing store might want to consider the possibility that it will add nonclothing items to its sales list. In this case, the company should make sure that the turnkey system can handle the additional sales items.

The third approach is the business blueprint approach used with the major ERP systems on the market today. SAP, for example, licenses its ERP system in the form of a "standard reference model," which is a predeveloped but highly customizable software system that is designed to comply with best business practices. Using the business **blueprint approach to systems development,** the developer begins with the predeveloped system as a starting point for the final system. The developer then focuses on customizing the areas of the system that will produce the most benefit. Those parts of the system that already closely fit with the company's processes are customized only a little if at all.

The business blueprint approach is suitable for all companies, but many small companies do not have the resources to do the customization work, and many of the ERP systems are expensive to license. Among large companies, the business blueprint approach has become popular because it results in a fully customized system without the full costs associated with the classic approach. Nevertheless, even with the business blueprint approach, costs can be high. For example, it is not uncommon for a large company to spend $100 million just to implement an ERP inventory system.

Summary

Accounting information systems (AIS) are so complex that accountants must work with their components, called *business processes,* which are sets of coordinated activities and tasks that accomplish some organizational goal. A distinctive feature of business processes is that individual business processes are not confined to a particular department or division within the company, and a single business process can easily span multiple departments or divisions.

There is no one right way to divide the company's AIS into business processes, but one traditional approach is to divide the operations-related processes into four transaction cycles: revenue, expenditure, production, and finance cycles. These four cycles overlap with the AIS functional areas defined by the SAP enterprise resource planning (ERP) system.

Internal control is a process, effected by management, the board of directors, and other personnel designed to reduce risk exposures to an acceptable level given the company's objectives and appetite for risk. Three primary objectives of internal control are to ensure the integrity and reliability of the financial statements; to ensure compliance with various laws, rules, regulations, and contractual obligations; and to promote strategic, tactical, and operational effectiveness and efficiency.

Internal control processes are part of an organization's enterprise risk management (ERM) system. As such, they provide a reasonable assurance that their objectives are met. They virtually never provide a perfect assurance because it is generally not cost effective to totally eliminate all risks.

The main components of effective internal control processes include the control environment, risk assessment, control activities, information and communication, and monitoring. The control environment represents the overall atmosphere in which employees operate. It consists of the management philosophy and operating style, ethics and corporate culture, clearly assigned employee responsibilities, an effective and independent audit committee, an effective and independent internal audit function, and effective human resource polices and procedures.

Risk assessment means that management must design its internal control processes in light of the company's ERM system. Management must first identify its opportunities and objectives, then define the risks for those opportunities and objectives, and finally design the internal control processes to manage the identified risks.

Control activities are the policies and procedures that help to ensure that management directives are carried out. The basic accounting control activities include segregation of duties, which is the foundation of all internal control processes. *Segregation of duties* means that no one person should perform more than one of the following functions: accounting, authorization, and custody. Additional control activities include adequate documentation and records, including an audit trail; independent accountability checks and reviews of performance; and approval and authorization.

Information and communication relate to the accounting system and the flows of information through the organization. Finally, monitoring involves good corporate governance from the board of directors and top management and their active participation in the design and management of the internal control processes, as well as the internal and external audits.

Transaction processing controls are those controls relevant to implementing good internal control processes within specific transaction cycles. The two types of transaction processing controls are general controls and application controls. General controls include the general plan of organization for data processing, general operating procedures, hardware control policies and procedures, and general access controls for data and hardware.

Application controls relate to input, processing, and output controls tasks. They help ensure the accuracy, integrity, and security of the processes of collecting input data, processing input data, and distributing processed data, respectively. *Accuracy* means that the data are free from errors. *Integrity* means that the data remain intact, and *security* means that only authorized persons are granted access.

The exact application of internal control principles depends on the specific design of the information system. For example, daily sales transactions could be batched together and posted to accounts received every night. In real-time systems, however, sales transactions are immediately posted to accounts receivable.

General and application controls can be applied to specific business processes to establish control points. For example, control points in a sales order system include checking the customer's credit and releasing the goods to the customer only upon approval of the customer order. Customers should be invoiced based only on an approved sales order and a shipping report. Segregation of duties must be maintained, and all paper documents must be prenumbered. All postings to accounts should be verified by batch control totals, and proper end-of-period reconciliations must be performed.

The primary control point in the expenditure cycle involves ensuring proper documentation before paying vendors. Vendors should only be paid by an independent treasury function that reviews and approves a purchase order, a vendor's invoice approved by accounts payable, and a receiving report. Adequate separation of duties should be maintained at all points, and proper batch control totals and reconciliations should be done.

Control over cash involves special procedures, including lockboxes, mail-opening procedures—including the use of remittance lists that are sent to accounts receivable—daily deposits and reconciliations, cash register controls, cash transferal controls, imprest accounts, and limited endorsements for checks received.

Systems development involves the process of analyzing, designing, and implementing accounting information systems. In the classical approach to systems development, the company designs systems from ground up. In the turnkey approach, the company buys fully working systems that can be rapidly deployed with little work beyond installation and training. The business blueprint approach is a combination of the classic and turnkey approaches in which the developer begins with an initial predeveloped system but then makes needed customizations.

The classic approach is the most expensive of the three approaches. The trend in large companies is toward the business blueprint approach, but for many small businesses, the turnkey approach is the most cost effective.

Glossary

accuracy Freedom from errors.

application control Control including input, processing, and output that apply to specific applications, processes, and transactions, and ensure the accuracy, integrity, and security of the processes of collecting input data, processing input data, and distributing processed data.

approval Acceptance of a transaction that has already been authorized.

audit trail Documentation or records that permit account balances to be traced back to their original sources.

audit work Accounting work concerned with verifying numbers in the financial statements.

authorization Permission to initiate a transaction.

blueprint approach to systems development Approach to systems development in which the developer uses a predeveloped system as the starting point for the final system and then focuses on customizing the areas of the system to produce the most benefit; system parts that closely fit with the company's processes are customized only a little if at all.

business process Set of coordinated activities and tasks that accomplish some organizational goal.

classical approach to systems development Approach to systems development in which the developer works with company employees to identify needs and priorities to produce a custom, original "blueprint" for the desired systems design implemented through hardware, software, and other resources.

collusion Breakdown in the segregation of duties for nefarious purposes.

control activity Major component of effective internal control processes; the policies and procedures that help ensure management directives are carried out.

control environment Major component of effective internal control processes; represents the overall atmosphere in which employees operate.

customer audit Process by which customers are encouraged to monitor each sales transaction, typically by offering customers rewards if they report the failure to receive a receipt or discover an error in it.

general control Control pertaining to the overall environment and application of all transactions.

golden rule of separation of duties Concept that the accounting staff should never have even temporary control over operational resources, including cash, checks, and other assets, or the authority to authorize sales, purchases, customer credits, or other transactions.

imprest fund Fund (such as petty cash) with a fixed balance at all times so that the cash on hand plus receipts for expenditures always equals the constant fixed balance.

integrity Incorruptibility; soundness; state in which data remain intact in that nothing is added to or removed from transaction data as they pass through the system.

internal control (internal control process) Process effected by management, the board of directors, and other personnel that is designed to minimize risk exposures to an acceptable level given the company's objectives.

lockbox service Service that collects payments, deposits them into the company's bank account, and then sends the company a remittance list; minimizes the risk of theft and embezzlement.

main components of effective internal control processes Control environment, risk assessment, control activities, information and communication, and monitoring.

reasonable assurance Principle that internal controls must reflect a balance between the benefits of reducing risk exposures versus the costs of implementing the controls.

risk assessment and management Major component of effective internal control processes with internal control processes designed by management in light of the company's risks, opportunities, and risk preferences.

risk exposure Event such as asset loss due to theft or spoilage, accounting error and its consequences, revenue loss, expense overrun, business interruption, fraud and embezzlement, fine and penalty, civil liability, and loss of competitive advantage that can adversely affect the company.

security Freedom from danger by following the policy of granting only authorized persons access to parts of the system.

segregation of duties Control activity that is the foundation of all internal control processes; involves the separation of the custody of assets, recordkeeping, and authorization.

specific objective of internal control   Goal that ensures the integrity and reliability of financial reports; compliance with applicable laws, regulations, professional rules, and contractual obligations; and promotion of strategic, tactical, and operational efficiency and effectiveness.

system engineering and development work   Accounting work concerned with creating systems as well as managing and optimizing system performance.

transaction cycle   Business process that repeats itself over and over; traditionally divided into four major transaction cycles: revenue, expenditure, production, and finance.

transaction processing control   Control relevant to implementing good internal control processes within specific transaction cycles; consists of general controls and application controls.

turnkey approach to systems development   Approach to systems development in which ready-made, prefabricated systems that include all needed software, documentation, training materials, and vendor support are used without any design or programming work.

Review Questions

1. A *business process* is a set of coordinated activities and tasks that
   a. Create secure systems.
   b. Constitute a transaction cycle.
   c. Accomplish some organizational goal.
   d. Do none of the above.

2. Generally accepted accounting principles (GAAP) dictate which of the following?
   a. The structure of the four basic transaction cycles.
   b. The structure of the three basic transaction cycles.
   c. The structure of the five basic transaction cycles.
   d. None of the above.

3. Which of the following is a term some business processes are called?
   a. Inbound or outbound transaction loops.
   b. Cycles.
   c. Iterative processes.
   d. None of the above.

4. SAP is organized in
   a. ERP groups.
   b. Cycles.
   c. Modules.
   d. None of the above.

5. In SAP, the revenue, expenditure, production, and finance cycles are incorporated into which of the following areas?
   a. Operations and ERP logistics supply chain.
   b. ERP operations and financials.
   c. Operations and ERP financials.
   d. Sales, services, and product deployment.
   e. None of the above.

6. In practice, which way do companies tend to develop their information systems?
    a. Life cycle.
    b. Modular.
    c. Cycle based.
    d. Grouped.
    e. None of the above.

7. Those auditing the financial statements are most concerned about which of the following?
    a. System optimization.
    b. Transaction cycles.
    c. Flow of transactions through the accounts.
    d. Overall operational effectiveness.
    e. None of the above.

8. On which of these does internal control focus?
    a. Processes.
    b. Processes outcomes.
    c. Process effectiveness.
    d. None of the above.

9. When properly implemented, internal controls
    a. Eliminate large loss exposures.
    b. Eliminate material risks.
    c. Minimize loss exposures.
    d. Prevent large losses.
    e. None of the above.

10. Which of the following is *not* a specific objective of internal control?
    a. Ensuring compliance with applicable laws, regulations, professional rules, and contractual obligations.
    b. Promoting strategic, tactical, and operational efficiency and effectiveness.
    c. Promoting ethics in the corporate culture.
    d. All of the above are specific objectives of internal control.

11. In many types of frauds, such as embezzlement, the cover-up is
    a. The easiest part of the fraud.
    b. The most difficult part of the fraud.
    c. The defining characteristic of the fraud.
    d. The primary characteristic of the fraud.

12. Segregation of duties relates primarily to which of the following?
    a. Control activities.
    b. Information and communication.
    c. The control environment.
    d. None of the above.

13. Approval applies to transactions that
    a. Have been not yet been authorized.
    b. Are pending authorization.

   c. Are fully authorized.

   d. All of the above.

14. Segregation of duties applies to separating which three functions?

   a. Sales, purchasing, and expenditures.

   b. Ordering, receiving, and accounting.

   c. Accounting, authorization, and custody.

   d. None of the above.

15. Audit trail permits auditors to

   a. Balance and reconcile accounts.

   b. Provide SOX-compliant documentation to the SEC.

   c. Trace of the flow of transactions backward from accounts to source documents.

   d. None of the above.

16. When fully operating, control processes

   a. Must be periodically monitored.

   b. Do not require monitoring.

   c. Must be continually monitored.

   d. Must be monitored when failures are evident.

17. Two types of transaction processing controls are

   a. Operating controls and planning controls.

   b. Application and environmental controls.

   c. Planning and efficiency controls.

   d. None of the above.

18. Application controls help ensure

   a. Data accuracy, integrity, efficiency.

   b. Elimination of errors.

   c. Accuracy, integrity, and security.

   d. All of the above.

19. An accountant opens the mail and posts checks to accounts receivable. What is the best way to describe this internal control?

   a. Normal.

   b. Borderline.

   c. Weak.

   d. Normal, borderline, or weak internal, depending on the company.

20. Which of the following functions is *not* compatible with managing the accounts receivable ledger?

   a. Opening the mail.

   b. Approving the write-off of bad debt.

   c. Depositing customer payments into the company bank account.

   d. All of the above.

   e. Only *a* and *c*.

21. The primary control in the purchasing side of the finance cycle is

   a. Ensuring that accounting maintains control of company checks.

   b. Having the chief accountant review and approve all payments.

    c. Having the treasury function make payments based on documentation from other departments.

    d. Requiring at least one corporate executive to review payments before they are made.

22. Lockboxes are used for

    a. Storing petty cash.

    b. Storing the combined receipts of multiple cash registers.

    c. Storing the payment collection.

    d. None of the above.

23. For ideal control over cash registers, there should be

    a. Two employees assigned to each register.

    b. One employee assigned to each register.

    c. At least one employee assigned to each register.

    d. None of the above.

24. In the classical approach to systems development, the developer

    a. Produces a custom blueprint for the desired system.

    b. Uses an industry-standard system blueprint.

    c. Starts with an industry-standard system blueprint and then makes adaptations.

    d. All of the above.

25. The turnkey approach to systems development is

    a. More expensive that the classical approach.

    b. Less expensive than the classical approach.

    c. Costs about the same as the classical approach.

    d. More or less expensive than the classical approach, depending on the systems life cycle.

Discussion Questions

26. How does the finance cycle overlap with the revenue and expenditure cycles?

27. Why do none of the SAP modules directly correspond to any of the four basic transaction cycles?

28. Explain how the focus differs for auditors and systems developers.

29. What focuses do auditors and systems developers share in common?

30. Is the concept of reasonable assurance relevant to controls for all types of security risks? Explain your answer.

31. What are the main components of internal control processes?

32. Should internal controls prevent financial statement fraud? Explain your answer.

33. Give several examples in which management's philosophy and operating style can support the control environment.

34. Are corporate ethics codes effective in preventing improper employee behavior? Explain your answer.

35. The principle of charge and discharge states that individual employees should be held accountable for their actions. Explain.

36. What things would you look for in inviting individuals to serve on an audit committee?

37. To whom should the internal auditor report? Why?

38. Is training employees in their normal job functions important to internal control? Why or why not?

39. In assessing risks, is it important to quantify possible losses in monetary terms? Why or why not?

40. Do cashiers perform any accounting functions? Explain your answer.

41. Why is the audit trail important to the internal auditor?

42. What role should the CEO play in developing and monitoring internal control processes?

43. Give at least three examples of financial transactions that would normally be approved by the accounting function.

44. How do auditors evaluate internal control processes?

45. Give an example of a problem with data integrity.

Cases

46. Assume that you are a forensic accountant consulting for the Mixed Veggies Company. The company has been suffering inventory losses for unknown reasons. Every inventory count for the last five years has shown a significant shortage. The CEO and controller have been debating possible causes for the problem including everything from theft to accounting errors. The controller thinks the investigation should take place strictly within the inventory department. The CEO, on the other hand, thinks a much broader investigation is needed and should include sales and billing.

   Given the information you have, state whether you agree with the CEO or the controller. Explain your position.

47. Green Gooey Company is evaluating all of its internal control processes. Betty Webit, the controller, believes that overall the processes are fairly decent, but she is concerned that there is a lack of integration between the internal control structure and Green Gooey's enterprise risk management (ERM) system. She turns to you, a forensic accountant, for advice on how to integrate the ERM system with internal controls.

   a. What type of general advice might you give to Betty Webit?

   b. How might ERM and the internal control structure be integrated at the organization level? Should the same person be in charge of both?

   c. What are some ERM considerations that are not directly relevant to internal control?

48. The concept of reasonable assurance applies to internal control, but Maria Salzo, the chief compliance officer of the ABC Company, says that she does not care about reasonable assurance. She wants absolute compliance in all matters relating to the financial statements. Here's what she said: "As long as I'm working here, we will have a perfectly tight system that ensures absolutely no fraud in our financial statements." Tom Cheepez, the controller, disagreed with Maria Salzo and argued that anything more than reasonable assurance is both financially and practically impossible.

   a. Do you agree with Tom Cheepez or Maria Salzo? Explain.

   b. Is absolutely preventing financial statement fraud an unrealistic goal?

   c. Could such a goal be even partially obtainable if the internal auditor reports to the CEO?

49. FastBuck Company has great internal controls, including extremely thorough internal and external audit programs. The problem is that the credit manager and the accounts receivable manager have been working together to defraud the company out of tens of

thousands of dollars in a scheme that involves fictitious customers, fictitious credit reviews, and secret write-offs of the related accounts. The accounts receivable manager has covered up the fraud by not including the related write-offs and overdue accounts in the periodic reports.

a. How could such a problem occur in a system with excellent internal controls?

b. How can such schemes be prevented and detected?

50. John Goodtime is the accountant for the XYZ Business Services Company. His company provides basic accounting and tax services to about 100 small business clients in the Coral Gables area of Miami, Florida. John's duties include managing accounts receivable, accounts payable, payroll, and cash disbursements. He pretty much handles everything to do with accounting and payments. John's boss, Marina Jefe, was playing golf with a partner from a local CPA firm, when an unusual conversation evolved.

"I hear that you have only John Goodtime doing all your accounting and financial work," said the CPA.

"He's great," said Marina. "I never have to worry about anything. He does it all."

"That's crazy," said the CPA. "You need separation of duties. You're an accounting firm, and you have a guy in charge of your accounting who doesn't even follow basic textbook segregation of duties."

"But we're making a lot of money. Things are going well," said Marina.

"Get rid of him. He's a walking time bomb," said the CPA. "Take my professional opinion."

Marina was terribly saddened after her golf game with the CPA. She liked John Goodtime and hated the thought of firing him, so she told him what the CPA said.

John responded that the CPA was "off his rocker." He added, "Your CPA friend is used to working with large clients. We're too small to have separate accounting and finance. Do you really want to pay a second person to do some of my work? You don't have anyone else who can do it. All our staff members are overloaded already, and it would be even worse to let one of them handle both clients and billing."

a. Who is right, John Goodtime or the CPA?

b. Should Marina consider firing John Goodtime?

c. Should she consider hiring another person? The money is there to hire someone else, but it would come out of the bottom line and her pocket.

51. Arexl Media Company owns several radio stations in the Chicago area. Most of Arexl's revenues come from on-the-air advertising, and some revenues come from banner advertising on Arexl's Web site. Arexl has an office staff consisting of five persons: an office manager, a secretary, a sales manager, a marketing manager, and a general manager. Liliana Byrd, Arexl's office manager, opens the mail each day and then does the following:

- Immediately separates any account payment checks from clients. She places the checks in the company safe until the end of the week.

- On Friday each week, she removes the checks from the safe and posts them to accounts receivable.

- Friday afternoon, before the banks close, she deposits all checks on hand in the company bank account.

- She returns to the office and files the deposit slip.

- At the end of each month, she reconciles the bank statement.
- After reconciling the bank statement, she reconciles total deposits for the month against total revenues from credit sales and total credits to accounts receivable.

Evaluate the internal controls for these procedures described, and make suggestions for improvements in the internal control processes.

52. Greenwood Rock Company quarries and sells limestone. The company operates its own stone quarries and makes various products used in construction and landscaping. Greenwood's construction products include chopped, cut, and crushed stone. The company prides itself on its quality. It uses only the best diamond saws in the cutting process and only hand loading instead of the usual method of scooping loads using front-end loaders, which often damages the stone. As a result of Greenwood's quality standards, it is able to deliver limestone that covers a larger area per ton than is covered by limestone of its competitors. Also, because it minimizes waste, it extends the life of the entire quarry.

    About 75 percent of the customer orders come from stone masons; the rest come from building contractors. Company trucks deliver orders within a 300-mile radius. Third-party carriers are used to deliver orders farther away.

    Greenwood employs 42 production workers, 12 truck drivers, 1 mechanic, an accountant, a full-time office manager, and a full-time salesperson. Homer Winston takes orders over the phone, via fax, and from the Web. When orders arrive over the phone, this process occurs:

    - He prepares a written sales order.
    - He sends one copy each to the customer and the production manager.
    - The production manager processes the order and sends it to delivery.
    - Upon delivery, the delivery manager sends a copy of the delivery slip to Homer.
    - Based on the delivery slip, Homer sends an invoice to the customer.

    Evaluate Greenwood's internal controls over the sales cycle, and make suggestions for improvements in the internal controls for its sales cycle.

53. Barbara Minker owns South Texas Falldown Construction Company that specializes in residential construction in new gated communities. Her staff consists of Wilson Straight (the office accountant), Georgia Mint (the secretary), 12 job managers, and about 200 workers including carpenters, plasterers, and licensed plumbers. New workers are hired using the following procedures:

    - The job managers hire new workers who show up at one of the job sites looking for work. This is a common practice in the industry in which turnover among workers is a constant problem.
    - A job manager who hires a new worker has the worker fill out and sign a brief form that includes the worker's name, social security number, and contact information.
    - Every Monday and Wednesday afternoon, the job managers give their completed new worker forms to Wilson Straight to ensure that the new workers are added to the payroll.
    - Late Thursday afternoon, each job manager gives Wilson Straight a payroll report that shows the time worked for each worker, which he uses to prepare pay slips for each worker.

- Wilson Straight gives the pay slips to Georgia Mint, who totals them; she then goes to the bank and makes a cash withdrawal for the total payroll for the workers. Finally, she gives each job manager the exact amount of cash needed to pay that job manager's workers.

Barbara Minker had often considered paying employees with checks instead of cash, but many of the workers complained that checks were often difficult to cash and that they needed cash right away to buy food and pay rent. This problem and a shortage of workers forced Barbara to continue to pay workers in cash.

Evaluate payroll-related internal controls for South Texas Falldown Construction Company and make suggestions for improvement in its payroll-related internal controls.

Chapter **Four**

Fundamentals II: The Auditing Environment

CHAPTER LEARNING OBJECTIVES

After reading Chapter 4, you should be able to:

- LO1: Define *auditing*.
- LO2: Describe the functions and benefits of auditing.
- LO3: Describe the regulation of auditors.
- LO4: Describe the effect of rule-making bodies on the auditing profession.
- LO5: Describe the roles of materiality and risk in the performance of an audit.
- LO6: Explain the function of audit reports and describe the various types of reports.
- LO7: Describe the audit assertions and explain their importance.
- LO8: Describe the types of evidence-gathering procedures used by auditors.
- LO9: Compare and contrast the types of audit tests.
- LO10: Explain the role of sampling in the performance of an audit.
- LO11: Describe the audit process.
- LO12: Explain the responsibilities of auditors and management with respect to the assessment of controls over financial reporting.
- LO13: Describe the auditor's responsibility to detect fraud.
- LO14: Describe other services provided by accountants and auditors.

The auditing environment offers opportunities for forensic accountants to use their skills of investigation. Scandals that have occurred over the years, such as at Enron, WorldCom, and Adelphia, highlight the necessity of using forensic accountants to investigate and substantiate suspected frauds. To adequately fulfill this role as an expert, the forensic accountant must understand the auditing environment, including the work performed by auditors.

This chapter describes the auditing process and the role that forensic accountants can play in the determination of the fairness with which the financial statements depict financial position, results of operations, and cash flows of the company being investigated. For example, if an employee has embezzled funds from the employer by skimming revenue, the financial statements are misstated because the revenue shown is understated. Because of the accepted practice of sampling, this fraud will not necessarily be uncovered by the audit. If the employer suspects embezzlement, the skills of a forensic accountant can be beneficial in determining who perpetrated the fraud and the amount of it.

AUDITING

LO1   **Auditing** is the process of gathering and evaluating evidence about information to determine the degree of correspondence between the information and the standards used to prepare the information. For example, the information could be contained in financial statements and the standards used to judge how appropriately they were prepared could be international accounting standards. In this situation, the **auditor**—the person performing the auditing activity—would issue an audit report that discloses the results of the audit.

Auditing is a distinct activity from accounting. Whereas **accounting** is the process of recording, classifying, and summarizing economic events in a manner that helps decision makers make decisions based on financial data, auditing is the process that determines whether the financial data that have been recorded, classified, and summarized are reliable.

DEMAND FOR AUDITING

LO2   The demand for auditing arises because the providers of capital often are not directly involved in the daily operations of the business and managers are usually compensated based on the financial results that they report. For example, assume that a medium-size business desires to obtain additional funds for expansion. The business submits financial statements to a banker from whom the CEO hopes to obtain a loan. In this situation, the manager has an incentive to report biased financial results that present financial position, results of operations, and cash flows depicting the business as being financially healthier than it really is. Because the banker is not as familiar with the CEO's company as the CEO is, she must make her decision as to whether to loan this business money based on her knowledge of the industry, economic conditions, and the financial statements given to her by the CEO. In other words, one of the most important factors that distinguish this company from other, similar companies is the result of operations reported in the financial statements provided by the CEO. If the financial statements are unaudited, the banker's confidence in them would be lower than it would if they had been audited.

Consider the CEO who is compensated for reaching a specific financial target (e.g., net income). The CEO may be inclined—if not consciously, then unconsciously—to accelerate earnings into the current reporting period that would otherwise be recognized in future periods or capitalize amounts paid that should normally be expensed currently. Even audited financial statements can contain a certain amount of earnings management. The presence of auditors, however, reduces the likelihood of earnings management because the possibility of detection is higher during the audit.

Other reasons for the demand for auditing include the complexity of business transactions, complexity of accounting standards, and tremendous volume of transactions in which companies engage. Complexity of business transactions has led to the existence of auditors who are industry specialists. The proliferation of complex accounting standards since the late 1970s, due partly to the increase in the complexity of business transactions, has made the recording and presentation of financial data increasingly difficult. Furthermore, the sheer volume of transactions that some companies engage in daily requires auditors to use sampling techniques to formulate conclusions about the populations on which they are to give an opinion.

For these reasons, auditors serve a vital role by providing a service that facilitates the movement of capital between investors and companies issuing stock or between lenders and borrowers. To protect the public, society has established a regulatory arrangement to increase the likelihood that only qualified persons perform the auditing function so that investors and lenders are not harmed. This protection is accomplished by licensing persons and firms that meet certain criteria.

LICENSING

LO3   States regulate U.S.-based auditing firms' expression of an opinion on financial statements through public accounting acts. No two public accounting acts are identical; thus, there are as many different public accounting acts as there are states (and the District of Columbia) and territories (e.g., Puerto Rico). According to these acts, accountants who wish to perform certain accounting functions, such as expressing opinions on financial statements, must meet specific requirements and apply for a license with the state in which they will practice. Typically, states require those who apply for a public accounting license to pass the Uniform Certified Public Accountant examination and to earn a specified number of college credit hours (usually 150 semester hours). Some states, such as Indiana and New York, require applicants to have experience in accounting before granting them a license. After obtaining a license, **public accountants** must engage in a specified number of continuing professional education (CPE) hours to maintain their licenses.

State boards of accountancy can discipline licensed public accountants by suspending their licenses to practice or, in more egregious instances of misconduct, revoking their licenses. Generally, if a person's license to practice is revoked, the person cannot use the title CPA or sign audit reports. The SEC regulates the practice of accountants by using Rule 2(e), which allows it to deny, temporarily or permanently, the right to practice before it. Often states also license public accounting firms. This enables states to take even more stringent regulatory action against producers of substandard work. Penalties against firms can range from suspension of a firm's right to perform certain work (e.g., audits) to the revocation of its license.

Auditors from other countries must meet standards established by the country in which they practice. For example, in Canada, the United Kingdom, and Australia, auditors of financial statements must meet the requirements of their respective Institute of Chartered Accountants. In Canada, for example, the Canadian Public Accountability Board (CPAB) oversees the performance of **chartered accountants,** persons who have met specific CPAB requirements. Auditors must be members in good standing of the CPAB before they can audit companies that raise capital from the Canadian investing public. One of the duties of the CPAB is to conduct inspections of public accounting firms in much the same manner as does the Public Company Accounting Oversight Board (PCAOB) in the United States.

RULE-MAKING BODIES

LO4   A number of rule-making bodies affect the auditing profession. Primary among them are the PCAOB, the Securities and Exchange Commission (SEC), the Financial Accounting Standards Board (FASB), the Governmental Accounting Standards Board (GASB), the American Institute of Certified Public Accountants (AICPA), and the Institute of Internal Auditors (IIA).

> The **PCAOB** defines itself as a "private-sector, nonprofit corporation, created by the Sarbanes-Oxley Act of 2002, to oversee the auditors of public companies in order to protect the interests of investors and further the public interest in the preparation of informative, fair, and independent audit reports." It is, however, subject to oversight by the SEC. The PCAOB has the authority to establish the standards by which auditing is

to be performed, perform inspections of auditing firms to determine whether they are following these standards, and impose sanctions against auditing firms that fail to fulfill their professional responsibilities when auditing public companies. In 2003, the PCAOB adopted the auditing standards that were in effect at that time and has since issued additional auditing standards, one of which addresses the audit of internal controls over financial reporting.

The SEC is an agency of the United States and oversees the administration of the Securities Act of 1933, the Securities and Exchange Act of 1934, and other acts, such as the Sarbanes-Oxley Act of 2002. The 1933 act regulates initial sales of securities to the public; one of its requirements is that audited financial statements be submitted on the SEC's S form. The 1934 act regulates all sales and exchanges that occur subsequent to the initial sale. According to this act, each company that has assets of more than $1 million and equity securities owned by more than 500 investors and that offers its securities for sale to the public must register with the SEC and submit audited annual financial reports (on Form 10K), a review (a *review* is a less intensive examination than an audit) of quarterly financial reports (on Form 10Q), and a report of any significant event of which investors should be aware (on Form 8K).

The FASB is responsible for issuing the financial accounting standards that companies must use when preparing their financial statements. Thus, auditors must have knowledge of these standards so that they can determine when these standards, collectively called **generally accepted accounting principles** (GAAP), have not been properly applied.

The GASB determines the governmental accounting standards that governmental units, such as states, counties, and local governments, are to use when reporting their results. Thus, auditors who audit these entities must follow GASB standards to determine whether these entities are complying with the reporting standards commonly accepted for governmental entities.

The AICPA is responsible for issuing auditing standards used to audit private U.S. companies. The Auditing Standards Board issued more than 100 Statements on Auditing Standards (SAS) that, until 2003, were to be followed by auditors who audit both public and private companies. In 2003, the PCAOB replaced the AICPA as the auditing standard setter for companies that are publicly held. The AICPA also promulgates a Code of Professional Conduct that affects most public accountants, including the accountants of the largest CPA firms.

The IIA is an organization that provides guidance to internal auditors through the issuance of Statements on Internal Auditing Standards (SIAS) and the establishment of a code of ethics. These standards, which are published in the *IIA International Standards for the Professional Practice of Internal Auditing,* are divided into attribute standards that the individual internal auditor must follow and performance standards that prescribe proper guidance for the practice of internal auditing. The IIA also oversees the administration of the certified internal auditor (CIA) designation.

INTERNATIONAL BOARDS THAT AFFECT THE ACCOUNTING PROFESSION

The following two boards are representative of those that affect the international auditing profession by issuing pronouncements and assisting in the harmonization of standards across countries.

building on its balance sheet is asserting that the building exists. Note that this assertion does not address ownership (the assertion of "rights" addresses ownership) but states that the company is merely asserting that the building exists.

Likewise, if sales are shown on the income statement, management is making the assertion that those sales occurred, just as the inclusion of supplies expense on the income statement represents the assertion that supplies were consumed during the period.

Completeness

The *assertion of completeness* addresses whether all assets, liabilities, and operational (e.g., income and expense) items are included in the company's financial statements. For example, assume that the company purposely did not record certain liabilities. Such a situation could occur if the company borrowed funds and recorded the proceeds as revenue. In this case, two assertions have been violated: (1) completeness because all liabilities were not recorded and (2) occurrence because the liability that was recorded as revenue was a statement by the company that revenue transactions occurred that, in fact, did not occur.

Note the difference between the assertion of existence or occurrence and completeness. *Existence or occurrence* addresses overstatements whereas *completeness* addresses understatements. If, for example, a fictitious entry was made during the year that inflated sales, the assertion of occurrence has been violated. In other words, too many sales were included in the income statement—an overstatement—because some of these "sales" were not valid sales. If, on the other hand, the Sales account were understated, the assertion of completeness is not true.

Valuation or Allocation

The *assertion of valuation or allocation* addresses the correctness of amounts in the financial statements. Allocation pertains to such items as depreciation, allowance for doubtful accounts, recognition of revenue on long-term construction contracts, and the determination of the amounts of overhead that should be divided between the cost of goods sold and inventory for manufacturing companies.

Statement on Auditing Standard (SAS) No. 106, *Audit Evidence,* added a few assertions and classified each assertion as a transaction-related assertion, balance-related assertions, or and presentation- and disclosure-related assertion, as shown in Figure 4.2. The addition of these assertions and classification of all assertions into categories was undertaken to assist the auditor in performing the audit. Prior to 2006, the additional assertions were considered subsets of the five primary assertions. For example, accuracy and cutoff were previously subsumed by valuation and allocation because accuracy and cutoff addressed the proper fiscal amount of a transaction.

The auditor tests the authenticity of these assertions by using the evidence-gathering procedures discussed in the next section.

FIGURE 4.2
SAS No. 106
Financial Statement
Assertions

Transaction-Related Assertions	Balance-Related Assertions	Presentation- and Disclosure-Related Assertions
Occurrence	Existence	Occurrence/rights and obligations
Completeness	Rights and obligations	Completeness
Accuracy	Completeness	Classification
Cutoff	Valuation and allocation	Accuracy and valuation
Classification		

EVIDENCE-GATHERING PROCEDURES

LO8   Seven primary evidence-gathering procedures are available to the auditor: confirmation, observation, physical examination, reperformance, analytical procedures, inquiry of the client, and documentation. Each of these is discussed in the following sections.

Confirmation

Confirmation is used when third parties (persons who are not the audit client or auditor) have knowledge of some aspect of the audit client and can be asked to provide this information. Confirmations are used to obtain information about accounts receivable, notes receivable, investments, bank accounts, and accounts payable, for example.

When auditing accounts receivable, the auditor selects customers whose balances he wants to confirm and provides the list to the audit client. The audit client prepares the confirmations and gives them to the auditor, who then checks the names, addresses, and balances (if included) provided on the confirmation requests before mailing them to the customers. The confirmation request usually includes a stamped envelope addressed to the auditor. The important point to note about accounts receivable confirmations is that once the audit client gives the confirmation requests to the auditor, the client has no contact with them. This rule increases the reliability of the evidence provided by the confirmations (otherwise, the audit client could change information to hide an overstatement before the confirmation request is mailed to the customer).

The three types of confirmations are (1) positive "in-blank," (2) positive, and (3) negative. The positive in-blank confirmation request does not contain the amount the recipient is to confirm. Response to this type of confirmation requires the recipient to consult its records to write in the amount requested by the auditor. The other type of positive confirmation—the one on which the amount is written—requires that the recipient indicate whether the amount shown on the confirmation is correct and, if incorrect, write in the correct amount. (Used in this context, the word *positive* means that the recipient is requested to return the request regardless of whether the recipient agrees with the amount listed or has no balance due.)

On the other hand, *negative* confirmations request that the recipient return the confirmation to the auditor only if the recipient believes that the amount on the confirmation is incorrect. In other words, if the auditor does not receive a negative confirmation from the recipient, the auditor assumes that recipient is confirming the amount as correct. However, this assumption may not be warranted; many other reasons could explain why the auditor did not receive a negative confirmation. These include the possibilities that the recipient did not receive the confirmation, the confirmation was lost after having been received, and the recipient decided not to respond to the request.

Therefore, the positive confirmation provides a higher level of reliable evidence than does the negative type because the auditor does not assume anything if the positive confirmation is not returned. Furthermore, the positive in-blank confirmation provides a higher level of reliable evidence than does the positive confirmation that contains the amount to be confirmed written on the request because the "in-blank" type requires the recipient to write the amount being confirmed on the request letter (with the other type of confirmation, the recipient could easily agree with the amount written on the request without verifying this amount).

If a response to a positive confirmation request is not received, the auditor is to perform alternative procedures by examining source documents that underlie the amount being confirmed. Note that because the audit client possesses the source documents, they could have been altered and thus are not usually believed to be as reliable as confirmation requests. On the other hand, responses received by auditors to confirmation requests can be misleading. For example, Parmalot has been called one of the largest confirmation frauds ever discovered. Its losses of almost $5 billion were facilitated by the return of confirmations that supported an overstatement of cash and investments.

Observation

Observation involves the use of the senses to assess the propriety of employee performance and other activities, such as business processes that have a tangible component (e.g., assembly lines). It is an excellent evidence-gathering technique for determining how well functions that do not leave a documentary trail are performed. For example, assume that the audit client established a requirement that two persons be present when mail is opened each day to lower the likelihood of embezzlement at the point of receipt. An auditor can easily observe the opening of mail to determine whether this control is being performed. Another example is the observation of counting inventory, an audit procedure specifically required by auditing standards.

Observation is best used when employees are not aware they are being observed. Otherwise, their reaction to being observed can affect their behavior in such a way that the auditor does not witness behavior that occurs when she is not present.

Physical Examination

Physical examination is the inspection of assets. For example, the auditor could examine an assembly line to determine the existence of equipment or a sample of vehicles by physically locating them by vehicle identification number. This procedure is also used to determine the existence of notes receivable by examining its physical representation—the note.

Physical examination does not indicate ownership, however. For example, assume that an audit client sells inventory on consignment for another retailer. The audit client does not own the consigned inventory it possesses and thus should not include it as an asset on the client's balance sheet. Thus, even though the auditor can physically examine the inventory, the inventory is not an asset of the audit client.

Reperformance

Reperformance is the act of performing a task that has been previously performed. It provides highly reliable evidence regarding how well the task was originally performed. For example, assume that an audit client's employee reconciles the bank account each month. To gather evidence as to how well the reconciliation is performed, the auditor can observe the employee as he performs this task. If the employee appears to perform it conscientiously, the auditor has some assurance that the task was performed well. However, the auditor can make a much better determination of the employee's performance by reperforming the task. This procedure is not used often because of the time it takes; however, it is a useful tool when highly reliable evidence is sought.

Analytical Procedures

Analytical procedures are comparisons of recorded amounts to expectations developed by the auditor. For example, assume that an auditor audits a company in an industry that, during the current year, has experienced difficulties as a result of a downturn in the economy. When the auditor begins the audit of the current year, she has a reasonable expectation of encountering a lower level of sales. If, however, recorded sales are higher than the auditor's expectations, she would most likely investigate this unexpected result to determine whether the higher level of sales is not materially overstated.

Many different types of analytical procedures are available. The five most common types are shown in Figure 4.3.

Analytical procedures in an audit are required at two points: the planning stage and the completion (final) stage. In the planning stage, they are performed to determine what areas

FIGURE 4.3
Common Analytical Procedures

- Comparison of recorded amounts with corresponding amounts from prior years
- Comparison of recorded amounts with the amounts expected by the auditor
- Comparison of recorded amounts with the amounts expected by audit client (e.g., budgets or forecasts)
- Comparison of recorded amounts with industry results (e.g., gross profit ratio)
- Comparison of recorded amounts with nonfinancial data (e.g., use of number of hotel rooms, room rates, and vacancy rates to determine expected revenue)

appear to be misstated so that an effective audit plan can be developed and an adequate amount of audit hours can be budgeted. Analytical procedures are required in the final stage to determine whether the financial statements, as a whole, are not materially misstated (i.e., determining whether they appear reasonable in light of the evidence collected) and whether the audited company will continue to exist for a reasonable period of time (the going concern assessment mentioned in the Audit Reports section).

Although not required, analytical procedures are often used in the middle of the audit as either a supplemental audit procedure or, in the case of accounts that have immaterial balances, the only audit procedure. For example, assume that Supplies Inventory has a balance that is not material relative to other current assets. The auditor may choose to compare this account's current year balance with its balances that existed in the five prior years. If the balances are not significantly different from these prior years, no other tests on this account are performed.

Inquiry of the Client

Inquiry of the client is a necessary procedure for obtaining information that does not exist in written form. For example, if the auditor determines with a high likelihood that an audit client will not continue to exist, the auditor may ask the client whether it has plans to decrease this likelihood; although written plans could exist, certain portions of them, particularly those still being formulated, may not be written.

Inquiry of the client can also be used to obtain clarification of matters that do not appear to be consistent. For example, if the auditor notices a discrepancy when comparing a source document to the recorded transaction, the auditor may ask the client for an explanation of the difference.

Documentation

Documentation is the act of examining source documents. For example, an auditor may select a sample of recorded sales transactions from the sales journal and match them with their corresponding sales invoices. An auditor could also inspect a contract that provides for the audit client's contingent payments. Documentation also occurs when an auditor opens a computer file and reads its contents.

The auditor uses all of these procedures in a typical audit. The extent to which each type is used is a matter of professional judgment and is often affected by the level of reliability desired by the auditor. For example, assume that the auditor is verifying whether an employee performed a comparison of two sources of information to determine whether the sources matched. Also assume that the employee was to initial one of the documents to indicate that the documents matched. In this situation, the auditor could look for the initials and, when found, use this *documentation* to rely on the initials to confirm that the documents matched. Alternatively, the auditor could *observe* the employee making the comparison to determine not only whether it was performed but also the extent to which the employee appeared to consciously perform it. However, the auditor would not have direct evidence that the task was performed correctly unless he *reperformed* the task. Thus, reperformance, relative to documentation, yields evidence of higher reliability.

TYPES OF TESTS

LO9   Whereas the auditor uses the procedures described to collect evidence, his or her objective determines the type of test used. The four primary types of tests are tests of controls, substantive tests of transactions, analytical procedures, and substantive tests of balances. Each of these tests is used for a particular purpose.

Tests of Controls

Auditors use **tests of controls** to determine whether controls are functioning well. According to professional standards, the auditor is to gain an understanding of internal controls to determine the nature, timing, and extent of tests to be performed including tests of controls, substantive tests of transactions, analytical procedures, and substantive tests of balances.

After obtaining an understanding of the internal controls, the auditor assesses how well the controls were designed and how well they appear to be functioning. This assessment is made for each business process (typically, sales and collection, acquisition and payment, inventory and warehousing, payroll and personnel, and capital acquisition and repayment) and area of financial reporting. The quality of internal controls can vary according to business processes. For example, for small businesses, controls over payroll are often better than they are over sales and collection.

This assessment is summarized by a quantitative or qualitative determination of control risk defined as the likelihood that misstatements that exceed a tolerable rate will not be prevented or detected in a timely manner by the audited company's internal controls. For many small companies, the control risk pertaining to certain activities in a business process may be 100 percent (or, in qualitative terms, *maximum*). An assessment of risk at 100 percent does not mean that there is a 100 percent likelihood that a misstatement will occur; rather, it simply means that the control cannot be relied upon. When the auditor assesses control risk at 100 percent, this assessment indicates that either the controls are not designed well or are not functioning well enough to reduce, to an acceptably low level, the risk that the company's objectives will not be achieved. Thus, tests of controls for this activity are not performed; instead, the use of other tests—such as substantive tests of transactions and substantive tests of balances (both discussed in following sections)—will be expanded.

In summary, the auditor first obtains an understanding of the internal controls for a business process and then assesses how well he believes they are designed and functioning. He then tests the controls to determine whether his assessment is correct. If the tests of controls indicate that the controls are not functioning as well as he thought they were, he increases control risk (perhaps not to 100 percent, but above the level initially assessed). The increase in control risk affects the nature, timing, and extent of tests of transactions and balances, and analytical procedures yet to be performed.

Substantive Tests of Transactions

Substantive tests of transactions or simply *tests of transactions* seek to determine whether transactions were recorded correctly. For example, an auditor can determine whether the amount of sales during the audit year were correctly recorded, a test of the management assertion of valuation. The auditor could test this assertion by selecting a sample of sales recorded during the year and vouching them to supporting documents, specifically sales invoices. By comparing the amount recorded for each sale (i.e., transaction) to the amount on the sales invoice, the auditor can determine whether the amount recorded matches the amount that should have been recorded (the amount on the sales invoice). If the amounts differ, this difference is called an *exception* or *deviation*. (An *exception,* then, can be defined as the absence of a characteristic that the auditor normally expects to find.) The auditor then determines the rate of exceptions that exist in the sample, projects this rate to the population (see the later section on sampling), compares this projected exception rate to the tolerable exception rate the auditor selected before beginning the test, and makes a judgment about whether the sales transactions were correctly recorded. Although the assertion of valuation is used here as an example, note that tests of transactions are used to determine whether other assertions, such as completeness and existence, are met.

The auditor's test of each transaction has one of two possible results: The transaction was either correctly recorded or not correctly recorded (an exception). Any time one of two possible results can occur, a rate can be developed. The tolerable exception rate referred to earlier is similar to the tolerable misstatement discussed in the section on materiality. The difference is that tolerable misstatement is a *dollar amount* (e.g., $10,000) that the auditor will allow to exist in a segment and still believe the segment is not materially misstated whereas the **tolerable exception rate** is a *rate* of exceptions the auditor will allow to exist and still believe the class of transactions is correctly recorded. The concept of *exception rate* is also used when determining whether internal controls are operating well; in this case, one of two possible findings occurs each time the control is tested: The control either is or is not functioning correctly.

Tests of transactions and of controls have other aspects in common. Some tests satisfy the determination of whether a control is functioning well (a test of controls) *and* whether a class of transactions (a test of transactions) is recorded correctly. For example, assume that the audit client has instituted a control by which sales cannot be recorded until each sales document is matched with a bill of lading (a shipping document). The auditor selects a sample of recorded sales and reperforms the control of matching, which achieves two purposes: She has determined whether, for each recorded sale, the sales invoice matches the bill of lading (the control), and whether the existence of these two documents substantiates the transaction (thus testing the assertion of occurrence). This test, which satisfied two purposes—testing both a control and an assertion—is called a *dual-purpose test*.

One additional point must be made with respect to tests of transactions. The *direction of testing* can determine the assertion tested. For example, assume that an auditor wants to test whether all sales have been recorded. He should select a sample from the population of all sales that occurred during the year (usually represented by sales invoices). He then traces the sales invoices into the sales journal to determine whether each sales invoice was recorded as a sale. If, on the other hand, the auditor wanted to determine whether all sales that were recorded are valid sales (i.e., they "occurred"), the auditor should select a sample from the recorded sales and vouch to source documents, the sales invoices. This concept, known as *directional testing,* is illustrated in Figure 4.4.

Analytical Procedures

Analytical procedures are attention-directing procedures. Their primary purpose is to determine whether an account balance or transaction appears unusual. However, they offer no concrete evidence that an account balance or transaction is misstated. Instead they often are used to identify balances and transactions that require further investigation. For example, assume that the unaudited financial statements of a company indicate that the

FIGURE 4.4
Directional Testing

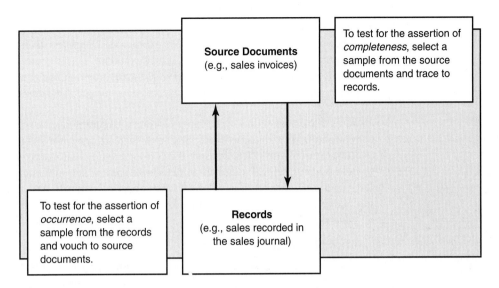

gross profit percentage for the current (unaudited) year is 42 percent but in each of the last three years was 35 percent. This information alone does not indicate any misstatement. The auditor recognizes that many causes besides errors or fraud could produce the 7 percent difference. For example, the company could have found a vendor that offers inventory at a lower price than it paid in previous years. The company could also have begun selling a new product that has a much higher profit margin than those sold in the three prior years. The auditor will most likely begin by asking the client for an explanation (the *inquiry of client* audit procedure). The auditor must not accept the client's answer at face value but must gather **corroborating evidence** that supports management assertions to determine whether the client's answer has substance. This evidence could be gathered by an audit procedure such as documentation or physical examination.

Substantive Tests of Balances

Substantive tests of balances, or simply *tests of balances,* provide evidence as to the correctness of account balances. Examples of these tests include confirmations of cash in bank balances and accounts receivable balances as well as the comparison of recorded accounts payable with vendors' monthly statements.

SAMPLING

LO10   As mentioned in the auditor's standard report, "An audit includes examining, on a test basis, evidence supporting the amounts and disclosures in the financial statements." Briefly, **sampling** is the examination of less than the entire population so that a conclusion can be formulated about the population. Its objective is to determine whether a recorded account balance is fairly stated or a class of transactions was recorded correctly without having to examine the entire population.

The sample size can vary from segment to segment and can differ for the same segment from year to year. The variation depends on several factors including the auditor's estimation of errors in the population, her belief that fraud has occurred, and the amount of errors she will tolerate in the population before concluding that the population is materially misstated.

Sampling Risk

When less than an entire population is examined, the risk exists that the judgment based on the sample differs from the judgment that would have been obtained had the entire population been examined. This risk is known as **sampling risk** and can be eliminated only if the entire population were examined; this risk decreases as the sample size increases.

Statistical sampling is a sampling method based on probabilities. Use of its procedures allows the auditor to obtain an estimate of sampling risk. Auditors, however, are not required to use statistical sampling and, instead, may use judgmental sampling. When **judgmental sampling** is used, the auditor has no quantitative estimate of sampling risk but uses professional judgment to determine sample size and interpret results.

Sampling for attributes—used when tests of controls and tests of transactions are conducted—differs from sampling for tests of balances. Each of these applications of sampling is discussed next.

Sampling for Attributes

Sampling for attributes is used when the auditor performs tests of controls and tests of transactions. It involves estimating the exception rate of the population based on a portion—the sample—of the population. The primary issues involved are determining the size of the sample and selecting the sample items.

Size of the Sample

The following items affect the choice of sample size for tests of control and tests of transactions: tolerable exception rate, acceptable risk of assessing control risk too low, estimated population exception rate, and population size.

The **tolerable exception rate** is the rate of exceptions (or deviations) from a prescribed control that the auditor is willing to accept and thus believe the control is functioning as well as initially believed. This concept applies equally to substantive tests of transactions; in this case, it is the exception rate the auditor is willing to accept and thus believe the class of transactions is correctly recorded. The lower the tolerable exception rate, the larger is the sample size; this reflects the auditor's desire for increased precision. The **acceptable risk of assessing control risk too low** (ARACR) is the level of risk the auditor is willing to accept that he is not overrelying on the internal controls. As the amount of risk the auditor is willing to accept decreases, the sample size increases. The estimated population exception rate is an estimate of the true but unknown population exception rate. As this estimate increases, sample size increases. Generally, sample size increases as the population size increases, although the effect of population size on sample size is not as great as the effect that each of the other three factors has on population size.

Typically, the auditor either selects a sample size using a program (or table) based on the acceptable risk of assessing control risk too low, the tolerable exception rate, and the expected population exception rate or uses judgment to determine sample size. Likewise, when interpreting the results of testing, the auditor uses a program (or table) to obtain a **computed upper exception rate** (CUER). This rate includes an amount for sampling risk and thus represents the maximum rate of exceptions that can exist in a population given a chosen confidence level, the sample size used, and the number of exceptions found in the sample.

The auditor compares the CUER to the tolerable exception rate (TER); if the CUER exceeds the TER, the auditor would conclude that the control is not functioning as well as she thought it was. If the objective of the tests performed is to determine whether transactions are recorded properly (tests of transactions), she would conclude that the transactions are not recorded correctly.

Note that the existence of an exception does not necessarily mean that the exception is a deviation; there could be acceptable reasons for the exception. The auditor should investigate the exceptions found to determine whether their effect on the CUER could be appropriately reduced. This reduction is a process known as *isolation* and requires professional judgment to implement.

If, on the other hand, the TER exceeds the CUER, the auditor would conclude that the controls are functioning as well as she thought they were when she initially planned the audit or—if transactions are being tested—that the transactions are correctly recorded.

If CUER exceeds TER for tests of controls and the auditor believes the exceptions are true deviations from prescribed controls, the auditor usually increases control risk. This increase affects the nature, timing, and extent of other tests—particularly substantive tests—the auditor has not yet performed. Furthermore, this test revealed a weakness in internal controls (because CUER exceeded TER) that should be communicated to management.

If CUER exceeds TER for tests of transactions, the auditor most likely requests that the audit client adjust the records for the errors that were found and carefully considers the effect of this result on the tests of balances to be performed.

Auditors can also use nonstatistical methods, called *judgmental sampling* (defined earlier) to draw conclusions about the population. Use of judgmental sampling to select a sample size determines size based on professional judgment and is most likely the result of past experience, the culture of the public accounting firm for which the auditor works, and the personality characteristics of the auditor (e.g., the extent to which the auditor is conservative). Furthermore, interpretation of results involves professional judgment because no CUER can be quantified with the precision determined using the statistical approach discussed earlier.

Selection of Items That Make Up the Sample

The auditor must also determine the individual items to make up the sample. The auditor prefers a sample that is representative of the population so that he is more likely to draw correct conclusions about it. One way to increase the likelihood that a representative sample is obtained is to select the items randomly. In fact, if statistical methods are used to interpret the results, each sample item *must* be selected randomly, that is, each item must have an equal chance of being selected. The reason for this is that the programs or tables used to interpret the results are based on probabilities obtained from repeated trials using items that have an equal probability of being selected.

Nonstatistical sampling involves selecting items judgmentally. If this approach is used, the auditor often selects items based on certain characteristics (e.g., those most likely to contain misstatements such as large dollar transactions). The auditor can also combine the two methods. For example, assume that for the first nine months of the fiscal year, sales transactions were recorded by the person who had performed this function for the last 12 years. Also assume that this person left the job and another, less experienced person recorded these transactions during the last three months. The auditor may want to consider the population of recorded sales transactions as two separate populations and obtain a random sample from each of these subpopulations (called *stratification*). By doing so, the auditor is more likely to develop a more nearly precise judgment about how well sales were recorded for the year.

Sampling for Substantive Tests of Balances

Sampling for substantive tests of balances (or simply, "tests of balances") is performed to determine whether an account balance, such as accounts receivable, is materially misstated. The objective of sampling for tests of controls and transactions was to produce an *estimate of the deviation rate,* but the objective of sampling for tests of balances is to produce a *dollar estimate* of a difference between the recorded balance (the amount shown in the financial statements) and the amount that should have been recorded (based on the sample).

In sampling for tests of controls and tests of transactions, the auditor must consider acceptable risk of assessing control risk too low. When sampling for tests of balances, the auditor considers the **acceptable risk of incorrect acceptance** (ARIA). The risk of incorrect acceptance is the risk that the auditor will conclude that the balance of the account being sampled is not materially misstated when, in fact, it is materially misstated. ARACR affects ARIA because an auditor who assesses control risk too low is overrelying on controls that ensure that transactions—and thus balances—are recorded correctly. The auditor considers these risks when determining sample sizes and interpreting the results.

The methods used to determine whether account balances are correctly stated include **variables sampling** (e.g., difference estimation, ratio estimation, and mean-per-unit estimation), monetary unit sampling, and judgmental sampling. Each of these methods produces an estimate of the difference between the recorded balance and a more nearly correct balance (based on a sample). This difference is then compared to the tolerable misstatement (TM) and, if the difference exceeds the TM, the auditor concludes that the balance is materially misstated.

Monetary unit sampling (MUS), sometimes called *dollar unit sampling (DUS), probability-proportional-to-size sampling (PPS),* or *cumulative monetary amount sampling (CMA),* is frequently used to determine whether assets, such as accounts receivable, inventory, and investments, are overstated. This method automatically selects the largest items in an account balance by selecting not only sample size but also individual items that make up the sample. The name *probability-proportional-to-size sampling* has been used because the probability that an item will be selected is the proportion of the size of the item (in dollars) to the size of the population (in dollars). Thus, the larger the item, the higher is the probability it will be selected. For example, the probability of selecting the $60,000 accounts receivable balance of customer A is 10 times the probability of selecting the $6,000 accounts receivable balance of customer B.

MUS is usually easier to use than variables sampling methods and produces a smaller sample size if no misstatement is expected. In addition, sample selection may begin before the entire population is available. However, it is not without its disadvantages; MUS can overstate the allowance for sampling risk, thus biasing in favor of finding that the account balance is materially misstated.

MUS provides the auditor an estimate of the maximum amount of overstatement of an account given a specified level of the risk of incorrect acceptance. This estimate of the misstatement is then compared to the tolerable misstatement. If the estimated misstatement exceeds the tolerable misstatement, the auditor most likely concludes that the account balance is materially misstated.

When MUS is used for auditing accounts payable, the auditor must exercise special care because this technique is better suited for overstatements than understatements. A separate sample of low dollar (and zero balance) items should be selected when understatements are a concern.

Nonstatistical Sampling for Tests of Balances

Increasingly, public accounting firms are using nonstatistical sampling to determine the appropriateness of book values of accounts. Consider this example. Madera Corp. is conducting an audit of Ariel Enterprises and decides to use a nonstatistical approach to determine whether accounts receivable are fairly stated. Assume that the book value of accounts receivable is $5,000,000. Madera has determined, based on tests of controls, that a moderate assessment of inherent and control risk is appropriate. The risk that other auditing procedures will fail to detect material misstatements is slightly below maximum. Madera has chosen a tolerable misstatement of $60,000, and the expected population misstatement is $30,000.

The sample size, using the table in *Audit Sampling* (New York: AICPA, 2001), is 175. The book value of these accounts is $1,000,000. Madera finds that the difference between the book value of the sample and its audited value is a $4,000 overstatement. This results in a projected misstatement of $20,000, according to the following calculation. The percentage of accounts receivable that was sampled is $1,000,000/$5,000,000 = 20%. Therefore, the projected misstatement is $4,000/0.20 = $20,000. In this case, because the projected misstatement of $20,000 is comfortably lower than the expected population misstatement of $30,000 and the tolerable misstatement of $60,000, the auditor can conclude that the accounts receivable account is not materially misstated.

As was the case when the auditor used sampling to test controls and transactions, the auditor will analyze the misstatements found in the sample to determine the reason for their occurrence and whether she can reduce their effects by isolating them.

Selection of Items That Make Up the Sample

If statistical methods are used, the items that make up the sample must be selected randomly; otherwise, interpretation of the results is meaningless. If statistical methods are not used, nonrandom selection is acceptable. As mentioned earlier, the use of the monetary unit sampling technique not only produces a sample size but also results in the selection of the items that make up the sample.

The auditor uses sampling and each type of test—tests of controls, substantive tests of transactions, analytical procedures, and substantive tests of balances—during the audit process to determine whether the financial statements are free of material misstatement.

THE AUDIT PROCESS

LO11   The audit process comprises four distinct yet integrated phases: planning and designing the audit, performing tests of controls and tests of transactions, performing analytical procedures and tests of balances, and completing the audit and issuing the audit report.

In theory, the first three phases are chronologically performed. That is, tests of controls and tests of transactions are performed prior to performing analytical procedures and tests of balances. In practice, however, these first three phases often are performed simultaneously, an approach that is more efficient. Economics and experience are two reasons for performing these phases simultaneously. With respect to economics, the more efficiently an auditor can perform an audit, the lower the cost of the audit. Also, performing audits more efficiently and at a lower cost increases the likelihood that the auditor will perform more audits, obtain additional experience, and thus add greater value to the financial statements being audited. This experience, in turn, can lead to even more efficiency—and, more importantly—effectiveness by the auditor.

Plan and Design the Audit

The first phase of auditing involves collecting information about the audit client. When auditing a client for the first time, the auditor must obtain extensive information about such items as corporate governance and business processes. For continuing clients, the auditor's knowledge must be updated for changes since the last audit was conducted. These changes could include key personnel changes, introduction or discontinuance of products manufactured or sold, and installation of new business reporting systems.

The planning phase is also important from the standpoint of determining the amount of audit firm resources that are expected to be allocated to this client. (If the auditor does not make this determination early in the audit, those resources may not be available later when the audit work is to be performed.) Typically, an audit will begin with an examination of the current (unaudited) financial statements. Analytical procedures are used to highlight areas that are of particular concern to the auditor. These areas usually require more auditor attention and thus should be considered when the auditor designs the audit so that these concerns are adequately addressed.

Performance of Tests of Controls and Substantive Tests of Transactions

Tests of controls and substantive tests of transactions are similar (see the earlier discussion of each type). They are performed in this phase to determine whether controls over safeguarding assets and recording transactions are functioning well enough to decrease the extent of tests of transactions and test of balances.

Performance of Analytical Procedures and Substantive Tests of Balances

Analytical procedures are used here as a supplemental or the only procedure applied to the audit of accounts that have immaterial balances. Substantive tests of balances are conducted to determine whether balances (particularly those of accounts that appear on the balance sheet) are not materially misstated.

Completion of the Audit and Issuance of the Audit Report

After the preceding phases have been completed, the auditor must determine the overall reasonableness of the financial statements. In particular, he must determine whether the financial statements, taken as a whole, fairly present the financial position, results of operations, and cash flows in accordance with the basis of accounting specified in the footnotes to the financial statements. The result of this determination is a judgment as to the type of audit report (unqualified, qualified) that the auditor believes should be issued.

Certain other activities occur during this period:

- Assessing the going concern status of the audited entity to determine whether an unqualified opinion with modified wording should be issued.
- Submitting an inquiry to the client's attorney (a request for information about contingencies that could affect the financial status of the audit client).
- Reviewing to identify subsequent events that could require adjustment to the financial statements or disclosure in the footnotes to the financial statements. Such events occur between the end of the fiscal year but prior to the issuance of the auditor's report. An example of a subsequent event that requires adjustment to the financial statements is the declaration of bankruptcy of a major customer that owes a material amount to the audit client; this information provides additional evidence as to the collectibility of the receivable listed on the balance sheet. An example of a subsequent event that requires only footnote disclosure is the destruction of a major asset by fire after the end of the fiscal year.
- Reviewing for contingent liabilities and commitments to be disclosed in the footnotes to the financial statements.

- Obtaining the management representation letter that formalizes statements made by management during the audit.
- Issuing a management letter, the objective of which is to inform the client of the auditor's recommendations as to ways in which the audit client can improve its business.

THE AUDIT OF INTERNAL CONTROLS OVER FINANCIAL REPORTING

LO12 According to Auditing Standard No. 2, issued by the PCAOB, the auditor of a company's financial statements must also perform an audit of the internal controls over financial reporting. This audit is to be integrated with the audit of the financial statements. Specifically, the auditor's responsibilities are to

- Conduct an integrated audit of the financial statements and of internal control over financial reporting.
- Issue an opinion on management's assessment of internal control over financial reporting.
- Issue an opinion on the effectiveness of internal control over financial reporting.

Management's responsibilities include

- Accepting responsibility for the effective operation of internal control over financial reporting.
- Evaluating the effectiveness using adequate criteria.
- Providing adequate evidence of the evaluation.
- Providing a written assessment of an evaluation of financial reporting controls as of the end of the fiscal year.

Design Deficiencies

The auditor is to design an audit program to identify internal control deficiencies, which occur when the design or operation of a control may not prevent or detect misstatements on a timely basis. Internal control deficiencies can be in either the design or operation. A **design deficiency** exists when a necessary control is missing or is not properly designed. An **operation deficiency** occurs when the control does not operate according to design or when the person performing the control does not have the authority or the ability to perform it. Note that a control deficiency does *not* have to result in a misstatement; it merely must be a deficiency that *could allow* a misstatement in financial reporting to occur. Deficiencies can be either a significant or material weakness, depending on their severity.

A **significant deficiency** is one or more control deficiencies that could affect the entity's ability to initiate, authorize, record, process, or report consequential external financial information in accordance with GAAP and results in a more than remote likelihood that a more than inconsequential misstatement would not be detected or prevented. A **material weakness** is a significant deficiency (or combination of deficiencies) that could result in more than a remote likelihood that a material misstatement of externally reported financial information could occur. (SAS No. 112, released after AS No. 2, similarly defined *significant deficiency* and *material weakness* and set the requirement to report these control deficiencies to the board of directors in audits of nonpublicly held companies.)

Auditor's Evaluation Process

The auditor must evaluate the process by which management assessed the internal controls over financial reporting. This evaluation begins by obtaining an understanding (typically through inquiry of the client, possibly through reading a policy and procedures manual) of management's assessment process. Gaining an understanding is often affected by several factors, including an understanding of company-level controls (e.g., general controls over IT), evaluating audit committee effectiveness (independence, involvement with internal control, etc.), understanding the period-end financial reporting process (significant because of its effect on external financial reporting), and walkthroughs—a technique by which the auditor follows the physical or virtual path of a transaction (or process) from beginning to end. (Walkthroughs are required of the auditor for each year and each major class of transaction, giving the auditor a chance to question those who perform controls.)

After the auditor has gained an understanding of management's assessment process and has identified the controls over financial reporting that she intends to test, she determines the nature, timing, and extent of tests to be performed. With respect to the nature of tests, recall that evidence represented by documentation does not always provide the highest level of evidence—in other words, the auditor could need to reperform the control indicated by the document. The time during which the auditor performs certain tests depends on whether the control is performed continuously or occasionally. Review and approval are more critical controls over nonroutine transactions; therefore, these controls should be thoroughly tested. These controls are especially critical for any adjustments made to the books just prior to the issuance of financial statements because fraudulent financial statements could be the objective of such an adjustment.

After the auditor has tested the controls over financial reporting, he forms an opinion on their effectiveness. The auditor must consider evidence he gathered in the regular financial statement audit in addition to the evidence collected through procedures specifically designed to assess internal controls over financial statement reporting. The auditor must obtain a written representation on the effectiveness of internal control over financial reporting from management and must document the items shown in Figure 4.5.

Reporting on Internal Control over Financial Reporting

The auditor's report on internal controls over financial reporting contains two opinions:

- The auditor's opinion on whether management's assessment of the effectiveness of internal control over financial reporting is reasonably correct.
- The auditor's opinion, based on his or her assessment, of whether the internal control over financial reporting is effective.

FIGURE 4.5
Auditor
Documentation
Requirements

- Processes, procedures, judgments, and results relating to the auditor's audit of controls over financial reporting.
- Audit understanding and evaluation of the design of each major component of internal controls over financial reporting.
- The points at which misstatement could occur within each significant account, major classes of transactions, and disclosures.
- Justification and extent to which the work of others was relied on when conducting audit.
- Description of known control deficiencies and a determination of whether these were major weaknesses or merely significant deficiencies.

An auditor who agrees with *management's assessment of effectiveness of internal control* issues an unqualified opinion. If the auditor disagrees, the opinion is adverse. With respect to the opinion on the *effectiveness of internal control over financial reporting,* the auditor's report can be unqualified, qualified (due to limited scope restriction), adverse, or disclaimer. The presence of significant deficiencies that are not likely to result in major weaknesses in internal controls will result in an unqualified opinion.

For the integrated audit, the auditor is allowed to issue two audit reports, one on the financial statements themselves and the other on internal control over financial reporting. On the other hand, the auditor may issue one report that contains an opinion on the financial statements and another opinion on internal control over financial reporting. The report shown in Figure 4.1 represents the situation in which the auditor is issuing two reports and merely refers to the report on internal controls over financial reporting in the audit report on the financial statements.

The PCAOB continues its efforts to improve the implementation of the internal control reporting requirements of the Sarbanes-Oxley Act of 2002. These efforts focus on emphasizing the efficient performance of the integrated audit, reinforcing auditor effectiveness through PCAOB inspections, and providing guidance and education to public accountants that audit small companies (especially education to help them audit internal controls over financial reporting). In addition, the Committee of Sponsoring Organizations (COSO) has issued *Internal Control over Financial Reporting—Guidance for Small Public Companies* designed to aid companies in establishing and maintaining effective internal control over financial reporting. The COSO document could also be helpful to management in assessing the effectiveness of these internal controls.

THE AUDITOR'S RESPONSIBILITY TO DETECT FRAUD

LO13   Auditors are to search for the existence of material misstatements in financial statements whether due to errors or fraud. SAS No. 99, *Consideration of Fraud in a Financial Statement Audit,* and a briefing paper, *Financial Fraud,* written by an advisory group of the PCAOB, provide auditors specific guidance on searching for fraud.

SAS No. 99, *Consideration of Fraud in a Financial Statement Audit*

SAS No. 99 specifies that auditors must explicitly consider the potential that fraud exists in the financial statements by discussion among the audit team of how fraud could have been committed by and against the audit client and how the financial statements could have been affected. SAS No. 99 stresses the importance of professional skepticism (especially the ill effects of overrelying on inquiry of the client) and contains a section describing fraud and a discussion of its characteristics.

SAS No. 99 provides examples of sources that auditors can use to gather information when identifying the risks of fraud. These include the client (especially management), analytical procedures to determine areas that could have been affected by fraud, consideration of fraud risk factors, discussion among those on the audit engagement team, information gathered as a result of determining whether to accept (or continue serving) the client, and the results of reviews of interim financial statements.

The statement goes beyond previous guidance provided to auditors by indicating that, as a part of the assessment process, auditors must connect the identification of fraud risk characteristics to their response. This connection is considered a synthesis of risk identification and involves incorporating various fraud risk characteristics to produce a holistic judgment of the likelihood that fraud has occurred and how it was concealed.

An auditor who suspects that a misstatement (including an omission of information) could be the result of fraud is required to do the following:

- Obtain additional evidence.
- Consider any effects on other areas of the audit.
- Discuss the auditor's suspicion and her or his plan to obtain additional evidence with a member of management who is at least one level above those suspected of perpetrating the fraud and with select persons including senior management and the audit committee if one exists.
- Consider suggesting that the client seek the advice of legal counsel.

Note that materiality is not a factor in determining whether additional evidence should be obtained and communicating concerns to affected parties such as the audit committee; often the initial evidence of fraud is only the tip of the iceberg and appears immaterial. Thus, the auditor is expected to investigate any suspected frauds. If the auditor obtains additional evidence that indicates the presence of fraud, she may consider withdrawing from the audit engagement particularly if senior management is involved. She may also desire to seek legal counsel on such matters as the consequences of her continued association with the audit client and, if necessary, the manner in which to withdraw.

Financial Fraud

A briefing paper, *Financial Fraud,* was issued as a result of a meeting of the Standing Advisory Group (SAG) of the PCAOB in September 2004. The paper is not an official pronouncement of the PCAOB and does not necessarily represent the views of its board. The meeting was conducted to generate discussion of fraud issues in anticipation of creating an auditing standard that pertains to the detection of fraud in audits of publicly held companies. In the briefing paper, the PCAOB provides examples of what the SAG believes are inappropriate disclaimers of responsibility for detecting fraud in SAS No. 99 and implies that any new standard issued by the PCAOB would emphasize the auditor's responsibility to protect public investors.

The Profession's Response to Fraud

In addition to the issuance of SAS No. 99 and the PCAOB briefing paper, the AICPA has embarked on an antifraud initiative, which includes cosponsoring the Institute for Fraud Studies with the University of Texas at Austin and the Association of Certified Fraud Examiners (ACFE). The AICPA has also developed an Antifraud and Corporate Responsibility Resource Center located on the AICPA's Web site; has designed antifraud criteria and controls intended for public corporations; has urged stock exchanges to require effective antifraud training for management of companies listed with it, their boards of directors, and audit committees; and has encouraged CPAs to allocate at least 10 percent of their CPE hours to fraud topics.

OTHER SERVICES

LO14   Although the audit of financial statements is one of the two services most closely identified with public accounting firms (the other being tax preparation), it is not the only assurance service performed by public accountants. Other services include providing reports on specified elements, accounts, or items; performing agreed-upon procedures engagements; preparing compliance reports and reviews; and offering specialty assurance services such as WebTrust and SysTrust. These services are briefly discussed next. In addition, the compilation service is discussed to increase awareness of this nonassurance service that often carries some assurance.

Reports on Specified Elements, Accounts, or Items on Financial Statements

An auditor may be engaged to audit parts of a financial statement. These parts could be specified elements, accounts, or items. For example, an auditor may be asked to audit the gross sales of a retail store to determine the correct basis for rental payments when rent is based on a percentage of gross sales. The auditor may audit the accounts receivable of a company as a prerequisite to **factoring,** which is selling accounts receivable. Generally, these audits are more detailed than the audits of these elements, accounts, or items as a part of a larger audit of the financial statements.

The auditor's report issued under these circumstances differs from the standard auditor's report. The scope and opinion paragraphs refer to the element, account, or item being audited, not the financial statements and, if the element, account, or item was audited to determine compliance with a contract, the auditor includes a separate paragraph restricting use of the report.

Agreed-Upon Procedures Engagements

An *agreed-upon procedures engagement* is one in which the auditor applies agreed-upon procedures and reports on the findings of these procedures. The report on this engagement does not contain an opinion. Furthermore, the user of the report bears the responsibility for determining whether the procedures agreed upon are sufficient. The report identifies the specified elements, accounts, or items the auditor tested, the specific procedures agreed to by the user, the findings, and the persons (entities) to whom the report is restricted.

Compliance Reports

An auditor may be requested to report on whether an audited entity is in compliance with certain contractual agreements or regulatory requirements. For example, an auditor could examine evidence that would provide some basis for reporting on whether the audited entity is in compliance with certain debt covenants that specify that the entity cannot exceed a certain debt-to-equity ratio.

The report issued provides negative, *not* positive, assurance. In other words, the language of the report indicates that "… nothing came to our attention that would cause us to believe that the Company failed to comply with the terms, covenants, provisions, or conditions of the agreement." Furthermore, the report is restricted to specified users.

Review

A review provides a lower level of assurance than does the audit. This lower level of assurance is termed "negative assurance" because the accountant states in the report, "… we are not aware of any material modifications that should be made to the accompanying financial statements in order for them to be in conformity with [the basis of accounting purported to be used by the company]." An example of a standard review report is presented in Figure 4.6.

A review consists primarily of inquiry of client and analytical procedures. Because these evidence-gathering procedures do not usually produce evidence of high reliability, the scope of the service and thus the assurance provided are substantially less than that of an audit. Often the financial statements of small to medium-size businesses and quarterly financial statements of publicly held companies are reviewed.

FIGURE 4.6
Standard Review
Report

To the Owners of Thebes Corporation

We have reviewed the accompanying balance sheet of Thebes Corporation as of December 31, 2016, and the related statements of income, retained earnings, and cash flows for the year then ended. A review includes primarily applying analytical procedures to management's financial data and making inquiries of company management. A review is substantially less in scope than an audit, the objective of which is the expression of an opinion regarding the financial statements as a whole. Accordingly, we do not express such an opinion.

Our responsibility is to conduct the review in accordance with Statements on Standards for Accounting and Review Services issued by the American Institute of Certified Public Accountants. Those standards require us to perform procedures to obtain limited assurance that there are no material modifications that should be made to the financial statements. We believe that the results of our procedures provide a reasonable basis for our report.

Based on our review, we are not aware of any material modifications that should be made to the accompanying financial statements in order for them to be in conformity with accounting principles generally accepted in the United States of America.

Tate & Young
January 20, 2017

Prospective Financial Statements

A public accountant may be requested to provide assurance on the preparation of financial forecasts and projections. The public accountant may even be involved in preparing these forecasts and projections. In any event, the accountant is never to issue a statement that indicates that he is vouching for the achievability of the forecasts or projections.

Specialty Assurance Services

Public accountants sometimes provide assurance services other than audits, reviews, agreed-upon procedures, and the examination of prospective financial statements. These services include WebTrust and SysTrust. WebTrust is a service that was jointly developed by the AICPA and the Canadian Institute of Chartered Accountants. If a Web site meets specific criteria that address transaction integrity, information processes, and business practices—as determined by a CPA—it is allowed to display the WebTrust seal. The criteria against which the Web site is evaluated, the Trust Services principles, are listed in Figure 4.7.

FIGURE 4.7
Trust Services
Principles

Principle	Objective
Security	The entity maintains security practices that protect the Web site or system against unauthorized access.
Availability	The Web site or system is available to meet the needs of users.
Processing integrity	The Web site or system processes authorized transactions in a complete, accurate, and timely manner.
Online privacy	Personal information collected during e-commerce activities is used, disclosed, and retained as committed or agreed.
Confidentiality	Information considered confidential is protected as committed or agreed.

SysTrust is a service provided to evaluate the integrity of a computer system by means of testing controls related to the system. The service, then, is a system application of the WebTrust service and utilizes the same Trust Services principles that are used when evaluating Web sites.

Compilation

The compilation service involves determining whether the financial statements appear reasonable without the performance of any type of examination. *Compilation* is the act of compiling, in the form of financial statements, information that is the representation of management, but the act of compilation does not have to involve the preparation of financial statements. For example, a company has prepared its own financial statements and requests that an accountant read them to determine whether they appear reasonable; this, too, is termed a *compilation.*

An example of a standard compilation report is presented in Figure 4.8. Note that the report states that the accountants "… do not express an opinion or any other form of assurance on them." Still, because a certified public accountant is the person who usually issues a compilation report on these financial statements and the AICPA is mentioned, an aura of assurance often surrounds them and, therefore, some assurance is conveyed by the accountants' compilation report. Compilations are usually performed for small businesses.

It is important that the forensic accountant understand the difference between an audit, a compilation, and a review. Whereas the audit provides positive (i.e., explicit) assurance as to whether the financial statements present financial position, results of operations, and cash flows in accordance with the basis purported by management, a compilation provides no such assurance, and a review provides limited assurance.

FIGURE 4.8
Standard
Compilation Report

To the Owners of Millstadt Corporation

We have compiled the accompanying balance sheet of Millstadt Corporation as of December 31, 2016, and the related statements of income, retained earnings, and cash flows for the year then ended. We have not audited or reviewed the accompanying financial statements and, accordingly, do not express an opinion or provide any assurance about whether the financial statements are in accordance with accounting principles generally accepted in the United States of America.

Management is responsible for the preparation and fair presentation of the financial statements in accordance with accounting principles generally accepted in the United States of America and for designing, implementing, and maintaining internal control relevant to the preparation and fair presentation of financial statements.

Our responsibility is to conduct the compilation in accordance with Statements on Standards for Accounting and Review Services issued by the American Institute of Certified Public Accountants. The objective of a compilation is to assist management in presenting financial information in the form of financial statements without undertaking to obtain or provide any assurance that there are no material modifications that should be made to the financial statements.

Tate & Young
January 15, 2017

OTHER AUDITING FUNCTIONS

Several other important areas of auditing exist, particularly those relating to internal auditing, operational auditing, and governmental auditing. These are discussed in the following sections.

Internal Auditing

According to the IIA, internal auditing is

> . . . an independent, objective assurance and consulting activity designed to add value and improve an organization's operations. It helps an organization accomplish its objectives by bringing a systematic, disciplined approach to evaluate and improve the effectiveness of risk management, control, and governance processes.

Internal auditing is typically broader than the auditing performed by public accountants (i.e., external auditors) when they audit financial statements. Internal auditors not only audit certain aspects of financial information before the information is evaluated by external auditors but also are often involved in the study and evaluation of company processes. They do this by collecting and organizing data so that management can be better informed when making decisions about the company's daily and long-term operations. For example, internal auditors may be involved in the collection, presentation, and evaluation of information pertaining to the geographical relocation of the company.

Internal auditing is performed in most medium and large-size companies. The persons who perform the auditing function are usually employees of the company, so they are not independent of the company they audit. These auditors' nonindependence requires careful consideration when determining the party to whom the internal auditors report. They should report to an audit committee composed of directors who are not a part of management because the auditors typically report on some aspect of management's performance. (If the company does not have an audit committee, the internal auditor should report to the board of directors or, in the case of a proprietorship or partnership, the owners.)

Some companies outsource the internal audit function. The outsourcing approach provides for greater independence of the auditors; as a result, the internal auditor could more likely express concerns about the company, especially those that involve management. As with internal auditors who are employees of the company they audit, these auditors should report to an audit committee or, if none exists, the board of directors.

In some companies, the internal audit function is performed by one person who does not have the title of internal auditor. What is most important is the competence of the auditor and the persons to whom this person reports.

The forensic accountant can be a tremendous asset to the internal audit department as a specialist member of the internal audit department or as an expert who is engaged when fraud is suspected.

Operational Auditing

The objective of operational auditing is to determine whether an entity's process is effective and conducted efficiently. Auditors performing operational audits may, for example, evaluate a process such as trimming excess material from a metal part to determine whether the amount of waste can be reduced or determine whether a city has met its charge to reduce the number of accidents experienced by its maintenance workers. Reports that contain the findings of an operational audit are typically restricted to management.

As with other types of auditing, an operational audit must establish criteria, and an evaluation of controls may occur as an attendant activity. For example, if a city is charged with reducing the number of accidents of its maintenance workers, a control related to reporting accidents may be subjected to testing before a conclusion can be reached on the accident level.

Operational auditing can lead to the discovery of fraud. For example, if the waste material produced by a manufacturing process is to be sold to a scrap dealer, fraud may occur if part of the waste material is diverted by an employee who later sells it for personal gain. At this point, the skills of a knowledgeable forensic accountant can be utilized to determine the effects of any **defalcation** or theft by an employee.

Governmental Auditing

The objective of auditors who audit governmental entities, such as federal, state, and local governmental units and higher education institutions, is to determine whether the audited entity is complying with the provisions of contracts, grant agreements, and laws (especially those pertaining to the financial use of monies allocated to the entity for specific purposes).

These governmental units and higher education institutions usually have their own auditors who perform audits of various programs and offices. Additionally, some CPA firms audit these entities. Regardless of whether the governmental auditors are internal or external, they must follow generally accepted governmental auditing standards (GAGAS), which are published by the Government Accountability Office (GAO) in the Yellow Book (named for its yellow cover).

The Yellow Book auditing standards are similar to the 10 generally accepted auditing standards with a few exceptions. The most notable exceptions follow.

- The emphasis is on compliance auditing.
- The level of materiality is usually lower than the level found in financial statement audits, consistent with the auditor's charge of protecting the citizens. (Note that use of a lower level of materiality generally results in a more detailed examination than would a higher level.)
- The audit report must state that the audit was conducted in accordance with GAGAS and either indicate the scope of the auditor's tests of laws and regulations and internal controls and the results of those tests or refer to a report in which this information is discussed.

Single Audit Act

The Single Audit Act of 1984 required a single audit that meets the requirements of all federal agencies. In 1990, this act was amended to extend the requirements to all higher educational institutions and certain other not-for-profit organizations through the issuance of OMB Circular A-133. A further amendment in 1996 exempted small entities from the act's requirements; currently, entities receiving less than $500,000 in federal funds are not required to comply with most of the act's provisions.

The 1996 amendment and OMB Circular A-133 require the auditor to obtain a sufficient understanding of internal controls over federal programs if control risk for major programs is assessed at a low level. It also requires the auditor to determine whether the entity being audited has complied with the laws, regulations, contracts, and grant agreements that have direct and material effects on each of the entity's major programs.

Required Reports

OMB Circular A-133 requires several reports including these:

- A report that includes an opinion (or a disclaimer) as to whether the financial statements are, in all material respects, presented fairly according to GAAP and an opinion (or disclaimer) on whether the schedule of expenditures of federal awards is presented fairly and is consistent with the financial statements.

- A report on the entity's internal controls over financial reporting and its major programs.

- A report on the entity's compliance with laws, regulations, contracts, and grant agreements for circumstances in which noncompliance could affect the financial statements.

- A schedule of findings and questioned costs.

These reports are issued to inform the entities that disburse funds to the audited unit (and interested citizens) of the use of these funds. Forensic accountants have been instrumental in investigating fraud against the federal, state, and local governmental units. GAO auditors, for example, investigate suspected misuse of funds. Howard Davia, a former GAO auditor, once remarked that the United States provides some of the best experience in uncovering fraud because it is one of the only entities that can have fraud committed against it repeatedly and not go out of business.

Summary

Auditing is a process that involves the collection and evaluation of evidence about financial information (and nonfinancial information in the case of internal, operational, and governmental auditing). In addition, it encompasses the communication of the results of the audit to interested and affected persons; this communication usually occurs by means of an audit report. Auditing exists for several reasons: the absence of owners and lenders, the complexity of business transactions and accounting standards, and the volume of business transactions engaged in daily by many companies. This demand for and importance of auditing have led to the establishment of a regulatory process that encourages the performance of high-quality audits. This process involves the licensing of U.S. auditors of financial statements by the states in which they practice. Those who practice in other countries must meet the requirements of those countries. Auditors in the United States are affected by several organizations including the PCAOB, SEC, FASB, GASB, AICPA, and the IIA. Some of these organizations are regulatory, and others promulgate standards—such as auditing standards—that auditors must follow. Materiality and risk underlie the conduct of auditing.

Auditors search for material misstatements, whether from errors or fraud, and recognize that the risk exists that they may not arrive at a correct conclusion. Therefore, auditors provide reasonable—not absolute—assurance that the financial statements are free of material misstatement. At times, auditors perform other types of audits, such as operational audits, and function as internal auditors. Governmental auditors determine whether entities that receive federal, state, and local funds use them according to the purpose for which they were intended. Forensic accountants function as experts who provide specialized skills in determining the effect of fraud on the financial statements.

Glossary

acceptable detection risk   Level of detection risk the auditor is willing to accept.

acceptable risk of assessing control risk too low   Accepted level of likelihood that the auditor is overrelying on internal controls.

acceptable risk of incorrect acceptance   Acceptable likelihood that the auditor will conclude that an account balance is fairly stated when, in fact, it is not fairly stated.

accounting   Process of recording, classifying, and summarizing economic events in a manner that assists decision makers when they make decisions based on financial data.

adverse report   Report that contains the opinion that the financial statements were not prepared in accordance with the basis specified in the footnotes.

analytical procedure   Test used to determine whether account balances appear reasonable.

audit assertion   Statement about a company's financial condition and results of operations that is implicitly contained in the financial statements.

audit risk   Likelihood that the financial statements will contain material misstatements after the auditor has issued an unqualified opinion.

auditing   Process of gathering and evaluating evidence about information to determine the degree of correspondence between the information and the standards used to prepare the information.

auditor   Person (or firm) performing auditing services.

chartered accountant   Person who has met specific requirements of the Canadian Public Accountability Board or the corresponding boards in Australia and the United Kingdom.

computed upper exception rate   Maximum rate of exceptions that exist in a population given an acceptable risk of assessing control risk too low.

control risk   Likelihood that misstatements that exceed a tolerable level will not be prevented or detected in a timely manner by the audited company's internal controls.

corroborating evidence   Evidence that supports assertions made by management.

defalcation   Theft by an employee.

design deficiency   State that exists when a necessary control is missing or a control was not properly designed.

detection risk   Likelihood that the auditor will not detect misstatements that exceed a tolerable level.

disclaimer report   Report issued when the auditor cannot form an opinion on the financial statements.

factoring   Selling accounts receivable.

generally accepted accounting principles   Standards by which financial statements are prepared.

generally accepted auditing standards   Standards by which the process of auditing is conducted.

independent   Description of an auditor who is separate, financially and otherwise, from the company being audited.

inherent risk   Likelihood that an account or class of transactions is materially misstated before considering the effects of internal controls.

judgmental sampling Selection of sample size and/or individual items that make up the sample by means of professional judgment.

material weakness Significant deficiency (or combination of deficiencies) that could result in more than a remote likelihood that a material misstatement of externally reported financial information could occur.

operation deficiency State that exists when a control does not operate according to design or when the person performing the control does not have the authority or the ability to perform it.

preliminary judgment of materiality Initial amount of materiality selected by the auditor for the financial statements.

professional skepticism Attitude of an auditor that causes the auditor to critically evaluate evidence (or lack of evidence).

public accountant Person who has passed the Uniform Certified Public Accountant exam and who is licensed to practice public accounting.

qualified report Report that contains the opinion that the financial statements contain a departure from the basis of accounting specified in the footnotes or an indication that the scope of the auditor's examination was limited.

reasonable assurance Level of confidence the auditor conveys as a result of performing an audit.

revised judgment of materiality Level of materiality that differs from the preliminary judgment as a result of new information discovered by the auditor.

sampling Examining less than the entire population so that a conclusion can be formulated about the entire population.

sampling risk Likelihood that the auditor's judgment based on a portion of the population would differ from the judgment based on an examination of the entire population.

scope limitation Restriction on the auditor's ability to gather evidence about the financial statements.

segment Account or group of accounts (e.g., Bonds Payable and Bond Discount).

significant deficiency One or more control deficiencies that could affect the entity's ability to initiate, authorize, record, process, or report consequential external financial information in accordance with GAAP; results in a higher than remote likelihood that a misstatement that is more than inconsequential would not be detected or prevented.

standard unqualified report Report that contains the opinion that the financial statements are free of material misstatements (i.e., are prepared in accordance with the basis of accounting specified in the footnotes).

statistical sampling Method of sampling based on probabilities.

substantive tests of balances Tests used to determine whether account balances (e.g., accounts receivable) are presented in the financial statements correctly.

substantive tests of transactions Tests used to determine whether a class of transactions (e.g., cash) is recorded correctly.

test of controls Test used to determine the operation effectiveness of internal controls.

tolerable exception rate Rate of exceptions (or deviations) from a prescribed control that the auditor is willing to accept and thus believes the control is functioning as well as initially believed; applies equally to substantive tests of transactions as the exception rate the auditor is willing to accept and thus believes the class of transactions is correctly recorded.

tolerable misstatement   Amount of misstatement (in dollars) that the auditor is willing to accept and thus believes the account balance is correctly recorded.

unqualified report   Report that contains the opinion that the financial statements are free of material misstatement.

unqualified report with modified wording   Report that contains the opinion that the financial statements are free of material misstatement as well as other information deemed useful to users of the audit report.

variables sampling   Statistical sampling methods used to determine whether account balances are materially misstated.

Review Questions

1. Which of the following best defines auditing?
   a. Process of gathering and evaluating evidence about information to determine the degree of correspondence between the information and the standards used to prepare the information.
   b. Process of gathering and evaluating evidence about information to determine the degree of correspondence between the information and the accuracy of the financial statements.
   c. The process of gathering and evaluating evidence about information to determine the degree of correspondence between generally accepted accounting principles (GAAP) and the standards used to prepare the information.
   d. None of the above.

2. The WorldCom case is an example of which of the following?
   a. Best practices in auditing techniques.
   b. Best practices according to generally accepted accounting principles (GAAP).
   c. Normal level of embezzlement in the auditing environment.
   d. None of the above.

3. Which of these best describes auditing?
   a. Process of recording, classifying, and summarizing economic events in a manner that helps decision makers make decisions based on financial data that determines whether the financial data that have been recorded, classified, and summarized are reliable.
   b. An important part of accounting.
   c. Distinct from accounting.
   d. None of the above.

4. Which of the following describes auditors?
   a. Government watchdogs.
   b. Eyes and ears of the SEC.
   c. Facilitators of the movement of capital between investors and companies issuing stock or between lenders and borrowers.
   d. None of the above.

5. Which of the following is *not* true regarding licensing of CPAs?
   a. Licenses are issued at the state level.
   b. Licenses are issued at the federal level.

c. Potential licensees must first pass the Uniform CPA examination.

d. None of the above is not true.

6. As a general rule, auditors in Canada and most European countries must do which of the following?

a. Obtain licensing in their respective countries.

b. Obtain licensing from the International Accounting Standards Board.

c. Both *a* and *b*.

d. Obtain licensing from the International Accounting Standards Committee.

7. Which of the following is *not* one of the primary rule-making bodies that affect the auditing profession?

a. PCAOB.

b. SEC.

c. FASB.

d. GASB.

e. None of the above is *not* a primary rule-making body that affects the auditing profession.

8. Which of the following organizations was/were created by the Sarbanes-Oxley Act?

a. PCAOB.

b. SEC.

c. FASB.

d. GASB.

e. All of the above.

9. Which of the following groups is the primary promulgator of financial auditing standards for private companies?

a. PCAOB.

b. SEC.

c. FASB.

d. GASB.

e. None of the above.

10. Which of the following organizations affects the international auditing profession by establishing standards on auditing, quality control, review, other assurance, and related services and encouraging similarity between national and international standards?

a. International Accounting Standards Board.

b. Transnational Accounting Standards Board.

c. Multinational Accounting Standards Board.

d. None of the above.

11. Which of the following is the reason that auditors audit companies?

a. To determine whether their financial statements (including footnotes) present financial position, results of operations, and cash flows in accordance with some accounting basis.

b. To determine whether their financial statements (including footnotes) present financial position, results of operations, and cash flows in accordance with international auditing standards.

   c. To determine whether their financial statements (including footnotes) present financial position, results of operations, and cash flows in accordance with applicable auditing standards.

   d. None of the above.

12. Which of these statements is *in*correct?

   a. The auditor's objective is to determine whether the financial statements are free of misstatement whether from error or fraud.

   b. Auditors have a responsibility to plan the audit to uncover material misstatements regardless of their character.

   c. A given amount of fraud is not as easy to find as is the same amount of error.

   d. None of these statements is incorrect.

13. The concept of *preliminary judgment of materiality* is defined in which of the following?

   a. Auditing standards.

   b. GAAP standards.

   c. Practice.

   d. All of the above.

14. What are the three conditions that auditors consider when making a preliminary judgment of materiality?

   a. Presence of fraud, consequences arising from equity obligations, and misstatements that affect the financial statements.

   b. Presence of fraud, consequences arising from contractual obligations, and errors that affect earnings trends.

   c. Likelihood of fraud, consequences arising from contractual obligations, and misstatements that affect earnings trends.

   d. Presence of fraud, consequences arising from contractual obligations, and misstatements that affect earnings trends.

15. The suspicion of fraud probably affects which of these?

   a. Audit procedures selected by the auditor.

   b. Amount of the testing.

   c. The timing of procedures selected by the auditor.

   d. Both *a* and *b.*

   e. None of the above.

16. Which of the following defines *tolerable misstatement*?

   a. Maximum amount of misstatement the auditor is willing to tolerate in a segment.

   b. Minimum amount of misstatement that the auditor is willing to tolerate before initiating fraud detection procedures.

   c. Maximum amount of misstatement that the auditor is willing to tolerate before initiating fraud detection procedures.

   d. None of the above.

17. How is a determination of whether a segment is materially misstated made?

   a. By comparing the tolerable misstatement to the results specified by generally accepted auditing standards.

   b. By comparing the maximum misstatement to the results of testing.

    c. By comparing the tolerable misstatement to the results of testing.

    d. By comparing the minimum misstatement to the results specified by generally accepted auditing standards.

18. *Risk* in the context of financial information is defined as which of these?

    a. Likelihood that a material misstatement will influence the decision of a reasonable user of the financial statements.

    b. Likelihood of significant errors in the financial statements.

    c. Likelihood of material misstatements in the financial statements.

    d. Likelihood that fraud will influence the decision of a reasonable user of the financial statements.

19. How many components of risk must the auditor consider?

    a. 1.

    b. 2.

    c. 3.

    d. 4.

    e. 5.

20. When is the assessment of inherent risk made?

    a. After considering the effects of internal controls.

    b. Before considering applicable audit procedures.

    c. Before considering the effects of internal controls.

    d. None of the above.

21. One assessment of acceptable audit risk is made for which of these?

    a. Entire audit.

    b. Each audit segment.

    c. High risk segments.

    d. None of the above.

22. Risks affect which of the following?

    a. Timing of testing.

    b. Extent of testing.

    c. Both the timing and the extent of testing.

    d. None of the above.

23. Acceptable detection risk depends on which of these?

    a. Inherent risk and control risk.

    b. Inherent risk, acceptable audit risk, and sampling risk.

    c. Inherent risk, acceptable audit risk, and control risk.

    d. None of the above.

24. Which of the following is a list of the different types of opinions expressed in audit reports?

    a. Standard, unqualified, qualified, negative, and disclaimer.

    b. Standard unqualified, unqualified with modified wording, qualified, adverse, and disclaimer.

    c. Standard unqualified, modified, qualified, adverse, and disclaimer.

    d. None of the above.

25. If the client has changed accounting principles during the current year, the auditor is required to do which of these?

    a. Add a paragraph that draws the audit report reader's attention to this change.

    b. Issue a qualified report and add a paragraph pointing out the change.

    c. Issue an adverse report.

    d. Issue a disclaimer report.

Discussion Questions

26. Assume that you are an auditor and as part of your routine audit, you discover a fraud being committed by the accounts receivable manager. The fraud is large enough to have a material impact on the financial statements. How does this finding affect the rest of your audit?

27. What is the impact of an auditor lowering his or her preliminary judgment of materiality?

28. Why would an auditor *not* want to allocate a degree of tolerable misstatement that is too high to any one segment?

29. How important is risk to the auditor? Why?

30. What are the major components of risk considered by auditors?

31. Why does acceptable audit risk not depend on the audit data?

32. In the equation, $ADR = AAR/(IR \times CR)$, does it make sense to rearrange the terms as follows: $AAR = ADR \times IR \times CR$? (Refer to the chapter for the meaning of these terms.)

33. What is the scope paragraph in an audit report?

34. What type of report would an auditor issue after finding that the client changes inventory methods from one year to the next to smooth income?

35. Do client departures from GAAP require the auditor to issue a qualified report? Explain.

36. What is the appropriate action for an auditor who believes the client will not be able to remain as a going concern for more than another year?

37. When does an auditor issue an adverse report?

38. What type of opinion would an auditor likely give for a retail firm that prevents the auditor from reviewing inventories and accounts receivable?

39. What are the seven evidence-gathering procedures?

40. What type of evidence-gathering procedures would normally be used for accounts receivable?

41. Why are analytical procedures applied during the initial phases of audits?

42. What does the auditor accomplish by testing controls?

43. Explain the following statement: "Analytical procedures may show that account balances are misstated but do not provide evidence they are misstated."

44. What is the difference between tracing and vouching?

45. What are substantive tests of balances?

46. Why do auditors use sampling?

47. What is sampling risk?

48. What is sampling for attributes?

49. What are the four audit phases?

50. Why does the PCAOB require a separate but integrated audit of internal controls?

51. What happens if the auditor disagrees with management's assessment of internal control?

52. Are auditors responsible for finding material fraud?

53. Can auditors audit less than the entire financial statements?

54. How does internal auditing differ from external auditing?

55. What is operational auditing?

Cases

56. Remco Gourmet Water Company produces and distributes bottled water in a variety of natural flavors. Jan Cancel, a partner in a local CPA firm, is conducting the first-time-ever audit of Remco. On the second day of her audit, she discovers that the CEO has acquired a large-screen television, a speed boat, and a Jacuzzi for his personal use. All three items were delivered to the CEO's personal residence, and they were booked into the accounting records as consulting expenses. Jan examined Remco's most recent federal tax return and noticed that the items had been included in deductible consulting expenses.

    a. What should Jan Cancel do about her finding?

    b. What impact should the finding have on how she proceeds with the audit?

    c. What impact should the finding have on her audit opinion report?

57. John Rella is a long-time auditor of a medium-size public accounting firm that serves clients in the Miami area. He is auditing Green Market Vitamin Company for the fourth year in a row, but this year Green Market has a new CEO, who has an unusual style of doing business.

    Margarat Boracha, the new CEO, likes to drink and party, and she insists that top employees and business associates drink and party with her. On the first day of the audit, she invites John to meet with her on her private yacht where she has her second office. He thinks nothing of it because he has met with clients on corporate yachts before.

    When John arrives at the yacht, he is in for a big surprise. Margarat is sitting outside on the rear deck in a skimpy bikini, talking with two men in Spanish. She tries to introduce John to the men, but neither of them speaks English. John studied Spanish in college, but he does not try to speak to them in Spanish for fear of showing his weak command of the language.

    A minute later a man appearing to be the captain (because of his white navy-style clothes) calls Margarat to the front of the boat, leaving John alone with the two men. The two begin a heated conversation, but John simply stares out over the water, not letting on that he understands.

    John listens as one of the men begins to describe what sounds like a small airplane arriving from Cartagena. They speak in somewhat coded language, but it does not take him long to figure out that they are speaking about a shipment of cocaine.

    The men leave as soon as Margarat returns. She then sits down with John and begins speaking about her company. She drinks a lot but does not push John to do the same. After a while, John finds she is not only charming but very knowledgeable about business, and he becomes convinced that she is a good leader and probably an effective CEO for Green Market Vitamin Company.

    John leaves the meeting with mixed feelings. On one hand, he would like to retain the engagement because Green Market has been a profitable client in past years and, under Margarat's leadership, will probably add an extra six figures to his personal annual income. On the other hand, he is worried about getting mixed up with someone affiliated with drug dealers.

a. How should John handle the situation?

b. Should he confront Margarat with his concerns?

c. Should John go to the police?

d. Assume that this year is the first year that John is the auditor of Green Market Vitamin Company. Does he need to issue a report if he walks away from Green Market? What might such a report say?

58. Karen Winkler is the senior partner in Three Rivers International Public Accounting firm, whose main office is in Pittsburgh. She is the partner in charge of a first-time audit of the financials for Weezo Beverage Company, which bottles and distributes soft drinks throughout the United States and Latin America.

After about two weeks into the audit, Dick Clemens, the senior audit manager assigned to the engagement, comes to Karen with some bad news: Weezo's internal controls are a total mess.

"They don't even do bank reconciliations," says Dick. "I don't see any way you're going to be able to give this company a clean opinion."

"Don't worry about it," said Karen. "It's a private company."

"Yes," says Dick, "but because there are no controls, we're going to need to quadruple our sample sizes, and when we find irregularities in an account, we'll probably need to audit every single transaction in it."

Karen does some quick math in her head. She had originally quoted Weezo $800,000 for the audit, but if Dick is correct, the cost will soar to several million dollars.

"Again, don't worry about it," says Karen. "We'll do our usual audit assuming a good internal control system. Then we'll look at our sampling results and estimate any errors in the accounts. If the errors are material, we'll simply ask the company to make a corresponding adjustment to earnings. That way we'll be covered from liability. Remember, we're dealing with a private company here. We don't have to worry about Sarbanes-Oxley and SEC reports. The main thing is that the bottom line is good."

Dick walks away scratching his head.

What do you think of Karen's approach to dealing with Weezo's lack of internal controls?

59. Sam Johnson is a new partner in Wilkerson, James, and Flores, an accounting firm. He is in charge of an audit for Zappo Electronics, which manufactures circuit board parts for major international electronics companies.

Zappo's main asset is its inventory, which is listed on the books at $742,000. After doing a complete audit of the inventory, however, Sam discovered that nearly half of it is obsolete and worthless. He reported to the senior partner that the inventory needs to be written down by $350,000 before the firm could sign off on a clean opinion.

The senior partner meets with Zappo's CEO, who argues strongly against any write-down of inventories.

"We'll find a market for every last item in the inventory," said the CEO. "It might take some time, but we'll sell everything."

The senior partner tried to disagree, but the CEO was adamant. "If you make us write down the inventory that much, we won't be able to get any more bank loans, and that will put us out of business."

The senior partner and the CEO haggled back and forth until they finally agreed to a $125,000 write-down.

"That will keep our credit intact," said the CEO.

The next day, Sam met with the senior partner.

"We've agreed to a $125,000 write-down," said the senior partner to Sam. "The company has already made the adjustment, and now I want you to sign the audit report without any qualifications or modifications. This is a good client, and I'm not going to let us lose it over something stupid like this."

Sam objected. His analysis of the inventory was solid, and he did not understand how an honest auditor could simply negotiate a write-off.

"Forget about it," said the senior partner. "The company is financially sound, so what does it matter? Where's our liability? We don't have to worry about getting sued unless the company fails, and you know it isn't going to fail. It's overflowing with military contracts. I wish I owned part of the company myself."

"But that's not how we're supposed to do auditing," said Sam.

"Look," said the senior partner, "Who's to say for sure what that inventory is worth? Just forget about it. Besides, we can get it to do more write-offs next year. If I listened to you, there would be no next year; the company would be cut off from its creditors and out of business."

a. Do you agree with Sam or the senior partner?

b. Defend your position.

c. Should auditors consider the impact of their opinions on clients? A negative opinion can sometimes destroy a company.

Fraud Examination
Theory, Practice, and
Methods

Chapter **Five**

Fraud Prevention and Risk Management

CHAPTER LEARNING OBJECTIVES

After reading Chapter 5, you should be able to

- LO1: Define and explain *information security deliverables.*
- LO2: Define the concept of *information security management system.*
- LO3: Define and explain key concepts relating to information security management systems.
- LO4: Explain the PDCA methodology and how it is applied to information security deliverables.
- LO5: Explain the major international standards that apply to information security.
- LO6: Describe how to evaluate and obtain assurance for information security deliverables.
- LO7: Apply information security concepts to developing information security management systems.

FRAUD PREVENTION AND INFORMATION SECURITY MANAGEMENT SYSTEM (ISMS)

LO1 One important function of forensic accountants and fraud examiners involves advising clients how to prevent fraud. In many cases preventing fraud is much more economical than it is to detect, investigate, and recover from it. That said, however, fraud prevention must be implemented on a cost-benefit basis, and in some cases the most economical approach is to detect fraud rather than prevent it. The economics of fraud prevention verses detection and investigation is discussed in Chapter 6.

The current chapter focuses on fraud prevention as a process in the form of a management system. Given today's complex information technologies, reducing fraud prevention to a list of do's and don'ts is no longer possible. Instead, organizations must rely on various international standards that provide guidance in order to achieve security. Thus, the focus has shifted to security systems. Consequently, the bulk of the discussion in the current chapter focuses on information security management systems from the point of view of international standards. This in turn involves the use of specialized terminology adopted by such standards. For this reason and because standards-based terminology will be used throughout the entire chapter, we begin by defining some basic terminology.

LO2   In many cases, as in Chapter 3, the word *security* simply means limiting access to authorized persons. This is one important meaning of security, but this chapter is concerned with the meaning of *security* in a much broader sense regarding information security deliverables. An **information security deliverable** is any type of security product, which in the broadest sense includes, for example, information-security-related processes, software and hardware products, systems, services, organizational units, environments, warranties, and even security-related personnel.

This chapter focuses primarily on one type of deliverable, the information security management system. An **information security management system (ISMS)** is an organizational internal control process that ensures the following three objectives in relation to data and information within the organization: confidentiality, integrity, and availability. These three objectives are so important that they are common to all information security processes and deliverables.

The definition of an ISMS is framed in terms of internal control because information systems security is merely the application of standard internal control principles to information resources. In fact, good internal control processes require good information security processes. Neither internal control nor information security can exist without the other.

Because internal control processes are very much about risk management, both they and ISMS processes are an integral part of management's overall **enterprise risk management (ERM)** process. ERM involves weighing various opportunities against related risks and managing the opportunities and risks in a way that is consistent with management's objectives and risk preferences. For this reason, as is discussed more thoroughly later, risk management lies in the heart of effective ISMS. An explanation of the three ISMS security objectives common to all information security processes and deliverables follows (see Figure 5.1):

- **Confidentiality**   is the concept that involves ensuring that data and information are made available only to authorized persons.

- **Integrity**   involves accuracy and completeness. *Accuracy* means inputting the correct data into the system and then processing it as intended without errors. For example, an individual must input the correct employee pay rates and other data into the payroll system to achieve accuracy in employee paychecks. Similarly, the payroll software must contain the correct formulas needed to compute employee net pay to achieve accuracy in employee paychecks. In summary, accuracy is achieved by avoiding input and processing errors. *Completeness* ensures that no unauthorized additions, removals, or modifications are made to data that have been inputted into the system. Examples of data integrity problems include accidental deletions of accounts receivable records,

FIGURE 5.1
**Information Security
Core Objectives**

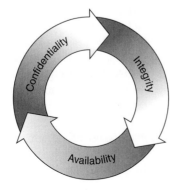

unauthorized additions of new customer credit accounts, and unauthorized increases in the credit limits in customer credit accounts.

- **Availability**   involves ensuring that data and information are available when and where they are needed. Timeliness is important because information tends to lose value over time.

Key Concepts in ISMS

LO3   The following set of interrelated concepts provides a background for the study of ISMS.

Organizational Embedding, Risk Management, and Internal Control

As is discussed, the ISMS is part of ERM and internal control processes. This means that the ISMS must be formally embedded into the company's ERM and internal control processes. The ISMS is not a stand-alone process.

Prevention, Detection, and Response

Prevention stops security problems before they occur. Some problems cannot be stopped, however, so they must be detected and then responded to in an appropriate way. Many systems place a great emphasis on prevention but lack adequate mechanisms for detection and, especially, response. A key ISMS issue for response is planning responses *before* incidents occur.

LO4   ### *The ISMS Life Cycle and PDCA*

Although the ISMS must be integrated into the organization's internal control and ERM processes, it must also be developed as a process in its own right as a major component of the overall information system. Therefore, development of the ISMSs should proceed through six ongoing phases: analysis, design, implementation, operations, continuous evaluation, and improvement. The *analysis phase* determines the needs for an ISMS based on the organization's environment and risk preferences. The *design phase* converts the ISMS needs into plans for concrete processes. The *implementation phase* converts the design phase plans into working processes. The *operations phase* provides the day-to-day operation of the ISMS. The *continuous evaluation phase* involves continuously monitoring the overall ISMS. In the *improvement phase,* results from the continuous evaluation are constantly fed back into the ongoing analysis and design phases, and changes are made as needed.

The overall result of the six phases is an ISMS that constantly adapts to changes in the organization's environment. The ability to adapt is essential because new security threats constantly arise in a rapidly changing world.

Corresponding to the multi-phase development process is the **plan-do-check-act (PDCA) methodology** often used in the security literature (see Figure 5.2). *Plan* corresponds to analysis and design, *do* to implementation and operations, *check* to continuous evaluation, and *act* to continuous improvement.

Risk Management and Threat and Vulnerability Analysis

Because ISMSs are part of the organization's information systems, security development requires a special focus on threats and vulnerabilities. **Threats** are systems-related individuals or events that can result in losses to the organization; they can be either active or passive. **Active threats** relate to the intentional acts of individuals, such as hackers or saboteurs. **Passive threats** relate to random events, accidents, or acts of nature. **Vulnerabilities** are weaknesses in the ISMS that result in exposures to threats.

FIGURE 5.2
PDCA Methodology versus the Systems Life Cycle

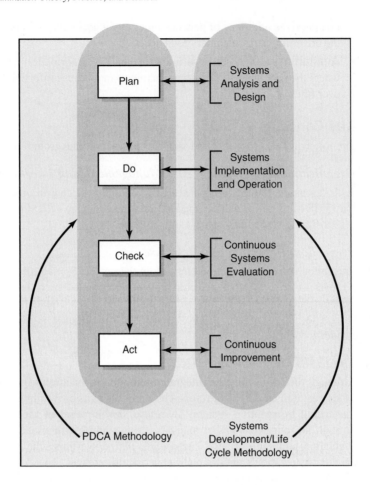

Active and passive threats are closely related, and in many cases, the distinction between the two is trivial, at least with respect to the consequences. For example, a hacker's destruction of the accounts payable files is an active threat. On the other hand, destruction of the same files by a flood is a passive threat. Either way, the files are destroyed. Therefore, given the conceptual similarity between active and passive threats, the current chapter focuses primarily on active threats. Remember, however, that security measures to protect against active threats also generally protect against passive threats.

Of course, threat and vulnerability analysis is not unique to ISMS management. It is also standard practice in the development of internal control processes. In fact, ISMS development merely involves carrying out the principles of internal control in detail in the areas of data and information. Therefore, the ISMS can be thought of as an advanced-level topic in internal control processes.

INTERNATIONAL STANDARDS ORGANIZATION SERIES 27000 RELATING TO INFORMATION SECURITY

LO5 The **International Standards Organization (ISO)** is the primary international group that promulgates standards relating to business processes. The organization constitutes a network of the national standards institutes in more than 150 countries. The ISO itself is nongovernmental, but many of its member institutes are government funded.

Because the ISO is a private organization, adherence to its standards is strictly voluntary, although member countries are free to make them internally mandatory. All standards passed by the ISO carry the ISO logo and bear the designation "international standard." Thus far, the ISO has promulgated more than 15,000 standards on matters ranging from screw threads to business-to-business quality management. The most well-known of all the ISO standards is ISO 9000 (quality management), which has been implemented by thousands of companies around the world.

The ISO promulgates standards in "families," or series, that are numbered in common ranges, such as ISO 9000, ISO 9001, ISO 9002, and ISO 9003. The latter three standards were then consolidated into a single standard, and later ISO 9004 was added. All of these standards relate to the common theme of quality control management.

The **ISO 27000 family** relates primarily to information security. The series consists of six standards, all of which are under continuous but different stages of development:

- **ISO 27000 (vocabulary and definitions)**   This standard defines a common vocabulary for use in the 27000 series.

- **ISO 27001 (ISMS requirements and implementation)**   This defines the main standard applicable for certification of ISMSs. The standard sets the processes for planning, building, implementing, operating, monitoring, reviewing, maintaining, and improving an ISMS within the context of an organization's ERM processes.

- **ISO 27002 (code of security practices)**   Also known as *ISO/IEC 17799,* this standard is a code of best practices in ISMS. It consists of 132 general security controls organized under 11 topics. The general security controls are broken down into more than 5,000 detailed controls. This standard is intended to be implemented within the context of ISO 27001, and organizations are supposed to select only the controls applicable to their given risks and risk preferences.

- **ISO 27003 (implementation guidance)**   This standard contains guidelines for implementing ISO 27000 series standards.

- **ISO 27004 (security management metrics and measurement)**   This standard deals with information security management measurement and metrics, which are useful in reporting on and assessing the effectiveness ISMSs.

- **ISO 27005 (information security risk management)**   This standard provides guidelines relating to the risk management aspects of ISO 27001 including the assessment and evaluation of risks, implementation of appropriate controls, monitoring of risks, and continuous improvement in controls.

The two core standards for implementing ISMSs are ISO 27001 and ISO 27002. *ISO 27001* provides the general framework for implementing an ISMS, and *ISO 27002* provides the specific controls to be implemented in light of the framework. Both standards work together, and both standards are harmonized to work with other standards such as ISO 9001 (quality management).

ISO 27001: Implementing ISMSs

ISO 27001 follows the PDCA methodology. Each element of it is discussed in detail.

The Plan Phase

This phase involves initiating the project, defining the scope of the ISMS, establishing an ISMS policy, performing a risk assessment, selecting risk treatments, selecting control objectives, and producing a statement of applicability.

Initiate the Project In initiating an ISMS, top management must establish acceptance or buy-in among the organization's leaders. A top-level executive must be appointed to manage the project.

Define the Scope of the ISMS The ISMS can be implemented for a single department or process or for an entire division of the organization. The project team must define the scope of the ISMS in terms of the applicable organizational areas or processes.

Establish an ISMS Policy This process involves the creation of a brief document that states goals for integrity, confidentiality, and availability in general terms. Special attention should be given to key areas, major threats and vulnerabilities, willingness to take or avoid risks, and major contractual, regulatory, or other key risks. For example, a credit card company would pay special attention to maintaining privacy of cardholder information. The security policy should be signed by the CEO and the controller or vice president of information systems. It should then be widely disseminated to key individuals within the organization and made part of their ongoing security training. Some important elements of a good organizational security policy follow:

- A statement of the organization's intentions and principles relating to information security. This should include a discussion of the importance of security to the organization.
- A statement of the scope of the security policy.
- A statement of the accountability of top management for information security.
- A statement that defines the roles, responsibilities, and duties of key employees that relate to information security.
- A statement of the organization's security goals.
- A summary list of critical information assets and a classification of each asset's security requirements.
- A summary of a program to educate, make aware, and train employees in relation to security. This should include a statement relating to how employees are to communicate regarding information security.

Large organizations are likely to need an overall security policy plus individual security policies for divisions, departments, and processes.

Perform a Risk Assessment Risk assessment follows a three-step process. The first step is to determine what assets need protection. The second step is to determine the threats and vulnerabilities for the identified assets. The final step is to analyze the losses that could occur to vulnerable assets.

Determining what assets need protection should consider the following general asset types:

- **Human resources** Employees and the organization's investments in their training, knowledge, and experience comprise these assets.
- **Information** These assets include data and information of all types, including data files, accounting information, plans and strategies, policies, intellectual property, documentation, user manuals, training manuals, policies, and procedures.
- **Documents** Legal documents such as contracts, deeds, and loan agreements make up this category.
- **Software** These assets include company-developed software, purchased software license codes, and purchased customizations to vendor-supplied software.
- **Physical equipment** Examples include personal computers, mainframe computer servers, modems, phone systems, routers, wiring, hubs, and support equipment.

- **Services** These include computing support, electricity, water, air conditioning, and maintenance services.
- **Company image and reputation** Examples include the quality of the company's products and services and its good name.

Each asset should also be classified according to its desired access security level:

- **Unclassified** Unrestricted access; the asset is available to the public.
- **Shared** Restricted access to specific groups of individuals including organizational insiders and outsiders.
- **Company only** Restricted access to organizational insiders.
- **Confidential** Restricted access to a specific list of individuals.

The second step of threat assessment involves determining all possible threats and vulnerabilities for each asset. Active threats include intentional attacks against assets by various types of individuals. Passive threats can be caused by individuals (accidents), or by acts of nature such as storms, fires, earthquakes, and floods. Individuals posing active and passive threats include the following:

- **Computer systems personnel** This group includes programmers, computer maintenance persons, network operators, and systems and database administrators. They tend to have privileged access to information system resources and could, in the absence of proper controls, cause major damage. For example, a computer programmer could put a patch in the accounts receivable software to omit billing for a specific account.
- **Computer users** This group includes individuals with authorized access to the assets at risk. For example, a billing clerk could have access to the company's customer account list. The clerk could steal this list and sell it to a competitor.
- **Intruders** This group includes all individuals who do not have authorization to access a given asset. Various intruders include hackers, ex-employees, eavesdroppers, wiretappers, and employee impersonators.

General active threats include the following:

- **Input manipulation** Incorrect or fraudulent transactions can be entered into the system. For example, in one case, a payroll clerk updated the pay rate tables and gave all of her friends a raise.
- **Direct file alteration** This threat differs from input manipulation in that the perpetrator does not use the normal software (e.g., the accounting system) to modify the contents of a file or database but edits a file directly with, for example, a disk sector–editing utility. This type of threat is minimized by encrypting the files.
- **Program alteration** Trusted computer programmers can make unwanted changes to the organization's software. For example, in one case, a programmer modified the payroll software to begin erasing files if it could not find his social security number anywhere in the system. After he left the company, his "logic bomb" deleted many critical files.
- **Data theft** The information system in numerous companies contains many types of valuable data that can be sold or used by competitors. For example, in several prominent cases, hackers have stolen customer lists that included credit card numbers.
- **Sabotage** Disgruntled present or ex-employees can carry out sabotage. For example, in many cases, employees have started fires in the computer data center, erased

magnetic media with magnets, and cut wires. In some cases, political radicals have bombed data centers. Network-related threats include denial-of-service attacks on the company's Web or mail servers and "malware" attacks such as those caused by computer viruses, worms, and spyware.

- **Misappropriation of information system resources** This type of threat includes employees using company information resources for their own personal purposes. In one case, an employee used his company's computers to run his own personal computer service bureau at night.

Vulnerabilities exist in the absence of adequate controls. Therefore, identifying vulnerabilities involves assessing procedural and technical controls. Such assessments can be made by comparing the existing controls to lists of controls in ISO 27002. **Gap analysis** focuses on identifying needed controls that are not already in place.

The normal way to assess controls is to use questionnaires and checklists based on the ISO standard. Of course, not every one of the thousands of controls in the standard applies to every organization. The relevant controls are those that best relate to the particular threats facing the organization.

The third and final phase of the risk assessment process involves identifying **loss exposure,** a condition of being subject to loss associated with vulnerabilities in the information system. This process identifies the possible loss(es) associated with the known vulnerabilities of each threatened asset. For example, a company could identify a $10,000 per hour loss exposure associated with its Web site being down. It could also identify likely losses associated with the site being down as a result of a hurricane, denial-of-service attack, or hardware failure. Each specific threat would result in a different loss computation.

The **quantitative approach to risk assessment** employs various mathematical and statistical methods for assessment. For example, the company can consider the maximum possible loss for a given event or the expected loss for the same event. The expected loss is computed by the dollar cost of the loss times the probability of the loss occurring.

Using the **qualitative approach to risk assessment** categorizes various losses according to their severity from trivial to threatening the organization's continuing existence.

Neither the qualitative nor quantitative approach is inherently superior. Many of the most serious events do not readily lend themselves to numerical analysis. For example, how can the probability of being hit by a category 5 hurricane in, say, Tampa, Florida, be calculated? What is the dollar value of the loss likely to be? A qualitative risk assessment could simply label such a hurricane risk as "barely survivable."

Select a Risk Treatment Risk treatment strategies (see Figure 5.3) must be created for identified loss exposures. Possible strategies include the following:

- **Accept the risk** This strategy applies especially to losses that companies can manage within their usual budgets. For example, a risk analysis could show that a single-owner hotel's reservation system is subject to power interruptions. One possible treatment for this risk is to install a backup generator, but the owner could decide simply to live with the risk of a power failure and not purchase one. The reasoning for the decision could be that the hotel can revert to a manual system to manage the reservations despite some inconvenience and problems.

- **Insure against the risk** The organization could purchase various types of insurance (fire, flood, windstorm, theft, vandalism, sabotage, etc.). Insurance companies often

FIGURE 5.3
**Risk Treatment
Strategies**

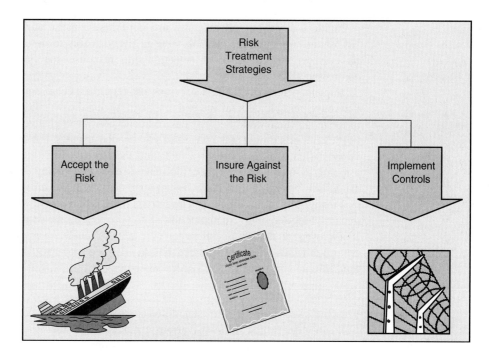

have risk management programs that require the insured to implement risk-reducing controls.

- **Implement controls** If risks cannot be accepted or insured against, the organization must implement security controls on a cost-benefit basis.

The general treatment strategies and selected control procedures should be summarized in a risk management report.

Select Control Objectives Control objectives define in specific terms what the controls are designed to accomplish. For example, "ensure the integrity of customer information when updating customer accounts" is a control objective. ISO 27001 provides lists of these objectives. General and application control objectives related to all internal control processes, as discussed in Chapter 3, should be considered. Specific controls can be selected from ISO 27002, discussed in Chapter 15, which lists more than 5,000 controls in 132 categories that fall under 11 general areas.

Produce a Statement of Applicability (SOA) The **statement of applicability (SOA)** is the end product of the risk assessment process. It lists the controls selected, the reasoning behind their selection, and the reason that other controls were not selected. The SOA should be consistent with the ISMS policy developed in the early stages of the PDCA process.

The Do Phase

Do-phase activities include applying the controls defined in the SOA, operating the ISMS, and ensuring that all employees are properly trained and competent to perform their security duties.

Implementation of the do-phase activities requires mechanisms for compliance monitoring and incident detection and response. *Compliance* means that the controls in practice correspond with the controls on paper. Controls should be considered worthless in the absence of adequate compliance monitoring.

Incident detection and response are important because controls are never perfect. No matter how good the control, there is always a way to defeat it. Excessive reliance on controls without incident detection and response can be as bad as having no controls at all.

Implementation of do-phase activities also requires mechanisms (in the form or reports) that make possible internal and external auditing and the overall evaluation of the success of the ISMS framework. Security environments constantly change, and incident and effectiveness reports should make it easy to spot needed changes. For example, an airline reservation system availability report could show the percentages of the system's availability on a month-by-month basis. This could make it easy to spot any degradation trends in the availability, which could require system upgrades and improvements.

Finally, employee training and awareness often represent the weakest link in the ISMS and do-phase activities. No matter how strong the controls are on paper, they will likely fail if employees do not practice them and take them seriously. A security-conscious corporate culture in which employees believe that security is a necessary and helpful component to their jobs and the organization's success is crucial.

The Check Phase

The final check phase ensures that all the control objectives are being met and that all controls are in place and working. Various check activities identified in ISO 27001 include intrusion detection, incident handling, learning from outside sources, internal and external audits, self-policing procedures, and management reviews.

The Act Phase

The act phase involves continually improving the entire ISMS based on analysis of incident reports and the overall efficiency and effectiveness of the ISMS processes.

PDCA Reports and the ISMS Deliverable

Key PDCA documents include an ISMS organization plan, a security policy document, a risk analysis report, an SOA, and a continuity plan. Collectively, these documents constitute a deliverable for the ISMS.

ISO 27002: Code of Security Practices

As mentioned, ISO 27002 lists the best security practices that should be implemented in a PDCA framework. The standard highlights the following controls as being of special interest.

Essential Controls Required by Legislation

These include controls related to the following:

- Data protection and privacy of personal information.
- Protection of organizational records.
- Intellectual property rights.

Controls in Common Practice for Information Security

These include controls related to the following:

- The ISMS policy document.
- Allocation of information security responsibilities.
- Information security awareness, training, and education.

- Processing of applications correctly.
- Management of technical vulnerability.
- Management of business continuity.
- Management of information security incidents and improvements.

IT SECURITY ASSURANCE

LO6 **Information security assurance (ISA)** refers to some type of evidence-based assertion that increases the certainty that a security-related deliverable can withstand specified security threats. Recall that, as discussed earlier in this chapter, an information system security deliverable is any type of information-security-related product, service, process, system, or organizational unit. ISAs are important to a wide range of individuals and organizations, some of which follow:

- Standard-setting bodies.
- Local, state, national, and international governments and organizations.
- Specific industries.
- Units within organizations.
- Organizational policy makers (e.g., for policies relating to security, personnel, procurement, and marketing).
- System owners.
- System accreditors (those that accredit and certify systems).
- End users (including consumer and business users).
- The general public.

ISAs are necessary because security-related deliverables, including ISMSs, can and do fail for a variety of reasons that include, for example, design flaws and changing environments. As a result, individuals and organizations demand assurances.

How Assurance Is Achieved

Information security assurance is achieved for a target of evaluation by performing assurance activities that satisfy a predefined security target or security protection profile. Explanation of this definition requires defining its component terms:

- **Target of evaluation (TOE)**   This is the information security deliverable, the object for which assurances are made.
- **Assurance activities**   These activities depend on the method of assessment. Various methods of assessment are discussed later.
- **Security target (ST)**   This is the set of security specifications and requirements used to evaluate the target of evaluation. The specifications are developed depending on the user's specific security needs and the specific deliverable. For example, the SOA would constitute a security target for a given ISMS. STs are normally created by the developers of security deliverables in anticipation of the likely security needs of end users. In the case of ISMSs, the developers and end users are the same, at least from an organizational perspective.
- **Security protection profile (SPP)**   Similar to a security target, this profile is much broader in scope. Unlike an ST, an SPP does not apply to any one particular deliverable but represents the security needs of a given individual or group of individuals. SPPs are

typically used for procurement specifications. For example, a given organization might develop an SPP to use in all its software purchases. SPPs are normally created by the end users of security deliverables.

Forms of Assurance

In general, assurances for specific deliverables may be given by internal auditors, external auditors, developers, certification authorities, or anyone in the position to make assurance assessments, even end users. They can come in many forms.

- **Informal or semiformal**   An internal project development leader could simply write a letter to management indicating that the product meets company security standards.
- **Formal certification by an accredited certification body**   Some ISO standards, such as ISO 27002, are designed so that organizations can be certified against them. Certification bodies, also called **certification registrars,** may receive credentials from various accreditation bodies, such as the ANSI-ASQ National Accreditation Board, the Japanese Accreditation Board (JAB), the United Kingdom Accreditation Service, and the German Association for Accreditation (TGA). However, all such bodies do not need to be accredited to be recognized. For example, Microsoft has various certification programs, including one for Microsoft Certified Systems Administrators (MCSAs) Security Specialty. (Recall the concept that an information security deliverable is very broadly defined to include personnel.)
- **Self-certification**   Some organizations perform their own internal certification process as part of their internal quality assurance process. Self-certification can be against internally developed standards or widely recognized standards.

Assurances also come in degrees. Part 3 of ISO 15408 (the **Common Criteria** for IT security evaluations, discussed later) sets seven increasing levels of assurance, called **evaluation assurance levels (EALs).** EALs are affected by various factors called **assurance classes.** ISO 15408 defines the following seven assurance classes:

1. **Configuration management (CM)**   This assurance class ensures control over changes to the TOE and its related documentation by determining that the evaluated TOE and the implemented TOE are one and the same.
2. **Delivery and operation**   This class defines evaluation requirements for the secure delivery, installation, start-up, and operation of the TOE. It ensures that the TOE is not compromised during any of these phases.
3. **Development**   This defines evaluation requirements for the iterative development and implementation of security functions based on the security target.
4. **Guidance documents**   This class defines evaluation requirements for the TOE's user and administrative documentation as provided by the developer.
5. **Life cycle support**   Evaluation requirements for the life cycle model used to develop the TOE are defined here. Attention is also given to procedures and policies for flaw remediation, the correct use of tools and techniques, and security associated with the development process itself.
6. **Tests**   Requirements for testing the TOE's security functions to ensure that the overall security target is achieved is defined in this class.
7. **Vulnerability assessments**   This assurance class defines evaluation requirements relating to the identification of exploitable vulnerabilities, which are considered at all levels, in the construction, operation, misuse, or incorrect configuration of the TOE.

These seven assurance classes provide a good inventory of the ways that weaknesses can exist in any type of deliverable. Consider, for example, the secure delivery aspect of the second assurance class, delivery and operation. If no attention is given to secure delivery, a developer could create a secure accounts payroll system only to have it compromised by a programmer's secret insertion of a "back door" into the program code before the system is installed and becomes operational. (A *back door* is program code that bypasses normal security and grants someone access to software or to a system.)

The seven Common Criteria evaluation assurance levels are as follows:

EAL1. Functionally tested This EAL provides some confidence in correct operation in low security environments. The TOE is tested to function in a manner consistent with its guidance documentation, and working protection must exist against identified threats. EAL1 evaluations can be provided by an end user without any help from the developer.

EAL2. Structurally tested This EAL provides for the analysis, evaluation, and testing of the high-level TOE design, functional security specifications, and vulnerability analyses. It also provides for a subjective review, evaluation, and selective verification of the developer's test results and for verification that the TOE's security functions can protect against publicly known threats. It also verifies that the developer's tests are consistent with the high-level design. Finally, it provides for a review of any configuration and secure delivery procedures. EAL2 evaluations require that the developer provide design specifications and test results.

EAL3. Methodically tested and checked This EAL adds to EAL2 by including analyses of the high-level design, the development environment (life cycle) controls, and configuration management.

EAL4. Methodically designed, tested, and reviewed Adding to EL3, this EAL includes a complete review of the interface specifications, the low-level design, a subset of the implementation, and an informal model of the TOE security policy. It also provides for an independent vulnerability analysis that shows resistance to low-level types of attacks and a more thorough configuration management review. Finally, it verifies that the developer's tests are consistent with the low-level design.

EAL5. Semiformally designed and tested This EAL adds to EAL4 by including a review and analysis of the security functions in the implementation, a formal TOE model, and a semiformal check to make sure that included security functions are consistent with the high-level design. The TOE is required to be designed in modules. Finally, it validates the developer's analysis of secure communication channels.

EAL6. Semiformally verified design and tested EAL6 adds to EAL5 by including an analysis of a structured presentation of the implementation, a semiformal presentation of the low-level design, and a semiformal verification for consistency between the high-level and low-level designs. The TOE design is required to be both modular and layered. The vulnerability analysis is required to demonstrate resistance to penetration by attackers with high attack potential. The development processes is required to be structured, and the configuration process must be completely automated. Finally, the developer must include a systematic analysis of secure communication channels.

EAL7. Formally verified design and tested This EAL adds to EAL6 by including a formal presentation of the functional specification and high-level design, a formal demonstration of the correspondence between the high-level and low-level designs, as applicable. A simple TOE design must be presented in addition to a modular and layered design. Testing must also be based on an implementation representation, and a complete independent verification must be made of the developer's test results, searches for vulnerabilities, and analyses demonstrating resistance to attackers with high-attack potential.

The lower-level EALs tend to focus more on correctness evaluation, whereas the higher-level ones tend to focus more on effectiveness evaluation. **Correctness evaluation** merely tests to see whether the deliverable meets the standards in the defined security target even if the security target is poorly defined and weak. **Effectiveness evaluation,** on the other hand, tests to ensure that the deliverable can withstand attacks that could be encountered in the deliverable's operating environment.

The scope of the assurances can be limited to almost any aspect of the deliverable rather than the deliverable as a whole. For example, it is possible to develop assurances only for the user login portion of an accounting security system.

Assurances can even be made for the deliverable's development process rather than for the deliverable itself. For example, it is possible to develop separate assurances for the design and implementation processes.

Assurance Authorities

When assurances are to be made for some deliverable, the process must involve an **assurance authority,** the person or organization that makes various assurance-related decisions. These decisions may include the following:

- Type of assurance to seek.
- Level of assurance to seek (e.g., from EA1 to EA7).
- Types of certification and accreditation to seek.
- Type of testing labs to use.
- Methods of assurance to use.
- Acceptance of a TOE based on assurances that have been received.

In many cases, multiple assurance authorities may be associated with a given deliverable.

Assurance Methods and Approaches

An **assurance method** is a recognized specification for assurance activities that yields reproducible assurance results. Assurance results are reproducible when different evaluators working independently of each other are likely to obtain similar assurance results.

To perform an assurance assessment, some assurance method must be selected. The selection of a particular method depends on the overall security policy, the TOE, the scope of the assurance, whether widely recognized certification is required, the degree of assurance required, and all costs and benefits associated with the assurance assessment.

The number of widely used assurance methods is large. Specialized assurance methods have been developed for many possible types of deliverables, such as hardware, software, management systems (including ISMSs), personnel, and so on. Various methods that target the life cycle process and that are based on usage and experience exist.

In practice, more than one assurance method is often applied to a deliverable. For example, in a life cycle assurance, one method could be applied to the design phase and another applied to the implementation and operation phases. When multiple methods are used, it is necessary to develop a **security assurance model,** which specifies how the various individual assurances and methods work together to yield an overall **composite assurance** for the deliverable.

ISO/IEC 15443 defines three general categories of assurance methods; each category focuses on a different type of assessment evaluation. These are called **assurance approaches:**

- **Methods that assess the deliverable** The deliverable itself is evaluated.
- **Methods that assess the deliverable's development process** The life cycle process used to produce the deliverable is evaluated.
- **Methods that assess the deliverable's development environment** The environment in which the deliverable is produced is examined.

Note that the second assurance approach directly involves only the life cycle and environment related to the *development* and production of the deliverable. It does not directly involve the life cycle and environment in which the deliverable is *deployed.*

ISO/IEC 15443 also defines four life cycle phases relating to security deliverables.

- **Design/Development** Creating and producing the deliverable.
- **Integration** Making the deliverable work with other deliverables and objects.
- **Transition** Putting the deliverable into operation including deployment and validation.
- **Operation** Actually operating and maintaining the deliverable.

Note that these four life cycle phases apply to the environment in which the deliverable is *deployed.*

Assurance methods vary with respect to the life cycle phases on which they focus. Consequently, ISO/IEC 15443 classifies assurance methods based on both the assurance approach and life cycle focus. This means that a given assurance method uses one or more of the assurance approaches combined with one or more of the life cycle phases.

ISO/IEC 15443 classifies a large number of assurance methods using this classification system. In the ISO/IEC 15443 classification scheme, each security method is represented by a single security standard. Assessment is performed by comparing the deliverable to the security standard. For example, ISO/IEC 15443 classifies ISO/IEC 27002 (best practices in information security) as primarily focusing on process assurance and the operations phase of the life cycle. This means that it does not primarily focus on the deliverable itself, the deliverable's environment, or the design, integration, and transition phases of the life cycle. This demonstrates one of the most important concepts in this chapter. *Single security standards, even when properly implemented, generally do not lead to complete security assurances in terms of all assessment approaches and life cycle phases.* Stated differently, in many cases, especially in ISMSs, adequate security may be achieved only by applying multiple security standards.

That being said, however, because a given security standard focuses on a given assurance method and life cycle phase does not necessarily mean that the standard will not perform well in areas on which it does not focus. For example, a standard that focuses on the deliverable and the process development environment could achieve excellent results in its operational phase. After all, a secure, high-quality development environment is likely to lead to a secure, high-quality deliverable.

Well-Known Information Security Assurance Methods and Their Primary Assessment Properties

We use the term **primary assurance properties (PAPs)** to refer to the classification assigned by ISO/IEC 15443 to a given assurance method according to its assurance approach and its relation to the deployment life cycle. For example, the PAPs for ISO/IEC 27002 focus on processes and the operations phase of the security life cycle. That is,

ISO/IEC 15443 classifies ISO/IEC 27002 as primarily focusing on process assurance and the operations phase in the life cycle.

The remainder of this section presents some well-known security standards and their related ISO/IEC 15443 primary assurance properties. These standards use a wide variety of models, specifications, general methods, and general approaches relevant to information security.

ISO 21827: Systems Security Engineering Capability Maturity Model (SSE-CMM®) and Security Engineering

ISO 21827 presents a process reference model for systems security engineering. A **process reference model** is a standardized model or framework for a given process or set of processes. One of the most well-known reference models is SAP R/3, which is in essence a working computerized information system that integrates all major information-related functions within the organization.

The **SSE-CMM** belongs to a class of process reference models that use a process-improvement framework called the **capability maturity model (CMM).** The CMM was originally developed by Carnegie Mellon University's Software Engineering Institute with more than 50 organizations to help the U.S. government evaluate its contractors. It is now used for a wide variety of applications and has become a widely recognized standard for assessing and improving processes.

The word *maturity* in CMM stems from the premise that processes exist in varying levels of maturity ranging from ad hoc and very immature to well defined, organized, and mature. One of the primary benefits of the CMM is in its use for assessing the maturity of a given process. That assessment can then be used as a starting point for process improvement such as helping the process become more mature. Maturity is typically achieved in stages or levels.

The term **security engineering** refers to the application of engineering concepts to the development of security processes. General engineering concepts applicable to all types of engineering include developing processes that proceed through concept, design, implementation, testing, deployment, operation, maintenance, and decommission. Goals of security engineering include the following:

- Identify and understand an organization's security risks.
- Understand and define an organization's security needs given identified risks.
- Transform security needs into security specifications and processes.
- Establish confidence in the security processes.
- Determine and manage residual security vulnerabilities that exist even with well functioning security processes.
- Integrate methods and approaches from various branches of engineering to assess and manage the overall reliability of the security processes.

The CMM defines five progressive levels of process maturity or capability: initial, repeatable, defined, managed, and optimizing. Each process level has its own **process areas** (PAs). The five levels are as follows:

- **Initial level**   Also called the *performed informally level,* this level is characterized by disorganized, ad hoc, chaotic processes, probably with poor or little formal documentation. Process results at this level are inconsistent and overall are of low reliability. For example, a sales order process without formal documentation and staff training could allow some orders to be approved without proper credit checks.

- **Repeatable level**   This level, also called the *performed and tracked level,* is characterized by processes that are organized through basic project management techniques that include documentation, training, and the consistent application of policies and procedures.

- **Defined level**   Characterized by processes that are not only well managed and documented but also integrated into the organization's processes in a standardized way, this level is also called the *well-defined level.* Organizational integration facilitates the timely and efficient exchange between different organizational processes. For example, the sales order process can be linked to both the production and product development processes so that sales data are used to define production and product development needs.

- **Managed level**   Also called the *quantitatively controlled level,* it is characterized by processes that are monitored and managed at the organizational level. Because process levels are centrally managed at a high level, problems with individual processes can rapidly be identified and repaired.

- **Optimizing level**   This level, also called the *continuously improving level,* is characterized by processes that undergo continuous improvement, and new, innovative processes are created to assist in adapting to changing needs.

Three primary benefits arise as organizations or processes reach the highest maturity level: process predictability, process control, and process effectiveness. **Process predictability** means that the process produces results that are consistent and according to plans. **Process control** refers to rapid and effective responses to deviations from planned results, which in turn lead to further increases in predictability. **Process effectiveness** refers to lower costs, shorter development times, higher quality, and higher productivity.

The SSE-CMM® defines 22 process areas, which in turn define practices that can be used to identify the maturity level of a given information security process. The 22 process areas are divided into two groups: security engineering activities and project and organizational activities. The security engineering processes relate to administering security controls, assessing the impact of risks, assessing risks, assessing threats, assessing vulnerabilities, building security assurances, coordinating security, providing security inputs, specifying security needs, and verifying and validating security. The project and organizational activities relate to process quality, managing security and project configurations, managing project risks, managing and controlling technical efforts, defining and improving the organization's security processes, managing the evolution of product lines, managing the systems engineering support environment, providing for ongoing skills and knowledge, and coordinating purchasing activities with suppliers.

Each of the process areas contains base practices that are common to many organizations and processes. The extent to which an organization implements these base practices determines its maturity level in a given process area. However, the SSE-CMM does not suggest that all practices must be implemented in every situation. Rather, each organization must choose those practices relevant to its own environment.

Baseline Protection Manual

The *Baseline Protection Manual* was developed by Germany's Federal Office for Information Security, Bundesamt für Sicherheit in der Informationstechnik (BSI, www.bsi.bund.de). *This method's primary assurance properties focus on the deliverable and the operations phase of the security deployment life cycle.*

The **Baseline Security Manual** is a standard that includes a combination of organizational, personnel, infrastructure, and technical security measures to counter a set of well-known vulnerabilities that exist for an "average" organization. The measures included are presented in checklist style, and the standard emphasizes continuous improvement through monitoring and acting on security problems. The manual is updated as new threats and vulnerabilities become known.

Penetration Testing

Penetration testing is a widely used method for assessing weaknesses in a deliverable. It is normally conducted after a correctness testing. The normal approach to penetration testing is to attempt to exploit all possible vulnerabilities.

Trusted Product Evaluation Program (TPEP) and the Trust Technology Assessment Program (TTAP)

TPEP was a National Security Agency program that evaluated commercial off-the-shelf security (COTS) products using trusted computer security evaluation criteria (TCSEC). TCSEC was one of the first sets of computer security criteria and was originally developed in 1967 and published in 1985 by the Department of Defense under the nickname of the "Orange Book" (referring to its orange cover). In 1999, the Department of Defense more or less abandoned TCSEC in favor of ISO/IEC 15408, mentioned earlier, also known as the *Common Criteria* for information security.

TPEP was replaced by the **Trust Technology Assessment Program (TTAP)**, which bases evaluations on the more modern ISO/IEC 15408 Common Criteria EALs discussed earlier. The program focuses on COTS characterized by Common Criteria EAL4 and higher. The EALs for evaluated products are posted on the Department of Defense's Web site at http://www.radium.ncsc.mil/tpep/tpep.html. *TPEP and TTAP focus primarily on the deliverable and the design and integration phases of the security phase of the life cycle.*

The Canadian trusted computer product evaluation criteria (CTCPEC) was a standard similar to TCSEC. It too was replaced by the ISO/IEC 15408 Common Criteria.

The **rating maintenance phase (RAMP)** is used to evaluate newer versions of products that already have EAL ratings. Rating maintenance is achieved by vendors' use of qualified vendor security analysts (VSAs) to oversee and monitor the development of product revisions. RAMP is a sister program that works with TTAP.

ISO/IEC 15408—Evaluation Criteria for IT Security (the Common Criteria)

The Common Criteria sets uniform standards for evaluating IT security deliverables. Part 1 includes definitions for standard terminology (e.g., for the TOE, ST, SPP). This important terminology is widely known and used throughout the IT security industry.

The Common Criteria includes three parts:

- **Part 1, Introduction and General Model** This part defines the common terminology and presents a general model for security evaluation. Guidance is included for writing STs and SPPs.

- **Part 2, Security Functional Requirements** This part establishes a set of functional security components that can be used to define TOE security requirements in a standardized way.

- **Part 3, Security Assurance Requirements** This part establishes a set of assurance components that can be used to express TOE assurance requirements in standardized terms. It defines all of the standardized EALs discussed earlier.

One reason that the Common Criteria have been so widely accepted is that they focus on the deliverable and all phases of the deployment life cycle.

Information Technology Security Evaluation Criteria

Information technology security evaluation criteria (ITSEC) was a forerunner document to the Common Criteria as was the related **Information Technology Security Evaluation Manual (ITSEM)**. They were originally developed by France, Germany, the Netherlands, and the United Kingdom and are widely recognized throughout Europe.

ITSEC is based on a modified version of TCSEC that focuses on correctness versus effectiveness evaluation. Its EALs range from E0 through E6 with E0 representing no assurance at all. EALs 1 through 6 roughly equate to Common Criteria EALs E2 through E7. *ITSEM* sets forth standards for applying the ITSEC criteria to evaluate TOEs. *ITSEC and* ITSEM *focus primarily on the deliverable and the design/development, integration, and operation phases of the security deployment life cycle.*

ISO/IEC 27000 Series

These standards focus primarily on processes and the operations phase of the security deployment life cycle.

The Trusted Capability Maturity Model (TCMM)

Much like the SSE-CMM, the **trusted capability maturity model (TCMM)** is another special version of the CMM that focuses on security in software development. It combines the CMM with the trusted software development methodology (TSDM). The military developed TSDM to enhance security for its software development processes. The methodology establishes 25 trust principles applicable to the various phases of the software development process. The trust principles are grouped into four broad areas:

- Management policy.
- Environment controls.
- Environment management.
- Software engineering.

Each trust principle is then rated on a five-level scale:

- T1 (minimal trust).
- T2 (moderate trust).
- T3 (preferred).
- T4 (malicious attack).
- T5 (ideal).

The TCMM and TSDM focus on the design and integration phases of the security deployment life cycle, not on the TOE.

ISO/IEC 13335—Management of Information and Communications Technology Security (MICTS)

ISO/IEC 13335—Management of information and communications technology security (MICTS) is a multi-part standard devoted to providing a general framework for developing and managing IT security. It includes a thorough discussion of basic security principles and concepts including, for example, those relating to security policies, assets, threats, vulnerabilities, and risk management. Much of the discussion is similar to that in ISO/IEC 27001 as discussed earlier. MICTS, which also recommends specific controls from ISO/IEC 27002, covers the following broad topics:

- Concepts and models for information and communications technology security management.

- Techniques for information and communications technology security risk management.
- Techniques for the management of IT security.
- Selection of safeguards.
- Management guidance on network security.

MICTS is process oriented and focuses on the integration, transition, and deployment phases of the security deployment life cycle.

Certified Information Systems Security Professionals (CISSP)

Certified Information Systems Security Professionals (CISSP) offers certification that provides assurance that an individual understands a broad body of common knowledge relating to information security. The CISSP certification examination evaluates the candidate's knowledge in 10 broad domains:

- Access Control Systems & Methodology.
- Applications & Systems Development.
- Business Continuity Planning.
- Cryptography.
- Law, Investigation & Ethics.
- Operations Security.
- Physical Security.
- Security Architecture & Models.
- Security Management Practices.
- Telecommunications, Network & Internet Security.

As an assurance method, CISSP focuses on the security development environment and all phases of the security deployment life cycle.

Federal Information Processing Standard 140 (FIPS 140)

Federal Information Processing Standard 140 (FIPS 140) is a standard published by the U.S. National Institute of Standards and Technology (NIST). It defines security requirements for cryptographic security modules contained in IT products that are used for sensitive but unclassified purposes. The standard uses a four-level security rating system that focuses on secure design and implementation. Product certification is available against the standard.

Control Objectives for Information and Related Technology (COBIT)

This standard suggests that IT delivers the information that management needs through 34 high-level objectives categorized into four domains: planning and organization, acquisition and implementation, delivery and support, and monitoring. The 34 high-level objectives are then separated into 318 detailed control objectives.

In many respects, COBIT is very much like ISO/IEC 27001/27002, but COBIT also uses a broader range of tools that include maturity models, critical success factors, key goal indicators, and key performance indicators. On the other hand, ISO/IEC 27001/27002 contains a much longer list of controls. Neither standard is inherently more comprehensive than the other, and the two complement each other, although ISO 27001 (and the rest of the ISO/IEC 27000 series) tends to be much more widely recognized in the information security world. *COBIT focuses on the deliverable and all phases of the security life cycle. It also focuses on processes in the design and integration phases of the security life cycle.*

Achievement of Total Security in ISMSs

In practice, no one security method or standard can yield total information security for ISMSs. A good starting point in developing a secure ISMS is ISO/IEC 15443 combined with the ISO 27000 series and COBIT.

APPLIED SECURITY CONTROLS

LO7 The preceding discussion of security standards indicates that it would be impossible to list in the space available here every important security control. ISO/IEC 27002 alone lists more than 5,000 security controls. Instead, the following discussion focuses on the 11 main areas covered in ISO/IEC 27002 as applied to ISMSs. The controls presented supplement and expand upon (rather than replace) those associated with basic internal control processes. This discussion also supplements the preceding discussion relating to ISO/IEC 27001.

ISO/IEC 27002 Areas Applied to ISMSs

Security Policy

The main issue here is that management must formulate an organizational security policy as indicated earlier. Additional securities policies could be required for individual organizational subunits or processes.

Organization of Information Security

This control requires security to be a formal part of the organization and headed by a chief information security officer. Special attention must be paid to organizational segregation of duties. Duties of computer personnel should be segregated from those of computer-user personnel. For example, the database administrator for the sales order system should not work in the sales department.

Asset Management

As stated earlier, all information assets must be inventoried. Each asset must identify threats, vulnerabilities, and loss exposures and must be assigned a security access classification that specifies exactly which persons or groups of persons are permitted access to it. Such access permissions can be expressed in detail: permission to view only, permission to edit or change the information, permission to append to the information and not view, and permission to delete information.

Human Resources Security

Persons with security responsibilities should be properly trained in security. Careful hiring practices should be followed to ensure employee loyalty, competency, and integrity.

Human errors can be minimized by systems that double-check work done by humans. For example, a clerk's manual payroll calculations should be checked by a second clerk. All employees must be aware of security policies as well as threats, vulnerabilities, and possible losses. All employees must be responsive to maintaining good security.

Physical and Environmental Security

Physical access to all information system resources should be restricted, on a cost-benefit basis, using biometric devices, locked doors, badges, security fences and gates, and so on. Proper physical protections for hazards relating to fires, floods, hurricanes, earthquakes, and so on should be in place.

Communications and Operations Management

Organizations should maintain off-site backups for critical data. Various possibilities exist: All data transactions can be mirrored in real time to a remote site. Backups of critical files can be made by the minute, hour, or day and carried to a remote site. Contracts can be put in place for alternate processing facilities in the event of a major failure of the network, processing facilities, or equipment.

Appropriate security software must be maintained to protect against malware including viruses, Trojan horses, worms, spyware, and so on. The latest security updates for all software, including Web servers, operating systems, and applications must also be maintained.

Access Controls

Access controls provide the primary line of defense against most intentional attacks. The best defense is a **layered approach to data protection** that requires an attacker to penetrate multiple layers of security to obtain access to data (see Figure 5.4).

- The first and outermost layer is the **network layer** that can restrict access to the entire network by means such as passwords, firewalls, and encrypted communications.
- The second layer is the **network domain layer** that can restrict access to authorized users who typically operate within the local-area network by using passwords, secondary firewall, and encrypted communications.
- The third layer is the **application layer** that would require a user to use a password to access, for example, an accounting program. The computer on which the application resides and the application itself can be protected by a third-level firewall.

FIGURE 5.4
The Layered Approach to Information Security

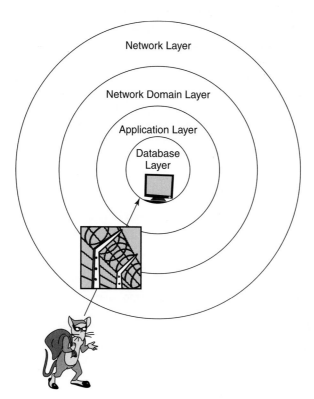

Network Layer

Network Domain Layer

Application Layer

Database Layer

- The fourth layer is the **database layer** in which the application program or database would grant the user password-based access only according to the user's predefined access privileges. For example, a given user could view the customer name and address but not the account balance. The database itself can be protected by encryption to thwart any direct access to the database with software that bypasses the application program normally used to access the database.

To be effective, network-type access controls must be accompanied by good physical access controls and employee education, awareness, and training. Network access controls will not help if someone leaves a critical computer open and unguarded or if someone gives away her password.

Varying degrees of password policies can be enforced. Ideally, passwords should consist of two unrelated words connected by at least one symbol. An example would be "dogdesk. Password policies can impose various restrictions. For example, passwords can be required to contain a minimum number of characters, to contain both alphabetic and numeric characters, and to be periodically changed.

Firewalls and access controls may be worthless if malware is permitted to run on an otherwise secure computer. For example, if an accounting system user browses the Web from his computer and picks up a Trojan horse keyboard logger program, everything the employee types, including passwords, could be surreptitiously transmitted to an outside hacker. Firewalls protect primarily against unwanted incoming traffic. They are much less likely to prevent unwanted outgoing traffic.

The best way to stop malware is to prevent its introduction into a computer in the first place. However, security-oriented software alone is generally not enough to prevent infections. For this reason, employees must be trained to avoid the types of behavior that lead to infections.

Information Systems Acquisition, Development, and Maintenance

Control must be maintained over IT projects at all stages of their development. Special attention must be given to "change controls." Changes to internally developed software should never be made directly to working versions of the software but to copies of the working versions and then reviewed and approved by a superior. Similarly, configuration changes to all software, whether internally developed, hosted by an application service provider (ASP), or purchased, should be made only after review and approval.

All purchased software and outsourced applications and support must meet appropriate security standards, either through evaluation or certification.

Information Security Incident Management

Operations must be carefully monitored for security incidents. Policies must be in place that automatically set responses into motion. Various forms of monitoring exist. Specialized network monitoring tools exist for detecting various types of attacks and intrusions. Auditing software that automatically scans transactions and databases for suspicious activity is available.

An incident-reporting system should be in place to log all incidents into a database for later analysis. It is especially important that all information relevant to an incident (log files, damage reports, network tracing information, and so on) be collected and entered into the database when the incident occurs. The incident-reporting system should serve as a basis for systematic analyses of incidents with the intent to continuously improve the security system.

Business Continuity Management

Formal written **disaster management and recovery** plans should be implemented to deal with responses to possible disasters and substantial business interruptions. Such plans should include the following elements:

- An **emergency response director** should be assigned the responsibility for emergency preparedness and response. That person should be in charge of an emergency response center and a supporting emergency response team.

- Policies and procedures should be implemented for the emergency response director to declare an emergency and communication of the emergency to employees, vendors, and customers.

- Employees should be familiar with special telephone numbers and/or Web pages to consult during emergencies when normal communications could be interrupted.

- All mission-critical resources should be inventoried and prioritized. These include data, software, processing equipment and facilities, power and maintenance requirements, communications equipment, building space, human resources, and vital records.

- Plans should be made to protect the mission-critical assets if there is advance warning of an impending disaster. Many resources (such as computers and equipment) can simply be moved out of harm's way or specially protected. For example, a company in Miami, Florida, facing an impending category 5 hurricane could plan to move critical computers, data, and records to an alternate office, say, in Jacksonville. Alternatively, these resources could be put into plastic bags and moved to an upper floor and away from windows to protect them from possible water damage. Postevent recovery plans should be made for critical resources that cannot be moved or protected. For example, a good plan contains provisions to transfer an organization's operations to an alternate location in the event that its facilities are destroyed. The plan should also provide for recovery from the loss of vendor-supplied products or services, such as phone, Internet, maintenance, software, temporary personnel, and so on.

- A salvage plan should include procedures to minimize damage after the disaster and salvage as many assets as possible. In many cases, most of the damage occurs after the disaster. For example, fires can erupt from broken gas lines after earthquakes. Rainwater can enter buildings through damaged roofs after hurricanes.

- The emergency response plan should be rehearsed and tested. Testing can be time consuming and expensive, but a plan that is not rehearsed and tested is likely to fail when it is really needed.

- Adequate insurance must be in place to cover disaster-related losses when possible. Not all risks may be insurable, however.

Compliance

Policies and procedures must exist to ensure all statutory, regulatory, and contractual obligations. This can be done only if those obligations are specifically inventoried.

Summary

An information security management system (ISMS) is an organizational internal control process that protects information integrity, confidentiality, and availability. ISMSs exist within the organization's internal control and risk management frameworks. Security is achieved only in the context of weighing various opportunities against related risks and managing the opportunities and risks in a way that is consistent with management's objectives and risk preferences.

Key concepts relating to ISMSs include organizational embedding (which places information security within the scope of the organization's risk management and internal control processes); prevention, detection, and response; the plan-do-check-act (PDCA) methodology; and risk management and vulnerability analysis.

The ISO/IEC 27000 standards are the most widely recognized information security standards. ISO/IEC 27001 defines the PDCA methodology, and ISO/IEC 27002 defines best security practices. Both of these international standards apply to ISMSs and all security-related deliverables. An *information security deliverable* is any type of security product, process, function, service, and security-related personnel (and their knowledge, experience, and training).

Regarding PDCA, the *plan phase* involves initiating the project, defining the scope of the ISMS, assessing risks, managing risks, treating risks, selecting controls, and producing a statement of applicability that identifies which controls were and were not selected and why.

Assessing risks involves inventorying information-related assets and identifying the threats, vulnerabilities, and loss exposures for each asset. Information-related assets include human resources, information, documents, software, physical equipment, services, and company image and reputation. Each asset should be classified according to its desired access security level such as unclassified, shared (specific groups of insiders and outsiders), company only (company insiders), and confidential (specific listed individuals).

Specific individuals who could pose threats include computer systems personnel, computer users, and intruders. General methods of attack include input manipulation, direct file alteration, program alteration, sabotage, and misappropriation of information system resources.

Vulnerabilities exist when threats are present in the absence of adequate controls. *Gap analysis* focuses on identifying needed controls that are not already in place. The normal way to assess controls is to use questionnaires and checklists based on the ISO standard. Only the controls relevant to the environment under consideration must be selected, and then on a cost-benefit basis.

Potential losses associated with each information asset should be estimated given the known vulnerabilities. Losses can be expressed in either quantitative or qualitative terms. Using the quantitative approach to risk assessment, various mathematical and statistical methods can be employed to express losses in numerical and dollar terms. Using the qualitative approach, various losses can be categorized according to their severity. Severity levels can range from trivial ones to those that threaten the organization's continuing existence. Neither the qualitative nor quantitative approach is inherently superior.

Risks can be managed or treated in several ways: They can be accepted, insured against, or controlled via security. Control objectives for each risk to be controlled should define in specific terms what the controls are supposed to accomplish. ISO/IEC 27002 and other standards can be helpful in identifying controls.

The *do phase* includes applying the controls, operating the ISMS, and ensuring that all employees are properly trained and competent to perform their security duties. Mechanisms for compliance monitoring, incident detection, and response must be included. Results from compliance and monitors should be used in structuring formal audits and in continuously improving the ISMS.

The *check phase* ensures that all control objectives are being met, are in place, and are working. Various check activities identified in ISO 27001 include intrusion detection, incident handling, learning from outside sources, internal and external audits, self-policing procedures, and management reviews.

The *act phase* ensures that the security processes are continually improving. Without continuous improvement, the ISMS is likely to become out of date and ineffective.

Information security assurance (ISA) refers to evidence-based assertions that increase the certainty that a security-related deliverable can withstand specified security threats. ISA is achieved for a target of evaluation by performing assurance activities that satisfy a predefined security target or security protection profile. The *target of evaluation* is the deliverable for which assurance is sought. The *security target* represents the security specifications and requirements for the target of evaluation. The *security profile* is similar to a security target but applies instead to users' needs rather than to a particular target of evaluation.

In general, assurances for specific deliverables may be given by internal auditors, external auditors, developers, certification authorities, or anyone in the position of making assurance assessments, even end users. ISO 15408 (the Common Criteria for IT security evaluations) defines seven increasing levels of assurance, called *evaluation assurance levels* (EALs).

Assurances can be limited to almost any aspect of the deliverable rather than the deliverable as a whole. For example, it is possible to develop assurances only for the user login portion of an accounting security system. Making assurances for some deliverable must involve an assurance authority, the person or organization that makes various assurance-related decisions. An *assurance method* is a recognized specification for assurance activities that yields reproducible assurance results. A large number of widely used assurance methods is available, and specialized methods have been developed for many possible types of deliverables, such as hardware, software, management systems (including ISMSs), personnel, and so on. In practice, more than one assurance method is often applied to a deliverable, resulting in composite assurance.

ISO/IEC 15443 defines three general categories of assurance standards called *assurance approaches.* Assurance approaches focus on the deliverable, its development process, and its development environment. Assurance methods can be further classified according to the phase of the security life cycle they focus on: design/development, integration, transition, and operation. ISO/IEC 15443 classifies a large number of assurance methods using this classification system.

Some of the standards classified by ISO/IEC 15443 include ISO 21827, the systems security engineering capability maturity model (SSE-CMM®), the *Baseline Protection Manual,* penetration testing, ISO/IEC 1540 (Common Criteria), the Trust Technology Assessment Program (TTAP), ITSEC/ITSEM, the ISO 27000 series, the trusted capability maturity model (TCMM), ISO/IEC 13335–management of information and communications technology security (MICTS), Certified Information Systems Security Professionals (CISSP), Federal Information Processing Standard 140 (FIPS 140), and control objectives for information and related technology (COBIT). Each has its own focus under the three-category and life cycle classification scheme. No one method provides total security.

ISO/IEC 27001 and ISO/IEC 13335 tend to represent the most thorough guidelines relating to establishing and maintaining ISMSs. ISO/IEC 27002, the *Baseline Protection Manual,* and COBIT tend to represent the most thorough set of controls; they are complementary, and no one is better than the others. COBIT has the benefit of also providing more organizational and environment guidance than ISO/IEC 27002.

The SSE-CMM® method is somewhat unique in focusing on the processes associated with the deliverable's life cycle. Basic, low-maturity processes are chaotic whereas the most mature processes are self-improving.

ISO/IEC 27002 sets controls in 11 main areas that include security policy; organization of information security; asset management; human resources security; physical and environmental security; communications and operations management; access controls; information systems acquisition, development, and maintenance; information security incident management; business continuity management; and compliance. The standard divides these areas into 34 categories and 5,000 specific controls.

Glossary

access control Control that provides the primary line of defense against most intentional attacks; normally implemented with a layered approach.

active threat Potential intentional attack on the information system.

application layer Data protection that restricts access to specific application programs, such as accounting programs.

assurance activity An activity set conducted as part of security assessment.

assurance approach A general category of assurance methods; organized by ISO/IEC 15443 into three general categories that assess the deliverable, the deliverable's development process, and the deliverable's development environment.

assurance authority A person or organization that makes various assurance-related decisions, including the type of assurance to seek and the desired level of assurance.

assurance class A factor that effects evaluation assurance levels. ISO 15408 defines seven assurance classes: configuration management, delivery and operation, development, guidance documents, life cycle support, tests, and vulnerability assessments.

assurance method Recognized specification for assurance activities that yield reproducible assurance results defined as obtaining similar assurance results when different evaluators are working independently of each other.

availability One of the three objectives of information security that involves ensuring that data and information are available when and where they are needed; timeliness is important because information tends to lose value over time

Baseline Security Manual Security assurance standard that uses a combination of organizational, personnel, infrastructure, and technical security measures to counter a set of well-known vulnerabilities that exist for an "average" organization; emphasizes continuous improvement through monitoring and acting on security problems.

capability maturity model (CMM) Class of process-improvement models defined in terms of the degree of sophistication for a given process; mature processes effect continuous improvement.

certification registrar Body that certifies deliverables against published security standards.

Certified Information Systems Security Professionals (CISSP) Professional organization that provides assurance that an individual possesses an understanding of a broad common body of knowledge relating to information security.

Common Criteria Another name for ISO/IEC 15408; represents a security assurance method and sets uniform standards for evaluating IT security deliverables in three parts: introduction and general model, security functional requirements, and security assurance requirements.

composite assurance Overall assurance achieved for a given deliverable as a result of using multiple assurance methods.

confidentiality One of three objectives of information security; involves ensuring that data and information are made available only to authorized persons.

correctness evaluation Type of security evaluation that tests only to determine whether the deliverable meets the standards in the defined security target.

database layer Layer of access controls that allows password-based access to application program or database only according to each user's predefined access privileges.

disaster management and recovery Process by which management plans for and responds to possible disasters and substantial business interruptions.

effectiveness evaluation   Type of security evaluation that tests to ensure that the deliverable can withstand attacks in the deliverable's operating environment.

emergency response director   Individual responsible for emergency preparedness and response; should be in charge of an emergency response center and a supporting emergency response team.

enterprise risk management (ERM)   Organizational process that involves weighing various opportunities against related risks and managing the opportunities and risks in a way that is consistent with management's objectives and risk preferences.

evaluation assurance level (EAL)   One of seven increasing levels of assurance set by the Common Criteria; each represents an increasing level of assurance for a given deliverable.

Federal Information Processing Standard 140 (FIPS 140)   U.S. standard published by the National Institute of Standards and Technology (NIST) that defines security requirements for cryptographic security modules in IT products used for sensitive but unclassified purposes.

gap analysis   Part of threat and vulnerability analysis that focuses on identifying needed controls not already in place.

information security assurance (ISA)   Evidence-based assertion achieved for a target of evaluation by performing assurance activities that satisfy a predefined security target or security protection profile; increases the certainty that a security-related deliverable can withstand specified security threats.

information security deliverable   Type of security product defined in the broadest sense to include, for example, information-security-related processes, software and hardware products, systems, services, organizational units, environments, warranties, and even security-related personnel.

information security management system (ISMS)   Organizational internal control process that ensures three objectives in relation to data and information within the organization: integrity, confidentiality, and availability.

integrity   One of the three objectives of information security; involves accuracy and completeness.

International Standards Organization (ISO)   Primary nongovernmental international group that promulgates standards relating to business (and other) processes.

ISO 27000 family   Group of ISO standards relating primarily to information security.

ISO/IEC 13335—management of information and communications technology security (MICTS)   Standards-based security assurance method that provides a general framework for developing and managing IT security.

ITSEC/ITSEM—information technology security evaluation criteria   Forerunner documents to the Common Criteria, widely recognized security assurance methods used throughout Europe.

layered approach to data protection   Approach to data security that requires an attacker to penetrate multiple layers of security to obtain access to data.

loss exposure   Condition of being subject to loss associated with vulnerabilities in the information system.

network domain layer   Level of data security that restricts access to authorized users who typically operate within the local-area network.

networklayer   Level of data security that restricts access by means such as passwords, firewalls, and encrypted communications.

passive threat Nonintentional threat against the information system, such as an accident and act of nature.

penetration testing Security assurance method widely used to assess weaknesses in a deliverable by exploiting all possible vulnerabilities; normally conducted after a correctness testing.

plan-do-check-act (PDCA) methodology Systems development methodology often used in the security literature; involves planning (analysis and design), doing (implementation and operations), checking (continuous evaluation), and acting (continuous improvement).

primary assurance property (PAP) Classification assigned by ISO/IEC 15443 to a given assurance method as defined by its assurance approach and relation to the deployment life cycle.

process area Element of the SSE-CMM® that can be used to define practices that identify the maturity level of a given information security process.

process control Primary benefit of applying capability maturity models that refers to rapid and effective responses to deviations from planned results and in turn to further increases in predictability.

process effectiveness Primary benefit of applying capability maturity models that results in lower costs, shorter development times, higher quality, and higher productivity.

process predictability Primary benefit of applying capability maturity models to produce results that are consistent and according to plans.

process reference model Standardized model or framework for a given process or set of processes; includes SAP R/3, which integrates all major information-related functions in the organization, and SSE-CMM.

qualitative approach to risk assessment Nonmathematical and nonstatistical approach to assessing IS threats, vulnerabilities, and loss exposures; categorizes possible losses according to their severity.

quantitative approach to risk assessment Mathematical and statistical approach to assessing IS threats, vulnerabilities, and loss exposures.

rating maintenance phase (RAMP) Security assurance method that works with TTAP; used to evaluate newer versions of products that already have EAL ratings.

security assurance model Model that specifies how multiple assurance methods work together to yield an overall composite assurance for a deliverable.

security engineering Application of engineering concepts to the development of security processes.

security protection profile (SPP) Protection typically used for procurement; represents the security needs of a given individual or group of individuals.

security target (ST) Set of security specifications and requirements used to evaluate the target of evaluation.

statement of applicability (SOA) End product of the risk assessment process that lists the controls selected and the reasoning for their selection and why other controls were not selected; should be consistent with the ISMS policy developed in the early stages of the PDCA process.

Systems Security Engineering Capability Maturity Model (SSE-CMM®) Same as ISO 21827, which presents a process reference model for systems security engineering.

target of evaluation (TOE) The information security deliverable, the object for which security assurances are made.

threat Impending event that can result in losses to the organization from systems-related individuals or events.

Trust Technology Assessment Program (TTAP) Security assurance method that bases evaluations on the ISO/IEC 15408 Common Criteria.

trusted capability maturity model (TCMM) Security assurance method that is a special version of CMM; focuses on security in software development.

vulnerability Weakness in the information system that exposes it to threats.

Review Questions

1. Which of the following is *not* a possible information system security deliverable?
   a. Software.
   b. Hardware.
   c. Personnel.
   d. None of the above.
   e. All of the above.

2. Which is an information security management system (ISMS) that ensures the three objectives of integrity, confidentiality, and availability in relation to data and information within the organization?
   a. Security system.
   b. Deliverable specification.
   c. Organizational process.
   d. None of the above.

3. Which of the following is the most accurate statement?
   a. Management's ERM is part of the company's control processes.
   b. Management's ERM is part of the company's ISMS.
   c. The ISMS is part of the ERM.
   d. None of the above is true.

4. What are the three objectives of information security?
   a. Integrity, efficiency, and effectiveness.
   b. Integrity, confidentiality, and availability.
   c. Integrity, confidentiality, and availability.
   d. None of the above.

5. Which of these are weaknesses in the ISMS that result in exposures to threats?
   a. Threats.
   b. Vulnerabilities.
   c. Both *a* and *b*.
   d. None of the above.

6. Which of the following are the two core standards for the ISO 27000 series?
   a. ISO 27000 and ISO 27001.
   b. ISO 27001 and ISO 27002.
   c. ISO 27002 and ISO 27003.
   d. ISO 27003 and ISO 27004.

7. Which of the following represents a code of best practices for ISMSs?
   a. ISO 27000.
   b. ISO 27001.

   c. ISO 27002.

   d. ISO 27003.

8. Defining the scope of the project is part of which phase in applying the PDCA methodology?

   a. Plan.

   b. Do.

   c. Check.

   d. Act.

9. Assessing risks is part of which phase in applying the PDCA methodology?

   a. Plan.

   b. Do.

   c. Check.

   d. Act.

10. Which of the following is *not* considered an asset when performing ISMS risk assessments?

   a. Human resources.

   b. Information.

   c. Software.

   d. The company's reputation.

   e. None of the above.

11. Program alteration is an example of which of the following?

   a. An active vulnerability.

   b. A passive vulnerability.

   c. An active threat.

   d. A passive threat.

12. Which of the following does gap analysis primarily identify?

   a. Controls that are in place but not working.

   b. Controls that are not already in place.

   c. Controls that may already be in place.

   d. Controls that are not working.

13. Which approach to identifying loss exposures is superior?

   a. Qualitative.

   b. Quantitative.

   c. Neither, both the quantitative and qualitative are equally good.

   d. There is not enough information to support any answer.

14. Which of the following is *not* a risk treatment?

   a. Minimize the risk.

   b. Accept the risk.

   c. Insure against the risk.

   d. Implement controls.

15. The end product of the risk assessment process is which of these?

   a. The statement of authority.

   b. The statement of action.

   c. The statement of applicability.

   d. None of the above.

16. Which of the following is often the weakest link in the ISMS?
    a. Employee supervision.
    b. Employee training and awareness.
    c. Employee procedures.
    d. Employee policies and procedures.

17. Incident handling applies primarily to which phase in the PDCA methodology?
    a. Plan.
    b. Do.
    c. Act.
    d. Check.

18. Information security assurance (ISA) refers to a type of evidence-based assertion that does which of the following?
    a. Increases certainty that a security-related deliverable is secure.
    b. Increases certainty that a security-related deliverable is ISO compliant.
    c. Increases certainty that a security-related deliverable can withstand specified security threats.
    d. None of the above.

19. A security target is which of the following?
    a. The deliverable for which security is desired.
    b. The standards used to evaluate a security deliverable.
    c. The same as the target of evaluation.
    d. None of the above.

20. To which of these do security protection profiles apply?
    a. Individuals.
    b. Single targets of evaluation.
    c. Multiple targets of evaluation.
    d. None of the above.

21. What are the seven increasing levels of assurance in Part 3 of ISO 15408 (the Common Criteria for IT security evaluations) called?
    a. Security evaluation classes.
    b. Security evaluation levels.
    c. Security test levels.
    d. None of the above.

22. Which of the following represents the highest security level under the Common Criteria?
    a. Formally verified, designed, and tested.
    b. Structurally designed and tested.
    c. Formally reviewed, tested, and checked.
    d. None of the above.

23. The Common Criteria higher levels focus primarily on which of the following?
    a. Correctness.
    b. Effectiveness.
    c. Assurance.

     d. Correctness and effectiveness.

     e. None of the above.

24. Which of the following would *not* be of primary interest to an assurance authority?

     a. Type of assurance to seek.

     b. Level of assurance to seek.

     c. Types of certification and accreditation to be sought.

     d. Type of testing labs to use.

     e. None of the above.

25. Which types of security assurance method yield the highest level of assurance?

     a. Methods that assess the deliverable.

     b. Methods that assess the deliverable's development process.

     c. Methods that assess the deliverable's development environment.

     d. No one type of assurance method generally yields the highest level of assurance.

Discussion Questions

26. Why is it true in many cases, especially in ISMSs, that adequate security can be achieved only by applying multiple security standards?

27. How does ISO/IEC 15443 classify assurance methods based on both the assurance approach and life cycle focus?

28. What are primary assurance properties? How might they be considered in developing an ISMS?

29. How is "maturity" achieved in terms of the capability maturity model (CMM)?

30. Can information security be adequately achieved in ISMSs with low levels of maturity?

31. Explain the benefits of an ISMS becoming mature under the CMM.

32. What are some deliverables that could be evaluated under the trusted technology assessment program?

33. What are the benefits of developing security assurance by focusing on the deliverable's development environment versus its deployment environment?

34. What are the benefits of developing security assurance by focusing on the deliverable's deployment environment versus its development environment?

35. Is it possible to achieve security assurance for a deliverable without testing and evaluating the TOE itself?

36. Why is IEC 15408 (the Common Criteria) so widely accepted?

37. From the standpoint of assurance properties, what is the weakness in relying on the 27000 series alone? (*Hint:* On what aspects of security assurance does the ISO 27000 series *not* focus?)

38. Explain how the designation Certified Information Systems Security Professional (CISSP) provides security assurance.

39. How does COBIT differ from the ISO 27000 series?

40. How could an organization use various security standards to achieve total security?

41. Security policy is one of the 11 main areas covered by ISO 27002. A security policy can be developed for organizations and organizational subunits such as divisions and departments. What is an example of a security policy that could be applied to a single department?

42. What are some ways that human resource security can be achieved under ISO 27002?

43. What forms the primary line of defense in a security system?

44. What are some security risks during the deployment phase of an ISMS?

45. How is business continuity management implemented?

Cases

46. Geox Company produces and sells a specialized software package used by valuation analysts throughout the world. The software contains a series of modules connected to online databases in such a way that valuation analysts can quickly and accurately calculate estimated market values for private companies. Geox uses a subscription model to sell its product. Subscribers pay an initial fee, which permits them to immediately download and begin using the software. At the end of one year, subscribers must pay an annual fee or the subscription expires and the software stops working.

    Geox began operations only several years ago with three brothers pitching in and working together in the garage of the oldest brother, Ricky. He developed the concepts behind the product and its marketing. Middle brother Zeek is a software engineer and did all the programming work. The youngest brother, Tricky, developed the Web site and did all of the work setting it up and billing customers. He manages everything to do with accounting.

    Geox has rapidly grown from only a handful of subscribers to more than 10,000. Because of this growth, Tricky hired three full-time staff members for technical support and service. He does all of the billing himself with the help of his wife and oldest son. His present billing system was designed for only a small number of subscribers. Customers input their payment information into a secure Web form on Geox's site. Tricky then receives the payment details via e-mail. He then e-mails the customer a code from his database, which the customer inputs into the software to make it work for one year.

    Tricky has become very good at handling the customer subscriptions and payments, despite the large number of transactions. Still, the large customer load often causes him to work too many hours, so he wants an automated system to handle all customer orders. He found an open-source shopping cart system that he likes on the Web. He prefers an open-source system so that Zeek can customize it as needed. Zeek is one of the world's best programmers, and he would never tolerate relying on any accounting system to which he could not make programming changes.

    Tricky is presently using the Isolex accounting system, which is also a completely open source. It handles all payroll and expenses. It also handles revenues, but Tricky enters them manually, in weekly totals. All main data files in the Isolex system are stored in MySQL databases. This means that Zeek can easily integrate the Isolex system with any of the many online shopping cart and billing systems that also support MySQL. Tricky is considering three open-source shopping cart and billing system packages. He is very worried about security because he has heard many stories of hackers breaking into online systems such as the one he is contemplating.

    a. Assume that you are called in as a forensic accountant to advise Geox. How would you suggest evaluating the contemplated open-source shopping cart systems?

    b. How does the fact that the systems are open source affect their security?

47. Rimco Automobile Company specializes in repairs and custom modifications for high-performance sports cars. Dana Peaker, the CEO, is a former race car driver. Over the last 10 years, she has managed to open 18 shops in major U.S. cities. Rimco has

been very profitable. Because it provides such specialized services for very expensive automobiles, it is able mark up both labor and materials at least four times cost and in many cases more than 100 times cost.

Rimco's operations have several divisions, each with it is own national division manager.

- Basic engine and automobile repairs.
- Collision repairs.
- Interior customization.
- Body customization.
- Parts procurement and distribution.
- Central office support.

Most of the profits come from the two customization divisions. Each division manager updates monthly budgets and plans for his or her area in each of the 18 stores. The central office support division includes the CEO, various administrative staff, accounting, internal auditing, IT, and security support.

The stores are connected to the main office through a network of VSAT satellite dishes, which permits all transactions to be centrally recorded in real time.

Donna Hacher, a member of the IT support group, is in charge of security. She constantly ensures companywide information security through a series of procedures that include the following:

- Checking to see that all of the latest security patches are applied to all company software.
- Telling all employees to notify her of any security problems.
- Teaching employees about not sharing their login passwords for the accounting system.

Overall, Donna feels pretty good about security because she recently moved all accounting functions to the latest version of the Zelical Accounting system, which has one of the best reputations in the industry for security features. She believed that with such a secure accounting system, her main concern would be ensuring that employees do not share their login passwords with others, for that would be the likely opening for any type of attack.

a. Describe Rimco's ISMS.

b. What weaknesses exist in the ISMS?

Chapter **Six**

Fraud Detection

CHAPTER LEARNING OBJECTIVES

After reading Chapter 6, you should be able to:

- LO1: Indicate the different ways in which occupational fraud is detected.
- LO2: Explain how fraud detection relates to enterprise risk management.
- LO3: Design an optimal fraud detection system.
- LO4: Develop a data-driven fraud detection model.

The **fraud detection process** involves identifying indicators of fraud that suggest a need for further investigation. The indicators in and of themselves are not evidence of fraud; they only suggest items of concern that, if investigated, might lead to the discovery of fraud. In many cases, fraud indicators simply lead to the discovery of errors or unusual events that can reasonably be explained upon further examination.

The objectives of fraud detection include not only catching fraud but also preventing it. Prevention is achieved by the deterring effect of early detection. Simply put, fraudsters are generally less likely to attempt fraud if they believe the risk of rapid detection is high. Furthermore, rapid detection, investigation, and follow-up action can prevent fraudsters from repeating a fraud. So, even if detection does not prevent a fraud from happening in the first place, it can lead to preventing it from happening a second time and thereafter.

Fraud detection can also be used as one of the many tools in fraud investigations. Although it does not produce evidence, it can help point investigators in the right direction, and in some cases, it can be used to help rule out the presence of certain types of fraud. The use of fraud detection as an investigative tool is discussed in Chapter 9. The current chapter focuses on pre-investigation fraud detection, although the same fraud detection methods are generally used for both pre-investigation and investigation scenarios.

WAYS IN WHICH OCCUPATIONAL FRAUD IS DISCOVERED

LO1   The various ways by which occupational fraud is normally discovered (Figure 6.1) include through the use of tips and hotlines, financial statement audits, internal audits, and by accident. Each of these areas is discussed.

Fraud Discovery from Tips and Hotlines

Various studies have shown that tips account for roughly 35 to 50 percent of frauds detected within organizations. Such tips come from employees, customers, vendors, and anonymous sources. Thus, because tips are so important, it is essential for a company to have a formal system in place that encourages them. One such system includes the hotline.

FIGURE 6.1
Rough Breakdown of the Different Ways in Which Occupational Fraud Is Detected

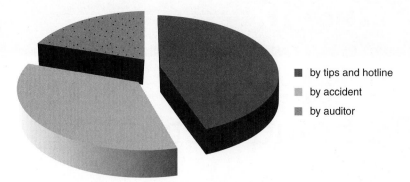

- by tips and hotline
- by accident
- by auditor

Hotlines can come in various forms. Telephone hotlines are phone lines dedicated to accepting tips. The typical hotline accepts calls anonymously, and some hotlines give the tipster a confidential identification number that can be used for subsequent follow-up by the tipster. Cash rewards may be offered as incentives to prospective tipsters.

Hotlines can also exist in the form of Web sites or even simple e-mail addresses dedicated to accepting fraud tips and reports. Good examples of Web-based hotlines can be found in the public sector. For example, the Office of the Inspector General at the U.S. Social Security Administration (SSA) hosts a Web site (http://www.ssa.gov/oig/hotline) devoted to accepting tips relating to social security fraud. The Web site gives tipsters three choices relating to disclosure of their identity:

Confidentiality and Anonymity Not Requested   If necessary, the investigator may contact the tipster for additional information, and the tipster does not place any restrictions on the release of her contact information.

Confidentiality Requested   The investigator may contact the tipster for additional information, but the tipster's name is to remain confidential and not shared outside of the Office of the Inspector General. The policy is to honor requests for confidentiality and not to release any data that would identify such individuals unless required to do so by order of law (e.g., a court order or subpoena).

Anonymity Requested   The tipster does not supply contact information; thus, the investigator will not be able to contact the tipster if additional information is needed to process the complaint.

These choices of identity disclosure raise two important points. First, the words *confidentiality* and *anonymity* differ although they are often confused; in many cases, anonymity is promised when in fact the intention is to promise only confidentiality. Second, the promise of confidentiality contains a qualifier: "unless required to do so by order of law." This qualifier is essential, for without it, the organization risks being sued by the tipster in the event that his name is disclosed to a third party as a result of a court order or subpoena.

The SSA site also contains a disclosure policy:

We cannot provide information regarding what action we have taken on any allegation reported to our office. Federal regulations prohibit the disclosure of information contained in law enforcement records even to the individual making the allegation. Unless you are contacted directly by one of our investigators, there will be no communication from our office. Under no circumstances will we provide you with the "status" of action taken on the allegation.

If you are an SSA employee, SSA may not take action against you solely because of your submission of an allegation to the SSA OIG [Office of the Inspector General] hotline. Federal laws protect employees from reprisals by their employers for "blowing the whistle" on illegal activity.

A *hotline disclosure policy* is important because it defines the privacy rights of the "accused" and protections available for the tipster. The organization's policies in both of these areas should be spelled out carefully.

The hotline site should contain a clear statement regarding the types of items for which it does and does not accept reports. For example, the SSA site indicates that it accepts reports for many types of fraud, including those committed internally, but it also indicates that reports relating to the misuse of social security numbers should be directed to the Federal Trade Commission.

Finally, the typical site accepts tips relating to all types of ethics violations, not only those violations relating to fraud. Examples of nonfraud violations include illegal discrimination and sexual harassment. Someone at the organization's top, typically in the legal department, must review incoming tips and refer them to other departments (e.g., to the internal auditor) as appropriate.

Hotlines Alone Insufficient

For hotlines to be effective, they must be combined with an ethics code, employee training, proper monitoring, good communication, and the right tone from the company's top management. Furthermore, hotlines need to be "advertised" in a variety of places such as on paycheck stubs and vendor invoices.

Fraud Discovery by Accident

Surprising as it may seem, the second most common detection of occupational fraud is accidental discovery. According to studies, accidental discovery accounts for roughly 25 to 35 percent of all occupational fraud detected. The incidence is likely much higher in small companies that do not have or benefit from hotlines or other detection measures. It is a sad fact that the "accidental" discovery in small business is frequently a result of managers trying to figure out why there is not enough cash to pay employees and bills.

Fraud Discovery by Financial Statement Auditors

SAS No. 99, *Consideration of Fraud in a Financial Statement Audit,* requires that auditors design financial statement audits in such a way as to have a reasonable chance of detecting misstatements in the financial reports. This requires auditors to follow a three-step process: (1) gather information relevant to risks of misstatements in the financial reports, (2) analyze and assess risks of misstatement in regard to the entity's programs and controls, and (3) apply the information gathered to the structure and application of the audit.

The application of SAS No. 99 in audits typically accounts for anywhere from 5 to 20 percent of the occupational frauds detected. Unfortunately, some very significant cases of financial statement fraud have escaped detection from auditors despite SAS No. 99.

SAS No. 99 also requires that members of the audit team formally discuss among themselves the potential for misstatement in the financial statements. This discussion must continue throughout the audit process and must be formally documented in the audit working papers.

An important part of the SAS No. 99 audit risk assessment involves studying and defining fraud indicators relevant to the particular entity and its programs and controls. In addition, SAS No. 99 charges the auditor with assessing and documenting the risk of management override of internal controls. Other required assessments include retrospective reviews of accounting estimates and business rationales for unusual transactions. Auditors are to presume that improper revenue recognition indicates a risk for fraud.

In addition to the use of specific fraud indicators, SAS No. 99 indicates that auditors should use the **fraud triangle** in assessing risks. The three "sides" of the triangle are pressure/incentive, opportunity, and rationalization/attitude. These three elements appear in almost all fraud cases. The fraud triangle is discussed in detail in Chapter 9.

At the level of the individual employee, pressure/incentive typically relates to situations in which an employee has an substantial unmet financial need, such as gambling debts, medical debts, excessive lifestyle, and so on. Opportunity is an obvious ingredient; without opportunity, fraud can become impossible. The final ingredient, rationalization/attitude, typically involves the employee's fabrication of a personal moral excuse for the fraud. Such excuses typically involve things such as "I was only borrowing it" or "My sick mother's surgery is more important than a little money for the company." Rationalizations typically take place before the crime is committed.

At the organizational level, pressure/incentives may relate to such things as undue pressure to perform, opportunities may relate to weak controls, and rationalizations/attitudes may relate to factors such as bad examples set by people at the top of the organization.

Finally, SAS No. 99 requires the auditor to report to the appropriate level of management any evidence found that fraud may exist. In general, auditors should not become too close to their clients and maintain a healthy attitude of suspicion throughout the audit.

Fraud Discovery by Internal Auditors

Within the organization, the internal auditor has the responsibility of actively monitoring compliance with policies and behavior relating to internal control. According to the Institute of Internal Auditors (http://www.theiia.org/),

> Internal Auditing is an independent, objective assurance and consulting activity designed to add value and improve an organization's operations. It helps an organization accomplish its objectives by bringing a systematic, disciplined approach to evaluate and improve the effectiveness of risk management, control, and governance processes.

Key elements of this definition include the following:

1. **Independent**   Independence is achieved by the internal auditor reporting directly to the board of directors. The independent internal auditor is free to investigate and report to the CEO without fear of reprisal.
2. **Objectives**   Risk management begins with the organization's objectives and appetite for risk.
3. **Systematic**   Internal auditing is an ongoing process that must be carried out in a planned, consistent manner.
4. **Improve the Effectiveness of Risk Management, Control, and Governance Processes**   With regard to fraud detection, this term means that the internal auditor not only detects and reports fraud but also oversees the design and operation of the processes that prevent, detect, and correct fraud.

Fraud Discovery by Inspectors General

Many government agencies have an **inspector general** whose job includes investigating possible frauds. The inspector general often works with the internal auditor in dealing with fraud-related issues. In the U.S. federal government, the main charge of the inspectors general is to audit various federal agencies and programs with an eye toward possible fraud; waste; and violations of laws, agency policies, and regulations. Inspectors general operate independently of each other.

Many of the federal inspectors general share information through the President's Council on Integrity and Efficiency (PCIE) and the Executive Council on Integrity and Efficiency (ECIE). Special PCIE agents are authorized to carry firearms and make arrests.

Fraud Discovery by Security Departments

Frauds committed against an entity by customers, vendors, and the public are typically detected by specialized functional-area security departments. The position of such security departments within the organization chart tends to vary by industry. For example, in the insurance industry, a department that prevents, detects, and investigates insurance claims fraud might be a branch of an insurance company's claims division. On the other hand, in the financial services industry, the department that deals with credit application fraud might be located in the lending division.

In addition to functional area departments dedicated to fraud management, companies may also have a separate information-security department that also performs fraud management functions that overlap those of the functional area security department.

FRAUD DETECTION AND ENTERPRISE RISK MANAGEMENT

LO2   Within the organization, fraud detection is part of the larger enterprise risk-management (ERM) process, and as such, it is also part of the internal control process (Figure 6.2). In the classical sense, the internal control process views fraud detection as a second line of defense with the first line being prevention. Furthermore, when both prevention and detection fail, the internal control process seeks to implement corrective measures. Therefore, detection is one integral part of a three-part defense process that consists of preventive, detective, and corrective subprocesses. This suggests that measures to detect fraud must be considered in conjunction with measures related to preventing and correcting fraud. The discussion that immediately follows explains the relative roles of prevention, detection, and correction in managing fraud. These three roles are then put in an economic context and applied to the optimal design of a fraud detection system.

Importance of Detection Relative to Prevention and Correction

Preventive Controls

In their strongest form, preventive controls frequently rely on security barriers to prevent fraud. For example, placing inventory in locked storage monitored by video cameras would represent a security barrier that prevents fraud by limiting access to the inventory. Note that security barriers yield a much stronger form of prevention than that produced by early detection. Security barriers prevent fraud by making its commission more difficult or impossible whereas early detection assumes that either preventive controls have failed or do not apply. Of course, not all preventive controls are based on security barriers. For example,

FIGURE 6.2
The Relative Role of Fraud Detection in the Enterprise Risk Management Process

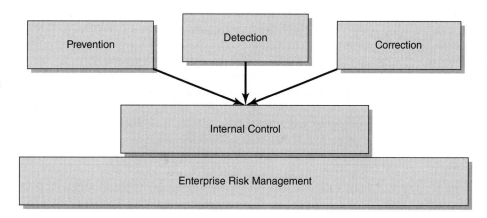

good employee training can prevent fraud by increasing compliance with control policies and procedures. In general, preventive controls seek to stop fraud before it happens.

Detective Controls

It is not possible or economical to stop all fraud before it happens. For example, the only way for a retail store to absolutely stop shoplifting might be to close and accept orders only over the Internet. Similarly, the only way for a bank to absolutely stop all loan fraud might be for it to stop lending money.

In general, increasing preventive security can reduce fraud losses, but beyond some point, the cost of additional preventive security will exceed the related savings from reduced fraud losses. This is where detection comes in; it may be economical when prevention is not. For example, one way to prevent a salesclerk from stealing from the register would be for the security department to carefully monitor, review, and approve every one of the clerk's sales. However, it would likely be much more cost–effective instead to implement a simple detective control: an end-of-shift reconciliation between the cash in the register and the transactions logged by the cash register during the clerk's shift. If refunds are not given at the point of sale, the end-of-shift balance of cash in the register should equal the shift's sales per the transaction logs minus the balance of cash in the register at the beginning of the shift. Any significant failure of these numbers to reconcile would amount to a fraud indicator. Of course, further investigation could show that the clerk simply made an error and did not commit fraud.

The cost–effectiveness of detective controls, like preventive controls, has limits. First, such controls are not cost free to implement, and improving detective controls may cost more than the results they provide. Second, detective controls produce both false positives and false negatives. A **false positive** occurs when a detective control signals a possible fraud that upon investigation turns up a reasonable explanation for the indicator. A **false negative** occurs when a detective control fails to signal possible fraud when one exists. Reducing false negatives means increasing the fraud detection rate.

In the same way, the cost–effectiveness of increasing preventive security has a limit as does the benefit of increasing the fraud detection rate. To increase the detection rate, it is necessary to increase the frequency at which the detective control signals possible fraud. The result is more investigations, and the cost of the additional investigations can exceed the resulting reductions in fraud losses.

Corrective Controls

Controls are essentially policies and procedures designed to minimize losses due to fraud or other events such as errors or acts of nature. Corrective controls are merely special control types involved once a loss is known to exist. With respect to fraud, an important corrective control involves the investigation of potential frauds and the investigation and recovery process from discovered frauds.

More generally speaking, fraud investigations serve not only a corrective function but also detective and preventive functions. Such investigations are detective of fraud to the extent that they follow up on fraud signals in order to confirm or disconfirm the presence of fraud. But once fraud is confirmed to exist, fraud examinations shift toward gathering evidence and become corrective by assisting in recovery from the perpetrator and other sources such as insurance. Fraud investigations are also corrective in that they can lead to revealing and repairing unknown weaknesses. For example, a fraud investigation of inventory shortages in a college bookstore reveals that an employee is secretly dropping new books into trash cans located throughout the store. The employee then returns after store hours and completes the fraud by removing the books from the outside trash Dumpster.

Upon being confronted, the employee confesses and makes restitution. The end result is that the fraud investigation functions to correct the original loss, and the related discovery of the fraud scheme leads to prevention of similar losses in the future. In summary, the fraud examination has served to detect, correct, and prevent fraud.

Thus, because fraud investigations can serve as a fraud-detection function, it is not really reasonable to call the fraud investigation a detective control. However, fraud investigations are not normally thought of as detective controls. This so is because fraud investigations tend to be much more costly than standard detective controls and therefore are normally used only when there is already some fraud indicator generated by a typical detective control. Therefore, the primary functions of fraud investigations are to correct existing frauds and prevent future ones.

In some cases, the primary benefit of a fraud investigation might be to prevent future frauds. Even when recovery is impossible or impractical (e.g., because the thief has no assets), unwinding the fraud scheme may still have the benefit of leading to the prevention of the same scheme in the future. Furthermore, a company might benefit from spending a very large sum of money to investigate and prosecute a very small theft in order to deter other individuals from defrauding the company.

Fraud versus Errors, Waste, and Inefficiency

There's never any guarantee that investigating a fraud indicator will lead to discovering fraud. Depending on the situation, an investigation might lead to nothing at all (i.e., a reasonable explanation for the indicator) or to the discovery of losses due to errors, waste, inefficiencies, or even uncontrollable events (Figure 6.3). If one is considering a loan application, a fraud indicator might indicate nothing, fraud, or an error. On the other hand, in regard to the possible theft of raw materials in a production process, a fraud indicator might indicate undocumented waste or scrap.

Two important factors to consider concerning the general design of a fraud detection process are not only the costs and benefits of detecting, correcting, and preventing fraud but also the costs and benefits of detecting, correcting, and preventing errors, waste, uncontrollable events, and inefficiencies. Of course, the particular costs that are relevant will vary from one type of business process to another.

For purposes of simplicity, the discussion that follows refers only to fraud-related costs. However, this simplification poses little restriction on the discussion because,

FIGURE 6.3
From an Economic Standpoint, Losses Due to Fraud Are Often Indistinguishable from Losses Due to Error

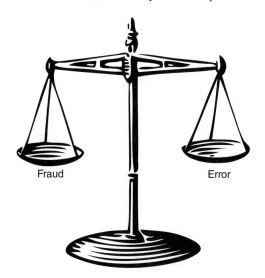

Fraud   Error

notwithstanding the limitation of fraud applying only to intentional acts, factors such as waste, uncontrollable events, and inefficiencies can be thought of as fraud in which a perpetrator's intention is not discernable. Furthermore, many acts that could appear to be fraud can easily be accidents.

Optimal Design of Fraud Detection Systems

LO3 To design a loss management system, one must consider the total costs of prevention, detection, and correction associated with the system. One must also consider the costs of losses associated with the operation of the system. Therefore, the total costs associated with a given fraud loss management system are as follows:

$$\textbf{Total Fraud Costs (TFC)} = \text{Prevention Costs} + \text{Detection Costs} \\ + \text{Correction Costs} + \text{Losses}$$

Given this relationship, the total loss management process can be economically optimized by using a two-step process: first, choose an acceptable level of risk, and then choose the right mix of prevention, detection, and correction measures that will minimize the TFC and achieve the desired level of risk.

The acceptable level of risk may be defined in terms of expected losses and the degree of certainty regarding those losses. For example, an insurance company may decide that its acceptable level of risk due to claims fraud and errors is a maximum of $1 million per year with a 98 percent certainty. It would then budget its expenditures for prevention, detection, and correction accordingly, say at the rate of $200,000 per year in total with allocation percentages of 90 percent to prevention, 8 percent to detection, and 2 percent to correction.

Alternatively, the insurance company could reverse the two-step process: It could first set the level of total loss management expenditures and then optimize the mix of prevention, detection, and correction to minimize the resulting level of risk. For example, the insurance company could budget only $100,000 for loss management and then allocate percentages of 95 percent, 4 percent, and 1 percent for prevention, detection, and correction, respectively. The result of this optimization process might be a maximum estimated annual loss of less than $2 million with 98 percent certainty. In other words, by cutting its total loss management expenditures in half, from $200,000 to $100,000, the insurance company doubles its maximum expected loss from $1 million to $2 million.

Both the forward and reverse two-step processes are acceptable as long as management sets a balance between costs and risks that is consistent with its appetite for risk and its overall ERM process. In the end, loss management is like purchased insurance: You get the coverage you pay for; your main decision is to pick the right coverage given your appetite for risk and your budget.

Of course, generating loss estimates that are conditioned on control expenditures may be difficult, but it can be done using actuarial-type analyses. Furthermore, it is not necessary to use a quantitative approach. In many cases, losses are too difficult to estimate with any precision, so combining intuition with rough estimates may work as well or better than a refined actuarial-type analysis.

Catastrophic losses are especially resistant to refined analysis. Consider the British Petroleum (BP) mishap that sent millions of gallons of oil spilling in to the Gulf of Mexico over a period of months. Who could have estimated the probability of such a disaster? There had not been a similar accident in more than 40 years in over 30,000 oil platforms worldwide. Second, who could have estimated the losses that rose into difficult-to-imagine billions of dollars? Perhaps BP could have estimated the maximum losses, but then any related cost-benefit analysis would have been no better than the estimated probability of such a disaster.

One might be tempted to ask what a BP oil spill has to do with fraud. The answer is that any loss that can be caused by an accident, for example, by human error or equipment failure, can just as easily be caused by some form of fraud. For example, the press reported that one of the safety mechanisms that could have immediately stopped the oil spill had failed because of a battery failure. Let's just say that the spill was caused by bad luck and a bad battery. But what if a vendor had fraudulently sold the company a bad battery, or what if a third party was being paid to check the battery but never did so while providing fraudulent document saying that it did? In theory, the disaster could have as easily been caused by fraud as by accident.

Relative Cost of Detection versus Prevention and Correction

As a general rule, we can say that both preventive controls and detective controls cost less than corrective controls. Corrective controls tend to involve hands-on, resource-intensive investigations, and in many cases, such investigations do not result in recovering the loss. On the other hand, preventive controls can also be quite costly. Banks pay armed guards and incur costs to maintain expensive vaults and alarm systems. Companies surround their headquarters with high fences and armed guards, and use security checkpoints and biometric key card systems inside. On the information technology side, firms use sophisticated firewalls and multi-layer access controls. The costs of all these preventive measures can add up to staggering sums in large companies. Of course, losses that are not prevented or corrected in a timely fashion can lead to the ultimate corrective measure: bankruptcy. In fact, some estimates show that about one-third of all business failures relates to some form of fraudulent activity.

One positive aspect of the cost of preventive controls is that unlike detective controls, they do not generate fraud indicators that lead to costly investigations. In fact, they tend to do their job in complete "silence" so that management never even knows when they prevent a fraud. For example, the thick door of a bank vault with a time lock prevents bank employees from entering the building at night to steal its contents. Similarly, passwords, pin numbers, and biometric data silently provide access to authorized individuals and prevent access from others.

The problem with preventive controls is that they are always subject to circumvention by determined and cunning fraudsters. There is no perfect solution to preventing acts of fraud, so detection is necessary as a secondary line of defense, and in some cases, as the primary line of defense. For example, consider a lending company that accepts online loan applications. It may be difficult or impossible to prevent fraudulent applications, but the company can certainly put a sophisticated (and expensive) system in place to analyze applications and provide indicators that suggest when an application may be fraudulent.

In general, the optimal allocation of resources to prevention versus detection depends on the particular business process under consideration. So, there is no general rule that dictates the optimal allocation of resources between prevention versus detection. But there is a general, heuristic approach that can assist in making the allocation (Figure 6.4):

1. Analyze the business process and identify threats and vulnerabilities.
2. Select reasonable preventive controls according to the business process and customs within the company's industry.
3. Estimate fraud losses given the assumed preventive controls.
4. Identify and add a basic set of detective controls to the system. (If returning to this step after completing Step 8, instead add additional detective controls to the basic set.)

FIGURE 6.4
Heuristic Approach for Optimizing Detection Controls

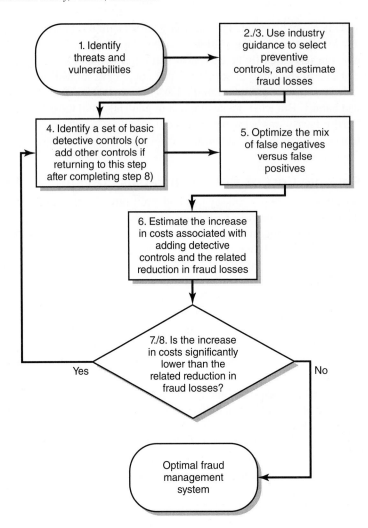

5. For a given set of detective controls, identify the optimal mix of false negatives versus false positives. The optimal mix depends on the costs of investigations versus the costs of losses. Large losses and small investigation costs favor relatively low false negatives and high false positives for fraud signals.

6. Given the assumed mix of false negative and false positive errors, estimate the incremental cost associated with adding the detective (and related corrective) controls, and estimate the resulting reduction in fraud losses.

7. Compare the reduction in fraud losses with the increase in costs associated with adding the optimal mix of detection and correction controls.

8. If increase in costs is significantly lower than the related reduction in fraud losses, consider returning to Step 4 to add more detective controls. Otherwise, accept the set of detective controls under consideration.

The entire process can be repeated for different sets of preventive controls. In addition, the cost-benefit comparison in Steps 7 and 8 can also consider the maximum possible losses and the probabilities of their occurrences.

The "trick" to this heuristic process is that detective and corrective controls are considered jointly because fraud indicators generate costly investigations. So, the cost of such generated investigations must be considered when choosing fraud indicators.

Example: Loan Applications

Detective control: Generate a fraud indicator if the applicant has no landline phone but has income of more than $150,000.

Rate that the fraud indicator is a positive rate: 3 percent

Rate that the fraud indictor is a false positive: 2 percent

Rate that the fraud indicator is a false negative: 1.5 percent

Cost of one investigation: $1,000

Typical loss from a fraudulent loan: $20,000

Volume of loans per year: 1,000

Cost of detective controls (the fraud signal): $10,000 but fixed (i.e., it does not depend on the volume of loans)

Cost of preventive controls: $50,000 (also fixed)

Based on these assumed numbers, there would be

Thirty investigations per year at a total cost of $30,000.

Twenty investigations per year that are false positives at a total cost of $20,000.

Ten investigations per year that are correct positives at a total fraud savings of $200,000.

Fifteen frauds per year that are not detected by the fraud indicator at a total loss of $300,000.

Total Fraud Costs (TFC) per Year = Cost of Investigations + Cost of Preventive Controls
+ Cost of Detective Controls + Cost of Fraud Losses

or

Total Fraud Costs (TFC) = $390,000 per Year ($30,000 + $50,000
+ $10,000 + $300,000)

Consider the following observations: (1) The use of the fraud indicator and investigations is cost beneficial. The joint effect of the fraud indicator and the investigations is to detect (and thus prevent) annual losses of $200,000 at a cost of $30,000. (2) The fraud indicator does not detect the majority of the frauds. It identifies only 10 of 25 frauds. (3) Given that frauds cost 20 times more than investigations, it would make sense to conduct more investigations as long as each new 20 investigations identifies at least one additional fraud.

Next, consider what happens if the fraud indicator is changed so that the $150,000 applicant income number is reduced to $100,000. This change is obviously likely to increase the number of investigations and, it is hoped, reduce the number of false negatives. The results might be something like the following:

Rate that the fraud indicator is positive: 5 percent

Rate that the fraud indicator is false positive: 3 percent

Rate the fraud indicator is false negative: 1 percent

Other assumptions: unchanged

This change results in the detection of an additional five frauds per year resulting in $100,000 in incremental loss savings. On the other hand, the incremental investigation costs are only $20,000 per year. At this rate of savings, it might appear beneficial to tweak the fraud indicator even more. See the following calculations:

Reduction in the number of fraud losses: 5 = 1000 × (1.5 percent − 1 percent)

Incremental costs of investigations: $100,000 = $1000 × (5 percent − 3 percent)

Consider this observation: The false positive rate per year has gone up by one-third (from 20 to 30). In general, the higher the ratio of the loss per fraud to the cost to investigate one fraud, the higher the optimal false positive rate will be.

Next, assume that further tweaking the fraud indicator does not produce any net incremental loss savings. For example, the company might discover that reducing the $150,000 applicant income number to $50,000 reduces the number of losses by only one but requires an additional 50 investigations. Therefore, the company would not further tweak the fraud indicator, and its total costs would be follows:

Total investigation costs: $50,000

Total fraud loss costs: $200,000

Prevention costs: $50,000 (unchanged)

Detection costs: $10,000 (unchanged)

$$\text{Total Cost of Fraud} = \text{Cost of Investigations} + \text{Costs of Preventions} \\ + \text{Cost of Detections} + \text{Cost of Losses}$$

or

$$\text{Total Cost of Fraud (TCF)} = \$310,000 = \$50,000 + \$50,000 \\ + \$10,000 + \$200,000$$

This compares to $390,000 before tweaking the fraud indicator.

Now that the company has the optimal mix of false positive and false negative fraud indicators, it can consider the effect of upgrading its preventive controls and its detection system. The effect of upgrading the preventive system would be to reduce the incidence of both fraud and fraud indicators. The general effect of upgrading the detection system would be to reduce both false positives and false negatives. The mix of false negative and false positive indicators would be reoptimized for each upgrade considered.

For example, assume that an upgrade to the preventive controls costs $20,000. This might then lead to no change in the detection costs, a $15,000 reduction in investigation costs, and a $60,000 reduction in fraud losses after reoptimizing the mix of false negative and false positive fraud indicators as a result of the upgrade prevention system. The result would be a net savings of $55,000, thus reducing total costs from $310,000 to $255,000. This would be a large savings compared to the original total cost of $390,000.

Alternative Cost Scenarios

One very simple cost scenario involves the case in which investigation costs are fixed over a wide range of volume. For example, assume that our loan company's investigation department requires a minimum of three full-time employees to investigate anywhere between 1 and 200 loan applications per year. If we also assume that the prevention and detection costs are fixed, then the entire heuristic process reduces to tweaking the fraud indictor. Furthermore, because investigations are essentially "free" (in an incremental sense, up to 200 per year because their costs are fixed), the optimal detection solution would be to tweak the fraud indicator so that it refers exactly 200 loan applications a year for investigation.

Definition of the Fraud Indicator

Composite Indicators

A typical approach is to define the fraud indicator as a single number (also known as a **composite fraud indicator** or **risk score**) that is computed from a formula that involves possibly many factors. This is a very common approach used in risk measurement. For example, there exists the well-known Altman Z-Score that predicts bankruptcy risk. Another example is the well-known FICO credit score (www.fico.com) used by many financial institutions in making credit decisions.

Risk scores are typically developed using statistical approaches such as linear regression analysis, discriminant analysis, or logistic regression analysis. In these models, the risk score is the dependent variable, which represents a composite fraud indicator that is based on a weighted sum of individual indicators. For example, a composite fraud indictor score for loan applications might be computed as follows:

$$\text{Composite Fraud Indicator Score} = b1 \times (850 - \text{Applicant's FICO Score})/850 + b2$$
$$\times (\$150{,}000 - \text{Applicant's Income})/150{,}000$$

where b1 and b2 are weights estimated using statistical techniques that rely on historical data. Once the weights have been estimated, they can typically be used for long periods of time subject to their periodic reevaluation.

The score would then be computed for each new loan application, and those applications that receive or exceed some minimum score would be referred for investigation. The minimum score would be set to optimize the mix of false negatives and false positives.

Single-Factor Indicators or Red Flags

The **single-factor fraud indicator,** or **red flag,** is just a special case of the composite indicator. It is made up of only one factor. Although composite indicators can be applied to almost any situation, in many situations a single factor, or red flag, generates sufficient concern or suspicion to trigger an investigation. The list of possible red flags is endless; examples for internal company misappropriation fraud include a cashier who fails to record a sale, a cashier who mishandles cash, an inventory clerk who is in the wrong place at the wrong time, and an accounts receivables clerk who fails to record a customer's payment on account. Other red flags could be unusual activities in accounts or unusual transactions or balances relative to previous periods or to other accounts or benchmarks. Even simple "errors" can be indicators of underlying fraud. For example, an error in posting a payment to a customer's account could easily be an indicator that the accounts receivables clerk is lapping accounts receivable.

Random Tests

Fraud indicators are an essential aid in identifying situations that deserve investigation. However, fraud indicators have one big weakness: At times they can be manipulated by fraudsters. In other words, fraudsters may manipulate the data used to generate the fraud indicators, thus rendering the indicators useless. For this reason, complete detection systems may include investigations of items selected at random. One type of random testing is the randomly timed surprise audit in which the investigator focuses on one attribute, such as verifying the amount of cash in each cash register at some moment in time. Another type of random testing is **discovery sampling** by which the investigator selects a random sample in such a way as to have a high probability of detecting a particular type and size error or fraud. For example, an investigator reviewing a file containing 1,000 invoices may use discovery sampling to determine the minimum number of invoices that she needs to investigate to be 95 percent certain that the total of all invoices in the file is not overstated by more than $500.

Obtainment of Cost Estimates

Implementing the heuristic fraud loss model requires reasonable estimates of the cost relating to prevention, detection, and correction. Such cost can be obtained through formal cost studies, which typically fall within the expertise of cost accountants. However, complete cost estimates are not always necessary. In many cases, one might simply consider incremental costs and benefits relative to an existing system. Such an approach would not require knowledge of existing costs although existing cost relationships would be important. For example, it would be necessary to know the relationship between investigative costs and the volume of cases investigated.

DATA-DRIVEN FRAUD DETECTION

LO4 *Data-driven fraud detection* involves the formal process of sifting through data in search of fraud indicators. It relies on four general sources of data: (1) internal control data, (2) basic tips and hotlines, (3) security breaches, and (4) pattern data tips and hotlines have already been previously discussed. The other sources of data are discussed here.

Sources of Data

Internal Control Data

Fraud indicators are generated by basic internal control violations that include the following, for example

1. **Reconciliation Failures**   For example, a bank reconciliation yields a deposit per the bank records that does not match the deposits per the accounting records.
2. **Control Total Failures**   For example, the amount posted to accounts receivables does not match the corresponding total of sales receipts.
3. **Exception Transactions**   For example, a customer is permitted to exceed his credit limit.
4. **Apparent Errors**   For example, a clerk makes an error in filling out a deposit slip. The company becomes aware of the error when the bank sends the controller a correction memo.

Security Breach Data

Security breaches can result from security access violations and security protocol violations. Security access violations occur when an individual accesses some entity resource without first being granted a sufficient privilege to do so. Examples of access breaches include the following:

1. A customer enters a secure inventory storage area.
2. An accounting clerk makes a bank deposit for a cashier when the cashier is too busy to perform her duty. The clerk should not have access to cash.
3. A bank employee uses another employee's account to access a client's loan data.

Security protocol violations involve failures to observe controls and security policies. Examples include the following:

1. A clerk skips her normal procedure of double-checking time cards.
2. An inventory clerk fails to record new inventory received.
3. A loan officer approves a loan without the normal careful review.

Pattern Data

Sometimes data from tips, internal controls, and security breaches are not enough to signal fraud. Normal monitoring systems can fail because of random error, or loopholes in the controls, the monitoring process, or the reporting process. Furthermore, standard fraud indicators can also fail because fraudsters intentionally circumvent them by manipulating the very data that are normally used to signal possible fraud. Examples of such manipulations include the following:

1. **Records and Inventory Falsification**   For example, shortages in inventory accounts can be covered up by falsifying inventory counts.
2. **Software Manipulation**   For example, a hacker breaks into a company's accounting system and installs a program patch that overrides billing for his purchasing account.
3. **Control Override**   A supervisor who is supposed to monitor employees' work hours permits an employee to report excess hours on her time card.

Pattern data include data items that tend to indicate fraud only when considered jointly. In many cases, pattern data can produce useful fraud indicators when simple fraud indicators do not. Pattern data can be based on almost any imaginable type of data item. For example, suppose fraudulent insurance claims are much more likely to occur near the Christmas holiday season, perhaps because that is a time when some people are desperate to buy presents and take vacations. If so, the time of year could be a relevant factor in a pattern analysis that produces indicators of insurance fraud. Also potentially relevant to pattern analysis is (when legally permissible) the personal history of potential suspects, including employment history, credit history, insurance claim history, education history, driving record, criminal history, and other personal information.

Pattern data analysis, also known as *data mining,* can be used to detect fraud as well as a tool to improve business processes and better compete in the market. A classical example of data mining is the "beer and diapers story," an urban legend often used to illustrate the power of data mining. As one version of the story goes, a convenience store clerk noticed that a lot of men were buying diapers on Friday evenings. The intelligent clerk carefully studied the pattern and soon figured out that men's main purpose in the store was to buy beer. It just so happened that their wives were asking them to pick up some diapers on the way home from work.

As a result of the clerk's data-mining effort, the store moved the diapers next to the beer cooler. Thereafter, diaper sales soared dramatically, and store profits increased. Data-mining systems are discussed in more detail in the next section.

Pattern detection and data mining have the power to uncover fraud indicators that would otherwise go without notice. Humans are only so good at monitoring and analyzing data. In fact, past research has indicated that in many cases, humans are not capable of processing more than a handful of data items when making decisions. Of course, with training and expertise, this number can be increased somewhat, but even then humans are not capable of processing the huge volumes of data typically associated with modern business processes. This is especially true for interactions between factors. For example, a human might view raw data and conclude that the risk of credit card fraud is elevated with new accounts, accounts that pay late, and accounts with no annual fees versus those with annual fees. But the same human would likely not be able to notice that card accounts in which the cardholder buys both laptop computers and fast-delivery pizza are at elevated risk for fraud. Such cardholders might be more likely to do business over the Internet with merchants who, for example, sell their card numbers to fraudsters.

There have been reports of credit card companies canceling cardholder accounts because of types of purchases the cardholders made. As an interesting exercise, ask yourself what types of credit card purchases might make a credit card company consider a cardholder's account to be at elevated risk for default. Perhaps a credit card charge for a bankruptcy attorney? How about a string of ATM charges made in casinos during normal work hours, or a cardholder who makes only the minimum payment every month?

Typical indicators for credit card fraud include purchases of items not usually purchased, purchases made in industries considered to be at high risk, and purchases made within a short time of each other that are geographically far apart. Indicators can also be generated from the bank number on the card, the purchaser's card number, and so on. Applications of fraud detection systems are discussed in the following section.

Data-Driven Fraud Detection Applications and Tools

The use of data-driven fraud detection applications is common in the public and private sectors. Examples of such systems include the following:

- **The U.S. Internal Revenue Service (IRS) Electronic Fraud Detection System** The IRS has spent hundreds of millions of dollars on its Electronic Fraud Detection System (EFDS). It uses complicated algorithms that incorporate data from tax returns filed by taxpayers in previous years as well as benchmark data from others' tax returns.

- **FraudPoint** LexisNexis (www.LexisNexis.com) provides FraudPoint, a service that continuously collects data from thousands of public and private sources. These data are analyzed to provide verification, authentication, and identity analytics for both consumers and businesses. The result is a three-digit risk score that can be used as a fraud risk indicator.

- **Experian Detect^{SM}** Experian (www.experian.com), one of the three top U.S. credit-reporting agencies, provides its Experian Detect fraud detection system. This system analyzes credit (and other types) of applications for indications of fraud. Some aspects of the analysis include more than 140 rules to detect application inconsistencies; cross checks against credit files, previous applications, and known fraud records; and data from fraud patterns across multiple industries.

- **Actimize Employee Fraud Solution** This banking industry system, provided by Actimize (www.actimize.com), monitors employees, accounts, and transactions in real time. It permits detection policies and thresholds to be adjusted in a simple Web interface. The initial set of detection policies was developed by subject matter experts and can be supplemented and revised as needed.

- **FraudLabs™ Fraud Detection Web Service** This service of FraudLabs, a Malaysian company with servers in the United States, provides a proprietary risk score for credit card fraud. The risk score is based on individual card transaction details that include the IP address, e-mail address, domain, delivery address, the card's bank identification number, phone number, and zip code.

In addition to dedicated fraud-detection systems, many internal auditing and control monitoring software products are available. These products can incorporate their own fraud detection indicators or work in conjunction with dedicated fraud detection systems. Examples include the following:

- **Approva One** Approva One is provided by Approva Corporation (www.approva.net) in the form of a Continuous Controls Monitoring (CCM) suite. The suite includes fraud risk scoring and analytics.

- **CCH TeamMate**   ARC Logics (www.arclogics.com) publishes the CCH TeamMate audit management system, an audit software platform used by more than 70,000 auditors from more than 1,800 organizations worldwide.
- **ACL**   ACL Services Ltd. (www.acl.com) provides continuous controls monitoring. The software uses a proprietary scripting language that can be used to program detection rules customized for the individual company or industry. ACL also provides ACL Audit Exchange, a team-based platform for managing and sharing fraud analytics.

A third class of software useful for fraud detection includes data-mining and business intelligence software. Such software can be added as a front end to an existing accounting or enterprise resource planning (ERP) system. The major data-mining/business intelligence products directly access existing enterprise and accounting databases to provide enhanced reporting and analytics. Examples include the following:

- **The MicroStrategy Business Intelligence Platform**   This software product, provided by MicroStrategy Inc. (www.microstrategy.com), can be configured not only to identify and report exceptions but also to build complex multi-dimensional profiles of different types of fraud. To build complex profiles, the software uses special database technologies, such as in-memory Online Analytical Processing (OLAP), that are not typically available in accounting systems. In-memory OLAP is capable of simultaneously analyzing the interactions of large numbers of data items thousands of times faster than conventional processing can.
- **SAP BusinessObjects**   This product is similar to the Microstrategy Business Intelligence Platform. It is marketed by SAP, one of the world's largest vendors of ERP software.
- **SAS Data Mining**   This product is published by SAS Institute Inc. (www.sas.com). SAS Data Mining facilitates the entire process of going from raw data to analytical models that can be used to facilitate fraud detection.

Data-Driven Applications for Small Businesses

Fraud detection systems are not just for big companies. Various fraud detection add-on products are available for many of the major accounting systems used by small and medium-size enterprises (SMEs). Examples include the following:

AuditMyBooks   This software product, published by AuditMyBooks LLC (www.auditmybooks.com), works directly with Intuit Quickbooks. AuditMyBooks provides software as a service (SaaS) and hosted by Intuit. Quickbooks is one of the world's most popular SME accounting systems.

AIM@Fraud Intelligent Fraud Detection   This product, published by Integral Solutions (Asia) PTE LTD integrates directly with Microsoft Dynamics, which is used by both small and large companies.

Ad Hoc Fraud Detection Tools

Various products on the market can be used as ad hoc, stand-alone tools. One good example is the Active Data add-in for Microsoft Excel published by InformationActive Inc. (www.InformationActive.com). This product adds more than 100 data analysis and worksheet manipulation features to Excel.

Another excellent stand-alone tool is IDEA, published by CaseWare International Inc. IDEA performs a wide variety of functions, such as extracting transactions, identifying gaps in sequences (e.g., in sequences of check numbers or invoices), and detecting duplicates. It also manipulates data using techniques such as stratifying and aging.

STEPS IN BUILDING A FRAUD DETECTION SYSTEM

Building a fraud detection system involves various steps. These include risk analysis (including threat and vulnerability analysis), the exploitation of expert knowledge, knowledge discovery, scoring and assessment, and implementation. Each step is discussed.

Risk Analysis and Control Development   As discussed in Chapter 5 and the first part of the current chapter, fraud detection is part of the larger ERM process. It must be considered jointly with the costs of prevention and correction. To develop a fraud detection system, basic controls should already be in place. Possible violations of these controls can serve as a starting point for identifying fraud indicators.

Exploitation of Expert Knowledge   A database of fraud indicators and detection rules should be developed based on existing sets of internal controls, security measures, audit checklists, professional literature, and so on. Individual indicators can be assigned severity levels. Databases of rules can be fed directly into fraud detection software. For example, the database of rules might be developed using the ACL scripting language.

Knowledge Discovery   Additional indicators and rules can be discovered through brainstorming, business processes reviews, and data mining. As depicted in Figure 6.5, the data-mining process involves five steps: sampling, exploration, modification, modeling, and assessment (**SEMMA**).

1. **Sampling**   One has to begin the process with some sample of data. This could be a sample of transactions or other data items. The sample should contain some cases of fraud. If real cases are not available, then the data can be massaged to simulate fraud.

2. **Exploration**   Various graphical and statistical techniques should be used to identify data items that are potentially relevant to the prediction of fraud. This is not an automatic process. It requires considerable judgment. Exploratory data analysis, a branch of statistics, can be helpful. The goal of the exploration process is to produce at least some sort of preliminary model for detecting fraud.

3. **Modification**   After exploration, changes may need to be made to the data sample. This may lead to additional changes in the preliminary fraud detection model. In addition, after the model has been developed and assessed, it may require modification and still more development and assessment.

4. **Model**   A model needs to be developed for testing. This includes selecting a modeling algorithm. Various types of modeling algorithms include linear regression, decision trees, market basket analyses, logistic regression, time series, gradient boosting, and neural networks. A detailed discussion of these algorithms and the many other algorithms available is beyond the scope of this text. Model parameters are estimated using one or more test data sets.

5. **Assessment**   This step involves testing the model. The model is applied to test samples that contain some fraud to see how well it predicts in terms of minimizing false negatives and false positives according to overall risk-management needs. As a general rule, the model's predictive accuracy should be tested on samples different from ones used in its development. After testing, it might be necessary to return to Step 3 and make changes to the model.

Implementation   To implement the model, documentation, training, and reporting are required. The model should undergo ongoing assessment.

FIGURE 6.5
Modeling Data-Driven Fraud Detectors (SEMMA)

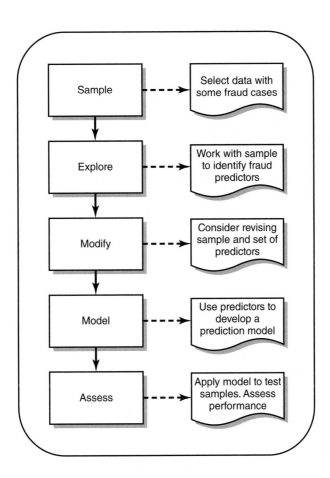

Special Modeling Techniques   Some modeling techniques are so different from the ones just mentioned that they deserve separate mention. One such technique is social networking analysis, which maps relations between individuals or entities. Relations can be defined in many ways, for example, in terms of phone calls, e-mail communications, funds transfers, financial exchanges, and memberships in groups or organizations.

The benefit of social network analysis is that it can sometimes identify all major players in a fraud scheme. Police investigators routinely analyze phone records to identify the relationships between suspects and others. For example, an identity theft ring may contain an identity document forger, a purse thief or hacker, and a person who forges and passes fake checks. In many cases, cell phone records of one of these suspects can quickly lead to the identity of the others.

Telephone records provide an especially good source of data needed to map a social network. Furthermore, many software applications on the market can quickly generate social network maps from raw telephone records. Examples include SAS's social networking analysis module and SPSS's (www.spss.com) IBM SPSS Modeler Professional product. Dozens of other social network modeling packages are on the market.

Social networking analysis has been used extensively to investigate terrorist rings. One Web site (www.orgnet.com) provides an interesting social networking map of the

911 terrorist network. The same type of map can be used just as easily for investigations relating to embezzlement, loan fraud, money laundering, and so on.

Content Analysis and Text Analysis Content analysis and text analysis involve using algorithms to automatically and without human intervention analyze and interpret the content of documents and conversations. Documents arise from many sources, including e-mail messages, Web pages, and legal documents. Conversations may arise from various sources that include wiretaps or surreptitiously recorded meetings.

The resulting analysis and interpretation can be used by itself or in conjunction with other tools. For example, a social network might be identified from the content of e-mail messages that refer to the common groups of persons, places, or subjects.

Benford Analysis Benford analysis presents another interesting approach to fraud detection. Its general use is to determine the likelihood that fraud exists in records. This technique is based on **Benford's law,** named after Frank Benford who realized that the likelihood that numbers 1, 2, 3, 4, 5, 6, 7, 8, and 9 will appear as the first digit in numbers occurring in a random data set conforms to a predictable pattern. That is, the number 1 is more likely to appear as the first digit in a number than is the number 2. The pattern of likelihood (Figure 6.6) continues with other digits: The number 2 is more likely to appear as a first digit than 3, 3 is more likely to appear as a first digit than 4, and so on. Note that just because the likelihood is higher that 7 will appear as a first digit than will 8 does not mean that a number that begins with 8 is due to fraud. Benford's law can be used to determine whether a higher risk than normal exists that a population of numbers—for example, a collection of vendor's invoices—contain fraud. Specifically, the invoice amounts can be analyzed by means of a Benford analysis to determine whether a higher than usual risk that the amounts were fabricated exists. If Benford's law identifies a high risk, the population itself can be examined in more detail. Several commercially available software programs contain the capability to run a Benford analysis.

FIGURE 6.6
The Incidence of Leading Digits 1–9 as Predicted by Benford's Law

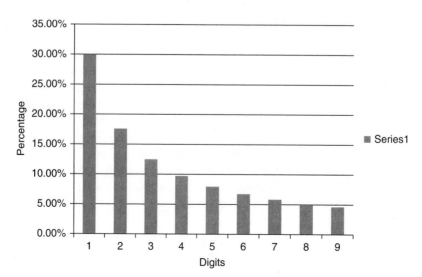

Summary

The fraud detection process involves identifying indicators of fraud that suggest a need for further investigation. The objectives of fraud detection include not only catching fraud but also preventing it. Fraud detection can also be used as one of the many tools in fraud investigations. Although it does not produce evidence, it can help point investigators in the right direction, and in some cases, it can be used to help rule out the presence of certain types of fraud.

Fraud is normally discovered in various ways. These include tips and hotlines, financial statement audits, internal audits, and by accident. Various studies have shown that tips account for roughly 35 to 50 percent of frauds detected within organizations. The main way of obtaining tips is through hotlines, which can be in the form of phone numbers, e-mail addresses, and Web sites. For hotlines to be effective, they must be combined with an ethics code, employee training, proper monitoring, good communication, and the right tone at the top of the company. Furthermore, hotlines need to be "advertised" in a variety of places such as paycheck stubs and vendor invoices.

According to studies, accidental discovery accounts for roughly 25 percent of all fraud detected within organizations. The incidence is likely much higher in smaller companies that do not benefit from hotlines or other detection measures.

Financial statement auditors also detect frauds. SAS No. 99 requires auditors to follow a three-step process: (1) gather information relevant to risks of misstatements in the financial reports, (2) analyze and assess risks of misstatement regarding the entity's programs and controls, and (3) apply the information gathered to the structure and application of the audit. Throughout the audit, auditors are required to discuss among themselves the possibility of fraud.

Within the organization fraud detection is part of the larger enterprise risk management (ERM) process, and as such, it is also part of the internal control process, which deals with fraud through preventive, detective, and corrective controls. It is not cost–effective to prevent all frauds; therefore, a need exists for detective controls. But the cost–effectiveness of detective controls also has limits and is not cost free to implement. Moreover, detective controls produce both false positives and false negatives, which in turn lead to unnecessary investigations (false positives) and losses due to failures to investigate (false negatives).

The total cost associated with a given fraud loss management system includes the sum of prevention costs, detection costs, correction costs, and losses. Given this relationship, the total loss management process can be economically optimized by a two-step process: first, choose an acceptable level of risk, and second, chose the right mix of prevention, detection, and correction measures that will minimize the TFC and achieve the desired level of risk.

As a general rule, we can say that both preventive controls and detective controls cost less than corrective controls because corrective controls tend to involve costly investigations. However, because detective controls are so closely linked to costly investigations, they and corrective controls must be considered jointly in minimizing TFC.

Various types of indicators may be used in implementing a fraud detection system. These include composite indicators and single-factor indicators (red flags). Single-factor indicators are merely special cases of composite indicators in which a single indicator has a sufficient effect on the risk score to signal a need for an investigation. In addition to indicator-driven investigations, there may be a need for random investigations. One example of a random investigation is the surprise audit.

Data-driven fraud detection involves the formal process of sifting through data in search of fraud indicators. It relies on four general sources of data: (1) internal controls (2) basic tips and hotlines, (3) security breaches, and (4) pattern data. Data-driven fraud detection applications are common in the public and private sectors. Also common are auditing and control-monitoring products, data-mining and business intelligence software products, fraud detection applications for small businesses that integrate with popular small business accounting systems, and specialized software tools that are useful for fraud detection.

Building fraud detection systems involves several steps: risk analysis (including threat and vulnerability analysis), the exploitation of expert knowledge, knowledge discovery, scoring and assessment, and implementation. Sources for exploiting expert knowledge include existing sets of internal controls, security measures, audit checklists, and professional literature. Knowledge discovery involves brainstorming, performing business processes reviews, and data mining. The data-mining process involves five steps: sampling, exploration, modification, modeling, and assessment (SEMMA).

Various modeling techniques ranging from standard regression analysis to social network analysis and content and text analysis are available. Modeling typically uses techniques from the statistics discipline.

Glossary

Benford's law   A fraud indicator that predicts the relative incidence of first digits of numbers in certain types of random data.

composite fraud indicator   A single-number fraud indicator that is computed from a formula that involves possibly many factors; also known as *risk score*.

content analysis and text analysis   Data-mining techniques that involve using algorithms to analyze and interpret the content of documents and conversations.

discovery sampling   A statistical technique in which the investigator selects a random sample in such a way to have a high probability of detecting a particular type and size error or fraud.

false negative   In fraud detection, the result that occurs when a detective control fails to signal possible fraud when one exists. Reducing false negatives means increasing the fraud detection rate.

false positive   In fraud detection, the result that occurs when a detective control signals a possible fraud that upon investigation indicates a reasonable explanation.

fraud detection process   Method that involves identifying indicators of fraud that suggest a need for further investigation.

fraud triangle   One means of assessing the risk that a particular individual may commit fraud. The three "sides" of the triangle are pressure/incentive, opportunity, and rationalization/attitude; they appear in almost all fraud cases.

inspector general   An individual in government agencies whose job includes investigating possible frauds.

pattern data analysis   An analytical technique that builds fraud indicators from data items that, individually speaking, appear to be unrelated to fraud; also known as *data mining*.

red flag   See *single-factor fraud indicator*.

risk score   See *composite fraud indicator*.

SAS No. 99, *Consideration of Fraud in a Financial Statement Audit*   Statement that requires auditors to design financial statement audits so they have a reasonable chance of detecting misstatements in the financial reports.

SEMMA   The five steps of the data mining process: sampling, exploration, modification, modeling, and assessment.

single-factor fraud indicator   A composite fraud indicator made up of only one factor; also knows as a *red flag*.

total fraud costs (TFC)   Cost calculated as: Prevention Costs + Detection Costs + Correction Costs + Fraud Losses.

Review Questions

1. Which of the following does fraud detection involve?
   a. Pinpointing the sources of the fraud.
   b. Detecting all frauds.
   c. Identifying fraud indicators.
   d. None of the above.

2. Which of these is the most common way that frauds, especially in large companies, are discovered?
   a. Through hotlines.
   b. Through financial statement audits.
   c. Through internal audits.
   d. By accident.

3. Which of the following provides the most protection for a tipster's privacy?
   a. Confidentiality.
   b. Anonymity.
   c. Both of the above provide equal protection.
   d. None of the above.

4. Which of the following best describes relative the likely incidence of fraud discovery by accident in small companies?
   a. Higher.
   b. Lower.
   c. Unknown.
   d. Similar.

5. SAS No. 99, *Consideration of Fraud in a Financial Statement Audit,* requires that auditors design financial audits in such a way to have a reasonable chance of which of these?
   a. Detecting misappropriation.
   b. Detecting embezzlement.
   c. Both *a* and *b.*
   d. None of the above.

6. SAS No. 99, *Consideration of Fraud in a Financial Statement Audit,* requires that auditors report any evidence found that fraud may exist to which of these?
   a. Inventory accounts
   b. Cash accounts
   c. Financial reports
   d. All of the above

7. The title *inspector general* applies mostly to
   a. Internal auditors.
   b. The head of the internal information security department.
   c. Government agents.
   d. All of the above.

8. In fraud detection, a false positive is said to occur when which of these occurs?
   a. A fraud indicator fails to indicate an ongoing or past fraud.
   b. A fraud indicator incorrectly indicates an ongoing or past fraud.
   c. A fraud indicator correctly indicates the absence of fraud.
   d. None of the above.

9. The best way to optimize a loss management system is to first do which of the following?

   a. Minimize total fraud costs and then minimize fraud risk.

   b. Budget total fraud costs and then maximize utility.

   c. Budget fraud risk and then maximize prevention effectiveness.

   d. Budget total fraud costs and then minimize risk.

10. Which of the following statements is typically correct?

    a. Corrective controls are more expensive than detective controls.

    b. Detective controls cost about the same as preventive controls.

    c. Corrective controls cost more than preventive controls.

    d. None of the above.

11. Which of these must apply to fraud indicators?

    a. Be defined in terms of one factor.

    b. Be defined in terms of at least one factor.

    c. Be defined in risk terms rather in terms of factors.

    d. None of the above.

12. Discovery sampling is a statistical technique that does which of these?

    a. Always detects fraud.

    b. Sometimes detects errors.

    c. Always detects errors or fraud.

    d. None of the above.

13. What general source of data does not apply to data-driven fraud detection?

    a. Reconciliation figures.

    b. Batch control totals.

    c. Missing invoices.

    d. All of the above apply.

14. Which of the following statements is true with respect to data mining?

    a. Exploration comes before sampling.

    b. Sampling comes before modeling.

    c. Assessment comes before exploration.

    d. None of the above.

15. Which of the following types of data would not be useful for social networking analysis?

    a. Phone records.

    b. Membership records for boards of directors for various companies.

    c. Employment records containing lists of past employers.

    d. None of the above.

16. Which of the following techniques/approaches would likely be most useful in determining whether a particular invoice is fraudulent?

    a. Benford's law.

    b. Text analysis.

    c. Social networking.

    d. None of the above.

Discussion Questions

17. Fraud indicators can indicate both errors and frauds. Would it be possible to develop indicators for fraud only?

18. Explain how the use of fraud indicators may be helpful in fraud investigations as opposed to only fraud detection.

19. Why are many frauds discovered by accident, not through systematic means?

20. What types of frauds are least likely to be detected through a hotline?

21. Explain the difference between *anonymity* and *confidentiality.*

22. How can an ethics code contribute to fraud detection?

23. Why is fraud detection not always relevant to applying SAS No. 99?

24. How does an internal auditor maintain independence?

25. How does fraud detection relate to the internal control process?

26. Preventive controls seek to stop fraud before it happens. What is the relative importance of preventive controls (versus detective and corrective controls) in the industry in which a business operates? For example, are detective controls relatively more important in the financial services industry versus the media services industry? Explain.

27. Explain false positives versus false negatives in fraud detection. What trade-offs are involved in their application? For example, what is the trade-off between false negatives and fraud correction costs?

28. Explain how fraud investigations can detect fraud.

29. Explain how fraud investigations can prevent fraud.

30. How important is the effect of deterrence in a fraud management system? What factors besides prosecutions deter fraud?

31. Is it ethical for a manager to permit an employee to continue working after finding the employee embezzling a significant amount of funds? Is it ethical for a manager not to report a subordinate caught in fraud to others in the organization?

32. Describe two different measures of acceptable risk in fraud detection.

33. Describe a situation in which an intuitive, nonquantitative measure of risk would work better than a formal quantitative measure.

34. Give two examples of an incidence that could be caused by either fraud or error.

35. Why must the total cost of fraud, as discussed in the text, include not only losses but also costs of prevention, detection, and correction?

36. What factors are relevant in creating a composite indicator of financial statement fraud?

37. What are some indicators that might signal a hacker attack on a company's Web-based accounting system?

38. Consider the fraud triangle. What does it suggest regarding fraud indicators in the case of a cashier who may be skimming sales receipts?

39. Are random tests needed in all fraud detection systems? Explain your answer.

40. Give an example of how pattern data might be used to identify fraudulent loan applications.

41. Is it practical for small businesses to build fraud detection systems?

42. How might social networking analysis be applied to preventing loan fraud?

Cases

43. The Veggie-Buffet Restaurant is a downtown expensive buffet-only restaurant that specializes in trendy vegetarian salads and soy-based meat substitutes. When customers first enter the restaurant, they immediately take a buffet tray and a large plate and pass though the buffet, selecting food items of their choice.

    The buffet is offered to all at a fixed price, and customers can eat as much as they can pile on their plate, but they cannot return to the buffet line once they have left it. At the end of the buffet line, customers are offered the option of purchasing nonfruit drinks or drinks in the fruit juice bar, which is located past the buffet line. Customers who purchase the juice bar option are given a plastic glass that is tinted slightly blue. Those who do not purchase the juice bar option are given the same plastic glass but without the blue tint.

    The juice in the juice bar is made from fresh fruit and fresh fruit juice but mixed with a good bit of water and raw sugar. Diluting the juice is necessary for cost-control reasons; pure fresh juice would cost too much to offer. In any case, those with the blue-tinted glass are permitted to return as often as they want for refills. On the other hand, those with the clear plastic glasses are offered filtered water and ice in the same fruit bar area.

    Midge Greenwafer, the owner, has noticed in recent months that profits appear to be down even though the customer count seems to be holding steady. Her first reaction is look to the juice bar because the weekly bill for fresh fruits and juice is much higher than she would like it to be. She does not spend a lot of time in the restaurant because she has several other businesses, so she has to rely on restaurant employees to help her figure out the problem.

    So, Midge asked Sanahoria Hambre, her favorite shift manager, about what might be causing the problem. Sanahoria had an immediate answer: "The problem is that many people are not paying for the juice bar but are filling their water glasses with juice. I see it all the time. Just yesterday, I saw a family of eight all freeloading on the juice bar."

    "That's theft," said Midge.

    "Yes, but there's not much we can do about it. We do not have the staff to constantly monitor the juice bar. Most of the time the problem just goes undetected. But when one of our staff does see a clear glass being used in the fruit bar, she politely reminds the customer that the juice bar is an extra charge."

    "Good," said Midge. "Now we just need a better way to detect customers doing this."

    a. Create a simple detection system that can be used to solve the juice bar crises.

    b. What do you think is the optimal role for detection in this problem?

44. Ashley Wesley is the assistant controller at the Walitin Construction Company. Walitin is headquartered in Miami, Florida, and has a general contractor's license in 30 different states. It is a privately held company with about 5,000 stockholders, with the majority of the stock being owned by the Walitin family.

    Roberta Walitin has been the CEO of Walitin Construction for the previous 12 years. Everyone considers her an excellent leader with excellent business skills. She has an undergraduate degree from the University of Illinois in engineering and an MBA from the same school with a concentration in accounting.

    Roberta has always insisted on ethical business practices, so two years ago she worked with Ashley to set up an ethics hotline, which Ashley personally manages on a daily basis. Anyone either inside or outside of the company can submit tips anonymously by e-mail, telephone, or a special Web page she had set up. There is a prominent link to the hotline on the home page of the company's Web site.

Since Ashley set up the hotline, she has received three tips, all via the Web. In every case, the tip was about a subcontractor overbilling the company for services rendered. In two of the cases, she was unable to confirm or disconfirm whether there was fraud, mainly because it is almost impossible to investigate the work of a subcontractor on a job that has already been completed. But in the other case, she caught a roofer billing for fictitious work. She did not report the fraud to authorities, but Roberta did immediately replace the subcontractor with another roofing company.

Ashley reports to Bob Benson, Walitin's controller. He's been with the company for many years and works very closely with Roberta. His main interest seems to be producing the financial statements and working with her to obtain new clients. Roberta and Bob spend large periods of their time going to lunches with clients, participating in civic meetings, and helping in small community-service construction projects.

Because Bob is busy so much of the time with outside activities, Ashley pretty much runs everything in accounting on her own except for the software and hardware, which Bob manages in conjunction with the head of the IT department.

Bob is not interested in details, and anytime Ashley tries to explain something to him, he simply waves a hand and says, "Don't worry me with operational issues. Just take care of it." Ashley has learned to live with his hands-off approach.

Overall, Ashley runs everything smoothly. Her main problem is that Betty Grabber, the senior accountant reporting to her, wants Ashley's job. To make things worse, Betty is a niece of Roberta Walitin's husband.

Betty is a very wily person. Her goal is to have Ashley fired, and she's been using her family connections to get the message to Roberta that Ashley is scheming to have Bob Benson, the controller, fired. Ashley also suspects that Betty has been spreading a rumor that she's planning to go to work for a competitor if she is not successful in taking over Bob's job.

Ashley is unsure as to whether Bob is aware of the rumors. He seems to be avoiding her recently, and there seems to an edge in his usually friendly voice. Ashley is feeling depressed just thinking about it. She's heard that Bob is having serious marital problems. Perhaps those problems are affecting the way he acts.

This morning Ashley had a major surprise when she started reading her e-mail, which contained a new anonymous tip. Someone had submitted it last night via the Web, and it had automatically been forwarded to her via e-mail. The tip read as follows:

> To: Walitin Tip System
>
> From: webuser@walitinconstructionservices.com
>
> Sent: Tuesday 8/1/2015
>
> Ms. Wesley,
>
> I'm sending this tip to help you. I understand what you are going through. You're working for a liar and a thief. Bob Benson is hacking the accounting system to produce fraudulent financial statements. He's doing it in such a way that you'll get the blame. It's going to be a big mess.

a. What should Ashley do? Should she try to investigate? Should she report the tip to Roberta?

b. Evaluate Walitin's hotline and make recommendations for its improvement.

Chapter **Seven**

The Fraud Investigation and Engagement Processes

CHAPTER LEARNING OBJECTIVES

After reading Chapter 7, you should be able to:

- LO1: Outline the fraud investigation process.
- LO2: Outline the fraud engagement process.
- LO3: Explain the fraud theory approach.
- LO4: Explain the four types of evidence.
- LO5: Explain the principle of reverse proof.

Aside from preventing fraud and possibly obtaining court-ordered restitution, punishing fraudsters may have little economic benefit to the entity. However, punishment tends to serve a larger societal purpose: If enough fraudsters are punished, the overall incidence of fraud may be reduced. Unfortunately, very few fraudsters are ever punished. Most cases are never reported, and among those that are reported, most are never prosecuted. The chances of most fraudsters ever going to jail are very low. However, when fraud is investigated, it should follow a specific process.

The **fraud investigation process** involves systematically gathering and reviewing evidence for the purpose of documenting the presence or absence of fraud. Fraud investigations normally commence as a result of some indication that fraud may have occurred: anything from an anonymous tip to anomalous data in the accounting system.

In virtually all cases, the fraud investigator must assume that the matter under investigation will eventually conclude in civil or criminal courts. As a result, fraud investigations must be conducted systematically and with the utmost care from the very beginning.

LO1 The fraud investigation process (Figure 7.1) involves a series of four steps: the engagement process, the evidence collection process, the reporting process, and the loss recovery process. The current chapter briefly outlines all four steps and then discusses the first step, the engagement process, in detail. The remaining four steps are covered in detail in Chapters 8 through 12.

FIGURE 7.1
The Fraud
Investigation Process

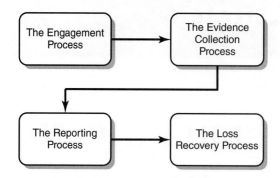

THE FRAUD INVESTIGATION PROCESS

The Engagement Process

LO2 As is thoroughly discussed in the next major section of this chapter, the **fraud investigation engagement process** is a series of steps that begins with the investigator's first contact with the case and concludes with a complete agreement regarding the fraud investigation services the investigator will provide.

The Evidence Collection Process

LO3 The **evidence collection process** involves the various steps in which evidence in support of the objectives and scope of the investigation is collected. The objectives and scope of fraud investigations are discussed in a subsequent part of this chapter.

Evidence collection is based on the fraud theory approach. The *fraud theory approach to fraud investigation* (Figure 7.2) follows four distinct steps: (1) analyze data, (2) create hypotheses regarding a possible fraud, (3) test the hypotheses, and then (4) refine and amend the hypotheses. The refined and amended hypotheses are then subject to additional testing and further refinement and amendment.

FIGURE 7.2
The Fraud Theory
Approach to
Evidence Collection

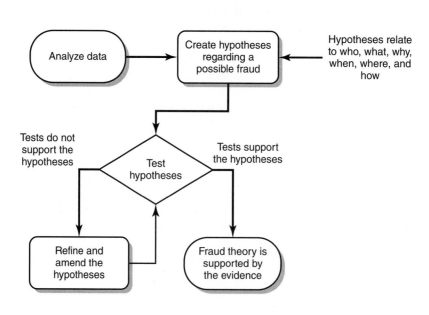

FIGURE 7.3
The Four Types of Evidence

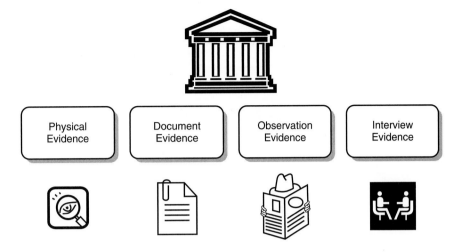

LO4 **Four types of evidence gathered in the evidence collection process** are physical evidence, documentary evidence, observational evidence, and interview evidence (Figure 7.3). The investigation process normally begins by examining physical and documentary evidence. It then proceeds to observational and interview evidence, and evidence from interviews normally is part of the final step. The evidence collection process is thoroughly covered in Chapter 8. Chapter 9 discusses physical, documentary, and observational evidence. Chapter 11 provides additional detail regarding physical evidence as part of forensic science.

The **interview process** involves specific steps. The initial interviews are conducted with the most remote suspects. The investigator then conducts additional interviews that are successively closer to the suspects, with the prime suspect being the last person interviewed.

Individual interviews also involve a specific sequence of steps. The focus of this sequence is obtaining a confession as the final step if the suspect is guilty. Details of the interview process, along with various interviewing techniques, are presented in Chapter 10.

The Reporting Process

The **reporting process** involves documenting and summarizing the results of the fraud investigation. Chapter 12 discusses the reporting process in detail.

The Loss Recovery Process

The **loss recovery process** involves civil and criminal litigation, expert testimony, and collection of insurance. These issues are discussed in Chapter 12.

THE FRAUD ENGAGEMENT PROCESS

The fraud engagement process begins with the investigator's first contact with the case and ends with a complete agreement regarding the services the fraud investigator will provide (Figure 7.4). In general, the professional fraud investigator can be an internal auditor, a staff accountant, an independent fraud examiner, an internal security specialist, an external auditor, or a law enforcement official. Regardless of who performs the investigation, the person must clearly understand the services he will perform and the scope of the investigation.

FIGURE 7.4
**The Fraud
Investigation
Engagement Process**

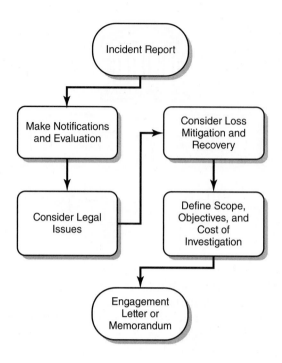

The actual unfolding of the engagement process varies depending on which type of investigative professional is involved. For example, the process is often very simple when the investigator is a law enforcement official: One simply calls the authorities, and a detective responds and begins gathering information and evaluating the case. The simplicity of the process arises from the fact the "rules of the investigation" are governed by procedures that are more or less dictated to the business. However, even police investigations involve some give-and-take between the business and the detective. Specifically, the detective might express her willingness to fully investigate only if the company is willing to support her with resources and information she may need.

The engagement process involves the following six steps: (1) create an incident report, (2) conduct the initial notifications and evaluation, (3) consider legal issues, (4) evaluate the loss mitigation and recovery considerations, (5) define the scope, objectives, and costs of the investigation, (6) and produce an engagement letter or memorandum.

The relative importance of each of the six steps depends somewhat on the fraud victim's point of view in the investigation. This is especially true for recovery/loss mitigation. This is almost always an important consideration for the fraud victim, but it is likely to be of much less concern to a fraud investigator or law enforcement official. In many cases, if a fraud exists, the fraud investigator or law enforcement official is primarily oriented to provide organized documentation that can be used to prosecute a fraud case in a civil or criminal court. On the other hand, the victim of the loss often seeks to be made whole through court-ordered restitution, the collection of insurance, or a civil judgment.

Although the fraud investigator might not have a direct interest in loss recovery, he can certainly assist the client in the loss recovery process. For example, he can answer insurance companies' questions, provide additional reports or details in support of insurance claims and litigation, do extended forensic accounting work in estimating lost income due to consequences stemming from theft and damage to financial records, and assist in improving the loss management system.

The fraud investigator can also assist in any needed reconstruction of accounting records. In cases in which embezzlers "cook the books" over an extended period of time, losses from the resulting damage to the accounting records can easily exceed direct losses from embezzlement (Figure 7.5). This is so because reconstruction of accounting records can be an extremely time-consuming and expensive process. Furthermore, such reconstruction may be absolutely necessary to continue to do business as normal, file correct tax returns, and so on.

Create the Incident Report and the Case File

As discussed in the previous chapter, fraud investigations are triggered by the presence of one or more fraud indicators. The first thing that happens when a fraud indicator signals a possible fraud is the generation of some type of **incident report,** which contains the initial information used to justify the investigation.

The scope and depth of the incident report depends on the type of suspected fraud and the extent of information in the fraud indicator. In the simplest case, the incident report might include only something such as an automated computer record of a single unusual item in a loan application. In a more complex case, it might include a detailed supervisor's report of suspected embezzlement.

For all fraud investigations, the creation of a **unified case file** is essential; the file should document all activities related to the investigation. The case file serves three main purposes: (1) to provide needed organization for administering and managing the case as it unfolds, (2) to document the investigation for future review and use in optimizing the fraud management system, and (3) to be a case information repository that can be used in subsequent civil or criminal litigation.

Given the sensitivity of the case file, access to it should be granted only on a need-to-know basis. Unwarranted disclosure of information in the case file can lead to the entity's being sued for defamation and can compromise an entire investigation by tipping off suspects.

In all cases of fraud investigation, no matter how routine or small, it should always be assumed that every step of the investigation and every activity associated with the investigation will end up in court. Therefore, the incident report has important legal significance because it is the foundation on which the entire investigation rests.

FIGURE 7.5
In Many Cases, Misappropriation Losses Are Not the Heaviest Losses

Misappropriation Losses

Damage to Financial Records

From a law enforcement standpoint, the incident report can serve as the probable cause that law enforcement needs to subpoena the suspect's financial or telephone records. In some states, such subpoenas are "silent" in that the suspect never knows they exist or are being implemented.

From an entity's standpoint, the incident report can serve as proof that a suspect is not being singled out because of illegal discrimination or in violation of collective bargaining rights. Suspects sometimes can and do sue their victims. It should always be remembered that fraudsters are often cunning and determined individuals who frequently seek ways to fight back and defend themselves. In fraud investigations, the hunters can easily become the hunted.

Conduct the Initial Notifications and Evaluation

The incident report must be evaluated by the proper persons (Figure 7.6). The primary objective in this phase of the engagement process is to determine who needs to be notified and whether the incident report justifies an investigation. For example, if the statement is a routine incident report that originates in an insurance claims department that receives many fraudulent claims, the report is likely to be evaluated only by the internal group that normally handles routine claim fraud investigations. In most cases, such groups may have a policy of reporting obvious and egregious cases to the state's Department of Insurance. Copies of such reports should be sent to the legal department before being sent to any other party. Copies should also be sent to the entity's risk management officer.

Nonroutine reports from a tip line may go directly to the legal department (or outside council). The legal department should in turn report all cases directly to the board of directors. In small and medium-size entities, nonroutine reports should be sent directly to the owner or CEO, who should in turn consult with legal counsel.

At the end of the notification and evaluation process, a decision as to whether to proceed with an investigation is made. For serious occupational fraud, the person who makes

FIGURE 7.6
Processing the Incident Report

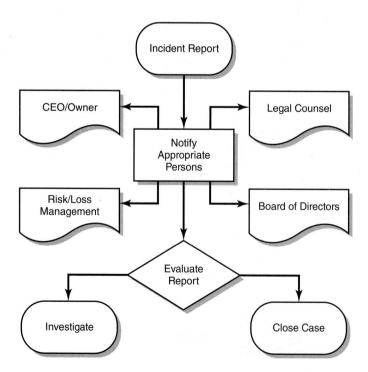

such a decision is likely a member of the legal team or a high-level manager. As a general rule, this person should not begin an investigation to decide whether to refer the case to the individual or group that will conduct the formal investigation. It is generally best either not to pursue the case further or to send it to a professional investigator. Investigations by untrained persons can ruin potential evidence and generate lawsuits against the company.

It is especially important in the initial notification and evaluation stage to keep the matter as quiet and secret as is legally possible. In many cases, especially in small businesses, the owner-manager's initial reaction is associated with anger and an overwhelming desire to confront the suspected employee. This temptation must be strongly resisted. Confronting the suspect too soon is one of the most damaging things that can be done in an investigation. It is much better first to secretly gather all the facts and understand the mechanics of the suspect's fraud scheme. It may then be possible to interview the employee and have her to go on the record with statements that either incriminate her or contradict the facts. At a minimum, keeping things quiet can permit the investigator to record the suspect in an interview with a sufficient degree of detail to make it much more difficult for the suspect to later attempt to concoct a story that conforms to the facts.

In one case, the business owner immediately confronted the bookkeeper when he strongly suspected that the bookkeeper had embezzled a significant amount of money by pocketing cash rather than taking it to the bank for deposit. The angry owner told the bookkeeper that he had her signature on many cash remittance advices that the bookkeeper was supposed to have deposited in the bank but did not. "I've got you cold," he said to her.

The bookkeeper walked out of the meeting with the owner and immediately quit. The owner then called the police and made a report. The next day the owner told the whole story to the detective and asked, "When are you going to make the arrest?"

"Forget it," the police officer said. "I already talked to her. She claims that she handed the money to you at your request."

That was the end of the police investigation.

In typical cases, police seek to make an arrest when they find a safe with its door blown off or if the suspect confesses. But police generally have no interest in becoming involved with accounting records. The expression among police is that "if it bleeds, it leads." The local police will have no problem sending in a SWAT team, police dogs, and helicopters if someone robs a convenience store for $100. But investigating obscure journals, ledgers, and computer files is a totally different matter.

It is not well known that victims do not posses any general or constitutional right to requires law enforcement to investigate crimes. Investigations are generally performed at the absolute discretion of law enforcement. In fact, when it comes to investigations of occupational fraud, it can sometimes be nearly impossible to persuade law enforcement to investigate in any depth. The best way to have the police make an arrest is by presenting them a videotape of the suspect stuffing money in her pockets or by getting a detailed confession. Getting either of these is impossible if the suspect is confronted too soon; the time for confronting the suspect is when the investigator already has all proof in hand except for a confession.

Consider Legal Issues

Before an investigation is launched, the entity must consider any legal issues that could affect the scope and manner of the investigation. Some examples follow:

1. **Rights of Workers or Other Suspects Under Investigation**   These include any rights created by applicable federal or state laws, employment contracts, and collective bargaining agreements that restrict or define ways in which investigations must be conducted.

For example, a collective bargaining agreement might require that the entity give formal notice to an employee under investigation with the right of union representation in any investigation-related interviews or meetings between the employee and the entity.

2. **The Possibility of Conducting the Investigation Under Attorney-Client Privilege** Depending on the legal jurisdiction, the work product of the corporate legal staff might be protected under attorney-client privilege. In some cases, it might be necessary to conduct the investigation under the general umbrella of an outside attorney in order to obtain attorney-client protection.

3. **Evaluation of the Evidence** The entity must determine whether there is sufficient evidence and legal justification to immediately fire a worker or to place the worker on administrative leave with or without pay.

4. **Rights of Investigating Employers** Employers have a general right to require their employees to assist in investigations and can terminate employees who refuse to cooperate. Unless there are specific laws or contractual obligations to the contrary, employers have a general right to search an employee's offices, office computers, and possibly even their briefcases and cars that are on company property.

5. **The Extent to Which a Government Entity May Be Directly or Indirectly Involved in the Investigation** To the extent to which a government agency is involved in an investigation or that the private entity acts on behalf of the government, the employee might have constitutional rights that limit the entity's powers of investigation. Failure to respect those rights could lead to a lawsuit by the employee or prevent evidence from being admissible in court.

6. **Reporting Obligations** Consideration should be given regarding any obligations to report the incident to law enforcement or government regulators.

Evaluate Loss Mitigation and Recovery Considerations

The entity must consider any immediate steps that may be required to mitigate losses related to the fraud, and to the eventual recovery of losses from insurance and through the legal system.

Loss Mitigation

An initial decision must be made as to whether it is necessary to immediately intervene to prevent the perpetrator from continuing with the fraud scheme. In an occupational setting, the entity may have various options: (1) immediately fire the employee, (2) change the employee's job responsibilities, (3) place the employee on administrative leave (with or without pay), or (4) permit the employee to continue in her current position, possibly continuing the fraud, thus giving the investigator the possibility of catching her in the act.

In some cases, it might be best to choose the fourth option. Obviously, this approach can be expensive because losses can continue to mount as the investigation proceeds. However, the costs of mounting losses need to be weighed against the benefits of catching the fraudster in the act.

Catching a fraudster in the act and getting a quick confession can save enormous amounts of investigation costs. Depending on the state of the financial records, investigating even a simple embezzlement fraud in a small or medium-size business can take a fraud examiner months with costs running into the six-figure range.

Investigations by independent fraud examiners can be time-consuming and expensive for two reasons: (1) the principle of reverse proof and (2) the need to reconstruct doctored financial records. The principle of **reverse proof** (Figure 7.7) states that in order to prove that an apparent fraud has occurred, it is necessary to prove that the apparent fraud cannot

FIGURE 7.7
The Reverse Proof Process

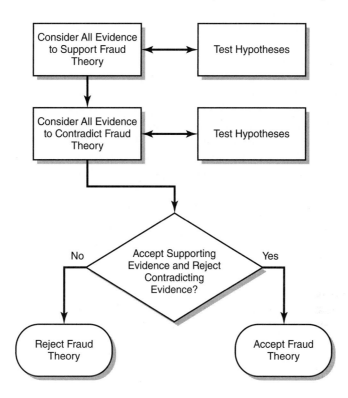

be explained by any means except fraud. In other words, fraud can be proved only by ruling out all reasonable explanations for an apparent fraud.

LO5 In courts, there are always two sides to a story with the plaintiff (or prosecutor) taking one side and the defendant taking the other side. In terms of fraud examinations, the principle of reverse proof means that the investigator must consider the evidence for both parties. In other words, the investigator must not only attempt to prove that a given fraud occurred but also attempt to prove that it did not. Therefore, the investigator must, to the extent possible, consider and rule out all evidence that would support the arguments of both the plaintiff and the defense.

Several standard defenses include the following:

1. Someone else did it.
2. It was done before or after the suspect worked for the entity.
3. Something is wrong with the computer software.
4. Had the fraud examiner reviewed 100% of the transactions, the apparent shortage would be accounted for.
5. The problems were simply errors, not fraudulent entries.
6. That's what the owner told the suspect to do.
7. A hacker did it.

Consider an example of what would be required for the second one of these standard defenses. Assume that a business owner believes that the bookkeeper has been pocketing cash receipts rather than depositing them. At first glance, unraveling such a fraud would seem to be an easy task for a fraud examiner: The only process needed is to reconcile the cash account with the bank account. But in the real world, things can be considerably more complex than this. Further assume that the bookkeeper batches together cash receipts (which include both cash and checks) for several days or longer and makes occasional deposits. In addition, the deposit slips contain only lump-sum amounts, no detail. Finally, assume that the bookkeeper makes batch-type entries in the cash receipts journal that do not coincide with actual batches of deposits.

Because the bookkeeper batches deposits together at irregular intervals, the investigator is not able to identify any specific deposits that were not made. Further, he is unable to simply compare adjusted monthly changes in the cash balance per the accounting records to the same month changes in the cash balance per the bank account because the batched entries to the cash receipts journal do not necessarily represent cash received in the month of recording and because funds deposited into the bank account do not necessarily represent funds received in the month in which they are deposited.

Under such circumstances, the investigator cannot even rely on the opening balance for any month in the cash ledger. There is always the possibility that it includes cash collected in the previous month. The result is that the investigator is left with little but arguments about account balances and timing to prove fraud—not the best type of evidence on which to build a court case.

To develop strong evidence, the investigator must contact the bank and obtain image copies of the deposit slips for the entire time period the bookkeeper was making deposits. Depending on the situation, it could span years. Next, the investigator would need to obtain reliable records of cash receipts from a source other than the bookkeeper's unreliable accounting records. Such records would include original source documents such as sales invoices, cash receipts logs, and register receipts. Given these documents and images of the deposit slips, the investigator could in effect reconstruct the account records and document specific deposits that were not made. This process could take months of work and would likely be complicated by missing documents, documents with errors, and unexplainable cash transactions. For example, there could be cash transfers to and from other bank accounts belonging to the same entity with the consequence that the investigator would have to include the other accounts as part of the investigation to rule out the possibility that missing funds were deposited to, or transferred to, the wrong account. In this case, the same problems could begin all over again with the other accounts.

In summary, fraud investigations can be time-consuming and expensive. Furthermore, the mere presence of fraud investigators in an organization, especially a small one, can unsettle employees, lead to months of internal finger pointing and suspicion, and devolve into infighting and the loss of employees. The result in some cases is that the costs of the investigation can easily exceed the direct costs of fraud. Therefore, an entity might be better off to let the fraud continue for a short time in order to catch the fraudster in the act and get a quick confession. The right balance between the possibilities of continuing fraud losses versus getting a quick confession must be made in consideration of the entity's overall risk management objectives. This is discussed in the next section.

Sometimes, however, a full fraud examination is indicated. First, if the fraudster has seriously damaged an entity's accounting records, their complete reconstruction may be required. The reconstruction process itself may provide sufficient evidence for litigation. Second, some organizations may have a regulatory or fiduciary obligation to fully investigate a suspected fraud. Examples of these organizations include charities, community services organization, estates and trusts, banks, insurance companies, religious organizations, and government entities. Third, security or auditing regulations may require an auditor and/or company officials to investigate suspected frauds that could affect the integrity of the company's financial reports. Fourth, governing boards or officers of some organizations may require full investigations as a matter of policy. Fifth, in some cases, a manager or officer might want to fully investigate a fraud simply as a matter of due diligence, especially if the person making the decision is worried that the fraud may be larger or more systemic than initially suggested by the incident report. Finally, suspected frauds may be fully investigated at random in organizations that routinely deal with customer fraud, such as those related to insurance claims or loan applications. Fraud investigations can give such organizations valuable insights into ways to better prevent and detect fraud.

Insurance Recovery

A second issue relating to recovery involves collecting insurance to cover losses. First, a decision must be made as to whether it is necessary to immediately report the loss to an insurer. Of course, this depends on the terms of the policy and the facts surrounding the suspected loss. Second, insurance policies typically require the policyholder to use all reasonable means to mitigate losses. This leaves the obvious problem that permitting a fraud to continue may cause the entity to violate its insurance policy's obligation to mitigate losses. Legal counsel should be consulted to resolve such issues.

Recovery through Litigation

Recovery can sometimes be made through criminal or civil litigation. In many situations, the prosecutor may require the fraudster to make restitution as part of plea bargain. In other situations, restitution can be a component of the fraudster's sentence upon conviction. In some districts, courts order restitution to be paid into a special account administered by the court for distribution to the victim.

Recovery can also be made by suing the fraudster in civil court. Public records searches can sometimes show that the fraudster has assets that can be targeted in a lawsuit. But in many cases, the fraudster does not have sufficient assets to justify the expense of a lawsuit. Furthermore, if there is insurance to cover the loss, the entity will subrogate the right to sue to the insurance company.

One Caution

The investigator should never tell the fraudster to make restitution or he will report the fraudster to law enforcement. Making such a demand could put the investigator in the position of committing the crime of extortion. Therefore, any settlement-oriented discussions should be handled only by competent legal counsel.

Determine the Objectives, Scope, and Costs of the Investigation

A fraud investigation can have many objectives other than catching and punishing a fraudster. Moreover, punishment might even be the least important objective in a given situation. Possible objectives include the following:

1. Stop the fraud from continuing.
2. Identify the loss for insurance purposes.
3. Identify the loss for tax purposes.
4. Make an example of a fraudster.
5. Minimize any embarrassing disclosures in the press.
6. Discover weaknesses in the internal control system.

Each of these objectives is discussed.

Stop the Fraud from Continuing

The exact way to stop a fraud from continuing depends on the type of fraud, but the general approach is to limit the fraudster's access in such a way that continuing fraud is no longer possible. In an occupational fraud setting, some ways to accomplish this include firing the suspect, putting the suspect on administrative leave, or changing or limiting the suspect's job responsibilities or access privileges.

An even simpler approach might be to simply repair a weakness in the internal control system that permitted the fraud to take place. For example, a bookkeeper who siphons off cash can be stopped by enforcing a proper segregation of duties. Of course, before changing the bookkeeper's duties, one would need to first consider how the bookkeeper might react to such a change. If it were felt that the person might react by destroying valuable accounting records, either using a different approach, keeping the investigation a secret, or completely removing the bookkeeper from the job would likely be better.

In nonoccupational fraud settings, the simplest way to limit a fraudster's access is by no longer doing business with the individual or company. If a vendor is committing the fraud, the solution is to use a different vendor. If It is a customer, refuse to sell to that individual. This can be as easy as canceling a customer's account.

In some cases, it might not be possible to limit a suspect's access until an investigation justifies doing so. For example, if a customer submits an insurance claim that suggests possible fraud, delaying or immediately denying the claim or dropping the customer might not be contractually or legally feasible. This scenario exists throughout the insurance and financial service industries in which consumers have fairly strong rights due to government regulations.

In still other cases, it might not be possible to avoid doing business with fraudsters. This especially includes case of Web-based e-commerce with large numbers of online customers. For example, online customers may present fraudulent credit card information. In such situations, investigations may be of little help, and the only solution is to seek ways to detect and block fraudulent credit card transactions.

Another consideration in determining whether to immediately stop a fraud from continuing is that it might be just the tip of the iceberg. Even billion-dollar frauds have to begin unraveling at some point. So, the investigator can never know for sure what lies behind a seemingly "small" fraud indicator. As a general rule, it is best to assume that frauds are much larger than initial indications suggest regardless of the type of fraud. The amount of embezzlement fraud is likely to be much higher than expected. Sometimes mortgage fraud that appears to be just a single case may in fact be just one of many being perpetrated by an organized crime ring. A single erroneous number in financial statement fraud might indicate massive manipulations of the accounting records and misrepresentation in the financial statements.

Identify the Loss for Insurance Recovery

It is fairly well known that insurance policies frequently cover losses due to employee dishonesty. What is not so well known is that such policies frequently require proof only of the loss through dishonesty, not proof that a particular person committed the dishonest acts.

In some cases, the threshold of evidence to prove a loss related to dishonesty can be substantially lower than the threshold required to prove that a particular person is guilty. For example, assume that three employees have access to a company's online wire transfer login credentials. Also assume that one of the three sent an unauthorized wire transfer of $5,000 to someone in a distant country. Finally, assume that the bank will not cover the loss because it was obviously caused by an authorized employee from a shared computer located in an office shared by the three suspects. In this case, the loss is clear, but the perpetrator is not.

Because the entity can recover from an insurance company, the cost of an investigation can be prohibitive, and an investigation can affect the morale of innocent employees, the simplest solution might be to collect the insurance and implement proper controls to prevent the fraud from happening again. This solution might be a very unpalatable one because it gives a fraudster a pass, but sometimes the best business decision is not emotionally satisfying. In any case, caution must be used to avoid launching a costly investigation based on emotional rather the business reasons.

Identify the Loss for Tax Purposes

Generally speaking, losses due to fraud are either tax deductible or can reduce reportable revenue. Furthermore, the required evidence for tax purposes is quite different from the beyond-a-reasonable-doubt burden required in criminal cases. The taxing authority (e.g., the U.S. Internal Revenue Service) may accept reasonable estimates of the loss in many cases, especially if an independent forensic accountant provides them.

Therefore, one simple approach to a fraud investigation is to estimate the loss for tax purposes. This could be combined with improving internal control or security without any detailed investigation to measure the exact amount of the loss and proving a suspect's guilt. The benefit of estimating the loss (versus documenting it with the normal precision of a fraud examination) is that estimation can frequently be done with much lower investigation costs because it does not have the forensic burden that courts require for proof.

This approach somewhat resembles what happens with employee thefts of inventory. The result is a lower ending inventory and a higher cost of goods sold. So, the thefts end up being written off for tax purposes as part of cost of good sold. It is not suggested here that this is the correct approach but that it does occur in practice. In many cases, losses are just "eaten." But in some of those cases, such as certain types of sales-skimming schemes, it is necessary to investigate the fraud to at least estimate the loss for tax purposes.

Make an Example of the Fraudster

If prosecuting a fraudster is important to deterring other fraudsters, an entity might be willing to spend much more on an investigation than the cost of the loss itself. However, as a general rule, the fear of punishment does not deter fraudsters: They generally do not plan on getting caught. Moreover, in asset misappropriation cases, it is common for embezzlers to rationalize and think to themselves that they are just borrowing the money with every intention of paying it back.

Most large banks have loss management departments whose main focus is preventing fraud or at least detecting it quickly. However, such departments routinely deal with stolen checks being cashed and unauthorized use of debit cards, for example. Such departments normally cooperate with local authorities, but they do not file a police report every time someone cashes a check stolen from a client's account. The banks just eat the losses as a cost of doing business.

Financial institutions are less concerned with lone-wolf fraudsters than organized check scam rings. The organized rings can repeatedly attack the same bank and cause serious financial damage over the long run. Furthermore, local law enforcement agencies like to devote their investigatory resources to crime rings.

On the other hand, prosecuting to make an example is a relatively common practice. One example is employee theft of inventory. Retail stores routinely prosecute shoplifters, so why not employees too? Another example is insurance claims fraud. Many states have insurance departments with the resources to investigate claims fraud. Furthermore, most large insurance companies have internal fraud investigation divisions. So, if the evidence is good, there is a reasonable chance of having the perpetrator arrested.

The U.S. Internal Revenue Service provides good examples of prosecuting to make an example. One such example involved Leona Helmsley. She was a flamboyant billionaire and real estate tycoon whose husband managed the Empire State Building in New York

City. The IRS claimed that she had evaded income taxes by charging off personal expenses to her hotel business. She was convicted and sentenced to 16 years in prison, although she served only about a year and a half of that time. In general, the IRS loves to prosecute public figures so that the average taxpayer will think that "if they can get someone that famous and wealthy, they can get me."

Minimize Embarrassing Disclosures in the Press

Quite a few occupational frauds are kept under wraps because owners, officers, and managers do not want their customers, vendors, and creditors to know about the entity's weak internal controls and/or the manager's poor judgment that permitted the fraud. In fact, most asset misappropriation frauds are never reported to law enforcement. In many instances, making a police report is as good as publishing a notice in the newspaper. Furthermore, many managers are aware of the futility of filing a police report.

It is common for dishonest bookkeepers in small and medium-size organizations to hop from one job to the next, each time after stealing as much as possible. They leave behind a wake of damaged businesses and sometimes bankrupt owners. In one case, one of the authors of this text was asked to investigate a bookkeeper in an attorney's office. When the attorney found out that he had lost a lot of money, he moaned and groaned his misery to the previous attorney the bookkeeper had worked for, whose comment was, "Oh, she got you too." The previous attorney had never reported the fraud to anyone or even had any type of investigation. Moreover, the previous attorney gave the bookkeeper a good recommendation after he fired her. He didn't dare mention the embezzlement, for without expensive forensic proof, she could have sued him for defamation.

Discover Weaknesses in the Internal Control System

One benefit of in-depth investigations is that they can reveal control or security weaknesses even if they do not find any evidence of fraud.

In many cases, weak internal control or security processes should serve as a good reason to investigate not only to discover possible fraud but also to gain an understanding of the weaknesses and how to fix them. After all, business processes with weak controls are more likely to fall victims to fraud. So, an entity with weak controls should have more to worry about and thus a relatively large need to investigate fraud indicators.

Create the Engagement Letter or Memorandum

Except for routine, frequently repeated fraud investigations, an engagement letter or memorandum should precede any fraud investigation. An engagement letter is necessary if the investigator represents an independent fraud examiner or accounting firm. A memorandum also is necessary if the investigator is performing an internal investigation. The memorandum is similar to the engagement letter, so only the engagement letter is discussed here.

The general objectives of the engagement letter are to set forth the services to be provided, the objectives and scope of the investigation, the methods to be used, the resources required, the responsibilities of the respective parties, the basis and methods to be used for charging professional fees and expenses, and the means for resolving disputes.

As a general rule, it is best for the engagement letter to be between the client's attorney and the investigator. This generally permits the work product results of the investigation to benefit from attorney-client privilege.

The Services to Be Provided

The obvious service to be provided is a fraud investigation. However, the description of services should include not only the services to be provided but also the services that will *not* be provided. Some services that might not be provided are reconstruction of damaged computer files or written/printed records, advice on improving business processes or controls, opinion of the financial statements, expert testimony in court, and determination of guilt. Of course, some of these services may be provided if that is the agreement between the investigator and the client.

One service that is *never* provided is a conclusion that points to one or more guilty persons. Decisions regarding innocence versus guilt should be left for the courts. The investigation seeks to gather evidence of the existence of fraud, the amount of the loss, and the actions of suspects as they may relate to a discovered fraud.

Independent investigators do not draw conclusions regarding guilt or innocence for two main reasons. First, guilt and innocence are generally a matter of opinion, even when one or the other appears obvious to all. In a court of law, those criminally accused are to be presumed innocent until proven guilty beyond a reasonable doubt. The investigator might be an expert, and experts' opinions are generally admissible as evidence in courts, but the ultimate "expert opinion," the one regarding guilt or innocence, is reserved for judges and juries. Second, an opinion regarding guilt could open up the investigator to a lawsuit for defamation. Moreover, there would be no benefit for the investigator to take a risk of being sued for defamation because an expert opinion regarding guilt is not likely to be admitted into evidence in a court proceeding.

Of course, the expert can come very close to indicating guilt. For example, an investigator could testify that she personally observed a suspect taking money from a safe and stuffing it into all his pockets. However, this would not be an expert opinion but a statement of fact based on personal knowledge. On the other hand, an expert could render an opinion that identifies by name the person in a video recording that shows someone stuffing money in all of her pockets.

The Objectives and Scope of the Investigation

The scope of the investigation serves to place limits on the breadth of the investigation. For example, an investigation of a treasury department could be limited to specific activities (such as bond purchases) and to a specific time frame (e.g., between 2018 and 2020). The objectives of the investigation could be any of the ones described previously.

Methods to Be Used

The methods to be used can include reviews of documents; interviews with employees; surreptitious surveillance of employees, vendors, and customers; reviews of computer records; and written confirmations of accounts. The important thing is that the client not object to a particular method once the investigation begins.

Resources Required

The independent investigator may require many different types of resources from the client. Some examples include the use of the client's accounting staff for document reviews or customer account confirmations, office space, telephone services, copying services, and travel support. It is perfectly normal to use client employees to assist in the investigation work. Of course, the investigator must be sure that those employees are not part of the possible fraud under investigation.

The Responsibilities of the Respective Parties

The investigator's primary responsibility is to complete the investigation as described in the engagement letter. Still, it can be helpful to include a paragraph in the letter that gives the investigator the right to disengage from the investigation if requested to do so by law enforcement or a court order, if remaining in the engagement would cause the investigator to commit an illegal or unethical act, if there is a lack of cooperation on the client's part, or if fees are not paid on time. This part of the letter should clearly state that the fees for the investigation are not in any way contingent on the results of the investigation.

A related provision that is typically included in engagement letters is a statement that the investigator's final written report cannot be given to a third party without the written permission of the investigator. This, along with attorney-client privilege, can help prevent the report from falling into the wrong hands and thereby cause problems for either the investigator or client.

One scenario in which the investigator would need such a restriction statement is when an attorney hires him to work in a "research mode" to obtain his opinion regarding which person he believes to be guilty in a known fraud. In this case and with the restriction, the investigator would then be free to render an opinion as to who is guilty without any fear of being sued for defamation by the suspect. Furthermore, the attorney-client privilege would likely prevent any third parties from using subpoenas to obtain copies of the report. Nevertheless, it's still not good practice to render an opinion of guilt, regardless the circumstances, and doing so may violate the investigator's professional code of ethics.

The Basis and Methods Used for Charging Professional Fees

Professional fees are normally charged on an hourly basis. Because the amount of work required in fraud investigations is uncertain, this part of the letter should indicate the frequency of billing fees, for example, on a monthly basis, and it must make clear that there is no guarantee that the investigation can be completed within any maximum number of hours or by a certain date.

Some investigations can be concluded very quickly with an early confession by a suspect; other investigations can drag on for long periods of time, especially when the scope is broad and the accounting records are in poor condition. Furthermore, a very long and expensive investigation can conclude with a finding of perhaps nothing more than sloppy accounting records that are loaded with errors.

This part of the letter should also include provisions for expenses for such items as travel and meals for the investigator, copying costs, telephone charges, and perhaps for hiring third-party professionals such as detectives, handwriting experts, and so on.

The Means for Resolving Disputes

To avoid excessive legal expenses and messy adverse public publicity, including a provision that requires any disputes to be settled through some form of arbitration, possibly with mediation, is generally desirable. Both mediation and arbitration are conducted in private and do not enter into the public record. They are discussed in detail in Chapter 20.

Summary

Fraud investigation is the process of systematically gathering and reviewing evidence for the purpose of documenting the presence or absence of fraud. Fraud investigations normally commence as a result of some indication that fraud may have occurred. Systematic fraud investigations undergo a series of five steps: the engagement process, the evidence collection process, the reporting process, and the loss recovery process.

The engagement process is a series of steps that begins with the investigator's first contact with the case and ends with a complete agreement regarding the fraud investigation services to be provided by the investigator. The evidence collection process involves various steps in which evidence is collected in support of the objectives and scope of the investigation.

Evidence collection is based on the fraud theory approach. It is an approach to fraud investigation that follows four distinct steps: analyze data, create hypotheses regarding a possible fraud, test the hypotheses, and then refine and amend the hypotheses.

Four types of evidence are gathered in the collection process: physical evidence, documentary evidence, observational evidence, and interview evidence. The investigation process normally begins by examining physical and documentary evidence. It then proceeds to observational and interview evidence with interview evidence normally being part of the final step.

The interview process involves specific steps. Initial interviews are with individuals furthest away from any suspects. The investigator then conducts additional interviews that are successively closer to the suspects, with the prime suspect being the last person interviewed. Individual interviews also involve a specific sequence of steps. The focus of this sequence is to obtain a confession as the final step if the suspect is guilty.

The reporting process involves documenting and summarizing the results of the fraud investigation. The loss recovery process involves civil and criminal litigation, expert testimony, and collecting insurance.

The complete engagement process involves the following seven steps: Create an incident report and case file; conduct the initial notifications and evaluations; consider legal issues; evaluate loss mitigation and recovery considerations; define the scope, objectives, and costs of the investigation; and produce an engagement letter or memorandum.

The relative importance of each of the seven steps depends somewhat on one's point of view in the investigation. This is especially true for recovery/loss mitigation. This is almost always an important consideration for the victim of the fraud, but it is likely to be of much less concern to a fraud investigator or law enforcement official.

The incident report contains the information used to justify the investigation. The scope and depth of the incident report depends on the type of suspected fraud and the extent of information contained in the fraud indicator.

For all fraud investigations, it is essential that a unified case file that documents all activities related to the investigation be created. Given the sensitivity of the case file, access to it should be granted only on a need-to-know basis. In all cases of fraud investigation, no matter how routine or small, it should always be assumed that every step of the investigation and every activity associated with it will end up in court. Therefore, the incident report has important legal significance because it is the foundation on which the entire investigation rests.

The incident report must be evaluated by the proper persons. The primary objective in this phase is to determine who needs to be notified and whether the incident report justifies an investigation.

At the end of the notification and evaluation process, a decision as to whether to proceed with an investigation is made. It is likely that the person who makes such a decision will be a member of the legal team or a high-level manager. It is generally best either not to pursue the case further or to send it to a professional investigator.

Any temptation to immediately confront the suspect must be strongly resisted. Confronting the suspect too soon is one of the most damaging things that can be done in an investigation.

Before an investigation is launched, the entity must consider any legal issues that may affect the scope and manner of the investigation. Some examples are the rights of workers, the possibility of conducting the investigation under attorney-client privilege, whether there is sufficient evidence and legal justification to immediately fire a worker or to place the worker on administrative leave with or without pay, rights of investigating employers, the extent that a government entity may be directly or indirectly involved in the investigation, and reporting obligations.

The entity must consider any immediate steps that may be required to mitigate losses related to the fraud and to the eventual recovery through insurance and the legal system.

In some cases, it might be best to permit an employee to continue with the fraud, thus possibly permitting the investigator to catch the employee in the act. Catching a fraudster in the act and getting a quick confession can save enormous amounts of investigation costs. Investigations by independent fraud investigators can be time-consuming and expensive for two reasons: (1) following the principle of reverse proof and (2) needing to reconstruct doctored financial records. The principle of reverse proof says that in order to prove that a loss related to fraud has occurred, it is necessary to prove that the supposed loss cannot be explained as anything but fraud. In other words, fraud can be proved only by ruling out all reasonable explanations.

A second issue relating to recovery involves collecting insurance to cover losses. First, a decision must be made as to whether it is necessary to immediately report the loss to an insurer. Of course, this depends on the terms of the policy and the facts surrounding the suspected loss. Second, insurance policies typically require the policyholder to use all reasonable means to mitigate losses. This leaves the obvious problem that permitting a fraud to continue might put the entity in violation of its insurance policy's obligation to mitigate loss. Legal counsel should be consulted to resolve such issues.

Recovery can sometimes be made through criminal or civil litigation. In many situations, the prosecutor may require the fraudster to make restitution as part of a plea bargain. In other situations, restitution can be a component of the fraudster's sentence upon conviction.

Recovery can also be made by suing the fraudster. Public records searches can sometimes show that the fraudster has assets that can be targeted in a lawsuit. But in many cases, the fraudster will not have sufficient assets to justify the expense of a lawsuit.

There are many possible objectives to a fraud investigation besides identifying and punishing a fraudster, which might be the least important objective in a given situation. Other possible objectives include the following: stopping the fraud from continuing, identifying the loss for insurance purposes, identifying the loss for tax purposes, making an example of a fraudster, minimizing any embarrassing disclosures in the press, and discovering weaknesses in the internal control system.

The final step in the engagement process is to create the engagement letter. The letter's general objectives are to set forth the services to be provided, the objectives and scope of the investigation, the methods to be used, the resources required, the responsibilities of the respective parties, the basis and methods to be used for charging professional fees and expenses, and the means for resolving disputes.

Glossary

evidence collection process   The four steps in which evidence is collected in support of the objectives and scope of an investigation.

four types of evidence gathered in the evidence collection process   Physical evidence, documentary evidence, observational evidence, and interview evidence.

fraud investigation engagement process   Series of steps that begins with the investigator's first contact with the case and ends with a complete agreement regarding the fraud investigation services to be provided by the investigator.

fraud investigation process   Steps in systematically gathering and reviewing evidence for the purpose of documenting the presence or absence of fraud.

incident report   Report that contains the initial information used to justify a fraud investigation.

interview process Steps in which the initial interviews are conducted with those furthest from any suspects. Subsequent interviews are conducted successively closer to the prime suspect, with the prime suspect being interviewed last.

loss recovery process Process with the object of recovering losses that involves civil and criminal litigation, expert testimony, and collecting insurance.

reporting process Process that involves documenting and summarizing the results of the fraud investigation.

reverse proof Principle of fraud investigations that requires the investigator to consider the evidence for both sides. To the extent possible, the investigator must consider and rule out all evidence that would support defense arguments.

unified case file File that documents all activities related to the investigation.

Review Questions

1. The fraud investigation process involves systematically gathering and reviewing evidence for the purpose of
   a. Providing proof in court that a fraud has been committed.
   b. Documenting the presence or absence of fraud.
   c. Satisfying the requirements of SAS 99.
   d. None of the above.

2. Which of the following is *not* a step in a systematic fraud investigation?
   a. Proving the loss.
   b. Collecting evidence.
   c. Reporting.
   d. Recovering the loss.

3. The series of steps that begins with the investigator's first contact with the case and ends with a complete agreement regarding the fraud-investigation services to be provided by the investigator is called:
   a. The systematic fraud investigation.
   b. The evidence collection process.
   c. The initiation process.
   d. None of the above.

4. The process that includes testing hypotheses regarding a possible fraud is called:
   a. The evidence collection process.
   b. The fraud theory approach.
   c. The hypothesis-driven approach.
   d. None of the above.

5. Which of the following is *not* one of the major types of evidence collected in the evidence collection process?
   a. Documentary.
   b. Interview.
   c. Forensic
   d. All of the above are major types of evidence gathered in the evidence collection process.

6. When should the primary suspect be interviewed?
   a. As the first person.
   b. As the last person.
   c. Somewhere between first and last person.
   d. When it becomes necessary to stop a fraud in process.

7. The fraud reporting process can be defined as:
   a. The process of submitting reports to authorities and insurance companies.
   b. The process of documenting frauds committed.
   c. The process of informing affected stakeholders.
   d. None of the above.

8. Which of the following is *not* a step in the fraud investigation engagement process?
   a. Create an incident report.
   b. Agree on the primary suspects.
   c. Produce an engagement letter or memorandum.
   d. All of the above are steps in the engagement process.

9. Which of the following statements is correct?
   a. The relative importance of the steps in the fraud engagement process is the same for all players involved (e.g., the police, the independent investigator, and the victim).
   b. The relative importance of the steps in the fraud engagement process varies among the players involved (e.g., the police, the independent investigator, and the victim).
   c. Completely different steps in the engagement process will be followed depending on what type of investigator is involved.
   d. None of the above is a correct statement.

10. Which of the following statements is correct regarding the role of the fraud investigator in the loss recovery process?
    a. The investigator definitely has an important role.
    b. The investigator may have an important role.
    c. The investigator never has an important role.
    d. None of the above statements is correct.

11. Which of the following is true regarding the use of a centralized case file in fraud investigations?
    a. It is not advisable because doing so makes it easier for legal opponents to subpoena documents.
    b. It is advisable because doing so does not make it easier to respond to subpoena requests of legal opponents.
    c. It is always advisable because doing so can be helpful in optimizing a fraud management system.
    d. It is not advisable because doing so can be deleterious in optimizing a fraud management system

12. From a law enforcement standpoint, an incident report may be important because it:
    a. Saves the officer from having to write his own report.
    b. May serve as the basis for an immediate arrest.
    c. May serve as probable cause needed to subpoena records.
    d. Guarantees habeas corpus for the suspect.

13. Which of the following does the principle of reverse proof say about proving fraud?
    a. All reasonable fraud schemes must be considered.
    b. All reasonable fraud schemes must be eliminated.
    c. All reasonable explanations for the apparent fraud must be ruled out.
    d. None of the above.
14. After an initial assessment, a good general rule is to:
    a. Thoroughly investigate all suspected frauds.
    b. At least partially investigate all suspected frauds.
    c. Investigate some suspected frauds.
    d. None of the above.
15. The primary objective in a fraud investigation should be to:
    a. Stop the fraud from continuing.
    b. Make an example of the fraudster.
    c. Punish the fraudster.
    d. All of the above are possible primary objectives.
16. A good general rule is that individual fraudsters are:
    a. Not deterred by prosecutions.
    b. The primary focus of law enforcement offices that specialize in economic crimes.
    c. Almost always flamboyant persons.
    d. None of the above.
17. Which of the following statements is *most* correct?
    a. Most frauds are reported to authorities but are not prosecuted.
    b. Most frauds are not reported to authorities and are not prosecuted.
    c. Most frauds are reported to authorities and are prosecuted.
    d. None of the above statements is correct.
18. In the absence of a confession, which of the following is true about the fraud investigator's report?
    a. Should not point to a guilty person.
    b. Usually points to a guilty person.
    c. Sometimes points to a guilty person.
    d. Almost always points to a guilty person.
19. According to the chapter, one important element to include in an engagement letter is:
    a. A mediation or arbitration requirement.
    b. A reasonable retainer fee.
    c. A prepaid expenses account.
    d. None of the above.

Discussion Questions

20. Why is fraud investigation considered a "process"?
21. What are the major steps in a fraud investigation?
22. What is the fraud theory approach to fraud investigation?
23. What are the four types of evidence?
24. How might the engagement process for an internal fraud investigator differ from that for an external fraud investigator?

25. In general, how do the objectives of a fraud investigation from law enforcement differ from those of a victim?

26. How does law enforcement use an incident report?

27. Explain why, ideally, it is best that the person initially receiving an incident report not collect evidence before deciding whether an investigation is warranted.

28. How can the victim's anger ruin an investigation?

29. Explain why police are reluctant to seriously investigate embezzlement cases.

30. What are some possible benefits of conducting an investigation under the attorney-client privilege?

31. When might it be beneficial to permit a fraud scheme to continue without any immediate intervention to stop it?

32. Explain how the principle of reverse proof places a burden on the fraud investigator.

33. How might a fraud investigation lead to the loss of employees?

34. How can a fraud investigator document a case against an embezzler who destroys the accounting records to the point that it is not possible to produce a reasonable estimate of a loss?

35. Why might it be reasonable to devote a disproportionately large amount of resources to an apparently small fraud?

36. When should the fraud investigator avoid negotiating with a suspect with respect to restitution for fraud?

37. From the standpoint of making a good business decision, how useful is the objective of punishment in pursuing a fraud investigation?

38. What is the proper action for an employer who knows a fraud exists but can only narrow the number of suspects to three?

39. One principle of fraud is that "fraud is hidden." What are the implications of this principle to the fraud investigator?

40. In an occupational fraud setting, why might it be unnecessary to catch the fraudster in order to recover through an insurance claim?

41. When might a business decide to ignore a fraud committed by an employee?

42. What are the possible tax implications of fraud against a business?

43. Of what importance are publicity concerns when formulating objectives for fraud investigation?

44. Why might a company file a police report even when it knows that the police will not investigate the fraud?

45. Why should a fraud investigation engagement letter describe services *not* to be performed as part of the fraud investigation? Give some examples of such services.

46. Assuming that the fraud investigator has absolute documentary proof that an employee committed a fraud, why should the investigator refrain from indicating the employee's guilt in the investigation report?

47. How might the scope of a fraud investigation be limited?

48. When would it be acceptable for an independent fraud investigator's fees to be contingent on identifying the fraudster?

49. Why might a fraud investigator want to include an arbitration clause in her engagement letter?

Cases

50. Joe Frecaso was recently hired as the controller for Larson Cement Company after the previous controller was killed in a boating accident in Biscayne Bay. That controller had been with the company since it first opened its doors. Joe spends most of his time in the back office that has a panoramic view of "the yard" where the company trucks constantly come and go throughout the day.

Larson is a privately held company owned by the same family for 40 years. The company delivers concrete to construction sites throughout Miami/Dade County area. Frank Larson, the son of the original CEO, runs the company. Joe and his two staff accountants; Betty Ladrone, the treasurer; and her three staff members support the company's operations. There is also a secretary, front-office staff of three, an operations supervisor, and a sales staff of seven.

Larson Company normally sells to most contractors on credit. Betty supervises the credit approvals and reviews and handles bill payments, collections, and the bank accounts. Joe has responsibility for the bank reconciliations, accounts receivables, and the accounting records in general including the financial reports.

This morning the company secretary thumbed through the incoming mail as was her custom. There was a stack of about 30 envelopes, many of them obviously containing checks from customers paying on their accounts. She mentally prepared herself to separate the envelopes into several different piles. She would route each pile to the appropriate person: Frank, Joe, Betty, and Sara Martillo, the head of sales.

One envelope caught her eye. It was from the bank, but it wasn't thick enough to be a bank statement. In fact, after feeling the letter, she concluded that it contained only a single page inside, part of which she tried to see through the small clear window on the front of the envelope that revealed the company's name and address.

She looked almost sideways through the envelope's window to get a better look. There was a message in red letters, but because of the angle, she couldn't read what it said. That was enough, however, for her to make a decision: The letter should go straight to Frank. He had given her strict instructions to route any unusual-looking mail directly to him.

About the time that the unusual looking enveloped arrived on Frank's desk, Joe was pouring over last month's combined bank statement. It was out of balance by $1,104.35. He just scratched his head, sighed, took a sip of his coffee, and remembered that the current month's bank statement had just arrived and was sitting unopened, propped up against his computer monitor. Then the phone rang. It was Frank calling.

"I want to know what's going on," said Frank in an almost accusatory voice. "Our operations bank account is overdrawn by some $14,000!

Frank was pretty sharp when it came to financial matters. His education included an MBA degree with an accounting concentration, and he had worked as the controller of Larson Cement when he was younger.

Within seconds after Joe hung up the phone, Frank appeared in his doorway looking angry. "I want the bank statements right now."

Joe tried to maintain his professional demeanor, but his chest tightened. "Don't look at me," he said. "I don't write the checks."

Frank returned to his office, opened the current month's combined bank statement, and began thumbing through canceled checks. He stopped at one check for $2,500 paid to a Mary Waters. "Mary Waters, who are you?" he mumbled to himself.

Frank was a hands-on CEO and knew all of the company's vendors, and he had never heard of Mary Waters before. He looked at the endorsement on the back of the check. The checked had been deposited into a New York bank account.

Nervously, Frank spread the checks out on the table. Right away, several other checks paid to Mary Waters popped out and stared at him. Now was is sure that something was wrong: No vendor is paid more than once a month. So, he grabbed the phone and called Joe again.

Joe answered on the first ring. In a thundering voice, Frank said, "Joe, we've got a problem."

Joe remained quiet and waited for what seemed like a long time and became more nervous because it appeared that he was supposed to know what the problem was. "That's not a good sign," he thought.

Frank pounded Joe with questions about Mary Waters.

"We'll call Betty," Joe finally said. "She's the one with the checkbook."

"No," said Frank. "I want you to do a complete audit of her office, and I want a hidden video camera set up in a position to record everything she does at her desk."

"But what if someone else in her office stole the checks?"

"That's not possible," replied Frank. "She keeps the checkbooks locked up at all times in her safe, and she's the only one besides me with the combination."

"Ok, I'll start the investigation."

a. Evaluate how well Frank and Joe have handled the problem.

b. Evaluate Larson Cement's internal control processes as they apply to this case.

51. Rich Skywark is the owner of Skywark Hardware and Electric, a family owned business, in the College Station, Pennsylvania, area. His business consists of over-the-counter retail sales and discounted sales of building materials to local contractors. Sales to contractors consist mostly of specialized lumber and electrical supplies that are not available through the area's larger suppliers of building materials and electrical parts.

Most contractor customers have established accounts and place orders over the phone or the Web. However, contractors also visit the store to make purchases, sometimes purchasing on account and other times paying in cash. Retail customers pay only in cash.

Next to the front door is a long glass counter area with items that are sold from both inside the counter and the wall behind it. Two cash registers sit on the counter, and at least one of the two is open and in operation at all times during business hours.

Skywark's bookkeeper is Mark Hansen, who works alone and maintains all accounting records, including accounts receivables and accounts payable. He also manages the checkbook, payroll, cash deposits to the bank, and all tax-related matters. He maintains all accounting records in Intuit Quickbooks®, the well-known computerized accounting system that is popular among small and medium-size businesses.

Rich was happy he had hired Mark the year before because before Mark, he had had a string of successive bookkeepers who each worked for a few months and then quit. In recent months, Mark had become moody and difficult to work with. Whenever Rich asked him a question about something, Mark would become irritated.

"I know how to do my job," Mark would say.

Rich just shrugged off Mark's irritable disposition, mainly out of fear of losing one more accountant.

Jill Evans worked the front cash register most of the time. She was a long-time trusted employee who knew the store and the business inside and out. At the end of each day,

Chapter **Eight**

The Evidence Collection Process

CHAPTER LEARNING OBJECTIVES

After reading Chapter 8, you should be able to:

- LO1: Explain the use of a fraud theory and give examples of it.
- LO2: Outline the steps in the evidence collection process.
- LO3: Apply the fraud theory approach to evidence collection.
- LO4: Explain the elements of a fraud scheme.

INTRODUCTION

Once a fraud investigation is launched, the evidence collection process begins. Generally speaking, **evidence** is anything (tangible objects, documents, and testimony) that relates to the truth or falsity of an assertion made in an investigation or legal proceeding. Of course, as discussed in Chapter 2, not all evidence is admissible in a court of law.

The goal of the fraud investigator is to collect evidence relevant to the fraud under investigation. Such evidence, when well organized, provides answers to the classic sleuth's questions regarding the possible fraud: who, what, when, where, how, and why. The very first question is what. That is, what happened? Was there a fraud? If so, what was the fraud? What was the loss? If there is no evidence of fraud, the remaining questions are irrelevant and need not be considered.

LO1 A **fraud theory** (Figure 8.1) is an organized set of suppositions related to the classic sleuth's questions of who, what, when, where, how, and why. From the standpoint of evidence, the fraud investigation is a process involving a series of evidence-gathering steps the investigator takes to obtain successively refined answers to these basic questions. *Answers,* as the word is used here, suggest more than mere evidence: rather evidence that can be organized and knit together in such a way as to paint a powerful picture of a fraud— a fraud theory—especially when combined with expert opinion.

Embezzlement Case Example

This example demonstrates how evidence can be woven together with expert opinion to construct a fraud theory and build a case for court. A **complete court case** typically includes a fraud theory, collected evidence, and expert testimony. The fraud theory includes answers to the classic sleuth's questions. Collected evidence (i.e., all evidence including

FIGURE 8.1
Fraud Theory

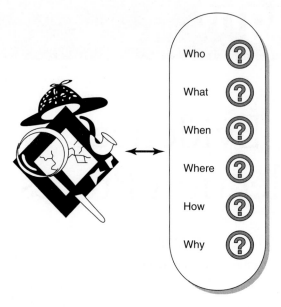

witness statements other than expert testimony) and expert testimony seek to provide proof that the fraud theory is correct.

Collected Evidence

For example, consider the case of a bookkeeper embezzling cash receipts. Furthermore, assume that the investigator gathers the following evidence:

1. The bookkeeper's résumé on file shows 10 years of experience with Intuit Quickbooks.
2. In Quickbooks, the cash receipts journal includes a large number of irregular and unexplainable journal entries. There are so many of these entries that the cash receipts journal is completely unreliable.
3. The irregular journal entries were made using the bookkeeper's login for Quickbooks during his normal working hours. Furthermore, they were made on a consistent basis over the period of one year.
4. The bookkeeper signs cash remittance advices when he receives cash to carry to the bank for deposit. He maintains custody of these documents, but half of them are missing. Without those documents, there is no definitive way to establish the amount of cash the business received. The business conducts sales strictly on a cash basis.
5. The bookkeeper is the only person to make bank deposits. Monthly deposits have declined every month for the previous 12 months. Deposits in the last 3 months are less than half of what they were at the beginning of the year and during the same period in each of the previous three years.
6. The company sells throw rugs. Purchase records indicate that the company's purchases of throw rugs has maintained steady for the previous three years. Profit margins on goods sold have also remained steady.

Expert Opinion

The evidence collected can be combined with expert opinion to form a picture of a fraud. The following items represent expert opinions regarding the evidence collected:

1. Only the bookkeeper could have made the irregular journal entries. This assumption is based on the fact that they were made on a regular basis, using the bookkeeper's login

and password, and during regular hours when the bookkeeper worked. Furthermore, the Quickbooks files were encrypted so that the cash receipts journal could not have been altered to make it falsely appear that the bookkeeper had made the irregular journal entries.

2. The nature and frequency of the irregular journal entries were such that given the bookkeeper's experience, he could not have made them by accident. Furthermore, there existed no legitimate business reason for such journal entries, and they are too egregious to be explained simply by sloppy bookkeeping.

3. The effect of the irregular journal entries was to render the cash receipts journal unusable.

4. The decrease in cash deposits can only be explained as a loss.

Fraud Theory: A Painted Picture of Fraud

The evidence gathered does not prove that a fraud took place. The defense could argue that inventory theft accounted for the drop in cash flows or that the bookkeeper never received the cash. However, a skilled attorney or prosecutor might still be able to prove embezzlement in court based on expert testimony regarding the irregular journal entries and an argument that they were made to cover up the embezzlement. Therefore, a conviction in this case would likely include a combination of basic evidence, fraud theory, and expert testimony.

The Investigator's Role in Building a Case

The role of the fraud investigator in collecting evidence, rendering expert opinion, and developing a fraud theory depends on the type of case and the scope and objectives of the fraud examination. Each of these three is discussed next.

The Fraud Investigator's Role in Collecting Basic Evidence

In virtually all cases, the fraud investigator has the primary responsibility for collecting the basic evidence needed to build a case.

Expert Opinion

The extent to which a fraud investigator renders an expert opinion in her investigation report depends on the objectives, scope, and type of case, and on the type of investigator.

Certified fraud examiners are bound by the Certified Fraud Examiner Code of Ethics, which states that "no opinion shall be expressed regarding the guilt or innocence of any person or party." On the other hand, fraud examiners can and do include expert opinions in their reports. For example, a fraud examiner could state that the cash receipts journal was in excellent condition prior to hiring the bookkeeper in the previous example.

Some investigators render opinions regarding guilt or innocence. For example, an entity's internal investigator working under the supervision of outside legal counsel may be asked, under the umbrella of attorney-client privilege, for an opinion as to whether an employee is guilty of asset misappropriation. In this case, the investigator, not bound by a code of ethics, might report back, "Yes, in my opinion the employee stole the money."

However, just because the investigator in this example is not bound by a code of ethics, is it a good idea to render an opinion that points to a suspect being guilty? If for no other reason than to avoid human error, it is probably much better to say instead something like, "In my opinion, the evidence of the person's guilt appears to be very compelling."

Fraud Theory

It is the attorney's responsibility to construct the theory of fraud to be used in court. The attorney's choice of theory depends on not only the strength of the evidence but also strategic decisions. For example, a prosecutor might decide to ignore certain important evidence to a fraud scheme in order to keep the case simple and easier for a jury to understand. This is especially true regarding a theory for the motive. In one case, a prosecutor had strong evidence that the defendant had committed the fraud to support an overly extravagant lifestyle with frequent weekend trips to casinos and large gambling losses that he did not have the income to support. However, the prosecutor had equally strong evidence that the defendant committed the fraud because he was passed over for a promotion. In the end, the prosecutor chose to focus only on the extravagant lifestyle and ignore the promotion motive.

Fraud investigators also develop fraud theories. In fact, a fraud theory is normally an essential requirement of a fraud investigation. Recall from the preceding discussion that the first question to be asked in an investigation is *what,* specifically, "What fraud, if any, has been committed?"

For practical purposes, it is impossible to investigate a fraud without some idea of what fraud is being investigated. For example, there is a big difference between a kickback scheme and one that involves cash receipts skimming. So, the fraud investigator's task is to posit some theory for the suspected fraud. As the investigation proceeds, the theory is then tested and modified as the evidence warrants. This process is discussed in detail in a subsequent section of this chapter.

THE EVIDENCE COLLECTION PROCESS

Types of Evidence

The general **sources of evidence** in fraud investigations include physical evidence, document evidence, observations, and interviews.

Physical and Document Evidence

Strictly speaking, physical evidence includes document evidence because all documents have some physical existence even if only inside a computer. However, for fraud investigation purposes, it is convenient to place document evidence in its own category because it is a mainstay of fraud investigations.

Physical evidence, as the term is used here, refers to a relatively broad category of evidence that includes items such as fingerprints and trace evidence. The various types of physical evidence are discussed in Chapter 11 as part of the discussion of forensic science. The various types of document evidence are discussed in Chapter 9. **Document evidence** includes not only documents collected as part of the investigation but also documents created in the form of charts, graphs, or other exhibits admitted into evidence as part of expert testimony.

Observations

Observation evidence is obtained by monitoring suspects. Such evidence may ultimately take the form of eyewitness testimony or various types of electronic or other recordings. Observation techniques can produce extremely powerful forms of evidence. A videotape of a clerk putting wads of money in her pockets can be worth all types of sophisticated expert analysis of accounting records. Observation techniques are discussed in Chapter 9.

Interviews

The ultimate item of evidence is a court-admissible recorded interview and signed confession. Interviews of individuals providing effective witness testimony with personal knowledge relevant to the alleged fraud can provide one of the most powerful types of evidence.

Interviews can also provide a powerful investigatory tool because they can provide information that helps narrow the evidence collection process.

The Steps in the Evidence Collection Process

LO2   The **evidence collection process** (Figure 8.2) begins with a review of the physical and document evidence. The process then proceeds to observations and interviews. These steps are separately discussed.

Review the Physical and Document Evidence

Depending on the case, the review of the physical and document evidence may involve items such as accounting records, application forms, credit reports, bank statements, and tax returns.

The objective of the physical and document review phase is to become as familiar as possible with the relevant business processes and individuals involved as well as the possible fraud scheme before conducting any interviews. This serves two main purposes:

1. A thorough knowledge of the business processes and the physical and document evidence helps the investigator to know whom to interview, the order in which to interview individuals, and the questions to ask.

2. In many cases, it is possible to keep the investigation secret while reviewing physical and document evidence. Once interviewing begins, it can be difficult to keep everyone, including perpetrators, from knowing that an investigation is underway. Once perpetrators know that an investigation is underway, they may destroy evidence, disappear, or fabricate false stories.

Observation

There is nothing better than catching a fraudster in the actions of the fraud. Moreover, in some types of frauds, especially those that involve identity theft, this is frequently the only way to catch and convict a fraudster. The reason for the difficulty in cases of identity theft is that the investigator might know the fraudster only by the fraudster's assumed identity. It is obviously difficult to take legal action against a person whose identity is unknown.

FIGURE 8.2
The Evidence-Gathering Process

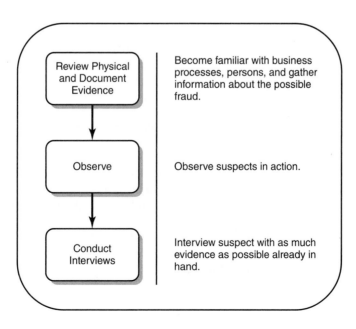

In cases of internal asset misappropriation, catching a fraudster in the act may result in substantial savings in the cost of the fraud investigation. For example, in one case, a bookkeeper made thousands of false entries into the cash receipts journal and completely destroyed the accounts receivable files. It took a fraud examiner many months to reconstruct the corrupted accounting records and unravel the fraud scheme. However, unknown to the fraud investigator, the bookkeeper had complete and uncorrupted copies of the records at his home. Had the fraud examiner caught the bookkeeper in the act at the beginning of the investigation, the chances would have been very good that the bookkeeper would have confessed and turned over his home copies of the accounting records, saving the fraud examiner months of work that were billed to the client at hundreds of dollars per hour. However, the investigator never had an opportunity to catch the bookkeeper performing the act because the business owner had confronted the bookkeeper before calling the independent fraud investigator. As a result, the bookkeeper immediately quit and hired a lawyer, who declined to permit the bookkeeper even to grant an interview to the fraud investigator.

The importance of catching a fraudster in the act by a video recording, if possible, cannot be overemphasized. As was previously mentioned, fraud investigations can be time consuming and expensive. Therefore, at the beginning of any investigation, serious consideration should be given to the possibility of catching the fraudster red-handed with the hope of simplifying the entire investigation. In some cases, this might require the assistance of a private detective with special equipment and skills useful for surveillance. In all cases, legal counsel should be consulted to ensure that any surveillance is conducted in a lawful way.

In considering the extent which to use observation, the investigator must weigh the benefits of catching the thief in the act versus the possibility of continuing losses. In many cases, the main priority is stopping the fraud scheme as soon as possible. For example, a fraudster who is an employee with wire transfer privileges associated with a company bank account whose balance is $10 million is in a position to do very serious damage in a very short time. In such a case, the company would not want to simply sit back and watch the employee transfer millions of dollars of funds into unauthorized offshore bank accounts.

Interviews

Interviews are conducted after the investigator has carefully studied all other types of evidence and has a fairly strong theory of the fraud scheme under consideration. The goal in interviewing is to obtain a confession if possible. If a confession is not possible, then the goal is to record the suspect in as much relevant detail as possible.

Ideally, it is best to record the suspect before she is aware that she is a suspect or is even aware that a fraud investigation is underway. This step increases the possibility of catching the suspect making inconsistent statements or telling outright lies.

Example

During reviews of physical evidence, records, and observations, the investigator may gain substantial amounts of information about the suspect's conduct and actions. Such information can be used to the investigator's great advantage during interviews. Consider, for example, the case of a bookkeeper who carries cash receipts in a money satchel to the bank for deposit. An investigator might surreptitiously follow this bookkeeper from the company office and photograph her handing the satchel to an unknown man who then carries the satchel to his car and drives away.

The investigator might then ask the following questions without the bookkeeper suspecting that the interview is anything more than a routine audit. The investigator reads the questions from a checklist, asking each one in a routine way, almost as if she is tired and bored and just wants to get the interview over with.

Investigator: So you are in charge of bank deposits?

Bookkeeper: Yes.

Investigator: Are you the only one who makes deposits?

Bookkeeper: Yes.

Investigator: What if you are sick on or vacation?

Bookkeeper: The money stays locked in my office safe until I return, and then I make the deposits. I'm the only one with the combination.

Investigator: Does anyone assist you in making the deposits?

Bookkeeper: No, it's just me.

Investigator: And so you have them picked up in an armored car?

Bookkeeper: No, I walk with them to the bank. It's only five blocks away.

Investigator: OK, OK. Aren't you concerned about being robbed? Does anyone accompany you or assist you?

Bookkeeper: No, I go by myself.

Investigator: I apologize. I asked two questions at once. So are you concerned about being robbed?

Bookkeeper: No, it's a safe part of town with tons of people on the sidewalk and cars and police everywhere.

Investigator: OK. And you always go alone?

Bookkeeper: Yes, just me.

Investigator: Do you ever stop for lunch or anything on your way to the bank?

Bookkeeper: No, I feel safe walking to the bank, but I wouldn't want to sit in a restaurant with a bank moneybag on my lap. It just wouldn't look right.

Investigator: (nodding with approval and looking at the checklist): This looks pretty good. I've just about finished. So then you carry the money bag straight to the bank?

Bookkeeper: Yes. Every time, like clockwork. When I'm carrying money, I never even stop for a second.

Analysis The bookkeeper is caught in a lie. She claims she goes straight to the bank when she does not. Furthermore, she has gone on record saying she is the only one who handles the money, which means she cannot later say that she gives the money to someone else.

Had this interview been conducted before the bookkeeper was observed handing the satchel to an unknown man, the investigator might not have asked the detailed questions about the bookkeeper carrying the satchel directly to the bank.

It is also significant that the bookkeeper was unaware that the investigator knew she had handed off the satchel to the unknown man. Because she was unaware, she felt comfortable lying about the handoff. On the other hand, if she had been aware, she might have made her story conform to what the investigator knew. For example, if the unknown man had been her husband, she could have replied that on occasion her husband helps her because she does not like walking five blocks in high heels. But as it was, she lied to the investigator, and lying is consistent with consciousness of guilt. A skillful interviewer will get the suspect on record telling as many lies as possible and then confront the suspect with the contrary evidence. In many cases, the suspect will then be unable to explain the lies and confess as a result.

Catching suspects in lies is only one aspect of interviewing. The main point here is that it is essential for the investigator first to gather and analyze as much relevant information as possible before conducting interviews. One of the worst mistakes that an investigator can make is to conduct interviews without the proper background information and preparation. Interview methods are covered in detail in Chapter 10.

The Order of Interviews

Interviews should generally be conducted in a specific order (Figure 8.3). The investigator should begin interviewing those furthest from the prime suspect and then work toward the suspect. If there is more than one suspect, the prime suspect would be saved for last.

By interviewing the prime suspect last, the investigator will be able to bring the maximum amount of information to the interview. This both maximizes the investigator's chance of getting a confession, if one is due, and the chance of getting all relevant details on record so that the suspect has a difficult time later making her story conform to any evidence that may later emerge or be disclosed to her.

APPLICATION OF THE FRAUD THEORY APPROACH TO GUIDE THE EVIDENCE-GATHERING PROCESS

The Fraud Theory Approach

LO3 The fraud theory approach provides the standard structure to fraud investigations. As mentioned at the beginning of the current chapter, it is practically impossible to conduct a fraud investigation without some theory regarding what type of fraud is being investigated. Without a fraud theory to guide the investigation, the process devolves into a mere "fishing expedition." This is not to say that fishing expeditions are never warranted but that fraud

FIGURE 8.3
Interviews Are Conducted in a Specific Order

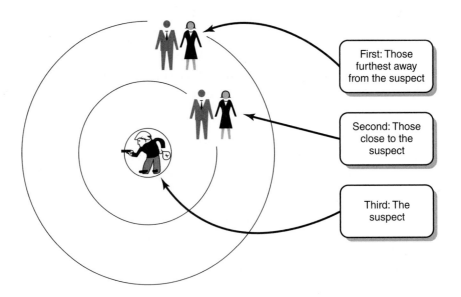

First: Those furthest away from the suspect

Second: Those close to the suspect

Third: The suspect

investigations and fishing expeditions are two different things. The focus of the current chapter is on fraud investigations. "Fishing" is more consistent with ordinary auditing, the subject of Chapter 4.

The **fraud theory approach** to fraud investigations is a process that posits a hypothesis regarding a fraud scheme, tests the hypothesis with evidence, and then accepts, modifies, or discards the hypothesis as the evidence warrants.

Example

Assume that a bank loan officer reports that he suspects that a mortgage loan applicant is using a false identity with the intent to defraud the bank for a large sum of money. Because the bank is very small and does not have its own investigation unit, the loan department hires an independent fraud investigator to look into the matter.

In this case, the initial hypothesis is that a loan applicant is using a stolen identity. Therefore, the investigator reviews the loan application, and, using public databases, verifies that the applicant's social security number belongs to someone who had died many years ago at a very young age. At the same time, there are active credit files open in this person's name.

To build a better case, the investigator asks the lending department to set up a "loan review" interview with the applicant. The investigator secretly videotapes the interview after making sure that all legal aspects had been addressed.

As a result of some of the applicant's answers in the interview, the investigator becomes concerned that she is just one person in an identity theft ring, leaving open the possibility that the bank is falling victim to multiple instances of loan fraud. The economy had been so bad recently that the bank has a substantial portfolio of foreclosed properties that has loan balances for less than the properties were worth. Perhaps some of those bad loans were a result of fraud.

Given the investigator's concern (which was supported by some of the comments made by the applicant during the interview), he decides to revise his fraud hypothesis to include a fraud scheme perpetrated by an organized crime ring.

Given the revised hypothesis, the investigator reviews all documentation for all foreclosed loans. There are 31 in total. He begins with the additional hypothesis that any fraudulent loan applications would have been supported by bogus property appraisals.

In reviewing the appraisals, the investigator discovers that the 31 loans involved a total of nine different appraisers, so he runs background checks on each of these appraisers. He finds that one appraiser currently has a $3 million home in foreclosure and several lawsuits against her relating to a business venture involving her.

As a next step, the investigator contacts a detective in the local economic crimes unit. The sergeant in charge immediately recognizes the name of the appraiser: This person is already under police investigation for loan fraud involving a different bank.

The result is that a group of more than a dozen persons are charged in the organized fraud scheme. Included in the arrests are attorneys, real estate brokers, one title company officer, two appraisers, and a group of foreign individuals who had been running the scheme. Many of the fraudsters had already left the county and cannot be pursued because they had entered and left the country illegally and had used false identities during their entire stay in the county.

Analysis   In this example, the investigator began with a fraud hypothesis (a single case of loan fraud), collected evidence (the applicant's interview), modified the hypothesis (to include a crime ring), gathered more evidence (from the foreclosure portfolio), and finally confirmed the fraud. However, the confirmation of the fraud was for the investigator's benefit only. It does not mean that her report will say that a given person is guilty of fraud. The evidence will speak for itself, and as was discussed, independent investigators generally avoid rendering an opinion that a specific person is guilty of fraud.

The Fraud Theory Approach to Fraud Investigation

The fraud theory approach to fraud investigation provides a way to structure the evidence collection process. As discussed, the collection process begins with physical, document, and observation evidence and ends with interviews. However, this process as described does not specify what evidence is to be collected or the specific order in which individual pieces of evidence are to be obtained.

To know what evidence to collect, investigators must first have a theory regarding what fraud may have occurred. They then collect evidence that either proves to be consistent or not consistent with the theory. The investigation continues until a reasonable amount of evidence has been collected to support, modify, or discard the theory given the scope of the investigation. If evidence gathered supports the fraud theory, the investigation is concluded. If the fraud theory is discarded, the investigation is concluded if no alternative theories deserve investigation. If the fraud theory is modified, the modified version is investigated, and additional evidence is collected to support, further modify, or discard the theory as modified. This process continues until there are no more modifications or alternatives to consider.

As previously mentioned, a fraud theory involves answers to the basic sleuth's questions (who, what, when, where, how, and why). Evidence, then, includes the organized pieces of information that support the answers to these questions for a given fraud theory. From an investigator's point of view, the notion of evidence has little meaning apart from a fraud theory.

Ideally, investigators begin an investigation with a correct theory of *what* fraud occurred if indeed one has occurred. If the initial theory is correct, the entire investigation involves answering the remaining questions to the extent possible. In some cases, however, the initial theory may need to be significantly modified or even abandoned. For example, an investigator might begin with an initial theory that an inventory clerk is systematically stealing goods from inventory. Because this is an initial fraud theory, the investigator might begin examining the accounting records relating to inventory purchases, sales, and requisitions. After examining those records and surreptitiously observing and making nighttime counts of the inventory, the investigator might conclude that the inventory shortages are real. However, the investigator might also conclude that the theory that the inventory clerk is responsible for the shortages is not correct; rather, a dishonest vendor siphoning off goods from deliveries is responsible.

Fraud Schemes

LO4 An important aspect of any fraud theory is the fraud scheme. A **fraud scheme** is a predefined set of answers to the questions "who, what, how, when, and where."

- **Who** A fraud scheme defines the "who," in a generic sense, such as "the bookkeeper" or "customer," without reference to a specific person. It also identifies the victim of the fraud.
- **What** A fraud scheme defines the "what" in terms of the classification of the fraud. For example, it could be cash sales skimming or accounts receivable lapping. Included in the definition of "what" is the objective of the fraud, such as to steal cash receipts, steal goods from inventory, or to obtain credit by deception.
- **How** A fraud scheme defines the "how" in terms of the mechanics of the fraud. For example, a loan fraud scheme may include a person applying fraudulently for a loan application with a stolen identity obtained from hacking employers' Web sites.

- **When**   A fraud scheme defines the "when" in terms of the conditions that must be present for the fraud to be committed. For example, an accounts receivable scheme may occur *when* the same person manages both accounts receivable and bank deposits.
- **Where**   A fraud scheme defines the "where" in terms of the possible locations of the fraud. In many cases, the "where" is explained in the "how" and "when."

The fraud scheme does not include the specific "why" the reason fraud is committed. The main benefit of answering this question is that doing so helps to identify the specific perpetrator. For example, a typical answer to the why question is that the perpetrator steals to live beyond his means. For this reason, investigators normally profile suspects to identify those most likely to commit fraud.

Predication and Investigation Risk

An important principle in the investigation of frauds is predication (Figure 8.4). The principle of **predication** dictates that there must be a reasonable justification for each step in the evidence collection process. If no reasonable basis exists to continue to collect evidence, this process must stop.

The opposite is also true: The principle of predication also dictates that evidence must be collected until no reasonable basis remains to continue collecting it. This is sometimes stated as the principle of **following the evidence.**

The first application of the predication principle to investigations involves the "what" question. Specifically, an investigation should begin with the question of what fraud may have occurred. Unless there is some reasonable basis to believe that a fraud may have occurred, the evidence collection process should be terminated.

The principle of predication is especially applicable to law enforcement officials, who are frequently constrained by the requirement to justify evidence-seeking requests (e.g., subpoenas and search warrants) via probable cause. Without probable cause, there

FIGURE 8.4
The Predication Principle

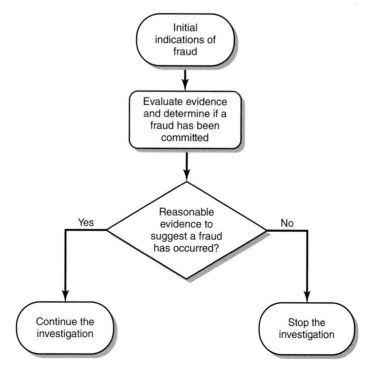

may be no reasonable basis for law enforcement officials to obtain evidence needed to sustain an investigation.

Private fraud investigators are often much less constrained by predication than law enforcement officials are. For example, business insurance policies frequently include provisions that require policyholders to cooperate with the insurer in ways that are very broadly defined. In the event of a claim for a loss, for example, insurance policies typically require that the policyholder give statements under oath, provide personal bank records, and so on. Specialized attorneys who sometimes interrogate policyholders for many hours at a time obtain required statements the policyholders make under oath. Of policyholders, they can simply refuse to cooperate and not collect on the claim, but they cannot simply refuse to cooperate without consequences. On the other hand, suspects can refuse to speak to law enforcement officers without consequences.

Predication may place ethical constraints on independent investigators who bill by the hour. Continuing to collect evidence without some reasonable basis for doing so could result in billing the client for unnecessary services. However, what constitutes a "reasonable basis" can be a matter of judgment, so a good understanding between the investigator and the client is essential.

Deciding in practice what constitutes a reasonable basis involves **investigation risk** of making less-than-optimal decisions in deciding what evidence to collect, how to collect it, and how to interpret it. For example, an investigator who suspects a fraudulent invoice scheme might decide that carefully investigating half of 1,000 invoices would produce a 95 percent chance of detecting any set of fraud losses that exceed $500 in total. Thus, there would be a 5 percent chance of failing to detect fraud losses that exceed $500. This 5 percent would constitute investigation risk with respect to the particular situation as to how much evidence to collect.

Fraud investigations can involve many questions relating to evidence collection, and each question has its own investigation risk. Furthermore, because investigations are sequential (i.e., they follow the evidence), investigation risks taken at one stage of the investigation can affect risks relating to later stages of the investigation. For example, in investigating the invoice scheme described in the previous paragraph, a failure to detect fraud losses exceeding $500 could result in a failure to interview the perpetrator who might be sitting on the edge of her seat ready to confess.

Hypothesis Testing

Each individual fraud scheme suggests particular pieces of evidence for the investigator to weigh. The process of weighing such evidence is sometimes called *hypothesis testing* (Figure 8.5). In fraud theory, a **hypothesis test** is an examination of a piece of evidence to decide whether it is consistent with a given fraud theory under consideration.

FIGURE 8.5
Hypothesis Testing in Relation to a Fraud Theory

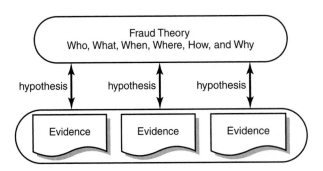

Testing a fraud theory may involve examining a set of related hypotheses. If enough of the tests support the fraud theory, the investigator would continue to collect evidence relevant to the theory. As discussed, at any point the investigator could consider the theory confirmed, modify it, or abandon it (and possibly begin considering an alternative theory).

Protocols for Investigating Fraud Schemes

Ideally, generally accepted, published professional protocols should be available to a fraud investigator in conducting investigations for each specific type of fraud scheme. But such a general set of protocols does not exist.

One reason that no general set of protocols exists is that the specific way in which a given investigation is conducted, especially in gathering evidence, is very much determined by the objectives of the investigation and the risk preferences of the client and investigator. For example, if the primary objective in an embezzlement scheme is to simply identify the source of the loss and stop it but not to prosecute a suspect, a relatively low amount of effort may be devoted to using the interview to collect evidence.

Much depends on the client. In one case, a small business owner spent $5,000 to investigate why the bookkeeper's trial balance was off by only $1. The business owner was preoccupied with the thought that a "missing dollar" may have only been the tip of the iceberg. The investigation continued until an error was discovered, and to everyone's relief, the bookkeeper was exonerated.

Fraud investigation protocols do exist within given industries and companies. For example, companies in the financial services and insurance industries and many government entities typically have fraud investigation units that routinely use consistent sets of protocols. For example, auto insurance companies have fraud investigators who are experts in analyzing crash reports and identifying evidence of fraud. Issues relating to investigating various specific types of frauds are discussed in Chapters 13 through 18. Furthermore, the Association of Certified Fraud Examiners (ACFE) (www.acfe.org) has an excellent (members-only) database of links to online articles that describe approaches to investigating various types of fraud.

In the absence of any pre-established protocols, the fraud investigator must establish protocols for each new investigation. The general rule in establishing such protocols is that each fraud scheme has its own "smoking gun" that represents not only evidence but also a weak point in a fraud scheme. Consider, for example, a scheme in which a cash register clerk pockets cash from his cash register and replaces it with phony checks. In this scheme, the cash register balances at the end of his shift because the ending register balance equals the beginning register balance plus the cash and phony checks received during his shift. However, the company ends up with the worthless checks.

The phony-checks-in-the-register scheme has its weak points. At first glance, a manager or owner might think that the company has been victimized repeatedly by identity thieves writing bad checks. Simply tracing the checks back to a single cashier, however, could unravel the scheme. Proof could then be confirmed by setting up a hidden camera to record the cashier switching checks for cash.

Almost all ongoing fraud schemes, no matter how sophisticated, have one weakness: the perpetrator is subject to being caught in the act. On the other hand, the nature of past fraud schemes could make establishing proof of guilt either impossible or impracticable. In some cases, it might not be possible to prove even that a loss, let alone a fraud, had taken place.

Consider, for example, a former employee from the information technology department who breaks into her former employer's computer network and steals bank access passwords. The individual then wires money to an account in a small country on the other side of the globe and finally accesses the system's logs and erases all traces of her access to the system. In this case, the loss may be completely untraceable to the former employee, leaving no possibility of proving guilt. Unfortunately, perfect crimes do exist when viewed from a practical point of view.

In any case, the fraud investigator should posit a fraud scheme and then focus on gathering evidence related to the weak points associated with the scheme under consideration. When this approach works well, it permits the investigator to rapidly confirm or deny the given fraud scheme. Then, once the fraud scheme has been reasonably confirmed, the investigator can focus on securing evidence that proves a given suspect's guilt. So, the general approach to hypothesis-driven investigations can be summarized as follows: Verify the fraud, identify the scheme, and find the evidence to prove guilt.

Summary

Once a fraud investigation has been launched, the evidence collection process begins. Generally, evidence is anything (including tangible objects, documents, and testimony) that pertains to the truth or falsity of an assertion made in an investigation or legal proceeding.

A *fraud theory* includes answers to the classic sleuth's questions of who, what, when, where, how, and why. Collected evidence (i.e., all evidence other than expert testimony) and expert testimony are used to provide proof that the fraud theory is correct.

The role of the fraud investigator in collecting evidence, rendering an expert opinion, and developing a fraud theory depends on the type of case and the scope and objectives of the fraud examination. In virtually all cases, the fraud investigator has the primary responsibility for collecting the evidence needed to build a case.

The extent to which a fraud investigator renders expert opinion in his investigation report depends on the objectives, scope, type of case, and the type of investigator.

Certified fraud examiners are bound by the Certified Fraud Examiner Code of Ethics, which states that "no opinion shall be expressed regarding the guilt or innocence of any person or party." On the other hand, fraud examiners can and do include expert opinions in their reports.

The attorney has responsibility for constructing the theory of fraud to be used in court. The attorney's choice of theory depends not only on the strength of the evidence but also on strategic decisions. Fraud investigators also develop fraud theories as an essential part of fraud investigations.

The general sources of evidence in fraud investigations include physical evidence, document evidence, observations, and interviews. *Physical evidence,* as the term is used here, refers to a relatively broad category of evidence that includes items such as fingerprints and trace evidence. Document evidence might include not only documents collected as part of the investigation but also documents created in the form of charts, graphs, or other exhibits admitted into evidence as part of expert testimony.

Observation evidence is obtained by monitoring suspects. Such evidence may ultimately take the form of eyewitness testimony or various types of electronic or other recordings. Observation techniques can represent extremely powerful evidence. A videotape of a clerk stuffing money in her pockets can be as effective as sophisticated expert analysis of accounting records.

The ultimate item of evidence is a court-admissible recorded interview and a signed confession. Interviews can produce one of the most powerful kinds of evidence: effective witness testimony from individuals with personal knowledge relevant to the alleged fraud.

The evidence collection process begins with a review of the physical and document evidence. The process then proceeds to observations and interviews. The review of the physical and document evidence may involve items such as accounting records, application forms, credit reports, bank statements, and tax returns. One objective of the physical and document review phase is to become as familiar as possible with the relevant business processes and individuals involved and the possible fraud scheme before conducting any interviews.

There is nothing better than catching a fraudster in the act. Moreover, in some types of frauds, it is frequently the only way to identify and convict a fraudster. This is especially true in cases that involve identity theft. Catching a fraudster in misappropriating internal assets may result in substantial savings in the cost of the investigation. However, in considering the extent to which to use observation, the investigator must weigh the benefits of catching the thief in the act versus the possibility of continuing losses. In many cases, the main priority is stopping the fraud scheme as soon as possible.

Interviews are conducted after the investigator has carefully studied all other kinds of evidence and has a fairly strong theory of the fraud scheme being investigated. The goal in interviewing is to obtain a confession. If this is not possible, the goal is to get the suspect's interview on record in as much relevant detail as possible.

Interviews should generally be conducted in a specific order. They should begin with those furthest from the prime suspect and then work their way to the suspect. If there is more than one suspect, the primary suspect would be saved for last. This enables the investigator to obtain the maximum amount of information during the prime suspect's interview. This increases the investigator's chance of both getting a confession, if one is sought, and recording all relevant details so that the suspect has a difficult time later conforming his story to any evidence that later emerges or is disclosed to the suspect.

The fraud theory approach provides the standard structure for fraud investigations. As mentioned at the beginning of the current chapter, conducting a fraud investigation is practically impossible without some theory regarding the type of fraud being investigated. Without some fraud theory to guide the investigation, the process may devolve into a mere "fishing expedition."

The fraud theory approach to fraud investigations is a process that posits a hypothesis regarding a fraud scheme, tests the hypothesis with evidence, and then accepts, modifies, or discards the hypothesis as is warranted by the evidence.

Evidence refers to the organized pieces of information that support the answers to the questions that apply to a given fraud theory. From an investigator's point of view, the notion of evidence has little meaning apart from a fraud theory.

An important aspect of any fraud theory is a *fraud scheme;* it is a predefined set of answers to the fraud theory questions.

The fraud scheme does not include the "*why*" the reason fraud is committed. The main benefit of answering this question is that doing so helps to identify the specific perpetrator. For example, a typical answer to the "why" question involves the perpetrator stealing to live beyond her means. For this reason, investigators normally profile suspects to identify those most likely to commit fraud.

An important principle of investigation frauds is *predication,* which requires a reasonable justification for each step in the evidence collection process. If no reasonable basis exists to continue to collect evidence, the process must stop. The opposite is also true: the principle of predication also demands that evidence must be collected until there remains no reasonable basis not to stop collecting it. This is sometimes stated as the principle of "following the evidence." Depending on the investigator, the client, and the client's risk preferences, predication can place varying degrees of constraints on evidence gathering.

Deciding in practice on what constitutes a reasonable basis involves *investigation risk.* It is the risk of making less-than-optimal decisions in deciding what evidence to collect, how to collect it, and how to interpret it.

Each individual fraud scheme suggests particular pieces of evidence for the investigator to weigh. The process of weighing it is sometimes called *hypothesis testing.* In fraud theory, a hypothesis test examines a piece of evidence to decide whether it is consistent with a given fraud theory under consideration. This process may involve testing a set of related hypotheses. If enough of the tests support the fraud theory, the investigator may continue to collect evidence relevant to the theory. At any point, the investigator may consider the theory confirmed, modify the theory, or abandon it (and possibly begin considering an alternative).

No generally acceptable set of protocols exists for investigating fraud. One reason that no such set of protocols exists is that the objectives of the investigation and the risk preferences of the client and investigator determine the specific way in which a given investigation is conducted, especially when gathering evidence.

In the absence of any pre-established protocols, the fraud investigator must establish protocols for each new investigation. The general rule in establishing such protocols is that each fraud scheme has its own "smoking gun."

Glossary

collected evidence   Evidence collected as part of an investigation; does not include expert testimony, which may also be admitted into court as evidence.

complete court case   Trial that typically includes a fraud theory, collected evidence, and expert testimony; actual litigation also involves legal strategies and tactics.

document evidence   Information that includes not only documents collected as part of the investigation but also those created in the form of charts, graphs, or other exhibits admitted as part of expert testimony.

evidence   Any information (including tangible objects, documents, and testimony) that relates to the truth or falsity of an assertion made in an investigation or legal proceeding; exists only to the extent that it relates to a fraud theory.

evidence collection process   Sequence of steps in evidence collection that begins with a review of the physical and document evidence and then proceeds to observations and interviews.

following the evidence   Principle in fraud investigations that dictates evidence must be collected until there remains a reasonable basis to stop collecting it.

fraud scheme   Predefined set of answers to the questions who, what, how, when, and where.

fraud theory   Organized set of answers to the classic sleuth's questions of who, what, when, where, how, and why.

fraud theory approach   Process in fraud investigations that posits a hypothesis regarding a fraud scheme, tests the hypothesis with evidence, and then accepts, modifies, or discards the hypothesis as the evidence warrants.

hypothesis test   Assessment of a piece of evidence to decide whether it is consistent with a given fraud theory under consideration.

investigation risk   Chance of making less-than-optimal decisions in deciding what evidence to collect, how to collect it, and how to interpret it.

observation evidence   Information obtained by monitoring suspects; may ultimately take the form of eyewitness testimony or various types of electronic or other recordings.

physical evidence   Relatively broad category of information that includes, for example, fingerprints and trace evidence.

predication   Principle in fraud investigations that requires a reasonable justification for each step in the evidence collection process.

sources of evidence   Origin of information in fraud investigations that includes physical evidence, document evidence, observations, and interviews.

Review Questions

1. Evidence is defined as:
   a. Anything that affects the truth or falsity of an assertion made in an investigation or legal proceeding.
   b. Anything that affects the truth or falsity of an assertion made in an investigation or legal proceeding, and that is admissible in a court of law.
   c. Both *a* and *b*.
   d. None of the above.

2. A fraud theory is similar to a fraud scheme except with respect to which of these questions?
   a. Who?
   b. Why?
   c. How?
   d. When?

3. An attorney pursuing a court case against a fraudster generally:
   a. Uses the same fraud theory as the investigator.
   b. Uses the same theory as the fraud investigator but adds a motive.
   c. Uses the same or different theory as the fraud investigator.
   d. Uses a "force of evidence" instead of a fraud theory.

4. To effectively use collected evidence in court, an attorney will also need which of these?
   a. At least one eyewitness.
   b. A signed confession.
   c. A fraud report.
   d. None of the above.

5. The primary person responsible for collecting the actual evidence to be introduced in court is:
   a. The attorney or paralegal.
   b. A private detective.
   c. A fraud investigator.
   d. None of the above.

6. When may Certified Fraud Examiners include an opinion of guilt or innocence in their fraud reports?
   a. Only when there is a clear-cut signed and properly obtained confession.
   b. When physical forensic evidence irrefutably ties the suspect to the crime.
   c. When the suspect is caught in the act.
   d. None of the above.

7. Whose responsibility is it to construct the fraud theory to be used in court?
   a. The attorney's.
   b. The client's.
   c. The investigator's.
   d. None of the above.

8. The first question asked in a fraud investigation is:
   a. Who?
   b. What?
   c. How?
   d. Why?

9. Strictly speaking, physical evidence includes which of these?
   a. Admissible evidence.
   b. Predicated evidence.
   c. Document evidence.
   d. None of the above.

10. Eyewitness testimony can best be described as a form of which type of evidence?
    a. Documentary.
    b. Physical.
    c. Expert.
    d. Observational.

11. Which of the following is the ultimate item of evidence that is admissible in court?
    a. Fraud investigation report pointing to the perpetrator.
    b. Video recording of the suspect appearing to commit the fraud.
    c. Set of solid, forensic physical evidence.
    d. None of the above.

12. An objective of the review of physical and document evidence is to:
    a. Become as familiar as possible with the business processes involved.
    b. Collect sufficient evidence to legally pursue the perpetrator.
    c. Both *a* and *b*.
    d. None of the above.

13. At the beginning of any investigation, serious consideration should be given to the possibility of catching the fraudster in the act because:
    a. Doing so can result in lowering investigation costs.
    b. Doing so can provide good evidence for court.
    c. Both *a* and *b*.
    d. None of the above.

14. When should interviews normally be conducted?
    a. Before documentary evidence is obtained.
    b. After a preliminary draft of the fraud investigation report is ready.
    c. Once a suspect can be identified.
    d. None of the above.

15. The best approach during interviews is for the investigator to:
    a. Be immediately open and let the suspect know at the beginning what evidence exists.
    b. Withhold knowledge of evidence for strategic or tactical reasons.
    c. Consult with legal counsel to preserve the admissibility of any statements made by the suspect.
    d. None of the above.

16. The fraud theory approach to fraud investigations does which of these?
    a. Posits a hypothesis, tests the hypotheses against legal norms, and then accepts, modifies, or discards the hypothesis as warranted by the evidence.
    b. Posits a hypothesis, tests the hypotheses against evidence, and then accepts, modifies, or discards the hypothesis as warranted by legal norms.

    c. Posits a hypothesis, tests the hypotheses against evidence, and then accepts, modifies, or discards the hypothesis as warranted by the evidence.

    d. None of the above.

17. The fraud theory approach to fraud investigation involves using a fraud theory to structure which of the following?

    a. The evidence collection process.

    b. The entire investigation process.

    c. The interview process.

    d. None of the above.

18. A fraud scheme is a predefined set of answers to which of these?

    a. Who, why, how, when, where questions.

    b. Who, what, how, why, where questions.

    c. Who, what, how, why, when, and where questions.

    d. None of the above.

19. Which of the following does the principle of predication require?

    a. A reasonable incident report exists before commencing an investigation.

    b. Interviews be conducted after collecting documentary evidence.

    c. A preponderance of the evidence at each step of the investigation.

    d. None of the above.

20. Which of the following best describes how the principle of predication can affect private fraud investigators compared to law enforcement officials?

    a. Provides less constraint.

    b. Provides more constraint.

    c. Provides equal constraint.

    d. Provides equal constraint but in different ways depending on the type of investigation.

21. An investigator has identified a fraud in one loan application and wonders whether the same fraud also exists in other loan applications. For budgetary considerations, the investigator is not able to check 100 percent of the loan applications and decides to check every 10th loan application for fraud. This decision is an example of the application of which of the following?

    a. Fraud risk.

    b. Enterprise risk management.

    c. Investigation risk.

    d. None of the above.

22. In fraud theory, hypothesis testing involves which of these?

    a. An application of discovery sampling.

    b. The examination of a piece of evidence to decide whether it is consistent with the fraud theory under consideration.

    c. The application of discovery sampling to examine evidence for consistency with the fraud theory under consideration.

    d. None of the above.

23. Which statement is true regarding protocols for investigating fraud schemes?

   a. A complete set of protocols is published by the American Institute of Public Accountants.

   b. A complete set of protocols is published by the Association of Certified Fraud Examiners.

   c. A complete set of protocols is published in the accounting literature.

   d. None of the above.

24. The general rule for establishing fraud investigation protocols is that each fraud scheme has which of the following?

   a. Three weak points.

   b. Something known as a "smoking gun."

   c. A central audit point.

   d. None of the above.

25. Almost all ongoing fraud schemes have one weakness in common:

   a. They leave an audit trail.

   b. The perpetrator is subject to being caught in the act.

   c. The perpetrator does not have enough time to destroy the evidence.

   d. All of the above.

Discussion Questions

26. Why is it important that evidence be tied to a fraud theory?

27. What is the relationship between a fraud theory and the steps in the evidence-gathering process?

28. What are the relative roles of fraud theory, evidence, expert opinion, and a court case in fraud investigations?

29. Are expert opinions formed during the fraud investigation or only after it is finished? Explain.

30. What are the investigator's primary roles in fraud investigations?

31. When is it acceptable for a fraud investigator to render an opinion that a suspect is guilty?

32. Why might the fraud theory used in court differ from the fraud theory developed and used by the fraud investigator?

33. Why is a fraud theory an essential part of a fraud investigation?

34. What are the primary sources of evidence in a fraud investigation?

35. Is a verbal confession by a suspect part of the evidence of a fraud case? Explain.

36. At what point in the investigation process is it important to develop a fraud theory?

37. In what type of fraud might it be possible to make a case against a fraudster without catching him in the act?

38. Give an example of how catching a fraudster in the act can save considerable investigation expenses.

39. Why are interviews conducted after physical, document, and observation evidence are collected?

40. In what order should individuals be interviewed?

41. Should only suspects be interviewed?

42. How does hypothesis testing in fraud investigations relate to the principle of predication?

43. How does the fraud theory approach structure the evidence-gathering process?
44. When should an investigation end?
45. How does a fraud scheme differ from a fraud theory?
46. How does application of the predication principle apply to the "what" question?
47. How does a fraud investigator control investigation risk?
48. How does an investigator test a fraud theory?
49. How does an investigator establish protocols for a given fraud investigation?

Cases

50. The Green Natural Wellness Company, aka GNWC, sells select, high-end nutritional and health and beauty products to small health food stores throughout the United States. Its headquarters and warehouses are located in Clear Lake, Texas, only a couple of miles from the NASA Space Center.

    GNWC's key success factor is its ability to quickly bring to market new products before other suppliers do. The company has two full-time buyers who spend all their time traveling around the world in search of unique "nutraceuticals." For example, one of the buyers recently discovered that when a common plant in the Brazilian rain forest is mixed with natural emollients, the result is a cream that eliminates even the most difficult cases of acne. After the discovery, GNWC took only six weeks to bring the product to market.

    GNWC has four sales divisions that report to the vice president of sales: skin care, hair care, nutritional supplements, and dried foods. Each division operates autonomously with its own revenue and expense budgets. The controller's office reviews and approves all divisional budgets.

    Barbara Larkin is the head of the skin care division. In recent years, her division has done spectacularly well with annual sales growth rates averaging in the 20 percent range and the most recent quarter's sales being just over $4 million.

    Until several years ago, Barbara's division was so independent that it managed its own collections of accounts receivable, although it forwarded all incoming customer checks to the central finance division for deposit, and all purchase orders had to be approved by the finance division before being forwarded to the purchasing division for additional approval.

    About two years ago, Barbara decided to turn over the collection of customer accounts to the collections department in the finance division. Because of the rapid growth in her skin care division, there was a shortage of staff, and she was having a difficult time keeping up with collections. Things were so bad that she wasn't even able to get good aging reports.

    Martin Mouse runs the collection department in the finance division; he is an up-and-coming star in the company. Rumor has it that he's in line for the vice presidency of finance as soon as the existing VP retires or leaves the company. Furthermore, he's a cousin of the CEO, so no one wants to get on his bad side.

    Under both the present and past system, Barbara's division has a single master budget account used for crediting all the division's incoming cash receipts and charging the division's payments. As a result, the master account should effectively reflect the balance in cash funds available to the division.

    Barbara has been having problems with Martin over the last year. First, he has been asking Mac Plata, the controller, to use his influence to permit Martin to charge Barbara's division 7 percent of it's revenues for the collection services. That fee would have a seriously detrimental effect on Barbara's master account and would hinder her ability to continue to grow. Second, Martin's collection department has not been doing a good job with Barbara's collections, especially in sending out bills on time and dealing with overdue accounts.

The problem with the collection efforts is that Martin periodically shifts his staff's efforts to the dried foods division and doesn't give proper attention to the skin care division. The obvious reason for this is that Betty Riley, the head of the dried foods division, has been with the company since it was founded 15 years ago. She regularly eats lunch with the CEO and knows everyone in the company, so Martin wants to win her favor in the hope of furthering his climb to the finance position.

Barbara is very careful with her division's budgets and her management of its master account. Because her division operates as an investment center, she maintains at least a $1 million balance in the master account at all times as a safety net. She needs this money to be available in case there is a sudden interruption or downturn in sales so that she could continue to operate and pay employees until she could resolve the sales issue.

On the first day of a new month, Barbara reviewed the balance in her master account; it was about $2.3 million. Following her normal practice, she attempted to reconcile this against her internal sales records. She couldn't reconcile the balance against actual cash receipts because Martin's collections department handles and processes all receipts. Furthermore, Barbara had to estimate collected sales because sales collection reports were about three months behind in the system, thanks to the fact that Martin inputs all collection data into spreadsheets and forwards them only sporadically to the accounting department.

Barbara took the beginning balance in the master account, subtracted new expenses (which she knew because she has to submit purchase requisitions and payroll authorization), and then added an estimate of newly collected sales. She had a pretty good idea of what the collected sales should be because when she handled her division's collections, 95 percent of accounts receivables were collected within 30 days of billing.

Barbara checked and rechecked her calculations. The balance in her master account should have been about $1.1 million, not $700,000 as the system reported. That meant that her account was short about $400,000.

Being a little afraid of Martin and mindful of their argument over the collection department's charging for her services, Barbara caught him in the hallway and casually asked him to look into the matter. She didn't immediately blurt out her request but inserted it into a casual conversation regarding an injury accident that had occurred in the warehouse the day before.

Over the following week, Barbara again mentioned the issue on the phone with Martin, but he seemed totally uninterested in helping. Finally, Barbara called him again and told him that if she didn't get an answer in one day, she would have to report the issue to Martin's boss, the VP of finance.

Barbara was absolutely sure that the $400,000 had disappeared. She was afraid that Martin had been embezzling incoming receipts. Furthermore, regardless of what happened to the missing funds, Martin had the responsibility for keeping up with collections and should have been able to explain what happened to the missing funds.

The next morning Barbara received a call from Myrna Wilson, the secretary to Victor Vaccio, the VP of finance. Myrna spoke as if Barbara were in trouble:

"Mr. Vaccio considers this to be a serious problem. He's looking into it."

Barbara was a little shaken because she hadn't even reported the problem yet.

Barbara had friends in various places in the company. One friend, who works in the assistant controller's office, told her that Martin was telling Victor and everyone else that Barbara had overspent her budget in the previous quarter.

Barbara then received an e-mail from the CEO's secretary advising her that her master account was frozen and that Victor must personally approve any expenditures except for continuing payroll. The CEO himself had told Victor to conduct a complete investigation. He wanted a complete audit of all sales and collections beginning with the previous quarter.

Barbara was stunned. The CEO had swallowed Martin's story about Barbara's having overspent her budget in a previous period, hook, line, and sinker. And Martin was doing the audit.

To make things worse, Barbara's sales analysis and reconciliation to her master account made her sure that the money had disappeared in the current quarter, not in the previous one. That meant that the investigation would go nowhere for some time, and in the meantime, her budget would remain frozen, and she would have to live with the embarrassment and disgrace that come with being suspected of irresponsible financial conduct.

Barbara called Martin and offered her help in locating the missing funds, but he refused. "I've been instructed to keep our investigation independent," he said. "Sorry, but this means we can't use any outside help."

a. From a process standpoint, evaluate how well this investigation began to unfold.

b. Should Barbara have done anything differently?

c. What changes, if any, would you recommend be made to the system?

51. Gabriela Pearson is a professionally certified independent forensic accountant. She has more than 20 years of experience investigating fraud and has testified numerous times in both state and federal courts in both civil and criminal cases. She was recently hired by WindSand Hotels, a closely held corporation, to investigate a company purchasing officer who was suspected of taking kickbacks on purchases.

Gabriela gave WindSand her standard engagement letter with the scope of the investigation to be limited to investigating the one suspect. It promised no guaranteed findings or results.

She deal directly with Sam Markoff, the company's controller, and Joanna Rodriguez, the outside attorney. Gabriela was working under attorney-client privilege.

At their first get-to-work meeting, Sam said, "We've had three different tips from our Web site about this. All three were short messages that simply said Tania Perez, our main purchasing agent, was taking kickbacks from our suppliers. One tip even named a particular supplier, the Whole Coast Seafood Supply, a company that supplied fresh and frozen seafood to our restaurants."

Gabriela responded, "Any documentation that supports her involvement in this?"

"Not yet," said Sam. "That's why we hired you. If she's selling us out under the table, it could be costing us a fortune."

Joanna, the outside attorney, jumped into the conversation. "I've already talked to several employees about Tania Perez, and I'm convinced that she's guilty. I heard from one reliable employee that one of your suppliers paid for her vacation on a Caribbean cruise ship. And there are rumors that she had bank accounts in the Cayman Islands and Brazil."

Gabriela thought about the situation. She knew that kickback schemes were difficult to break.

"Don't worry," said Sam. "I've known her since she was a little kid. She'll confess if we confront her and tell her we have the evidence against her."

"What evidence is that?" asked Gabriela.

"All we have to do is bluff," said Sam. "I know her. She'll buckle right away. All she needs to do is believe that a forensic accountant has the goods on her."

"It's against my ethics to lie to suspects," said Gabriela.

"But the police lie all the time to catch suspects, don't they?" asked Sam.

"You'll have to let me run the investigation," said Gabriela.

a. What steps might Gabriela follow to proceed with her investigation?

b. What mistakes, if any, have already been made in the investigation?

Chapter **Nine**

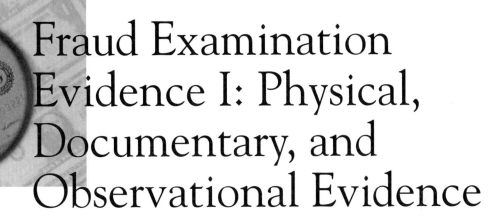

Fraud Examination Evidence I: Physical, Documentary, and Observational Evidence

CHAPTER OBJECTIVES

After reading Chapter 9, you should be able to:

- LO1: Define *evidence* from relative to investigations versus relative to a court of law.
- LO2: Explain the importance of the care, protection, and organization of documents.
- LO3: Describe various sources of evidence that can be used to build a profile of a suspect.
- LO4: Identify sources of information available to the public.
- LO5: Identify sources of information not generally available to the public.
- LO6: Discuss analytical procedures that can be used to locate areas of fraud.
- LO7: Describe audit techniques that can be useful in gathering evidence.
- LO8: Discuss the objectives and limitations of using indirect methods.
- LO9: Discuss the reasons for document analysis and identify various analyses that can be used in examining documents.
- LO10: Describe the methods of obtaining observational evidence and the benefits and disadvantages of such methods.
- LO11: Identify factors that should be considered when choosing the appropriate evidence-gathering technique.

INTRODUCTION

LO1   Chapter 8 defined *Evidence* from the point of view of an investigator: anything that relates to the truth or falsity of an assertion made in an investigation or legal proceeding; it includes physical objects, documents, observations, and interviews. The current chapter focuses on the first three of these types of evidence. Chapter 10 focuses on interview evidence.

     As discussed in Chapter 2, not all evidence will be admitted in a court of law.

For evidence to be useful in court, it must be relevant, reliable, and valid. *Relevant* means that the evidence must have some connection to the fraud hypothesis; in other words, it must be persuasive in either proving or disproving the case (i.e., the fraud theory). *Reliable* refers to the extent to which the source of the evidence is consistently credible. For example, a witness—as a source of evidence—who changes his story is not reliable. *Valid* (and *validity*) refers to the veracity (i.e., truthfulness) of the evidence. If, for example, a document that appears to absolve the fraudster of guilt is shown by opposing counsel to be fraudulent, the evidence does not have validity. Evidence can be valid without being relevant; for example, if the first president of the United States is George Washington and all expert witnesses (historians) testify that he was the first president, the source would no doubt be considered reliable and the fact valid but usually would not be relevant in a fraud case.

Evidence, then, only has meaning as evidence when it is defined in some context. In an investigation, evidence is defined in the context of some assertion relating to some fraud theory posited by the investigator. In an investigation, "evidence" has absolutely no meaning at all unless it relates to some fraud theory. In a court room setting evidence is defined in terms of the courts' rules of evidence, what is admissible in court, trial strategy, and how it is viewed by judges, juries, and attorneys. One significant task of attorneys is to convert an investigator's evidence into court-based evidence in light of a trial strategy. Attorneys may, and commonly do, use evidence in trials that is in addition to evidence developed by the fraud investigator.

Given that evidence only has meaning when defined in some context, unique definitions for various types of evidence are sometimes applied relative to a court of law. Relative to a court of law, *physical evidence* includes documents and other tangible evidence that does not require expert testimony. *Testimonial evidence* is courtroom testimony from witnesses which can include testimony from expert witnesses and the fraud investigator. Courtroom testimony can be based on investigation interviews and additional witnesses not interviewed in the investigation (e.g., the fraud investigator). *Documentary evidence* can include various types of observational evidence recorded in investigations, and tangible evidence collected by investigators that requires explanation in court by an expert witness. *Demonstrative evidence* includes things like charts and graphs that are usually prepared by expert witnesses or attorneys and are more demonstrative in nature. Such charts, graphs, and other aids might include or be in addition to those included in the fraud investigation report. The remainder of the current chapter focuses on evidence as defined within the context of an investigation, but it is important to remember that sometimes attorneys operate in a different context and may define evidence relative to a court of law.

PHYSICAL EVIDENCE

Physical evidence is evidence that is tangible. For example, a person was detained at an airport recently because her luggage contained laminating sleeves, a hair dryer, and a flat iron—all items that are used in creating fake ID cards. These items and the fraudulent checks found in her luggage represent physical evidence. *Physical evidence* refers to a relatively broad category of evidence that includes fingerprints and trace evidence. Except for physical evidence related to documents (e.g., forgeries), the various types of physical evidence are discussed in Chapter 11 as part of forensic science.

One of the most important aspects of physical evidence is that forensic accountants must be aware of the importance of not disturbing it so that it is preserved as evidence for court. Even using gloves might not be adequate: If the accountant touches surfaces on which fingerprint evidence exists, the impression made by the suspect's fingerprints can be degraded to the point that they cannot provide evidence that is as beneficial as it could have been. Engaging an expert in a timely manner can increase the likelihood that this evidence will be preserved.

Often the existence of trace evidence is not apparent to the naked eye. Having a physical evidence expert available in such situations becomes important in preserving, for example, the dioxyribonucleic acid (DNA) of suspects. Because most of us are not physical evidence experts, we recommend that a suitable physical evidence expert be retained when the need arises.

Although physical evidence includes documents because all documents and records have some physical existence even if only inside a computer, we place document evidence in its own category because it is one of the most often used types of evidence in fraud investigations.

DOCUMENTS AND RECORDS

Documents (including records in electronic format) are the most often used type of evidence in forensic accounting investigations. This type of evidence includes not only documents collected as part of the investigation but also those created by the forensic accountant such as charts, graphs, and other exhibits admitted into evidence as part of expert testimony. Documents include files that reside on hard drives, flash drives, and servers. They can take the form of paper (e.g., personnel files contained in a filing cabinet) or Web pages (e.g., Facebook). In short, documents are representations of information about persons, places, or things. Usually, they provide circumstantial—not direct—evidence. In forensic accounting, circumstantial evidence may be the only evidence available.

LO2 Care must be exercised when handling documents. For paper or any perishable documents, the forensic accountant should follow a few basic rules:

1. Obtain original documents if possible (the credibility of a case is enhanced by having original documents).
2. Keep them in a secure location so that access is restricted.
3. Make copies of the original documents; use copies in the investigation, originals in court.
4. Handle originals as few times as possible; they might later be used for fingerprint analysis.
5. Maintain appropriate chain of custody information.

In some cases, copies of original documents are *not* allowed as evidence in court. Copies are allowed when the originals are in the possession of a public official or a person outside the jurisdiction of the court, an adverse person who has not produced the document when asked to do so in writing, or are lost or destroyed by persons other than those seeking to use the document to support a case and when there are too many documents to allow careful analysis (in this case, a summary may be allowed by the court).

If the appropriate chain of custody is not maintained, opposing counsel can allege that the evidence has been altered. In this situation, the custodian of the evidence (usually the person who is introducing the evidence in court) must show that it has been preserved appropriately. Maintaining information on the appropriate chain of custody information can be accomplished by (1) placing certain information on the outside of a transparent, sealed envelope containing the document and (2) keeping a record of this information in a place separate from the evidence itself. In the second example, the information should include a description of the content, each date (and preferably the time of day) the evidence was transferred to and from another party, and the name and contact information of the party to whom (or from whom) the information was transferred.

These documents not only must be gathered and handled with care but also should be organized so that they can be located easily. For example, if a hard-to-contact suspect calls a forensic accountant on the phone, the ease of retrieving documents that are necessary to successfully communicate with the suspect can be critical to the investigation. In a court of law, the quick retrieval of crucial documents can mean the difference between winning and losing a case, especially when the examination (or cross-examination by opposing council) takes an unexpected turn. One method of organizing and tracking documents is by using **Bates numbers.** Use of Bates numbering involves assigning to each page a unique identifier that may be numeric, alpha, or alphanumeric (a combination of letters and numbers). No standard method exists for identifying documents. For example, the identifying number of the 10,031rd document of 12,000 documents used in a case assigned to the Miami office of Forensic Consultants, Inc., could be coded Miami 10031.

Documentary evidence is usually obtained in any one of four ways: (1) searching public records, including commercial Web sites and the trash of those thought to be in possession of evidence, (2) obtaining consent from those who have custody of the evidence to release evidence, (3) obtaining subpoenas, and (4) obtaining search warrants. All of these methods are discussed later. Although interested parties other than victims can voluntarily come forward and offer evidence, evidence is usually not collected in this manner.

SOURCES OF DOCUMENTARY EVIDENCE

Numerous sources can be helpful in building a profile of a suspect and establishing a case to support the allegation of fraud. These documents are beneficial particularly in determining motive: the result of pressure or one of the legs of the fraud triangle. Several of these sources (e.g., social networking sites) are easily accessed and provide helpful information that the suspect himself divulges. Although some sources are available to the general public, others are restricted to persons or entities such as local, state, or federal employees. Access to some sources, such as information contained in state databases, can depend on state law. In this section, we explore various sources of documentary evidence and the use of each.

Personnel Files

LO3 These documents can be examined when an employee is suspected of committing fraud against her employer. For example, information in a personnel file can be helpful in determining a suspect's motive. A pattern of increasing grievances filed by the suspect can indicate discontent with either his work environment or general dissatisfaction in his personal life; in either situation, the pattern can be a clue to less visible forms of retribution (e.g., embezzlement). Increasing the number of exemptions on Form W-4 can indicate increasing responsibilities and thus an increasing need for funds.

Résumes

Another source of information in a suspect's personnel file is her résumé. Keep in mind, however, that a suspect might not list incriminating information on the résumé. For example, Albert Dunlap, commonly known as "Chainsaw Al" did not list his employment at Nitec, Inc., when he applied for the position as chief executive officer at Sunbeam. According to one source, he was fired from his position at Nitec after his use of questionable accounting practices was discovered. Despite this limitation, résumes can be a good starting point in gathering information about a suspect. By matching information obtained from a postemployment background check against the suspect's résumé, the forensic accountant can build a better profile of the suspect than that readily available in his résumé. Similarly, applications for positions can provide information about former employers, for example, and can lead to other sources (e.g., former co-workers who can provide details that are missing from suspect-created documents).

Current Co-Workers

Current co-workers, too, can be of help. A forensic accountant can begin collecting this type of evidence by questioning co-workers. If the investigation is not public, the forensic accountant does not usually begin by asking about the suspect. For example, an initial question can be about the general friendliness of her co-workers. If, however, information about the suspect is not forthcoming, the accountant can ask about the individuals in the group of co-workers that includes the suspect and listen for any clues—for example, shifts in her behavior.

Friends and Acquaintances

Investigators can also ask friends and acquaintances about the suspect by using any one of a number of pretexts (e.g., the suspect is being considered for an award at work or a forensic accountant who poses as an employee of a consulting firm charged with the responsibility of increasing employee recognition wants to ask a few questions). One of the questions could be, for example, whether the friend believes the suspect has honestly told the friend how he feels about his workplace conditions and his employer.

Postemployment Background Checks

Checking an employee's background while employed can be helpful, for example, in determining whether the suspect has had brushes with the law. For example, Andrew Taber has been employed by Pinetop, Inc., for the last three years. Two months ago, a judge gave him a suspended sentence for possession of controlled substances. His employer was unaware of this incident because Andrew's family posted bail when he was arrested and because this was the first time he had been arrested, the judge did not sentence him to jail. The day Andrew appeared in court, he called in sick so his employer would not suspect anything. He continued using the drugs illegally and, despite random drug testing, had not been caught. He embezzled from Pinetop to fund his habit. A background check would have revealed the suspended sentence and provided the employer with a motive for the embezzlement.

Sites Other Than the Suspect's Home State

In some cases, the suspect could be committing crimes in another state. This can occur, for example, when she lives near the state border. Therefore, limiting the search to the state in which the suspect lives might not be an effective way to gather evidence.

Social Networking Sites

Social networking sites such as Facebook and MySpace can be sources of evidence. These sites can be very beneficial in providing evidence for court cases that involve divorce, custody battles, and insurance fraud. The physical separation from others can cause people to disclose information they would not divulge in person.

Records Available to the Public

LO4 An excellent place to begin a search for evidence is in public records because of their availability. Real estate records, court records, assumed name indexes, Uniform Commercial Code filings, and other records can be of immense help in locating owners of assets and establishing connections between persons or business entities.

Real Estate Records

Documents such as title certificates and deeds of ownership are usually maintained in the county in which the related real estate exists. These records are beneficial because they identify current and past owners of property and, in some states, include the consideration paid for property. In addition, the tax assessor's office maintains records of the persons who pay property taxes on real estate within the county.

Court Records

Transcripts of hearings and judicial decisions of criminal and civil lawsuits are available in court records. They are maintained by the clerk of courts. Examples of these documents are divorce decrees, bankruptcy petitions, and property settlements. To efficiently locate these documents, the forensic accountant must know whether the legal action was taken in local, state, or federal court.

Assumed Name Indexes

Sometimes referred to as *fictitious names indexes,* assumed name indexes are helpful in identifying the owners of entities, especially businesses. Businesses that operate under a name that differs from the name that appears in the incorporation documents are required to register the assumed name in the city, county, or state in which the business was organized. Often business owners operate a business under an assumed name to indicate a specialty or as a means of capturing the public's attention (wouldn't you pay more attention to Superfast Cleaning! than you would Arthur Brown's Cleaning Company?). The purpose of the law requiring the registration is to protect the general public by making owners' identities available so that the public can use this information to determine the reputation of the business owners.

Uniform Commercial Code (UCC) Filings

When an investigator is trying to determine whether mortgages on items other than real estate exist, Uniform Commercial Code (UCC) filings can be helpful. Individuals and businesses use these types of mortgages—called *chattel mortgages*—to purchase assets such as equipment, furnishings, and automobiles. UCC filings are made at the county or state level.

Motor Vehicle Identification Number (VIN)

Information such as the current state of a motor vehicle title, the title issue date, and the previous state of the motor vehicle the title can be obtained by searching for the VIN at the National Motor Vehicle Title Information System sponsored by the Department of Justice.

Commercial Databases

Investigators may find commercial databases helpful in establishing a suspect's profile and history and providing leads to locating others who are related to the suspect so that they can be questioned. For example, sites such as Intelius provide information including ages, birth dates, address history, phone numbers, household members, home values, and income. Another example is IntegraScan, which advertises its capability to do a complete scan of official records that can disclose felonies, misdemeanors, and federal charges; sex offenders; arrest records; warrants; wanted people; civil records including bankruptcies, tax liens, lawsuits, and judgments; alias names; 25-year address data; and other information.

Other types of public records can be beneficial to the investigator. Various types of filings—voter registrations, change of name filings, business operating licenses, and fishing and hunting licenses—are almost always made with the county recorder. Other public records include birth and death certificates and marriage licenses, which are maintained by the county clerk.

Restricted Records

LO5 The following records may be restricted to limited groups of persons such as federal and state employees and law enforcement personnel. The records include databases on which drivers' licenses and boat and aircraft licenses are recorded.

Motor Vehicle Records

Information on motor vehicle transactions can be an excellent source of information for the investigator. Using a database available through the office of secretary of state, the VIN can be used to identify registered owners of vehicles (be aware that these persons may not be the true owner of the vehicles). The database also can be searched using the names of persons to determine whether they own vehicles and, if so, the type of vehicles owned. If the vehicle was financed, the financier's name is also shown in the records. Access to these records through the secretary of state's offices is often restricted to federal, state, or local government agencies (including law enforcement); a business or its agents, employees, or contractors during the normal course of business; an insurer or self-insured entity in connection with an investigation of claims, antifraud activities, or underwriting. These records may also be restricted for use as part of a civil, criminal, administrative, or arbitration proceeding in any court, government agency, or self-regulatory body; by a licensed private investigator or security service for purposes authorized by law; or by an individual to obtain his own motor vehicle or vessel record.

Dealership Vehicle Records

The vehicle records that dealerships keep can also provide excellent information on the activities of persons. Examples include sales contracts, loan documents (if purchaser's acquisition was financed through credit providers available to the dealer, such as General Motors Acceptance Corporation), copies of receipts given to the customer, copies of checks submitted by the customer, documents used to determine appraisals of vehicles traded for vehicles purchased from the dealership, and service request forms detailing subsequent service performed on the vehicles. Information useful to the investigator includes type of vehicle purchased (e.g., luxury or economy) and whether the customer made a substantial down payment for it and, if so, whether it was made with cash, check, or credit card. If payment was by credit card, the type of card used (e.g., Visa or MasterCard) and, if possible, the card number (or last five digits) and the authorization date can be particularly helpful in connecting a person and purchase.

Financial Crimes Enforcement Network

Reports regarding currency transactions and suspicious activities must be filed with the federal government. The Financial Crimes Enforcement Network (FinCEN) is charged with assessing penalties for failure to file a correct and complete form on time (or filing false forms). These reports are required so that the government can be aware of certain types of behavior that may be associated with illegal activities. Examples of these reports will be discussed here. The reports are accessible electronically to every U.S. Attorney's office and to law enforcement agencies such as the FBI and Secret Service. No court order, warrant, subpoena, or even written request is needed for these agencies to obtain these reports.

Currency Transaction Reports

Financial institutions are required to file currency transaction reports (FinCEN Form 104) when a customer deposits more than $10,000 in currency. The form identifies the customer by name, address, date of birth, social security number, and the identity of any person who conducts the transaction on behalf of the owner of the currency. The definition of *financial institution* includes not only banks but also brokers or dealers in securities, currency exchangers, check cashiers, issuers of money orders and traveler's checks, auto dealers, and real estate businesses. Financial institutions are allowed to exempt certain high-volume cash businesses that routinely receive currency in amounts of more than $10,000. However, these financial institutions must maintain a list of these businesses.

Report of International Transportation of Currency or Monetary Instruments

Any person who physically transports, mails, or ships currency or monetary instruments of more than $10,000 into or out of the United States or any person who receives payments from a source outside the United States must file a Report of International Transportation of Currency or Monetary Instruments (FinCEN Form 105).

Report of Cash Payments over $10,000 Received in a Trade or Business

Businesses that receive more than $10,000 in one transaction or in a series of related transactions must file a report of cash payments of more than $10,000 (FinCEN and Internal Revenue Service [IRS] Form 8300). For example, if a car dealer received $9,000 today from a customer and $8,000 the next week for the purchase of a car, the transactions are related, and the dealer must file Form 8300 within 15 days of receiving the $8,000.

This report and others can be used to link the movement of money to those who control the funds.

Tax Returns

Investigators can find information on a perpetrator's sources of income, which could lead to information on hidden assets. For example, deductions for home mortgage interest or a safe deposit box on Schedule A of an income tax return can indicate assets that were purchased by funds fraudulently obtained. Generally, the IRS, federal agencies that obtain these records by subpoena, the tax preparer, and the taxpayer have access to these returns. A forensic accountant who desires this data but is not a member of at least one of these four groups must obtain copies of the returns through the discovery process or by obtaining the voluntary consent of the taxpayer. Be aware that the tax return provided by the taxpayer might not have the same information that the tax return filed with the IRS contained. In addition, the information on the tax return that differs from information provided to banks in anticipation of obtaining a loan can be an indication of intent to defraud. Sales tax returns can provide information about the gross sales of an entity; when coupled with the use of industry ratios, this information can provide an approximation of the net earnings of the business.

Social Security Death Index (SSDI)

The Social Security Administration (SSA) maintains an index of social security numbers of persons who have been reported as deceased if their death occurred after 1962. In addition to being available from the United States Department of Commerce's National Technical Information Service (NTIS) by means of a subscription, access is also available through several genealogy Web sites. The database is not infallible: One government audit revealed that the SSA had incorrectly listed approximately 23,000 people as dead within a two-year period.

Other Restricted Records

County governments usually maintain bankruptcy filings, divorce filings, marriage certificates, and death certificates. All of these can be helpful in determining motives for crimes. For example, bankruptcy filings would indicate financial need, a common motivating factor in the commission of crimes.

The use of certain methods of evidence production is limited to those who work for governmental agencies such as the FBI; the Bureau of Alcohol, Tobacco, Firearms, and Explosives (ATF); sheriff's offices; and local police. These techniques include subpoenas and search warrants.

Methods for Obtaining Restricted Records

Use of the Subpoena

Subpoena duces tecum—often simply called a **subpoena**—is a written order typically issued by an officer of a court and is used to compel the production and delivery of documents, records, or other information Another type of subpoena, called the subpoena ad testificandum, can be used to order a person to testify. A subpoena can also be used to compel a witness to submit to a **deposition,** a record of a person's answers posed by opposing counsel. At times a "forthwith subpoena" is served when the court believes that documents and records will be destroyed or altered if they are not obtained quickly. Subpoenas are typically issued by a court or by an attorney acting as an officer of a court.

Use of the Search Warrant

Search warrants are often necessary because a person who perpetrated fraud may have consciously hidden information and other evidence sought by forensic accountants. A search warrant is a written order that allows a specified place (including a geographical location, vehicle, or person) to be searched and specified items to be seized. It is issued by a judge (or magistrate in certain jurisdictions) who is briefed on evidence that suggests a crime was committed or will be committed.

A search warrant is issued only if probable cause exists, which a judge determines according to the facts and circumstances the investigator presents. The evidence of probable cause is time sensitive; that is, the evidence indicating that the crime the investigator suspects was committed (or is about to be committed) must be recent. Furthermore, the evidence must be reliable (i.e., trustworthy) and reasonable. In other words, the evidence must be sufficient to persuade an impartial judge to issue a warrant.

Some jurisdictions may place restrictions relating to the manner and timing of search warrants. For example, some jurisdictions may require that search warrants be served between 6:00 A.M. and 10:00 P.M. After the search warrant has been served, a detailed inventory of the items seized must be recorded. A copy of this listing and the search warrant must be left at the place searched (or given to the person searched). The original warrant and a list of the inventory are given to the judge who authorized the search warrant, and the court holds the inventory until the case is closed.

To obtain a search warrant, a law officer (including authorized IRS personnel) must prepare an affidavit and present it to a judge. The purpose of the affidavit is to show probable cause. If the judge, after reviewing the affidavit, believes probable cause exists, the law officer must swear that the affidavit was prepared truthfully. After the oath of the officer has been witnessed, the judge will issue the search warrant.

The affidavit includes three parts: a summary of the credentials of the investigator (the "affiant"), a summary of the evidence that suggests that probable cause exists, and a detailed list of the persons and places to be searched as well as the evidence that the officers expect to seize. A search warrant for financial records (including tax returns) must also include the investigator's conclusions, which need not be about the guilt of any party; they are merely reasonable assumptions as to why the warrant for financial records is requested. For example, if a person who owns a bar is suspected of income tax evasion, the investigator may request financial records that include the personal records of the owner to establish the activity of skimming income (see later discussion); this investigator would provide a written conclusion that the personal lifestyle of the owner indicates that she may have underreported taxable income.

The type of search warrant in which forensic accountants are most interested is called a **search warrant for financial records;** it empowers law enforcement personnel to search for books and records believed to be involved in financial frauds.

The documentary evidence discussed here is often one of the most valuable tools to the forensic accountant and, coupled with information gathered through interviews, usually leads to the successful resolution of a case by linking suspects with assets fraudulently acquired or other criminal actions. In the next section, we discuss another type of linking mechanism that can be used to establish associations among individuals so that evidence can be obtained to support a forensic case.

Link Analysis

Link analysis is a process that allows information in various databases and files to be evaluated and integrated in such a way that associations become apparent. This process is accomplished by using software programs that are commercially available. For example, associations that exist between owners of property can be uncovered so that assets can be traced or persons of interest can be interviewed. Items of information that can be used to connect persons or entities include VINs, vehicle licenses plates, and telephone numbers. Even financial transactions can be linked to show relationships among persons and entities.

Typically, the program constructs an association matrix after the data have been analyzed. This matrix is a visual map of the potential associations that exist. After the forensic accountant creates the matrix, he must then gather evidence to support the suspicious associations. Thus, link analysis can be thought of as a sophisticated type of analytical procedure (recall that forensic accountants use analytical procedures to focus their attention on areas, accounts, and transactions that require more investigation).

Example An analysis of telephone records indicates that calls were made between the following telephone numbers (the number of times each telephone number was called is shown in bold).

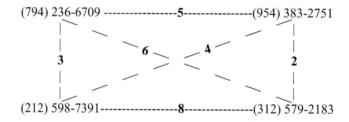

This type of analysis is possible because telephone records provided a trail that could be followed. In the next section, we discuss another type of linking process: the audit trail.

ANALYTICAL PROCEDURES AND AUDIT TECHNIQUES

When a suspected fraud is either, for example, an embezzlement or the misstatement of financial statements, the forensic accountant can use certain techniques to gather evidence that can lead to the determination of who, what, when, and why regarding the fraud. Note that the discussion in this chapter is confined to situations in which fraud is suspected; methods to prevent and detect fraud are discussed in other chapters. At times, one method (e.g., analytical procedures) can be used as a detection tool and later as an investigation tool of frauds already suspected.

Analytical Procedures

LO6 In determining the areas of financial statements that are most likely to have been affected by fraud, **analytical procedures** can be particularly useful. Keep in mind that analytical procedures do not confirm that fraud exists; rather, they provide evidence of areas that are likely to contain fraud. See Table 9.1 for five common types of analytical procedures.

TABLE 9.1
Five Common Types of Analytical Procedures

- Comparison of financial data with prior period financial data
- Comparison of financial data with industry data
- Comparison of expected financial results with nonfinancial data
- Comparison of financial data with results expected by the entity itself
- Comparison of data with results expected by the forensic accountant (e.g., expected decline due to downturn in economy)

These comparisons are often made by using ratio analysis to determine whether over-statements or understatements of revenue (and assets) and expenses (and liabilities) appear to exist. Some common types of ratios that are used to perform analytical procedures are presented in the appendix to this chapter.

Comparison of Financial Data with Prior Period Financial Data

Comparing current financial data with prior period financial data can provide evidence of possible fraud and can be used to locate areas in financial statements affected by fraud. However, an area in the financial statements can appear consistent with prior year results yet not be accurate. For example, Waste Management was alleged to have capitalized certain expenditures that should have been expensed; this act of departing from generally accepted accounting principles was used to make net income appear higher than it would have had the capitalization not occurred. The asset accounts into which the expenditures were placed did not appear excessively. Waste Management had not made as many capital expenditures as it normally had in previous years; thus, by increasing the capital accounts that otherwise would have decreased, the capital accounts appeared to be reasonable.

Ratio Analysis and Historical Financial Data

Ratio analysis and historical financial data are often used in fraud investigations. Two common approaches are horizontal and vertical analysis. **Horizontal analysis** is a side-by-side comparison of financial statements or data. **Vertical analysis** is an analysis of relationships within a particular financial statement. See Table 9.2 for examples of these two approaches for Analytics, Incorporated.

As data in Table 9.2 indicate, the gross margin percentage increased by 87.5 percent. A forensic accountant could investigate this increase and determine whether it was due to company changes such as the production of a new product that has a higher gross margin than existing products or to fraud such as the inclusion of fictitious sales in the revenue account. Another area that may require the accountant's attention is the account Other Expenses because it increased by 63.64 percent. The advantage of using percentages is that identifying anomalies in the data is much easier than using the raw data (in dollars).

Benford analysis is another technique that forensic accountants can use to determine the likelihood that fraud exists in the historical records and is based on the relative likelihood that lower digits (e.g., 1 and 2) are more likely to appear as the first digit in a number in data that are naturally occurring than are higher digits (e.g., 8 and 9). This method is usually used as a detection method; therefore, it is discussed more thoroughly in Chapter 6.

Comparison of Financial Data with Industry Data

Comparing client information, such as percentages, to industry data can aid the detection of fraud as well as the estimation of the amount of fraud loss experienced by the victim.

Example Carl Anderson, a forensic accountant, has been engaged to estimate the loss experienced by Topaz Co., a small start-up company that has been in business for two years. Topaz already has evidence that inventory has been taken fraudulently but needs an

TABLE 9.2
Horizontal and
Vertical Analysis of
Analytics, Inc.

Horizontal Analysis				
Statement Item	**2008**	**2007**	**Change**	**Change in Percentage**
Net sales	$100,000	$80,000	$20,000	25.00%
Cost of goods sold	70,000	64,000	6,000	9.38
Gross margin	30,000	16,000	14,000	87.50
Selling expenses	5,000	4,000	1,000	25.00
Other expenses	18,000	11,000	7,000	63.64
Pretax income	7,000	1,000	6,000	600.00
Income tax expense	2,100	300	1,800	600.00
Net income	4,900	700	4,200	600.00
Vertical Analysis				
	2008		**2007**	
Net sales	$100,000	100.00%	$80,000	100.00%
Cost of goods sold	70,000	70.00	64,000	80.00
Gross margin	30,000	30.00	16,000	20.00
Selling expenses	5,000	5.00	4,000	5.00
Other expenses	18,000	18.00	11,000	13.75
Pretax income	7,000	7.00	1,000	1.25
Income tax expense	2,100	2.10	300	0.38
Net income	4,900	4.90	700	0.88

estimate of the loss. Due to poor internal controls, the perpetrator has destroyed the company's disbursement records. In addition, the difficulty of estimating the loss is compounded by the fact that some of the inventory purchases were made in cash because the firm lacked a good credit rating. Because cash sales were only a small amount of Topaz's total sales and most sales were by credit card, Carl has determined that he will estimate the inventory loss by using sales. Because he has limited cost information to guide him, he obtains the industry gross profit percentage and uses it to determine an estimate of the proper amount of ending inventory. He compares this estimate to a physical inventory taken and considers the difference to be an estimate of the loss.

Comparison of Expected Financial Results with Nonfinancial Data

An example of nonfinancial data includes the number of units produced or purchased. This comparison is a reasonableness test that can be used, for example, to accept or reject an insurance claim for loss of inventory.

Example Assume that Jersey Joe, Inc., submitted an insurance loss claim on which it asserted that it had lost a warehouse full of inventory when a fire occurred. A deposition of the warehouse foreperson revealed that the inventory was always stored on pallets (3″ high) and that the inventory on each pallet (including the height of the pallet) was never more than 6′ 3″ high. The only product that Jersey Joe sold came packaged in 2′ by 2′ by 2′ boxes. The pallets were 4′ wide by 4′ long; the warehouse had an interior storage space of 300′ by 500′. Jersey Joe claimed that 470,000 boxes of product were stored in the warehouse when the warehouse was destroyed by fire. This amount is not reasonable, however. By using the information provided by the warehouse foreperson, there could not be more than 112,500 boxes in the warehouse [(300′ × 500′)/(4′ × 4′)] × 12 boxes per pallet = 112,500].

Comparison of Financial Data with Results Expected by the Entity Itself

Successful use of this method of comparison to generate evidence is based on the presumption that the results expected by the entity (e.g., budgets) are attainable; if they are not (i.e., they are unrealistic), this method of evaluating records will not be as useful (although relative differences between expected and actual can still be identified by comparing the differences). If previously published budgets indicate results that are significantly not consistent with the actual results in a particular area, this evidence could suggest that fraud had occurred in this area. This method can also be used to provide evidence of fraud on behalf of the entity: If, for example, cash collections are much higher than the amount forecasted, another source of revenue (e.g., illegal) might account for the difference; another potential explanation of this difference is the activity of money laundering.

Comparison of Data with Results Expected by the Forensic Accountant

If, for example, a business being investigated by the forensic accountant is doing very well while similar businesses are not (e.g., due to a downturn in the economy), the business being investigated could be involved in illegal activities (e.g., drug dealing). Assume, for example, that a video store has 3,000 unique movie titles to rent and video stores of that size and locale rent an average of 850 movies each day at $5 per movie. Assume further that miscellaneous sales (e.g., soft drinks, candy) amount to $10,000 annually. If the store is open 360 days a year, the expected revenue is $1,540,000 ([850 × $5 × 360] + $10,000 = $1,540,000). If the amount reported by the store is $3,200,000, the difference could be due to drug money that is laundered through the store.

Tracing versus Vouching

LO7 Simply put, an *audit trail* is a connection of one item of information to one or more other items of information. When, for example, the suspected fraud is believed to affect a company's financial records, forensic accountants can begin with the financial statements and follow the information contained in the statements through the ledgers to their source documents (e.g., invoices, receiving reports). This process is called **vouching.** On the other hand, the accountant can begin with the source documents and trace the information through the ledgers to the financial statements (**tracing**). Each of these "directions" has a purpose: vouching is associated with determining the *overstatement* of assets, liabilities, revenues, expenses, gains, and losses. Tracing, on the other hand, is associated with determining the *understatement* of these items.

Example Assume that a company suspects inventory fraud. The informant has divulged that the missing inventory was received at the dock by the suspect and immediately placed in his truck. Thus, the company no longer holds the inventory listed on the balance sheet (i.e., an overstatement). Assume that each item of inventory has a unique identifying number and that the company uses the specific identification method to value inventory. The first step would be to compare the items (by unique number) in the ledger (the basis of the balance sheet) to a physical inventory (listed by unique number). The receiving reports for each item of missing inventory should be examined to obtain documentary evidence as to who received the inventory and perhaps the identity of the suspect.

There have been numerous instances of "top-side" journal entries (journal entries made by employees who have more authority than those who usually make these entries) made by companies at or near the end of the accounting period to increase net income and the balances of assets. Often these entries are for large, round dollar amounts (a red flag). In some cases, no supporting documents were created to substantiate these entries; therefore, the astute forensic accountant should not assume that a company would not make an entry unless supporting documents exist; crooks don't play by the "rules." A good forensic accountant must think like a crook (without, of course, acting like one).

Example Assume that Cathy Martinez, a forensic accountant, is investigating suspected **financial statement fraud.** Although she knows, based on a few factors including an anonymous tip, that the statements are fraudulent, she is unsure of the area (or areas) that are affected. She first determines whether the financial statements agree with the general ledger balances and then determines whether the general ledger accounts agree with subledger accounts. For example, does the total in the accounts receivable subledger equal the general ledger accounts receivable account balance? The third step would be to investigate the details of the accounts themselves. For example, if the financial statements are those of retailers and wholesalers, do shipping documents exist for each sales transaction and did these shipping documents generate sales invoices that, in turn, support recorded sales?

Financial statement fraud, however, is not always discovered from missing documents. At times, fictitious documents can be used to cover up fraud. For example, an accounts payable clerk may create false vendor invoices to bill his employer (a theft of cash) for merchandise never received, a fraud that can lead to the overstatement of cost of goods sold. Often the vendors' names and addresses shown on fictitious invoices are similar to those of legitimate vendors so that the transactions represented by fictitious invoices are not likely to be noticed and thus flagged by forensic accountants when they conduct their examination. There are various methods—none infallible—to increase the likelihood of detecting a scheme involving fictitious documents. One of these is searching for addresses of vendors that are post office boxes or that match employee addresses.

Surprise Counts

Surprise counts are unexpected counts of inventory or other assets. The results of these counts, when compared to the entity's records, can provide evidence of an unexplained difference. This method can especially be helpful when investigating suspected inventory fraud. The difference can be examined by preparing an analysis of the purchases, sales, and sales returns that have occurred in the last month or two (depending on the rate of turnover of the items believed to have been stolen). If, for example, inventory that is missing is not recorded as sold and no sales invoice or shipping document can be located for it, the inventory is likely to have been stolen. If the records to which the surprise counts are being compared are maintained by those suspected of the theft or by persons who could be sympathetic to those suspected (e.g., close friends or relatives), other methods of investigation (e.g., surveillance) should also be used. The usefulness of surprise counts depends, then, on the strength of the internal controls, especially separation of duties and whether the records are accurate.

Statistical Sampling

Forensic accountants can use **statistical sampling** to either (1) detect fraud or (2) estimate the loss from fraud when an estimate will suffice. The sampling process does not examine every item in an account balance or class of transactions. Instead, it examines a portion of the population so that conclusions about it can be made. Forensic accountants who use statistical sampling do so often because the client does not have a sophisticated system whereby all documents are digitized and thus can be analyzed by using a computer.

When forensic accountants wish to detect fraud, the use of sampling allows them to make a reasonable decision as to whether the population contains indications of fraud. The obvious problem with using sampling to detect fraud is that fraud is usually not evenly distributed throughout the population (if it were, a random selection of population items would, most likely, contain some—and, it is hoped, a representative portion—of the fraud).

To sample, an auditor can use statistical or judgmental sampling (which is not addressed here; see Chapter 4 for a discussion of this method). Statistical sampling is preferred because it allows the auditor to obtain an estimate of sampling risk (the likelihood that the accountant's judgment based on a portion of the population differs from the judgment based on an examination of the entire population). Sampling involves determining an adequate sample size for the population that will be tested. This is done by using a computer program or tables. After the sample size has been selected, the auditor randomly selects (by means of the computer program or table) the individual items from the population (if random selection is not used, interpretation of the results is difficult if not impossible).

The most common *detection* sampling technique used by forensic accountants is known as *discovery sampling.* After the accountant has selected items to be included in the sample, she will begin to examine them for fraud. If one item contains fraud, she usually stops the sampling process and examines the complete population.

If, however, the forensic accountant already knows that fraud exists in the population, the parties involved (e.g., those involved in arbitration including the perpetrator and victim) may decide to accept an estimate of loss so that the costs of investigation can be minimized. The forensic accountant, then, can use sampling as a means of determining an *estimation* of the loss. This estimate is determined by using the fraud found in the sample to project (i.e., estimate) the loss from fraud that exists in the population.

Example   In one case, a medical fraud investigator examined a random sample of 230 claims from the total population of suspected health care fraudulent claims. He determined that all but 14 of the claims were fraudulent. A statistician testified that the extrapolation (i.e., the court's term for *projection*) of these findings to the total number of claims produced a loss of $6,330,298 at a 90 percent confidence level. Upon appeal of the suspect's conviction for fraud, the appellate court noted that extrapolation is an acceptable method to use when making a reasonable estimate of the amount of loss under sentencing guidelines.

Reconciliations

Reconciliations are performed to explain differences between two or more accounts, items, or counts of assets. For example, a search by a forensic accountant reveals $351,000 of liabilities, yet the general ledger and the balance sheet show only $150,000 of liabilities. An analysis reveals that $10,000 of liabilities was credited to Additional Paid-in Capital and the rest of the difference ($191,000) was credited to Sales. As a result of reconciling the accounts, correcting entries can be made to reduce Additional Paid-in Capital and Sales. An investigation could help determine whether the incorrect accounting was accidental or purposeful (i.e., fraudulent).

A common type of reconciliation is the bank reconciliation (a reconciliation between the account balance shown on the books and the balance shown on the bank statement). It can provide evidence of embezzlement. If, for example, a perpetrator is writing checks to herself, she can remove the checks from the bank statement or, if the checks are not returned with the statement, can alter the payee on copies provided by the bank. Another way to hide this type of embezzlement is to indicate that the check written to the employee is "void." If, however, the check listed as "void" in the accounting records actually cleared the bank, a reconciliation performed by an independent individual such as a forensic accountant would identify a potential problem. If the fraudster had simply changed the payee on the check and debited the check to an account into which payments to the altered payee would normally be found, the embezzlement would be more difficult to discover. Forensic accountants should always ask that the victim request a duplicate bank statement from the bank because embezzlers might have altered the original one so that the amount on the bank statement corresponds to the bank reconciliation and the accounting records. Because theft of cash by employees is a common type of embezzlement, bank reconciliations should always be performed.

Confirmations

Confirmations are used when third parties (persons other than the client) know some aspect of a financial or nonfinancial matter and can be asked to provide this information. Confirmations are used to obtain information about assets and liabilities such as accounts receivable, notes receivable, investments, bank accounts, consigned inventory, and accounts payable. A confirmation is simply a letter in which the client asks that the third party confirm the balance of an account or the existence of an asset or liability with the investigator. There are three types of confirmations: positive "in-blank", positive with the information written on the form, and the negative confirmation. Each of these types is discussed below.

Before sending confirmation letters, the forensic accountant should, at a minimum, check the work of the person who prepared them; otherwise, that person might engineer the results. This rule increases the reliability and validity of the evidence provided by the confirmations.

Example   Assume that the forensic accountant wishes to confirm the existence of liabilities of Northbrook Inc. because the company had received an anonymous tip that an employee had obtained a loan in Northbrook's name. If the employee suspected of obtaining the loan is allowed to prepare and mail the confirmation letters, he has the opportunity to falsely "respond" to the confirmation that was to be sent to the bank at which the employee fraudulently obtained the loan. Thus, the forensic accountant could receive a confirmation letter—supposedly from the bank—that indicates that the loans to Northbrook agreed with the amount shown as the loans in the general ledger.

Of the three types of confirmations, the positive "in-blank" confirmation provides the best evidence because it does not contain the amount the recipient (the person or entity responding to the confirmation) is to confirm. As a result, the recipient must consult her records to determine the amount to report on the form. Another type of confirmation (termed "positive with information written on the form") has the amount to be confirmed written in the letter and the recipient is to respond by indicating whether the amount is correct or incorrect. The third type provides the least amount of evidence; called the "negative" confirmation, it also has the amount written on the form but the recipient is to respond only if the amount is incorrect. Thus, the forensic accountant who does not receive a response from the recipient is to assume that the client's records are correct.

One drawback to using confirmations is that the number of them returned (especially the two types of positive confirmations) can be low. If this occurs, the forensic accountant should follow up with alternative procedures (e.g., inspection of documents). Note, however, that because the source documents are in the client's possession, they could have been altered by perpetrators and thus are not usually believed to be as reliable as confirmation requests. On the other hand, even if responses to confirmations are received, they might not be valid. At times, confirmations that were alleged to have been deliberately misleading have been returned to auditors of financial statements indicating no exceptions (i.e., that nothing is wrong). Forensic accountants should consider the extent to which the source is independent (i.e., reliable). Confirmations that are returned quickly and those that appear to have certain anomalies (discussed in the following section on questioned documents) should increase the forensic accountant's professional skepticism.

Indirect Sources of Evidence

LO8   Indirect methods are useful when a perpetrator is believed to have substantial amounts of unexplained income. There are several types of indirect methods, such as net worth method, the expenditures method, and the bank deposit method. These methods provide circumstantial evidence that a suspect acquired assets from unknown sources. The net worth method is illustrated next. Other methods, such as the expenditures method, the bank deposit method, the markup method, and the unit and volume method, are discussed and illustrated in Chapter 16 on tax fraud.

The **net worth method** is a process that compares the current net worth of the suspect to his net worth at the end of the prior year to arrive at a change in net worth for the year. Recall the basic accounting equation: Assets = Liabilities + Owners' Equity. The term *owners' equity* is sometimes called *net worth.* By substituting Net Worth for Owners' Equity and solving the accounting equation for Net Worth, we have:

$$\text{Net Worth} = \text{Assets} - \text{Liabilities}$$

By recognizing that Assets − Liabilities is considered Net Assets, we obtain:

$$\text{Net Worth} = \text{Net Assets}$$

Recall that we are trying to determine the *change* in net worth for the year. We can do this by comparing the net assets of an individual (or corporation) as of the end of the prior year to the net assets of the same individual (or corporation) at the end of the current year.

The net worth method can be represented by the following computation:

	Assets at end of year
−	Liabilities at end of year
	Net worth (net assets) of year being investigated
−	Prior year net worth (net assets)
=	Increase in net worth
+	Identified expenses*
=	Total net worth increase
−	Funds from known sources†
=	Funds from unknown sources

*These are expenses that did not increase assets or decrease liabilities. They were used to pay for things such as personal expenses. Only documented expenses should be used, and suspects should be given the benefit of the doubt when this item is estimated.

†These items include wages, interest, and other items that are known at the time of the net worth calculation.

Keep two things in mind: (1) the change in net worth can be provided only by income, liabilities, or such items as inheritances (this is why you will hear some perpetrators say that their sudden increase in wealth is due to an inheritance) and (2) the beginning balances of assets and liabilities must be established with care; otherwise, a suspect might assert that a smaller amount of "funds from unknown sources" exists than the amount computed because the prior year net worth amount was inadvertently understated.

Example Sam Thug's assets and liabilities today are $300,000 and $100,000, respectively. His assets and liabilities one year ago were $150,000 and $30,000, respectively. Sam's change in net worth is $80,000 [($300,000 − $100,000) − ($150,000 − $30,000) = $80,000]. However, Sam contends that the $150,000 of assets pertaining to the prior year is understated and that the correct amount is $230,000. If Sam is correct, his change in net worth is zero [($300,000 − $100,000) − ($230,000 − $30,000) = $0]. Can you think of a reason (or reasons) Sam might give to explain the large discrepancy between the $230,000 and $150,000?

If the change in net worth is significantly higher than the income for the year (i.e., the "funds from unknown sources" is a positive and significant amount), additional evidence must be gathered to determine the source of the additional, unexplained, increase in net worth.

Net worth method begins with a financial profile of the suspected perpetrator and is performed for the year prior to the year in which the perpetrator is suspected of acquiring assets fraudulently. The correct computation of beginning net worth is crucial to the performance of the net worth method. If the financial profile is not correctly determined, the credibility of the net worth method may be questioned in court by the perpetrator's attorney. The most important asset to be determined in the financial profile is "cash on hand" because the most frequent assertion made by a suspect in reaction to a net worth method is that the suspect had additional cash on hand. This "cash hoard" argument can be compelling for a judge or jury, especially if the perpetrator can present evidence not uncovered by the forensic accountant during his examination. If this argument is made by the person being investigated, she should be questioned extensively as to why the cash on hand is believed to be understated, where the additional cash was kept, and how it was acquired; the forensic accountant should follow up by using the answers to these questions to investigate the allegation of the understatement.

In addition, establishing the amount of cash in bank accounts—not a part of cash on hand—is another item that requires careful analysis. Bank statements may not have a cut-off date that corresponds to the end of the taxpayer's year. Large transactions that occur at the end of the year should be analyzed to determine whether they should be included or excluded from the net worth method. A consistent treatment of similar transactions is extremely important in maintaining credibility. Other assets should be valued at cost, not market value. Therefore, depreciation and appreciation of assets is ignored in net worth analyses.

Example Consider the information in Table 9.3 pertaining to Tom Springfield and the results of using the net worth method to compute an increase in his net worth (see Table 9.4).

TABLE 9.3
Financial Information for Tom Springfield

	Year 1	Year 2	Year 3
Assets			
Cash on hand	$ 500	$ 750	$ 900
Cash in bank	3,000	3,500	4,000
Certificates of deposit	40,000	30,000	30,000
Stocks and bonds	20,000	25,000	28,000
Vehicles	30,000	60,000	60,000
Real property	120,000	320,000	320,000
Total assets	$213,500	$439,250	$442,900
Liabilities			
Vehicle loan	$ 20,000	$ 40,000	$ 30,000
Mortgage	70,000	150,000	60,000
Total liabilities	$ 90,000	$ 190,000	$ 90,000
Income			

Salary	$ 65,000	$ 70,000
Interest income	1,200	1,100
Total income	$ 66,200	$ 71,100
Expenditures		
Vehicle payments	$ 15,000	$ 15,000
Mortgage payments	20,000	20,000
Additional living expenses	75,000	85,000
Total expenditures	$110,000	$120,000

TABLE 9.4
Net Worth Method Analysis for Tom Springfield

	Year 1	Year 2	Year 3
Total assets (from Table 9.3)	$213,500	$439,250	$442,900
Less: Total liabilities (from Table 9.3)	90,000	190,000	90,000
Net worth	123,500	249,250	352,900
Prior year net worth		123,500	249,250
Increase (decrease) in net worth		125,750	103,650
Add: Additional living expenses (from Table 9.3)		110,000	120,000
Total income		$235,750	$223,650
Less: Known sources of income		66,200	71,100
Income from unknown sources		$169,550	$152,550

Note that the process of gathering evidence on many of these assets and liabilities can take considerable time and effort. At times, the perpetrator is not cooperative and additional investigation work is necessary.

QUESTIONED DOCUMENT ANALYSIS

LO9 A forensic accountant must realize that documents might be altered or forged and, although she is not expected to have the skills of a document examiner, the accountant must be astute enough to know when to engage such an expert. Forensic accountants should be suspicious when one or more of the following exists:

- Signature appears to be contrived.
- Date on document is not consistent with other evidence.
- Paper does not seem to be the type usually used for the purpose.
- Document is a copy when original was expected.
- Erasures or a covering agent, such as a fluid correction cover-up, is present.
- If document is in electronic form, different styles or sizes of fonts were used.
- Document numbers appear to be out of sequence.
- Checks have second endorsements.

Questioned Documents

Documents (or files) on which these types of anomalies exist are usually referred to as *questioned documents*. They are contested because their authorship or authenticity (or both) is not established. When documents are questioned, **document examiners** may be consulted to confirm or refute the document's authorship and authenticity. Often document examiners are engaged to determine whether a document was altered in some manner to facilitate a fraud. In addition to determining whether documents have been altered, document examiners are often requested to analyze handwriting, printer output, and the ink and paper used in questioned documents. They are sometimes requested to aid in the restoration of documents. Document examiners' services are discussed next.

Identification of Alterations of Documents

Altered documents are usually classified as having additions or deletions. Additions are any marks on documents that were made subsequent to the time the document was created. These additions can be one or more words, letters (such as the addition of the letter *s* to a word), numbers, a signature, or initials. Additions can include legitimate additions as well as those made to further fraud. For example, a document examiner in Miami, Florida, used an electrostatic detection apparatus to establish that a medical doctor added a notation advising against surgery *after* the patient died during it.

Deletions exist when words or symbols have been removed from documents. This can occur through erasures, chemical removal of type or ink, or the covering of the areas of a document that the perpetrator wants hidden and then photocopying the document. Discovery of deletions made by sophisticated means may involve the use of laser or ultraviolet light techniques to detect alterations not visible to the naked eye.

The advent of computers has made the detection of alterations both easier and more difficult. Detection can be easier because of the electronic trail left by computers when a file is created, accessed, modified, or deleted. On the other hand, if the hardware (including storage disks) cannot be located, a file could have been modified and the altered document substituted for the original without creating an obvious trail of evidence.

On a related note, desktop publishing programs have made the forgery of documents even easier to perform. The existence of these programs has enabled perpetrators of fraud to create a wide array of documents that are so nearly similar to those being forged that document examiners possessing knowledge of technology are becoming an even more important part of the forensic team of experts. At a minimum, desktop publishing has made the forgery of documents easier for a person to perform.

Authorship Analysis

Authorship analysis is performed to determine the identity of the person who wrote a series of words, numbers, or signature. For example, this type of analysis has been used to show that the initials placed on a document to indicate acceptance of changes to the document (such as a contract) are not those of the person they were meant to represent. The document examiner typically obtains an **exemplar** (sometimes referred to as a *standard*)—a handwriting sample of the person suspected of authoring or altering the document—and compares it to handwriting that appears on the document. Because a person's handwriting (and, to a certain extent, signature) can vary depending on factors such as time of day, day of the week, and even the vicissitudes of life, variations can occur. One judgment a document examiner must make is whether normal variation accounts for any difference between the exemplar and the person's actual handwriting. Document examiners use nonrequested and requested exemplars. Nonrequested exemplars are handwriting samples written by a person that have been obtained under normal situations. Requested exemplars are handwriting samples written at the request of the document examiner and, as a result, have a high likelihood of being contrived. The advantage of requesting an exemplar is that the examiner can have samples of the very words, numbers, and symbols that the suspect is believed to have written in documents used in the fraud.

Other handwriting experts—called *forensic stylists*—take a different approach to determining the identity of the author of a questioned document by studying the author's choice of words, syntax, spelling, and phrasing.

In most cases of forgery, the identity of the forger is difficult to determine. Therefore, the expert may be able to ascertain only that the person whose writing is being forged is not the document's author. Document examiners rarely ever state in court that they are certain that the document examined was signed by the suspect. Instead, they will often state their findings in qualitative terms (e.g., the suspect is *probably* the person who wrote the letter using someone else's identity).

Analysis of Printer Output

To determine whether printed matter was produced by a particular printer, analysis of printer output is conducted. The ancestor of this technique is the analysis of typewriter type for the purpose of identifying whether a document was produced on a particular typewriter. Typewriter analysis was easier than computer printer analysis because each typewriter—even others of the same model—could be distinguished because of its unique letter (or number) strike.

Ink Analysis

Ink analysis is performed to determine the type of pen used on documents and the approximate date of the writing relative to other written words and numbers on the document. Chemical analysis is performed by means of infrared, florescence, and spectrochromatography to establish the difference between inks appearing on the same paper. Graphite analysis is similar; pencil analysis can determine whether the words, numbers, or signatures were added by using the same pencil.

Paper Analysis

Paper analysis can identify the thickness, texture, color, and opacity of the document paper so that a connection can be established between persons who use a type of paper document and the fraud. Watermarks and the date the paper was manufactured (sometimes placed on the paper) can also provide a connection to perpetrators of fraud.

Restoration of Documents

Restoration of documents can be performed if they are torn, shredded, spoiled (marked on), and even burned. Care must be exercised when handling damaged or partially destroyed documents, and the restoration process is best performed by persons who possess the necessary experience and skill.

Connecting persons to documents they have created, altered, or destroyed is an important activity and by using scientific methods, document examiners can identify documents that represent valuable items of reliable and valid evidence.

OBSERVATIONAL EVIDENCE

LO10 *Observation* involves the use of the senses to assess the propriety of the behavior of persons (e.g., employees' performance) and other activities such as business processes that have a tangible component (e.g., assembly lines). Observational evidence can be gathered as a result of surveillance, invigilation, and co-worker testimony. Evidence provided through observation is often the most convincing and the easiest evidence to understand for juries who often lack the background necessary to fully understand evidence in the form of accounting analyses.

Example   Karnak Corp. received a tip that one of its employees was stealing money from the cash register. After reviewing video camera evidence on which the employee was seen pocketing cash on numerous occasions, the company was able to identify the person who took the cash. This evidence was much more compelling to the jury than was the analytical comparison (e.g., comparison of the amount of cash in each employee's register to the amount of cash in every other employee's register; the analytical comparison provided supporting evidence in this case).

For observational methods to be compelling, the perpetrator should be witnessed either (1) a number of times or (2) by two or more individuals who are objective. If a fraudster is caught taking cash from a register only once, he can more easily provide an excuse for his behavior, such as "I was making change from the register." If, however, a witness sees the behavior occur repeatedly, the fraudster is less likely to be successful in offering a believable excuse for his behavior.

This type of evidence is sometimes called **surveillance** and may be conducted by either law enforcement personnel (including government employees) or private citizens, although some restrictions pertain to the admissibility of certain types of evidence obtained by private citizens through the use of undercover operations.

Surveillance is conducted covertly and continuously to gather information about persons, places, or things to determine the activity and identity of persons suspected of behavior that may (or may not) be a violation of civil or criminal law. Investigators use this technique to gather information that is not readily available through other means. The advantage of using this technique is that the persons of interest or activities are observed as they naturally occur (i.e., they are less likely to be contrived); therefore, the evidence is very likely to be valid. (This technique, then, is much like the observation used on audits of financial statements; however, while auditors' observation is *sometimes* performed surreptitiously, forensic investigators *almost always* observe surreptitiously.)

Surveillance can be used for many purposes including gathering evidence to support probable cause for the issuance of a search warrant, to identify individuals involved in crimes activities, and to apprehend perpetrators.

Surveillance can be stationary, active, or electronic. *Stationary surveillance* is conducted when neither the investigator nor the target moves from one location. For example, if an investigator watches a building to determine when a suspect enters or exits, the surveillance is considered stationary. *Active surveillance* involves watching while following a moving target. For example, the act of following a suspect in a car is active surveillance. *Electronic surveillance* occurs when any electronic device is used to record the activity or identify a suspect. For example, using a voice recorder to record a suspect's conversation is considered electronic surveillance. If a person is aware that her voice is being recorded, the surveillance is considered to be consensual monitoring. In some states, voice recording without the agreement of the party being recorded is illegal; therefore, it is wise to be knowledgeable about peoples' rights in the geographical area in which the surveillance is to occur.

While watching a suspect, the investigator may see the suspect throw away paper or other potential forms of evidence. It is lawful for the investigator to retrieve such items, especially if they are in the suspect's trash. This technique was an invaluable lead when an investigative organization, Trinity Foundation, Inc., engaged in surveillance of bank personnel in the investigation of claims of fraud against televangelist Robert Tilton. Trinity's team staked out behind the bank to which Tilton had contributors send their prayer requests and donations. He had told viewers that he would pray over the prayer requests. The lockbox system that Tilton used would have been free of any allegations of fraud had Tilton not allegedly allowed the bank to throw away prayer requests before he had seen them. Trinity was able to recover prayer requests from trash dumpsters. Furthermore, the investigative team followed the Dumpsters to the dump to determine that the prayer requests were actually disposed of, not delivered to Tilton. The allegation of fraud was that Tilton did not do what he said he would do.

Extracting paper and other debris from trash can be done lawfully without obtaining a search warrant. Investigators find this technique quite helpful, especially because it may yield telephone numbers, records (such as credit card receipts, billing statements, or financial documents that have been altered), or even evidence of drug use (a possible motive for the commission of fraud). Regarding the disposer's right of privacy, an investigator generally cannot take something that is within an area marked by boundaries that would, to a reasonable person, mark the line within which a resident would normally expect privacy. This area is referred to as **curtilage.** Boundaries could be sidewalks, shrubs, gates, and so on.

In short, once information or physical items are placed in an area in which they may be read or observed by persons unrelated to the person of interest, the information is not privileged. This rule extends, for example, to faxes received when there is no attempt to limit exposure of the contents of the transmission to attorneys and their support staff. Therefore, investigators can gather information from the outside of envelopes (such as return addresses or postmarked stamps) or any faxes they notice. This information-gathering technique can be of immense help when investigators are seeking evidence that establishes contacts between persons or are looking for leads that provide additional evidence.

At times, evidence may include information provided by informants—persons who have specific information about the investigation. This information has been so crucial that some cases could not have been solved without the involvement of the informants. Informants typically provide information either because they believe they can obtain significantly reduced punishment (including shorter sentences) for themselves, they seek retribution by seeing those who were involved in a fraud suffer what the informants believe to be proper consequences, or they are motivated by a sense of justice. Note that the informant is not always motivated by a sense of justice but could be a jilted lover or a competitor of the perpetrator. Because the informant is often not without blame himself, the information he provides must be corroborated to increase its reliability. The informant should be questioned as to possible leads to corroborate the information; the method of conducting interviews of these informants is the subject of Chapter 10.

Invigilation is a technique that can be useful in providing evidence of whether an employee is stealing from an employer no matter how it is being done. This method often involves using the techniques of observation and documentation. For example, assume that management suspects that one of its employees is stealing inventory. The forensic accountant's presence and often purpose (to determine why inventory levels are declining) is announced to employees, especially those suspected of the theft. After a period of time, the announcement is made to these employees that the forensic accountant is no longer investigating the business. The forensic accountant, then, compares data from the three periods (preannouncement, announcement, and postannouncement) to determine whether any change in behavior—as measured by inventory levels—occurred as a result of the announcement (see Figure 9.1).

Invigilation can be expensive because of the heightened controls that must be implemented. It is typically used in high-risk areas in which theft of assets can cause great economic harm to the company (e.g., that has expensive inventory or is a cash-only business) and areas in which there are insufficient controls.

FIGURE 9.1
Invigilation

Preobservation Period	Observation Period	Postobservation period
	Usually at least 14 days	

Co-worker testimony can aid an investigation by providing an eyewitness account of embezzlement or other asset-based frauds. The fact that co-workers are usually in the best position to observe nefarious acts by other employees should come as no surprise; co-workers are usually the persons closest to other employees. Co-worker observation is one of the best types of evidence that can be obtained (signed or videotaped confessions and video surveillance of embezzlement are usually better). The usefulness of observation by a co-worker depends on that individual's credibility. If opposing counsel can establish that the co-worker is biased in any way against the fraudster, the evidence is not as useful. Additionally, co-workers can provide testimony that the suspect appeared to be living beyond her means (e.g., driving an expensive automobile to work, wearing expensive clothing and jewelry to work, and bragging about vacations taken). If the true nature of the investigation is still being kept secret, inquiries of co-workers can be phrased to avoid arousing suspicion. For example, employees can be asked, "Have you noticed anything unusual lately?" or "Have you noticed any changes in your workplace, including any by your co-workers?"

CHOICE OF THE APPROPRIATE EVIDENCE-GATHERING TECHNIQUE

LO11   Choosing the appropriate evidence-gathering technique can be critical to the success of the investigation. Evidence can sometimes exist only for short periods of time, particularly when the fraudster is aware of it and that it can incriminate him. To choose the appropriate technique, the forensic accountant should consider the following factors: the type of fraud believed to have been perpetrated; the fact that the fraud is or is not ongoing; the extent of the fraud; the extent to which the investigation can be kept secret; the condition of the financial records, other source documents, and physical evidence; the sophistication of the suspect and whether collusion exists; the cost of applying a given method; the psychological and organizational impact of applying the given method; and the objectives of the investigation. These factors are discussed next. Just as evidence collection should continue as long as sufficient predication exists to justify accumulating it, the technique used to collect evidence should periodically be reevaluated in relation to the fraud theory currently being used. For example, different types of frauds (**skimming**—taking cash receipts before they are deposited or reflected in any way in the financial records versus taking money from a register) and the persons involved (e.g., CEO versus a lower-level employee) suggest a preference for the use of certain evidence-gathering techniques relative to others. For example, if the primary objective of the fraud is to misstate the financial statements, the techniques chosen will involve using analytical procedures, tracing and vouching, and reconciliations. If, however, the fraud is embezzlement, the techniques will involve observation and reconciliation.

Note that the same type of technique can be used for different types of fraud but that the emphasis on the techniques used will differ. When assets are being taken, the best method is observation—particularly surveillance—because it is one of the strongest types of evidence for use in court. For example, if skimming is occurring, observation (through surveillance) can be used to establish the act or invigilation can be employed; in addition, a supporting technique such as the use of analytical procedures (e.g., comparisons to the amounts collected by other employees) can be used to determine who is most likely the guilty party (this evidence can be used to encourage confession, a subject of Chapter 10). If, however, a perpetrator is engaging in financial statement fraud, observation of the perpetrator making top-down journal entries is nearly impossible. In this situation, the testimony of credible co-workers can be beneficial as can documentation by examining the journals and revealing the journal entries. A search for supporting documents (e.g., invoices) can be undertaken to determine whether the entries are indeed fraudulent.

Whether the fraud is ongoing is a critical factor in the selection of techniques, particularly when the fraud is embezzlement. This is true because an ongoing fraud offers the opportunity to catch the perpetrator in the act—the best type of evidence. In addition, if a fraud is ongoing, the investigation period may be shortened in order to collect the appropriate amount and quality of evidence as quickly as possible and to stop the fraud and thus to reduce the losses due to the fraud.

The extent of the fraud is a critical factor—if it is large, the forensic accountant might choose the techniques that will resolve the fraud as quickly as possible so that the adverse effect of the losses is mitigated. For example, the forensic accountant might not choose document analysis because the needed documents could be in the hands of a third party and might take some time to obtain. In this situation, the accountant could rely more on interviews to further refine the fraud hypothesis in order to collect relevant and reliable evidence as quickly as possible.

The extent to which the investigation can be kept secret is important for various reasons, one of which is the preservation of documents and other evidence that either are in the hands of the suspect or are controlled by the suspect. Another reason is that the person or entity making the allegation of fraud might be sued for defamation of character if information about the investigation was leaked. In these situations, the methods that allow for the most secrecy usually involve documents (from in-house records, online searches, and governmental offices) and various analyses. When conducting investigations on premises, investigators should avoid using words such as *investigation* and *audit* (unless, perhaps, when an invigilation is performed); instead, they should characterize the investigation as a "routine check-up" so that individuals do not feel threatened and thus less likely to be cooperative. Be aware that the more humans involved, the higher is the likelihood that an investigation will become public knowledge.

Another factor to consider is the condition of the financial records, other source documents, and physical evidence. In any investigation, one objective is to preserve and protect documents and physical evidence that represent relevant, reliable, and valid support for a case. At times, adverse parties possess these documents, which could be lost, altered, or destroyed. If documents (including files) are unreadable, document examiners or computer forensic professionals can be helpful in restoring them so that they can be useful. However, if they are lost or destroyed, their use becomes more difficult, if not impossible, although technology can help: Software has been developed to reassemble shredded documents. In these cases, the forensic accountant might have to use alternative methods such as contacting persons who have knowledge of the fraud so that they can be questioned. If, for example, the fraud investigated is employee theft of inventory and the source documents have been lost or completely destroyed, confirmation can be made by communicating with vendors as to the amounts paid. If an employee is suspected of fictitious vendor fraud, link analysis or a search for addresses of employees that are similar to vendor addresses can be undertaken.

In some cases, financial records have had to be reconstructed. Consider, for example, the alleged financial statement fraud that occurred at WorldCom during the years 1999–2001. The restatement of WorldCom's financial statements, said to have cost approximately $365 million, involved the help of more than 500 WorldCom employees, more than 200 KPMG employees, and a supplemental workforce comprising almost 600 Deloitte & Touche employees (at one point in 2003, approximately 1,500 people worked on the restatement).

The sophistication of the suspect and whether collusion exists can have an impact on the evidence-gathering technique(s) used. Sophisticated suspects are not as likely to leave a trail. For example, documents could be shredded and disposed of in various Dumpsters in several towns, making reassembling them nearly impossible, or they could be destroyed by fire. Some suspects are clever at avoiding surveillance cameras. Catching sophisticated suspects can mean paying closer attention to documents for alterations (or created fake documents) and stepping back and questioning the existence of documents and the reasonableness of certain acts committed by the suspects. Similarly, collusion can pose a challenge in selecting the best evidence-gathering techniques to use. As the number of persons colluding increases, so does the likelihood that the fraud is well thought out. However, when collusion occurs, the opportunity to catch the perpetrators can increase. With more than one person to observe, the chances of catching at least one of the perpetrators in the act can increase. Also, one of the suspects might be willing to provide evidence against the others if she becomes disgruntled. Thus, observation is still a good technique to use as is talking with co-workers not suspected of being involved.

The cost of applying a given method should not be ignored; some techniques, for example, are expensive (e.g., invigilation) and might not provide benefits that outweigh the costs incurred. In a world of limited resources, the forensic accountant must make decisions that are business oriented. This is not to say that expending $300,000 to investigate a fraud for which the losses are approximately $100,000 should never be undertaken; in some situations, expending more than the approximate loss is prudent (e.g., the results of the investigation can be used to prevent similar frauds and the message sent to employees can deter them from committing fraud in the organization). Most often, though, the accountant must carefully consider the approximate costs of applying a particular method relative to the expected benefits. In general, any method that requires a large amount of human labor (e.g., examination of documents and observation) will be more expensive than methods requiring less labor (e.g., ratio analysis [see the appendix] performed by a computer).

The psychological and organizational impact of applying a given method should be considered. As an extreme example, consider an employer who has some evidence that a few of its employees are stealing inventory. If the employer searches each employee and his or her car as he or she exits company premises each day, the method is not only disruptive and expensive to implement but also is likely to lead to employee resentment, decreased productivity and, quite possibly, more fraud. In this case, video surveillance or surprise counts could be used to determine the identity of the fraudsters.

Finally, the objectives of the investigation must be considered. If the objective is to go to court (or to arbitrate), the techniques chosen should be those that provide more detail than those that would be utilized if the victim was not planning to prosecute (e.g., will use the information to implement controls to decrease the possibility of fraud in the future). If the matter is to be litigated, direct methods of proof that can be easily understood by juries are better than other methods such as the net worth, expenditures, and bank deposit methods.

Summary

Evidence is anything that relates to the truth or falsity of an assertion; it includes physical objects, documents, observations, and interviews. Evidence represents facts or representations of facts that can be used to convince a judge or jury of one party's belief. For evidence to be useful in court, it must be relevant, reliable, and valid.

Physical evidence refers to a relatively broad category of evidence that includes fingerprints and trace evidence. Forensic accountants must be aware of the importance of not disturbing physical evidence so that it is preserved to use as evidence for court.

Documents (including records in electronic format) are the most often used type of evidence in forensic accounting investigations and include not only documents (including ones in electronic form) collected as part of the investigation but also documents created by the forensic accountant such as charts, graphs, or other exhibits admitted into evidence as part of expert testimony. Care must be exercised when handling documents and maintaining the appropriate chain of custody so that they are preserved as reliable evidence. Documents should be organized so that they can be easily located.

Documentary evidence is usually obtained by searching public records including commercial Web sites and the trash of those thought to possess evidence; acquiring consent to release evidence by those who have custody of it; and using subpoenas and search warrants. Numerous sources of documents can be helpful in building a profile of a suspect and establishing a case to support the allegation of fraud including personnel files, résumés, co-workers' information, facts supplied by friends and acquaintances, post-employment background checks, and information contained on social networking sites. When building a case against a suspect, certain records that are available to the public— such as real estate records, court records, assumed name indexes, and Uniform Commercial Code filings—can be helpful. Other records—motor vehicle records, FinCEN reports, and tax returns (the latter can be requested from the suspect) are restricted to limited groups of persons, such as federal and state employees including law enforcement personnel. At times, governmental agencies, such as the FBI, ATF, and local sheriff's office, can request that the court issue a subpoena or search warrant to obtain evidence from persons believed to possess it.

Analytical procedures, such as comparisons and ratio analysis as well as audit techniques (e.g., tracing; vouching; making surprise counts; and using statistical sampling, reconciliations, and confirmations) can aid the investigation and provide estimates of the dollar loss of the fraud.

Questioned document analysis can be a critical part of an investigation when documents are not what they appear to be. Instead of relying on documents as representations of the truth, the documents themselves can become exhibits of fraud.

Certain indirect sources of evidence exist including the use of methods such as net worth method. These techniques are useful to support the allegation of fraud but are not as useful as observation methods such as surveillance, invigilation, and eyewitness accounts by co-workers.

Observation involves the use of the senses to assess the propriety of the behavior of persons and other activities such as business processes. Observational evidence can be gathered as a result of surveillance, invigilation, and co-worker testimony. This evidence is often the most convincing and the easiest evidence to understand by juries who often lack the background necessary to fully understand evidence in the form of accounting analyses.

Choosing the appropriate evidence-gathering technique can be critical to the success of an investigation. The best evidence-gathering technique can depend upon the type of fraud believed to have been perpetrated; whether the fraud is ongoing; the extent of the fraud; the extent to which the investigation can be kept secret; the condition of the financial records, other source documents, and physical evidence; the sophistication of the suspect; whether collusion exists; the cost of applying a given method; the psychological and organizational impact of applying the given method; and the objectives of the investigation.

Glossary

analytical procedures   Methods such as tests that often involve making comparisons and using ratios to determine whether account balances, line items in financial statements, and other financial information appear reasonable.

Bates numbers   Unique identifying numbers, letters, or both assigned to documents so that the documents can be easily located and tracked.

curtilage   Area that a person inhabits in which the person can reasonably expect privacy.

deposition   Sworn testimony taken before a trial begins that is a record of answers given to questions asked by opposing attorneys.

document examiners   Fraud investigators who examine documents to determine whether they have been altered and the validity of claims made about them; often use an exemplar to determine authorship of a handwriting sample in their examination.

exemplar   Sample of a known person's handwriting.

financial statement fraud   Intentional misstatement of financial statements so that they do not present fairly the financial position, results of operations, and cash flows of an entity.

horizontal analysis   Comparison of line items (or accounts) across time periods; for example, comparing the amount of the current year balance of sales to the amount of sales for each of the five previous years.

invigilation   Investigation technique that notifies suspects that they (and others) will be watched for a period of time; thus, three periods of activity are generated for comparison: the period prior to the notice, the period in which the activity of notice occurs, and the period that begins after the persons are told they are not being watched.

link analysis   Method used to establish a connection between information in databases and files.

net worth method   Indirect method used to determine unsubstantiated increase in wealth that could be from fraudulent activities.

search warrant for financial records   Authorization of law enforcement personnel to search for books and records believed to be involved in a financial fraud.

skimming   Taking cash receipts before they are deposited or reflected in any way in the financial records.

statistical sampling   Applying statistical theory to select, interpret, and project results from a subset of a population to the entire population so that a decision about the population can be made.

subpoena   Written order issued by a court to compel a person to give a deposition, testify in court, or submit documents or records.

surprise count   Process of making an unexpected count of inventory or other assets; used to document unexplained differences between the physical assets and the accounting records.

surveillance   Observation—both visual and auditory—usually done to obtain evidence for which no documentary trail is available.

tracing   Act of comparing information in the accounting records (e.g., ledgers and journals) to information in the financial statements or reports.

Vertical analysis   Comparison of accounts within a financial statement to a base account by restating each account in terms of the base account (e.g., if sales is used as the base account, it is assigned a value of 100 and all other accounts are stated relative to that account).

vouching   Comparing information in the financial statements or reports to information contained in the accounting records (e.g., ledgers and journals).

Appendix

Common Analytical Procedures

REVENUE AND ASSET ANALYTICAL PROCEDURES

Gross profit margin represents the percentage of net sales after considering the direct costs of producing sales. Identifying this amount is helpful in determining the possibility of misstatements of revenue as well as the cost of sales.

Gross Profit Margin = (Net Sales − Cost of Goods Sold)/Net Sales

Net sales represent total sales less sales discounts and sales returns.

If, for example, the gross margin percentage is lower than usual, the reason could be that sales are understated as a result of skimming (which would lower total sales) or theft of inventory (and thus increase the cost of goods sold). If the gross margin percentage is higher than usual, the reason could be that fictitious sales are recorded with no attendant increase in cost of goods sold. For example, assume that during the year, Company X has $100,000 of sales and $60,000 of cost of goods sold; the gross margin percentage is ($100,000 − $60,000)/$100,000 = 40. However, if Company X records an additional $20,000 in sales without recording the corresponding cost of goods sold, the gross margin percentage becomes ($120,000 − $60,000)/$120,000 = 50.

It is important to understand what the word *usual* means: what has commonly been considered normal or ordinary in the past. Thus, to determine what is usual for a company often involves analyzing past financial statements and records. For example, to determine the usual gross profit margin, a fraud investigator could calculate the gross profit margin for each of the five years preceding the year under examination. Note that the gross profit margin for each year should be calculated and compared with that of the other years to determine whether the gross margin percentage in any one year appears unusual. If it is similar in each of the years, the average of these gross profit margins can be compared to the gross profit margin for the year being examined. Care must be exercised when relying on these base-year gross profit margins because they could be inflated (or deflated) as a result of fraud.

It is also important to understand that just because a company experiences a gross margin percentage that is higher (or lower) than it has in the past, this information by itself does not mean that the company is fraudulently stating its financial statements. A legitimate reason for a significant increase in gross margin percentage is that the company could have begun selling a new product that had a higher gross margin percentage than those of other items it has sold in the past.

Percentage of sales discounts indicate whether sales discounts are misstated or sales are understated. For example, if an employee is improperly granting sales discounts to a customer (possibly to receive a portion of the reduction in price), the percentage of sales discount would be higher than usual. Another reason for the elevated level of percentage of sales discounts is the understatement of sales, which could occur as a result of skimmed sales.

Percentage of Sales Discounts = Sales Discounts/Total Sales

Percentage of sales returns is similar to percentage of sales discounts but pertains to sales returns rather than sales discounts. Fraud can exist if this percentage is higher or lower than usual. If fictitious returns are reflected in the records, this percentage would be higher than usual. Fictitious returns could occur when an accounting entry is made to increase the amount in this account and decreasing the amount in accounts receivable. (For valid returns, two other adjustments would be made to the records: inventory would be increased and cost of goods sold would be decreased.) The motivation for these fictitious increases could be a kickback from the customer whose account was reduced.

At times, the percentage of sales returns could be lower than usual, indicating the diversion of returned products by employees. For example, when inventory is returned, employees could take it for their personal use or sell it for personal profit. Thus, because the returned merchandise was not recorded on the books, the percentage of sales returns for the period during which this fraudulent activity was taking place would be lower than usual.

$$\text{Percentage of Sales Returns} = \text{Sales Returns/Total Sales}$$

If the percentage appears to be higher than usual, a sample of increases to the Sales Returns account could be made to determine whether proper support exists (e.g., a sales return memo) and the addition to the inventory confirmed by the inventory manager.

Accounts receivable turnover provides an indication of how well accounts receivable are being collected.

$$\text{Accounts Receivable Turnover} = \text{Net Sales/Average Accounts Receivable}$$

A lower than usual turnover rate may indicate overstated sales and accounts receivable and thus the possibility of fraud. For example, assume that net sales are $100,000 and the average accounts receivable for the year is $20,000. The accounts receivable turnover ratio is $100,000/$20,000 = 5. Further assume that an additional $5,000 of fictitious sales is added at the end of the period by making an accounting entry. This would decrease the accounts receivable turnover ratio so that it is now less than 5. (If, however, the initial accounts receivable turnover ratio is less than 1.0, the addition of fictitious sales increases this ratio.)

Percent of uncollectible accounts can also indicate the presence of fraud. If, for example, fictitious accounts receivable are allowed to remain on the books for an extended period of time (i.e., for more than 120 days) without reflecting the fact that they are not collectible (by expensing a portion of the fictitious accounts by means of bad debts), the percent of uncollectible accounts will decrease. (Note that the accounts receivable amount used to calculate the percent of uncollectible accounts is not reduced by the allowance for uncollectible accounts.)

$$\text{Percent of Uncollectible Accounts} = \text{Allowance for Uncollectible Accounts/Accounts Receivable}$$

Number of days in receivables is the number of days the business takes to collect accounts receivable. If the number of days is large, the likelihood is high that fictitious receivables exist in accounts receivable. This procedure uses the accounts receivable turnover ratio already presented.

$$\text{Number of Days in Receivables} = 365/\text{Accounts Receivable Turnover}$$

Current ratio indicates the relative size of current assets to current liabilities. A decrease in the current ratio may signal embezzlement of funds. On the other hand, if the ratio increases, the entity could be reducing liabilities inappropriately by, for example, debiting an amount as a "payment" and crediting expenses.

$$\text{Current Ratio} = \text{Current Assets/Current Liabilities}$$

Quick ratio provides a relative measure of liquid assets to current liabilities. A decrease in this ratio, like the current ratio, may indicate a theft of current assets; an increase could indicate a fraudulent decrease of liabilities.

$$\text{Quick Ratio} = \text{Current Assets (less Inventory)/Current Liabilities}$$

EXPENSE ANALYTICAL PROCEDURES

Bad debt percentage indicates the relative size of bad debts arising from accounts receivable. If, for example, this ratio increases, controls over the extension of credit may not be working well.

$$\text{Bad Debt Percentage} = \text{Bad Debt Expense/Total Sales}$$

or

$$\text{Bad Debt Percentage} = \text{Bad Debt Expense/Average Accounts Receivable}$$

Cost of good sold percentage highlights the amount of cost of goods sold—usually an entity's largest expense—relative to the amount of sales. An increase in this ratio could indicate theft of inventory.

$$\text{Cost of Goods Sold Percentage} = \text{Cost of Goods Sold/Net Sales}$$

Inventory percentage shows the amount of inventory relative to that of total assets. An increase in this percentage could indicate inflated or nonexistent inventory; a decrease could indicate the theft of assets or a manipulation of income to show a lower net profit (and thus lower taxes).

$$\text{Inventory Percentage} = \text{Inventory/Total Assets}$$

Inventory turnover is a ratio that indicates the efficiency of an operation. If the ratio decreases, inflated inventory values may be the culprit.

$$\text{Inventory Turnover} = \text{Cost of Goods Sold/Average Inventory}$$

DEBT ANALYTICAL PROCEDURES

Debt percentage indicates the amount of liabilities relative to assets. An increase in this ratio may indicate that cash has been diverted from the payment of liabilities. A decrease could indicate a misclassification of liabilities (e.g., recording loan proceeds as sales) or an inappropriate reduction of liabilities.

$$\text{Debt Percentage} = \text{Total Liabilities/Total Assets}$$

Debt to equity reveals the size of debt relative to the owners' interests. An increase in this ratio, like an increase in the debt percentage, may indicate that cash is not being used to reduce debt. If this occurs and the company has a debt covenant as a part of a loan agreement with a financial institution, the consequences can be onerous for the company.

$$\text{Debt to Equity} = \text{Total Liabilities/Stockholders' Equity}$$

Review Questions

1. Evidence is:
   a. Useful in court only if the plaintiff and defendant can agree on its admissibility.
   b. Allowed in court only if it is truthful.
   c. Most useful if it is relevant, reliable, and valid.
   d. Allowed if it passes the Vorhees test of veracity.

2. Reliability of evidence refers to:
   a. Its truthfulness.
   b. Its accuracy.
   c. The extent to which it is consistently credible.
   d. All of the above.

3. Which of the following does physical evidence include?
   a. Observation and surveillance.
   b. Fingerprints and DNA.
   c. Tire tracks and passkey.
   d. *b* and *c*.

4. Documents are not usually used because of the possibility of alteration or falsification.
   a. True.
   b. False.

5. Which of the following is *not* a basic rule of handling evidence?
   a. Keep documents in a secure location.
   b. Maintain appropriate chain of custody information.
   c. Handle original documents whenever possible.
   d. All of the above are basic rules of handling evidence.

6. Which one of the following items of evidence must be obtained by voluntary consent?
   a. Trash outside a suspect's residence placed on the curb.
   b. Tax return.
   c. Videotape (no audio) of suspect shopping.
   d. None of the above items requires voluntary consent.

7. Which item of information from an employees' personnel file might indicate a source of pressure to commit fraud?
   a. Signature indicating agreement to abide by a code of ethics.
   b. Six exemptions on a W-4 form.
   c. Award for commendable service to the company.
   d. None of the above indicates a source of pressure to commit fraud.

8. Which records are normally not available to the public?
   a. Assumed name indexes.
   b. Uniform Commercial Code filings.
   c. Currency transactions reports.
   d. Real estate records.

9. A search warrant can be issued if predication does not exist, but only by a court.
   a. True.
   b. False.

10. Comparing financial data with results the entity itself expected requires:

    a. Consistency of data among periods.

    b. An attainable budget.

    c. Estimate the amount of inventory lost due to fire.

    d. Data from similar entities to use as a comparison.

11. Which of these does vertical ratio analysis involve?

    a. A columnar approach to analytical review.

    b. A within-statement approach to analytical review.

    c. A year-to-year approach to analytical review.

    d. None of the above.

12. Analytical procedures are comparisons of recorded amounts to which of the following?

    a. Standard amounts as determined by generally accepted accounting principles.

    b. Similar amounts known not to contain errors.

    c. Amounts expected by auditors.

    d. None of the above.

13. Which of the following does tracing involve?

    a. Following the flow of information beginning with the financial statements and going back through the system to the source documents.

    b. Following the flow of information beginning with the source documents and following the flow of information forward through the system to the financial statements.

    c. Applying analytical procedures to the financial statements.

    d. Using surveillance to observe the steps of a suspect as he commits the crime.

14. Making a surprise count is a technique that can be used to:

    a. Account for understated liabilities.

    b. Determine why inventory is missing.

    c. Determine whether a difference exists between tangible assets and accounting records.

    d. Locate overstated inventory.

15. The likelihood that a forensic accountant's judgment based on a sample differs from the judgment based on an examination of the complete population is called:

    a. Difference estimation.

    b. Discovery sampling.

    c. Sampling risk.

    d. Judgmental risk.

16. Confirmations are:

    a. Always a reliable source of evidence.

    b. A process used to determine an understatement of liabilities.

    c. A good indicator of fraud if the recipient does not respond.

    d. All of the above.

17. The net worth method can be used as:

    a. A direct form of evidence.

    b. An indirect form of evidence.

   c. Conclusive evidence that an embezzlement has taken place.

   d. An indication that collusion between employees has occurred.

18 Alterations of documents are usually classified as:

   a. Changes.

   b. Additions.

   c. Deletions.

   d. Both *b* and *c*.

19. Which of the following issues with documents would *not* normally be considered as a possible indicator of fraud?

   a. Duplicate payments.

   b. Photocopied documents.

   c. Unrecognized handwriting.

   d. All of the above could normally be taken as a possible indicator of fraud.

20. *Questioned documents* are documents that are contested for what reason?

   a. They exhibit one of the document-related indicators of fraud.

   b. They are declared fraudulent by a document examiner.

   c. They are questioned by an auditor.

   d. None of the above.

21. What do most document examiners study?

   a. The author's choice of words, syntax, spelling, and phrasing.

   b. An exemplar of the person suspected of authoring or altering a document.

   c. Both *a* and *b*.

   d. None of the above.

22. Which of the following must file currency transaction reports?

   a. Any person who physically transports, mails, or ships currency or monetary instruments of more than $10,000 into or out of the United States or any person who receives payments from a source outside the United States.

   b. Financial institutions when a customer deposits more than $10,000 currency.

   c. Businesses that receive more than $10,000 in one transaction or in a series of related transactions.

   d. Answers *a* and *b* only.

23. How many observation periods are needed for invigilation?

   a. 1.

   b. 2.

   c. 3.

   d. 4.

24. The observation period used in invigilation should be approximately how long?

   a. 10 days.

   b. 7 days.

   c. 30 days.

   d. 14 days.

25. Surveillance is *not* typically used for which of the following?

    a. Gathering evidence to support probable cause for the issuance of a search warrant.

    b. Gathering evidence leading to the identification of activities and individuals involved in crimes and the apprehension of perpetrators.

    c. Gathering evidence of crimes.

    d. All of the above.

Discussion Questions

26. Give an example of an item of evidence that is valid and relevant but not reliable.

27. Give a reason why forensic accountants do not usually evaluate physical evidence.

28. What is the basis for not accepting copies of original documents in a court?

29. Of the four ways documentary evidence can be obtained, which can be performed without the suspect being aware of the investigation?

30. A suspect lists former employers on an employment application contained in her personnel file. What might the forensic account do with this information?

31. Google your name (or the name of a friend) and location (e.g., state). What information can you find on yourself (or this person)? Is this information correct?

32. A manager is suspected of making top-side journal entries to increase the income of the company because his bonus depends on the company's achieving at least a certain level of income. What would you, a trained forensic accountant, look for when investigating this type of fraud?

33. You just received a tip that a substantial amount of inventory is being stolen from the dock area of the company for which you work as an internal auditor. What techniques might be useful in determining whether this allegation is true (i.e., collecting evidence of this fraud)?

34. Discuss how you might resolve a suspect's allegation that the amount of cash on hand in your net worth method is understated.

35. When might questioned document analysis be used as part of identity theft?

36. When might document restoration be useful in a forensic investigation?

37. Give an example of how link analysis might be used to investigate mortgage fraud.

38. What is required to obtain a search warrant?

39. When would a search warrant *not* be used to investigate an employee fraud?

40. Give examples of situations in which a search warrant could be used to investigate employee fraud.

41. Give an example of a situation in which surveillance could be used to justify seeking a search warrant.

42. For what types of fraud would the technique of invigilation be used?

43. Give an example of how opposing counsel might seek to discredit a co-worker's testimony.

44. Give a reason for the increase in the cost of goods sold percentage that is not the result of fraud.

45. Discuss what a company subject to a debt-to-equity ratio covenant might to do to reduce the ratio so that it does not exceed the bank's stipulated ratio. (*Hint:* Abandon conformance to GAAP when thinking of answers.)

Cases

46. Cary and Elle Bronson had been married for 15 years when trouble arose in their marriage. Cary's long hours of working had taken a toll on it; he was rarely around even for family functions. The last straw came when Elle found lipstick on the collar of Cary's shirt and the unmistakable scent of a very expensive woman's perfume; this wasn't the first time she had noticed the telltale signs of what appeared to be a clandestine affair. The next day, Elle visited an attorney to begin divorce proceedings. After some small talk, the attorney, Mark Smithson, asked Elle about the major assets accumulated during the marriage.

"Oh, there are the cars—a Jeep Cherokee, a Chevy Suburban, and a Bentley," she answered.

"A Bentley?" he queried, somewhat surprised.

"Yes," said Elle. "Our restaurant, The Roasted Duck, has done very well over the years. We began the business with almost nothing and both worked there until Karen, our second child, was born. At that point, I became a stay-at-home mom and left everything to Cary."

"I've eaten at The Roasted Duck—the food is excellent," Mark said.

"Thank you," replied Elle.

"Is this the only source of income for you and your husband, Mrs. Bronson?" he asked.

"Yes, other than some interest and dividends," she answered.

She and the lawyer discussed other matters pertaining to the divorce. He told Elle that he would obtain information from Cary's attorney so that an equitable division of assets could occur and the issue of the custody of their children would be settled.

Two weeks later, Elle received a call from Mark. Through the discovery process, Cary's attorney had submitted a valuation of the restaurant that seemed unusually low and had not listed any other assets that could account for the house and vehicles that the Bronsons had acquired and the private education that they had provided for their children.

"That can't be right!" Elle exclaimed.

"Well, it certainly doesn't look right," Mark said, "I'll look into this some more and let you know what I find."

After he hung up the phone, Mark called Cary's attorney. "This value placed on the restaurant doesn't make any sense. What's your take on this?"

After a short pause, the attorney replied, "Cary told me that the restaurant business is not doing well and, thus, the value has declined."

After Mark hung up the phone, he pondered the situation: There must be an answer to this mystery. One thing's for sure; if Cary isn't telling the truth, he might as well change the name of his restaurant to The Cooked Goose.

a. What evidence (i.e., physical, documentary, and observational) could be collected to determine whether the valuation is correct? How could you go about collecting this evidence?

b. Assume for a moment that the valuation is correct. What other sources of money could Cary have to maintain his family's lifestyle? How would you test your theories?

47. Andrus Bettenhaus had worked at Ye Old Troubadour for 15 years and had been given increasing levels of responsibility until he reached the position of manager. One evening, Sharon Ellis, an employee at the Troubadour, asked to speak with Carmela Rodriguez, one of the managers in the internal audit division of the company.

"I think Andrus has been taking cash from the register," said Sharon.

"Thanks for letting me know about this, Sharon. Can you tell me what made you suspect that he was doing this?" Carmela replied.

"I came to his office just after Kim, one of the cashiers, dropped off her register tray, and he was trying to hide something in his desk drawer. He looked a little sheepish and seemed flustered. I don't know . . . maybe it's nothing."

"Well," Carmela replied, "we don't know that yet, so I'll look into this. In the meantime, please don't say anything about this to anyone. If it does turn about to be nothing, no one is hurt."

After Sharon agreed and left, Carmela's thoughts turned to a conversation she had earlier with her supervisor, Karen Turner. She recalled that Karen had said that an analysis of the cash collections had indicated that they hadn't been as high for the last three months as they had been previously. "But Andrus is such a well-liked and trusted employee. I just can't imagine why he would do such a thing," Carmela thought. "There must be a reason."

a. List some reasons why an employee might embezzle cash from his employer and the evidence that would determine which reason (or reasons) could provide the pressure to motivate a person to embezzle. Note which evidence, if any, is obtainable only if the employee voluntarily makes it available.

b. How would an opposing attorney try to discredit the evidence that Carmela thinks is relevant to the case?

48. Talia Finn is working as an analyst for the Drug Enforcement Agency (DEA) and has been assigned to a case in which the suspect is believed to be engaged in a rather large drug-dealing operation behind the sham business Nutritional Supplements. Her first assignment is to perform a net worth method on Clyde Barrow Jr., the sole proprietor of the unincorporated business.

a. Talia prepared a net worth method using the information she had collected that follows.

Financial Information for Clyde Barrow Jr.			
	Year 1	**Year 2**	**Year 3**
Assets			
Cash on hand	$ 500	$ 750	$ 900
Cash in bank	3,000	12,500	15,000
Vehicles	30,000	90,000	120,000
Real property: Store		250,000	250,000
Real property: Homes		350,000	575,000
Total assets	$33,500	$703,250	$960,900
Liabilities			
Vehicle loans	$20,000	$ 70,000	$ 85,000
Mortgages		290,000	450,000
Total liabilities	$20,000	$360,000	$535,000
Income			
Income from business		$ 85,000	$ 97,000
Total income		$ 85,000	$ 97,000

(Continued)

(Continued)

Expenditures

Vehicle payments	$ 15,000	$ 15,000
Mortgage payments	55,000	190,000
Additional living expenses	100,000	135,000
Total expenditures	$170,000	$340,000

b. After Talia completed her analysis, Clyde's attorney raised an objection. Talia asked to meet with Clyde again, and at that meeting Clyde told her that he believes that the cash on hand amounts that were used in the projection were too low. Although he had provided the amount to her earlier, he now believes that it was much higher than the amounts used and seems to recall that he had about $200,000 "stashed away" in case the economy crashed. When Talia asked him about the source of the $200,000, Clyde shrugged and said, "Part of it was an inheritance from my dear old Aunt Hattie, and the balance was just some money I had saved."

c. How should Talia respond to this new information (i.e., would she want additional information from Clyde), and what are the sources of evidence that she needs to follow up on his assertion?

49. As a certified fraud examiner, Laura Wu has been retained by an attorney to investigate an overstatement of revenue fraud at Unlimited Growth Ltd. All sales to the company are on credit (i.e., there are no cash sales). Laura has found an entry in the records debiting accounts receivable and crediting the Sales account on the last day of the fiscal year.

a. Would confirmations help her gather evidence in preparing for prosecution of financial statement fraud? Why?

b. Laura employed a novice fraud examiner to help her in the investigation. After an employee of Unlimited Growth had prepared the confirmation letters (using the positive "in-blank" type), her novice fraud examiner reviewed the letters and asked another employee (who had worked at Unlimited Growth for 12 years and had a character that was beyond reproach) to mail them for him. The confirmations were all returned, and all recipients had indicated that the information provided in the letter agreed with their records. Should Laura be concerned about the process her fraud examiner used and the results?

Chapter **Ten**

Fraud Examination Evidence II: Interview and Interrogation Methods

CHAPTER OBJECTIVES

After reading Chapter 10, you should be able to:

- LO1: Describe the interview and explain its importance.
- LO2: Define *interviewing.*
- LO3: Describe how the interviewer should prepare for an interview.
- LO4: Describe the importance of the order in which multiple persons are to be interviewed.
- LO5: Describe the types of questions used, their order, and the persons to whom they should be asked.
- LO6: Describe and discuss the importance of the final questions to ask nonsuspects.
- LO7: Describe the verbal and nonverbal cues of interviewed subjects and the hidden meanings they can convey.
- LO8: Discuss the two main categories of nonverbal behavior and how they can indicate guilt.
- LO9: Describe how admission-seeking questions are usually asked.
- LO10: Discuss the benefits and detriments of recording an interview.
- LO11: Discuss the benefits and detriments of taking notes during an interview.
- LO12: Describe the proper setting and room in which interviews are to be conducted.
- LO13: Describe the various structures of interview questions and the reasons these structures are used or avoided.
- LO14: Describe the various methods of persuading subjects to provide information.
- LO15: Discuss various reasons for which subjects offer to avoid being interviewed and proper responses to these reasons.
- LO16: Discuss various reasons for which subjects avoid answering specific questions and how the interviewer should respond to these reasons.
- LO17: Describe the essential information contained in a signed confession.
- LO18: Discuss the need for a release of information and how it can be obtained.

INTRODUCTION

LO1   Conducting effective interviews and interrogations can be one of the most important evidence-gathering techniques in forensic accounting. Interviewing skill is of paramount importance for the forensic accountant. In fact, it is the most frequently employed type of evidence-gathering method used by forensic accountants, particularly when performing fraud examinations. While documents can provide facts, they cannot be questioned and sometimes do not possess the broad array of evidence that interviewees can. Verbal and nonverbal cues observed during interviews can provide an interactive give-and-take that can produce additional evidence, lead to the identity of the perpetrator, and yield one of the most useful forms of direct evidence: the confession. Even in the absence of a confession, credible information obtained from interviews coupled with documentary evidence can cause a judge or jury to convict a suspect based on circumstantial evidence alone.

In previous chapters, physical, documentary, and observational evidence was discussed. In this chapter, we discuss the process of conducting effective interviews that can be used as evidence in court.

THE INTERVIEWING PROCESS

LO2   An **interview** is conversation in which persons are questioned and their responses noted. Responses can be verbal as well as nonverbal. At times, interviewees' nonverbal responses are just as important as verbal ones.

Interviewing is sometimes used to refer to an activity more appropriately called *interrogation.* The distinction between interviewing and interrogation is not always clear. Each involves asking questions of persons (subjects), and the objective of each is to obtain relevant information that leads to the discovery of truth. Interviewing typically is a more casual form of asking questions, is usually performed away from the forensic accountant's office, and does not require reading Miranda rights to the person(s) being interviewed.

Interrogation, on the other hand, is an information-seeking questioning technique that law enforcement uses to obtain information about a crime from those who are suspected of committing it and is, therefore, more likely to involve confrontation. Interrogation is usually conducted in the investigator's office and, like interviewing, involves soliciting specific information that can be used as evidence in a court of law. For the remainder of this chapter, the word *interviewing* will be used to represent both interviewing and interrogation because, except for the more formal custody and setting of an interrogation, these two techniques are nearly identical.

Whether interviews or interrogations are conducted, the desired objectives are more likely to be achieved if the proper process is followed: preparing for the interview, conducting the interview, and obtaining confessions if necessary.

Preparing for the Interview

LO3   Before the interview, the interviewer should prepare for it by becoming as familiar as possible with the individual being interviewed, the type of fraud that he is investigating, the suspect, and the victim. Usually, the interviewer becomes familiar with any physical evidence collected, analyzes the documentary evidence, and, if possible and appropriate, has observed the suspect. In other words, evidence other than interviews—physical, documents, and observation—have been collected and analyzed before any interviews are begun. This is not to say that additional physical, documentary, and observational evidence will not be obtained after interviews; they might very well provide leads to additional evidence of this nature.

The forensic accountant should build a profile of the individual suspected of committing the fraud using the evidence-gathering techniques discussed in Chapter 9. This profile should include the following about the suspect:

- Position in the firm.
- Job functions.
- Length of time with the firm.
- Salary and benefits.
- Any promotions that may have been expected but not received.
- Work-related interaction with co-workers.
- Age and marital status.
- Interests and hobbies.
- Assets.
- Outstanding bills, including recent purchases of items such as cars and real estate.

Armed with this knowledge, the forensic accountant can formulate a strategy for the initial interview by using the information gathered about the suspect and fraud triangle. By taking this approach in the initial interview, she can gather information, much of which can be confirmed or refuted, about the suspect's likely pressures, perceived opportunities, and rationalization—particularly if she is informed about the suspect. Be aware, however, that although gathering information about the suspect prior to the initial interview can be immensely helpful, the forensic accountant must guard against tunnel vision and seek to keep an open mind and be an active listener.

One reason for this tunnel vision is the fundamental human tendency to trust, which can be both a benefit and a detriment to the interviewer. On one hand, using an interview strategy that encourages the subject to trust the interviewer is beneficial. Humans are more likely to divulge confidential information to those they trust (eliminating from consideration, of course, the extraction of information by force). On the other hand, if the interviewer trusts the subject, she is less likely to question the subject adequately. Listening for truthful statements may cause the interviewer to miss verbal and nonverbal cues that indicate untruthfulness or the withholding of information. The interviewer's tendency for placing too much trust in the subject is more likely to occur if she is inexperienced or if the subject appears very courteous. Interviewers who have several years of experience (have "seen it all") are less likely to accept subjects' responses at face value.

An approach for minimizing the effects of this tendency to trust is to conscientiously practice the habit of being skeptical. An investigator, especially a less experienced one, using active skepticism may require at least one follow-up interview. Responses made by the subject should be scrutinized for their lack of truthfulness. Having a more experienced interviewer present during the interview may help because he can interject questions in response to the subject's answers (be aware, however, that it is usually better for only one person to ask the questions so to avoid creating a "them-against-me" environment). There is no substitute for reflecting on answers provided in an interview after it has taken place. Afterward, the interviewer can analyze the responses by keeping the possibility of guilt in mind much easier than when in the presence of a subject who may be quite adept at convincing others of her innocence.

Before we discuss the mechanics of interviewing each individual, we discuss the determination of when to interview a particular person when more than one individual might have information about the perpetrator or the fraud.

Conducting Multiple Interviews

LO4 When more than one person is to be interviewed, care must be exercised to determine the order in which each person is to be interviewed. Usually, the forensic accountant first interviews those persons who, although knowledgeable about some aspect of the suspect or of the fraud, are not suspects. The interviews, then, begin with individuals who are not suspects and then those who are least culpable and finally the most culpable (i.e., suspects). The reason for this is simple: By the time the investigator has interviewed the suspects, he is better informed about the suspect and the fraud itself. When collusion has occurred, the suspects should be interviewed in the order of their responsibility—the suspect believed to be most responsible is to be interviewed last.

In addition, when multiple persons are to be interviewed, the interviewer usually requests that each person being interviewed not discuss the matter with anyone. This helps accomplish two purposes: (1) to preserve evidence (a suspect could destroy evidence if she believes a fraud she committed is being investigated) and (2) to give the suspect less opportunity to think of a plausible **alibi,** a defense she offers to support her assertion of innocence.

Conducting the Individual Interview

LO5 The individual interview involves asking the right questions, listening, and responding appropriately. The questions to ask are typically one of five kinds: introductory, informational, assessment, admission seeking, and concluding. As discussed in a following section, assessment and admission-seeking questions are only used when the interviewee is considered a suspect. The questions are asked in an order that facilitates the information-gathering process and generally follows the order shown in Figure 10.1.

FIGURE 10.1
The Interviewing Process

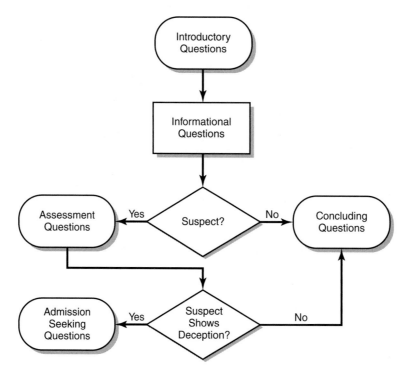

Initial Questions for Suspects and Nonsuspects

The questions to ask depend on whether the interviewee is not a suspect (i.e., simply a person from whom information is collected) or a suspect. When interviewees are not suspects, the interviewer asks introductory, informational, and concluding questions. However, when he is a suspect, the interviewer will ask introductory, informational, assessment, and admission-seeking questions. These types of questions are discussed next.

Introductory questions are asked to solicit the interviewee's cooperation. Before asking these questions, the interviewer should shake his hand upon greeting him. This act, and others such as mirroring (discussed later), usually engenders a feeling of connection—called **rapport**—between the interviewer and the subject that can increase the likelihood that the subject will answer the questions posed.

After the interviewer has introduced herself and engaged in some small talk (usually about benign topics such as the weather) to further the connection to the subject, the interviewer should state the purpose in general terms (e.g., "I'm here to collect some information about the area in which you work so that we can make improvements"). The interviewer should next ask the person interviewed if he would help by answering a few questions. His response should be definite—a nod of the head is too weak because he has not committed himself as strongly as he would have had he voiced a reply. Thus, if the interviewee merely nods his head, the interviewer should ask the question again, "So you would be willing to help by answering a few questions?" Persons who are asked a question a second time often provide an answer in a different form, thinking that the person who asked the question might not have understood the answer.

During this phase of the interview (and the next phase, the informational phase) the interviewer should avoid using sensitive terms such as *audit* and *investigation;* instead, she should use words such as *assignment* and *inquiry.* For example, she can say "I've been given an assignment by my boss. Would you mind if I asked you a few questions?" If words such as *investigation* are used, the interviewee might feel threatened or, if not a guilty party, could be even more reluctant to divulge information that could be the basis for retaliation by the person about whom the questions are asked.

While introducing oneself, making small talk, and asking for the interviewee's cooperation, the interviewer should be watching the suspect's demeanor closely. The purpose of this close observation is called **calibration,** which fine-tunes an interviewer's perception of a person's behavior when he is asked nonsensitive (i.e., nonincriminating) questions so that she can contrast that behavior with the subject's behavior when he is asked sensitive questions. His behavior during the time when he is asked nonconfrontational (i.e., nonsensitive) questions can be compared later with his behavior when he is asked more sensitive questions.

Informational questions are designed to collect information that is relevant to the investigation. Therefore, they represent the most important and most frequently used type of questions an interviewer can ask. These questions can be about the interviewee's work environment, such as internal controls (or, more specifically, lack of controls or violations of controls), co-workers, and documents such as records, bank accounts, and loan applications. Examples of these questions are "Who performs the bank reconciliation around here?" and "Have you noticed any changes in any of your co-workers' behaviors?" The interviewer is not to ask these questions in an accusatory manner; the purpose of informational questions is to collect information.

The interviewee should be asked—if he knew the purpose of the interview—whom he believes committed the fraud and why. Often a co-worker or victim of the perpetrator is knowledgeable about who committed a fraud.

Final Questions to Ask Nonsuspects

LO6   If the person being interviewed was a suspect at the beginning of the interview but has since been eliminated as a suspect by means of verbal and nonverbal responses during the interview, he is asked **concluding questions.** These questions are used to (1) confirm information received by the interviewer during the interview, (2) obtain information that has not yet been gathered, and (3) seek the subject's agreement that he will continue to cooperate.

The interviewer is performing a number of tasks when interviewing: asking questions, listening carefully, observing nonverbal communication, and adapting to new information that she might not have known prior to the interview. It would not be unusual, then, for the interviewer to misinterpret information the suspect provides. Therefore, one purpose of concluding questions is to confirm the interviewer's understanding of the important facts collected during the interview. Closely associated with this task is to clarify the meaning of any statements made by the subject about which the interviewer is unsure.

New information can be obtained by asking concluding questions. This is usually accomplished by asking "Is there anything you'd like to add that would help me to look into this matter we've been discussing?" Even though an experienced interviewer will be well prepared before interviewing the subject, she might overlook the importance of asking certain questions because she is not privy to *all* the facts. The interviewer should never assume that she knows everything about the investigation; she is interviewing because she does not have enough information including evidence.

The interviewer should end the interview on a positive note. This is especially helpful if she needs to contact the subject again should she gather evidence not known at the time of the interview. As she did at the beginning of the interview, the interviewer strives to elicit a verbal "yes" in answer to the question, "If I need to contact you again, would you be willing to speak with me?"

Also at this time, an interviewer might want to solicit the subject's agreement to keep the matter discussed quiet. This can be accomplished by asking, "Would you not discuss this matter with anyone? I'd like the matter to be kept quiet so that no one is hurt by the disclosure of the information we've discussed."

Additional Questions to Ask Suspects

Besides introductory and informational questions, suspects are also asked assessment questions and, if the interviewer is still convinced of the interviewee's guilt, admission-seeking questions. Up to this point, the various types of questions (introductory and informational) usually will not have provoked confrontational behavior from the interviewee. Even though suspects are more likely to be defensive, they usually hold their behavior in check (consistent with their covert behavior) when they are asked introductory and informational questions. However, assessment questions, and especially admission-seeking questions, can raise the ire of even the most disciplined of suspects. These questions represent a threat to their survival and can result in various responses—most likely fear, which can appear as anger.

Assessment questions are asked to determine whether the interviewee is a suspect and are asked only when the interviewer believes that the interviewee is a suspect based on evidence collected before the interview began or because of answers provided during the interview, or both. Answers provided during the interview can indicate guilt if they are inconsistent with reliable, valid evidence collected prior to the interview or if the subject provides contradictory answers during it.

Verbal and Nonverbal Responses

LO7   Subjects' **verbal responses** (oral or written answers to questions) and **nonverbal responses** (physiology-based reactions to questions, statements, and physical evidence) become even more important during this phase of the interview. Verbal replies to assessment questions can indicate the subject's attitude. Assessment questions are, for the most part, similar to the analytical procedures discussed in Chapter 9: They are *indications* of guilt, not a determination of the person's guilt or innocence. That determination is more fully explored in the admission-seeking phase.

The interviewer can begin, for example, with the following: "We are aware that fraud has been committed by an employee at this location. As I understand, you're a person who's knowledgeable about what goes on around here. Have you heard about this fraud?" The interviewer will not only listen to the subject's answer but also watch the subject closely to assess any nonverbal cues (discussed later) such as nervousness.

Subjects who are not trying to hide anything usually provide direct answers to questions without hesitation. They do not seem distracted (perhaps, in large part, because they are not trying to formulate a story to tell) and may even appear interested in helping her. Exceptions to these general rules exist. For example, if the subject is aware that the reason for the interview is the investigation of an embezzlement of cash and knows that his supervisor is a suspect in the crime, he may be reluctant to volunteer any information that would lead to the supervisor's conviction.

Subjects who are trying to hide something usually do not furnish helpful information. For example, if a suspect is asked a typical assessment question such as "What do you think should happen to the person who committed this fraud?" a guilty person's answer is more likely to convey a belief that the person committing a fraud should be treated leniently (e.g., "Perhaps the person should be given a second chance") or that the punishment should depend on the reason the person committed the fraud, meaning that the commission of a fraud can be justified.

Asking guilty persons why someone would have committed a fraud can also be helpful because guilty persons have probably had sufficient practice at rationalizing their behavior. In fact, their rationalizations might be their own reasons for committing fraud or at least related to them. Persons who are not guilty are not as likely to provide rationalizations; instead, they are more likely to say something such as, "I don't think there's a good reason to commit fraud." Besides asking about the reasons (i.e., rationalizations) perpetrators commit fraud, the investigator can use the fraud triangle to determine the identity of the perpetrator by asking, "Who would have the opportunity to do this?" Guilty people seldom want to implicate anyone, so that the pool of suspects should be as large as possible (and thus the suspicion is directed as far away from the subjects as possible); therefore, a guilty person might respond by saying, "Well, it could be anyone here," a response reminiscent of the "everybody-does-it" assertion often used to justify guilty actions.

Another indication of deceptive behavior exists when a subject attempts to treat the crime (e.g., financial statement fraud) being investigated as unimportant. This attempt to reduce the egregiousness of the crime may be an attempt to convince the interviewer that the perpetrator should not be punished severely for the crime. More obvious **verbal cues** (indications of guilt that should be investigated) occur if the subject attacks the interviewer verbally. Fear is the basis for this type of response and is a natural reaction when survival is threatened. When an animal (the human animal in this case) is cornered, it makes a fight-or-flight response. The fight response may materialize as accusations regarding the interviewer. In this situation, the interviewer should respond calmly to the subject and attempt to reestablish rapport. This approach is directed at making the subject feel more comfortable and less threatened. In extreme cases, when rapport cannot be reestablished, termination of the interview may be necessary; if it is, an effective interview with the subject in the future may be best conducted by someone else who is familiar with the case.

To better understand verbal cues and their use, we must consider the sensory orientation of humans. Information about a human's environment is registered through one or more of the five senses: hearing, sight, smell, taste, and touch. Each person assesses his environment by predominantly using one of these senses. Remember: other senses are used as well and a sophisticated forensic accountant can utilize this knowledge to expand the amount of information obtained from a subject. Persons usually speak, however, in terms of one of three senses: sight, auditory (hearing), and touch (sometimes called *kinesthetic* but also associated with feelings or emotion). These three senses will provide clues as to which of the senses predominates for a particular person.

An interviewer typically would determine which sense predominates by being aware of the use of words by the person being interviewed. For example, if a person uses phrases such as "I see" or "It looks like," the person is probably a sight-dominated person. Consider the following example.

> Look here. I didn't see anything. If you think you're gonna put me under the microscope so that you can clearly see what's going on, you're not. Why don't you look elsewhere? I'm sure you'll find a lot more reasons to focus on another person. I'm not the one you're looking for.

Can you "see" the sight words in this paragraph? *Look, looking, see, microscope,* and *focus* all indicate that this person "thinks" in terms of sight and uses this sense more than others. An astute interviewer could tap into what this person saw because this sense is more likely to be the person's more highly developed sense.

A person who uses phrases such as "It sounds to me" or "I hear what you mean" is a likely an auditory-dominated person. Consider the following example.

> Don't you hear what I'm saying to you? To anyone else, it would sound as though you're trying to make some big noise about what you think I did. I didn't hear anything, and I'm not gonna talk about this because you're not listening to me.

This person appears to use the sense of hearing to interact with the world—to accumulate as well as disseminate information. She could be questioned to determine what she heard about the fraud or what she heard while committing the fraud.

A person who uses phrases such as "I feel that . . ." or "My heart nearly broke" more likely than not has touch as the predominate sense. The following example demonstrates this type of person.

> I'm not sure about what was going on, but I feel that whatever it was, it wasn't fair. Life's been kind of rough and I do not know . . . perhaps I've not gotten in touch with the right people—made the right connections, I guess. But I know one thing: I was not about to go through times like these again. I was going to get a handle on life and grab on to whatever I could, even if it meant stepping on other people's toes.

This person senses the world through feeling, through touching. To speak his language, the interviewer must listen closely and use similar words.

Why is it important for interviewers or interrogators to determine the predominant sense? The answer lies in what has to be done in order for the objective—the gathering of relevant information—to be accomplished. The subject must be persuaded to become a willing participant in the evidence-gathering process. An investigator who can determine an interviewee's predominant sense can "tune in" to it to establish rapport to increase the likelihood that a subject provides information the investigator seeks.

Interviewers should also pay close attention to the words subjects use even though they are not consciously choosing their words. Use of words such as *you, your,* and *they* (rather than *I, my,* and *me*) to describe their own behavior may be an attempt to shift some responsibility from themselves to others. Consider the following interview example in which a member of management is suspected of intentionally misstating financial statements.

You know how the market interprets a decline in earnings. It kills you. And you feel that pressure to protect your employees. Some of these people have families with small children and they could not afford to lose their jobs. Have you ever seen worried looks on the faces of faithful employees? Believe me—you don't have any choice but to help these people.

Here the subject is shifting responsibility from himself to the market. Whether consciously or unconsciously, he wants to distance himself from any improprieties that have occurred.

If the subject typically uses the words listed in the preceding paragraph to refer to his behavior, their use may simply be a habit. Still, the display of habit does not necessarily mean that the subject is not subconsciously using these words to purposely absolve himself from the consequences of his behavior. Another reason the subject may use these words is to engender sympathy from the interviewer. In other words, by talking in terms of the interviewer (the reference to *you*), the subject may consciously or unconsciously be attempting to get the interviewer to step into his shoes and identify with him.

Other words to be aware of are *qualifiers.* A **qualifier** modifies the meaning of a sentence so that the subject can make a truthful statement while providing an exception that often represents the opportunity to commit fraud or is an excuse for the subject's behavior. For example, if a subject who has not followed the prescribed internal control of listing checks says, "We prepare a list of the checks received almost all the time," the word *almost* is a qualifier because it changes the meaning the sentence would have if it did not contain the qualifier. The word *almost* allows the subject to avoid making a statement that she knows is untrue. The sentence without the qualifier would appear as follows: "We prepare a listing of the checks received all the time." On the other hand, a subject who is innocent and very conservative may use the word *almost* to be more nearly precise. This illustrates an important point about evidence. Rarely will one evidence-gathering technique provide all evidence needed to solve a case; instead, evidence from multiple sources is generally required for identification of the fraudster.

At times, a subject may use phrases such as "To the best of my knowledge" as a means of having the option to recant later by means of an apparent improvement in memory. Other phrases used as qualifiers include "That's about it" and the words *sometimes, often, maybe, possibly, typically,* and *normally.* Use of these words and phrases may represent attempts to hedge, thus enabling her to avoid making definite statements that can be shown to be untrue. At times, a subject may use qualifiers to enhance the credibility of her statements. Examples of these qualifiers include "The truth is . . ." and "To be perfectly honest . . . ." The words that follow these phrases may indeed represent the truth if for no other reason than to intersperse some truth among false statements in attempting to draw attention away from her deceptive statements. In other cases, the words that follow the qualifiers may represent untruthful statements.

Other qualifiers operate by association. They are used in attempts to increase the credibility of statements by associating the statements with references to authorities or to what many persons may believe are representations of honesty. For example, a subject might say, "I'm a decent, hard-working person. You can check with my minister; he'll tell you that." In other cases, she might say, "As God is my witness . . ." or "I swear on a stack of Bibles." Peppering responses with these compensating phrases is a ploy to associate the ideals conveyed by the compensating phrases with her character in an attempt to reduce the similarity between her and dishonest acts.

Sounds that are not words also may be a clue to the truthfulness of the subject's statement. These sounds include "ah" and "um" and serve the same purpose that beginning a sentence with *well* serves: providing the subject additional time to think of a plausible response (as does repeating the interviewer's question). These sounds and words represent signposts that point to statements the subject is making up as she speaks rather than being a factual recount of events that occurred. Again, the signpost of truthfulness is the *change* or *lack of change* in the subject's method of speaking.

Another indication of a potentially deceptive response is a response that is overly specific. A subject who has had sufficient time to formulate a story to tell can give such a response. When provided with a very specific response, the investigator can use the information to demonstrate that the subject intended to deceive (by proving the information was false) or that the subject had knowledge that only the perpetrator would possess. This technique underscores the importance of documenting subjects' responses carefully so that any later objection raised by her regarding her responses can be effectively countered.

Nonverbal cues are just that; they are not spoken or written. These can include the failure to deny an allegation as well as the failure to answer an interviewer's question. Besides the nonverbal cue that exists when the subject does not convey information the interviewer believes should be communicated orally or in written form (i.e., the absence of information), two nonverbal cues are of primary importance: eye movements and body language. The former can be used to determine (or confirm) the subject's dominant sense, and the latter can provide clues as to the truthfulness of the subject's spoken words.

LO8   *Eye Movements*   Movement of the eyes can indicate the truthfulness of a subject's response. A subject who is Sight-dominated when asked a question usually (1) looks up and to the left, (2) straight ahead, or (3) uses both of these movements. They allow a subject to more easily access visually stored memories. These eye characteristics, coupled with the language the subject uses, provide an indication that her dominant sense is sight.

At times, a subject must visually construct (Figure 10.2) an image of a situation that has not occurred. This would happen, for example, when a guilty subject is asked, "What would top management think about you if it was discovered that one of your subordinates was embezzling funds?" When asked a question such as this, a sight-dominated person would most likely look up and to the *right.*

How can you use this information as an interviewer? If a subject you believe is sight-dominated is asked a question that should elicit the recounting of a factual situation and looks up and to the right, he may be speaking of things that did not occur and thus may be changing history. Prior to asking a question such as this, the forensic accountant should ask a question to which she knows the answer and expects the subject to respond truthfully. By doing this, she will have a higher level of assurance that the subject is sight-dominated and will likely respond by using typical eye patterns of sight-dominated persons. In interviewing, the key information is often contained in *changes* in the subject's behavior, not any one particular habit.

A subject who is primarily auditory will exhibit memory recall by either (1) looking down and to the left or (2) horizontally and to the left. Sounds the subject recalls hearing from external sources are associated with the eyes looking down and to the left. If the subject is recalling internal sounds—sounds he made—he will be more likely to look horizontally and to the left. Similar to the visual construction of the sight-dominated person, the interviewer would expect a different pattern if the subject were asked how a particular scenario would sound. In this case, the auditory-dominated person would most likely look horizontally and to the right. Again, being alert to changes will reveal clues as to the truthfulness of a subject's response. See Figure 10.3.

For a touch- (or feeling-) dominated person, the eye patterns are slightly different. This type of person will either (1) look downward and to the right, (2) look downward, (3) blink rapidly, or (4) close his eyes. Of course, the subject could (and probably will) exhibit a

FIGURE 10.2
Visual Memory Eye
Positions

Visual Construction Eye Position

combination of these eye movements. Recall that one of the interviewer's objectives is to move an unwilling subject to a more willing position. For a feeling person, this can be accomplished by establishing an emotional rapport with him. Because this person reacts more often by what he *feels*—instead of what he *thinks*—recreating an ambiance that leads him to feel that he is doing what is best for him often encourages him to cooperate with the interviewer. A person who usually experiences the world through feelings exhibits certain characteristics when he is receptive to questions posed by the interviewer. For example, deep breathing accompanied by a relaxation of the major muscle groups (those of the arms, legs, abdomen, and chest) is often a sign that he is more willing to cooperate. If, however, he exhibits any tenseness, he may indicate that he is not in a willing position. A change in behavior, whether toward a more relaxed position or away from it, indicates to the interviewer the relative willingness, and thus receptiveness, of the subject to the interviewer's attempts to gather evidence.

Body Language   A subject's body language can tell the interviewer things he is not willing to disclose verbally. This includes sitting in a "fleeing position" in which his face and torso are facing the interviewer but his legs and feet face the door. A shift or almost any discernable changes by the subject—particularly when the topic of conversation changes—can signal subtle yet revealing clues to the truthfulness of his responses. For example, if he allows a significant pause to occur between the time he is asked a question and his verbal response, he could be taking additional time to think of an answer to the

FIGURE 10.3
Auditory Memory
Eye Positions

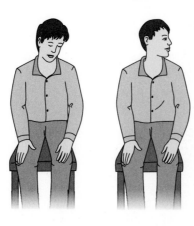

Auditory Construction Eye Position

question. Other body language that can indicate deception includes reaching for nearby objects, scratching, adjusting clothes, and picking lint off clothes. These acts not only can provide additional time for the subject to think of a deceptive response but can also offer him a chance for mental respite from the tremendous stress of being interviewed. Such acts can cause the interviewer to focus on nonessential activities that can increase the likelihood that the interviewer will accept the answers the subject provides without rigorous evaluation. Other behavior that may indicate untruthful responses include swallowing, biting lips, pursing (i.e., closing tightly) his lips, covering his mouth with his hand (or hands), and perspiring.

Be aware, however, that there can be reasonable explanations for a subject's behavior. For example, a subject being interviewed might be cold natured; crossing her arms is a normal response to being in a cold environment. If, however, the arm crossing suddenly occurs when the interviewer begins to ask sensitive questions, this *change in behavior* can indicate guilt. Thus, the most important aspect of reading body language is the attention paid to the *change* in behavior. For example, if the suspect had made eye contact with the interviewer until the topic of skimming (of which she was suspected) was brought up, the lack of eye contact becomes a very important indicator of guilt.

Over time, interviewers become more adept at recognizing cues and thus are more likely to recognize even subtle messages contained in the subjects' physical and verbal responses. Being alert for these messages is very important. Subjects who are guilty or who have information they are not willing to share have an informational advantage over interviewers who try to obtain this information. Humans can speak at about 125 words per minute and can think about 10 times that speed; therefore, subjects who are deceptive can anticipate questions and have time to mentally prepare responses designed to satisfy the interviewer without disclosing all information the interviewer desires.

Admission-Seeking Questions

LO9 If, based on responses (both verbal and nonverbal) to the assessment questions, the subject displays a sufficient indication of guilt or if the interviewer has a reasonable amount of evidence that suggests the subject is guilty, the forensic accountant should ask **admission-seeking questions** that are designed to encourage confession from someone strongly suspected of playing a role in the fraud being investigated.

When seeking an admission to a fraud, the forensic accountant doing the interview often directly accuses the subject if he is almost certain the subject has committed the offense. When making this accusation, the interviewer should avoid the use of emotionally charged words such as *fraud, crime, theft, steal, embezzle,* and *embezzlement, manipulation, lie,* and *cheat.* Furthermore, he should not ask the subject whether she acted wrongly but tell her that he is aware of the fraud and that she committed it. For example, if the interviewer is conducting an interview of a person suspected of embezzling money, he could state, "We are aware that you have been taking money from the company."

The suspect should then be asked a question that, if answered, is tantamount to an explicit confession. The interviewer's objective is to make confession as painless as possible; people do not usually change their behavior (e.g., confess) unless the pain of continuing their behavior (e.g., not confessing) is greater than the pain of stopping it. These questions should not be structured so that the suspect is asked whether she committed the fraud but so the answer is an admission of guilt. For example, if she is believed to have embezzled money, a question can be "Is this the first time you took the money?" Note that he is not asking the suspect if she took the money; he asks if this time was the *first time* she took it. By answering "yes," the suspect has confessed. If the answer is "no," then the follow-up question should be "When was the first time you took some money?" The suspect can provide an approximate date or state that she has never taken any money. By this time, however, the interviewer should have evidence that strongly suggests that the suspect has committed embezzlement and must make a decision as to whether he should divulge some of the evidence to her or to respond to the denial by saying, "We have evidence that you took the money. Right now, we're giving you the opportunity to cooperate. If you refuse, I'll have to terminate the interview and report that you failed to cooperate." As mentioned earlier, guilty persons usually do not want an interview to end because if it does, they are unsure how much evidence the interviewer has against them. This attempt by the suspect to know the extent of the evidence against her is an effort to regain control, stemming from the inborn desire to survive.

Instead of asking whether a specific incidence of fraud was the first time the suspect had committed fraud, the interviewer can ask the admission-seeking question by providing alternatives; the choice of either is again tantamount to a confession. For example, the interviewer could ask, "Did you take the money because of financial hardship or to teach [employer's name] a lesson?" The alternatives here—financial hardship or revenge—vary from investigation to investigation. The structure, though, is the same: To ask a question that contains two alternatives so that whichever one the subject chooses indicates an admission of guilt. The question must be structured as a leading question and phrased so that she must respond with either a "yes" or a "no." Although leading questions are discouraged in court, they are appropriately used when asking admission-seeking questions in interviews. Here the leading question approach makes it easier for the suspect to respond affirmatively by providing an opening for her to rationalize her behavior. However, when she suspect has signed a confession, the investigator avoids this approach in favor of what is acceptable in court: a direct, unequivocal admission of guilt that is not tied to a reason for the illegal behavior.

Subjects may attempt to deceive by responding to questions with questions of their own. In a situation such as this, the interviewer must be careful not to relinquish control to the subject. For example, if he asks a subject, "Did you take the money?" and she replies, "Why would I do something as foolish as that?" her indignant behavior (which, of course, may be feigned) is meant to imply that she did not take the money. Notice that in this situation, the subject has not answered the question. At the same time, she may respond to his question with a statement such as "I'm a well-respected member of the management team at this company." The subject is providing the interviewer a reason to drop the question. In such a case, the interviewer should first explain to the subject that he needs a "yes" or "no" response and should then repeat the question.

When accused, innocent persons are rarely silent. Guilty persons, on the other hand, often react by becoming silent or, if they speak, offer weak denials. If the subject does deny the accusation and the interviewer has evidence that indicates her guilt, she should not be allowed to continue to make denials. She should be interrupted because with each occurrence of a denial, she is making any subsequent confession more difficult. At this point, she has not only committed the offense but also has lied. In this situation, the interviewer should quietly remind the suspect that protesting her innocence may only make the situation worse and assure her that he wants to report that she was cooperative. Just as a subject uses qualifiers (e.g., almost, nearly always) to avoid telling a lie, she usually does not say, "I didn't do it" but attempts to explain why she did not do it or try to divert the interviewers' attention to others who may have committed the offense.

The suspect may give an alibi in an attempt to convince the interviewer of her innocence. At this point, he may have to disclose some of the evidence that indicates her guilt. It is important not to disclose all the evidence; much like the poker player, the interviewer must not show his hand before full disclosure of the evidence is necessary. The evidence that should be shown first is the least important. If necessary, increasingly important evidence may be shown until the suspect's denials cease. At times, the evidence may be testimony obtained from earlier interviewers with others who know about the fraud. However, the disclosure of too much testimony, besides tipping the interviewer's hand, may also inform the suspect of the identity of witnesses and therefore should be avoided. Thus, the decision to divulge evidence to the suspect is not to be done without carefully weighing its impact on coaxing a confession from the suspect against the unwanted consequence of giving her knowledge of information concerning the evidence the forensic accountant possesses. After all, the reason for seeking a confession is to build a stronger case than the one he has without the confession. The evidence without the confession might barely be adequate (and in some cases, is inadequate) to prosecute the suspect in court. The confession can be a critical factor in determining success in court.

In seeking a confession, the interviewer can make confessing easier for the suspect by helping her find a morally acceptable reason for committing the fraud. This reason is not one that would excuse her from legal consequences; it is only a reason that, for herself, reconciles her illegal behavior with her ideal self. Reducing this cognitive dissonance by having a person such as the interviewer not reject the reason as a morally acceptable one is an important step in eliciting the confession. In some cases, finding the morally acceptable reason can be accomplished by asking the suspect, "Can you tell me why you did this? I just want to know." If she does not respond immediately, he can offer common reasons and, if one of those does not seem to be the reason, progress to less common ones.

The most common reasons for committing fraud include being underpaid, experiencing inadequate recognition (nonfinancial) at work, drug and alcohol abuse (i.e., these substances altered her personality and ability to think to the point at which she behaved in an unusual manner), financial difficulties such as the need to pay medical bills including those of family members, and other financial needs created by an addiction to drugs or gambling. The suspect can even give reasons that are seemingly unjustifiable to the interviewer. For example, assume that Lisa is married and has two young children. The interviewer suspects that she has been embezzling money to fund family vacations. An astute interviewer can ask the following question to establish a face-saving reason: " Lisa, did you take the money to help your family?" Most parents would do anything they could for their family and our society respects those who (legitimately) do. In other words, the suspect would like to be seen as someone who tried to solve her own problems (i.e., she was a victim herself because she was not paid enough by her employer to provide a family vacation).

Expressing sympathy with the subject can make confessing easier. By appealing to her circumstances (e.g., difficult financial stress because of the illness of a family member), the interviewer may make answering truthfully less difficult for her. Expressing sympathy will work best if he can share with her a similar hardship that he experienced. This is another example establishing rapport with the subject and of its importance to both him and her. He can empathize with her but not convey that her behavior is excusable legally—that is a decision to be made by a judge or jury.

The morally acceptable reason a suspect gives is often the rationalization she used to excuse her behavior to herself. Thus, finding this key piece of evidence is important for building the case that the crime was committed with intent and that the suspect knew that the behavior was wrong.

Once the suspect has confessed, the interviewer can then ask, in a considerate manner, about the details of the fraud. For example, questions regarding an embezzlement should include those that elicit information concerning when the activity first occurred, when it ceased, approximately how many times it occurred, approximately how much money was taken, how any assets were taken, where are the stolen assets, and whether others were involved. These are facts that are known only to the perpetrator and will collaborate evidence already in his possession. Also at this time, the motive should be established. Although repeated acts, such as the perpetrator's pocketing cash, can indicate intent, the investigator needs to know why the fraud was committed so that defense counsel is less likely to be successful at refuting the charges.

Using Interview Techniques

In this section, we discuss certain aspects of interviewing that the forensic accountant should consider as she plans and conducts the interviews.

Recording the Interview

LO10 An interview should be recorded only if the information expected to be conveyed during it will be very detailed and is not easily susceptible to note taking or later recall (or, in the case of law enforcement, when proper protocol is to record interrogations). If the interview is to be recorded, permission from the subject usually must be obtained. Often, audio recording individuals who are not aware that they are being recorded is against state law. In this case, checking with an attorney on the legality of surreptitious audio recording before attempting it is prudent. Besides the benefit provided by creating a record of details and of a confession when one occurs, factors to consider before audio recording include the possibility that the knowledge of recording might inhibit a subject's disclosure of certain facts and opinions. If in doubt, the interviewer is better off not audio recording an interview.

Taking Notes

LO11 Instead of making an audio recording of the interview, a forensic accountant can write brief notes during the interview and (time permitting, of course) can later rewrite a more complete version that can include items that the interviewer recalls but did not write down during the interview. People remember by connecting bits of information to other bits of information. Thus, if they put certain information on paper, they can recall other information by their association with the written notes. This association, however, does not last for long; therefore, rewriting a more nearly complete version of information as soon after the interview as possible is a technique that will greatly increase the effectiveness of interviewing.

If notes are taken during an interview, the interviewer should begin them for each interview on a separate piece of paper. Some interviews will be used as evidence in court and others will not; notes taken during interviews not used in court should not be a part of the evidence admitted. The reason for this is simple: Information that one subject gave during an interview might not be supported by information given by other subjects interviewed and/or evidence from other sources. The jury might therefore misunderstand the evidence or have its attention diverted by opposing counsel if this information is a part of subpoenaed evidence. As a result of a doubt created in the minds of jury members, the perpetrator might not be convicted.

If notes are taken during an interview, the interviewer should exercise care so that she does not provide the subject—especially if a suspect—any indication that would indicate her evaluation of his spoken word or behavior. If she telegraphs her evaluation to the subject, later answers can be affected (either fabricated or omitted) because he will have more information as to what appears to be important to the interviewer.

Using Written Questions

Bringing a list of written questions to the interview is not usually a good idea for two reasons. First, it can encourage the tunnel vision discussed earlier because the interviewer's focus is on a set of predetermined questions to be asked. A good interviewer must be prepared to analyze new information quickly during an interview and formulate questions about this information. Writing a predetermined set of questions beforehand can be an anathema to this process.

Second, if the subject sees the set of written questions and can read them, he is in a better position to respond to the questions with contrived answers. Receiving answers that were designed to cover up the truth is not consistent with the objective of the interview: to obtain the truth. Instead of writing a set of questions, a better approach is for the interviewer to write a list of general topics. Even if the subject sees the topics, he is not as likely to formulate a fictitious answer to a question that the interviewer could ask. If the interviewer can use abbreviations or other type of shorthand, she could reduce further the possibility of being given untruthful responses.

Choosing the Interview Setting

LO12 If the subject is not a suspect, the interviewer can conduct the interview at her office where she has easy access to files that might be helpful to the investigation. If, however, the subject is a suspect, he should be interviewed at a neutral location. One reason for using a neutral location is to purposefully place him in a setting that is not familiar to him. Not being in a familiar setting can interfere with the recall of previously rehearsed alibis and thus increase the likelihood that the suspect will have to create fictitious answers. Fictitious answers can lead to inconsistencies in the suspect's story, which can be the predication and opportunity for an interviewer to begin asking admission-seeking questions. As an alternative, the interview can be conducted on a surprise basis; this, too, can reduce the recall of previously rehearsed answers.

When being interviewed, the subject should be seated without any obstruction between him and the door, which should remain unlocked during the interview. The subject should also not be seated behind a desk so that the interviewer can see his entire physical form. The interviewer should be looking for signs of deception such as fidgeting, toe-tapping, crossing and uncrossing the legs, or nervousness such as bouncing the leg. If the subject is interviewed in his office, as many nonsuspects are, he may already be behind a desk. Although nonsuspects do not usually display as much nervousness as suspects, having the subject not sit behind a desk is still preferable because in some cases, nonsuspects become suspects.

The temperature of the room should not be too low or too high. If it's too low, the subject might not be as likely to exhibit physical symptoms that can be distinguished from the symptoms produced by the temperature. For example, if he is too cold, he might have already folded his arms across his chest; therefore, arm folding is not a reliable symptom of guilt. If the temperature is too high, he might not be able to concentrate on the questions due to the unpleasantness of the heat and might not take time to respond to narrative-type questions. He might also use the high temperature as a distracter by constantly complaining about the temperature of the room.

Preferably, the interview room will contain few distractions. Guilty persons become adept at using pictures, memorabilia, books and other items as a means to distract the interviewer from her agenda or to dilute the significance of certain answers he has provided. In reality, the interviewer will have to deal with a certain amount of potential distracters in the room and might, then, have to refocus the subject on the questions asked.

Determining the Number of People to Interview

Normally, one interviewer is sufficient. However, for interviews that involve admission-seeking questions, two interviewers should be present so that if the suspect alleges that he was coerced into confessing or otherwise mistreated, the charge can more easily be repudiated.

Interviewers should not sit together across from the suspect; if they do, the suspect may feel he is outnumbered and may be even less amenable to answering questions. The suspect might also feel oppressed if both interviewers ask questions; thus, the best approach is to have one of the interviewers ask the questions while the other takes notes. The suspect need not be informed of his Miranda rights unless he is being questioned by law enforcement personnel and is in custody.

If possible, no other persons other than the two interviewers should be allowed to witness the interview; if others are present, the flow of questioning could be disrupted, causing the suspect to regress to a less persuasive position. If the attorney for the suspect or a union representative is present, the interviewer should request that he or she not ask questions or object to specific questions.

Mirroring

An interviewer uses the process of **mirroring** to establish rapport by mimicking the subject's body language. For example, assume that the interviewer and subject are sitting directly across from each other. If the subject crosses his left leg over his right leg, the interviewer should cross her right leg over her left leg (see Figure 10.4). If the subject cups his chin with his right hand, the interviewer should cup her chin in her left hand. The purpose of this, of course, is for the interviewer to appear as similar to the subject as possible so that she appears to identify so closely with the subject that he feels as though the interviewer is on his side. In short, friends confide in friends, and even though the interviewer and subject logically know they are not "friends," mimicking is used to produce the emotional feeling of closeness that unconsciously recalls the rudimentary feelings of friendship.

FIGURE 10.4

And then how did you react?

Establishing Interviewer Demeanor

The interviewer's objective of gathering information is more likely to be accomplished if she is in control of the interview. It is important then, that she never becomes angry (note that *appearing* to be angry as an interviewing tactic is quite different from *actually* becoming angry). If the interviewer becomes angry, she transfers control from herself to the subject. In this situation, he can more easily determine the amount and quality of information he provides. It is important, then, for the interviewer not to take the actions (present or past) of the subject personally. A subject, particularly one that is a suspect, is engaged in a battle for his survival. Usually, any animosity the subject feels toward the interviewer occurs because she represents a threat to the suspect's freedom (or wealth, if fines could be imposed). In other words, he usually does not become angry at the interviewer, but does become angry at the authority the interviewer represents. This anger, however, may be focused on the interviewer because the interviewer is a tangible representation of the authority.

Applying Structure to Questions

LO13 The investigator can use several different types of question structures when interviewing a subject. Questions with these structures are commonly referred to as *closed-ended questions, forced-choice questions, open-ended questions, connecting questions, positive reaction questions, clarifying questions, confrontational questions,* and *secondary questions.* The interviewer's knowledge of these question structures and when they are best used increases the likelihood of obtaining information beneficial to the investigation.

Closed-ended questions are those to which a response is either "yes" or "no" or a brief response. An example is "Did you take money from your employer?" If the subject answers this type of question with anything other than a "yes," "no," or brief response, the interviewer should pay close attention because the answer may be evasive; for example, the subject may answer this question by saying, "Why would you ask me a question like that? I've been working for my boss for eight years. Don't I deserve more respect than this?" Notice that the subject did not answer the question but posed two questions of his own. An investigator should respond to this question by saying, "You do deserve respect. This is why I'm asking you such a simple question. Now, did you take money from your employer?"

Forced-choice questions are similar to closed-ended questions but do not result in a "yes" or "no" response. Instead, they give the subject limited (usually two or three) choices. For example, an interviewer could ask, "When you took the money, was it because of something your employer said or something that he did?"

Open-ended questions are those that encourage the subject to respond with more than a simple "yes" or "no" response. An example of this type of question is "What do you know about the situation?" The advantage of using such a question is that the investigator does not impose her perspective on the subject; instead, she allows him to mention details of which she may be unaware. Also, the longer a subject is allowed to speak—uninterrupted—the greater the likelihood that the investigator can observe the body language and, of course, "read" the subject for his dominant sense and signs of lying.

Connecting questions are used to "connect" details and events. For example, the investigator could ask a connecting question such as, "You mentioned that you were in the office on Monday. Was that the day that you overheard the conversation?"

Positive-reaction questions are used to elicit an agreement from the subject so that a pattern of agreement and willingness is more likely to continue. Positive reaction questions are also used to make answering easier for the subject. An example of this question structure is "You saw the person who took the money, didn't you?" Notice that the question is designed to produce a positive response (i.e., a "yes") from the subject. In other words, answering "yes" is much easier for the subject than stating that she saw the embezzler in response to an open-ended question.

Clarifying questions are used to encourage the subject to provide additional details that clarify a particular point of interest to the investigator. If, for example, the subject has just indicated that he has had difficulty with other employers, the investigator could ask, "What type of difficulties are you referring to?"

Confrontational questions are not really questions; they are actually statements designed to highlight contradictory evidence. The contradiction is usually between an answer provided by the subject and evidence that the investigator has obtained from other sources. An example of this is "You mentioned that you were at work between 9:00 A.M. and 10:00 A.M. Is that correct? [If the subject confirms, the interviewer proceeds.] I have an eyewitness who saw you park in the parking lot at 10:30 A.M." The last sentence, a statement, is the confrontational element. Confrontational questions are usually asked partly to determine whether the subject will change his story but, more importantly, whether his pattern of speech and body language will change in response to the question. If, for example, the subject speaks haltingly or appears to be making up a story as he answers, the interviewer may be able to follow up by asking clarifying questions. Often the use of clarifying questions in situations such as these further indicates a fictitious response.

Secondary questions, or second-hand questions, are used to elicit an expanded response from a subject and, like confrontational questions, are really statements rather than questions. Typically, the interviewer restates a sentence spoken by the subject as a means to encourage elaboration on the point he made in the sentence. For example, if a person in a managerial position is suspected of misstating the financial statements and says, "The accounts receivable were not correct," the interviewer may repeat the statement by saying, "The accounts receivable were not correct." At a minimum, this invites the subject to respond in the affirmative (by saying "yes"). If the interviewer does not obtain elaboration, she may use an open-ended, follow-up question such as "What do you mean when you say 'The accounts receivable were not correct'?"

The interviewer should avoid certain types of questions that allow the subject the chance to convey vague, even untruthful answers. These types of questions are *compound questions, leading questions,* and *negatively phrased questions.*

Compound questions are two or more questions contained in the same sentence. The reason their use should be avoided is that any answer provided by the subject cannot be easily connected to any specific question asked in the single sentence. For example, assume the investigator asks a subject, "Are you aware of any misstatements of the financial statements that have occurred in the past and have you made changes to your year-end financial statement preparation procedures in the last two years?" An answer of "no" could allow him to later contend that he was responding to the last question asked—the question about changes to the year-end financial statement processes. The rule here is for the interviewer to be specific by asking one question and waiting until the subject has answered the question before asking another one.

Leading questions prejudice a subject's response and are similar to compound sentences because the interviewer cannot determine the meaning of the subject's response. For example, assume that she asks, "Did you increase your allowance for bad debts because you wanted to show lower net income?" This question is actually two: One question is whether the subject increased the allowance and the second one is *why* the allowance was increased. This type of question is best asked by using two different questions. The first question would be "Did you increase the allowance for bad debts?" to allow the subject to respond that he did—or did not—increase the allowance, thus creating an opportunity to provide a response for the record as to his involvement. The second question would be "Why was the allowance for bad debts increased?" Another reason for not using this type of question is to reduce the likelihood that anyone who analyzes the video or transcript of the interview could later allege undue pressure.

The answer to **negatively phrased questions** is ambiguous. For example, assume that the interviewer asks the subject, "You are not aware of any financial statement fraud that has occurred, are you?" The answer "no" could mean that the subject *is not* aware of any financial statement fraud or that he *is* aware of financial statement fraud. A better way to ask this question is simply, "Are you aware of any financial statement fraud?"

How does an interviewer use her knowledge of the types of questions and verbal and nonverbal cues to gather evidence? The answer is to have a plan including the questions to be asked before the interview begins. Note that the questions and the question structure the interviewer uses in the interview may differ from those she originally chose. Still, having a plan more easily allows her to control the interview and obtain the evidence she needs.

The interview is much like a dance in which the interviewer and subject assume different positions and stances during it. A skilled interviewer who can sense the subject's position can adjust her approach and question type depending on the tone of the interview. Interviewing is a dynamic process and can turn quickly as a result of the words used and the manner in which questions are asked and answers are provided.

Using Persuasion

LO14 As mentioned earlier, the objective of the forensic accountant's interview is to obtain useful information. In most civilized societies, obtaining information involves the use of persuasion, not violence. Therefore, the subject who is either willing to cooperate or can be persuaded to cooperate will be more likely to provide information that can be used as evidence than a subject who is not. The subject who is willing to provide information from the time the interview begins does not pose the same challenge as that of an unwilling subject. However, the interviewer must still be aware of the possibility that a subject can appear willing yet provide misleading and even untruthful information. Nonverbal cues, discussed earlier, can indicate the truthfulness of the subject's statements.

The major challenge, then, is to persuade the unwilling subject to become a willing participant in the evidence-gathering process. One of the most important things to remember when attempting to persuade a subject to cooperate is to determine her motivation for committing the fraud and to sincerely attempt to convey an understanding of this motivation to her. Persons are more likely to respond when shown kindness and sympathy. In addition, the interviewer can use several approaches to persuade the subject to provide evidence he desires. These include the *direct approach, indirect approach,* and *combined approach.*

The **direct approach** is often effective when there is little doubt as to the suspect's guilt, she does not have a history of criminal behavior, and she can be influenced by appealing to her sympathy for others. Using this approach usually produces results more quickly than the **indirect approach** (see the following discussion) because the interviewer does not reason with the suspect and exercises more control over the interview, not allowing the suspect to meander when answering. When using this approach, the interviewer may point out to the suspect the overwhelming evidence that implicates her or the answers she has given that conflict with evidence available to him. The direct approach is often used when the suspect is unwilling to provide more than cursory answers to the interviewer's questions, which, most likely, will be structured as closed-ended questions. This type of approach is likely to be used when, for example, the investigation involves embezzlement by an employee not suspected of having engaged in this activity before.

The indirect approach is often employed when interviewing subjects who are either not believed to be those involved in the fraud or who are involved but are willing to answer questions, are persons who have been involved in similar activities in the past, or do not possess a sense of fairness and sympathy for others. The indirect approach works well when the interviewer is dealing with a person who realizes that her guilt can be established by evidence other than her answers to the interviewer. Open-ended questions are more likely to be used when the indirect approach is employed; answers to these questions provide the basis for a less controlled dialogue between the interviewer and subject—who is usually more sophisticated in her thinking—either because of her intelligence level or past convictions—than is the first-time offender. In this situation, a more suggestive and less emphatic manner of persuasion, such as reasoning, can be used. This approach is more likely to be used, for example, when conducting interviews of persons suspected of intentionally misstating financial statements.

The **combined approach** involves using parts of each approach or even changing from using one type to the other (e.g., from the indirect to the direct approach). The ability to do this is learned from experience and requires the interviewer to be acutely aware of the subject's mood.

Other approaches include influencing the subject's perception, by, for example, causing her to believe that much more is known about her misdeeds than actually is known; identifying her use of silence means that her belief that she can avoid prosecution is not correct; appealing to her emotional state; and using techniques such as rapid questioning that interfere with the subject's recall of rehearsed responses. See Table 10.1 for other approaches (which can be used singly or in combination).

It is important for the interviewer to keep in mind that the objective is to obtain helpful information from the subject in order to obtain a conviction or to obtain leads created by this information that can be pursued. Subjects who feel threatened will do what they can to survive. Thus, good interviewers have developed the ability to sense the attitude of the subject and adjust accordingly. Asking the right questions the right way increases the likelihood that the subject will be persuaded to provide the necessary information.

Overcoming Objections to Being Interviewed

LO15 Persons the interviewer wants to interview might not agree to be interviewed for various reasons, most of which fall into one of two categories (when the person does not want to incriminate herself, these reasons are better called *excuses*). The theme of the first category is "Do not bother me." Requests for interviews are usually met with such responses as "I don't want to be bothered" or "I don't have the time." The interviewer can counter such responses by saying that the interview will be short and that the answers the subject provides could be very helpful. If the subject insists on not talking, the interviewer should simply state, "I'd like to schedule a time to talk with you within the next two days." The time period—here two days—should be precise, not a distant time in the future. The definiteness

TABLE 10.1
Other Persuasive
Approaches

Name of Approach	Description
Everything is known	Investigator is very familiar with evidence in his possession and can respond with details so that subject believes he has substantial evidence on subject.
Folder	Investigator brings to the interview what appears to be a substantial amount of evidence in a folder so that the subject is more likely to cooperate by answering questions and, in the case of a suspect, to confess.
Silence	Interviewer is silent. If used at the beginning of an interview, the subject may lose self-confidence; if used after individual questions have been asked, the silence may prompt the subject to respond with more information.
Emotion	Subjects are usually motivated to commit misdeeds by some emotional stimuli (e.g., providing for family); the interviewer uses the emotional stimuli to motivate her to cooperate.
Rapid questioning	Interviewer poses questions quickly and with little time between them. This rapidity may increase the subject's truthfulness of responses due to the small amount of time she has between questions. To be effective, the interviewer must begin with questions that are seemingly innocuous to be able to achieve a momentum.
Change of location	Interviewer chooses a particular setting to encourage the subject to cooperate by, for example, providing a reminder of the environment in which the fraud occurred or an unfamiliar location to impair her ability to recall previously fabricated responses.

and short time period convey the impression that the interviewer *will* be back and could even encourage the subject to allow him a few minutes immediately in hopes of getting the issue out of the way.

The second category of responses is characterized by the theme "I can't help"; typical of these responses is the dismissive statement "I don't think I could help you." The best response to this statement is, "I'm confident that you can; just let me ask a few questions— that's all I ask." Whether the subject can help should be apparent not long into the interview. If she can help, she may obtain intrinsic satisfaction from helping. If the subject is a guilty person, she will most likely want to continue the interview to learn what evidence and knowledge the interviewer possesses.

Overcoming Objections to Answering Specific Questions

LO16 Besides having to overcome objections to being interviewed, the interviewee will occasionally not want to answer a specific question. Besides pressing her for the reason for not answering, the approach the interviewer should use to handle these objections depends on whether the subject is or is not a suspect. If she is not a suspect, the objection could be the result of fear that the suspect or others will retaliate (recall that SOX Section 806 provides a measure of protection but only if the subject is an employee of a public company and reports fraudulent financial reporting). If this is the case, the interviewer should assure the subject that the information divulged in the interview will be kept as quiet as possible. Under no circumstances should the interviewer guarantee confidentiality; the information the subject provides should be available for use in a court.

Perhaps the subject might have been raised not to criticize (i.e., told that "If you can't say something good about a person, don't say anything at all"). The interviewer should stress the amount of good the subject would be doing if she cooperates. Alternatively, he could stress the amount of harm that she could continue to do if she is not stopped or brought to justice so that the victim can be treated fairly. Casting the victim as a person (or, for example, a company having many innocent employees who have been harmed by the fraud) often triggers the sense of fairness that most people possess.

Some responses can be thinly veiled objections. For example, a subject who does not want to answer a question or who might want more time to create a fictitious answer might respond by saying something socially acceptable (e.g., "I don't remember anything about that"). The interviewer can respond by saying, "I'm not surprised. You're a very busy person. How about I give you a couple of minutes to think about it?" After several minutes, he can résume questioning about the event. If the subject truly could not recall the event in question and is not guilty, the extra time can enable her to recall something about the situation. The interviewer can then begin probing for more details. If she does not remember anything, he can jog her memory by asking her where she was or what she was doing on the day the event in question occurred. Sometimes, the interviewer can do little other than ask the subject to call him if she does recall anything. If the subject is a suspect, the interviewer should press her for information because she probably does recall but is not sharing this information with him.

The interviewer should be aware of a subject who tells him that she will check on the answer and get back to him in a couple of days. Such responses are often used as delaying tactics in the hope that the interviewer will become frustrated in his attempts to obtain the information. If she responds this way, he works with her to set a specific date for her to have the information by saying something such as "Very well, then, how about I drop by next Tuesday and you give me the information then?" If the investigator had not set the specific deadline of Tuesday, the subject most likely would indefinitely put off providing the information. Another example of vague references is to the ambiguous "someone" who either is responsible for a misdeed or has the information that the interviewer desires. In this case, the subject should be asked about the identity of the "someone."

If the subject is a suspect, her objections could be more vigorous. At times, suspects have attacked either the question or the interviewer or both. For example, she could ask, "What do you mean by asking that?" The tone of voice distinguished mere inquiry from a subtle threat. Whether the subject is inquisitive and thus requires clarification of the question or is displaying anger, the interviewer should respond by elaborating on the question, including rephrasing it by using different words.

If, however, the subject asks, "Why would I do that?" which is a thinly veiled assertion that the interviewer is questioning the suspect's character, the interviewer could respond by saying, "I don't know. Why would you do that?" This response holds the suspect accountable. If she continues by asking, "Are you accusing me?" the interviewer can respond by asking, "Should I?" At this point, the suspect is more likely to respond to the questions and end the circular answer-a-question-by-asking-a-question game.

In any event, the interviewer should not become angry; if he does, he effectively transfers control of the interview to the subject. If this does occur, the interviewer is not as likely to obtain the evidence he needs to prosecute. To guard against becoming angry, the interviewer should concentrate on the mission at hand: gathering information. He can also remind himself that by losing control, he has effectively reduced his source of evidence and, ultimately, harmed himself.

A subject—usually a suspect or a person who has something to hide or someone to protect—sometimes attacks the interviewer by questioning his competence. This might be done by asking, "Why are you bothering me?" The interviewer should simply respond, "My intention is not to bother you; just like you, I'm just trying to do my job." A typical retort to his response is something like, "Well, you are getting in the way of me doing my job." At that point, the interviewer is better off not arguing about interfering. Instead, a good approach is to simply say, "This will take only a few minutes and then I'll be out of your way." If the subject becomes angry, however, a different approach is needed.

When a subject becomes angry or feels threatened, she often does not think clearly. These emotions not only can interfere with her ability to control her physical responses but also can interfere with her ability to process information. Anger usually produces an attack; do not defend or attack in response. The interviewer should do something that is unexpected to break the fight response the subject exhibited. This interruption of behavior is used to cause the person to be less emotional and more rational. For example, the investigator should look for opportunities to agree firmly (rather than fight, which is expected) with the subject so that the two achieve at least a minimum level of rapport. Usually, when two persons lack agreement, each feels isolated; this feeling of being isolated leads to an "us-against-them" mentality. Reducing the disagreement can increase the level of cooperation.

The interviewer should focus on enlisting the angry person's help. Doing this is a show of respect and satisfies a fundamental human need. By showing respect to the interviewer, the subject is more likely to respect him and is more likely to answer his questions. For example, the interviewer could ask, "Would you help me understand this situation? It seems that you have a good understanding of it, so I need your help." This approach is also one that a subject who is angry or feels threatened does not expect. A related approach that can be used when the subject is adamantly opposed to answering questions is to ask for her opinion. For example, he can ask, "If you were me, what would you recommend that I do?"

The fundamental basis for the approaches discussed here is respect for the subject. If interview subjects do not feel respected, they will object to answering questions and, at worst, might even attempt to sabotage the investigation. Showing respect for others might not get what the interviewer wants, but it will get more than he would otherwise obtain.

SIGNED CONFESSION AND RELEASE OF INFORMATION

LO17 Once the interviewer has overcome objections, established a morally acceptable reason, and obtained an oral confession from the suspect, the next step is to have the person sign a confession. While oral confessions are just as binding as signed confessions in a court of law, they are more easily renounced. Therefore, signed confessions are always preferable to oral confessions.

The signed confession should be a concise statement regarding the guilt of the perpetrator. It should include a statement indicating that the confession was voluntarily made, an acknowledgment that he knew the act was wrong, the approximate dates on which the offenses occurred, and an approximate amount of the losses. If he committed more than one type of crime, he should sign a separate confession for each one. The signed confession can include a paragraph in which he provides a reason for his behavior and that he is contrite. Finally, the confession should contain an acknowledgment that he has read the statement (if the statement is longer than one page, he should initial each page to indicate that he was aware of each page). The confession should also contain a statement that indicates that the perpetrator believes the statement is true to the best of his knowledge.

Because the confessor could quickly change his mind about signing a sworn statement, the interviewer should come to the admission-seeking interview with a hard copy of the expected statement and, if possible, a copy in electronic format on a laptop computer so that any changes can quickly be made and the statement printed. If no computer is available and the hard copy must be used, changes can be made to it by using an ink pen. Initials of those present (including the confessor) can be added above the changes as an indication that the changes were accepted by the confessor and that they occurred prior to the time the confessor signed the confession.

See Figure 10.5 for an example of a signed confession.

At times, the suspect is the person who has information needed by the forensic accountant. This information should be requested, in writing, from the suspect. For example, in cases when cash was taken, the investigator may want to obtain the perpetrator's permission to examine his bank account records, including checking, savings, and investment accounts as well as income tax returns. Because of the privacy of such records, the investigator should obtain this permission in writing. The suspect may feel so strongly about voluntarily surrendering this information that the request for it could increase the likelihood that he will balk at signing a confession. Therefore, the interviewer may prefer to make this request after the signed confession has been obtained. This request, in the form of an authorization by the suspect, should set forth the information requested by the forensic accountant and can be a part of the signed confession although the preferred approach is that it be separate from it. The authorization should be signed and dated by the suspect and witnesses.

FIGURE 10.5
Example of Signed Confession

July 18, 2017

Ft. Lauderdale, Florida

I, Edison P. Hotchkiss, freely and voluntarily provide the following statement to Sam the Man Music Store, Inc. I hereby state that no threats or promises of any type have been used to cause me to make this statement.

I am the treasurer at Sam the Man Music Store, Inc. My duties at this company include being responsible for keeping merchandise inventory safe. Beginning in March 2014 and continuing until today, I have taken approximately $15,000 in merchandise inventory from Sam the Man Music Store, Inc. At the time I took the merchandise, I knew it was not mine.

I took the company's merchandise inventory by creating false sales invoices with the help of Alice M. Roswell, an employee in the accounting department. An account receivables was set up for each fictitious sale and written off after the account became four months old. I took the merchandise and sold it for prices that were less than market. Some of the proceeds were deposited in my checking account at the Sixth Republic Bank (account number 569-8901-6224). Approximately $10,000 was paid on medical bills incurred at Broward General Hospital to care for my sick mother. Alice received approximately $3,000 for her help in obtaining this money.

No one other than Alice knew what I was doing. I understand that my actions are illegal and are a violation of the policies of Sam the Man Music Store, Inc. I would not have taken the money if my mother had not been ill. I realize my actions were wrong. I am very sorry for my conduct and intend to repay the money I've taken.

I have read this statement that is wholly contained on this page. By signing my name below, I indicate that this statement is true and correct to the best of my knowledge.

_____   _____

Edison P. Hotchkiss   Witness

_____   _____

Date   Date

Summary

Conducting effective interviews is one of the most important evidence-gathering techniques in forensic accounting and is the most frequently employed type of evidence-gathering method used by forensic accountants, particularly when they perform fraud examinations.

Interviewing is the act of questioning persons and listening to their responses, which can be verbal as well as nonverbal. Interviewing is a more casual form of asking questions relative to interrogation and does not require reading Miranda rights to the person(s) being interviewed. Before the interview, the interviewer should prepare for the interview by becoming as familiar as possible with the individual being interviewed, the type of fraud that he is investigating, the suspect, and the victim so that information about the suspect's pressures, perceived opportunities, and rationalization can be confirmed or refuted.

When more than one person is to be interviewed, care must be exercised to determine the order in which the various persons are to be interviewed. Usually, the forensic accountant first interviews individuals who, although knowledgeable about some aspect of the suspect or of the fraud, are not suspects. By the time the investigator interviews the suspects, he is better informed about the suspect and the fraud itself.

The individual interview involves asking the right questions, listening, and responding appropriately. The questions to ask are typically one of five kinds of questions: introductory, informational, assessment, admission-seeking, and concluding. Assessment and admission-seeking questions are used only when the subject is considered a suspect. The questions are asked in an order that facilitates the information-gathering process. The questions to ask depend on whether the interviewee is not a suspect (i.e., simply a person from whom information is collected) or a suspect. When interviewees are not suspects, the interviewer asks introductory, informational, and concluding questions. However, when the interviewee is a suspect, the interviewer asks introductory, informational, assessment, and admission-seeking questions.

Introductory questions are asked to solicit the interviewee's cooperation, to establish rapport between the interviewer and subject, and to closely observe the subject in order to engage in calibration, the act of establishing a yardstick by which the subject's behavior can be measured when sensitive questions are asked. *Informational questions* are designed to collect information that is relevant to the investigation and represent one of the most important and most frequently used types of questions an interviewer can ask. If the person being interviewed is not a suspect, she is asked *concluding questions*. These questions are used to confirm information received by the interviewer during the interview, to obtain information that he has not yet gathered, and to seek the subject's agreement that she will continue to cooperate. The interviewer should end the interview on a positive note so that he can contact the subject again as a result of gathering evidence not known at the time of the interview. At this time, the interviewer might also want to solicit the subject's agreement to keep the matter discussed quiet.

Besides introductory and informational questions, suspects are also asked *assessment questions,* which are designed to determine whether the subject appears guilty. Both verbal and nonverbal responses of subjects are analyzed to determine the likelihood of guilt. If the interviewer is still convinced of the interviewee's guilt, he asks the suspect *admission-seeking questions,* which are designed to encourage a confession from guilty persons.

Innocent persons, when accused, are rarely silent. Guilty persons, on the other hand, often react by becoming silent or, if they speak, offer weak denials. If the subject does deny the accusation and the interviewer is convinced of her guilt, he should not allow her to continue to make denials because with each occurrence of a denial, she is making any subsequent confession more difficult.

Just as a subject use qualifiers (e.g., almost, nearly always) to avoid telling a lie, a suspect usually does not say, "I didn't do it" but attempts to explain why she did not do it or try to divert the interviewer's attention to others who may have committed the offense. To persuade the suspect to confess, the interviewer may have to disclose some of the evidence that indicates her guilt. It is important for him not to disclose all of the evidence but to show first the least important evidence.

In seeking a confession, the interviewer can make confession easier for the suspect by helping her to find a morally acceptable reason for committing the fraud. Note that this reason is not a legally acceptable reason; it is only a reason for the suspect to reconcile to herself her illegal behavior with her ideal self. The most common reasons include being underpaid at work, experiencing inadequate recognition, using drugs and alcohol, which altered her personality, and financial difficulties such as the need to pay medical bills. The morally acceptable reason is often the rationalization the suspect used to excuse her own behavior; determining this reason can greatly aid the effort to build the case that the crime was committed by a person having intent and the knowledge that the behavior was wrong.

Recording an interview should be done only if the information expected to be conveyed during the interview will be very detailed and is not easily recorded by note taking or later recall (or, in the case of law enforcement, when proper protocol is to record interrogations). If notes are taken during an interview, the interviewer should begin the notes for each interview on a separate piece of paper so that if notes pertaining to the interview of a particular subject are subpoenaed, only those notes are admitted into evidence. The interviewer should take care not to give the subject any indication that would indicate his evaluation of her spoken word or behavior.

Bringing a list of written questions to the interview usually is not a good idea because it can unduly fix the interviewer's focus on a set of predetermined questions to ask. Furthermore, if the subject sees the written questions and can read them, she is in a better position to respond to them with contrived answers.

If the subject is not a suspect, the interviewer can conduct the questioning in his office where he has easy access to files that might be helpful to the investigation. If, however, a subject is a suspect she should be interviewed at a neutral location to increase the likelihood that the unfamiliar location will interfere with her ability to recall a previously formulated story. The subject should be seated without any obstruction between her and the door, which should remain unlocked. The subject should not be seated behind a desk in order to give the interviewer an unimpeded view of the physical signs of deception such as fidgeting, toe-tapping, and crossing and uncrossing legs. The room's temperature should not be too low or too high; if it is, the subject's nonverbal behavior might be the result of being uncomfortable rather than a reaction to questions posed by the interviewer. Preferably, the interview room should contain few distractions because guilty persons become adept at using pictures, memorabilia, books, and other items as a means to distract the interviewer from his agenda or to dilute the significance of certain answers she has provided.

Normally, one interviewer is sufficient. However, for interviews that involve admission-seeking questions, two interviewers should be present so that if the suspect alleges that she was coerced into confessing or otherwise mistreated, the charge can more easily be repudiated. Interviewers should not sit together across from the suspect; if they do, the suspect may feel that she is outnumbered and may be even less amenable to persuasion.

It is important that the interviewer never become angry during an interview. If he does, he transfers her control to the subject and allows her to determine the amount and quality of information she provides.

The investigator can use several different types of question structures when interviewing a subject. Use of these structures result in questions commonly referred to as *closed-ended, forced-choice, open-ended, connecting, positive-reaction, clarifying, confrontational,* and *secondary questions.* Knowledge of these question structures and when they are best used increases the likelihood that the forensic accountant can obtain information beneficial to the investigation.

The subject who is either willing to cooperate or can be persuaded to cooperate is more likely to provide information that can be used as evidence. Thus, the interviewer sometimes attempts to persuade subjects to cooperate. Besides establishing rapport with the subject, the interviewer can use several approaches to persuade her to provide evidence the interviewer desires. These include the direct approach, the indirect approach, and a combined approach.

Some persons the interviewer would like to interview raise objections to being interviewed. Most of these reasons fall into one of two categories. The first category is "Don't bother me." Requests for interviews are usually met with such responses as "I don't want to be bothered" or "I don't have the time." The second category of responses used by subjects is "I can't help." Potential interviewees will say something such as "I don't think I could help you." Even those subjects who agree to be interviewed will sometimes object to answering specific questions.

Once the interviewer has overcome objections and the suspect has provided an oral confession, he can obtain a signed confession, which is a concise statement regarding the suspect's guilt. It should include a statement indicating that the confession was voluntarily made, an acknowledgment that the act was wrong, the approximate dates that the offense occurred, and an approximate amount of the losses. If the suspect committed more than one type of crime, a separate signed confession for each one should be prepared. The confession should contain an acknowledgment that the confessor has read the statement and a statement that indicates that she believes the statement is true to the best of her knowledge. In addition, information the forensic accountant needs from the confessor should be requested in writing.

The interview can be one of the most powerful tools of the forensic accountant if conducted properly. This technique, along with others described in this textbook, can produce evidence that will be beneficial in obtaining convictions in a court of law or resolutions in arbitration.

Glossary

admission-seeking questions   Inquiries designed to solicit a confession from persons strongly suspected of playing a role in the fraud being investigated.

alibi   Defense offered to support the assertion of innocence of the person making it.

assessment questions   Queries asked of persons being interviewed to determine if those persons are guilty of the fraud being investigated.

calibration   Act of fine-tuning an interviewer's perception of a person's behavior when the person is asked nonsensitive (i.e., nonincriminating) questions so that the interviewer can contrast that behavior with the subject's behavior when asked sensitive questions.

clarifying questions   Inquiries designed to obtain information that elaborates on information provided earlier in the interview.

closed-ended questions   Queries designed to elicit a "yes," "no," or brief response.

combined approach   Synthesis of two approaches to interviewing: the direct approach and the indirect approach.

compound questions   Two inquiries contained in the same sentence.

concluding questions   Queries asked of persons not suspected of being involved in a fraud.

confrontational questions   Inquiries used to highlight the difference (i.e., conflict) between information provided by the subject and information provided by another source.

connecting questions   Queries used to connect two or more details or events.

direct approach   Manner of questioning used when the interviewer is reasonably certain of the suspect's guilt.

forced-choice questions   Inquiries designed to cause the subject to choose from one of several answers provided by the interviewer.

indirect approach   Manner of questioning used when the subject's thinking is reasonably sophisticated.

informational questions   Queries asked to solicit additional evidence.

interrogation   Information-seeking questioning technique that law enforcement uses to obtain information about a crime that has been committed from those who are suspected of committing the crime.

interviews   Nonconfrontational dialogues between two persons, one of whom (the interviewer) is interested in obtaining information, including perceptions, of other persons, places, or aspects of the fraud being investigated.

introductory questions   Questions that set the tone of an interview and provide information about the reason the subject is being interviewed.

leading questions   Queries designed to elicit a predetermined response.

mirroring   Process by which the interviewer attempts to appear as similar to the subject as possible to cause the subject to identify with the interviewer.

negatively phrased questions   Inquiries that tend to be ambiguous and for which the answer could be interpreted in one of two ways.

nonverbal cues   Signals that are not spoken or written; usually involve movement of the body including the subject's head and eyes.

nonverbal responses   Physiology-based reactions to questions, statements, and physical evidence.

open-ended questions   Queries designed to encourage subjects to answer with more than a "yes" or "no" response.

positive-reaction questions   Inquiries asked to elicit agreement from a subject so that agreement with statements the investigator later makes is easier to accomplish.

qualifiers   Words or phrases that change the meaning of a sentence, usually by allowing the speaker to be less precise and thus provide less self-incriminating information.

rapport   Relationship characterized by mutual understanding, trust, and agreement.

secondary questions   Queries that are actually statements of information made to elicit confirmation of the information heard by the interviewer.

verbal cues   Reactions that indicate guilt that should be investigated.

verbal responses   Answers that include oral or written responses to questions.

Review Questions

1. The difference between interviews and interrogations is that:
   a. Interrogations do not involve planning.
   b. Interviews, but not interrogations, involve reading a suspect her Miranda rights.
   c. Interviews are usually more informal than interrogations.
   d. None of the above.

2. Tunnel vision:
   a. Is the result of the human tendency to trust.
   b. Should always be avoided.
   c. Can be a benefit and a detriment to the interviewer.
   d. Both *a* and *b*.

3. When multiple persons are to be interviewed:
   a. Interview the least culpable persons first and then progress to the most culpable.
   b. Interview them in a random order to reduce the likelihood of bias.
   c. Interview the most culpable persons first and then progress to the least culpable.
   d. None of the above.

4. The correct order of questions to ask subjects who are not suspects is best represented as:
   a. Introductory, assessment, informational, and concluding.
   b. Introductory, informational, assessment, admission seeking, and concluding.
   c. Introductory, informational, assessment, and admission seeking.
   d. Introductory, informational, assessment, and concluding.

5. The feeling of rapport can be enhanced if the interviewer:
   a. Makes small talk with the subject.
   b. Shakes hands with the subject.
   c. Engages in the act of mirroring.
   d. All of the above.

6. Which of the following words should be avoided during the introductory and informational phases of the interview?
   a. *Assignment.*
   b. *Examination.*
   c. *Inquiry.*
   d. All of the above words are acceptable.

7. The interviewer uses concluding questions to:
   a. Provide the interviewer's opinion on the likelihood of guilt to the subject.
   b. Request a final opinion from the subject as to the guilt of another person.
   c. Gather additional information not provided earlier.
   d. None of the above .

8. Subjects who are not guilty usually respond to assessment questions:
   a. Slowly, carefully considering the questions and the implications of their answers.
   b. Without hesitation.
   c. Indirectly, so that the interviewer has more information.
   d. Reluctantly due to a desire to show kindness toward others.

9. A guilty person is likely to respond to the question "What is the reason a person might take money from the cash register?" by saying:
   a. "Maybe she needs to feed her children and she's not being paid enough."
   b. "I don't know; he probably had a good reason."
   c. "There's no good reason to take money that's not yours."
   d. Both *a* and *b*.

10. An example of a sentence that includes a qualifier is:
    a. "I'm not sure."
    b. "She's at the teller window just about all the time."
    c. "I'm certain the person who committed the fraud is Jim."
    d. None of the above sentences contains a qualifier.

11. During an interview, a subject consistently looks up and to the left when providing answers that are known to be true. This likely indicates that:
    a. The subject is constructing visual images.
    b. The subject is accessing visually stored memories.
    c. The subject is showing signs of guilt.
    d. None of the above.

12. During an interview, a subject who consistently looks down and to the left when providing answers that are known to be true is likely:
    a. Sight dominant.
    b. Hearing dominant.
    c. Feeling dominant.
    d. Intuitive dominant.

13. During an interview, a subject who blinks her eyes when providing answers that are known to be true is likely:
    a. Sight dominant.
    b. Hearing dominant.
    c. Intuitive dominant.
    d. Touch dominant.

14. Crossing his arms is a sure sign of a subject's guilt.
    a. True.
    b. False.

15. An inappropriate way to accuse a suspect is to ask:
    a. "When was the first time you took money from the register?"
    b. "You took the money because you needed to help your mother, didn't you?"
    c. "You took the money, didn't you?"
    d. All of the above are appropriate ways to accuse a suspect.

16. During an interview, the interviewer should:
    a. Never show anger.
    b. Never get angry.
    c. Never show anger or get angry.
    d. Get angry only if the crime is especially offensive.

17. During an interview, confrontational questions are typically asked to:
    a. Determine whether the subject will change his story.
    b. Determine the pattern of the subjects' speech and body language in response to the question.
    c. Verify inconsistencies in the subject's story.
    d. Discover inconsistencies in the subject's story.

18. If the subject of an interview is willing to cooperate, the interviewer is better off using:
    a. An induction approach.
    b. A deduction approach.
    c. A casual approach.
    d. An indirect approach.

19. When there is little doubt of a subject's guilt, an interviewer is better off using:
    a. A direct approach.
    b. An indirect approach.
    c. A deduction approach.
    d. An indirect approach.

20. Subjects are more likely to respond when they are shown:
    a. Firmness and evenhandedness.
    b. Kindness and sympathy.
    c. Toughness.
    d. Impartiality.

21. The indirect approach to an interview is relatively more likely to use:
    a. Open-ended questions.
    b. Close-ended questions.
    c. Forced-answer questions.
    d. Passive-ended questions.

22. Which of the following questions should be avoided?
    a. "What do you know about the situation?"
    b. "Did you leave the building immediately after he told you that?"
    c. "You didn't go the store after that, did you?"
    d. "What type of problems are you referring to?"

23. If a subject does not want to be interviewed, the interviewer should:
    a. Respect her privacy and not bother her.
    b. Reapproach her in a few days.
    c. Set up a definite time in the near future with the subject to interview her.
    d. Place a bug (a recording device) in her office.

24. When might interviewer silence best be used?
    a. When the subject is silent.
    b. Sometime after the beginning of the interview.
    c. Whenever the interviewer wants to assess the subject's visual cues.
    d. In the first 5 minutes of the interview.

25. A signed confession need not contain:
    a. A statement that the confessor knew the act he committed was wrong.
    b. The approximate dates of the offenses and an approximate amount of the loss.
    c. A reason for his commission of the crime.
    d. The signed confession should include all of the above items.

Discussion Questions

26. Discuss the importance of interviewing.

27. What should be done before interviewing a suspect?

28. How is the fraud triangle helpful in interviewing?

29. What should be done in the first 5 minutes of an interview?

30. Suggest one technique that an interviewer can use to establish rapport with a subject.

31. Discuss the procedures that should be considered when more than one person are to be interviewed.

32. Define *calibration* and discuss how and why it is used in interviews.

33. Discuss the importance of each type of question (e.g., informational) to the investigation.

34. What are the purposes of concluding questions, and why are they important?

35. Discuss the differences between verbal responses of suspects and nonsuspects to assessment questions.

36. Analyze yourself to determine whether you primarily speak in terms of the sight, auditory, or touch sense. Without disclosing your determination to anyone else, ask a friend or family member to provide his or her opinion on your primary sensory orientation.

37. What are some body language indicators that suggest that a subject is lying during an interview?

38. What information or indications could provide predication for asking assessment questions?

39. Discuss common reasons for committing a fraud against an employer.

40. When would an interviewer want to use confrontational questions?

41. Describe some common approaches that can be used to make confessing easier for a suspect.

42. Discuss the reasons for and against audio recording an interview.

43. What should the interviewer be aware of when taking notes during an interview?

44. Why should the interviewer not write a set of detailed questions to ask the subject?

45. Refer to Table 10.1, Other Persuasive Approaches. Which of these approaches do you believe is most effective? Why?

46. Construct a compound question. Discuss how a subject might answer one of the questions and divert attention from the other one.

47. Discuss the various ways a subject can avoid answering specific questions.

48. What can the interviewer do to calm a subject's anger?

49. Describe the various items that a signed confession should contain and the reasons they should be included in it.

50. Describe items of information that the forensic accountant might need, that are in the possession of the confessor, and for which a signed release of information might be appropriate.

Cases

51. Rob Ellis is a forensic accountant who has been engaged to investigate a case of electronic fraud at Weezer, a company that operates a chain of wholesale restaurant supply stores in the Houston area.

Sonya Goyos, Weezer's controller, first contacted Rob. She tells him that she's discovered that one of several employees working in the main office has been stealing company blank checks.

The main checkbook is normally kept locked in the office desk of the CFO's secretary. Only the CFO, the secretary, two accountants, and the company janitor normally have access to the CFO's office suite.

Sonya discovered the problem in a routine reconciliation of the bank statement against the cash disbursements ledger. The reconciliation revealed two paid checks in the amounts of $1,324 and $1,726, both made payable to and cashed by Maximo Gomez.

Sonya's follow-up investigation revealed that both checks had been cashed in the drive-thru window of Weezer's bank, and on both occasions the teller had written Maximo's driver's license number and address on the back of the checks.

Sonya reported the two checks to the check fraud division of the local district attorney's office. Two weeks later, she received a call from one of the investigators. He had visited Maximo's residence and found that he had been very ill and immobile for several months. It seemed apparent that Maximo was the victim of identity theft and had nothing to do with cashing the stolen checks.

"We see this all the time," said the investigator. "We have the videos of the person cashing the checks." He was obviously wearing a wig and sunglasses. He also knew exactly how to position his head to minimize his exposure to the bank's surveillance camera.

"What about a license plate number?" Sonya asked. "Did that show up on the video?"

"Yes, but it was unreadable. This guy was a real professional. It appears that he put some kind of reflective coating on the license plate to confuse the camera."

Sonya was really frustrated. Her preliminary conversations with the bank led her to believe that Weezer would have to eat the losses because a company employee was obviously involved in the scheme. Even worse, she had a strong feeling that the problem would happen again. There was really no way to keep the bank from cashing the checks, and next time the losses could be even worse.

Sonya discussed the problem with Harry Winkler, the CEO. He strongly insisted that Sonya focus on catching the crook because doing that was more important than taking a chance that the problem might happen again. She replied that she wanted to place a hidden surveillance camera in the CFO's office, but Harry refused because he was afraid of the possible consequences of spying on his CFO whose family connections were important to Weezer's survival.

"No, I want you to gather evidence from what you have already," Harry said. "Hire a forensic accountant and let the accountant provide some evidence as to who did it. If that evidence is good, then I'll consider installing a spy camera."

Rob was hired to conduct a preliminary investigation that involved a handwriting analysis of the checks. He was not a handwriting expert, but he quickly found that there was no obvious correspondence between any of the handwriting on the bad checks to the handwriting of any of the employee suspects. He concluded that he needed to interview each of the suspects and perhaps obtain a confession.

Rob decided to conduct the first interview with Maria Ladronia, the CFO's secretary. Both he and Sonya considered Maria to be the prime suspect. Rob conducted the interview in an empty conference room. She sat directly across from him on the other side of the table.

"Hello, I'm Rob Ellis," he said to her. "I'm a certified fraud examiner from the Wilson and Larson Accounting Firm." I need to ask you only a few questions.

Maria stiffened.

"Please don't worry; you're not being accused of doing anything wrong. I'm just here for a routine investigation."

His reassurance did not seem to help, and Maria only looked more nervous. Rob wondered if Maria was acting guilty.

"Do you know what I am investigating?" Rob asked.

Maria shook her head back and forth, still sitting straight up in her chair like a lamppost.

"Someone stole checks from your boss's desk," Rob told her.

"Are you a policeman?" she asks.

Rob tried to speak in a calm and reassuring voice, "No, just an accountant."

Maria began to cry softly, but she still remained upright and stiff.

"Why are you crying?" Rob asked.

"I don't want to lose my job. I have two kids in private school, and my husband and I can barely make ends meet."

Rob decides that Maria was acting very guilty and decided to get right to the heart of the matter.

"Ok," he said. "We do have information that points straight to you. You might as well confess. Help me out, and I'll see if I can convince your boss not to press charges."

Maria became very quiet, and for a time Rob heard only the hum of the overhead florescent lights. Finally, Maria spoke. "You're accusing me. I want a lawyer, and I'm not going to talk to you. And I'll sue both you and my company if anything happens to me." She got up and walked out of the room.

a. How well did Rob handle the interview?

b. How well did Rob handle the overall investigation?

c. What might Rob have done differently?

d. What is Rob's assessment of Maria's responses?

52. Denise Stubbs, the Nancy Drew of forensic accounting, sat in her office pondering yet another financial mystery. Her client, Candace Goodwell, owns Salon Select and the building and land on which the building sits. The retiree, who spends her winters in Florida and her summers in New York, had just left Denise's office after discussing a matter that was particularly troubling. Candace had relied on her office manager, Dick Maxwell, who had been with her for years, to obtain bids to resurface the parking lot at Salon Select while she was in New York. He had told her that he had obtained the bids and had engaged the lowest bidder to do the job.

Candace had recounted to Denise the conversation she had just last week with a representative of an asphalt company. She had been pleased with the resurfacing job when she had returned from New York on August 2 until Nick Woods, the representative, had stopped by the salon. Candace had happened to be in, and he had asked her if she needed her lot resurfaced. "Why, I had it resurfaced just three months ago," replied Candace.

"That's interesting," said Nick. "I looked at the lot before I came in and, although it has the sheen of a new lot, the edges tell a different story."

"What do you mean?" asked Candace.

"Well," Nick continued, "the edge can indicate whether the lot is newly surfaced by the thickness and layers that exist. Of course, only drilling down and taking a sample will tell us for sure, but due to the relative thinness, I think you've been had." "Egad!" exclaimed Candace. "I don't understand how this could have happened. Where's Dick? I need to ask him some questions!"

Dick was in the back office when Candace found him. "Dick, what happened? The man who was just here said that the lot might not have been resurfaced."

"No," replied Dick, "he's mistaken. Here, you can look at the paperwork."

"You know I don't like to look at that stuff," retorted Candace. "I just don't know what to do. I can't do anything now; I've got to run to attend a charity event in West Palm."

With that, she left. But the information was still bothering her. That's why she mentioned it to Vic Rickenbacker when she was in his office to discuss another matter. He had encouraged her to see Denise and, after some discussion, had solicited Candace's permission to set up an appointment.

"Denise can do some preliminary investigation to determine whether you've received the service and product for which you have paid," Vic told Candace.

During the call to set up an appointment, Vic set up a fee arrangement whereby Denise, a CPA and CFF, would practice, for purposes of this matter, as his agent.

A few days later, Candace was in Denise's office.

"Hmmm," said Denise. "I need your permission to interview your employees. Also, please don't mention that you've come to see me. Sometimes it puts people on the defensive and I can't get the information I need to do a good job for you. Just tell your employees that an office consultant—that's me—might need to interview them for a project to improve the business and that they are to cooperate with her. Do you understand?"

"Yes," replied Candace.

"Then I'll get to work. By the way, when does Dick come in each day?"

"Oh, usually not until the afternoon," replied Candace.

"Good," thought Denise. "I'll interview a couple of staff members in the morning and catch Dick when he arrives in the afternoon."

After Candace left the office, Denise began to think about a plan to collect the information she needed to draw a conclusion. "The lot may have been resurfaced and, then again, it might not have been." She contacted a friend who owns an asphalt paving company and asked him to take some core samples at the salon after it closed at 7:00 P.M.

A few days later, the results were in: Five different core samples taken from different areas of the lot indicated that it had not been resurfaced. Denise had evidence.

Her next step was to ask Candace to allow her to search the salon's files for the invoice from the asphalt company. Once she had the name of the repaving company, she would do some searching to verify that the company existed. A quick search of the Internet did disclose the company, RJ New Look, along with its address and phone number. Denise slowly dialed the number and, when a voice answered, inquired about whether the company would be interested in repaving her lot.

"Could you give me some references—some jobs that you've done in my area so that I can decide whether to use you?"

She was hoping that Salon Select would be mentioned but, even if it wasn't, she was prepared. When Salon Select was not mentioned, she brought it up. "There's a business in my area whose parking lot looks great. I believe it's . . . uh . . . Salon Select; yes, I'm sure of that. Do you know who did its lot?"

"Yes," said the voice on the other end of the line, "we did that lot."

"It must have been recent. Can you tell me when it was done?" asked Denise.

"Just a moment and I'll check on that," said the voice.

Within a few minutes, the voice returned. "It was done two months ago on July 22."

"Thanks," replied Denise, "I may be getting back with you soon about doing my lot. Goodbye."

Denise arrived at Select Salon a few days later and interviewed a couple of employees. Both said the same thing: The asphalt job was done quickly on a Sunday. One of the employees said she'd driven by the salon going and coming from a friend's house and said that the job could not have taken more than two hours. She was surprised that it took so little time.

When Dick arrived, Denise introduced herself as an office consultant and asked if she could ask him a few questions.

"I guess so," replied Dick, "but make it quick. I have a lot of work to do."

"I'll do my best," replied Denise. "By the way, the parking lot looks nice; did you have it repaved recently?"

"Oh yes," he replied., "It was done early in June. The New Look Company did it for us. I was very pleased with the job."

"Interesting," replied Denise. "I was a consultant on a job recently. The job was to look into some fraud that had occurred. It seems that the company that was to resurface a parking lot simply put on a layer of thin coating so that it looked as though it had been resurfaced."

Dick sat back abruptly in his chair. "Well, that certainly didn't happen here!" he exclaimed, visibly shaken. "What was the name of the company you said resurfaced, or . . . er . . . pretended to resurface the lot?"

"I can't mention names, Dick, but it was a local company. It works with insiders who receive kickbacks from the company," replied Denise.

"Let's get back to what you want to discuss, Denise, and leave the tawdry gossip for others," said Dick.

"Actually, Dick, I'm here to talk about the parking lot. I know it wasn't resurfaced. If you tell me what happened, I'll let Candace know that you were cooperative. If you don't, you will face harsher consequences."

Dick began to protest. "I did not . . ." but Denise cut him off immediately.

"Yes, you did," Denise said firmly. "I have the evidence. Protesting only makes your situation worse. Right now, I'm just trying to understand why you did this. I know we all need additional money. Was it because you needed the money?"

   a. Did Denise handle the events leading up to the interview correctly?

   b. Did Denise handle the interview correctly?

   c. Should Denise have approached the resurfacing company before she interviewed Dick?

   d. What do you think will happen next in the interview?

   e. What should Denise bring with her to the interview with Dick?

53. Tom Quick, an investigator who had received his training from a mail-order school that claimed to have been founded when it opened its first post office box location three years ago, had been interviewing Ace Malone, an employee of Bookmakers, Inc., a corporation located near a major horse track in a well-known, large Midwestern city

that shall remain nameless. The interview, which was conducted at Ace's place of employment, had lasted three hours and Tom, who always works alone (because, he says, other people get in the way) was quickly becoming impatient with Ace.

Suddenly, Tom stood up. He slammed and locked the door, which had previously been wide open. Tom sat down right in front of Ace and, inches from his face, declared, "You're not gettin' out of here til I get the truth from you. I know you took the money and you're not goin' anywhere until you confess. Now, tell me what happened beginning at 10:30 P.M. on the night you took the money. You said you remembered that night well. So tell me; I'm all ears."

"So, you wanna know what happened from 10:30 that night on?" replied Ace. "OK, I'll tell ya."

"That's right," growled Tom, "and tell me quick. I'm tired of messing around with you. Did you or did not you not take the money and stash it at your house somewhere?"

"The answer to your second question is 'no,'" replied Ace. "After 10:30, I finished my shift and got outta here so that I could meet some buddies at The Drunken Lush."

"All right, now we're gettin' somewhere. I'm gonna talk to your buddies about being at The Drunken Lush. But you'd better confess," Tom commanded, again moving inches from Ace's nose, "or I'm not letting you outta here any time soon."

"I'm tellin' you the truth. I didn't take any money then," replied Ace.

a. What did Tom do wrong?

b. Do you think Ace was telling the truth about his actions after 10:30 P.M. on the evening in question?

54. Quality-Best, the company for which Christie Bowers works, manufactures and sells components for the aerospace industry. In her position as chief internal auditor, she has investigated several suspected frauds over the years and she was reviewing a new one. The current case began when a tip was submitted through an anonymous hotline. The tipster said that Johnnie Grant, an employee in the purchasing department, was receiving money from a supplier of Quality-Best.

Christie's first step was to review the personnel structure of the purchasing department. Just as she suspected, Johnnie was the person in charge of ordering components for all manufacturing processes. She wasn't surprised; Johnnie had been at Quality-Best for more than 20 years and had risen in the ranks to become supervisor.

Johnnie had three assistant buyers. Christie decided to interview these buyers before she interviewed Johnnie. The first buyer, Donna Malone, who was the most recent hire in the purchasing department, was rather quiet and seemed to answer questions in a straight-forward manner. The second buyer, Alan Fuentes, had been at Quality-Best for six years. He explained that each buyer had been assigned 10 unique parts to order. Each buyer was to purchase an adequate amount of high-quality parts that are used in the manufacturing processes. His supervisor, Johnnie, reviewed the purchases of these buyers and must sign off on the orders to indicate that he approved them.

The third buyer, Karen Rosen, has been at Quality-Best for 12 years. Portions of the interview with her follow.

After introducing herself, Christie proceeded to ask Karen about her work.

"I work here at Quality-Best in the internal audit department," Christie said. It's the one that usually does the analysis of whether to buy equipment around here. Today, I've been looking into the ordering function to determine whether it can be improved, so I'd like to talk with you about your position and what you and others in ordering department do. If you have any suggestions for improving its function, let me know. Even after our chat, my door is always open, and I'd be interested in your views.

"First, please describe your duties here in the department."

"I'd be happy to. I'm one of four buyers here at Quality-Best. Alan, Karen, and I are responsible for purchasing 10 different parts for various manufacturing processes. We have an approved vendor list that we use and can't purchase from any company not on the list unless we ask for approval from Johnnie."

"You mentioned four buyers. Who is the other one?"

"Oh, that would be Johnnie. A few years ago, he took on some of the parts I was handling and then, as new ones were added, he took responsibility for those, too."

"How many unique parts do you think he purchases?"

"Now?" asked Karen.

"Yes," Christie replied.

"Well, I think he orders for about 15 different parts. I'm not really sure because only he knows."

"You mentioned that Johnnie must approve your purchases. Have there been any times that Johnnie hasn't approved them?"

"Well, yes," replied Karen, as she shifted positions.

"Would you tell me about one of those times?"

"Could we talk about this later? I really have a lot of work to do."

"Just a couple more questions, Karen. I promise. Now, would you tell me about one of the times that Johnnie has not approved your purchases?"

"Ok, ok. It's usually about quality. Sometimes Johnnie says that a particular vendor doesn't provide a part that has the quality that another vendor has. Sometimes he's even recommended a vendor who's not on the approved list."

"And did you question him about ordering from a vendor who's not on the approved list?"

"Yes, and he always says he'll add the vendor later."

"Does he?"

"Most of the time, yes, but there were a couple of times that he did not. I didn't ask him about these. After all, he's my boss, and he's the one who does my personnel evaluation."

"You mentioned that sometimes the issue is the quality of a part provided by a particular vendor. Would you tell me about that?"

"Yes," said Karen. Christie could sense a feeling of reluctance to answer. "I know Johnnie is trying to save money, but I don't think these parts have nearly the quality that the parts that I had chosen have."

"What about the cost—how does that compare between the items?"

"Now that's the strange part. The parts that I don't think are as good as those I've recommended cost more, not less."

Abruptly, Karen says, "I've talked enough. I have to get back to my work."

"May I talk with you again if I have additional questions?"

"I . . . I . . . yes, I suppose that would be fine. But I really don't know anything more, so I don't think I could help you."

"One last thing, Karen: Please don't mention what we've talked about here today to anyone. Can you do that?"

"Yes, I suppose I can," replied Karen.

Christie left Quality-Best that day thinking that Karen knew more than she was saying but was reluctant to talk.

a. Before interviewing Johnnie, is there any information from his personnel file that you would like to know?

b. Before interviewing Johnnie, would you like to ask Donna and Alan any additional questions?

c. Before interviewing Johnnie, what documentation would you like to see and why? (*Hint:* Think of information that might indicate vendor fraud.)

d. Before interviewing Johnnie, is there anything else you might have wanted to know about him that perhaps Donna, Alan, and Karen could tell you because they see him almost daily?

55. Edsel Edison, an employee of Go Fast & Play Hard, has been with the company since it opened four years ago. Go Fast is a company that is still experiencing growing pains, and current management believes that the company can make money if costs are kept low. This is the reason "Easy" Smith, the operating manager, has given for not implementing more internal controls. In particular, he has rejected the recommendation to add additional employees to produce better separation of duties as unnecessary. As a result, Edsel is the only person who does the accounting, including the billing and collection, for Go Fast.

"Easy" had become a bit uneasy lately. He'd noticed that within the last two years, cash collections on accounts receivable do not seem to have been as high as he would have expected. Business, though, had been booming, and "Easy" has been able to negotiate several new contracts over the last year. He'd asked Edsel about the lower level of collections and told Victoria Bass, a forensic accountant, "Edsel says it's the economy. You know . . . times are tough. I've experienced tough times even when the economy is going well."

"Easy" filled Victoria in about various aspects of the business such as the fact that there are three other persons who work in the shop: Theresa Parks, the receptionist/secretary; Andre Green, the assistant salesperson; and Patrick Fine, who is in charge of promotions and advertising. She learned that on Fridays, Edsel, Theresa, Andre, and Patrick, who have all been with the company since it began, go out to lunch together.

a. What documents/files would Victoria want to see before interviewing anyone?

b. What other procedures from Chapter 9 (the evidence chapter), if any, should Victoria consider using to determine whether her suspicions of "Easy" are valid?

c. Should she consider interviewing Theresa, Andre, and Patrick? Why or why not?

Chapter **Eleven**

Fraud Examination Evidence III: Forensic Science and Computer Forensics

CHAPTER LEARNING OBJECTIVES

After reading Chapter 11, you should be able to:

- LO1: Define *forensic science*.
- LO2: Explain which areas of forensic science are important to forensic accountants.
- LO3: Identify the major players in forensic investigations.
- LO4: Explain forensic evidence and how it is used to identify suspects and criminals.
- LO5: Explain the requirements for expert testimony to be admitted into court.
- LO6: Identify the major issues in a forensic computer investigation.
- LO7: Explain how to conduct forensic computer investigations.
- LO8: Describe various law enforcement networks and databases.

FORENSIC SCIENCE

LO1 **Forensic science** is the application of science to legal matters. One of the earliest applications of forensic science dates back to the 7th century when fingerprints on loan documents were used to prove debtors' identities. Since that time, forensic science has become much more sophisticated, especially with the explosion of scientific knowledge in the 20th century.

Forensic science has numerous branches, many of which are important to forensic accounting. Some forensic science branches are shown in Figure 11.1.

LO2 The specialty areas of particular interest to forensic accounting include computer forensics, criminalistics, **dactylography,** forensic evidence, forensic identification, forensic **palaeography** (also called **diplomatics,** or *questioned document examination*), forensic psychology/psychiatry, and information forensics. The other specialties are also of interest but apply more to murders, armed robberies, and so on, than to forensic accounting.

Participants in Forensic Science Investigations

LO3 Forensic science investigations involve various types of forensic specialists. These include criminalists, forensic scientists, and crime labs.

FIGURE 11.1
Forensic Science
Specialties

Forensic Science Specialty	Primary Focus
Forensic ballistics	Firearms
Computer forensics	Computer technology
Criminalistics	Collection, processing, and analysis of crime scene evidence
Dactylography	Fingerprints
Forensic anthropology	Human skeletons
Forensic chemistry	Explosives, poisons, controlled substances
Forensic engineering	Materials, products, structures, and components that either fail to operate or do not operate properly
Forensic entomology	Insects as they relate to identifying the time and location of death
Forensic evidence	Any physical thing than can be used as evidence in a legal proceeding
Forensic genetics	DNA analysis to identify subjects
Forensic identification	Object identification from trace evidence
Forensic odontology	Dental evidence to identify bite marks and dead bodies
Forensic palaeography, also called *diplomatics*, or questioned document examination	Documents to determine origin and authenticity
Forensic palynology	Pollens and minerals as they relate to the time and location of a crime
Forensic pathology	Wounds, injuries, fluid samples, and tissue samples as they relate to the cause of death or various aspects of crimes
Forensic psychology/psychiatry	Mental competency as related to a participant in a legal proceeding, the mental state of someone when he committed a particular act, and criminal profiling
Forensic toxicology	Drugs, alcohol, and poisons, and their effects
Information forensics	Organizational information systems focusing on fraud, abuse, negligence, and accidents
Serology	Blood evidence

Criminalists

Criminalists are crime scene technicians or investigators who specialize in finding, collecting, and preserving physical evidence at crime scenes. The typical criminalist has a college degree with substantial coursework in areas such as biology, chemistry, and physics. Some colleges and universities offer specialized degree programs in criminalistics.

Criminalists are especially good at performing certain activities, such as collecting blood, DNA, fingerprints, footprints, trace evidence, and so on, in homicide cases. However, these types of evidence are often only peripherally important in financial and computer-related crimes, although fingerprints are discussed later.

Some criminalists have special training in computer and information systems, which is becoming more important as computer criminals become more sophisticated. In the absence of a specially trained criminalist, law enforcement officers are likely to seize computers using standard search warrant procedures. However, as discussed later, valuable evidence can be lost if a computer is simply shut down, unplugged, and carted away.

In some cases, traditional criminalists and specialists work together at the crime scene. For example, an arsonist might burn a building to cover up a financial crime in which case both arson investigators and computer-specialized criminalists need to work together.

Forensic Scientists

A **forensic scientist** tends to work in the laboratory rather than at crime scenes. Furthermore, a forensic scientist focuses on interpreting evidence gathered by criminalists although some experienced criminalists develop interpretive skills. Forensic scientists tend to have graduate degrees, and some have doctorate degrees in areas such as genetics, biology, and chemistry. Forensic scientists specializing in information technology may have graduate degrees in computer science.

Criminalists generally work at the beginning of cases; forensic scientists typically work at the end of cases, and they are the individuals who normally give expert testimony in the courtroom (see Figure 11.2).

Crime Labs

The United States has hundreds of crime labs. Approximately 80 percent of them are affiliated with a police agency. The better labs are accredited by one of the main accrediting organizations such as the American Society of Crime Laboratory Directors or the National Forensic Science Technology Center. Specialized labs can receive additional accreditation.

At the state level, a crime lab typically includes a single parent lab and several regional labs. This ensures that in most cases a nearby crime lab is available for all law enforcement jurisdictions.

The typical crime lab has five divisions or departments: serology (fluids), unknown substances (including drugs and poisons), trace evidence (small items examined under a microscope, including hairs and fibers), ballistics, and fingerprints.

FBI Lab

The FBI lab, which is much more sophisticated than a typical state lab, provides lab and related forensic services in the following areas:

- Chemistry.
- Combined DNA index system (CODIS).
- Computer analysis and response team (CART).
- DNA analysis.
- Evidence response team (ERT).
- Explosives.
- Firearms and toolmarks.
- Forensic audio, video, and image analysis.
- Forensic science research.
- Forensic science training.
- Hazardous materials response.

FIGURE 11.2
**The Criminalist
versus the Forensic
Scientist**

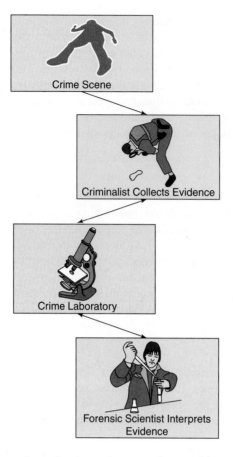

- Investigative and prosecutive graphics.
- Latent prints.
- Materials analysis.
- Questioned documents.
- Racketeering records.
- Special photographic analysis.
- Structural design.
- Trace evidence.

Of special interest to the forensic accountant are the **computer analysis and response team (CART),** evidence response team (ERT), questioned documents unit, investigative and prosecutive graphics, and racketeering records. Each of these is discussed in the following sections.

Computer Analysis and Response Team (CART) CART consists of a group of individuals who are highly trained in information technology and networking. Included in the group are forensic computer examiners with expertise in nine areas:

1. **Content** Determining the content of computer files.
2. **Comparison** Comparing the content of computer files to known reference files and/or documents.
3. **Transactions** Determining the exact time and sequence in which files were created or modified.

4. **Extraction** Extracting data from computer storage.

5. **Deletion** Recovering deleted data files.

6. **Format conversion** Converting data from one format to another.

7. **Keyword searching** Finding data (possibly in deleted files) that contain keywords or phrases of interest.

8. **Password recovery** Finding or recovering passwords that have been used to encrypt files or that limit investigators' access to important IT resources.

9. **Limited source code** Studying computer programs to identify processing steps that can be of interest to investigators.

Evidence Response Teams (ERTs) ERTs are groups of FBI special agents who focus on evidence recovery. They are experts in the latest techniques for finding and collecting evidence. ERTs normally include a team leader and six additional support specialists, including an evidence custodian, sketch preparer, photographer, evidence log recorder, evidence collector/processor, and specialist such as bomb technician or forensic anthropologist.

Questioned Documents Unit The questioned documents unit examines paper documents, surface impressions on paper documents, and other types of surface impressions such as shoeprints and tire tread impressions. Document examination typically involves comparing questioned documents with other types of evidentiary materials. Examiners also evaluate the characteristics of the documents themselves, including watermarks and safety fibers. The unit is capable of evaluating many types of paper surface impressions, including those originating from handwriting, typewriting, printing, and hand printing. The unit also analyzes typewriter/printer ribbons, photocopiers, faxes, graphic arts, and plastic bags. Various databases are maintained within the unit, including the anonymous letter file, bank robbery note file, national fraudulent check file, watermark file, and shoeprint file.

Investigative and Prosecutive Graphics Unit This unit specializes in crime scene survey and documentation, forensic facial imaging, and demonstrative evidence. *Demonstrative evidence* is generally of the most interest to financial investigations. In regard to this evidence, the unit provides charts, maps, diagrams, link analyses, flow and check kite charts, time lines, and technical renderings. Of course, accountants are also very skilled in providing graphics.

Racketeering Records Unit This unit contains four subunits: gambling, drug, money laundering, and cryptanalysis, each of which specializes in the examination of financial, property, taxation, real estate, and other types of records relating to specific types of crimes. The gambling subunit focuses not only on gambling records but also on the examination of records relating to sports bookmaking, loan sharking, prostitution, illegal lottery, video gambling machines, and Internet gambling. The drug subunit examines records relating to illegal drug-trafficking operations. The money-laundering subunit examines financial records relating to all areas including international terrorism. Finally, the cryptanalysis subunit "breaks" coded messages found in letters, e-mail messages, diaries, and financial records often used by organized crime and gang members, prison inmates, and terrorist groups.

Types of Evidence Used in Court

From the perspective of the forensic scientist and a court-room setting there are four types of evidence: physical, documentary, testimonial, and demonstrative. These four types of evidence are consistent with the types of evidence discussed in Chapter 8 relative to fraud investigations except that the focus here is on evidence used in court as opposed to evidence gathered as part of an investigation. Note that observational evidence is not included here, because forensic scientists and attornyes typically don't have an opportunity to observe crimes in progress. However, observational evidence becomes testimonial evidence or documentary evidence in a court setting.

- **Physical** This type of evidence includes tangible objects that can be physically carried into a courtroom and shown to a jury. It is said to speak for itself. Examples include a handwritten journal, a computer storage unit accompanied by a printout of its contents, a wire transfer slip, and a telephone log. Note that what is document evidence to a fraud investigator becomes physical evidence in a courtroom. This is because documents can by physically carried into court.
- **Documentary** This evidence type normally includes recorded information, such as an audio or video recording or a transcript of a telephone intercept. Unlike physical evidence, documentary evidence does not speak for itself but requires support from an expert witness.
- **Testimonial** This evidence includes testimony made under oath by eyewitnesses, expert witnesses, and character witnesses as well as confessions and hearsay evidence.
- **Demonstrative** As discussed earlier, such evidence includes charts, graphs, and computer reconstructions that attorneys or expert witnesses can prepare for use in either direct testimony or cross-examination.

Physical and Documentary Evidence

LO4 Forensic scientists and attorneys generally rely on all types of evidence to win cases. However, most cases involving financial crimes are won using physical evidence, including computer records, bank records, and charge card records. Good physical evidence often makes obtaining pre-trial settlements or plea bargains easier, and witnesses can be more cooperative when they are aware of strong physical evidence.

In general, financial records are the most important type of physical evidence to forensic accountants. Most financial crimes leave either money trails or record trails, or both. Moreover, the importance of financial records applies to a wide range of crimes, for it has been said that "the love of money is the root of all evil." For example, bank robbers can leave a record trail by depositing stolen money in their bank accounts, or they can make large cash purchases that leave money trails. Similarly, those trafficking in illegal drugs leave a record trail when they launder their ill-gotten money.

The subject of forensically examining financial records was discussed in Chapter 9. The focus in the present discussion is on forensic identification as it relates to traditional crime scene physical evidence such as fingerprints, trace evidence, blood evidence, and so on. Although such types of evidence are of secondary importance to forensic accountants, they are discussed here in general terms because forensic accountants need a general knowledge of them.

Fingerprints Fingertips have ridges that are normally covered with oil, sweat, amino acids, and various biological compounds. As a result, ridges on the fingertips leave a residue pattern when they come in contact with a surface. In some cases, these residue patterns are easily identifiable to the naked eye such as when they are made on glass or in blood, but most of the time they are latent, or hidden, and can be revealed only by special forensic techniques. The most basic of these techniques involves using a nylon brush to lightly dust the prints with black powder, which enhances the contrast of the ridges. The prints are then photographed and "lifted" with adhesive tape.

Black powder dusting works only on nonporous surfaces and when the prints are fresh. In many cases, other methods are used, such as the **superglue method,** which involves basking the fingerprint in gasified superglue. The gasses in the superglue have an affinity for the amino acids in prints, so they reveal the latent prints that are then powdered, photographed, and lifted via adhesive tape.

In some cases, sophisticated methods, such as using florescent powders and lasers, may be used to lift even old prints from porous surfaces. Therefore, the forensic accountant should always assume that fingerprints can be lifted from a given surface no matter what it is and how old the prints are.

Handwriting Handwriting comparisons are made by comparing handwriting from an **exemplar,** or known subject, to some disputed sample to determine whether the handwriting from the disputed sample is from the author of the exemplar. As with other forensic identification methods, various points of comparison are made. Some points of comparison include letter size, proportions, pressure, density, hesitations, and pen lifts.

The court admissibility of handwriting evidence has varied over the years and is still subject to debate. There has been a general tendency for courts to permit handwriting evidence as scientific evidence although it has been excluded in some cases. In still other cases, it has been considered to be an expert opinion but not scientific evidence. The process of collecting and analyzing an exemplar is best left to an expert. Various organizations such as the National Association of Document Examiners certify document examiners.

As a general rule, an existing date-appropriate exemplar should be used if it is available. Bank checks make excellent exemplars because they contain not only signatures but also handwritten dates, words, and numbers. If an exemplar must be obtained from a subject, certain procedures should be followed. First, the material to be written should be dictated, and the subject should never be shown the exemplar. Second, unless a particular writing instrument is important, the subject should use black or red ink to ensure readability in court. Next, the exemplar must be relevant, so the subject should write the data in question, including someone else's signature. The process should be rushed so the writer has no time to think. Everything, including any "mistakes," should be kept. If the exemplar exists on some form (such as a bank check), have the subject complete a blank copy of the form. Finally, have the subject write a combination of things, including the data in the exemplar. When the process is finished, have the subject sign and date each page of the exemplar.

Forensic Identification

The ultimate goal result of good physical evidence is **forensic identification** (see Figure 11.3), which occurs when the physical evidence can be specifically and unequivocally linked to a particular object or person. A famous statement relating to forensic identification is the **Locard exchange principle,** which says that "every contact leaves a trace." This principle has been used, for example, to identify bank robbers by their fingerprints, murderers by their DNA, and pistols by their expelled bullet cartridges. In financial investigations, the Locard exchange principle has been applied, for example, to identify embezzlers by their handwriting, racketeers by their bank deposits, and terrorists by their money transfers. The possibilities for forensic identification are nearly endless. Investigators can obtain information from each of the following, for example:

- **Paper shredder** Each paper shredder leaves unique cut marks on the paper it shreds.
- **Typing pattern** Each person types in a unique pattern. The pattern involves the speed of typing various characters, patterns of errors, habits involving the way errors are made, unique pauses, and so on. On computers, an individual's keystrokes can be recorded with hidden keystroke logging software.
- **Computer network identifying Information** Individual computers can be identified on computer networks by the unique addresses on the network adapter cards stored inside computers.

FIGURE 11.3
Forensic
Identification

Forensic identification occurs only when some characteristic, set of characteristics, or pattern of characteristics can be said to apply uniquely to an object or individual. The unique applicability of characteristics is established by comparing the object or individual to the characteristics of a reference specimen. For example, the handwriting characteristics of a suspect could be compared to the handwriting characteristics of an unknown person who made fraudulent entries in an accounting journal. If the suspect's handwriting characteristics are sufficiently close to those of the unknown person, a match is said to occur and a forensic identification has been made.

The study of individual characteristics involves the concept of class matching based on points of identification. A **class** is a group of persons or objects with similar characteristics; an individual or object is said to be a member of a class if he, she, or it shares common **points of comparison** (characteristics) with those included in the class.

Assume that it is discovered that someone has placed a destructive patch in one of the company's accounting programs that erases important data. In this case, investigators can determine certain characteristics, or points of identification, of the individual who has committed the crime as someone who has (1) access to the accounting software, (2) sufficient knowledge in computer programming, and (3) some motive to commit the crime.

Although the motive aspect can be difficult to determine, investigators can readily determine a class of suspect individuals with access to the accounting software and sufficient knowledge to commit the crime. To continue the example, assume that investigators find that six individuals have access to the software and the requisite knowledge. Assume also that one of these six individuals is a strong suspect because she has been repeatedly passed up for promotion because of discipline problems. Now investigators have one suspect in a class of six possible suspects. Unfortunately, this is not good enough to establish forensic identification. Forensic identification requires a set of points of comparison that reduces the class of suspects to one. *That is, to establish forensic identification, the suspect's points of comparison must uniquely correspond with those of the person who committed the crime.* In other words, forensic identification occurs when the group of suspects is reduced to a class of only one member.

To continue with the example, assume that by reviewing system log files, investigators discover that the destructive software patch was placed at 11:00 P.M. on a given Wednesday. A review of the records shows that only one employee was in the office when the crime was committed; the person is the same employee who had been repeatedly passed up for promotions. The result is that the class of suspects has been reduced to one, and investigators have made a forensic identification.

Although a forensic identification has been made, it cannot be stated with absolute certainty that the identification is correct. It is always possible that some unknown person made the change and made it appear that the suspect did it. For example, perhaps one of the other employees who has high-level programming skills unknown to the company hacked into the computer system when he knew the suspect would be in the office.

Forensic identification is never 100 percent certain, even with physical evidence such as fingerprints and DNA. In the case of fingerprints, the forensic scientist compares physical points of reference to compare a suspect's fingerprints with the fingerprints of the unknown perpetrator of the crime. The more points that match, the higher is the degree of certainty, but the process is not infallible regardless of the number of points matched.

DNA comparisons are generally considered to be less subject to error than fingerprint comparisons but are still subject to error. For example, in one burglary case in Great Brittan, a sample of crime scene DNA was forensically identified as belonging to an individual in a police database that contained DNA profiles of 700,000 persons. The suspect was a man with Parkinson's disease so advanced that he could barely dress himself. He lived 200 miles away from the crime scene, could not drive a car, and had a good alibi.

The forensic identification for the man was based on six points of comparison (loci) on the DNA molecules. Given such a comparison, the odds of an error were said to be 1 in 37 million. No error had been made in handling or processing the samples. There was in fact a valid six-point match.

After the man had spent months in jail, his attorney convinced the authorities to retest the DNA. The retest was done with 10 points of comparison, with 4 new points being added to the first test. The result was that the additional 4 points of comparison did not match, and the man was excluded and released from jail. The retest was said to be accurate.

After that case, the British government changed to a 10-points-of-comparison test. The odds of an error for this test are said to be 1 in 1 billion, but experts argue that such odds are mere estimates and could be greatly under- or overstated. Some experts argue that DNA comparisons are subject to false identification even when 13 points of comparison are used.

Evidence Identification   Forensic scientists use a wide variety of techniques (such as spectography, chromatography, neutron scanning, and x-ray dispersion) to identify almost any kind of substance. Both organic (e.g., hairs and blood) and inorganic (e.g., paint, poisons, glass) substances can be identified.

Evidence Identification by Minutia   All types of minute evidence including DNA, hairs, fibers, pollen, and dirt can be identified by comparing one object to another by using multiple points of comparison. In many cases, these types of comparisons result in **class identification** rather than definitive forensic identification. For example, a fiber comparison may identify the fiber as having come from a particular type of carpeting rather than the particular carpeting in a suspect's office. In other cases, comparing minutia can lead to unique forensic identification. For example, ballistics experts are able to compare **striations** (i.e., minute markings) on bullets to the inside of pistol barrels to establish a "match" between a bullet and the pistol from which it was shot.

Striations can be used to identify an almost unlimited number of objects. As examples, a pipe wrench can leave unique striation patterns on pipes; a sheet of paper can have patterns of microscopic striations that identify it as having come from a particular printing press. One robber was convicted based on a unique pattern of striationlike marks in the seams of his denim jeans captured by a security video camera taken during the robbery. The pattern was later matched to the suspect's actual jeans.

As discussed, there is no such thing as a perfect match. In fact, the word *match* is often misused. For this reason, *similarities* is typically used when points of comparison are similar. Matches are never 100 percent but are matters of probabilities that experts often debate in court.

Testimonial Evidence

LO5   Rule 702 of the federal evidence rules governs *expert testimony:*

> If scientific, technical, or other specialized knowledge will assist the trier of fact to understand the evidence or to determine a fact in issue, a witness qualified as an expert by knowledge, skill, experience, training, or education, may testify thereto in the form of an opinion or otherwise, if
>
> 1. the testimony is based upon sufficient facts or data,
> 2. the testimony is the product of reliable principles and methods, and
> 3. the witness has applied the principles and methods reliably to the facts of the case.

The phrase "reliable principles and methods" in requirement 2 in effect sets a legal standard for defining what becomes scientific, technical, or other evidence.

For 70 years, the legal standard merely required that an expert witness's principles and methods be generally accepted in the scientific community. That standard is referred to as the **Frye test,** named for one of the litigants in a Supreme Court decision. A subsequent Supreme Court decision, however, created what is now called the **Daubert test,** which sets specific requirements for a technique or theory to be considered scientific:

*   The technique or theory has been subjected to scientific testing.
*   The technique or theory has been published in peer-reviewed scientific journals.
*   The error rate for the technique is reasonably estimated or known.
*   The technique or theory is accepted in the relevant scientific community.

This test applies only in federal courts and in those states that have adopted it. The Supreme Court intended the test to be flexible with respect to the requirements, meaning that not all of them must be met in a given case. Nevertheless, some courts may rigorously apply all of the requirements to prevent possible problems with appeals.

In another case heard by the Supreme Court ***Kumho Tire Co. v. Carmichael,*** the Court made mandatory a Daubert determination in all cases involving expert testimony. The Court further refined the flexible requirements by indicating that they should not necessarily be applied to all forms of expert testimony with the same degree of strictness but should be applied strictly only to those forms of expert testimony for which their strict application is possible.

A Daubert determination is normally made in a "minitrial" held before a judge but outside the presence of the jury. The judge rules on whether the witness qualifies as an expert and whether the expert can represent a given body of evidence as being scientific. An expert who is not permitted to present the evidence as being scientific may still be permitted to introduce it as personal expert opinion.

What the courts are willing to accept as scientific evidence is an ongoing open question. Some courts accept a given method while others reject it. Moreover, even if the vast majority of courts accept (or reject) a given method, they can reverse themselves at any time because scientific knowledge and methods are constantly changing and new arguments can be made. It is therefore important that any expert witness be prepared to argue that the method employed meets the Daubert test. While some states use a combination of the Daubert and Frye tests, others use some version of the Frye test.

Investigatory Tools in Forensic Science

The preceding section discussed forensic science primarily in the context of court-admissible physical evidence that links a suspect to a crime. Forensic science can be useful as an investigative tool, however, even when it does not lead to court-admissible evidence. It can elicit testimonial evidence by using scientifically developed methods for questioning and interrogation.

A polygraph (lie detector test) is a good forensic-science investigative tool. Courts generally reject polygraphy (because it tends to measure stress more than honesty), but police frequently use it as an investigative tool. New investigative tools are constantly being developed. One example is **brain printing,** which monitors the pattern of the subject's brain activity with special instruments while showing her a photo. The pattern of brain activity is then used to determine whether the subject is familiar with the content of the photo. For example, a suspect could be shown a photo of a crime scene, and her resulting brain patterns could then be used to assess whether she is familiar with the scene.

Other methods are being developed to assess honesty in interrogations, including the analysis of mannerisms, body language, posture, and voice features. In fact, the entire area of interrogations is becoming somewhat of a science.

The area of **biometrics** (identifying persons by physical characteristics) is under development. Computers are being used to identify people by the irises in their eyes, the shapes of their ears, their "voice prints," and so on. Video biometrics is becoming especially important as police continue to place video cameras in more and more public locations. Computer software now can instantly compare facial features acquired from real-time video surveillance cameras to large databases of terrorists or criminals.

Many types of **profiling methods** are being developed and used today. Terrorist organizations or organized crime groups could be identified by mathematical, structural analyses of social networks. Profiles of criminals (including their age, marital status, education, living community, income, personality factors, and so on) are being developed and used to solve various crimes. *Psychogeographical profiling* analyzes patterns of spatial, geographical, and psychological crime-related data to help identify criminals. In some cases, geographical profiling software has been used to identify precisely where a criminal is at a specific moment.

Profiling techniques are part of the more general science of **data mining** (discussed in Chapter 5), which uses statistical techniques and artificial intelligence to analyze large volumes of data by considering the relationships between individual data items. For example, by analyzing large volumes of bank transactions, income tax data, and credit card charges for many companies, data mining could identify a terrorist or drug trafficking organization.

COMPUTER FORENSICS

Computer forensics involves applying computer science techniques to assist in investigations relating to a wide range of legal matters. Examples include theft, alteration or destruction of data, fraud, organized criminal actions, murder, drug trafficking, and terrorism. Almost any crime can involve a computer in some way. It has become almost standard for police to include computers in many search warrants regardless of the crime involved.

Computer forensic specialists are typically called on to study computers and computer networks to discover and preserve computer-related evidence and to achieve objectives in the following three areas:

1. Identify the perpetrator(s) of a crime or other type of malfeasance.
2. Locate and recover data, files, or e-mail messages relating to a crime or civil matter.
3. Reconstruct damaged databases and files.

Other computer security areas of risk management, prevention, and detection were covered in Chapter 5.

Each of these three areas is discussed individually after a discussion of considerations applicable to all computer forensic investigations.

Essential Considerations in Computer Forensic Investigations

LO6   The first consideration in any investigation includes collecting and preserving evidence and maintaining the **chain of custody.** These matters present special problems in computer-related investigations. The computer forensic professional must carefully handle all computer-related equipment to ensure the following:

- Evidence is not altered, damaged, contaminated, or destroyed by the investigative procedures. As discussed later, the mere act of inspecting data on a computer can itself destroy valuable information on it.
- No malicious software is permitted to infect or corrupt either the subject computer, the investigator's computer, or other computers on the subject computer's network.
- All possible relevant evidence extracted from the subject's computer or network is fully preserved.
- An unbroken chain of custody is established, documented, and maintained.
- Minimal interruptions to the operations of the business under investigation occur.
- The privacy and confidentiality of all data on the subject's computer and network are properly maintained.

Special Issues in Preserving Computer Evidence

The computer forensic professional must be especially careful when investigating a computer. As noted, interacting with the computer in any way risks the loss of evidence. When files, messages, database records, and log entries are deleted from computers, the actual related data are not actually deleted from the computer, but they no longer appear to be available to users. However, the storage space for those data is then made available for use by other applications; this means that using any software on the computer can cause the erased data to be overwritten by new data.

Many applications have built-in safeguards to protect against the accidental data erasure. Such applications normally provide for separate **logical versus physical erasure/ deletion of data.** Data that are only logically deleted are protected, and the deletion can be reversed any time before the user chooses the option to physically delete it. In some database systems, physical removal can be done either manually or by automated database utilities that periodically "compress" or "clean" the database. The act of compressing or cleaning often means physically removing deleted data. This suggests that in some cases, investigators could recover a data item simply by using the undo function or undeleting it, although the undo function might not work after the application has been closed. It also suggests the importance of time and the likelihood of data being deleted automatically or overwritten.

As mentioned, even when data are said to be physically deleted, they can still exist on the storage device as part of the pool of free storage space available. This fact implies that the forensic computer professional must not start browsing on a subject computer because doing so could overwrite physically deleted data that still exists in the pool of free storage space.

A second issue of data preservation relates to cache storage. Most operating systems have limited amounts of high-speed internal random access memory (RAM). As a result, they constantly swap large chunks of data in RAM to slower but more abundant mass storage devices such as hard drives. The swap is only for short periods of time and then the data are swapped back into RAM when the central processing unit (CPU) needs it for processing. While swapped into mass storage, the data are stored in hidden system **cache storage** files that temporarily store these data from RAM. Virtually all operating systems use system cache storage.

The problem with system cache storage is that its contents constantly change as the computer is used. Furthermore, data stored in the cache are routinely discarded and even overwritten when they are no longer needed by the CPU and host programs. This means that any of the forensic computer professional's use of the subject computer could lead to the loss of valuable data in the system cache. In some operating systems, shutting down the computer can delete the system cache file.

Individual application programs often have their own their own cache files. Such applications typically use them either for optimizing performance, undo functions, and recovery in the event of a power outage or hardware failure.

Antiforensics, Countermeasures, and Advanced Data Recovery As discussed, data in deleted files can be overwritten with new data. **Antiforensic software** programs overwrite empty spaces on hard drives in attempts to prevent data recovery. It is sometimes possible, however, to use advanced recovery techniques to recover data of interest that have been written over. Because the hardware process of writing data to a hard drive is not exact, the old data are not completely covered. Therefore, special techniques such as **magnetic-force microscopy** and **magnetic-force tunneling microscopy** can recover data overwritten many times. For this reason, some security experts recommend that data be overwritten up to 35 times in order to completely prevent it from being recovered. The **Department of Defense (DOD) "wipe" standard** calls for at least seven passes over every sector to overwrite it with new data.

The Forensic Accountant as Computer Forensic Professional

Much of this chapter assumes that a forensic computer specialist is the investigator. However, many times the forensic accountant serves as the computer forensic professional. The forensic accountant often begins the initial investigation and then decides whether to call in a specialist in computer forensics for a number of reasons. The forensic accountant should be familiar with computer forensic procedures if they are needed.

Before beginning any investigation, the forensic accountant should ensure that he has the proper legal authority and is not invading someone's privacy without authorization. In general, corporations and business owners can give permission to inspect items under their ownership and control, but some exceptions exist. For this reason, every forensic accountant should have access to and consult legal counsel familiar with laws applicable to the jurisdiction in which she works.

Steps in Forensic Investigation of Computers

LO7 Because of the special issues in preserving computer data, the forensic professional must follow an organized series of steps in dealing with a computer that could contain evidence. Great care and discipline must be exercised, for any mistakes are likely to lead to irreversible loss of evidence.

Step 1: Size Up the Situation

In sizing up the situation, ask questions such as these: What type of incident is being investigated? Who are the likely perpetrators, and how sophisticated are they? Which computers were likely used or affected? When did the incident probably happen? The answers to each of these questions should be recorded in the forensic professional's notes.

How the questions are answered will affect how the investigator proceeds. The seriousness of the matter and the sophistication of the perpetrator(s) will have the largest impact on the approach taken. If the matter is already known to be serious, consideration should be given to immediately restricting access to the suspected computers and relevant areas, and the issue should be discussed with law enforcement authorities, who could bring in criminalists to process the crime scene. The forensic professional should never contaminate a likely police crime scene. Of course, the forensic accountant or computer forensic specialist could already be a member of law enforcement, in which case the investigation will proceed after processing the crime scene if necessary.

The degree of the perpetrator's sophistication is important because it suggests possible countermeasures that she could have put in place. Some possible countermeasures are physical booby traps inside the computer, software-based self-destruct systems, and encryption. The more sophisticated the perpetrators, the more likely it is that these countermeasures are in place. The likelihood of countermeasures affects the degree of sophistication applied to the investigation. As a general rule, the most sophisticated available investigatory methods should be used unless there is good reason to believe that unsophisticated perpetrators are involved.

Step 2: Log Every Detail

The forensic professional should keep an accurate log of every step followed. It should contain precise details, including names, dates, times, and computer serial numbers.

Step 3: Conduct the Initial Survey

In conducting the initial survey, the forensic professional must immediately secure the site, including any offices and computers that could be relevant to the investigation. It is also necessary to secure any computer servers, video security camera recordings, computerized phone records, centralized e-mail databases, relevant paper files, and so on. The objective in securing the site is to restrict access to it to those participating in the investigation; it is especially important to deny access to possible suspects.

Any relevant computers and the immediate sites around them should be photographed. Items of possible interest, such as sticky notes containing passwords, computer disks, and so on, should be photographed individually with number cards placed next to them. Each item should logged in the forensic specialist's notebook with the date, time, and item number. In situations judged to be serious enough, all investigators should wear plastic gloves during the on-site investigation to avoid damaging possible evidence.

Items collected should be placed into tamper-proof evidence bags. These bags contain various features including serialized control numbers, removable receipts with control numbers, tamper-proof seals, and chain-of-custody listings.

Step 4: Assess the Possibility of Ongoing Undesirable Activity

If at the time of the investigation the computer could still be involved in some crime or other activity of interest, it could be desirable to install a **packet sniffer,** a hardware device that intercepts and records the computer's communications over any networks it is connected to. The wiretap is connected to the packet sniffer device that records all packets passing through the communication link. Even with packet sniffing or log tracing, however, a sophisticated person may still remain unidentifiable by communicating through a chain of anonymous proxy servers spread all over the globe. Therefore, tracing communications through one anonymous proxy server could lead to another anonymous proxy server in some tiny country half a world away. Such monitoring devices are routinely used in company networks to identify and solve technical problems. Before using such a device, the specialist should consult legal council to ensure that using them does not break wire-tapping or other laws.

An alternative to the packet sniffer is remote keyboard logging/monitoring software. Such software can record and send to a private web site all internet activity on a surveilled computer, including incoming and outgoing email, chat sessions, social networking communications, and web browser activity. Such software is widely available and for sale on the Web, and the higher-quality versions install as rootkits and are virtually undetectable by most anti-virus and anti-spyware software. Versions exists for both computers and mobile devices.

In some cases, the computer could contain some type of active Trojan horse, worm, virus, spyware, or other type of "malware" that is actively involved in sending out spam or fraudulent e-mail or spreading itself to other computers. First consideration must always be given to minimizing any damage caused by an intrusion or hostile incident. In this case, it could be necessary to immediately unplug or disconnect the computer from the network. However, a sophisticated perpetrator could have installed countermeasures that are activated if a computer is disconnected from its network. If such countermeasures are considered possible, it could be necessary to either pull the plug on the computer or shut it down using the procedures discussed in the next section.

Step 5: Power Down

If the subject computer is already off, it should absolutely not be turned on. If it is on, some minimal work could be needed before shutting the machine down or pulling the plug. As a general rule, it is much safer to shut down or unplug a machine than to do any work on it. Once the forensic professional starts working on the machine, data can be lost, and the investigator becomes responsible for the machine's status. That could lead to later claims that the investigator contaminated the data on the machine.

However, given the seriousness of an incident, the length of time since it occurred, and the investigator's assessment of the perpetrator's sophistication, doing some minimal work on the computer can be advisable before shutting it down or pulling the plug. The primary action is to use the operating system's task or process manager to obtain a list of all processes running on the system, the locations of their related programs, as well as any characteristic information available about them, such as priority, memory size, related processes, CPU utilization, and so on. All of this information should be carefully logged in the forensic professional's notes.

Information on processes is important because they represent all programs actively running on the computer, and one or more of the active programs could be involved in the incident under investigation. However, some sophisticated perpetrators might install rootkit-type software that runs within some known processes or invisibly so that it cannot be identified by using the usual system utilities for process viewing and management.

The next step is to shut the machine down. This can be done by either pulling the plug or using the operating system functions to shut it down (see Figure 11.4). The general rule is to pull the plug from the wall or uninterruptible power supply except in the case that

FIGURE 11.4
Pulling the Plug—Generally the Best Option in Investigations Involving Most Modern Operating Systems

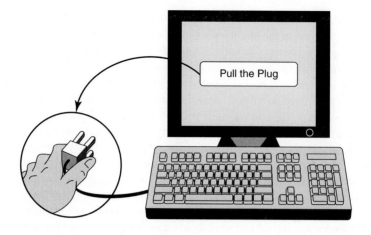

Pull the Plug

there is a good reason to believe that critical information, such as data not yet saved, exists only in RAM. This general rule applies to most late-version operating systems.

Because all data in RAM are lost when the plug is pulled, it is sometimes best to use the application program to save critical data before pulling the plug. It is also possible that other valuable information, such as passwords and encryption keys, are stored in RAM only.

Some software programs can dump the contents of RAM, including the keyboard buffer that contains the last 1,024 keystrokes entered into the computer, to permanent storage, but they must first be installed on the computer in question, which could destroy data in deleted files, as discussed. Therefore, the forensic professional must balance the risk of one problem versus the other. If it is known that critical information exists only in RAM, then the focus is on obtaining it. This supports the selection of the exact steps to follow according to the situation.

Ideally, any program that dumps RAM should occupy the smallest amount of RAM and permanent storage possible to minimize the possible destruction of any deleted data or files that are still recoverable. Furthermore, such software should dump RAM to an external device, such as a USB or firewire storage device that can be connected to the computer and is active with no software installation.

In some cases, it is also desirable to dump files to an external device before pulling the plug. This is especially true for encrypted files that are available in their unencrypted state when the machine is first inspected but would require an encryption key if the computer is restarted. Standard encryption techniques can easily put the encrypted files out of reach to the forensic professional.

Some operating systems support hibernation as an alternative to shutdown. This mode generally writes the entire contents of RAM to a special paging file. This in effect preserves the entire state of the system while shutting it down. The paging file is not normally readable directly, but it can be accessed if the permanent storage unit on which it resides is read from a different operating system. Therefore, putting a machine in hibernation mode could be an alternative to simply pulling the plug. However, that said, there still remains the possibility than any type of operating system shutdown can invoke countermeasures that have been added by a sophisticated perpetrator. Moreover, some countermeasures can "security wipe" a storage device and make it impossible to recover deleted data.

Finally, some hardware devices that can be physically attached to the inside of a computer to capture the contents of RAM are said to exist. A device that could do this would obviously be of great help to the forensic professional. It is likely that such devices exist at the National Security Agency, the Central Intelligence Agency, and the Federal Bureau of Investigation.

Step 6: Check for Booby Traps

After the computer has been shut down but before physically opening it to expose the main chassis and internal parts, the forensic professional must consider the possibility that it has an internal booby trap triggered to activate if it is opened. The booby trap could be a device rigged to destroy the computer's internal contents or a bomb (see Figure 11.5). If there is any possibility of a booby trap, the forensic professional should use a fiber optic probe to examine the computer's internal contents.

Step 7: Duplicate the Hard Drive or Other Permanent Storage Unit

When the computer is open, the investigator should photograph its inside and then remove the hard drive and log its make, model, and serial number. It should be placed in a sealed evidence bag and then immediately and directly transported to a secure off-site office or laboratory setting.

When the evidence bag is opened, the following steps as well as the hard drive's serial number should be documented in the notes. The forensic professional should next duplicate the hard drive using a system guaranteed not to write even a single bit to the drive being duplicated. The best approach is to use a hardware write blocker, which physically prevents any data from being written to the original disk. The duplication should be done using a sector-by-sector or bit-by-bit (i.e., an **imaging method**) method as opposed a file-copy method.

The duplication system should independently generate a **checksum** (a hash number created for a disk or a file) for the both the original disk and the duplicate. This number guarantees that the original and the duplicate are exactly the same; it should be matched at least twice. When the duplication process is completed, the original hard drive should be placed in a new bag with appropriate notes and the original bag. The serial number of the duplicate drive also should be logged, and the original drive should be bagged until it is to be studied. More than one copy of the original drive might be made, depending on the situation.

Step 8: Analyze the Hard Drive

Various methods for analyzing a hard drive exist. The drive can be placed in a machine and then booted. This should be done only if more than one duplicate copy exists because booting from the hard drive alters its contents. The strategy in booting a drive is to be able to explore it without concern for changing its contents and afterward to verify any findings using a second duplicate copy that was not booted and whose contents are not altered in any way.

FIGURE 11.5
Computer with Booby Trap

To explore the booted hard drive, the investigator can open the various programs and browse and search within them. It is also possible to use a desktop search program that indexes all viewable files, including e-mail messages, on the hard drive. The investigator can then search the entire hard drive using various keywords or phrases that could relate to the investigation. In a significant incident, a team of investigators could be assigned to read the many millions of words on the hard drive.

The duplicate hard drive can also be searched by mounting it as a second, nonbootable hard drive on a machine running a different operating system. For example, mount a Windows-based hard drive as a second hard drive on a Linux computer. Doing so will make some files accessible that could not otherwise be accessed because operating systems tend to protect their own system files.

Once the hard drive is mounted on an alternative operating system, it can then be explored, and searched, using **sector editing software** that completely bypasses the file structure of the hard drive to search it from beginning to end, including data in both hidden system files and normal user files.

Viewing data at the sector level is completely different from viewing at the normal file level. The advantage is that data from system files, such as the system cache file, and deleted files (that have not yet been overwritten) can be recovered.

Alternative Sources for Data Recovery If the desired data cannot be recovered from one computer, it could be recovered from another. The investigator should consider backup hard drives, network-level archives, and other computers that might have been used by any suspects. It is also possible that the perpetrator communicated valuable information via e-mail, so it is good practice to consider checking out computers belonging to individuals in the perpetrator's e-mail address book. Other information could also be found on the computer to assist in the investigations.

Some files may be protected by password or sophisticated encryption techniques, although this is usually not a problem for files related to most common office-type applications. Although many password recovery programs available on the Internet will recover passwords from such files, a sophisticated perpetrator could have encrypted files with elaborate encryption techniques. The contents of files encrypted with a sufficient degree of sophistication cannot be viewed. In certain situations, however, such as cases of national security, some government agencies may be able to use supercomputers and classified techniques to break encryption on otherwise unbreakable files.

If none of the standard password-recovery software can break the password for a given file, the investigator can make some educated guesses. Because people tend to use the same passwords for multiple purposes, the investigator could be able to obtain, possibly by subpoena, any passwords used by suspects for other purposes, such as for bank accounts or e-mail accounts.

The examiner should also investigate the system and individual program log files that could contain valuable information relating to who accessed the computer, when, what software was used, and any security violations.

Identify Individuals in a Network Environment In many cases, the forensic computer professional needs to identify the source of a hacker or an e-mail. Each of these possibilities is discussed in turn.

The best way to track a hacker is through his **IP address** (or, more briefly, IP), the unique number assigned to each computer on the Internet. A computer can have a dedicated IP (also called *static IP*), meaning that its IP address is always the same or a **dynamic IP,** meaning it obtains a unique, new "borrowed" IP address every time it establishes a new connection to the Internet. Each dynamic IP address is borrowed from an Internet service provider (ISP) or local network and then returned to the ISP or local network when the Internet connection is ended.

IPs are important because they route each *packet,* the form in which virtually all data transmitted over the Internet travel, in the form of discrete messages, to the correct destination. For example, here are the processing steps involved when a person enters the URL www.microsoft.com into a Web browser (see Figure 11.6).

- The Web browser retrieves (via the computer's operating system) the IP address for www.microsoft.com from the local **distributed name server (DNS),** which is a database, usually hosted by the user's Internet service provider, that contains Web addresses and their related IPs.
- The user's Web browser then sends a message in the form of packets that contain both the user's IP and the IP for www.microsoft.com using the IP as the destination address.
- The Web server at www.microsoft.com then responds by sending the user the requested Web page. The response is in the form of a series of packets that are routed using the user's IP address.

Each packet in the two-way communication process includes the source and destination IPs. Many software programs record sources and destinations for Internet traffic on a given computer. For example, most Web servers automatically log the IPs for all incoming requests. Results from packet sniffing could be the only source of information available to identify and locate an outside hacker.

Investigating log files of IPs is effective in tracing the IP address of anyone who directly communicates with a given computer via a Web browser, file sharing, and remote access.

FIGURE 11.6
URL to IP
Translation

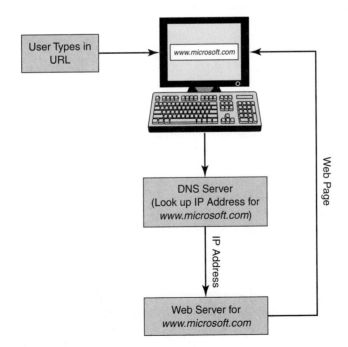

It does not help in investigating e-mail communications because e-mail does not travel directly from the sender's to the receiver's computer.

E-mail communications follow an indirect path as follows:

- When the sender presses the Send button, the e-mail message is uploaded to the sender's **simple mail transfer protocol (SMTP) server.**
- The SMTP server, also called the *relay server,* then relays the e-mail message to the receiver's incoming mail server. The SMTP server finds the IP address of the receiver's incoming mail server by doing a DNS lookup. The mail exchange (MX) record in the DNS database supplies the desired IP address.
- The e-mail message recipient then uses an e-mail client program to retrieve the message from her incoming e-mail server.

In summary, the typical e-mail message changes hands three times: first, from the sender to the sender's SMTP server; second, from the sender's SMTP server to the recipient's incoming mail server; and third, from the recipient's incoming mail server to the recipient. Each time the message changes hands, a complete record of the handover can be added to the mail header, a hidden part of the e-mail message that is not normally viewed by the recipient. The header typically includes the date and time of the handover and the IP of the e-mail client or server making the handover. What actually goes into the mail header depends on the specific e-mail servers through which the e-mail message passes.

Most e-mail programs have an option to reveal the full e-mail header; however, e-mail headers are sometimes a bit cryptic, in which case the forensic accountant could use one of the many available programs that analyze e-mail headers for tracing e-mail messages to their source.

When the subject's IP address has been identified, either through log files or an e-mail header, it is possible to access one of the many widely available Web sites through which a Web-based reverse IP lookup of the owner's known IP address can be performed. In many cases, the reverse lookup yields the IP of a company or Internet service provider (ISP), which could be asked, possibly with a subpoena, to find who used the given IP address on a given date and time.

Unfortunately, IP information is not always helpful because sophisticated individuals can use various methods to **spoof** (i.e., fake) their IP addresses. They can also hide their IPs by communicating though an anonymous **proxy server,** which is an intermediary for Web traffic. For example, for a person to use a proxy sever to access www.microsoft.com, the person's Web browser would not communicate directly with that address but would communicate only with the proxy server. The proxy server would communicate with www.microsoft.com and then relay information back to the user's Web browser.

Proxy servers become anonymous when they do not keep any logs of the traffic that flows through them. This means that the investigator who traces an IP to an anonymous proxy server may reach a dead end unless a court order is obtained to require the anonymous proxy service to keep a log. Also, with proper authority, a wiretap can be placed on the communications links that connect the anonymous proxy sever to the Internet.

Another way to identify an IP address is to search for its previous occurrences in any existing logs or e-mail archives. For example, assume that a company finds the IP address of a hacker but cannot get a subpoena for the hacker's ISP. The company could search all of its e-mail archives to possibly find the IP.

LAW ENFORCEMENT DATABASES AND NETWORKS

LO8 Law enforcement professionals have access to many databases that can be helpful in investigations. This section discusses some of these national databases and networks. The FBI's Criminal Justice Information Services Wide Area Network (CJIS-WAN) is typically used as the national communications system for access to its national databases.

Automated Fingerprint Identification System (IAFIS)

The **automated fingerprint identification system** (**IAFIS;** sometimes called *AFIS*) is a database that can match a suspect's whole or partial fingerprint against fingerprints in it. The system produces a list of candidates for matches whose fingerprints are then examined by a fingerprint specialist to make a final determination for any identification.

The FBI maintains the largest AFIS database, which contains fingerprints from more than 40 million individuals that include, for example, criminals and military personnel. Many states and cities also maintain their own individual IAFIS fingerprint databases.

National DNA Index System (NDIS)

NDIS is an FBI-run database system that contains DNA profiles of convicted criminals and forensic profiles of DNA collected from crime scenes. A large percentage of states participate in the NDIS system. All 50 states have laws that mandate collecting DNA profiles from those convicted of specific crimes, such as burglaries of residences and sex offenses.

Combined DNA Index System (CODIS)

CODIS is a database that contains DNA profiles instead of fingerprints. It is used to search the NDIS database. Individual states also have their own CODIS databases.

National Integrated Ballistics Information Network (NIBIN)

NIBIN is a system that matches bullets, bullet casings, and firearms. It uses integrated ballistics identification system (IBIS) equipment to compare firearms-related evidence (images of fired bullets and cartridge cases collected from crime scenes and recovered firearms) stored in a joint FBI–Bureau of Alcohol, Tobacco, Firearms, and Explosives (ATF) database.

National Law Enforcement Telecommunications Systems (NLETS)

NLETS is a nationwide criminal justice communications network that connects all 50 states and various federal agencies including virtually all police agencies (large and small), prosecutors, parole officers, and probation departments. Participants in the NLETS system have access to a wide variety of information, such as vehicle registrations, drivers licenses, criminal history records, and prison records, from member states. Participants also have access to various national databases, such as the ATF gun tracking database, Federal Aviation Administration tracking and aircraft registration databases, and the National Impound Vehicle database.

National Crime Information Center (NCIC) Network

Most state law enforcement agencies also have access to the FBI's **NCIC** network, a real-time system that is a national index of theft reports, warrants, fugitives, missing persons, gang membership data, and other data submitted by participating members. The system processes millions of transactions each day.

Financial Crimes Enforcement Network (FinCEN)

FinCEN is a Treasury Department agency (www.fincen.gov) whose original mission is, in its own words, "to provide a government-wide, multi-source intelligence and analytical network to support the detection, investigation, and prosecution of domestic and international money laundering and other financial crimes." FinCEN focuses primarily on money laundering, which continues to make its mission relevant to a wide range of financial crimes and investigations. It provides case support to federal, state, and local agencies.

Summary

Forensic science is the application of science to legal matters. Various areas of special interest to forensic accounting include computer forensics, criminalistics, dactylography, forensic evidence, forensic identification, forensic palaeography (also called *diplomatics,* or questioned document examination), forensic psychology/psychiatry, and information forensics.

Various persons and entities are important in forensic science–related investigations: criminalists, forensic scientists, and crime labs. *Criminalists* are crime scene technicians or investigators who specialize in finding, collecting, and preserving physical evidence at crime scenes. *Forensic scientists* work primarily in the laboratory rather than at crime scenes. Furthermore, they focus on interpreting evidence gathered by criminalists, although some experienced criminalists develop interpretive skills.

Most crime labs are affiliated with police agencies. The better ones are accredited by one of the main accrediting organizations such as the American Society of Crime Laboratory Directors and the National Forensic Science Technology Center.

The FBI lab is the largest and most sophisticated crime lab in the United States. The FBI crime lab provides various special services, such as those provided by the computer analysis and response team (CART), the evidence response team (ERT), investigative and prosecutive graphics, the questioned documents unit, and racketeering records.

Investigators generally rely on physical evidence, witnesses, and confessions to solve crimes. Most financial crimes are solved using physical evidence, including computer, bank, and charge card records. Good physical evidence can make it easier to obtain confessions, and even witnesses can be more cooperative when they are aware of strong physical evidence.

The ultimate goal of good physical evidence is forensic identification, which occurs when the physical evidence can be specifically and unequivocally linked to a particular object or person. Identification occurs only when some characteristic, set of characteristics, or pattern of characteristics can be said to apply uniquely to an object or individual. To establish forensic identification, the suspect's points of comparison must uniquely correspond with those of the person who committed the crime. In other words, forensic identification occurs when the group of suspects is reduced to a class containing only one member.

In general, there are four types of evidence in court cases: physical, documentary, testimonial, and demonstrative. The most important type of evidence to forensic accountants tends to be physical (i.e., financial records). Most financial crimes leave either money trails or record trails or both.

Forensic evidence sometimes requires testimonial evidence from experts. One legal standard for expert testimony to be considered "scientific" is the Daubert test, which is "passed" when the expert's technique has been subjected to scientific testing, has been published in peer-reviewed scientific journals, has an established or measurable error rate, and is accepted in the relevant scientific community. These criteria must be applied as relevant to the particular situation.

Chapter **Twelve**

The Fraud Report, Litigation, and the Recovery Process

CHAPTER LEARNING OBJECTIVES

After reading Chapter 12, you should be able to:

- LO1: Explain the different uses of fraud investigation reports.
- LO2: Outline the elements of a fraud investigation report.
- LO3: Outline the different options for fraud loss recovery.
- LO4: Contrast and compare serving as an expert consultant versus as an expert.
- LO5: Explain the role of the forensic accountant in expert testimony.
- LO6: Explain the legal standards for expert testimony.
- LO7: Explain issues and strategies relating to expert testimony.

When the fraud investigation has been completed, the investigator writes a formal report. The report itself plus expert opinions and testimony are then used as needed to support the resolution of any issues that may relate to taxes, employment, regulatory reporting, litigation (civil and criminal), and insurance claims.

Because the report is used for such important purposes, it must be constructed under the assumption that it will be challenged in court. This requires that the report meet very high standards; any errors or misstatements in it may be used to undermine the credibility of both the report and the investigator who wrote it.

The next section discusses various uses of reports (Figure 12.1). The following section discusses expert testimony.

FRAUD INVESTIGATION REPORTS

Uses of Fraud Investigation Reports

Taxes

LO1   Frauds typically result in business losses. For income tax purposes, such losses may be classified as either deductions or offsets to reportable revenues depending on the type of loss and the taxing authority. In cases of misappropriation, almost any type of asset can be fraudulently converted, and in some cases, a valuation expert might be needed to determine the dollar amount of the loss.

FIGURE 12.1
Fraud Investigation Reports Have Many Uses

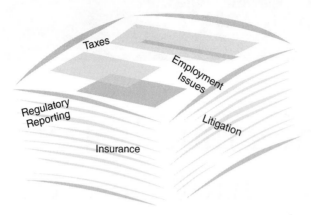

In cases of occupational fraud, the financial records can be so damaged from the fraud scheme that an exact determination of the loss is impossible. In such cases, the report may attempt to estimate the loss using any reasonable means available because taxing authorities often permit estimation of losses in cases of destroyed records.

Some occupational fraud schemes result in so much damage to the financial records that the entity will not have enough information to file tax returns. This can happen, for example, if the revenue records are either destroyed or rendered unreliable as a result of fraudulent transactions and journal entries. In such cases, it might be necessary to conduct a major reconstruction of the accounting records before losses can be determined, reliable financial statements can be generated, and tax returns can be filed. In fact, in some cases, the fraud investigator's report might need to focus on the loss due to destruction of the financial records and leave open the issue of misappropriation pending reconstruction of the financial records. Of course, depending on the scope of the investigation and the available information, the investigator might both reconstruct the financial records and report on any misappropriation losses.

Another tax-related issue involves the embezzlement of funds set aside to pay payroll taxes. The U.S. federal tax system sometimes refers to such funds as **trust fund taxes** because under tax law, these funds belong to the Internal Revenue Service (IRS) from the moment they are collected. The business and the owners merely serve as trustees in collecting the taxes on behalf of the IRS.

The U.S federal tax laws permit owners and officers to be held personally liable for embezzled trust fund taxes. If for any reason the trust fund taxes are not remitted to the IRS when due, it can assess a **trust fund recovery penalty (TFRP)** against anyone it considers to be a "responsible person" in regard to the unpaid taxes. In many cases, the IRS considers business owners, officers, and supervisors to be "responsible persons" simply because they should have been aware that the taxes had not been paid but were indifferent to ensuring that the taxes were remitted on time.

The TFRP is equal to the amount of the unpaid taxes. Once the IRS determines that an individual is a responsible person and serves notice, that person has 60 days to respond. After that, the IRS can immediately begin filing liens against that person's property and take levy and seizure actions. The TFRP cannot be removed in bankruptcy.

In many cases, especially with small businesses, misappropriation frauds ultimately lead to the complete failure of the business, and also an accompanying failure to remit trust fund taxes. The result is that the business owners can end up being held personally liable for funds embezzled by a dishonest employee.

In some cases, the fraud investigator's report can assist the business owners (or managers or officers) in fighting TFRPs assessed against them personally. For example, if appropriate, the report can indicate that funds from a segregated trust fund account were withdrawn without the owner's knowledge or consent, that reasonable internal controls were in place, and that the owner actively supervised the employee who withdrew the funds without authorization.

However, even with such a report, business owners and managers should expect the IRS to aggressively assess the TFRP against them. If that happens, the report may still help those assessed to receive favorable settlements with the IRS via an *offer in compromise,* an agreement between a taxpayer and the IRS that settles the person's tax liabilities for less than the full amount owed, or helps provide her defense in court. It might also be helpful for the owners and managers to report the fraud to the IRS by filing **IRS Form 3949-A** (Information Referral). Doing so can help strengthen an argument that the owners and managers were victims.

Employment

Employers who terminate an employee for committing fraud can eventually battle the employee in litigation. In some cases, the former employee may sue for wrongful termination of employment, defamation, or discrimination. In other cases, an employee who is to be fired might have collective bargaining rights that require an arbitration process with a right of appeal.

Fired employees may attempt to claim government unemployment compensation benefits. As a general rule, employees who are fired for serious misconduct (e.g., fraud) are not entitled to benefits. However, employees may argue that their termination was not deserved and may request a hearing to argue their side of the story. If this occurs, a fraud investigation report could serve as important evidence.

Whether a fired employee receives unemployment benefits may be important in determining the amount the company is required to pay for unemployment insurance. As a result, an employer who fires employees runs the risk of incurring considerable increases in the cost of unemployment insurance. To make things even worse, if a fired employee was the one in charge of making unemployment insurance contributions but did not make them on time, a penalty rate of 150 percent could be applied to the employer's future contributions. The exact consequences depend on the particular state involved because rules for unemployment insurance for state and federal governments differ.

As a result of the possible tax and legal consequences as well as possibly embarrassing publicity, employers are frequently reluctant to fire dishonest employees. Instead, they do things to encourage dishonest employees to leave voluntarily after taking measures to prevent them from continuing the fraud. In some cases, employers actually give dishonest employees favorable recommendations for future jobs.

Employers who think that an independent fraud report will help them fight their legal battles usually are only partially correct. The problem is that, as is discussed in previous chapters, independent fraud investigators generally avoid stating in their reports that a specific suspect is guilty of fraud. As a result, if the employer is to win any type of legal case, much case building and expert testimony may be required in addition to the fraud report.

A related issue is that a fired employee who is denied unemployment compensation can typically demand an administrative hearing. That hearing might take place before the fraud investigation is complete. The result is that the employer can be required to reveal his case against the employee before the investigation is complete. Furthermore, depending on state law, a finding of fact in an unemployment hearing could in theory become binding in future litigation in courts. Thus, an employer's failure to win an unemployment compensation hearing could place him in jeopardy in a defamation suit if the court prevents him from arguing that he had good reason to fire the employee. This actually happened in one case in which an employee of Kmart in Pennsylvania was fired for allegedly stealing a bag of potato chips. The employee who was denied unemployment compensation, appealed in an administrative hearing, and won. The former employee then sued Kmart for defamation. The trial court then prevented Kmart from asserting the defense that the employee had stolen the bag of potato chips because that issue of fact had already been decided in the administrative hearing. The employee received a $1.5 million judgment. But in the end, the state Supreme Court reversed the award, ruling that unemployment hearings are too informal to be considered final arbitrators of fact. The decision was binding on lower courts in Pennsylvania but not on those in other states and not in other types of state administrative hearings, such as worker's compensation or discrimination.

Even though the employer eventually won, the Kmart case demonstrates risks of "going legal" with an incomplete investigation. Unfortunately, the employer may be forced into this position, and even if she wins, any testimony or documents produced as part of the former employee's unemployment compensation appeal can be used against her in future litigation. This is something that must be considered before, during, and after firing an employee for fraud.

Regulatory Reporting of Fraud

In some cases, a fraud investigation report may trigger mandatory reporting of the fraud to a government agency. For example, §1233.3 (a) of Title 12 (Banks and Banking) of the U.S. Electronic Code of Federal Regulations states the following:

> A regulated entity shall submit to the Director a timely written report upon discovery by the regulated entity that it has purchased or sold a fraudulent loan or financial instrument, or suspects a possible fraud relating to the purchase or sale of any loan or financial instrument.

A fraud investigation report can sometimes be more helpful in ruling out fraud than in ruling it in. For example, a report might read, "A detailed examination of the financial records did not reveal any intentional irregularities or evidence of fraud or misappropriation."

On the other hand, when there is fraud, the report might read something like, "There was a series of irregular computerized journal entries made in the accounts receivables ledgers and corresponding shortages in the Cash account. The employee in charge of the computerized journal entries left the company before this investigation began and was not available for an interview. The owner states that only she and the former employee had access to the journal in question."

The wording in this report suggests that the former employee may have embezzled funds from collections on account by making irregular journal entries. But the report cannot guarantee that he did so, nor can it definitively conclude that a fraud occurred.

As a general rule in advance of an occupational fraud investigation, interested parties should not assume that the investigation will result in a report that gives a definitive answer to whether a fraud occurred. A more reasonable outcome is a report that identifies missed or damaging records or missing assets.

Litigation

Fraud reports can be very helpful in both criminal and civil litigation. However, they can be less than satisfying in trying to persuade authorities to prosecute a suspect. What happens too often is that police or prosecutors browse through a fraud investigation report looking for a clear statement that identifies the guilty person. But, of course, such statements generally don't appear in independent fraud investigation reports.

In many cases, a fraud investigation report is enough to at least persuade authorities to look at a case, especially with the hope of getting a quick confession. But if the suspect denies everything or "lawyers up," law enforcement quickly realizes that they will need to hire a forensic accountant (because it is unlikely that they have one of their own) and will be forced to try to understand what they consider to be arcane and obscure accounting concepts.

The saying in law enforcement circles is "if it bleeds, it leads." In a metropolitan area, police quickly send a dozen squad cars, a SWAT team, and a helicopter to pursue someone who robs a liquor store of $100 with a penknife. But the same police respond with glassy eyes if the owner of the same liquor store reports that his accountant has robbed the business of $100,000 using a computer to manipulate the accounting records.

Police sometimes devote resources to fraud investigations in cases in which "high-value targets" (such as politicians) are the suspects. Police also are relatively more likely to investigate frauds against religious, charitable, and community service organizations. In any police investigation, a good fraud investigation report can be of immense help.

Before a fraud report can be used in court, the prosecutor normally requires an expert witness to interpret it. This witness may or may not be the investigator who wrote the report. If the expert witness is someone other than the original investigator, the original one may need to be available to testify in support of the issues such as chain of custody, the methods used, and so on.

Although it does happen, most victims do not sue their fraudsters, primarily because fraudsters are typically judgment proof, meaning they do not have sufficient assets to repay their victims. However, criminal courts can and do order restitution, which can provide a strong motive for the victim to prosecute the perpetrator. In some jurisdictions, courts order convicted fraudsters to make regular restitution payments directly to the court, which then distributes them to the victim.

Insurance Claims

Many companies have insurance with coverage for losses related to fraud. This coverage can include losses such as those due to the costs of preparing a proof of loss, losses due to embezzlement, losses of valuable papers and records, and loss of income.

Independent fraud investigation reports can be very helpful in supporting insurance claims. Furthermore, one nice thing about embezzlement coverage is that some polices are written so that it is necessary only to prove that a loss has occurred, not who the guilty party is.

The usefulness of a fraud investigation report with respect to losses of valuable papers and records, and loss of income, depends on the scope of the investigation. In many cases, the scope does not include determining the amount of losses of income or damage to valuable papers and records.

Elements of a Fraud Report

LO2   A fraud investigation report typically includes the following sections:

1. **Address section**   This section indicates whom the report is from and whom it is addressed to. If the report is to be maintained under attorney-client privilege, it should be addressed to the attorney. Any restrictions regarding distribution of the report should be mentioned.

2. **Background information**   This section should very briefly describe what triggered the investigation.

3. **Executive summary**   This summarizes in a few paragraphs the entire investigation: the methods and tests used, any professional standards followed, and its results.

4. **Scope and objectives**   This section should indicate what the investigation sought to accomplish and any limitations placed on it.

5. **Approach**   This section should provide general information about the members of the fraud investigation team, the procedures and methods used, the tests performed, and the evidence collected. The report does not normally label evidence as such but refers to it directly in terms of documents reviewed, observations made, and interviews conducted, for example.

6. **Findings**   This part provides details regarding the methods used, the tests performed, and the evidence collected. It should include a simple one- or two-sentence statement of the findings of the investigation. This statement should be consistent in wording and content with the executive summary.

7. **Recommendations**   This section, if it exists, typically contains recommendations regarding repairing any internal control weaknesses that led to a fraud. It may also contain recommendations in referring the matter to legal counsel and reporting it to authorities.

8. **Exhibits**   Exhibits may include copies of documents, interview transcripts, a brief résumé of the fraud investigator, and so on. The résumé serves to establish the fraud investigator's expert credentials and lend authority to the report.

The Investigator's Liability in Writing a Fraud Investigation Report

In writing a fraud report, the investigator must give special consideration to the possibility of being sued by any suspect who does not appear favorably in the report. For this reason, she should be very careful in wording the report.

Avoid Any Inferences or Opinions That Suggest a Suspect's Guilt

Two things to be avoided in relation to the possible guilt of a suspect are *inferences* and *opinions*. There is no problem at all stating facts that point to guilt; the problem is only with inferences and opinions. For example, it would be perfectly acceptable to state "Exhibit B is a videotape of the bookkeeper putting the day's receipts in her coat pockets." It could also state, "The suspect confessed to stealing the money. A copy of the signed confession is attached as Exhibit B."

On the other hand, in the absence of a confession, it is not acceptable to state, "Exhibit B is a videotape of the bookkeeper stealing the day's receipts by putting the money into her coat pockets." This statement is improper because it involves an opinion and inference regarding the meaning of the bookkeeper's actions. In theory, it could be possible that the bookkeeper was putting the money in her coat pockets before leaving to deposit it in the bank.

In some cases, the fraud report can result in tension between the investigator and the client. On one hand, the investigator wants to avoid pointing to a suspect's guilt. On the other hand, the client wants a strong statement indicating that a fraud occurred and that a particular person is guilty. In some cases, a middle ground can be taken: The investigator can include in the report that a loss has occurred and that the facts surrounding the loss are consistent with fraud.

Note the use of the word *consistent*. This one word permits the report to suggest fraud without actually saying that it took place. The phrase "consistent with fraud" merely says that it looks like fraud, not that it is fraud.

On the other hand, it would be quite another thing to state, "The suspect's actions appear consistent with guilt." Technically speaking, the use of the word *consistent* in this case merely states the appearance of guilt, language that should not enable a suspect to sue the investigator for falsely accusing him of fraud. In practice, however, this statement can inflame the suspect and give him cause to sue the investigator for defamation. In many cases, guilty suspects feel "cornered" as an investigation closes in on them. As a result, they may seek to defend themselves by attacking anyone they can: not only the employer but also the investigator.

The investigator would probably win in such a lawsuit, but the cost of defense in such a suit could be prohibitive, resulting in negative publicity, litigation costs, and possible damage to the relationship between the investigator and her professional liability insurance company.

On the surface, if the investigator is not at fault, one would not anticipate a problem with her professional liability insurer. But in practice, insurers frown on policy claims for any reason. In such cases, they do not renew the policies of clients who have what they consider an excessive "frequency of claims." In practice, this means that insurers might decline to renew the policies of clients who file only a single claim. Furthermore, insurance companies are very good at sharing information with each other, so filing a claim with one insurance company could make it more difficult and expensive to find new insurance with a different company.

The bottom line is that the investigator should write the report in such a way as to avoid litigation.

Consult with Professional Liability Insurer

A good practice is for the investigator to discuss any doubtful wording with her insurance company before releasing it to the client. Many insurance companies have loss management departments that are more than happy to help their clients take measures to avoid the need to make claims.

FRAUD LOSS RECOVERY

LO3   The fraud loss recovery process includes the actions taken to make the victim whole again to the extent possible. In general, the various recovery options for fraud losses are as follows: accept the loss, collect insurance if available, or litigate (Figure 12.2). Each option is discussed.

Accept the Fraud Loss

Fraud losses often are accepted as a cost of doing business. Shoplifting losses are one example: Retailers accept a certain level of these losses as an alternative to incurring the cost of excessively tight security, which can be more damaging than fraud. In one case, excessively tight security led a credit cardholder to cancel his credit card account with a major bank after having his card was repeatedly declined at the point of sale. Each time his card was declined, he was able to speak with the issuing bank and have the transaction approved after answering various questions, but the inconvenience was so great that he changed to a different credit card. In the end, the bank lost a perfectly good customer because of excessive security.

Collect Insurance

Typical business insurance for occupational fraud includes coverage for the following items: proof of loss, loss of valuable papers and records, embezzlement loss, and loss of income due to an embezzlement loss. To successfully collect on such coverage, the insured must meet all of the policy's requirements.

Typical policy requirements include a policyholder obligation to notify the insurer as soon as there is some reasonable belief that a loss may have occurred, make all reasonable

FIGURE 12.2
Fraud Loss Recovery
Options

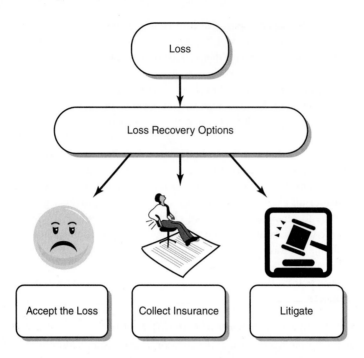

efforts to mitigate continuing damage related to the loss, provide a proof of loss statement, submit to one or more examinations under oath, and comply with all reasonable information requests. On the surface, these requirements seem simple enough, but in practice, the entire process can sometimes be murky and even take on the characteristics of litigation.

Fraud investigations frequently begin without information as to the exact nature and amount of the loss and the person(s) responsible. The means that until the fraud investigation is complete, filing a sufficiently complete proof of loss statement with the insurer might be impossible for the business. The typical proof of loss statement includes details of the loss including dates and amounts.

Depending on the policy, filing a proof of loss statement that indicates misappropriation may be necessary to trigger coverage. The result is that the insurer might not make any disbursements to the policyholder until the investigation is complete and misappropriation is certain. This can be a serious problem for a small or medium-size business faced with a major loss, especially if a fraudster has done major damage to the financial records, embezzled a large sum of money relative to the size of the business, or seriously interrupted the normal operation of the business. In such cases, the insured might not be able to continue in business without money from the insurer.

The problem is made worse by the fact that fraud investigations of misappropriation can take many months, especially if a substantial reconstruction of financial records is the necessary first step. The result is that the business can go bankrupt before it can provide the insurance company a sufficient proof of loss statement. Alternatively, the business might not have the funds to pay for the investigation and its bills as they come due. The final result is that the insurance coverage could have little practical value to the company.

Given an urgent need to provide a rapid proof of loss, the business may place considerable pressure on its independent fraud investigator to provide a statement quickly for the insurance company. Doing so is contrary to the normal investigation practice of getting all facts before writing a report. Therefore, the investigator must resist the pressure, at least to the extent that making a statement quickly requires making speculative statements or those not clearly supported by solid evidence.

The problem with the investigator's making statements before an investigation is complete stems from the principle of *reverse proof.* This principle dictates that to prove that an apparent loss is real, the investigator must in effect prove false all reasonable explanations that it is *not* real.

In terms of investigations, it is often relatively easy for the investigator to prove that an *apparent* loss exists—that is really the first step in weighing evidence. But that alone does not provide sufficient grounds for an investigator to tell an insurance company that a fraud (or even a loss) has occurred. The investigator can make such a strong statement only after gathering sufficient evidence to prove that no other reasonable explanation exists. The process of gathering such evidence typically does not end until the investigation ends. Hence, it may be impossible for the investigator to make any type of definitive statements regarding the existence of a loss or fraud until the investigation has ended.

Consider, for example, an apparent shortage in deposits of customer receipts. The investigator can very quickly show that an apparent shortage exists because of a failure of the bank statement to reconcile with the cash receipts records. But that reconciliation failure alone is not sufficient to conclude that there is a loss or fraud. The loss remains merely an apparent loss unless the investigator can rule out various reasonable explanations such as that the money was deposited into the wrong account, that it was deposited late and appeared on the next month's statement, that the cash receipts records are in error, that the person who made the deposits did not receive the full amount of cash, or that the owner took part of the money for use in the business. Until the reverse proof process is complete, the investigator cannot draw any conclusions as to whether the apparent loss is a real loss.

However, an investigator can make some statements prior to the completion of an investigation in situations with clear violations of company policies, documented incidences of irregular accounting entries, documented incidences of errors, failures of batch totals and sequence checks, and damage to the accounting records. In some cases, statements regarding these types of things may be sufficient to trigger coverage in a business policy.

Litigate

Sometimes it is desirable to pursue the perpetrator in civil or criminal court. As previously mentioned, suing a perpetrator in civil court can be a dead end, because in many cases fraudsters are judgment proof (i.e., without assets). Still, there are cases in which pursing restitution can be fruitful or in which the business wishes to set an example and deter other employees from committing fraud.

The investigator should be prepared to explain and defend his report in a court proceeding. But much more than the report is needed for a trial. In all likelihood, it must be supplemented by additional documents and exhibits as well as expert opinion that perhaps draws inferences not explicitly stated in the report. Expert testimony is discussed in the following section.

In typical litigation, the plaintiff's attorney or prosecutor will likely ask that a complete chronology relating to the fraud be prepared. In many cases, the fraud investigator is the best person in the position to prepare it. Of course, in some cases, the fraud report itself contains such a chronology, but a detailed one is not a required element of a fraud report because it is generally organized on a topical rather than chronological basis. Furthermore, even if the fraud report is organized on a chronological basis, the attorney may require much more detail and information than is included in the fraud report.

Another area for which the plaintiff's attorney or prosecutor may request additional information involves consequential damages. As previously mentioned, in many cases, misappropriation frauds can result in serious damage to the business in the form of lost income or damage to the financial records or to the company's reputation as a result of fraud-related business interruptions. In such cases, the fraud report may explain the fraud but not include valuation estimates of the consequential damages. Whether such estimates are included in the report depends on the scope of the investigation, but the scope typically does not involve the sophisticated analyses required to value consequential damages. As a result, supplemental work and reports are necessary to argue consequential damages in court.

EXPERT TESTIMONY

LO4   Forensic accountants serve two primary roles as experts in forensic matters: expert consultants and expert witnesses. In some cases, the forensic accountant may serve in both roles. As previously discussed, the fraud investigator must be prepared to serve as an expert witness in court. This section deals with expert testimony from the general point of view of the forensic accountant and consultant as well as the fraud investigator. The *expert consultant* is an independent accounting contractor who provides expert opinions in a wide array of cases, such as those relating to divorces, mergers and acquisitions, fraud investigations, employee-employer disputes, insurance disputes, and so on.

The forensic accountant consultant performs many of the services already discussed. For example, in a corporate acquisition, the forensic accountant could study the seller's final balance sheet and identify problems that in turn could lead the buyer to renegotiate purchase price. In a fraud case, the forensic accountant could identify and document all fraudulent transactions. This in turn could lead to reaching a plea bargain with a guilty employee. In both cases, the forensic accountant helps solve a problem before any expert trial testimony is needed.

Forensic accountants provide expert consultation services in various areas that include the previously discussed general areas of disputes and the alternative dispute resolution services (discussed in Chapter 20) as well as the following, for example:

- Business valuation calculations.
- Economic damage calculations.
- Lost profits and wages.
- Disability income analysis.
- Fraud investigations and management.
- Economic analyses and valuations in matrimonial (prenuptial, postnuptial, and divorce) accounting.
- Adequacy of life insurance.
- Analysis of contract proposals.

Expert Consultants and Discovery

As a general rule, at least under the federal rules of civil procedure, the pretrial work of the expert consultant is not subject to discovery by the opposing party if the expert consultant is not expected to testify at trial. Of course, the exact rules of discovery vary at the state level, and exceptions may exist. For example, if the consultant finds the murder weapon for the case at hand, there is likely an obligation to report the finding to the opposing side.

The courts have held that for an expert consultant's work to be privileged and exempt from discovery, there must be "more than a remote chance of litigation" at the time the work is performed. When the expert consultant is the employee of a company engaged in litigation, the privilege holds only if the employee's primary purpose for preparing materials is to assist in the litigation. In one case, an accountant's reports were held to be discoverable because the primary purpose for their preparation was to produce the company's financial reports, not to assist in litigation.

In some cases, the expert consultant could first be a fact witness before becoming an expert consultant. For example, an accountant could witness a fire and then be hired to estimate business interruption damages. In this situation, the accountant's factual knowledge of the fire could be subject to discovery.

A second exception to the expert consultant's privilege exists when there are "exceptional circumstances." This is normally interpreted to include situations in which the consulting expert possesses important evidence that the opposing side cannot obtain by any other means. For example, an expert consultant who takes photographs of the crime scene that is destroyed the next day by a fire could be forced to turn over the photographs to the prosecution if it had not already taken photos of the crime scene.

In some cases, the privilege may be inadvertently waived. If some of the expert consultant's work is given to the opposing side, a court could rule that the act was an implied waiver of the privilege. There is a tendency for courts to consider privileges that are waived "a little" to be waived in total.

Expert Witnesses

LO5 In many cases, expert services may extend into litigation, and forensic accountants often serve as expert witnesses. As was discussed in Chapter 2, expert witnesses are granted a privileged status in court trials: They are permitted to render opinions or conclusions based on facts admitted into evidence and other information on which they choose to reasonably rely. The expert's privilege is a major exception to the "personal knowledge rule," which normally limits witness testimony to matters of personal knowledge. For example, in an embezzlement case, a computer forensic expert could review various computer logs and testify that in his opinion, Jane Doe electronically transferred money from a particular company account. The expert can testify to this in court even though he did not actually witness her making the transfer. A nonexpert, however, could not directly point the finger at Jane Doe without actually seeing her make the transfer.

As previously mentioned, experts are permitted to base their conclusions not only on facts admitted into evidence but also on anything on which they can reasonably rely. That permits experts to base their conclusions on their own experience, their technical knowledge, and sometimes even hearsay evidence that would not directly be admitted into evidence. The result is that a convincing expert witness can be a powerful force in a court trial.

Admission of Expert Testimony into Evidence

Before experts can testify in trials as experts, they must first demonstrate their expert qualifications. Some factors that are typically involved in a court's assessment of an expert's qualifications follow:

- Education, including degrees, specialized training, and professional certifications.
- Experience in the subject area of testimony.
- Publication of books, proceedings, technical papers, and so on.
- Special awards and recognition in the field of expertise.
- Memberships in professional organizations.
- Professional speaking engagements.

Professional certifications are especially important, so forensic accountants very often earn various professional certificates. Some examples follow:

- Accredited business accountant (ABA).
- Accredited in business valuation (ABV).
- Accredited financial examiner (AFE).
- Accredited tax adviser (ATA).
- Accredited tax preparer (ATP).
- Accredited valuation analyst (AVA).
- Automated examination specialist (AES).

- Certification in control self-assessment (CCSA).
- Certified in Financial Forensics (CFF)
- Certified bank auditor (CBA).
- Certified bookkeeper (CB).
- Certified business manager (CBM).
- Certified cash manager (CCM).
- Certified divorce financial analyst (CDFA).
- Chartered financial analyst (CFA).
- Certified financial examiner (CFE).
- Certified financial services auditor (CFSA).
- Certified in financial management (CFM).
- Certified financial planner (CFP).
- Certified forensic accountant (Cr.FA).
- Certified forensic consultant (CFC).
- Certified forensic financial analyst (CFFA).
- Certified fraud deterrence analyst (CFD).
- Certified fraud examiner (CFE).
- Certified fraud specialist (CFS).
- Certified government auditing professional (CGAP).
- Certified government financial manager (CGFM).
- Certified healthcare financial professional (CHFP).
- Certified information systems auditor (CISA).
- Certified information security manager (CISM).
- Certified information technology professional (CITP).
- Certified insolvency and restructuring advisor (CIRA).
- Certified internal auditor (CIA).
- Certified management accountant (CMA).
- Certified payroll professional (CPP).
- Certified professional environmental auditor (CPEA).
- Certified public accountant (CPA).
- Certified public finance officer (CPFO).
- Certified quality auditor (CQA).
- Certified risk professional (CRP).
- Certified valuation analyst (CVA).
- Elder care specialist (ECS).
- Enrolled agent (EA).
- Forensic certified public accountant (FCPA).
- Personal financial specialist (PFS).

It is helpful for forensic accountants to obtain professional certification in each area in which they wish to testify. Especially good general certifications for the forensic accountant to have are the CFE and/or the CPA, although other certifications could also be as important. Finally, some organizations offer specialized training for expert witnesses. One is New Technologies, Inc. (www.forensics-intl.com), which offers specialized expert training in computer forensics.

Before someone is permitted to testify as an expert, the opposing side is permitted to examine and challenge that expert's background and credentials. This can mean asking detailed questions about the expert's publications or even a line-by-line questioning of each item on the expert's résumé. The opposing side may probe for skeletons in the expert's closest. In many jurisdictions, anticipated witnesses are subject to pretrial depositions, so it is common for the expert's credentials to be examined in detail before the trial begins.

In some cases, the opposing party could make a pretrial motion *in limine,* which is a request to prevent all or part of the expert testimony. The judge can then hold a mini-hearing on whether to permit the expert testimony. The legal standard to permit or deny the expert testimony varies from one jurisdiction to the next. However (as was discussed in

Chapter 11), the federal court system is governed by **Rule 702 (Testimony by Experts)**, which states the following:

LO6

If scientific, technical, or other specialized knowledge will assist the trier of fact to understand the evidence or to determine a fact in issue, a witness qualified as an expert by knowledge, skill, experience, training, or education, may testify to it in the form of an opinion or otherwise, if:

1. *The testimony is based upon sufficient facts or data.*
2. *The testimony is the product of reliable principles and methods.*
3. *The witness has applied the principles and methods reliably to the facts of the case.*

The key phrase in this rule is "reliable principles and methods," which sets the general standard for what is admitted as expert testimony. For 70 years, the legal standard merely required that an expert witness's principles and methods be generally accepted in the scientific community. That standard is referred to as the Frye test, named for one of the litigants in a Supreme Court decision. A subsequent Supreme Court decision, however, created what is now called the Daubert test, which sets specific requirements for a technique or theory to be considered scientific:

- The technique or theory has been subjected to scientific testing.
- The technique or theory has been published in peer-reviewed scientific journals.
- The error rate for the technique is reasonably estimated or known.
- The technique or theory is accepted in the relevant scientific community.

This test applies only in federal courts and in those states that have adopted it. The Supreme Court intended the test to be flexible with respect to the requirements, meaning that not all of them must be met in a given case. Nevertheless, some courts may rigorously apply all of the requirements to prevent possible problems with appeals. In another case heard by the Supreme Court, *Kumho Tire Co. v. Carmichael*, the Court made mandatory a Daubert determination in all cases involving expert testimony. The Court further refined the flexible requirements by indicating that they should not necessarily be applied to all forms of expert testimony with the same degree of strictness but should be applied strictly only to those forms of expert testimony for which their strict application is possible.

A Daubert determination is normally made in a "minitrial" held before a judge but outside the presence of the jury. The judge rules on whether the witness qualifies as an expert and whether the expert can represent a given body of evidence as being scientific. An expert who is not permitted to present the evidence as being scientific may still be permitted to introduce it as personal expert opinion.

What the courts are willing to accept as scientific evidence is an ongoing open question. Some courts accept a given method while others reject it. Moreover, even if the vast majority of courts accept (or reject) a given method, they can reverse themselves at any time because scientific knowledge and methods are constantly changing and new arguments can be made. It is therefore important that any expert witness be prepared to argue that the method employed meets the Daubert test. While some states use a combination of the Daubert and Frye tests, others use some version of the Frye test. The Frye test (also see Chapter 11) preceded the Daubert test and is still applicable in some state courts (see Figure 12.3).

The application of the Daubert and Frye tests varies from one jurisdiction to the next. All federal courts and some state courts use the Daubert test, but other state courts use the Frye test, a combination of the Daubert and Frye tests, or some other test. Furthermore, the way the particular test is applied can vary from one court to the next, even within the same

FIGURE 12.3
Daubert versus Frye Tests

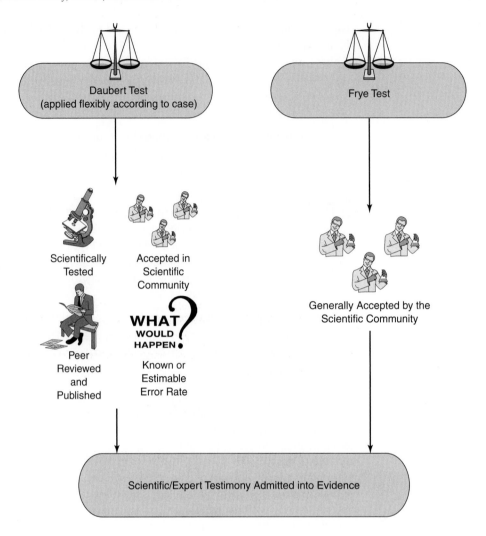

jurisdiction. For example, some courts might rigorously apply all of the Daubert conditions while others apply them selectively.

Jurisdictions generally do not maintain lists of court-approved experts (although courts do appoint their own experts), so as a rule, each expert must be qualified in each case. For this reason, forensic accounting expert witnesses must always be prepared to face rigorous Daubert challenges to their testimony. This means being questioned not only about their personal and professional backgrounds but also about the techniques, theories, and methods that they use to formulate their expert opinions.

Although the Daubert conditions are defined in scientific terms, the Supreme Court in the *Kumho Tire Co. v. Carmichael* case ruled that the four Daubert conditions were merely illustrative and applied to nonscientific expert testimony as well. Although the high court did not give illustrative conditions for nonscientific expert testimony, the general import of the decision is that all types of expert testimony are subject to Daubert-type testing.

The two Supreme Court decisions suggest that the forensic accounting expert witness must be prepared to do more than simply defend her methods based on their being generally accepted in the academic and professional areas of testimony. The forensic accounting expert witness must also be prepared to present evidence that her methods have been, to the extent possible, tested, published in peer-reviewed journals, and are of known or estimable reliability.

Courts generally limit experts' opinions to subject-matter areas for which they qualify as expert witnesses. For example, a court could a permit forensic accountant to testify regarding what computer logs say about which employee accessed a particular computer on a particular date and time, but the same court could forbid the same expert witness from testifying about an issue relating to a company's audit procedures. For this reason, it is very important for the expert witness to understand the exact scope of the expert testimony to be given to properly prepare for a Daubert or Frye challenge.

Pretrial Issues for Expert Witnesses

Pretrial Reports

LO7 The forensic-accountant expert witnesses could be asked to prepare written pretrial reports. Because such reports are subject to discovery and may be used at trial, the forensic accountant and counsel must be able to communicate well with respect to the scope of the report. The report should contain at least the following essential elements:

- The reason for which the report was prepared.
- The scope of the report, including the matters covered.
- Any conclusions drawn by the forensic expert.
- The information, observations, and rationale used by the forensic accountant to support any conclusions made in the report.

The report should not include any extra information or comments. Extra information unnecessarily increases the "target area" that can be used to attack the report.

Depositions

Expert witnesses are generally subject to pretrial depositions. For this reason, attorneys often use both nontestifying experts and testifying experts. Only the testifying experts are subject to discovery.

It is generally best for expert witnesses to testify in a deposition or at trial only if ordered to do so by a court or a subpoena. This helps ensure a sense of objectivity because voluntary testimony can give the impression that the expert witness is trying to help the side that asked him to testify.

As a general rule, the expert forensic accountant should bring to the deposition or trial only documents or files that are specifically named in the subpoena or court order. Anything brought to the deposition or trial could be subject to detailed inquiry by the opposing attorney or the court.

Preparation for Opposing Experts

In most jurisdictions, the two opposing sides must give each other lists of anticipated witnesses. The expert witness should review the credentials of any opposing witnesses. In consultation with counsel, the expert witness should also review depositions and testimony from the current and previous cases in which the opposing expert witness has testified.

Expert Witness Preparation for Testimony

Needless to say, an expert witness must be well prepared for testimony. Mistakes or omissions can damage his credibility in the negotiations or trial. That in turn can do major damage to the client's case and the forensic accountant's future as an expert witness.

Trial Strategy and Expert Testimony

- As mentioned, expert witnesses are generally subject to pretrial depositions. For this reason, attorneys often use both nontestifying experts and testifying experts so that only the testifying experts are subject to discovery.

- Depositions can serve multiple purposes. If the case is supposed to go to trial, the opposing attorney will seek to ask the expert witness many questions. This creates a record that the opposing attorney can go over with a fine-tooth comb for contradictions and weaknesses that can be attacked at trial. Under these circumstances, the attorney for the party that the expert witness "represents" may want the expert witness to give out the absolute minimum of information required by the questioning. On the other hand, if the case is not expected to go to trial, the deposition becomes part of a bargaining process. If that is the case, the optimal strategy could be for the expert witness to volunteer information to convince the opposing side that it is facing a strong case.

- It is generally not in the best interest of the opposing counsel to attack the expert witness during depositions. If that happens, a weak witness will likely be replaced by a stronger one for the trial. It is better for the opposing counsel to see a weak witness proceed to trial.

- Attorneys often shy away from hiring more than one expert witness in the same area. That adds the possibility that the one expert witness could contradict another when both are supposed to be on the same side.

- In some cases, courts may permit opposing counsel to put an expert on the stand without prior notice to the side the expert witness represents. When this happens, counsel should insist on very carefully and slowly qualifying the surprise expert. Counsel should request from the court the same ability to question the surprise witness as would have existed had the questioning taken place during a deposition. With a little luck, the questioning will take long enough for counsel to find an expert to counter the testimony of the surprise witness.

Trial Tactics and Principles Concerning Experts

The most important considerations at trial for experts are credibility, demeanor, understandability, and accuracy. Credibility is not something that can be controlled in and of itself but is a result of the factors that are under the control of the expert witness. Experts should follow these guidelines:

- **Answer questions in plain language** Judges, juries, arbitrators, and others tend to believe experts more when they truly understand what the expert says. It is best, therefore, to reduce complicated, technical arguments to plain language.

- **Answer only what is asked** Expert witnesses should not volunteer more than what is asked even when not volunteering more testimony could suggest that the expert's testimony is giving the wrong impression. It is up to counsel to clear up any misimpressions through follow-up questions. That is, it is up to counsel to "rehabilitate" an expert witness who appears to have been impeached. That said, however, experienced expert witnesses sometimes volunteer information to protect their testimony from being twisted. Experience is needed to know when and how to do this. The best thing for an inexperienced expert witness is to work with experienced attorneys who know how to rehabilitate witnesses.

- **Maintain a steady demeanor** It is important for the expert witness to maintain a steady, smooth demeanor regardless of which questions are asked and which side's attorney asks them. It is especially undesirable to do something such as assume defensive body language when being questioned by the opposing side.

- **Be friendly and smile at appropriate times** Judges and juries are just people, and it helps to appear as relaxed but professional.
- **Remain silent when there is an objection by one of the attorneys** Let the attorneys fight it out. Continue speaking only when instructed to do so.
- **Tell the truth** The expert witness should tell the truth plainly and simply. As noted, the expert's testimony should not become more complicated or strained when it appears to be harmful to the client the expert represents. The expert witness should not try to answer questions to which she does not know the answer but should simply say that she does not know or does not have enough information to form an opinion.
- **Control the pace** The opposing attorney can sometimes attempt to crush a witness by rapid fire questions. The expert witness should avoid firing back answers at the same pace. This can avoid giving the appearance that she is arguing with the examining attorney. It also helps prevent her from being rushed and overwhelmed to the point of making mistakes.

Professional and Ethics Guidelines for Expert Witnesses

Forensic accounting experts may belong to professional organizations that impose ethical requirements relating to expert testimony. Such requirements could impose credentialing and confidentiality standards for their members as well as conflict-of-interest rules and working paper requirements. Such requirements or rules can be either mandatory or voluntary.

For example, CPAs must comply with the relevant sections of the following:

- The AICPA Code of Professional Conduct.
- The Statement on Standards for Consulting Services No. 1.

In certain cases, the CPA must also comply with the following:

- Statements on Auditing Standards.
- Statements on Standards for Attestation Engagements.
- Statements on Standards for Accounting and Review Services.

Finally, the Litigation Services and Applicable Professional Standards–Special Report provides voluntary guidelines.

In some cases, testifying in court could violate professional confidentiality standards. The forensic accountant should clarify in advance whether the confidentiality is protected.

Many ethics questions such as the following can arise:

- Can the forensic accountant's fee be based on the outcome of the case?
- Can the forensic accountant serve as an expert consultant and write an expert report if the client does not permit him access to some information that could be important to the case?
- How should the forensic expert respond to the client when pressured to change a report or reconsider an opinion?
- What factors constitute a conflict of interest for a forensic expert?

The questions are only posed here. It is beyond the scope of this text to discuss ethics guidelines for any of the many possible professional organizations applicable to forensic accountants.

The expert forensic accountant should give the client an engagement letter that sets forth the responsibilities of the forensic accountant and the fees expected.

Legal Liability of Expert Witnesses

Expert witnesses are generally immune from libel and slander claims arising from their testimony. This is true even in cases when expert witnesses make errors, as long those errors are not caused by maliciousness or gross negligence. In general, it is difficult to sue an expert witness successfully because of the witness's testimony.

Summary

When the fraud investigation has been completed, the investigator writes a formal report. The report plus expert opinions and testimony may then be used in support of the resolution of any issues that may relate to taxes, employment, regulatory reporting, litigation (civil and criminal), and insurance claims.

For income tax purposes, fraud losses may be classified as either deductions or offsets to revenues, depending on the type of loss and the taxing authority. In misappropriation, almost any type of asset can be fraudulently converted, and sometimes a valuation expert is needed to determine the value of the loss.

Another tax-related issue involves embezzlement of trust fund taxes. U.S. tax laws allow holding owners and officers personally liable for embezzled trust fund taxes. If for any reason the trust fund taxes are not remitted to the IRS when due, the IRS can assess a Trust Fund Recovery Penalty (TFRP) against anyone it considers to be a "responsible person" with respect to the unpaid taxes. The TFRP amount equals the amount of the unpaid taxes and cannot be removed in bankruptcy. Frequently, especially with small businesses, misappropriation frauds ultimately lead to the complete failure of the business and an accompanying failure to remit trust fund taxes. The result is that the business owners can be held personally liable for funds embezzled by a dishonest employee. In some cases, the fraud investigator's report can assist business owners (or managers or officers) in fighting TFRPs made against them personally.

Employers who terminate an employee for committing fraud can eventually battle the employee in litigation. Sometimes former employees sue for wrongful termination of employment, defamation, or discrimination. In other cases, the to-be-fired employee might have collective bargaining rights that require an arbitration process with the right of appeal.

Fired employees may attempt to claim government unemployment compensation benefits. As a general rule, employees who are fired for serious misconduct (e.g., fraud) are not entitled to the benefits. However, employees may argue that their termination was not deserved and may request a hearing to argue their side of the story. If this occurs, a fraud investigation report could serve as important evidence.

In some cases, a fraud investigation report may trigger a mandatory reporting of the fraud to a government agency. The report can sometimes be more helpful in ruling out fraud than in ruling it in. Consequently, interested parties should not assume in advance that the investigation will result in a report that gives a definitive answer to whether a fraud occurred. A more reasonable outcome is a report that identifies missed or damaging records or missing assets.

Fraud reports can be very helpful in both criminal and civil litigation. However, they can be less than satisfying when trying to persuade authorities to prosecute a suspect. Too often police or prosecutors browse through a fraud investigation report looking for a clear statement that the suspect is guilty. But, of course, such statements generally don't appear in independent fraud investigation reports.

Independent fraud investigation reports can be very helpful in supporting insurance claims. Many companies have insurance with coverage for losses related to fraud. As previously indicated, coverage can include losses such as those due to the costs of preparing a proof of loss as well as losses due to embezzlement, of valuable papers and records, and of income.

A fraud investigation report typically includes these sections: the address section, background information, executive summary, scope and objectives, approach, findings, recommendations, and exhibits. In writing a fraud report, the investigator must give special consideration to the possibility of being sued by any suspect who does not appear favorably in the report. For this reason, the investigator should not suggest guilt of any particular suspect. A good practice is for the investigator to discuss any doubtful wording with her professional liability insurance company before releasing it to the client.

The fraud loss recovery process includes taking actions to make the victim whole again to the extent possible. In general, the various recovery options for fraud losses are to accept the loss, collect insurance if available, or litigate.

Businesses often accept fraud losses as a cost of doing business. In other cases, insurance may cover all or part of the loss. To successfully collect on such coverage, the insured must meet all requirements of the insurance policy.

Depending on the policy, filing a proof of loss statement that indicates misappropriation may be necessary to trigger coverage. Because of its urgent need to provide proof of loss, the business may place considerable pressure on an independent fraud investigator to quickly provide a statement for the insurance company. Succumbing to this type of pressure runs contrary to the normal investigation practice of first obtaining all the facts and then writing a report. Therefore, the investigator must resist pressure, at least to the extent that it requires making speculative or other statements not clearly supported by solid evidence.

In still other cases of fraud losses, it might be desirable to pursue the perpetrator in civil or criminal courts. The investigator should be prepared to explain and defend her report in a court proceeding. But often much more than the report is needed for a trial. In all likelihood, the report must be supplemented by additional documents and exhibits as well as expert opinion that perhaps draws inferences not explicitly stated in the report.

As experts, forensic accountants serve as expert consultants and expert witnesses. In both roles, forensic accountants provide expertise in areas such as business valuations, economic damage calculations, lost profits and wages, disability income analysis, fraud investigations and management, matrimonial accounting, adequacy of life insurance, mergers and acquisitions, and contract negotiations and disputes.

Under the federal rules of civil procedure, the pretrial work of expert consultants is not subject to discovery by the opposing party if the expert consultant is not expected to testify at trial. Company employees may also enjoy the same privilege when there is at least "more than a remote chance of litigation" at the time their work is performed. When the expert consultant is the employee of a company engaged in litigation, the privilege holds only if the employee's primary purpose for preparing materials is to assist in the litigation. A second exception to the expert consultant's privilege exists when there are "exceptional circumstances," which normally exist in situations in which the consulting expert possesses important evidence that the opposing side cannot obtain by any other means.

Forensic accountants often serve as expert witnesses who are permitted in court to render opinions or conclusions based on facts admitted into evidence and other information on which they choose to reasonably rely. The expert's privilege is a major exception to the "personal knowledge rule," which normally limits witness testimony to matters of personal knowledge.

Before experts can testify as experts, they must first demonstrate their expert qualifications. Factors that are typically involved in a court's assessment of an expert's qualifications include education and certifications, experience, publications, special awards, professional memberships, and professional speaking engagements. Many types of certifications are relevant to the forensic accountant. Some basic certifications include the certified fraud examiner (CFE) and certified public accountant (CPA).

Before someone is permitted to testify as an expert, the opposing side is permitted to examine and challenge that expert's background and credentials. This can mean intensive questioning about the witness's background and expertise. This examination is typically done through depositions, and challenges to the expert testimony normally are made through pretrial motions *in limine* or in mini-trials that apply Daubert, Frye, or other tests. In the federal court system, Rule 702 (Testimony by Experts) sets forth four criteria that require expert witness testimony to be based on reliable principles and methods:

- The technique or theory has been subjected to scientific testing.
- The technique or theory has been published in peer-reviewed scientific journals.
- The error rate for the technique is reasonably estimated or known.
- The technique or theory is accepted in the relevant scientific community.

The Supreme Court has ruled that these criteria are only illustrative and should be applied flexibly. Not all criteria need be applied in all cases, and the degree of strictness need be applied only to the extent possible in the given area of expert testimony.

The Daubert test contrasts with the older Supreme Court Frye test, which requires only that the expert testimony be based on "principles and methods that are generally accepted in the scientific community." The Supreme Court in the *Kumho Tire Co. v. Carmichael* case ruled that the Daubert conditions are applicable to nonscientific expert testimony as well. Individual states have their own standards for expert testimony; some have adopted the Daubert test, others the Frye test, and still others various other tests and standards. Finally, the Supreme Court decisions imply that the forensic accounting expert witness must be prepared to present evidence that his methods have been, to the extent possible, tested, published in peer-reviewed journals, and are of known or estimable reliability.

The forensic accountant expert witnesses could be asked to prepare written pretrial reports. Such reports should at least state the following: the reason the report is prepared, its scope including the matters covered, any conclusions drawn by the forensic expert, and the information, observations, and rationale used by the forensic accountant to support any conclusions made in the report. The report should not include any extra information or comments that unnecessarily increase the "target area" that can be used to attack the report.

Various considerations apply to depositions: (1) Attorneys often use both nontestifying experts and testifying experts so that only the testifying experts are subject to being deposed. (2) To promote the appearance of Independent, it is generally best if expert witnesses testify at deposition; they should testify at trial only if ordered to do so by a court or a subpoena. (3) As a general rule, the expert forensic accountant should bring to the deposition or trial only documents or files that are specifically named in the subpoena or court order.

Needless to say, an expert witness must be well prepared for testimony. Mistakes or omissions can damage the expert's credibility in the negotiations or trial. That in turn can do major damage to the client's case and the forensic accountant's future as an expert witness. Part of the preparation involves reviewing the credentials and records of any opposing expert witnesses.

Various trial strategy issues arise with respect to expert witnesses. In depositions, the attorney working with the expert witness may want the witness to go on record with the minimum amount of required testimony, especially if the case is expected to go to trial. This minimizes the amount of testimony the opposing attorney can attack during the trial. On the other hand, if the case is not expected to go to trial, the expert witness could be encouraged to do everything possible to convince the opposing side that it is facing a strong case.

Attorneys generally do not attack expert witnesses during depositions but usually prefer that weak expert witnesses proceed to trial. Beating off an expert witness in depositions merely results in the expert being replaced by a stronger one for the trial.

Finally, forensic accountants should consider ethics guidelines applicable to their practice of expert testimony. Forensic accountants are normally members of organizations with ethics codes that require and recommend conduct relating to credentials, confidentiality, conflicts of interest, and work paper requirements.

Glossary

IRS Form 3949-A   IRS form that can be used for reporting someone who has misappropriated funds, which generally constitute taxable income for the fraudster who frequently fails to report the misappropriated gains to the IRS.

Rule 702 (Testimony by Experts)   A federal rule of evidence that states the following: If scientific, technical, or other specialized knowledge will assist the trier of fact to understand the evidence or to determine a fact in issue, a witness qualified as an expert by knowledge, skill, experience, training, or education, may testify thereto in the form of an opinion or otherwise, if (1) the testimony is based upon sufficient facts or data, (2) the testimony is the product of reliable principles and methods, and (3) the witness has applied the principles and methods reliably to the facts of the case.

Trust Fund Recovery Penalty (TFRP)   Penalty that can sometimes be assessed against anyone that the IRS considers to be a "responsible person" with respect to unpaid payroll taxes; TFRP amount is equal to the amount of the unpaid taxes.

trust fund taxes   Payroll taxes collected and held by the employer on behalf of the taxing authority; failure to remit them to the taxing authority in a timely manner may result in criminal and/or civil penalties.

Review Questions

1. Which of these describes the use of the formal fraud investigation to support the resolution of loss recovery issues?
   a. Alone.
   b. In conjunction with expert opinions and testimony.
   c. As physical evidence.
   d. None of the above.

2. Regarding the fraud investigation report, the investigator should:
   a. Assume it will be challenged in court.
   b. Prepare a different report for the court.
   c. Assume that the investigation report will be protected under attorney-client privilege.
   d. None of the above.

3. For income tax purposes, fraud losses may be classified as:
   a. Deductions.
   b. Offsets to adjusted gross income.
   c. Both *a* and *b.*
   d. None of the above.

4. Reconstructing financial records as part of a fraud investigation is:
   a. Normally within the scope of the investigation.
   b. Never within the scope of the investigation.

    c. May be within the scope of the investigation.

    d. Not an issue in fraud investigations.

5. Which of these is correct regarding trust fund taxes?

    a. Must be remitted to the IRS the moment they are collected.

    b. Belong to the company except in bankruptcy.

    c. Belong to the employees and vest immediately in any company-offered pension plans.

    d. None of the above.

6. The Trust Fund Recovery Penalty can be assessed against:

    a. Business owners.

    b. Business managers.

    c. Business accountants.

    d. All of the above.

7. As a general rule, employees who are fired are:

    a. Not entitled to unemployment compensation.

    b. Not entitled to unemployment compensation until after a routine hearing.

    c. Entitled to unemployment compensation but with reduced benefits.

    d. None of the above.

8. In regard to obtaining a criminal conviction, the fraud report is:

    a. Always sufficient.

    b. Sometimes sufficient.

    c. Usually sufficient.

    d. Usually not sufficient.

9. An unemployment compensation hearing may do which of the following?

    a. Represent an opportunity to prove a suspect's guilt.

    b. Expose parts of an incomplete fraud investigation.

    c. Resolve the fraud investigation and case.

    d. None of the above.

10. Fraud reports generally can be expected to:

    a. Convince authorities to prosecute the fraudster.

    b. Permit authorities to prosecute without expert testimony.

    c. Convince police to refer the case to a prosecutor.

    d. Convince authorities to consider investigating further.

11. Victims of frauds:

    a. Usually do not sue the fraudster.

    b. Sue the fraudster almost 100 percent of the time.

    c. Sue the fraudster when they are large companies.

    d. None of the above.

12. Which of the following types of losses would usually be estimated in a fraud investigation report?

    a. Losses of valuable papers and records.

    b. Loss of income.

    c. Both *a* and *b*.

    d. Neither *a* nor *b*.

13. In general, fraud investigators:
    a. May be at risk for being sued by a perpetrator.
    b. Are protected from being sued by a perpetrator if they act in good faith.
    c. Are protected from being sued by a perpetrator under the federal Whistleblowers Act.
    d. None of the above.

14. The effect on the investigator's professional liability insurance as the result of a perpetrator's lawsuit against the investigator is:
    a. Not an issue if the investigator is found not to be liable in a court of law.
    b. Not an issue if the investigator is found not to be liable in a court of laws and pays the litigation costs.
    c. Possibly negative even if the investigator is completely innocent and wins in court.
    d. None of the above.

15. Which of the following is *not* part of the fraud recovery process?
    a. Collecting insurance if it exists.
    b. Recovering from the fraudster through a civil action or restitution ordered by a criminal court.
    c. Reviewing and repairing any internal control weaknesses that may have permitted the fraud to occur.
    d. All of the above are part of the fraud recovery process.

16. To avoid overly tight security, fraud losses are sometimes:
    a. Accepted.
    b. Counteracted.
    c. Prevented.
    d. None of the above.

17. Which is true of a small business waiting to collect insurance on an embezzlement claim, assuming substantial fraud and destruction of the financial records?
    a. At the beginning of a fraud investigation, the business is likely to immediately file a proof of loss statement and receive prompt payment under the insurance policy.
    b. At the beginning of a fraud investigation, the business is likely to immediately file a proof of loss statement, and after 90 days it receives payment under the insurance policy.
    c. The business may have a significant chance of failure before it collects the insurance.
    d. None of the above.

18. Suing a fraudster in civil court may be futile because of which of these?
    a. The fraudster is likely to obtain a high-powered defense attorney.
    b. The fraudster is likely to be without assets vulnerable to a civil action.
    c. It is necessary to obtain a criminal conviction before filing a civil suit.
    d. None of the above.

19. A detailed chronology is:
    a. Sometimes a part of fraud reports.
    b. Always a part of fraud reports.
    c. Never a part of fraud reports.
    d. Only a part of fraud reports when the case is expected to go to court.

20. To argue fraud-related consequential damages in court, lawyers often find that which of the following is true?
    a. The fraud report alone usually suffices.
    b. The fraud report plus the investigator's testimony usually suffices.
    c. Completely separate reports may be required.
    d. The fraud investigator will generally need a signed confession in most states.

21. The saying "if it bleeds, it leads" refers to:
    a. Ink on evidentiary documents that is affected by some type of aqueous solution.
    b. Many types of violent versus nonviolent crimes.
    c. The initial part of an investigation that drains investigation funds.
    d. None of the above.

22. Which of the following is most likely *not* to be included in coverage of many insurance policies that protect businesses?
    a. Losses of valuable papers and records.
    b. Costs of preparing proof of loss.
    c. Legal fees paid to prosecute a fraudster.
    d. All of the above are equally likely to be included.

23. As a rule, insurance policies that cover losses related to misappropriation require:
    a. At least an arrest of someone for the fraud.
    b. A criminal conviction of someone for the fraud.
    c. A civil action against someone for the fraud.
    d. None of the above.

24. How does the scope of a fraud investigation relate to the usefulness of the resulting fraud report?
    a. The usefulness and the scope are related concepts.
    b. With no report, there can be no scope.
    c. The scope is determined by the report's content.
    d. The report's content determines the scope.

25. Which of the following is *not* a section in a typical fraud investigation report?
    a. An analysis of the relevant state or federal statutes and their applicability to the fraud investigation.
    b. An analysis of the relevant state or federal statutes and regulations as well as their applicability to the fraud investigation.
    c. An analysis of the relevant regulations and their applicability to the fraud investigation.
    d. None of the above.

26. As a general rule, at least under federal procedures, whose pretrial work is *not* subject to discovery by the opposing party?
    a. Expert witness.
    b. Expert consultant.
    c. Expert witness and the expert consultant.
    d. Neither the expert witness nor the expert consultant.

27. In some cases, the opposing party in court litigation could do which of the following that is a request to prevent all or part of the expert testimony?
    a. Invoke Federal Rule 404.
    b. Make a motion *in limine*.

    c. Invoke the Frye test.

    d. None of these.

28. The Daubert test differs from the Frye test in that the Daubert test does which of the following?

    a. Focuses on reliable principles and methods.

    b. Is applicable in all state courts.

    c. Focuses on principles and methods that are generally accepted in the scientific community.

    d. None of these.

29. The Supreme Court in the *Kumho Tire Co.* v. *Carmichael* case ruled that the Daubert conditions were merely illustrative and applied to which of these?

    a. All scientific testimony.

    b. Nonscientific testimony.

    c. Applicable nonscientific testimony in some state courts.

    d. Applicable nonscientific testimony in federal courts.

30. Which strategy is an opposing attorney likely to apply in deposing a weak expert witness?

    a. Attack the witness vigorously to destroy his or her credibility.

    b. Ask questions that show the expert witness the strength of the opposing attorney's case.

    c. Ask many question but go easy on the expert witness.

    d. None of these.

31. Which of the following is *not* true?

    a. If the client's case is weak, a single expert witness for a given area of testimony is generally preferred.

    b. If the client's case is strong, a single expert witness for a given area of testimony is generally preferred.

    c. If the client's case is weak, multiple expert witnesses for a given area of testimony are generally preferred.

    d. None of these.

32. Which of these describes the best way for expert witnesses to answer questions?

    a. In plain language.

    b. In formal technical language.

    c. In legally framed language, according to professional ethics.

    d. None of these.

33. The CPA expert must comply with which of the following?

    a. The AICPA Code of Professional Conduct.

    b. The Statement on Standards for Consulting Services No. 1.

    c. Statements on Auditing Standards.

    d. All of the above.

34. What generally applies to expert witnesses in regard to libel and slander claims arising from their testimony?

    a. Responsible for.

    b. Immune from.

    c. Immune from when no errors are made.

    d. None of these.

Discussion Questions

35. What is needed besides the fraud investigation report to resolve issues related to taxes and insurance?

36. Why is the fraud investigation report alone not sufficient to use in litigation?

37. Give an example of a loss that would require a fraud investigator to seek the assistance of a valuation specialist.

38. When might it be impossible for a fraud investigator to determine the amount of losses due to misappropriation?

39. Explain the Trust Fund Recovery Penalty.

40. Why is it likely that the owner of a small business that fails due to misappropriation by a trusted bookkeeper ultimately is likely to be assessed the Trust Fund Recovery Penalty?

41. What types of lawsuits do fired employees tend to file against their former employers?

42. How can a fired employee's compensation claim compromise a fraud investigation?

43. Why are employers frequently reluctant to fire dishonest employees?

44. How helpful is a fraud investigation report in legal battles with employees fired for misappropriation?

45. How should the executive summary in a fraud investigation report relate to the findings section?

46. Describe what might be included as exhibits in a fraud investigation report.

47. Is it ethical for a fraud investigator not to include something in a report that she believes to be true and that would help her client but would increase the chances of the perpetrator filing a lawsuit against her? Explain.

48. Why should fraud investigators refrain from drawing conclusions about guilt in their fraud reports?

49. When might it be acceptable for a fraud report to render an opinion of guilt?

50. How is use of the word *consistent* helpful in fraud reports?

51. Is it good practice for a fraud investigator to include an opinion of guilt in a fraud report when the suspect has given a signed confession?

52. Is it good practice for a fraud investigator to indicate a definite finding of fraud in the investigation report?

53. What role should the investigator's professional liability company play in developing fraud investigation reports?

54. Can the investigator's professional liability policy be put in jeopardy if he is sued by a fraudster but wins the suit?

55. When is accepting losses a reasonable business practice?

56. What must a business do to collect insurance on a misappropriation fraud?

57. Why might a fraud cause a business to fail even when the business recovers related losses from insurance?

58. Why might an investigator discover a fraud with 98 percent certainty but then have to perform months of additional investigatory work before being able to state in a report that the evidence appears highly consistent with fraud?

59. What statements can an investigator make prior to the final report?

60. Why is it likely that suing a fraudster is a futile process?

61. What might an attorney ask for in litigation that might not appear in the fraud report?

62. How should a fraud investigator deal with pressure to render major opinions regarding the fraud but before the investigation is complete?

63. What is the difference between an expert consultant and an expert witness?

64. Are expert consultants subject to discovery? Explain.

65. What is mean by the expert's "privilege" with respect to court testimony?

66. What is the difference between the Frye test and the Daubert test?

67. What must happen in federal courts before someone is permitted to testify as an expert?

68. How must the Daubert test be applied in individual cases?

69. How should an expert witness deal with opposing experts?

70. Explain how depositions can serve multiple purposes.

71. Why should experts generally avoid answering more than was asked?

72. What are some subtle ways in which an expert witness can show an unsteady demeanor?

73. How can an expert witness deal with a barrage of rapid-fire questions from an opposing attorney?

74. What ethics considerations apply to CPAs with respect to expert testimony?

75. How could testifying in court violate professional confidentiality requirements?

76. What are the limits of expert testimony with respect to charges of defamation of character?

Cases

77. Max Warren, a fraud investigator, was in the middle of a case for a small family-owned clothing store. He had some fairly strong preliminary evidence pointing to an embezzlement fraud and powerful indicators that pointed to the bookkeeper's guilt.

    Mary Hilson, the client company's CEO, was attempting to collect insurance for the fraud loss, but the insurance company would not pay for the loss without Max providing a letter that certifies a loss. The insurance company also wanted to question him under oath.

    To complicate the matter, Mary told Max that without an immediate settlement from the insurance company, the business did not have sufficient funds for operations to continue and the business would be bankrupt. Max wondered whether he would be paid for the work he had done to date.

    How should Max respond to Mary's request that he help her provide the insurance company the information it needs?

78. Laura Connor just completed a fraud investigation during which she discovered that the bookkeeper had embezzled $103,240.25. The bookkeeper would not confess, but she had an airtight case against him.

    In her final report, Laura wrote, "An analysis of the accounts receivables records and bank records indicates that $103,240.25 in funds cannot be accounted for."

    Carlos Bowles, the CEO, was very unhappy with the report. He was trying to get the police to investigate the case, but they would not because the statement in the report was so weak. He wanted Laura's report to clearly indicate that the funds were stolen and that the records suggested the guilty person.

    Furthermore, a police investigator asked Laura for her opinion regarding the suspect's guilt off-the-record.

    How should Laura respond?

79. Harry Mendelson began his fraud investigation with great optimism. He was investigating a simple embezzlement from accounts receivables, in a small business with only one employee, and only the bookkeeper had ever had access to the Intuit Quickbooks accounting files. The bookkeeper was fired the day before Harry arrived.

   When Harry opened the Quickbooks system, he immediately noticed all kinds of strange entries that made no sense at all. After several hours of carefully studying the cash and accounts receivables, he concluded that the Quickbooks records were of no help.

   Next he discovered that there were no paper statements or deposit records for the company's bank account. After obtaining the online access credentials for the company's bank account, he was able to log in and view bank statements for the last 12 months, but all deposits simply showed up as lump sums with no reference to which portions were made in cash or in checks from customers.

   His client was a small insurance agency. Many clients of the agency made their payments at the agency's front desk, sometimes with cash and sometimes by check. Other clients sent their checks by mail. The bookkeeper opened all the mail. The front desk kept a list of all incoming payments before passing the checks on to the bookkeeper, but the list was only maintained sporadically and was, therefore, not reliable.

   The owner was certain that the bookkeeper had embezzled a lot of money, but Harry is wondering if he should withdraw from the engagement due to the lack of data needed to conduct a reasonable investigation.

   Required:

   What do you think Harry should do? What can he do? Is any kind of reasonable investigation possible?

80. Janet Markleson ran a profitable used-car business until the business failed as a result of an embezzling financial manager. The officers of the company were as follows: Janet was the president and treasurer, and her husband (now her ex-husband) was the secretary. All ownership equity in the business had been lost when the company's financial manager cleaned out all the bank accounts, including one trust account whose balance was to be remitted to consignment customers. In all, the financial manager managed to run away with over $432,000 from those accounts. Rumors circulated that he had left the country.

   The financial manager also cleaned out the company's trust fund account that was being used to remit payroll taxes to the IRS and to state tax authorities. The loss in that account amounted to $74,221.54.

   Janet hired a forensic accountant, whose final report clearly indicated the losses, although it only identified the financial manager as a suspect and not a guilty party. No guilty party was clearly identified in the report.

   Janet's husband, Mark Merkleson, never had had any involvement in the business. He worked as a salesman in a local department store, and after years of hard work he had managed to save up enough money to make a down payment on his first house, which he had planned to share with his new wife and raise a family.

   Janet was bitter. Despite the forensic report the police wouldn't seek an arrest warrant. She was told that even if they did prosecute, it would be impossible to get the suspect extradited from another country. She learned that extraditions can be expensive, and that local authorities didn't have the budget to even pay the plane fare required to repatriate criminals in extradition proceedings.

About a month after the business failed, Janet woke up one day to find that someone had filed a complaint with the state revenue office, saying that she had stolen the payroll trust fund due to the state. She heard from a friend that it was the financial manager who had filed the complaint.

She tried to tell the criminal investigators from the revenue department that the financial manager had stolen the money. She showed them the forensic accounting report, but they seemed unimpressed by it and advised her that she was a target of a criminal investigation.

A few months later things got much worse. Her ex-husband Mark called her, furious, and told her that the IRS had just frozen his bank account, one day before he was supposed to close on buying his first house. He was close to crying, because his real estate sales contract had a clause that required him to close on time or lose a $10,000 deposit he had used as part of the sales agreement. So he was going to lose both his deposit and dream house.

Required:

Is there anything Janet can do to help her ex-husband? Why was his bank account frozen? Would it help if the financial manager were arrested?

81. Jason Blair is a CPA who has been asked to serve as an expert witness in a civil case involving theft of employee secrets. His client, Rexmem, has filed suit against its former IT director, alleging that the former employee stole proprietary information relating to Rexmem's products, product strategies, and marketing plans and conveyed the stolen information to her new employer.

Rexmem intends to make its case by showing that the former IT director had access to the information in question. Furthermore, as soon as the IT director started working for her new employer, the employer began announcing new products that were identical to products that Rexmem had been planning to announce. Moreover, the competitor also began to run adverting campaigns that exactly matched those planned by Rexmem.

Jason has an extensive expert background in information systems and information technology.

a. How could Jason Blair prepare to serve as an expert witness?

b. What type of research should he do?

c. Is his IT background sufficient for a case that involves marketing issues?

Part III

Occupational and Organizational Fraud

Chapter **Thirteen**

Employee, Vendor, and Other Frauds against the Organization

CHAPTER LEARNING OBJECTIVES

After reading Chapter 13, you should be able to:

- LO1: Describe the seriousness and extent of the problem of employee and vendor fraud.
- LO2: Describe some characteristics of employees who commit employee fraud.
- LO3: Explain some of the major organizational factors related to internal fraud.
- LO4: Describe the major methods employees use to commit fraud.
- LO5: Identify some of the key factors in identifying employees who commit fraud.
- LO6: Explain the major types of vendor fraud.
- LO7: Explain ways frauds are committed in electronic information systems.

From a broad perspective, fraud must be viewed within the context of the organization's internal control and information security processes. Therefore, the profiles covered in this chapter should be viewed as supplementary to the general discussion of internal control (Chapter 3) and fraud prevention and risk management (Chapter 5).

THE FRAUD PROBLEM IN PERSPECTIVE

LO1 Organizations in the United States lose hundreds of billions of dollars per year to fraud. The problem is so large that every year many companies fail because of fraud, and some companies do not even realize that fraud caused their undoing. Fraud takes many forms, so it is impossible to list every type of fraud in this chapter. Instead, we present several categories of frauds and give examples within each category.

Much of what is known about fraud is from anecdotal experiences and scattered newspaper reports. Many believe that most frauds against organizations are never reported to law enforcement authorities to avoid negative publicity and legal liability. Few companies want newspaper and magazine stories published about how their accountants manipulated their accounts receivable, overbilled their customers, and then wired the absconded funds to some secret bank account in the Cayman Islands. Because good internal control prevents most types of fraud, the revelation of a fraud tends to point to weak internal control processes, which few companies want made public. Furthermore, in some types of fraud, the company lacks the means to quickly repair a given weakness, so news stories about problems could make the company a target for other criminals to do more damage to the company.

In addition, as strange as it sounds, many companies actually consider employee or vendor theft as a cost of doing business. Some fraud examples based on real cases follow:

- The main bartender at a large popular Florida beach hotel gave large numbers of free drinks to customers. Obviously, this made him popular with the customers and earned him great tips. The owner knew about the practice and did not like it but was afraid that firing the bartender would cause him to start working for a nearby competitor and take business with him.

- The store manager of an Italian restaurant and pizzeria regularly stole money by not properly ringing up delivery sales. The owner knew about the thefts but was afraid to do anything about it because she had such difficulty finding employees who would even show up for work on a regular basis. The restaurant consistently lost money, but the owner did not attribute the losses to the unfaithful manager. However, several years later, when the manager quit, the restaurant suddenly became very profitable. Only then did the owner realize the scope of the losses but still did not consider reporting the matter to authorities.

- The manager of an auto paint shop regularly stole paint and supplies from the shop. The shop owner, who happened to be a CPA, simply accepted the stealing as a cost of doing business. In fact, he included a 20 percent theft allowance in his cash flow budgets. When asked about the allowance, he said, "This is a rough business. My best painter was just killed in a bar fight. That's just the business. I've had a bunch of managers, and they all steal. So I just accept the stealing as a cost of doing business, and I don't do anything about it as long as the shop is running well and the manager doesn't steal too much."

- In one buffet-style restaurant, customers tell the cashier whether they want water or sodas to drink. The cashier then adds the cost of any sodas to the customers' tabs. The customers then pay, take an empty glass from the cashier, and proceed to the self-serve soda fountain, which operates on an honor system. Customers who do not pay for sodas are supposed to take water from the fountain. The problem is that large families come into the restaurant and pay for only one soda but then all members fill their glasses with it. The manager tried various tactics to stop the problem, but the customers would always make excuses, such as "I didn't understand," or "I forgot." The manager became so frustrated that one day he called the police on one woman and her four young kids. This made a big scene in the store, and the woman and the children cried loudly. Finally, the police refused to do anything about it, saying that they were not going to arrest little children for drinking sodas. The next day the woman complained to company headquarters, which resulted in the manager's being reprimanded for not being diplomatic with the customers. After that, the manager never even looked in the direction of the soda fountain.

The bottom line is that most frauds against organizations tend to go undetected, and those that are detected usually go unreported to the police. When they are reported to the police, prosecution is unlikely.

The economic crime division of most local law enforcement agencies, especially in large metropolitan areas, tends to be overloaded with cases. The caseloads are often so heavy that the authorities do not even want to take a report for economic crimes unless they are fairly large. Prosecuting many types of fraud, such as embezzlement, requires complex investigations, forensic analysis of accounting records, and expert testimony in court. Accordingly, law enforcement is likely to choose not to pursue an embezzlement case involving only a few hundred or even thousand dollars. The authorities instead prefer to focus on individuals who exhibit a pattern of illegal activity. For example, they might take a report for a single check forgery case, but they are unlikely to do significant investigatory work on a single case unless there is evidence that it is part of a series of related cases.

On the other hand, the authorities are relatively more likely to prosecute cases in which there is an obvious "smoking gun" such as a surveillance tape. Examples include shoplifting and cash register theft caught on videotape. Such cases easily can be handled by a single police officer and prosecutor and pass through the court system.

Another problem is that getting a conviction without a confession can be difficult in many fraud cases, especially in those involving computerized accounting records. The difficulty arises because such cases cannot be proved by traditional tangible evidence, such as fingerprints, videotapes, blown-off safe doors, and so on. The only evidence is frequently data inside computers that cannot be definitively traced to one individual. For example, if Jane Doe's account was used to alter the accounts receivable records, it might be impossible to prove that it was Jane Doe, not someone else using her account, who made the account alterations. Although such a crime can sometimes be proved by using log files, video records, building access logs, and so on, many companies do not have a system sophisticated enough to provide the necessary proof that one person and only one person could have committed the crime.

People Who Commit Fraud against the Organization

LO2   There is no simple profile for employees who commit fraud. However, some statistics are available. Research has shown that about 10 percent to 15 percent of employees are fundamentally dishonest and are likely to steal from the company if given the opportunity (see Figure 13.1). About 66 percent of employees are likely to steal under the right circumstances, such as when under pressure, or when "everyone is doing it," and the opportunity exists. In contrast, about 20 percent to 25 percent of employees are fundamentally honest and are unlikely to steal under any circumstances.

FIGURE 13.1
Honesty of Employees

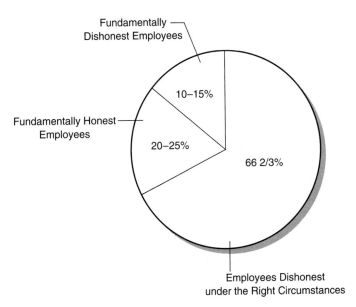

Furthermore, those employees who do steal from the company are unlikely to have a prior criminal record, and those with a good education, family background, and work record can be just as likely to steal as anyone else.

On the other hand, research shows that the fraud triangle is helpful in explaining which employees may defraud the company. As was briefly discussed in Chapter 2, the three elements of the **fraud triangle** are present in many cases of fraud against the company:

- **Pressure**   Usually related to financial pressure such as large medical bills, gambling problems, drug habits, and extravagant living.
- **Opportunity**   Required to commit fraud.
- **Rationalization**   Likely depends on the type of criminal and the criminal's personality type or possible personality disorder.

The rationalization component of the fraud triangle suggests three possible types of individuals who may commit fraud:

- **Fundamentally dishonest employee without a personality disorder**   This person could habitually be dishonest but does not have a personality disorder. Rationalization comes easily because the person is accustomed to dishonesty. Therefore, the rationalizations are likely to include statements such as "I need it more than they do" and "They won't miss it."
- **Fundamentally dishonest employee with a personality disorder**   Various personality disorders may contribute to the ability of the employee to rationalize fraud. Psychiatry uses the diagnosis **antisocial personality disorder** and the related diagnosis dissocial personality disorder. The following are characteristics that apply to persons with these types of mental disorders:

  - Nonconformist behavior; tend to be misfits.
  - Habitual lying and dishonesty.
  - Impulsiveness.
  - Irritability and aggressiveness.
  - Insensitivity to harming self or others.
  - Strong disregard for the needs of self and others.
  - Tendency to blame others for personal faults and mistakes.
  - Lack of responsibility.
  - Difficulty in establishing and maintaining close relationships.
  - Absence of the ability to feel emotions or the full range of normal emotions.

The deceitfulness dimension of these disorders could enable the person to hide some or all of his antisocial characteristics. This type of person is often able to steal without giving much conscious thought to rationalizations. The crime could simply arise out of a mental disturbance.

- **Normally honest employee who steals given pressure and opportunity and rationalizes theft**   A person who does not normally steal is likely to give serious thought to rationalizing the theft. One common rationalization is that the person is only borrowing the money; often the person takes money with the intent to pay it back, and many times does in fact pay it back. The result is that the corporate till can become the employee's personal lending institution; however, in many cases, the person is never able to pay back the ill-gotten loan. The normally honest employee is likely to steal out of a sudden financial need or because of a problem with a financially excessive lifestyle.

In summary, although no simple profile exists to identify potential perpetrators of employee fraud against the company, some measures can be taken based on the fraud triangle to prevent such fraud. First, stealing cannot take place without opportunity. Good internal control processes can eliminate opportunity. Second, companies should attempt to mitigate problems of pressure by performing careful background checks on potential employees, being especially sensitive to lifestyle or financial problems. Furthermore, good company medical plans can help prevent medically induced financial crises (and hence pressures), and companies can offer nonpunitive, private counseling services to help employees reduce pressures related to problems such as substance addiction, gambling, and general life crises. Finally, companies can attempt to minimize hiring individuals likely to rationalize fraud by giving prospective employees personality tests.

Employee Fraud and Corporate Culture

LO3 The corporate culture can actually supply the pressures that could drive employees to commit fraud (see Figure 13.2). The following factors in the corporate culture can contribute to these pressures.

- **Poor employee compensation** Employees could steal to make up for what they think the company owes them. They could have financial problems that pressure them to commit fraud.
- **Excessive pressure to perform** This can generate hostility toward the company, providing rationalizations for employees to cheat customers, vendors, and the company itself and to violate health and safety laws and regulations.
- **Hostile work environment** This situation can generate animosity toward the company, which can be a rationalization to commit fraud.
- **Corporate financial troubles** Financial disorder tends to produce general chaos within the company, leading to a wide range of problems including employee dishonesty.
- **Negative examples set by top management** Dishonest behavior by superiors with customers, vendors, shareholders, lenders, or the government creates an environment in which fraudulent acts appear to be accepted.

FIGURE 13.2
Employee Fraud and Corporate Culture

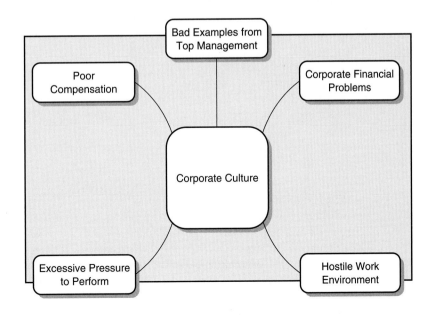

EMPLOYEE FRAUD SCHEMES

LO4 The general rule is that the more liquid the asset, the more likely it is to be a target of employee fraud. This tends to make cash and inventories the top targets for employee fraud. However, because they are obvious targets, they may be the areas that have the strongest controls, forcing dishonest employees to search for secondary targets from paper clips to major items of plant and equipment. Almost anything can be stolen. In one case, employees stole a large mainframe computer system from their employer by smuggling it out the back door a piece at a time.

Although there is no standard classification scheme for employee frauds, it is convenient for the discussion here to classify such frauds according to the basic transaction cycles: revenue, expenditure, production, and finance. For convenience in the present discussion, the finance cycle is included in the revenue and expenditure cycles.

Revenue Cycle Fraud

Cash Collection Fraud

Cash can easily "disappear" anytime between the moment of its collection and the time it is securely deposited in the bank. Discussion of some cash sales fraud schemes follows.

Basic Sales Skimming To engage in **basic sales skimming,** the employee does not record the sale but pockets the cash. This problem can be detected and discouraged by the use of the "customer audit," which gives rewards to customers who report transactions without proper sales receipts. Implementation of the customer audit includes the use of cash registers that display the amount for each item as it is rung up and cash registers that do not open unless a sale is being recorded and then make noises when they are opened. It is also important to ensure that all cash registers are managed on an imprest basis and promptly reconciled. Two employees should never share the same cash register.

Advanced Sales Skimming With **advanced sales skimming,** the employee collects the money from the customer, fails to record the sale, and gives the customer a forged receipt. In one case, an employee of a termite exterminator had his own moonlight business that operated under his employer's name. He gave customers official-looking but forged receipts and kept all of the money for himself. The company discovered the scheme when a dissatisfied customer sued after her house had been overrun by termites.

Companies can minimize advanced sales skimming by carefully prenumbering and controlling all sales forms and by restricting after-hours access to all resources that employees might use to run an illicit moonlight business. However, this fraud is prevalent in service-oriented industries.

Another form of advanced sales skimming occurs when employees make discounted off-the-books deals with customers who are unlikely to talk because they benefit from the deal.

Checks Swapped for Cash The fraud of **swapping checks for cash** involves an employee's removal of cash from the cash drawer and replacing it with phony checks, sometimes even adding false customer identification information (e.g., driver's license number) on the check. The employee hopes that the employer will attribute the bad check to a dishonest customer. One way to control this problem is to use an electronic cash box (i.e., point-of-sale terminal) that is integrated with an automated check approval system. The point-of-sale terminal records the check details, including the bank routing number and customer bank account number. This leaves an audit trail that shows all check-based transactions, which can be reconciled against the contents of the cash drawer.

Cash Box Robbery   If the employer does not reconcile sales and collections for the cash box at the end of each shift, the cashier could be **robbing the till,** that is, stealing from the cash box without restraint.

Shortchange Sales   A "skilled" cashier can confuse or distract customers while short-changing them. In these **shortchange sales,** the cashier pockets the amount shortchanged. Distraction techniques for shortchanging customers include anything from simple "mistakes" to complicated schemes. One complicated scheme is to begin to give the customer change in large bills, and then, while in the middle of counting the change, ask the customer to exchange some of the larger bills for smaller ones because the cashier is running short of large bills. The cashier then takes advantage of the confusion created to shortchange the customer. The slick cashier knows that this scheme works best with customers who are already distracted, perhaps with children or family, and who appear to have considerable paper money in their wallet. This scheme can be minimized by the video surveillance of cash registers and by having strict cash-handling procedures that disallow the cashier from doing anything but making simple change.

Mail Room Theft   Companies should have a policy that prohibits accepting cash in the mail. However, some customers still send cash, creating the possibility of cash theft in the mail room. This problem is best solved by having two employees open the mail together. The two employees should then prepare and forward to accounts receivable a cash remittance list. This procedure establishes an audit trail that can be used to locate the source of any missing cash or checks.

Cash Processing   Losses of cash may occur anytime after the initial receipt (see Figure 13.3, for example). Some methods follow:

- **Cash stolen in transmission**   "Leakage" can occur anytime cash exchanges hands. That is, either the person giving up the cash or the person receiving it can steal some of it. The only way to prevent this is for both the giver and the receiver to count the cash, agree on the count, and then sign a transmittal memorandum that can later by used to identify the source of any shortage.

FIGURE 13.3
Examples of Cash Register Fraud

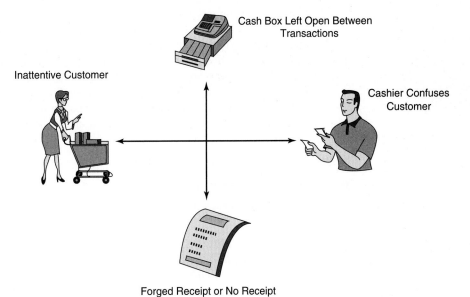

Cash Box Left Open Between Transactions

Inattentive Customer

Cashier Confuses Customer

Forged Receipt or No Receipt

- **Lapping of accounts receivable** The somewhat complex fraud of **lapping of accounts receivable** occurs when an accounts receivable clerk steals incoming payments and hides the theft by manipulating the customer account records. The clerk begins by stealing one incoming payment and not crediting it to the customer's account. Before the customer has a chance to complain about not being credited, the clerk uses a second incoming payment to cover the first customer's stolen payment. The process continues on and on. Lapping can occur only when the accounts receivable clerk is given access to incoming payments. This violates segregation of duties, one of the most basic internal controls. As was discussed in Chapter 3, segregation of duties requires separating functions relating to the custody of assets, recordkeeping, and authorization.

- **Short bank deposits** The person making a bank deposit can make a **short bank deposit** by failing to make a full deposit. This is easily detected by reconciling bank deposit slips against amounts that are supposed to be deposited. Because bank deposit slips are easily forged or altered, it is important to reconcile the deposit slips against deposit credits on monthly bank statements.

- **Noncustodial theft of money** Theft of cash is not limited to employees with custodial responsibilities. When a company has lax security, someone with a combination, key, or code can get into a locked safe or cash box. Noncustodial theft of money can result in several schemes including the following ones:

  - **Check tampering** **Check tampering** involves altering stolen customer checks and then cashing them using false or stolen identities.

  - **Check washing** An advanced form of check tampering, **check washing** involves the use of chemicals to remove payee names, dates, and/or amounts from customer checks that are typically turned over to organized crime (see Figure 13.4). The process provides blank checks that can be cashed in ways that are difficult to trace to the individuals who cash them.

  - **Check Laundering** **Check laundering** can occur because banks typically do not verify payee names on deposited checks for large commercial customers. In other words, a person could pay her telephone bill with a check made out to the electric power company. In all likelihood, the processing bank would not notice the discrepancy. This makes it possible for someone who possesses a stolen check to submit it as a payment for almost any type of account. Eventually, the payer of the check will discover that the check was processed by the wrong payee, but without a strong audit trail, the wrong payee might not even be able to identify the payer account to which the check was applied. Furthermore, even if the wrong payee does know to whose account the check was applied, the wrong payee might not disclose that information to the payer for privacy reasons. A police investigation might be required to obtain that information, and there is no guarantee the police will investigate any given case. Then, even if the police do get involved, their investigation could lead them to a stolen or fake identity.

Noncustodial theft of money is best prevented by good physical security.

Accounts Receivable Fraud

Frauds in this category center on improper credit approvals, improper credits, and improper write-offs.

- **Fraudulent credit approvals** Dishonest employees could intentionally engage in **fraudulent credit approval** by granting credit accounts to fictitious customers. The employee or a designated person then uses the accounts to make purchases without ever paying. Credit can be granted to unqualified individuals from whom the dishonest employee gets a kickback. This problem is prevented by requiring all credit approvals to come from an independent credit department.

FIGURE 13.4   Check-Washing Scheme

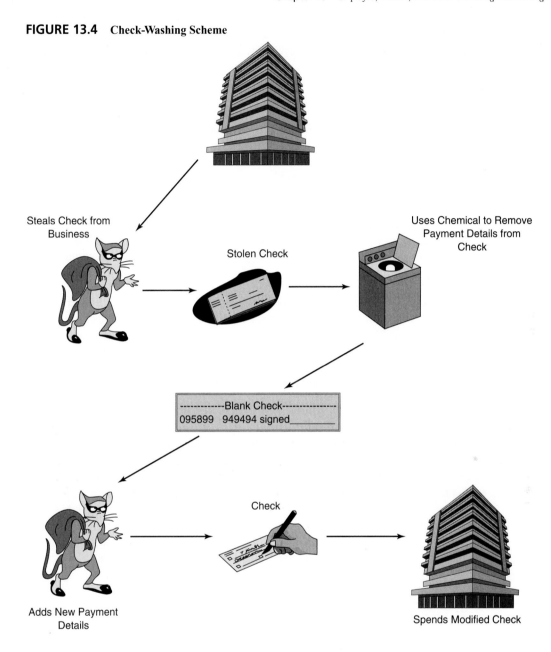

Steals Check from Business

Stolen Check

Uses Chemical to Remove Payment Details from Check

--------------Blank Check----------------
095899   949494 signed_____

Check

Adds New Payment Details

Spends Modified Check

- **Improper credits** Accounts receivable clerks could make **improper credits** to friends' accounts. This can be prevented by requiring supporting documentation for all credits to customer accounts. Refund credits should have credit memos from a separate refund department. Credits that require bookkeeping corrections should be supported by signed memorandums from the accounting supervisor. Other credits, such as goodwill credits, should be supported by documentation from the authorizing department.
- **Improper write-offs** Employees also could make **improper write-offs** to friends' accounts instead of sending the accounts to collection. This problem can be prevented by requiring written authorization from an independent credit department for all write-offs of customer accounts.

Expenditure Cycle Fraud

There are many types of expenditure cycle frauds. This section discusses the major expenditure cycle fraud schemes.

Improper Purchases and Payments

Any type of purchase or payment that is not consistent with company policy is improper. Fraudsters use many different types of improper purchase to cheat the company.

Unauthorized Purchases

Without proper purchasing controls, employees in the purchasing function could make purchases for their own personal use. For example, an employee might secretly use company funds to purchase a big-screen TV for home use. Such purchases are prevented by using a voucher system and having independent purchasing, receiving, accounting, and payment departments. In a voucher system, accounting sends a payment voucher to the payment department after matching a company purchase order, vendor invoice, and receiving report.

Fraudulent Purchases to Related Parties

An employee might purchase from a related party at a price that is too high to do the related party a favor or to obtain a **kickback** from the related party. Another problem is **bid rigging,** which occurs when a company insider gives an outside contract bidder privileged insider information so that the outside bidder obtains a bidding advantage. Fraudulent purchases to related parties are not always easy to prevent. The forensic accountant could be able to uncover these problems by obtaining alternate price quotations for past purchase orders.

Misappropriation of Petty Cash

A *petty cash fund* is an amount of cash, usually in small amounts, that is kept to be used to reimburse employees for miscellaneous business-related expenses, such as parking fees incurred while engaged in company business. Misappropriation of petty cash is best controlled by managing petty cash on an imprest basis. This involves periodically funding the petty cash with a fixed sum of money. When the money is spent, the cash receipts should total the original amount in the fund. At any given time, the sum of the cash and the receipts in petty cash should equal the fixed amount that established it. Periodic surprise audits of the fund and a careful inspection of the receipts can minimize any problems.

Abuse of Company Credit Cards or Expense Accounts

This self-explanatory problem can be controlled by a careful after-the-fact review of credit card and expense account purchases. Good control for certain expenditures on the company's credit card or expense account requires preapproval.

Unauthorized Payments

In the absence of a functioning voucher system, employees could make payments for fictitious or nonexistent purchases, for amounts larger than indicated on the purchase order or vendor invoice, for altered invoices, or even for valid purchases but to someone other than the actual payee. These problems can be controlled by having an independent purchasing department and a voucher system. As discussed, in a voucher system, the finance function reviews a voucher package (copies of the purchase requisition, purchase order, vendor's invoice, and receiving report) before paying the vendor.

It is necessary to periodically audit the voucher packages and reconcile authorized payments against actual payments per the bank statements. This last step serves as a check on the paying department. Additional safeguards include having physical security over checkbooks, requiring multiple signatures on some checks, and using imprest checking accounts with balances only large enough to make the needed payments.

Theft of Company Checks

Check payments to vendors or customers can be diverted. The fraudster possessing the diverted checks can then launder and alter them. In addition to having physical control over checks and outgoing mail, the use of checks that are difficult to alter or forge is the primary prevention against fraud.

Fraudulent Returns

Employees could issue refunds for fictitious returns or for incomplete or substituted returns. These types of problems are controlled by good physical security and careful monitoring and auditing of the returns department.

Theft of Inventory and Other Assets

Once purchased, any asset in the company can be stolen or converted to personal use by employees. This can generally be prevented by good physical security and a record of custody, proper employee supervision, asset disposal management, and internal auditing.

Payroll Fraud

When it comes to the payroll, there are as many ways to cheat as there are employees. Common areas of payroll fraud include the following:

- **Improper hiring**   Employees could hire friends or relatives who do not have proper training, hire them at a pay rate that is too high, or even hire phantom employees. These problems are generally prevented by requiring all hires to be approved by management and by an independent personnel department that verifies employee background information. Internal auditing is needed to ensure compliance with internal control policies and procedures.

- **Improper changes to employee personnel files for pay raises**   Payroll clerks have been known to give their friends pay raises. This problem is prevented by requiring all changes to personnel files (including wage rates) to be approved by both management and an independent personnel department. Again, internal auditing is needed to ensure compliance with internal control policies and procedures.

- **Improper work-related reporting**   Employees can report hours they do not work, fail to fill out the paperwork for leave time, or submit exaggerated sales reports to increase the amount of commissions. Such problems can be solved by proper supervision and approval of time cards, leave forms, reports, and so on. Internal audits are necessary to ensure compliance with internal control policies and procedures.

Production Cycle Fraud

Production cycle fraud involves theft of raw materials and finished goods. Most such thefts can be prevented by good physical security and authorization controls.

Waste, Scrap, and Spoiled Goods

Employees sometimes discard valuable raw materials or finished goods that they later retrieve from the garbage and convert to their own use. The simple solution is to carefully manage waste, scrap, and spoiled goods. Disposal of these things should follow carefully defined policies and procedures.

Other Types of Employee Fraud

Financial Statement Fraud

Employees, especially high-level ones, could obtain bonuses by exaggerating reported income or sales. This topic is discussed in Chapter 14, which covers financial statement fraud.

Insider Trading

Employees could illegally use inside information, which only people inside an organization could know, to make decisions related to buying or selling company stock. This in effect robs other shareholders, which in turn hurts the company. Insider trading is discussed in Chapter 14.

Employee Fraud in General

Many other employee fraud schemes are not discussed here. For example, the corporate treasurer could register company securities in her own name and then use them as collateral on a personal loan. One department could overcharge another department for its services. The list is endless. Regardless of the fraud scheme, however, good basic internal control is the route to prevention. Issues relating to detection are discussed next.

THE AUDIT PROCESSES IN DETECTING AND PREVENTING EMPLOYEE FRAUD

LO5   Chapters 9 and 10 detail the processes relevant to forensic auditing. The following principles relate to the detection of fraud, the identification of those who commit it, and some ways to prevent it.

Audit Trail

The **audit trail** is the most important element in detecting fraud. Use of proper accounting procedures that leave an audit trail enables the internal auditor or the forensic accountant to discover frauds and trace them to their origin. The audit trail is used to trace any amount in any account back to one or more original source documents that support all debits and credits to that account. Without a proper audit trail, detecting frauds could be impossible. Not all frauds can be prevented, but a good audit trail makes it possible to detect them.

Chain of Custody

The *chain of custody* in accounting is part of the audit trail. The forensic accountant should always be able to trace an asset's chain of custody to the point at which a fraud occurred. The chain of custody identifies the person who is responsible for the asset when the fraud occurred. This does not mean, however, that the person identified is guilty of the fraud. It reveals only the person under whose watch the fraud occurred.

Authorization and Approval

Authorizations and approvals are also important parts of the audit trail. Systems with good control processes require an **authorization** each time a transaction is initiated or an asset changes hands. When investigating a fraud, the forensic accountant considers who authorized any fraud-related transactions and whether the authorization is valid. **Approval** is similarly important to the forensic accountant when investigating fraud. Approval represents the review and acceptance of a transaction that has already been authorized. For example, the general accounting department may review and approve purchase orders after they are authorized by the purchasing department.

Internal Audit

The **internal audit** helps ensure that the audit trail is generated. Of course, the amount of the internal audit effort devoted to detecting frauds must be decided on a cost-benefit basis. It is generally not cost effective to attempt to eliminate all frauds.

Physical Security and Monitoring

Assets are most vulnerable to fraud before they are first entered into the company's accounting system. Once assets have been entered into it, the audit trail and chain of custody make it possible to pinpoint losses. For this reason, the receipt of goods and cash requires the highest level of security. An example of this heightened security is the video surveillance of cash registers. The video record in effect extends the audit trail before cash is entered into the accounting system.

Fraud Reporting Hotlines, Training, and Education

It is also helpful to encourage employees to anonymously report suspected frauds to company hotlines or Web pages. Hotlines, combined with good employee training and education, can promote good fraud deterrence and reporting.

VENDOR FRAUD

LO6   Vendors can also defraud companies or other organizations. However, such frauds are usually possible only when the company or other organization has weak internal control processes. This situation is somewhat similar to employee fraud because even with strong control processes, trusted employees can abuse their positions of trust. Most vendor-related frauds occur when companies put their vendors in a position of trust. For example, a company opens itself up to vendor billing fraud if it relies on the accuracy of vendors' monthly statements and pays whatever vendors request. Examples of vendor fraud schemes follow:

- **Short shipments**   A company is susceptible to paying for goods not received if it does not count its incoming shipments and match the counts against purchase orders and vendors' invoices.
- **Balance due billing**   Some vendors send their customers statements that show only the balance due. Companies whose vendors bill this way are at high risk for being overbilled. The problem is that without any transaction detail on the statements, the company has no way to document what it is paying for. If a billing dispute arises, determining the correct amount owed can be very difficult. Companies avoid this problem by paying only for specific invoices that match issued purchase orders.
- **Substandard goods**   Vendors can ship substandard goods if the receiving company does not have a method of receiving and inspecting goods.
- **Fraudulent cost-plus billing**   Under some contracts, especially ones involving the government as the procurer, vendors bill on a cost-plus-profit basis. Costs can include direct costs plus overhead. Such contracts are readily subject to fraud because the supplying company keeps the cost records. As a result, the U.S. military has at times paid for things like thousand-dollar toilet seats.

FRAUDS FROM CUSTOMERS AND COMPETITORS

Customers and competitors are often in a position to steal from or defraud companies with weak controls. Therefore, good overall internal controls represent the best defense against fraud from customers and competitors. Chapter 3 discusses internal controls in detail.

EMPLOYEE FRAUD METHODS IN ELECTRONIC ACCOUNTING INFORMATION SYSTEMS

LO7 This section discusses concepts relating to employee fraud within the context of computerized accounting systems. Various computer-related frauds deserve special attention because the nature of computerized systems is such that frauds can completely bypass standard controls or destroy, eliminate, alter, or obscure the audit trail related to the fraud. In other words, the principles discussed earlier for identifying employee fraudsters might not apply. For this reason, the forensic accountant must not only understand individual fraud schemes but also be able to recognize and deal with situations in which there is a compromised audit trail. Of course, not all computerized attacks compromise the audit trail, but the forensic accountant needs to recognize when they do and when they do not. The focus of the discussion in this section is on the schemes themselves and their impact on the audit trail rather than the issues and methods relating to detecting the schemes and to identifying the responsible individuals, which is the subject of Chapter 6 and the latter part of Chapter 11 on computer forensics.

In electronic accounting systems, employee frauds tend to involve attacks against the computers and computer databases. These attacks can be classified in five categories: input manipulation, direct file alteration, program alteration, data theft, and sabotage (see Figure 13.5). Each of these categories is discussed next.

Input Manipulation

Input manipulation is the most common mode of attack in computer fraud. In many cases, the fraud is as simple as the employee typing in a small amount of data into the system.

Abuse of Access Privileges

In this type of fraud, an employee with legitimate access to a portion of the system enters fraudulent data. For example, someone in the credit department could enter into the system a new credit account approval without the proper supporting documentation. If the system has an appropriate audit trail, the related approval details will appear in the customer's account record. However, if the supporting documentation is not electronic but on paper, it could end up in some distant warehouse after the account is inactive for a year or two. Then the company could have no practical means to verify the account approval. The account could then be abused by another dishonest employee without putting the credit department employee at risk of being caught.

FIGURE 13.5 **Major Modes of Electronic Fraud**

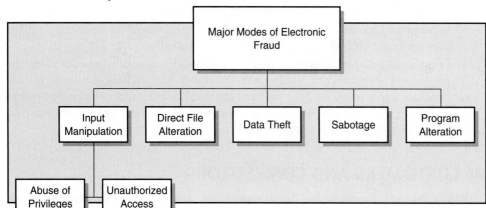

Simple automated reconciliations detect several types of access privilege abuse. For example, an accounts receivable clerk who issues an unauthorized cash receipt credit to a customer's account is likely to be identified if and when the system reconciles total cash receipts posted to the Cash account versus the total credits to customers' accounts. Many times, employees are not aware of such reconciliations, and so they commit crimes they cannot possibly get away with.

Unauthorized Access

An even worse case involves one employee who gains unauthorized access to another employee's account and then abuses that account. This fraud can render the audit trail useless in catching the perpetrator. For example, assume that someone in sales gains access to the cash payment system and sends a large electronic payment or wire transfer to a co-conspirator who uses a fake or stolen identity. The forensic accountant investigating such a case could have nothing to go on in investigating the fraud. In some cases, the accounting system logs could provide the IP address of the computer that entered the fraudulent transaction, but as discussed in Chapter 11, the IP address is not always helpful in identifying even the location of the computer used to commit the crime. Video surveillance records and building access logs could be helpful.

The situation can be worse when the compromised computer accounts belong to a computer system administrator who has "super-user" privileges. In this case, fraudsters could possibly erase the very logs that comprise the audit trail, leaving investigators little to go on. Another situation involves the fraudster's creation of a phony audit trail that points to another employee.

Direct File Alteration

Employees normally need an account login and password to access accounting databases and files, and this access method normally leaves an audit trail. In some cases, however, sophisticated employees manage to use system-type tools to directly access and modify accounting records without using the accounting system. This type of fraud leaves no audit trail in the accounting system, but it could leave an audit train in the general computer system logs. Of course, a sophisticated user might be able to doctor the general system logs.

Direct file alteration fraud is generally difficult or impossible to commit if the accounting files are properly encrypted. However, some encryption schemes, especially those based on simple passwords, can be broken. In addition, encrypted systems store temporary data in random access memory in unencrypted format. This means that a sophisticated enough attacker might substitute fraudulent data for real data in random access memory. This substitution would amount to piggybacking fraudulent data into a legitimate transaction. In this case, the audit trail would be misleading, and the unfortunate originator of the legitimate transaction could even be considered the perpetrator. The important point is that audit trails can be meaningless when a sophisticated fraudster is involved. Fortunately, however, the average company employee is not able to perform such sophisticated schemes.

Program Alteration

Program alteration occurs when a programmer makes unauthorized changes to the accounting software. The most famous case of program alteration involved the "round-off thief" who put a patch in the payroll processing code that rounded off payments to the nearest penny and transferred the fractional pennies to an account that he controlled. This happened in a large company that had large numbers of round-offs to steal, and the programmer ended up stealing thousands of dollars.

A forensic accountant might not easily spot program alteration fraud in the normal audit trail or miss it completely. Consider, for example, a fraudulent program patch that incorrectly computes one employee's paycheck to be higher than it should be. Depending on the situation, this fraud could go unnoticed unless someone double-checks the employee's payroll calculations, something that might or might not happen in an audit situation. Because audits focus only on samples of transactions, in many cases the audit concentrates on transactions that substantially differ from the norm.

In cases of program alteration, the audit trail of special importance to the forensic accountant is the program change log. In well-controlled systems, all changes to programs are made to nonworking copies of the programs. The changes are then reviewed, tested, approved, and entered into a program change log before they are implemented.

Data Theft

Data theft is usually easier to prevent than to identify, trace to a perpetrator, and prosecute. Corporate information systems usually hold high-value information such as customer lists, trade secrets, internal budgets, employee profiles, and strategic plans. Even with sophisticated security systems, there is often little that can be done to stop trusted employees from stealing valuable data and selling it to competitors or others.

In a well-designed system, users are not permitted to access or print more data than required for their job functions. This means that data access logs reveal only normal access patterns. That is, there may be nothing helpful for the forensic accountant in the audit trail.

An investigator could study a suspect's old e-mail, phone logs, computer logs, building access records, on so on, for telltale signs of guilt. With a little bit of luck, the investigator might find something like a smoking-gun e-mail message in which the suspect simply e-mailed stolen data to someone.

Sabotage

Sabotage, especially electronic sabotage, is usually carried out by disgruntled or recently fired workers. In one case, a programmer added a piece of malicious programming code to the payroll program to check each pay period to see whether the programmer was still an employee. If it found that he was no longer an employee, it began erasing critical files.

Summary

A forensic accountant must understand various schemes to be able to investigate fraud. Each year, employee and vendor frauds cost organizations billions of dollars, and much of what we know about fraud is from anecdotal experiences and from scattered newspaper reports because companies are often reluctant to report frauds to authorities. Companies do not like the negative publicity and embarrassment that comes with reporting fraud cases. Furthermore, many companies actually consider theft by employees, customers, or vendors as a normal cost of doing business.

When frauds are reported, the authorities often do not pursue them. Many types of fraud are complex and expensive to investigate, and economic crime divisions of local law authorities often have such heavy caseloads that they do not want to take reports for economic crimes unless the crime involves fairly large amounts of money. The authorities are relatively more likely to prosecute cases in which there is an obvious "smoking gun" such as a video surveillance tape.

Another problem is that obtaining convictions can be very difficult in many fraud cases, especially those involving computerized accounting records. Often the evidence is not tangible but exists only in complicated computer files and a weak audit trail.

percentage of the project completed. In this scheme, employees overstate the percentage that projects are completed and thus overstate revenues.

- **Unauthorized shipments or channel stuffing** Employees create sales orders at the end of the accounting period by shipping goods that have not been ordered to record the shipments in the current period's sales. When the goods are returned in the next period, they will be charged against the next period's sales. **Channel stuffing** is a similar process, but the company has a relationship with the customer to which it automatically ships goods according to the company's estimates of the customer's demand. The company takes advantage of this relationship and ships too many goods toward the end of the accounting period.

- **Consignment sales** Employees ship goods to customers on a consignment basis but record the shipments as normal sales. As with unauthorized shipments, this is done at the end of the accounting period to record the sale in the current period. When the goods are returned in the next period, they are charged against the next period's sales.

Overstating Assets

- **Inventories** The most common inventory fraud involves the overstatement of ending inventories. Many companies compute cost of goods sold from the formula $BI + P - EI = $ cost of good sold, where $BI = $ beginning inventory, $P = $ inventory purchases during the current period, and $EI = $ ending inventory. The beginning inventory amount must match the ending inventory amount from the previous period, so this number is not readily subject to fraud. The current period purchases (P) number is somewhat subject to fraud, but to overstate P, a company must create fictitious purchases, which requires making fraudulent entries into the accounts payable, Cash, and purchases accounts. On the other hand, overstating ending inventories is a fairly simple matter because it involves miscounting the inventories on hand without creating fraudulent transactions. Its simplicity is no doubt the main reason that inventory fraud is so common.

- **Accounts receivable** Accounts receivable are overstated by understating allowances for bad debts or falsifying account balances.

- **Property, plant, and equipment** In this scheme, depreciation is not taken when it should be, or property, plant, and equipment is simply overstated. A corresponding overstatement is made to the revenues.

- **Other overstatements** These involve other accounts such as loans/notes receivable, cash, investments, and so on. In some cases, expenses may also be understated.

Improper Accounting Treatment

- Recording an asset at market value or some other incorrect value rather than cost.
- Failing to charge proper depreciation or amortization against income.
- Capitalizing an asset when it should be expensed.
- Improperly recording transfers of goods from related companies as sales.
- Not recording liabilities to keep them off the balance sheet. For example, a company purchases inventory goods without recording the related liability to inflate the ending inventory, decrease the cost of goods sold, and inflate net income.
- Omitting contingent liabilities (e.g., pending product liability lawsuits, pending government fines) from the financial statements.

Fictitious and Fraudulent Transactions

- Recording sham transactions and legitimate transactions improperly. For example, the company purchases a machine for $800 with cash but records it as follows:

Debit:	Machine	$1,000	
Credit:	Cash		$800
Credit:	Sales		$200

Fraudulent Transaction Processing

- Intentionally misprocessing transactions to produce fraudulent account balances. For example, accounting software is modified to incorrectly total sales and accounts receivable so that all transactions in the account are real but the total is overstated.

Direct Falsification of Financial Statements

- Producing false financial statements when management simply ignores account balances.

Characteristics of Financial Statement Fraud

LO3   Financial statement fraud typically has certain known characteristics. Some of these include the following:

- Fraud tends to involve a misstatement or misappropriation of assets that is a substantial portion of total assets. The median amount of the fraud is approximately 25 percent of the median total assets.
- Most frauds span multiple fiscal periods with the average fraud time being approximately two years.
- The majority of fraud involves overstating revenues by recording them fictitiously or prematurely. It is common for misstatements to occur near the end of a quarter or fiscal year. Overstated revenues are frequently accompanied by related overstatements of assets such as inventories; property, plant, and equipment; and accounts receivable after allowances for bad debts. In some cases, fictitious assets are created.

The SEC publishes its enforcement actions on its Web site in the form of **Accounting and Auditing Enforcement Releases (AAERs).** Research focusing on AAERs has shown the following in relation to alleged cases of FSF (see Figure 14.2):

- FSF is much more likely to occur in companies whose assets are less than $100 million.
- FSF is much more likely to occur in companies with decreased earnings, earnings problems, or a downward trend in earnings.
- In a large majority of cases, either the CFO or CEO is involved in the fraud.
- In many cases, the board of directors has no audit committee or one that seldom meets, or none of the audit committee members has the required skills to perform as intended.
- The members of the board are frequently dominated by insiders (even related to managers) or by those with financial ties to the company.

In addition, the following facts relate to FSFs, audit reports, and audit firms/external auditors of firms that commit FSFs.

- Nearly half of audit reports indicate some type of anomaly, such as a change of auditors, doubts about the company's ability to continue as a going concern, a change in accounting

FIGURE 14.2
Accountants Sometimes "Cook the Books"

principles, or a litigation issue. Problems with departures from GAAP seldom occur, however.

- The size of the audit firm does not seem to matter. FSF occurs frequently in companies audited by both large and small audit firms.
- Nearly one-third of the enforcement action cases that name individuals allege wrongdoing on the part of the external auditor. About half the time, the auditor is accused of participating in a fraud; the other half of the time the auditor is accused of negligence.
- Auditor changes occurred about one-fourth of the time in and around the time of the fraud.

Motives for Management to Commit Financial Statement Fraud

Management has various motives for committing financial statement fraud.

Poor Income Performance

Most FSFs, especially in large companies, are committed to make the income statement look better. Poor income performance can cause managers to lose their jobs and/or salary bonuses as well as devalue managers' stock options or shares in the company.

Impaired Ability to Acquire Capital

Management produces fraudulent financial statements to facilitate capital acquisition. Poor financial results can impair a company's ability to raise capital through financing and other types of equity offerings.

Product Marketing

Management seeks to hide financial problems to keep buyers, who tend to shy away from companies that are having financial problems. Buyers are often afraid of entering into long-term relationships with companies that could be going out of business.

General Business Opportunities

Everyone likes to do business with a winning company. This applies to opportunities such as joint ventures and mergers. Managers sometimes commit financial statement fraud to make their company look better and increase their access to business opportunities.

Compliance with Bond Covenants

Fraud is performed to hide the company's inability to meet bond or other covenant conditions.

Generic Greed

Management produces fraudulent financial statements as a way to get ahead or keep their positions, increase salaries and other management benefits, and meet terms of incentive-based contracts.

Theft, Bribery, or Other Illegal Activities

Management needs to cover up the misappropriation of large amounts of money by issuing fraudulent financial statements. For example, the Foreign Corrupt Practices Act specifically requires companies to have proper internal controls and recordkeeping to prevent management from mischaracterizing bribes as legitimate expenses.

Bad News/Good News Example

This section demonstrates how management's hiding of bad news or good news can defraud and injure shareholders.

Management Hides and Trades on Bad News

Consider, for example, the following facts and events relating to bad news for XYZ Company. It is stable and has consistently reported "normal" earnings per share of $4 for the last 10 years. The market value of the company's stock has been consistently "normal" at $60 per share after adjusting for changes in the S&P 500 Index. In other words, if the S&P 500 Index goes up by 10 percent, XYZ's stock price also rises by 10 percent, from $60 to $66. At the end of the current fiscal year, the price of XYZ's common stock is exactly $60 per share.

XYZ's financial statements are followed closely by many financial analysts who regularly publish their opinions about XYZ in a wide range of financial news publications. At the end of the current fiscal year, the analysts predict that XYZ's earnings per share will again be the usual $4.

XYZ's top management secretly knows, however, that sales were down significantly in the most recent quarter. The drop was so bad that the annual earnings per share, according to GAAP, will be only $2 rather than the usual expected $4. Management decides that it does not want to disappoint shareholders with the bad news that earnings per share are only $2, so the CEO and controller overstate revenues and report earnings of $4 per share. The market is pleased with the announcement, and the stock price continues at the usual $60 per share.

One week after the annual earnings are announced, Jane Sorry purchases 100 shares of XYZ stock at the normal price of $60 per share for $6,000. Over the next several weeks, the CEO and CFO sell off much of their personal shares in XYZ at $60 per share. Sales do not rebound, and management accepts permanently lower sales.

Over the next several quarters, the CEO and controller continue to overstate revenues and earnings, but each quarter the amount of the overstatement is lower and lower, and reported earnings per share decline until they reach $2. At the same time, the price of the company's stock steadily declines until it levels off at $30 per share.

Jane Sorry finally gives up on her 100 shares of XYZ and sells them for $30 per share, taking a loss of $3,000. According to the preceding facts, Jane Sorry is a victim of financial statement fraud. If management had honestly reported earnings of $2 per share rather than $4 per share, Jane would not have purchased her shares at $60 and should not have lost $3,000.

To make things worse, the CEO and CFO dumped their stock shares at the $60 price when they knew that the price would decline. That means that the CEO and CFO directly "robbed" the persons to whom they sold their shares of stock. Moreover, anyone who purchased the company's stock during the period of the price decline lost money to those who sold it during the same period. Of course, any sellers not aware of the secret bad news were innocent of any wrongdoing, but they nevertheless sold their stock at a price that management knew was too high, and the buyers paid a price that management knew was too high.

This example leads to the conclusion that management defrauds anyone who buys shares during the time in which it keeps bad news secret. Anyone who buys during this time will pay too much for the stock. Conversely, anyone who sells during this period will gain at the expense of those who buy.

Management Hides and Trades on Good News

At first glance, one might be attempted to assume that dishonest management might be tempted to hide only bad news, but such is not the case. Consider the following facts:

- ABC Company's normal earnings per share total $2, and the normal stock price is $30 per share.
- Management secretly knows that sales have doubled and earnings per share have risen to $4.
- The CEO and CFO each buy 100 shares on the open market at $30 per share.
- Management falsely announces annual earnings per share at $2 and keeps the increase in sales a secret.
- At the end of the following fiscal year, management announces the correct earnings of $4 per share. The stock price immediately jumps to $60 per share.
- The CEO and CFO sell their stock at the higher price of $60 per share, realizing a $3,000 profit for each.

This case is the reverse of the bad news case, but again the CEO and CFO rob shareholders. This time each makes a $3,000 profit at the expense of the shareholders who sold to them.

This example leads to the conclusion that management defrauds anyone who sells shares during the time in which it keeps good news secret. Anyone who sells during this time will not receive the amount reflecting the true value of the stock sold. Conversely, anyone who buys during this period will gain at the expense of those who sell. Note that in these examples, it is not necessary for management to trade shares for them to defraud shareholders. In the bad news example, buyers pay too much for their shares if management does not trade any shares because the earnings overstatement alone causes them to pay too much for their shares. Similarly, in the good news case, the earnings understatement alone causes sellers to sell the shares at a price that is too low.

Fraud-Created Insider Information Period

As the preceding examples indicate, a key element to financial statement fraud analysis is the fact that fraud-related losses accrue to shareholders between the dates the company publishes the fraudulent information and the date it corrects the information. We refer to this period as the **fraud-created insider information period (FCIIP),** the time period in which unaware buyers and sellers trade their stock at prices that would be different in the absence of the fraud. Some generalizations can be made:

- Fraud-related losses *do not* accrue for those who *both* buy and sell their stock during the FCIIP. For actual losses to occur in the bad news case, the buyer must buy *within* the FCIIP and sell *after* it. In the good news case, the actual losses occur only for those who buy *before* the FCIIP and sell *during* it. Traders who both buy and sell completely outside the FCIIP can incur losses without fraud being involved.

- Normally, management has little incentive to hide good news for long. After all, good news makes managers look good, which can favorably affect their raises and bonuses. Therefore, most cases of fraud, especially those that are perpetrated over a long period, are likely to be related to bad news.

- Many cases of fraud occur when management fraudulently creates good news. The fraudulent creation of good news has the same impact as management's hiding bad news: Anyone who buys shares during the FCIIP and then sells after the FCIIP will lose money as a result of the fraud.

Effects of Financial Statement Fraud on Company and Management

FSF affects the company and management in several ways. They include the following:

- In the majority of cases, an SEC enforcement action for FSF is associated with bankruptcy or a change in ownership.

- In many cases, companies are delisted from a national stock exchange. Delistings tend to be associated with large declines in companies' market values.

- Managers accused of FSF are often named in class-action civil suits.

- Accused managers are often fined or their employment with the company is terminated.

- Jail sentences occur relatively infrequently, but this is changing as a result of the Sarbanes-Oxley (SOX) Act.

- SOX empowers the SEC to permanently bar offenders from serving as corporate officers or directors.

FINANCIAL STATEMENT FRAUD, THE STOCK MARKET, AND INSIDER TRADING

LO4 Financial statement fraud is harmful not only to individual investors but also to financial markets and society as a whole (see Figure 14.3). The stock market can be viewed as a mechanism that assigns gains and losses to individual shareholders on a risk-reward basis. Market participants take risks when buying and selling shares, and the market rewards investors who make good decisions (winners) by transferring wealth to them from those who make bad decisions (losers). Financial statement fraud artificially interferes with the stock market's determination of who is a winner and who is a loser, punishing good decision makers and rewarding bad ones.

Artificially interfering with the stock market's rewarding of winners and losers hurts the economy and the financial markets because rewards are in effect a signal to produce more. When the market rewards a particular activity, product, or service, more of that activity, product, or service is likely to be produced. On the other hand, when the market punishes a particular product, service, or activity, less of it will be produced. Therefore, the effect of financial statement fraud is to reduce the supply of valuable services and products that are available to society.

FIGURE 14.3
Example of Insider Dumping Shares for an Illegal Profit

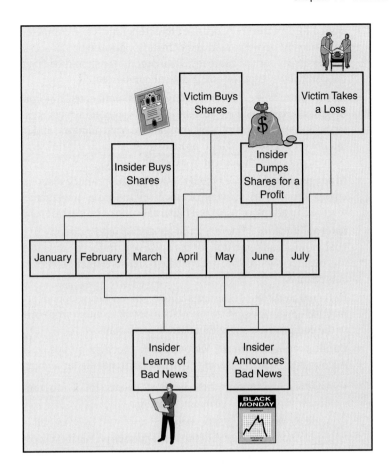

Losses relating to trading within an FCIIP are special cases of trading losses relating to trading in any period in which there is *inside information* regardless of whether there is financial statement fraud. For example, using the bad news example, the CEO and CFO might publish an honest financial report that shows earnings per share of $2. However, they could still perpetrate **insider trading** fraud by selling their shares one day before they publish the bad news. In that way, they would be transferring their losses to others. Insider trading is illegal in the United States except when done by company officials who file special SEC reports and comply with special SEC rules. Laws relating to the Securities Exchange Act seek to ensure that all market participants have access to the same information at the same time.

PREVENTION OF FINANCIAL STATEMENT FRAUD

Sarbanes-Oxley Act

LO5 The Sarbanes-Oxley Act (SOX) focuses on preventing financial statement fraud. Compliance with this act is mandatory for publicly traded companies, but much of its application can be useful for private companies.

The general philosophy behind SOX is to minimize FSF by promoting strong **corporate governance and organizational oversight** through the oversight of the following six organizational groups.

- **Board of directors** A board of directors must have competent, experienced members who actively participate in the company's governance process. They have the ultimate responsibility for the company. Board members should be financially independent from the company except for board-related compensation.

- **Audit committee** The audit committee should consist of board members with knowledge and experience in accounting and accounting systems. The committee should work closely with the internal auditors, external auditors, and management to ensure the integrity of external audit processes. It should carefully investigate any problems pointed out by management or external auditors.

- **Management** The CEO and CFO have the primary responsibility for implementing enterprisewide internal control processes and ethics management. Both must be actively involved in all major aspects of internal control process development.

- **Internal auditor** Internal auditors should report directly to the audit committee. The goal of this requirement is for the audit committee to serve as an independent check on top management and to independently ensure quality internal control processes and compliance.

- **External auditor** External auditors should be independent of the company in both fact and appearance. SOX prohibits external auditors from providing nonaudit services to the company except within narrow constraints.

- **Public oversight bodies** Various public oversight groups, such as the Public Company Accounting Oversight Board (PCAOB), set standards for auditors, some of which follow:

  - Auditors must retain their working papers for a minimum of seven years (even though for only five years under SOX).

  - Audit reports must be reviewed and approved by a second audit partner (the reviewing partner) in addition to the audit partner primarily responsible for the audit.

  - Audit reports must include a review and evaluation of whether the client's internal control structure and procedures include records that accurately reflect the transactions and dispositions of the client's assets.

  - Audit reports must include a review and evaluation of whether the client's receipts and expenditures are made only with authorization of the client's management and directors.

  - Audit reports must include a description of any material weaknesses in (or noncompliance with) internal controls.

  - Audit firms must adopt internal standards relating to professional ethics, the firm's independence from its clients, supervision of audit work, internal consultations, internal inspections, acceptance of and continuation of audit engagements, and other standards the PCAOB sets.

  - Neither the primary or reviewing partner can audit the same client for more than five consecutive years.

Among the six groups (see Figure 14.4), the audit committee is the one that is the most critical in the immediate sense. It has primary responsibility for selecting, hiring, and communicating with the external auditor. These functions are critical because a good external audit is a strong defense against financial statement fraud. The audit committee also oversees the internal auditor(s), who provides one more layer of security against FSF.

If the audit committee does its job well, financial statement fraud can occur only if there are three independent failures involving management, the internal auditor, and the external auditor. This situation is unlikely if all three of these functions in fact operate independently and the audit committee takes seriously its oversight function.

FIGURE 14.4
The Six Pillars of Corporate Governance

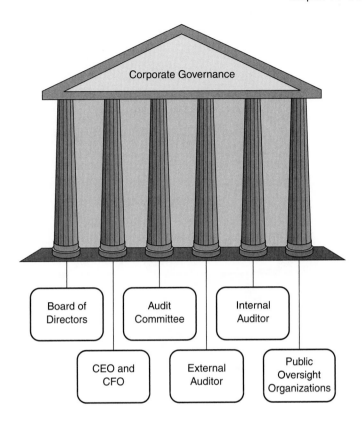

Red Flags: Indications of Possible Financial Statement Fraud

Research has identified a number of red flags associated with FSF. Some of these indicators are present in a large percentage of FSF cases, although their presence in no way means that fraud is actually present in a particular case.

Various red flags (see Figure 14.5) are discussed here.

Lack of Independence, Competence, Oversight, or Diligence

- Any lack of independence between management, internal auditors, and external auditors undermining the basic structure designed to prevent FSF.
- Any lack of competence, oversight, or diligence on the part of the audit committee or the internal auditor.

Weak Internal Control Processes

- Weak internal control processes or failure of top management to participate actively in developing and overseeing internal control.
- Lack of a corporate code of conduct with no related employee training and awareness.

Management Style

- Excessive pressure on employees to perform.
- Excessive focus on short-run performance, which could cause employees to cheat to achieve goals.
- Excessively authoritarian style that can cause employees to blindly agree to participate in fraudulent schemes.
- Excessive decentralization resulting in management oversight that is too lax.

FIGURE 14.5 **Red Flags Often Indicate Financial Statement Fraud**

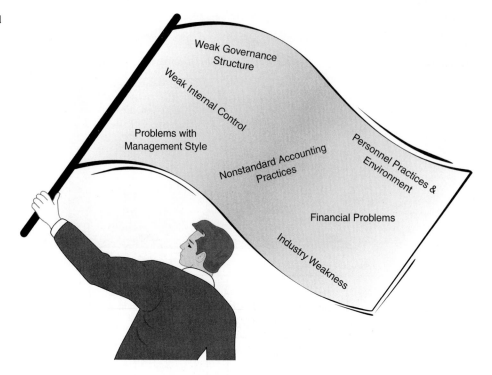

- Crisis management.
- Missing or poor strategic and operational planning.
- Excessive risk taking.

Personnel-Related Practices
- High employee turnover, especially among top management.
- Hiring unqualified employees or hiring without screening the background of potential employees.
- Inexperienced top management.
- Inadequate employee compensation.
- Low employee morale.

Accounting Practices
- Restatements of prior year reports.
- Aggressive accounting methods (discussed later).
- Weak audit trails.
- Losses of accounting records.
- Weak or poorly organized accounting information system.
- Overly optimistic or inadequate budgets.
- Arguments with auditors or lack of cooperation with auditors or the audit committee.
- Late or last-minute financial reports.
- Large or unusual end-of-year accounting adjustments or transactions.
- Frequent changes of the external auditor.
- Large or frequent accounting errors.

Company's Financial Condition

- Deterioration in the company's financial condition associated with a large percentage of financial statement frauds.
- Extremely high earnings or sudden increases in earnings.
- Declining net income.
- Declining cash flows from operations or low cash flows relative to net income.
- Declining sales or market shares.
- Increases in debt leveraging.
- Inadequate liquidity.
- Product obsolescence.
- Lagging collections in accounts receivable.
- Tax problems.
- Serious legal or contractual problems.
- Significant failure to meet analysts' earnings expectations.
- Doubt about the company's ability to remain a going concern.
- Insider sale of stock shares.
- Excess accumulation of inventory relative to sales.

Industry Environment and Conditions

- Volatility, especially when other firms in the same industry have problems.
- A one-product company in a declining industry.

MANAGEMENT DISCRETION, EARNINGS MANAGEMENT, AND EARNINGS MANIPULATION

Management Discretion

LO6   With respect to accounting discretion, its legitimate use does not violate any ethics guidelines although some individuals complain about its use and would like it eliminated. GAAP deliberately gives a certain degree of discretion to allow for differences between circumstances, companies, and industries. This discretion includes a wide degree of latitude with respect to **legitimate accounting choices** and **legitimate economic choices** that can affect earnings either way.

Use of Discretion in Making Accounting Choices
Accounting choices are discussed next.

Selection of Depreciation Methods
Accounting principles allow management discretion in choosing among several different methods of depreciation. Straight-line depreciation charges an equal dollar amount to expense in each year of an asset's life. Declining-balance depreciation, on the other hand, charges higher dollar amounts to expense in the earlier years of an asset's life but lower dollar amounts after the earlier years. Management can manage income according to the method it chooses. For example, choosing to use straight-line depreciation with newly acquired assets can "boost" income. Management also has some discretion in deciding the useful life of depreciable assets; the longer the useful life, the lower the annual depreciation expense and the higher current income. Management cannot, however, simply switch

depreciation methods (or other accounting methods) from one year to the next without generating at least a notation in the auditor's report. When the audit report does include a notation regarding a change in accounting method, the notation is likely to occur only in the year that that the change occurs although it affects income in future years.

Selection of Inventory Methods

The last-in, first-out (LIFO) inventory method assumes that the most recently purchased inventory goods are sold first. The first-in, first-out-(FIFO) method, on the other hand, assumes that the goods purchased first are sold first. In times of rising prices, the most recently purchased goods cost more than those previously purchased, and the use of LIFO results in a higher cost of goods sold and a lower income. At the same time, the use of FIFO produces a higher income.

Use of Discretion in Making Economic Choices

Examples of economic choices over which management can use discretion include the following:

- **Deferred expenses**   Management can boost its earnings simply by deferring one year's expenses to the next year. Many types of expenses can be deferred, including marketing campaigns, maintenance, research and development, training, and so on. Some may argue that deferring expenses to boost earnings is unethical; however, cutting expenses during economic downturns is a common practice and even considered to be a desirable business practice.

- **Accelerated revenues**   Management can also boost earnings by accelerating revenues. Offering end-of-year discounts, inventory liquidations, and other promotions are examples.

Management Discretion and Accrual Accounting

The predominant model of accounting today is accrual accounting, and accruals by their very nature require a certain amount of estimating, judgment, and discretion. The alternative is to eliminate accruals and simply report cash transactions, but a large body of research has shown that financial market participants are much more interested in accrual accounting income than in simple changes in cash balances. It is not that cash flows lack relevance—they do not—but that accrual-based income is believed to better indicate the company's economic future. The fundamental accounting principle of *matching* requires revenues to be matched with their related expenses on the income statement, which requires accrual accounting. When applied to inventory purchases, matching requires that inventory purchases be recorded as assets. The inventory asset values are then transferred to an expense account only in the period in which the inventory is sold in order to match the inventory expenses with their related revenues.

Consider the following facts:

- A new company purchases 100 units of inventory for $1,000 in December 20X1 and has no other expenses.

- The company sells all 100 units in January 20X2 for $2,000 and has no other expenses.

In this case, under cash accounting, the company would recognize a $1,000 loss in 20X1 and a $2,000 profit in 20X2. On the other hand, under accrual accounting, the company would recognize a profit of $0 in 20X1 and of $1,000 in 20X2. Now consider the two profit numbers for 20X2. Which seems to be a better indicator of future economic performance?

Many would say $1,000, the accrual profit. Of course, it is a matter of perspective, but what is certain is that the users of financial statements want accrual accounting.

Over the life of a company, accrual accounting merely reports the change in cash from beginning to end. Specifically, if a company begins with all cash and later liquidates to all cash, its accounting income equals the difference between the beginning and ending cash balances (adjusted for any dividends and other capital changes). In other words, over the life of a company, accrual income and cash flow are the same.

The real economic income is the cash flow, and accrual accounting decides only the timing of the recognition of that cash flow. GAAP is based on accrual accounting methods, and the accrual method has no effect on the total income or cash flows over the life of the company. Therefore, earnings manipulation that operates within the framework of accrual accounting and GAAP has no effect on total income over the life of the company but merely moves income from one period to the next.

Nonaccounting persons often believe that any use of discretion is a matter of abuse or fraud. In fact, some individuals believe that the accounting profession should change accounting rules to allow management much less, or even no, discretion. However, eliminating management discretion is practically impossible because a rigid cookie-cutter, one-shoe-fits-all approach to accounting is likely only to decrease the usefulness and relevance of financial reports.

The main point in regard to accounting discretion is that its application potentially involves a gray area that lies between legitimate discretion and the fraudulent abuse of discretion. In practice, it is not always easy to determine at what point legitimate discretion becomes aggressive discretion, or at what point aggressive discretion becomes abusive and fraudulent. The judgment is made by auditors, regulatory authorities (such as the SEC), and the courts.

Earnings Management

The term *earnings management* is frequently confused with *earnings manipulation.* The term **earnings management** refers to management's routine use of *nonfraudulent* accounting and economic discretion. It is well known that a high percentage of large companies legally engage in earnings management. **Earnings manipulation,** however, has a more nebulous meaning. It can refer either to the legitimate or aggressive use, or fraudulent abuse, of discretion. By definition, then, earnings management is legitimate, and earnings manipulation can be legitimate, marginally ethical, unethical, or illegal, depending on its extent. How management uses or exceeds its discretion is the crucial factor.

In some cases, management uses **aggressive accounting techniques** that are questionable but perhaps not fraudulent. As an example, assume that the company purchases a new group of machines for which the controller estimates a useful life of seven years. The CEO does not want such heavy annual depreciation expenses and insists that the machines will be useful for 10, not 7, years. The controller gives in and sets up a 10-year depreciation schedule. Both the CEO and the controller know that the auditor could complain but hope that she will be too busy thinking about other things.

In this case, the discretionary use of an aggressive accounting technique could be questionable but probably not to the extent that an outsider would call it fraudulent abuse of accounting discretion. On the other hand, the agreement of the CEO and controller to use a 40-year depreciation schedule clearly would be fraudulent abuse of discretion.

Ethics and Earnings Management   Is the practice of earnings management ethical? To answer this question, it helps to separate the use of economic versus accounting discretion. With respect to economic discretion, for example, few question the propriety of cutting expenses when times are bad or spending more when times are good. On the other hand, people do question management's use of economic discretion that helps the firm in the short run but hurts it in the long run. Some examples of such undesirable behavior related to economic discretion follow:

- Cutting equipment maintenance expenses could produce short-run costs savings but harm or destroy the equipment's long-term survival.
- Cutting safety or environmental practices could lead to future liability, lawsuits, government fines, and negative publicity.
- Offering large year-end product discounts could boost current year income but seriously damage the next year's income.

With respect to the aggressive use of discretion, many more consider it unethical or at least undesirable. However, the ethics issue might possibly be mitigated by clearly disclosing aggressive accounting assumptions in the financial statement footnotes.

Earnings Manipulation

Earnings manipulation does not include the outright falsification of the accounting records through fictitious transactions, the fraudulent alteration of legitimate transactions, or the intentional permanent failure to record transactions, which are always fraudulent regardless of their degree or extent. Several types of earnings manipulation are discussed next.

Earnings Smoothing

Management engages in earnings manipulation not only to *increase* earnings but also to *decrease* them. There are considerable incentives for management to manipulate earnings. **Earnings smoothing** is the manipulation of earnings to reduce their volatility. In simple terms, this means using manipulations to increase earnings in years when they are weak and to lower them in years when they are strong.

Earnings smoothing functions are based on **accounting's fundamental law of conservation.** This law says that as a general rule, GAAP-compliant accounting manipulations neither create nor destroy earnings; they merely shift them from one period to another. This means that manipulating earnings downward in the current year will increase earnings in one or more future years. Conversely, it means that manipulating earnings upward in the current year will decrease earnings in one ore more future years. A conservation effect applies because earnings are the same over the life of a company, regardless of any manipulations. That is, manipulation does not create or destroy earnings over the life of a company; it merely shifts earnings from one year to another. This is true no matter how the GAAP rules change. GAAP is based on accrual accounting methods, and the accrual accounting used has no effect on the total income or cash flows over the life of the company. Consequently, because GAAP-compliant earnings manipulation operates within the framework of accrual accounting, it merely moves income from one period to the next. Because of this, it follows that any current-period manipulations that increase current income must also decrease future income. This way, increases and decreases cancel each other out so that there is no lifetime effect on income over the life of the company.

The implications for reducing earnings volatility are simple. If management uses manipulations to reduce earnings in a very good year, there will automatically be more income available for a subsequent bad year. It does not really matter what type of accounting manipulation management uses; management's lowering of income in good years will make more income available for bad years. This can be demonstrated by a simple example:

- Management buys a new machine for $1,000 with a 2-year estimated life.
- Management decides that the current year is a very good year but expects the next year will not to be so good and so abuses its discretion and immediately charges the entire $1,000 to expense instead of charging $500 depreciation in the current year and $500 in the next year.

The effect of management's decision is to cause a $500 net decrease in the current year's earnings and a $500 net increase in the next year's earnings. This is so because management charges $1,000 to expense in the current year and $0 to expense in the next year; this is done instead of charging $500 in both years. The net result is that management's manipulation shifts $500 from the current year's income to that for the next year.

It is very well known on Wall Street that investors prefer steadily increasing earnings that consistently meet or exceed financial analyst expectations. This stems from the general economic principle that investors are risk averse.

In financial terms, risk aversion is associated with earnings volatility. Consider, for example, the following scenario:

- Two firms, A and B, have earnings that consistently average $5 per share.
- Firm A's earnings per share are smooth and never deviate by more than a few cents from $5. On the other hand, firm B's earnings per share are much more volatile, sometimes as low as $1 and sometimes as high as $9.
- Both firms are identical in all material ways except for earnings volatility. Risk-averse investors prefer firm A with the lower volatility.

In regard to accounting discretion, consider the use of the cookie jar and big-bath accounting discussed next.

Cookie Jar Accounting   One type of earnings management is sometimes called **cookie jar accounting,** an accounting practice by which a company uses generous reserves from good years against losses that might be incurred in bad years. The practice treats the balance sheet as a cookie jar: In good years, the company stores cookies (reserves) in the cookie jar (the balance sheet) so that it can take them out and eat them (place them on the income statement) when management is hungry (needs extra income to look good).

As discussed, any manipulation that affects current income has a reverse effect on future income, so it has a cookie jar effect. However, some companies have elevated cookie jar accounting to a formal science through the use of special reserve accounts.

Reserve accounts are used to charge anticipated future costs to current income. The costs are debited to current expense and credited to a reserve account (which acts as a liability). Companies use these accounts by adding to them in good years and then drawing from them in bad years.

Big-Bath Accounting   When a company makes a large one-time write off, it is said to take a **big bath** to improve future earnings (often in the form of restructuring or inventory write-downs) when earnings performance is poor. Management reasons that it is going to look bad anyway, so it will not make much difference how bad it looks. The benefit of higher future income outweighs any negative short-term appearance. A new CEO may be tempted to take a big bath to place the blame for poor performance on the previous CEO and to make her, as the new CEO, look much better in future years.

CASES OF FINANCIAL STATEMENT FRAUD AND MANIPULATION

LO7 This section presents several well-publicized, large fraud cases. Remember, however, that the majority of frauds occur in relatively small companies, many of which do not receive the enormous amount of public attention given to the cases presented here.

McKesson & Robbins: Financial Statement Fraud 101

This early fraud took place in the 1930s. McKesson & Robbins was a drug company that not only sold pharmaceutical alcohol to the mob but also created fictitious customers as well as inventories in fictitious warehouses and sales.

The Great Salad Oil Swindle

This is one of the most famous inventory fraud cases of all time. It happened during the 1960s when a vegetable oil company hired a highly respected accounting firm to audit its inventory of 1.8 billion pounds of salad oil. The salad oil firm needed the inventory audit to be able to use the inventory as security for bonds that it wanted to issue.

The salad oil was in large storage tanks. The auditors climbed to the top of each tank, opened the hatches, and put their fingers in to verify the presence of the salad oil. The only problem was that the tanks were full of water with only a thin layer of salad oil floating on the surface. The auditors "passed" the inventory, the bonds were issued, and many people lost a lot of money.

Equity Funding: They Made a Movie About It

This 1970s fraud was so large and infamous that the story was made into a movie, *The Billion Dollar Bubble.* Equity Funding created and sold a large number of fake insurance policies at their present value and misreported them on its financial statements. The scheme lasted for nine years and involved as many as 100 company employees until one employee blew the whistle. The result was the collapse of one of Wall Street's darling companies and billions of dollars in losses.

Cedant Corporation: Manufacturing Revenues

An ex-official of what is now Cedant Corp. (previously CUC International) was sentenced to 10 years in prison and ordered to personally pay more than $3 billion (yes, billion!) in losses. The alleged scheme involved the creation of $500 million in fictitious revenues. When the accounting irregularities became public, the company's stock price fell from its 52-week high of about $41 per share to nearly $13 per share.

Zzzz Best: The Teenager Who Fooled Wall Street

Zzzz Best is the story of Barry Minkow, a teenager who created a $200 million public company that was nothing less that a big pyramid scheme. The company's basic product was carpet cleaning and restoration, and the basic fraud involved fictitious sales revenues. After being convicted and receiving a 25-year prison sentence, he explained in interviews how easily he misled accountants and bankers with fictitious documents, claiming that everyone who was making money from his business wanted to believe him and that made it relatively easy for him to deceive them.

Sunbeam Corp.: Channel Stuffing

In a complaint drawn for the United States District Court (Southern District of Florida), the SEC accused Sunbeam Corp. employees of illegal channel stuffing. The following are items 2 and 3 of the complaint:

> 2. The illegal conduct began at year-end 1996 with the creation of inappropriate accounting reserves. These reserves artificially and improperly lowered Sunbeam's reported 1996 performance, which would make the Company's 1997 results appear better by comparison. They also served as a cookie-jar into which management could and did dip its hand to artificially and improperly inflate income in 1997, further contributing to the picture of a rapid turn-around. In addition, to boost income in 1997, and also to create the impression that Sunbeam was experiencing significant revenue growth, Defendants Dunlap, Kersh, Gluck, Uzzi, and Griffith (collectively the Sunbeam Defendants) caused Sunbeam to recognize revenue from sales that did not meet applicable accounting rules. As a result, for fiscal 1997, at least $60 million of Sunbeam's reported (record-setting) $189 million in earnings from continuing operations before income taxes (income) came from accounting fraud.
>
> 3. Also in 1997, the Sunbeam Defendants were responsible for a critical disclosure failure: they reported Sunbeam's significant 1997 revenue growth without informing investors that this increase had been achieved not only by illegal accounting, but also at the expense of future results. The Company had inflated its revenues by channel stuffing, i.e., overloading channels of distribution by offering discounts and other inducements in order to sell product now that would otherwise be sold in the future. Sunbeam had so stuffed its customers with product that the Company's future results would suffer.

The channel stuffing complaint related to $1.5 million in barbecue grills that the company shipped and booked into revenue. The grills were returned just a few months later.

The CEO agreed to pay the SEC a $500,000 fine and agreed never again to serve as the head of a public company.

Nortel: The Ultimate Big Bath

In one quarter, Nortel Networks Corp. announced that it was taking $18.4 billion in charges for restructuring costs, bad customer debts, and obsolete inventory. This became the world's record at the time for the largest big bath, and many argued that the reserves relating to the restructuring were excessive. Nortel used the reserves over a three-year period, improving income during that period.

WorldCom: Boosting Earnings in a Big Way

WorldCom improperly capitalized billions of dollars of costs that should have been charged to the income statement as expenses. The company sought to conceal the fraud by sprinkling the expenses over a large number of different capital accounts.

Enron: Lessons in Creative Accounting

The well-known Enron fiasco involved complicated accounting schemes, many of which violated GAAP and/or were illegal:

- More than $8 billion in loans were misclassified as "trades of energy futures." The borrowed funds were labeled cash flows from trading activities; the related liabilities were labeled price risk management liabilities and buried in an enormous derivatives trading budget that ran in the hundreds of billions of dollars. Readers of the financial statements had no way to know that Enron was borrowing such large amounts of money simply for basic operating funds.
- Enron abused *mark-to-market (MTM) accounting*. MTM is typically used in the financial securities industry to include in income unrealized gains and losses in security positions.

In other words, income is recognized when increases in value occur in a company's securities assets, and a loss is recognized when decreases in value occur. This does not follow the accounting principle of matching in which gains and losses are associated with the actual sales of a company's security assets. In any case, the SEC gave Enron permission to use MTM accounting for its natural gas trading business, but Enron abused the practice by applying it to business activities other than those relating to natural gas securities. It immediately recognized as current income the amounts of estimated future income from contracts signed. It also recognized as income "increases in value" from investments that were based on complex assumptions. For example, Enron used MTM to mark up the value of its investment in Mariner Energy (a private oil and gas exploration company) from $185 million to $367 million, thus creating $182 million in revenue. Enron later admitted that the markup had been greatly overstated.

- Enron used "special-purpose entities" (SPEs) to hide enormous MTM losses by creating hedge agreements with the SPEs that were supposed to cover Enron's MTM losses. The problem was that the SPEs were funded with revenue from sales of Enron's stock, so they were unable to cover MTM losses when Enron's stock price declined. Eventually, Enron's share prices dropped, and the SPEs became insolvent.

- Enron sold future income streams at their present value to generate cash and reported these proceeds as revenue. The problem was that Enron guaranteed the future income streams, thus creating accounting sales without real economic substance. Some of the guarantees were part of secret side agreements.

Qwest and Global Crossing: Swap Sales

Swap sales involve two companies that exchange business with each other to inflate both the sales and expenses of each to make their revenues look better. For example, two electric power companies agree to swap services by providing each other the same amount of power. Both could record sales proceeds as revenue and the related costs as expenses. This arrangement would not actually increase either's profits if the swap is done in the same year.

Swap sales also are used to transfer income from one year to the next if one company provides its swap services in one year and the other company does so in the next. In this case, the company providing the services in the first year would lower its income in that year and increase it in the next. A company could desire such an arrangement if it had excess income in the first year but needed more income in the second.

According to news reports, Qwest Telecommunications, Inc., allegedly boosted or attempted to boost its revenues by selling capacity on its fiber optic network while buying the same amount of capacity on another carrier's network. Similarly, congressional hearings raised the question of whether Global Crossing had engaged in similar revenue swaps to meet its publicly announced revenue targets.

Summary

Financial statement fraud (FSF) is any intentional or grossly negligent violation of generally accepted accounting principles (GAAP) that is undisclosed and materially affects any financial statement. Fraud can take many forms, including hiding both bad and good news.

Research shows that FSF is relatively more likely to occur in companies with assets of less than $100 million, with earnings problems, and with loose governance structures. In a large majority of cases, the CEO or CFO is involved.

Most FSFs involve revenue or asset overstatements; revenue overstatement is the most common method. The two most common methods of revenue overstatement involve sham sales and premature revenue recognition. Other overstatement methods include recognition of conditional sales, improper cutoff of sales dates, improper treatment of consignment and percentage of completion sales, and channel stuffing. Other general methods include improper accounting treatments, fictitious or fraudulent transactions, and fraudulent transaction processing.

Asset overstatement is the second most popular method of FSF; the most common type is inventory overstatement because it requires only overstating the count of ending inventories, but no fictitious transactions or elaborate cover-up schemes.

FSF frequently causes severe financial damage to investors and creditors. Large frauds sometimes produce damages in billions of dollars. Managers accused of FSF are often named in class action civil suits, terminated from their employment, fined, and sentenced to prison terms.

Frauds are committed for a variety of reasons such as to cover up poor performance to obtain capital, market products, obtain business opportunities, and comply with bond covenants. Other reasons relate to general greed and cover-up misappropriation of company funds.

Financial statement fraud can best be prevented by a strong and diligent governance structure that includes an independent audit committee, an independent internal auditor, an independent external auditor, and a management that sets the appropriate tone and culture from the top of the organization. The Sarbanes-Oxley Act sets forth governance standards.

Various red flags can indicate an increased possibility of FSF. They include declining net income, declining sales, increases in leverage, lack of liquidity, and volatility or weakness in the company's industry. Others include a weak governance structure, weak internal control processes, autocratic management, overly detached management, too much pressure to achieve immediate success, high employee turnover, low morale, aggressive accounting methods, restatements of previous period results, late financial reports, and financial problems.

Accounting rules provide management a wide degree of discretion and latitude with respect to legitimate accounting and economic choices that can affect earnings. Accounting choices can be legitimate, aggressive, or fraudulent. The terms *earnings management* (routine use of *nonfraudulent* accounting and economic discretion to smooth earnings) and *earnings manipulation* (use or abuse of accrual accounting methods to either increase or decrease accounting income; may be legitimate, marginally ethical, unethical, or illegal, depending on the circumstances) are frequently confused.

It is relatively common for management to use accounting and economic choices to smooth income. Within the context of GAAP and accrual accounting, the effect of accounting manipulation is generally to shift income from one period to another. Such manipulation neither creates nor destroys income but only moves it from one period to another. The practice of smoothing involves cookie jar accounting to lower income in very good years and shift it to future years. In some cases, firms take a big bath and write off a large amount of expenses in one year, which has the effect of increasing future income.

Glossary

Accounting and Auditing Enforcement Release (AAERs) SEC reports of alleged violations of the provisions of the Securities and the Securities Exchange Acts and its enforcement actions on its Web site.

accounting's fundamental law of conservation Law that within the context of accrual accounting and GAAP, accounting manipulations neither create nor destroy earnings; they merely shift them from one period to another.

aggressive accounting techniques Accounting practices that are questionable but perhaps not fraudulent.

big bath Large one-time write-off of expenses.

channel stuffing   Vendor practice of shipping customers an excess amount of goods near the end of its accounting period, boosting the vendor's revenues in the current accounting period, although these revenues are likely to be reversed in the following accounting period when customers return the excess goods.

cookie jar accounting   Pattern of accounting practices that treats the balance sheet as a cookie jar so that in good years, cookies (reserves) are stored in it (the balance sheet) so that they can be taken from it and eaten (placed on the income statement) when management is hungry (in need of extra income to look good).

corporate governance and organizational oversight   Best general way to prevent financial statement fraud; achieved by the monitoring from six groups: management, board of directors, audit committee, internal auditors, external auditors, and public oversight groups.

earnings management   Practice of routine use of nonfraudulent accounting and economic discretion to smooth earnings.

earnings manipulation   Use or abuse of accrual accounting methods to either increase or decrease accounting income; may be legitimate, marginally ethical, unethical, or illegal, depending on the circumstances.

earnings smoothing   The use of accounting manipulations to increase earnings in financially weak years and decrease earnings in strong years.

financial statement fraud (FSF)   Any undisclosed intentional or grossly negligent violation of generally accepted accounting principles (GAAP) that materially affects the information in any financial statement.

fraud-created insider information period (FCIIP)   Time period in which unaware buyers and sellers trade their shares at prices that would be different in the absence of some financial reporting fraud.

insider trading   Illegal trading of stock based on information known only to employees of a corporation.

legitimate accounting choices   Management choices of accounting methods within GAAP that affect earnings.

legitimate economic choices   Management's financial choices that affect earnings without accounting manipulation. For example, managers may defer research expenses until the next year in order to boost the current year's earnings.

Review Questions

1. To which of the following does fraud created by insider information period refer?
   a. The time frame management has to correct fraudulent information disclosed.
   b. The time frame within which insider trading is prohibited.
   c. The time frame between the disclosure of fraudulent information and the information as corrected.
   d. The time frame within which fraud is committed.
   e. None of the above.
2. Which of the following is more likely to be involved with the financial statement fraud of a company?
   a. The treasurer.
   b. The chairman of the audit committee.
   c. The chairman of the board of directors.

    d. The CEO.

    e. The largest shareholder.

    f. All of the above are equally likely to be involved.

3. Who is more likely to be involved in the fraud of misappropriation of assets?

    a. The CEO.

    b. The largest shareholder.

    c. The executive secretary.

    d. The audit committee.

    e. All of the above are equally likely to be involved.

    f. None of the above are generally likely to be involved.

4. Which of the following is a normal economic choice available to management?

    a. Dividend policy.

    b. Deferral of expenses.

    c. Nonpayment of lease obligations.

    d. Bonuses paid to upper level management.

    e. None of the above.

5. Which of the following types of company is least likely susceptible to fraud?

    a. A company that has only cash sales.

    b. A construction company that recognizes income by the percentage of completion method.

    c. A calendar year company that conducts most of its business at year-end.

    d. A company with an IT system developed and maintained by the auditors.

    e. A company that maintains an inventory.

    f. All of the above are equally likely.

    g. None of the above.

6. Which element in inventory computation is most likely to lead to fraud?

    a. Beginning Inventory.

    b. Purchases.

    c. Cost of Goods Sold.

    d. Ending Inventory.

7. To which of the following does *improper accounting treatment* refer?

    a. Misclassifying a capital asset as an expense.

    b. Recording the purchase price of an asset at market price, not cost.

    c. Neglecting to amortize an intangible asset.

    d. Failing to disclose the results of a recent judgment against the company.

    e. *a, b,* and *d.*

    f. Only *b* and *c.*

    g. All of the above.

    h. None of the above.

8. A manager with an incentive-driven employment contract could be more likely to do which of the following?

    a. Inflate revenue.

    b. Capitalize items rather than expense them.

    c. Maximize dividends to the stockholders.

    d. Expense stock options.

    e. All of the above.

9. Which of the following can motivate a manager to commit fraud?

    a. A debt covenant agreement that requires the company to maintain a certain percentage of assets as cash.

    b. Compensation through a set salary.

    c. An illegal agreement with a supplier.

    d. *a* and *b*.

    e. *a* and *c*.

    f. All of the above.

    g. None of the above.

10. Which of the following entities is *not* a primary focus of SOX in preventing financial statement fraud?

    a. The board of directors.

    b. The audit Committee.

    c. The PCAOB.

    d. The SEC.

    e. External auditors.

    f. Internal auditors.

11. Which of the following is best at catching an undetected financial statement fraud?

    a. The CEO.

    b. The CFO.

    c. The audit committee.

    d. The external auditor.

    e. The PCAOB.

    f. The stock market.

Please revise any false statement to make it true.

12. Research has shown that fraud is more likely to occur in a company with assets of less than $100 million.

13. Audits by a large auditing firm are more likely to be subject to fraud.

14. Aggressive earnings management always indicates financial statement fraud.

15. Earnings smoothing is a legitimate tool available to management to equalize the income of the business from year to year.

16. According to the concept of accrual accounting, the deferral of an expense today has no effect on tomorrow's revenues.

17. Channel stuffing usually occurs at the beginning of an accounting period.

18. Most financial statement fraud occurs through the deferral of expenses.

19. According to PCAOB standards, accountants are to keep their working papers for a minimum of five years.

20. The use of discretion in an accounting method is an abuse of discretion.

Discussion Questions

21. What is a *big bath*? When would management be inclined to use it?

22. Do deviations from GAAP always indicate financial statement fraud?

23. Is management more likely to disclose "good news" or "bad news"?

24. How does the audit committee fight financial statement fraud?

25. What are three different types of revenue recognition fraud, and what does each involve?

26. What role(s) does the external auditor play in fighting fraud? Is (Are) the role(s) primarily proactive or reactive?

27. What is the distinction between management discretion and the intentional falsification of accounting records?

28. What is the concept of earnings smoothing?

29. How can the use of depreciation methods be used to perpetuate asset fraud?

30. Identify three red flags that indicate the potential for financial statement fraud.

31. Explain why flash-in-the-pan companies are risky for financial statement fraud.

32. What are the differences between financial statement fraud that occurs on the balance sheet and that which occurs on the income statement? In your answer, discuss the different types of financial statement fraud, the timing of the fraud, and the recognition of the fraud by the marketplace.

33. Many management contracts include pay incentives. Are these incentives an invitation to commit fraud? Who determines whether management has achieved its goals? Are there certain types of incentives that would be less likely to be associated with fraud?

34. How long does it take the stock market to react to good news? To bad news? What time interval would you use to monitor the stock price of a company that you suspect is involved in earnings management?

35. Contrast the effect of financial statement fraud on the following:
    a. The stockholder.
    b. The corporation.
    c. The corporation's executives/directors.
    d. The market as a whole.
    e. Society in general.

36. The concept of fraud involves the legal concept of intent. What intent must be shown for there to be financial statement fraud? Would the same standards apply in other settings? In other words, is there a lower threshold for fraud in a financial statement setting than in other legal matters?

37. Which is more difficult to conceal, fictitious revenue recognition or premature revenue recognition? In answering this question, consider the timing of the fraud (i.e., which is more likely to occur at year-end).

38. What is the connection between the overstatement of assets and overstatement of revenue? Are they different sides of the same fraud?

39. Discuss how an audit committee can help combat financial statement fraud. What are the disadvantages and advantages of allowing members of the audit committee to serve indefinitely?

40. The concepts of ethics and earnings management are not necessarily mutually exclusive. Discuss how these two concepts can coexist.

41. Why is so much discretion given to management when it comes to earnings management? What functions does management fulfill when disclosing financial information?

42. In what ways do financial statement *usefulness* and *relevance* differ? In answering this question, consider the impact that usefulness and relevance have on the disclosure and the timing of disclosure of financial information.

43. What two steps could be taken to minimize each type of revenue recognition fraud?

44. Why is the audit committee the key to fighting financial statement fraud? Examine the steps in preparing the financial statements that lend themselves to instituting controls. What are the most effective controls for combating financial statement fraud?

45. How can you distinguish between accounting decisions that are permitted by GAAP and misleading financial statements? Consider whether the method of disclosing variances from GAAP has any to financial relevance to users of the financial statements.

46. What are the five major areas that COSO identified that are most open to financial statement fraud? What challenges apply in attempting to combat each of these types of fraud? Create audit steps that would detect the specific type of fraud identified.

47. Create examples showing a spectrum with strict adherence to conservative accounting policies at one end and aggressive and misleading earnings management at the other end. How far along the spectrum can a business go before it crosses the line into fraud? Is this spectrum the same for all businesses? If not, discuss the differences and the similarities.

Cases

48. The *positive accounting theory* is a well-established principle of accounting theory. Do an Internet search of it and then answer the following questions: What are the three main hypotheses of the positive accounting theory? How does each of these hypotheses fit into the concept of financial statement fraud?

49. Go to the SEC Web site and look for the AAERs reported. Look for examples of earnings manipulation that resulted in financial statement fraud. Identify the specific facts of the case that caused the SEC investigation. Identify how the SEC handled the complaints. How did the company react to the investigation? Were any sanctions imposed? What steps did the company take to rectify the situation?

50. List factors that could impact the presence of financial statement fraud in a real estate business and in a high-pressure sales organization. What are common to both lists? List other types for businesses for which a particular characteristic could be a red flag for fraud.

51. The Sunbeam Corporation is a famous case in which the CEO Al "Chainsaw" Dunlap was charged with utilizing earnings manipulation to achieve fraudulent financial goals. Find information about this case on the Internet and discuss the earnings management methods used in this case. Did the company "take a big bath" by taking a large deduction for prepaid expenses in 1996? How were accruals used to achieve management's goals?

52. In Zzzz Best, Inc., Barry Minkow wowed Wall Street with his carpet cleaning company. What methods of concealment and fraud did he use? How could this fraud have been prevented? Discuss the safeguards that need to be implemented to avoid this manipulation. What do auditors need to do differently to avoid audit failures like Zzzz Best, Inc.?

53. Mary Milken is the CFO of the Rbeck Company in Miami, Florida. The company is a closely held custom yacht builder with about 200 technical workers (engineers, marine architects, mechanics, boat workers, and so on), and 12 employees in its main office staff. Her primary job is to prepare the financial statements with the assistance of two full-time accountants. She normally follows generally accepted accounting principles, but she sometimes ignores them when she thinks they do not lead to what she considers best practices for the small number of her company's shareholders.

In the previous decade, the company was owned by three sisters, each of whom served on the board of directors. One of the three, Vanessa Rbeck, served as the CEO during that period. The other two have always deferred to her with respect to her operational management decisions.

Only a month ago, however, Vanessa's sisters were killed when their private plane crashed en route to the Bahamas, which they frequently visited on weekends for relaxation. Upon their death, all of their shares in the Rbeck company transferred to a single trustee in one of the large South Florida banks. Each sister had held her shares in revocable living trusts with the same bank named as successor trustee.

As soon as the funerals were over, Mary and Vanessa met with the trustee, Annie Crusher. The meeting did not go well. Annie had grown up working in a family-owned retail boat business, and she thought her knowledge of the industry transferred to the yacht-building business. She began asking Vanessa a rapid succession of unfriendly questions in an adversarial tone of voice. Her questions strongly implied that a yacht-building business did not belong in South Florida but offshore where labor is cheaper. After the meeting, both Mary and Vanessa became afraid that Annie would do something crazy like fire them both or liquidate the business.

For the previous five years, Rbeck's stock had sold for a steady $12 per share, with $8 per share in dividends. Vanessa received a good salary, but she depended on the dividends to send her children to private schools and to pay the large mortgage on her waterfront home in South Beach. She immediately realized that she was now at Annie's mercy; she could easily cut off Vanessa's dividends, lower her salary, or put her out of work.

To make things worse, Mary was almost finished with the most recent annual report, and it appeared that earnings were down for the first time ever. Her preliminary calculations showed earnings per share somewhere near $8.

The problem with earnings had been caused by large bad debts from three clients who had been arrested for drug trafficking. Rbeck had entirely financed luxury yachts for the three clients because of their excellent credit history and prominence in the business community. However, the federal government seized all of the clients' assets, leaving nothing for Rbeck but the three half-built yachts.

After thinking things over, Vanessa asked Mary to find a way to avoid having to report lower earnings because of her concern as to how Annie might respond to the decline in earnings. Mary considered various options:

- Increase the estimated percentage of completion on all yachts in work-in-process inventory by 15 percent. This would wipe out most of the loss. Work in process estimates have always been very conservative anyway.

- Recognize revenue on the three yachts in default. It would be very difficult to sell them at a good price, but she could always argue that they could be sold if she could keep a straight face. The best strategy would be to find new buyers for them, but that could take a couple of years.

- Switch to mark-to-market accounting for some of the yachts in progress so the company could recognize all of the profit when contracts with other clients are signed.

a. Is any option that Mary is considering acceptable under generally accepted accounting principles? Why or why not?

b. Do any of the options being considered by Mary constitute financial statements fraud?

c. How would you handle the entire situation if you were in Mary's shoes?

Chapter **Fifteen**

Fraud and SOX Compliance

CHAPTER LEARNING OBJECTIVES

After reading Chapter 15, you should be able to:

- LO1: Explain the overall objectives of the Sarbanes-Oxley Act (SOX).
- LO2: Describe the legal and institutional context in which SOX is implemented.
- LO3: Explain the major provisions of SOX.
- LO4: Discuss issues and approaches to SOX compliance.
- LO5: Explain ways small public companies can become SOX 404 compliant.

INTRODUCTION

LO1   In 2002, the 107th Congress passed the Sarbanes-Oxley Act of 2002. The full official title of the act is Public Company Accounting Reform and Investor Protection Act of 2002. Other titles used by Congress for the act are also descriptive of its purpose: Corporate and Criminal Fraud Accountability Act of 2002 and White Collar Crime Penalty Enhancement Act of 2002.

> An original bill to improve quality and transparency in financial reporting and independent audits and accounting services for public companies, to create a Public Company Accounting Oversight Board, to enhance the standard setting process for accounting practices, to strengthen the independence of firms that audit public companies, to increase corporate responsibility and the usefulness of corporate financial disclosure, to protect the objectivity and independence of securities analysts, to improve Securities and Exchange Commission resources and oversight, and for other purposes.

When he signed the bill into law, President George W. Bush commented:

> My administration pressed for greater corporate integrity. A united Congress has written it into law. And today I sign the most far-reaching reforms of American business practices since the time of Franklin Delano Roosevelt. This new law sends very clear messages that all concerned must heed. This law says to every dishonest corporate leader: you will be exposed and punished; the era of low standards and false profits is over; no boardroom in America is above or beyond the law.
>   This law says to honest corporate leaders: your integrity will be recognized and rewarded, because the shadow of suspicion will be lifted from good companies that respect the rules.
>   This law says to corporate accountants: the high standards of your profession will be enforced without exception; the auditors will be audited; the accountants will be held to account.

This law says to shareholders that the financial information you receive from a company will be true and reliable, for those who deliberately sign their names to deception will be punished.

This law says to workers: we will not tolerate reckless practices that artificially drive up stock prices and eventually destroy the companies, and the pensions, and your jobs.

And this law says to every American: there will not be a different ethical standard for corporate America than the standard that applies to everyone else. The honesty you expect in your small businesses, or in your workplaces, in your community or in your home, will be expected and enforced in every corporate suite in this country. (Office of the Press Secretary of the President of the United States, July 30, 2002)

The Sarbanes-Oxley Act (SOX) grew out of a decades-long trend toward more regulation over the accounting profession. Beginning decades before SOX, the Securities and Exchange Commission (SEC) and the accounting profession added new accounting/auditing requirements after each new major scandal. Finally, SOX was added after the 2001 recession and a massive collapse of the NASDAQ stock index, which fell from a high of around 1600 to a low below 400. The period was also fraught with major corporate scandals involving financial meltdowns in large companies such as Enron and World-Com in which thousands of employees lost their retirement savings.

The public outcry from the scandals was enormous, and Congress responded with SOX, which involves, as described by President Bush, "the most far-reaching reforms of American business practices since the time of Franklin Delano Roosevelt." The main idea was to restore public confidence in corporate America. However, such a broad objective could not be achieved without considerable cost, and reports showed that first-year implementation costs averaged around $2 million for all affected companies and nearly $8 million for large companies.

OVERVIEW, ENFORCEMENT, AND RULES AND REGULATIONS

LO2 As a general rule, the provisions of SOX apply to any company that files a 10K report with the SEC. The **10K report** is an annual report that contains the company's annual financial statements plus a substantial amount of other information. The specific provisions of SOX typically use the term *issuer* to refer to companies to which they apply. In the remainder of this chapter, the term *publicly traded company* is used interchangeably with the term *issuer.*

Many of the provisions of SOX require the SEC to create specific rules (see Figure 15.1). For example, according to Section 404, "The Commission shall prescribe rules requiring each annual report . . . to contain an internal control report. . . ." Other provisions simply amend the United States Code. For example, Section 203 states, "Section 10A of the Securities Exchange Act of 1934 . . . is amended by adding. . . ." In either case, whether a SOX provision directs the SEC to create a rule or simply amend an existing statute, the net practical effect is the same because rules created by the SEC under the act have the force of law. For this reason, no distinction is made between mandated rules and statutory amendments discussed in the remaining sections of this chapter.

Despite the fact that both SEC rules and related statutes carry the same force of law, the distinction is somewhat important because in the final analysis, SOX is only a basic legal template that cannot be implemented without an ongoing rule-making effort by the SEC. SOX clearly recognizes the need for this rule-making process in a number of ways. First, as mentioned earlier, the act directs the SEC to make rules. Second, the act explicitly establishes a new rule-making agency, the Public Company Accounting Oversight Board

FIGURE 15.1
Sarbanes-Oxley
Legal and Regulatory
Frameworks

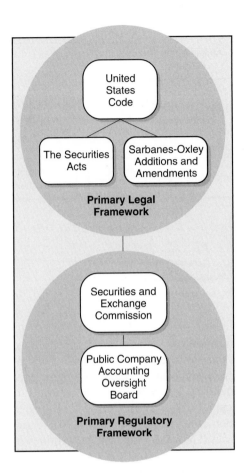

(PCAOB) discussed later in more detail. Third, many of the act's provisions are amendments to the Securities Act of 1934, which already falls under the SEC's rule-making authority.

In general, most of the provisions of the act fall under the scope of the SEC's oversight and enforcement functions. It is therefore important to discuss the organization of the SEC in relation to the act.

The SEC and the Sarbanes-Oxley Act

The SEC (see Figure 15.2) is administered by five commissioners appointed by the president; they serve staggered five-year terms. The SEC's organizational structure includes four divisions, 18 offices, and 11 regional and district offices throughout the United States. The four divisions include the Division of Corporation Finance, the Division of Enforcement, the Division of Market Regulation, and the Division of Investment Management.

The Division of Corporation Finance reviews accounting reports (and other documents) of publicly traded companies. It also monitors the accounting profession, including the Financial Accounting Standards Board (FASB) and other groups that contribute to generally accepted accounting principles (GAAP). Finally, this division makes administrative interpretations of securities-related laws (including SOX) and works closely with the SEC's Office of the Chief Accountant in making regulations.

FIGURE 15.2
Structure of the SEC

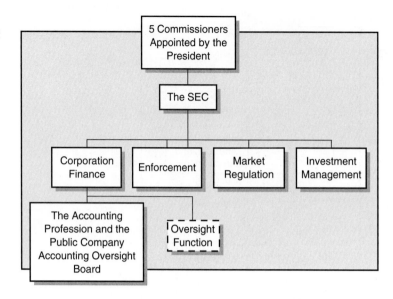

The Division of Enforcement can obtain a formal order of investigation from the SEC, which gives it the power to issue investigative subpoenas and can bring civil and criminal violations before a federal district court or before an administrative law judge.

The Division of Market Regulation oversees and regulates the major market participants, including, for example, broker-dealer firms and self-regulatory organizations such as the National Association of Securities Dealers. It also oversees the Securities Investor Protection Corporation, which provides insurance for securities-related account holders in member firms.

The Division of Investment Management oversees and regulates the investment management industry, including investment companies, mutual funds, and investment advisers. Its oversight functions include reviewing public accounting disclosures of the companies it regulates. It also oversees certain utility holding companies under the Public Utility Holding Company Act of 1935.

Of the SEC's 18 offices, the one most important to accounting is the **Office of the SEC Chief Accountant.** The chief accountant advises the SEC on accounting and auditing matters and works closely with various accounting and auditing standards-setting bodies, including the FASB, the International Accounting Standards Board (IASB), the American Institute of Certified Public Accountants (AICPA), and the PCAOB. The Office of the Chief Accountant also works with the public and the various SEC offices and divisions regarding the application of accounting standards and financial disclosure requirements.

THE SARBANES-OXLEY ACT

LO3 SOX contains 11 titles, each dealing with a different subject, and each title comprises multiple sections. The title and section numbers in the act in no way correspond to the title and section numbers in the United States Code. However, the language in the act's individual sections spells out various amendments to many sections of the United States Code.

FIGURE 15.3   **SOX and the PCAOB**

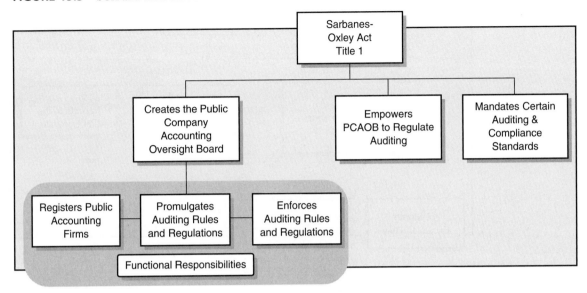

Title 1—Public Company Accounting Oversight Board

Title 1 establishes the **Public Company Accounting Oversight Board** (www. pcaob.org) under the oversight of the Securities and Exchange Commission (see Figure 15.3). The PCAOB consists of five members, only two of whom are permitted to either be or have previously been certified public accountants (CPAs). Furthermore, its chairperson cannot have been a practicing CPA anytime in the five years before serving on the board.

Title 1 is divided into Sections 101, 102, and so on up to 109. Collectively, Sections 101–109 accomplish three major objectives: (1) establish the PCAOB, (2) give the PCAOB power to regulate auditing and discipline auditors, and (3) mandate certain auditing and compliance standards.

Establishment of the PCAOB and Its Regulatory Powers

Under Title 1, the PCAOB's regulatory power is implemented by requiring that all accounting firms that audit SEC-listed companies register with the PCAOB, which then periodically audits registered firms for compliance. Audit firms that provide audit reports for more than 100 issuers must be audited annually. Other audit firms are audited every three years.

Mandated Standards

The mandated audit-related standards under Title 1 include the following:

- Auditors must retain their working papers for a minimum of five years.
- Audit reports must be reviewed and approved by a second audit partner (called the *reviewing partner*) in addition to the audit partner primarily responsible for the audit.
- Audit reports must include a review and evaluation of whether the client's internal control structure and procedures include records that accurately reflect the transactions and dispositions of the client's assets.
- Audit reports must include a review and evaluation of whether the client's receipts and expenditures are made only with authorization of the client's management and directors.

FIGURE 15.4
The Structure of SOX
Title 2

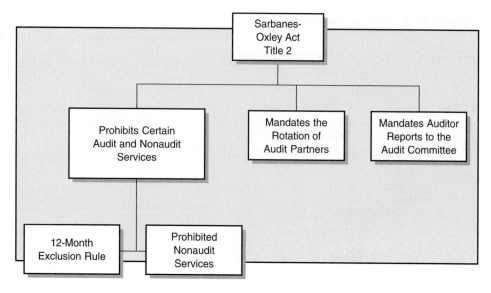

- Audit reports must include a description of any material weaknesses in (or noncompliance with) internal controls.
- Audit firms must adopt internal standards relating to professional ethics, the firms' independence from their clients, supervision of audit work, internal consultations, internal inspections, acceptance and continuation of audit engagements, and whatever other standards the PCAOB may set.

Title 2—Auditor Independence

Title 2 sets a series of rules that focus on ensuring that auditors are independent from their audit clients (see Figure 15.4). Collectively these rules have three major objectives: (1) prohibit auditors from providing certain audit and nonaudit services to their clients contemporaneously with audits, (2) require the rotation of audit partners, and (3) require auditors to report certain information to their clients' audit committees.

Prohibited Audit and Nonaudit Services

Title 2 is divided into numbered sections 201 through 209. Regarding audit services, Section 206 prevents a public accounting firm from auditing a client if the client's CEO, chief accountant, or chief financial officer worked for the public accounting firm and participated in auditing of that client in the 12 months prior to the beginning of the audit.

Although Section 206 does not prevent the former client executives from participating in the client's audit, it makes it impractical for them to do so because to recoup first-year start-up audit costs, auditors generally need to audit the same client for multiple years. However, an audit firm that triggered Section 206 would be permitted to audit the client for only one year.

Section 201 includes a list of nonaudit services that auditors may *not* provide their clients contemporaneously with audits:

- Bookkeeping or other services related to the accounting records or financial statements of the audit client.
- Design and implementation of financial information systems.
- Appraisal or valuation services, fairness opinions, or contribution-in-kind reports.
- Actuarial services.
- Internal audit outsourcing services.

- Management functions or human resources.
- Broker or dealer, investment adviser, or investment banking services.
- Legal services and expert services unrelated to the audit.
- Any other service that the PCAOB determines by regulation.

Sections 101 and 201 do permit nonaudit services (such as those relating to tax returns) not listed to be provided contemporaneously with audits if there is prior approval by the client's audit committee. However, the prior approval may be waived when the amount paid for the nonaudit services is no more than 5 percent of the total fees paid to the auditor, such services are not recognized as nonaudit services at the time of the audit engagement, and the services are promptly reported to the audit committee and properly approved prior to the completion of the audit.

Rotation of Auditor Partners

Section 203 prohibits either the primary or reviewing audit partner from providing audit services to a client that she audited in each of the five preceding years. In other words, neither the primary nor the reviewing partner can audit the same client for more than five consecutive years.

Mandatory Auditor Reports to the Audit Committee

Section 204 basically requires auditors to report to the audit committee all material written communications between the audit firm and the client. This section also requires that verbal discussions relating to alternative accounting treatments be reported to the audit committee. Finally, the auditor must also inform the audit committee of all critical accounting policies and procedures used in relation to the audit.

Title 3—Corporate Responsibility

Title 3, also known as the *Corporate Responsibility Act,* contains three numbered sections as discussed next.

Section 301, Public Company Audit Committees

Section 301 requires compliance with its provisions as a precondition for companies to publicly trade their stock. Companies not in compliance with Section 301 can be placed on probation or be delisted by the SEC.

The primary requirement of Section 301 is that each publicly traded company fund an audit committee that has the authority and responsibility to engage and compensate auditors and exercise general oversight over their work. The audit committee must also be given the authority and responsibility to consult external advisers and manage internal (named and anonymous) complaints relating to internal controls and accounting issues. Members of the audit committee must be independent; that is, they cannot accept any compensation from the company other than in their capacity as members of the audit committee.

Section 302, Corporate Responsibility for Financial Reports

Section 302 probably contains the most publicized of SOX provisions, namely the requirement that the CEO and CFO certify their company's financial statements. The certification is accomplished by requiring the CEO and CFO to file a separate report with each annual and quarterly report that certifies three things:

- The signing officer has reviewed the report.
- Based on the officer's knowledge, the report does not contain any untrue statement of a material fact or omit to state a material fact necessary to make the statements, in light of the circumstances under which such statements were made, not misleading.

- Based on such officer's knowledge, the financial statements and other financial information included in the report fairly present in all material respects the financial condition and results of operations of the issuer as of, and for, the periods presented in the report.

Section 302 also charges the CEO and CFO with designing an internal control system so that they become aware of all information relevant to the reports. Furthermore, within 90 days before each financial report, these executive officers are responsible for evaluating and reporting on their conclusions relating to internal controls. The officers are then required to report internal control deficiencies to the auditors. They must also report any incidents of fraud, whether material or not, that involve employees who have a significant role in the company's internal controls.

Sections 303–307

The remaining sections of Title 3 focus on the conduct of officers and attorneys. Section 303 makes it unlawful for any executive or director to improperly influence the audit firm in the course of an audit. Section 304 requires CEOs and CFOs to disgorge themselves of any profits from the sale of the company's securities, bonuses, or general incentive compensation when there is any misconduct-related restatement of the company's financial statements. Sections 304 and 305 together grant the SEC the authority to permanently bar executives who violate securities laws (which include SOX-related laws) from serving as officers or directors of publicly traded companies. Section 305 also grants the SEC the power to seek equitable relief in federal court when appropriate to help investors. Section 306 creates a complicated set of rules that prevent insider trading during certain blackout periods related to pension plans.

Section 307 requires attorneys to report "evidence of a material violation of securities law or breach of fiduciary duty or similar violation by the company or any agent thereof, to the chief legal counsel or the chief executive officer of the company." The report must be made to the company's chief legal counsel or CEO. If the CEO or chief legal counsel does not respond with the appropriate corrective actions, the reporting attorney must refer to matter to the company's audit committee.

Section 308, Fair Funds for Investors

This section permits the SEC to redirect civil penalties to defrauded investors. Prior to SOX, civil penalties were paid into U.S. Treasury funds, but in the first year of SOX, more than $1 billion in civil penalties was paid to defrauded investors. For example, WorldCom, Inc., satisfied its civil penalty obligation by paying $500 million to investors.

Title 4—Enhanced Financial Disclosures

This title contains nine numbered sections, 401 through 409. The general effect of these sections is to forbid certain personal loans and to mandate certain financial disclosures:

- Section 401 requires the disclosure of all material off-balance-sheet transactions and reconciliation of pro forma financial statements to the financial statements issued under generally accepted accounting standards.
- Section 402 forbids personal loans to directors and executives. Some exceptions are permitted, including those made by insured depositories if they do not violate Federal Reserve insider-lending restrictions.
- Section 403 requires that senior management and directors report changes in securities ownership within 2 days. Before SOX, the rule was 10 days.

- Section 404 is one of the most publicized sections of SOX. It literally created an entire cottage industry of "404 compliance" consultants, costing many firms millions of dollars each. Section 404 requires that the annual report contain a statement that management is responsible for maintaining and establishing an adequate internal control structure and procedures. It also requires that the annual report contain an assessment of internal control structures and procedures. Finally, it requires the auditor to attest to and report on management's assessment of the internal control structure and procedures.

- Sections 405–409 require that companies disclose whether they have adopted an ethics code for senior management (Section 406) and whether the audit committee includes at least one financial expert. These sections also mandate the SEC review of period disclosures of publicly traded companies and grant the SEC authority to make rules that mandate real-time (immediate) disclosure of material events.

Title 5—Analyst Conflicts of Interest

This title has only one section, 501, that seeks to ensure that the reports and recommendations of financial security analysts (also called *research analysts*) are not adversely affected by conflicts of interest. Specifically, this title does the following:

- Limits investment bankers' ability to preapprove research reports.

- Prevents securities research analysts from being supervised by persons who are involved in investment banking activities.

- Protects research analysts who write negative reports from retaliation by their employers.

- Creates blackout periods for dealers or brokers participating in public offerings. During blackout periods, they are not permitted to issue reports related to the offerings.

- Requires structural or institutional safeguards to ensure that research analysts can work independently from the brokerage side of business. It also requires a series of disclosures by securities brokers, dealers, and research analysts who make public appearances. Reports provided by these individuals must include the following: security interests held by the analyst, broker, or dealer in the subject company; compensation received from the subject company; and compensation paid to the analyst by the dealer or broker that depends on investment banking revenues.

Titles 6 and 7—Commission Resources and Authority and Studies and Reports

These two titles provided oversight funding, commissioned certain reports and studies, and enhanced the SEC's enforcement powers by permitting it to censure individuals who engage in unethical behavior. The specific provisions also give federal courts the power to bar those who violate security laws from participating in penny stocks.

Title 8—Corporate and Criminal Fraud Accountability

This title is also known as the *Corporate and Criminal Fraud Accountability Act of 2002*. It protects whistle-blowers and prescribes serious prison terms for those who obstruct justice or defraud shareholders. It also sets the penalties and fines for such acts not dischargeable in bankruptcy.

- Section 802 provides for up to 20 years in prison and fines for anyone who knowingly commits or attempts to commit one of the following acts with an intent to impede, obstruct, or influence an investigation by any department or agency of the U.S. government: alter, destroy, mutilate, conceal, cover up, falsify, or make a false entry in any record, document, or tangible object.

- Section 802 also requires auditors to retain their working papers for a 5-year period after the audit; failure to do so is subject to fines and 10 years in prison.

- Section 803 sets nondischargeable fines, penalties, and certain civil debts arising from violations of state and federal securities fraud laws.

- Section 806 provides protection to certain whistle-blower employees against retaliation, including the employee's reinstatement to a previous position, back pay, interest, and litigation costs.

- Section 807 sets a punishment of a fine or imprisonment of up to 25 years for knowingly defrauding shareholders of publicly traded companies.

Title 9—White-Collar Crime Penalty Enhancements

This title increases previous maximum prison sentences for mail and wire fraud from 5 to 20 years. Maximum prison sentences for violations of the Employee Retirement Income Security Act of 1974 are increased from 1 year to 10 years.

Section 906 perhaps yields the most salient provision in Title 9, making it a criminal offense for officers to willfully and knowingly certify financial reports not in compliance with the act. This provision distinguishes between those acts that are done "knowingly" versus those that are done both "knowingly" and "willfully," with the former act leading to a possible 10 years in prison and the latter act leading to 20 years in prison.

Title 10—Corporate Tax Returns

Title 10 is probably the simplest provision in the entire Sarbanes-Oxley Act. It merely says that it is the "sense of the Senate" to require that the CEO sign the corporate tax return.

Title 11—Corporate Fraud and Accountability

This title is also referred to as *The Corporate Fraud Accountability Act of 2002.* It does the following:

- Establishes a potential 20-year prison term for anyone who alters, destroys, mutilates, or conceals a record, document, or other object or otherwise impedes an official proceeding.

- Empowers the SEC to petition federal courts for temporary injunctions to freeze pending "extraordinary payments" to certain individuals under investigation for possible violations of federal securities law.

- Empowers the SEC to bar from serving as corporate officers any individuals who violate certain rules that govern certain manipulative, deceptive devices and fraudulent interstate transactions.

- Increases penalties for violations of Section 32(a) of the Securities and Exchange Act of 1934 to up to $25 million and up to 20 years in prison. Section 32(a) makes it a crime to willfully and knowingly provide false and misleading information in any application, report, or document that is required to be filed with the SEC. The maximum penalties had been $2.5 million and 10 years in prison.

SOX Rules, Regulations, and Standards

SOX itself is only the beginning of an evolving regulatory process because many of its provisions direct the SEC and the PCAOB to enact rules and regulations to implement SOX. For example, PCAOB Auditing Standard No. 5 established rules relating to the need for controls

workforce consists of only three brothers. The secret to the tremendous growth is in the brothers' smart outsourcing of almost all of their business activities. The brothers have decided to take their company public with the expectation of raising billions of dollars in equity money. To do that, however, they will have to become SOX 404 compliant. At present, the brothers are also the members of the board of directors and the officers of the company. One brother, a computer engineer, manages the Web site. The other brothers have degrees in management and engineering.

Is it possible for a three-person company to become SOX 404 compliant? What general steps should the brothers take to do so?

Part IV

Specialized Fraud Areas

Chapter **Sixteen**

Tax Fraud

CHAPTER LEARNING OBJECTIVES

After reading Chapter 16, you should be able to:

- LO1: Define *tax fraud.*
- LO2: Describe the types of tax practitioners who are allowed to represent taxpayers before the IRS.
- LO3: Describe the functions of the IRS and the role played by IRS personnel in the administration of tax law.
- LO4: Describe the types of taxes levied by federal, state, and local governments.
- LO5: Describe the format of the Internal Revenue Code.
- LO6: Discuss the principal tax evasion crimes found in the Internal Revenue Code.
- LO7: Recognize the existence of related Title 18 offenses.
- LO8: Discuss civil tax fraud penalties and the appropriate standard of proof.
- LO9: Compute a civil fraud penalty.
- LO10: Explain the statutes of limitations for tax fraud and the assessment and collection of underpaid taxes.
- LO11: Explain the methods of proof used by the IRS.
- LO12: Describe the types of tax protesters and discuss typical arguments made by protesters.

OVERVIEW OF TAX FRAUD

In this chapter, we discuss the types of tax fraud, often referred to as **tax evasion** (*tax evasion* is a legal term; in this chapter, we will use the terms interchangeably) and the investigation of it. The study of tax fraud is important for several reasons. First, when the frauds discussed in other sections of this book are committed, tax fraud is often present because the taxpayer either does not report the income derived from the fraud or misreports it on tax returns. Second, tax evasion can be the vehicle by which some persons satisfy their desire (a motive) for more money. Finally, the defense of a suspect and federal and state agencies such as the Internal Revenue Service (IRS) employ forensic accountants in tax investigations. Often, because the IRS and other agencies that employ forensic accountants—such as the FBI and the ATF—work together to solve crimes, forensic accountants who work for these agencies should be aware of the issues involved in tax evasion cases.

LO1 What exactly is fraud? The Tax Court, in *Mandt v. Comm'r,* TC Memo, 1955-226, states:

> Fraud connotes bad faith, a deliberate and calculated intention at the time the returns in question were prepared and filed, to defraud the Government of taxes legally due . . . [it involves] the personal intent of the taxpayer, and intent being a state of mind, seldom can one isolated act or omission be singled out as evidencing a fraudulent intent. Such intent is to be found by viewing a taxpayer's entire course of conduct.

The Internal Revenue Manual (IRM) assists IRS agents in carrying out their duties and provides this definition of **tax fraud,** in IRM § 25.1.1.2: "Tax fraud is often defined as an intentional wrongdoing on the part of a taxpayer, with the specific purpose of evading a tax known or believed to be owing" and states that tax fraud requires both an underpayment of tax and fraudulent intent.

To determine whether fraud is present, the courts look for objective manifestations of fraudulent intent called *badges* or *indicia.* These indicia have been developed over time, are found in case law, and are encapsulated in the IRM. According to IRM § 25.1.1.3, fraud indicia can be one or more acts of intentional wrongdoing by the taxpayer with the specific purpose to evade tax. Furthermore, fraud indicators can be divided into two categories: affirmative indications and affirmative acts. However, a taxpayer cannot be charged with tax fraud unless at least one affirmative act is present.

Affirmative indications represent signs or symptoms of actions that *could* have been performed for the purpose of deceiving or concealing. Indications, by themselves, do not establish that a particular process was performed with the intent to defraud. Instead, they are much like the results of analytical procedures performed by auditors; they point to anomalous events or relationships but do not offer proof as to what caused the anomalies. According to the IRM, examples include material unexplained increases in net worth, a substantial amount of personal expenditures over available resources, and bank deposits from unexplained sources that substantially exceed reported income.

Affirmative acts are actions that provide evidence that a process *was* deliberately done to deceive, undermine, or conceal the true nature of events. IRM § 25.1.1.3 includes examples such as omissions of specific items when similar items are included and concealment of bank accounts and the true source of receipts.

Therefore, a taxpayer who is to be charged with committing tax fraud must have committed an affirmative act and have violated the law willingly. These elements are discussed later and distinguish the crime of tax evasion from tax avoidance, the practice whereby taxpayers arrange their affairs so that they legally reduce the amount of tax they pay.

In the following sections of this chapter, we discuss tax practitioners, the Internal Revenue Service, the major Internal Revenue Code sections that pertain to tax fraud, types of taxes, criminal and civil tax fraud and the statute of limitations regarding such crimes, computation of civil fraud penalties, methods of proof, and common arguments of one group of tax evaders, tax protesters.

TAX PRACTITIONERS AND THE IRS

Tax Practitioners

LO2 Accountants, enrolled agents, tax preparers, and attorneys are those who practice tax in various capacities. Accountants—including CPAs and enrolled agents—prepare returns, assist in tax planning, and defend taxpayers before the IRS (accountants who are not CPAs or enrolled agents may not do so unless the taxpayer specifically designates). To be licensed as a CPA, a person must meet certain requirements and engage in a number of continuing professional education hours specified by the states in which she practices. CPAs are subject to the rules of tax practice outlined in IRS Circular 230, *Regulations Governing the Practice of Attorneys, Certified Public Accountants, Enrolled Agents, Enrolled Actuaries, and Appraisers before the Internal Revenue Service.*

Whereas CPAs pass an exam that is not regulated by the government and are licensed by the states in which they practice, enrolled agents must pass a rigorous two-day exam administered by the federal government; the exam is waived for persons who have worked for the IRS in a position that requires interpretation of tax code provisions. The exam tests applicants on detailed sections of tax law. Enrolled agents must engage in 72 hours of continuing professional education during each three-year period and, like CPAs, are subject to the rules outlined in Circular 230.

Attorneys must pass a bar exam that is administered by the states in which they intend to practice. Most often, they engage in the practice of tax law either as tax planners (the role played by many attorneys who are also CPAs) or as defenders of taxpayers who are facing assessments of tax; they may also be employees of governmental agencies such as the IRS, Department of Justice, and U.S. Attorneys Office. Attorneys must engage in a specified number of continuing legal education hours to maintain their license to practice and, like CPAs and enrolled agents, must abide by the rules contained in Circular 230.

The IRS

LO3 The IRS is the largest of the 12 bureaus of the United States Treasury Department. It is responsible for determining, assessing, and collecting the taxes that Congress imposes. The IRS encompasses four major divisions, according to type of taxpayer:

- **Wage and Investment Division**   Serves persons who file individual and **joint returns.**
- **Small Business/Self-Employed Division**   Serves small business and self-employed taxpayers.
- **Large and Mid-Size Business Division**   Serves corporations that have more than $10 million in assets.
- **Tax-Exempt and Governmental Entities Division**   Serves employee benefit plans, tax-exempt organizations, and governmental units.

Other divisions within the IRS include Appeals, Communications and Liaison, and Criminal Investigation.

The Criminal Investigation (CI) Division, called the law enforcement arm of the IRS, investigates potential criminal violations of the Internal Revenue Code. CI's mission is to encourage voluntary taxpayer compliance with the tax laws and to foster public confidence by means of effective enforcement of criminal statutes that apply to tax administration and financial crimes. Roughly half of all CI employees are special agents who as duly sworn law enforcement officers use criminal investigation skills coupled with financial acumen to solve complex cases involving both legal and illegal sources of income. Their duties include investigating not only possible violations of laws that relate to taxes but also **money laundering** activities and violations of the **Bank Secrecy Act.** In addition to following paper trails, special agents use their skills to obtain electronic evidence that could have been hidden by means of passwords, encryption, or deletion.

Other personnel who work for the IRS in the area of **compliance auditing** include office auditors and field agents. Office auditors are proficient in determining whether individual taxpayers owe additional amounts due to misapplication of law. Field auditors are most likely to be assigned to audit medium and large business returns, such as large proprietorships, partnerships, and corporations.

TYPES OF TAXES AND THE INTERNAL REVENUE CODE

LO4 Taxes are a means to raise revenue so that the government can provide goods and services. Tax types include taxes on income and goods and services (e.g., sales taxes). Several of these taxes are discussed next.

Individual Income Tax

The U.S. individual income tax is a tax based on gross income such as salaries and wages, interest and dividends, business income, gains and losses (e.g., due to sales of real estate), and rental income. The law allows adjustments to gross income for items such as moving expenses, contributions to retirement accounts, and alimony paid. Furthermore, the adjusted gross income (AGI) is reduced either by a standard deduction based on filing status (e.g., single, married filing a joint return) or by deductions the taxpayer itemizes such as mortgage interest, property taxes, charitable deductions, and employee business expenses. The income tax computed on the resulting taxable income is then reduced by credits for items such as child care and foreign tax payments. Finally, the tax after any credits is reduced by amounts already paid in the form of withholding payments and **estimated tax** payments. The taxpayer receives a refund if the amount of these payments exceeds the net tax due or pays the balance due if the net tax due exceeds the amount already paid.

Most states also impose an income tax on their citizens or those doing business within their borders. In fact, all but seven states—Alaska, Florida, Nevada, South Dakota, Texas, Washington, and Wyoming—levy an income tax, and two other states have a restricted income tax. New Hampshire has an income tax only on interest and dividend income, and Tennessee's state income tax is applicable only to income from stocks and bonds.

The income tax of most states is a flat rate tax that is based on the AGI from the federal income tax return. Many states offer a few deductions, such as interest income on federal government bonds, and allow an exemption amount for taxpayers and their dependents. States, like the federal government, usually require withholding of state income tax and/or remittance of estimated tax payments.

It should be clear, then, that any underreporting of gross income or overreporting of deductions on the federal income tax return affects the computation of state income taxes because the tax of most states is computed on a taxable income that begins with the federal adjusted gross income.

Corporate Income Tax

The U.S. corporate income tax is a tax on the income of corporations. The calculation of corporate taxable income follows closely the calculation of pretax income shown in corporate income statements: corporate gross income (i.e., gross income from its main operations) is reduced by cost of goods sold, if any, and then from this gross profit amount is added interest, dividends, rents, royalties, capital gains, and business gains (losses) to arrive at total income. From this total income amount, deductions (e.g., salaries, wages, utilities, and rent) are subtracted to arrive at an amount termed "Taxable income before any **net operating loss (NOL)** deduction." After reducing this taxable income amount by any NOL deductions to which the corporation is entitled, the corporate income tax is computed. This tax is then reduced by any credits and payments of tax the corporation has already made.

Most states levy a corporate income tax. This tax is sometimes called a *franchise tax* (in some cases, however, only a state intangibles tax is labeled a franchise tax). Often, the state return begins with the federal taxable income and makes certain modifications to that amount. Each state usually allows corporations to apportion the federal income to the state based on the amount of sales and expenses that are allocable to the state. In some states, a corporation that is a partner with other business entities in a state in which it is not incorporated may still be required to file a state return in that state. For example, if a Missouri corporation is a partner in a joint venture that does business in Florida, it must file Florida Form F-1120, *Corporate Income/Franchise and Emergency Excise Tax Return.* (Similarly, a partnership that does business in Florida must file Form F-1065 if one of the partners is a corporation.)

Sales and Use Taxes

Sales taxes are collected on retail sales of tangible personal property. Some states (e.g., Minnesota and Texas) also impose a tax on consumer services such as lawn care. Certain states exempt some items, such as food and medicine, from sales taxes. Sales tax rates can vary considerably from state to state and even within states.

Use tax is assessed by the state in which an asset is used. For example, when an asset is acquired in Kentucky for use in Illinois, the purchaser may be exempt from paying sales tax in Kentucky and, if so, will have to pay use tax in Illinois. Typically, sales and use tax rates are similar.

Employment Taxes

Employment taxes include social security (Federal Insurance Contributions Act, or FICA) and federal and state unemployment compensation taxes.

FICA

FICA is assessed only when persons who qualify as employees are paid (this tax, plus federal withholding, is reported quarterly by employers on Form 941). The employee portion of FICA comprises two parts: (1) old-age, survivors, and disability insurance (OASDI) and hospital insurance (HI). The OASDI portion is imposed on annual wages and salaries up to a specified ceiling that is indexed for inflation; no ceiling, however, exists for the HI portion. An equal amount is imposed on the employer for each employee. For example, if an employer paid $10,000 of qualifying wages during the year and the FICA rate was 7.65 percent, the employer would be required to withhold $765 from the employees' wages and remit $1,530 to the federal government—the $765 withheld from the employees' wages and the $765 that the business paid.

For self-employed individuals, a self-employment tax is imposed on net self-employment income (this tax represents both the OASDI and the HI). The rate imposed on self-employed persons is double the rate employees have withheld from their wages. The ceiling rates are identical to those that pertain to employees.

FUTA and SUTA

Federal unemployment taxes (Federal Unemployment Tax Act, or FUTA) are filed on Form 940 and state unemployment (State Unemployment Tax Act, or SUTA) taxes are imposed on employers to pay for unemployment benefits paid (or to be paid) to former employees who are unemployed. The amount of unemployment taxes paid to the state depends on the amount and frequency of the unemployment compensation drawn by the employer's former employees. In other words, an employer who has a history of hiring employees who rarely draw unemployment is rewarded by being granted a larger credit against the unemployment tax than the credit the employer would have been granted if the employer had former employees who drew unemployment frequently or for long periods of time.

Payroll Tax Avoidance

Some employers have tried to avoid paying payroll taxes by inappropriately classifying employees as self-employed individuals. The objective, of course, is to evade the employer's share of social security and the payment of federal and state unemployment taxes. For example, one owner and operator of a small business was sentenced to 27 months in prison and ordered to pay $471,690 in restitution on **conspiracy** and tax fraud charges. The owner and his bookkeeper/office manager paid cash wages to employees to avoid paying approximately $470,000 in employment taxes to the IRS. The owner also admitted that he and his bookkeeper actively attempted to avoid detection of the underreported cash wages paid to employees. The bookkeeper pleaded guilty to conspiracy and admitted that, at the direction of the owner, she kept two sets of books—one that reflected the true income and expenses of the company and a second set that reflected the income and expenses that were reported to the IRS.

Other Taxes

Other taxes, such as the estate and gift tax, present fewer opportunities for tax evasion. Because the estate and gift tax is assessed on the value of property transferred, the principal manner in which these taxes can be evaded is by undervaluing gifted or bequeathed property.

Another type of tax is the property (**ad valorem tax**) based on the value of real and personal property. Most counties, for example, assess a real property tax that must be paid annually and some states, such as Indiana, assess an annual tax on personal assets such as automobiles.

Thus, several types of taxes exist and can be evaded by potential taxpayers. The remainder of this chapter focuses on the federal income tax because it is the largest and one of the best examples of the taxes that U.S. citizens pay.

The Internal Revenue Code

LO5 After the Sixteenth Amendment was ratified in 1913, Congress began passing a series of revenue acts that resulted in a patchwork of statutes. Thirty-six years later, the statutes pertaining to tax law were reorganized as the Internal Revenue Code of 1939, and still later, as the Internal Revenue Code of 1954. Finally, the tax acts that were passed by Congress in the 1980s resulted in the most recent reorganization and resulted in the Internal Revenue Code of 1986.

The Internal Revenue Code (IRC) is contained in Title 26 of the U.S. Code, which is divided into subtitles A through I. Subtitle A, for example, addresses income taxes; subtitle B addresses estate and gift taxes. Each subtitle is further divided into chapters. For example, Chapter 1 contains the law pertaining to normal taxes and surtaxes, and Chapter 2 pertains to the self-employment tax.

Chapters are further divided into subchapters, which are further divided into parts. For example, Part I of Chapter 1, Subchapter A contains the law pertaining to the tax on individuals, and Part II of Chapter 1, Subchapter A contains the law on corporate tax. Parts are further organized as subparts, then sections, and finally subsections.

When we refer to *specific code sections,* normally we do not state the title, subtitle, chapter, subchapter, and part. For example, Title 26, Subtitle A, Chapter 1, Subchapter B, Part VI, § 179 is simply referred to as IRC § 179. However, any subsection, paragraph, subparagraph, and clause are cited. For example, IRC § 179 (b)(3)(B)(i) is read "Internal Revenue Code Section (or simply "Section") 179, subsection b, paragraph 3, subparagraph B, clause i." (This section, by the way, contains the law on limitations on deducting more than the usual cost recovery deductions for capital assets.)

Although most code sections follow this very structured citation form, some do not. For example, a section that pertains to the preparation of willfully making and signing a false statement is IRC § 7206(1). (Note the absence of a subsection number.)

PRINCIPAL TAX EVASION CRIMES

LO6   A taxpayer can commit various tax crimes. These include willfully evading tax or willfully failing to pay a tax (income tax as well as other taxes such as estate, gift, and excise taxes), making false statements on any return that is to be filed with the federal government, or aiding in the preparation of fraudulent tax returns. These crimes are discussed in the following sections.

Once a criminal tax investigation has begun, full payment of taxes, penalties, and interest will not prevent prosecution. While the filing of an amended return is not considered an admission of guilt with respect to a crime (because intent must exist before a charge of a crime can be sustained), it can be used to determine the amount of the underpayment.

Although some taxes are imposed only once (e.g., estate tax), most taxes are assessed annually. For annual taxes, each year the tax is evaded (for example, by the willful understatement or nonpayment of the tax) is considered one count. Therefore, a taxpayer who has willfully understated his tax for the years 2004, 2005, and 2006 can be charged with three counts of tax evasion.

Conviction of a **felony** tax offense usually results in the assessment of a sentence and penalties. For example, the following sentence and penalties can be assessed for *each count* of evasion (IRC § 7201):

- Imprisonment up to five years.
- Fine of up to $250,000.
- Civil fraud penalty of 75 percent on the portion of the underpayment due to fraud.
- Costs of prosecution.

In addition to these penalties, the taxpayer would owe interest on the underpayment for the period beginning on the due date of the return and ending on the date on which payment of the underpayment occurs.

The taxpayer is precluded from challenging the imposition of the civil fraud penalty because the IRS met the higher **standard of proof** required for criminal conviction. If a civil fraud action is begun before the criminal trial begins—something that does occur on occasion because matters could come to the attention of the IRS during the civil phase that indicate criminal wrongdoing—the civil phase is usually stayed until the criminal matters are settled.

Willful Attempt to Evade or Defeat the Imposition of Tax

According to IRC § 7201, any person who willfully attempts to evade or defeat any tax imposed by the Internal Revenue Code or the payment of the tax will, in addition to other penalties provided by law, be guilty of a felony and, if convicted, may be fined not more than $100,000 ($500,000 in the case of a corporation) or imprisoned not more than five years, or both, in addition to paying the costs of prosecution. (The $100,000 limit on the fine for individuals is now $250,000 per Title 18, § 3571.)

What if the person who commits tax fraud is married? Is the spouse liable for the tax and—worse yet—will the spouse suffer penalties? Spouses can be held liable for their share of the taxes evaded as well as their spouse's share of the taxes evaded if a joint return is filed because the liability is a joint liability. So, for a joint return, a spouse can be charged with evading payment of the tax that the other spouse fails to pay. If each spouse files a separate return, the nonevasive spouse can generally escape penalties. If, however, a joint return is filed, the nonevasive spouse can escape liability for payment and penalties if she is considered an "innocent spouse" who must not have suspected that tax fraud was committed.

Three elements of IRC § 7201 must be proven to sustain a charge under this section. The government must prove the existence of a tax liability that is substantially more than the liability that was shown by the taxpayer for a particular tax year, that an attempt was made by the taxpayer to evade the tax or payment of the tax, and that the taxpayer was willful in his attempt to evade the tax or payment.

Substantial Tax Liability

No dollar amount has been given to define the term *substantially,* and the courts have indicated that it is a relative term. Therefore, whether an understatement of tax or nonpayment of a tax liability is substantial is a matter for the government and the courts to decide.

Attempt to Evade the Tax

The taxpayer's evasion or defeat of the tax must be an affirmative action. This attempt need not be the filing of a false return; it could be, for example, not filing a return. The concept of "attempt" under IRC § 7201 differs from that under common law, which defines an *attempt* as an act that is directed at completing an offense and that results in a penalty that is generally less than the penalty that results from completion of the offense. For purposes of IRC § 7201, the *attempt* is the crux of the crime; whether the attempt was successful or unsuccessful is of no consequence to the taxpayer's guilt. Some examples of attempt include keeping a double set of books, destroying books and records, making false entries in the books, creating fictitious invoices, and engaging in a large number of cash transactions in a business not normally known to have such transactions.

Willful Intent

How is willfulness proven? In other words, how can intent be shown? The taxpayer's lack of filing (for years before or after the year of offense) or attempt to conceal income, for example, can show willfulness. Courts have routinely rejected arguments by the taxpayer that failure to file should be excused because of pressures of business and personal matters, fear that filing will cause the government to notice the taxpayer had failed to file in previous years, and intent to file in the future. While not an excuse for failure to file, **good faith beliefs**—such as the belief that returns could not be filed unless payment accompanied them, coupled with an inability to pay—have been found to be a sufficient defense against willfulness.

Willfully Attempting to Evade   The attempt must be more than merely an act; it must be carried out with intent to understate a tax liability. As with other types of fraud, intent is usually shown through a series of actions that create a pattern of behavior consistent with committing fraud. The preceding examples of attempt encapsulate this concept of intent. Other examples include substantially understating sales or overstating expenses, overstating the basis of capital assets for the purpose of lowering the tax associated with capital gains (or increasing the amount of cost recovery deductions taken), not reporting political bribes as income, and characterizing dividends as salaries. In other words, the attempt must be carried out with a willfulness to evade a tax or the payment of a tax. In *Cheek v. United States* (498 US 192, 201 (1991)), willfulness was defined as a "*voluntary and intentional* violation of a *known* legal duty" [emphasis added].

Knowledge of the law must exist before a taxpayer can be considered to have willfully attempted to evade a tax or the payment of a tax. Furthermore, a good faith misunderstanding of the law or even a good faith belief by the taxpayer that she is not violating the law will prevent a finding of willfulness. (But a good faith belief that the income tax is unconstitutional is not a valid defense to willfulness, and thus will not establish a successful defense in a tax fraud case.) If a taxpayer acts willfully to avoid obtaining knowledge, he has not acted in good faith; furthermore, he will have difficulty establishing that any underpayment (or nonpayment) was due to a good faith misunderstanding because exposure to information is necessary before a misunderstanding can be formed.

Although ignorance of the law generally is no excuse, criminal tax cases are usually recognized as an exception to this rule. The basis is that tax law is often so complex that even recognized experts can differ in their opinion of its application. Ignorance or a misunderstanding of tax law is excusable if the law itself is vague or ambiguous or the taxpayer relied, in good faith, on the advice of a tax adviser—but only if the taxpayer disclosed all relevant facts to the adviser.

Willfully Failing to Collect or Remit Tax   According to IRC § 7202, any person who has a duty to collect, account for, and remit any tax imposed by the Internal Revenue Code and who willfully fails to do so is guilty of a felony and, if convicted, in addition to other penalties provided by law, can be fined not more than $10,000, imprisoned not more than five years, or both, and pay costs of prosecution. 18 USC § 3571 has now raised the maximum fine under IRC § 7202 to $250,000 for individuals ($500,000 in the case of a corporation).

The taxes to which IRC § 7202 applies include federal income, social security, and FUTA. Violations can be classified in the following two categories:

- Willful failure to collect the taxes.
- Willful failure to account for these taxes and to remit them.

To be convicted for the willful failure to *collect tax,* the taxpayer must have had the duty to collect, account for, and remit the tax; have failed to collect the tax; and must have done this willfully. To be convicted of the willful failure to *account for and remit the taxes* that the taxpayer had a duty to collect, the taxpayer must have had the duty to collect, account for, and remit the tax; failed to truthfully account for the tax; failed to remit the tax; and acted willfully. Few prosecutions have occurred under this section.

Instead of being charged under IRC § 7202—which requires proof of willfulness—taxpayers are more likely to be charged under IRC § 7215 for either failing to collect, account for truthfully, or remit taxes held in trust or for failure to make deposits, payments, or file returns relating to taxes held in trust. (The "taxes held in trust" are often payroll taxes.) The penalty for committing this crime is a sentence of up to one year imprisonment and not more than a $100,000 fine for an individual ($200,000 for a corporation).

The taxpayer has the burden to prove that no liability existed. Defenses of the taxpayer include showing that there was reasonable doubt that the law required collection or that the taxpayer was not the person who should have been responsible for collecting it. Another reasonable defense is that the taxpayer's failure to comply was due to circumstances beyond the taxpayer's control.

Willfully Failing to Pay Tax, File Return, or Supply Information   According to IRC § 7203, any person required by the Internal Revenue Code to pay tax (including estimated tax) and who willfully fails to pay this estimated tax or tax, file a return, keep records, or supply requested information will, in addition to other penalties provided by law, be guilty of a **misdemeanor** and be fined not more than $100,000 ($200,000 for a corporation), imprisoned not more than one year, or both, in addition to paying costs of prosecution.

According to 18 USC § 3571, the maximum fine for misdemeanors punishable by imprisonment of more than six months is now $100,000 for individuals and $200,000 for corporations.

IRC § 7203 specifies four punishable offenses:

1. Willful failure to make (i.e., file) a return.
2. Willful failure to supply information.
3. Willful failure to pay tax and estimated tax.
4. Willful failure to maintain records.

The offense most frequently charged under IRC § 7203 is the willful failure to file a return. To be convicted under this statute, the taxpayer must have had a legal duty to file a return for the taxable year for which she was charged and willfully failed to file a timely return.

Whether the defendant had a legal duty to file a return is an issue of fact: Did the defendant have an amount of gross income that exceeded the filing threshold found in IRC § 6012? If so, this element is satisfied. Whether the defendant failed to file a timely return is satisfied by testimony by an IRS representative that a diligent search for the return in question has been completed and no return has been found. What if the defendant alleges that he filed a return, but the IRS alleges that the document filed is not a "return"? To be considered a return, the document filed must contain adequate information regarding the defendant's income and deductions so that the IRS can determine the tax liability.

A similar issue exists when a taxpayer wishes to avoid self-incrimination by asserting the Fifth Amendment privilege. The Fifth Amendment privilege cannot be used to excuse the taxpayer from filing a return; however, the privilege can be asserted with respect to specific questions on the return. Furthermore, a "good faith" claim of the privilege is an adequate defense to the charge of willfulness.

The taxpayer's failure must have been willful for him to be prosecuted successfully. The concept of "willfulness" in IRC § 7203 is the same as that found in IRC § 7201: a voluntary, intentional violation of a known legal duty (that is, to file a timely return). An erroneous belief formulated in good faith is a successful defense to willfulness, but a good faith belief that the law is unconstitutional is not a defense as discussed later.

Under IRC § 7203, taxpayers can be charged for willful failure to supply information. For example, the failure to provide a partnership balance sheet (a required part of the partnership return) after repeated requests for it was considered a willful failure to supply information under the statute that preceded IRC § 7203. If the information the taxpayer failed to supply is on a return the taxpayer failed to file, the taxpayer cannot be charged with two separate offenses—the failure to supply information and the failure to file.

IRC § 7203 also is used to charge taxpayers with the willful failure to pay tax and estimated tax. If the failure to pay is of estimated taxes, IRC § 7203 does not apply if a civil penalty under IRC § 6654 (pertaining to individuals' underpayment of estimated tax) or IRC § 6655 (pertaining to underpayment of corporate estimated tax) applies. Therefore, IRC § 7203 does not apply in the case of small underpayments. Furthermore, IRC § 7203 does not apply with respect to the failure to pay if there is no addition to tax under IRC §§ 6654 or 6655. (IRC §§ 6654 and 6655 relate to the exceptions to the estimated tax underpayment penalties.) For example, if the income tax withheld from a taxpayer's salary for the current tax year is equal to or more than the total income tax liability of the preceding tax year, no penalty applies. Therefore, if the taxpayer has met the minimum amount to be paid as estimated tax as specified in IRC §§ 6654 or 6655, the taxpayer cannot be charged with the more serious charge under IRC § 7203.

The failure to pay must be willful; the courts have said that the defendant who had the ability to pay must have intentionally and deliberately refused to do so. More recent cases have held that financial inability (due to lack of liquid assets) at the time the tax was due does not excuse the defendant from criminal penalties for willful failure to pay. Of course, there can be exceptions to this rule; a taxpayer with financial inability to pay taxes could escape prosecution under IRC § 7203 if the inability was the result of a compelling situation, such as the payment of medical bills.

According to the **lesser included offense doctrine,** if a defendant has been charged under IRC § 7201 and IRC § 7203 and one of the facts to be determined by the jury is the affirmative act required for prosecution under IRC § 7201, the jury can **acquit** on the IRC § 7201 offense and still find the defendant guilty under IRC § 7203. This is so because IRC § 7203 is the lesser included offense. For example, assume that a taxpayer is charged with violating IRC § 7201 and IRC § 7203. The IRC § 7203 charge was asserted because the taxpayer failed to pay the tax shown on the return filed. Also assume that the government could not prove that the taxpayer willfully evaded the tax (the IRC § 7201 charge) because it could not show that the taxpayer committed an affirmative act. If the government could show that the taxpayer willfully failed to pay the tax, the defendant could be found guilty under IRC § 7203. If, however, the defendant is found guilty of both IRC § 7201 and IRC § 7203, the offenses merge for purposes of sentencing, and separate convictions and sentences for violating the two statutes are not imposed.

Under IRC § 7203, the taxpayer can be convicted of the willful failure to maintain required records. However, there are no known cases of prosecution under this section.

Delivering Fraudulent Returns, Statements, or Other Documents According to IRC § 7207, taxpayers who willfully deliver or disclose any list, return, account, statement, or other document, that they know to be fraudulent or false as to any material matter shall be fined—as modified by 18 USC § 3571—not more than $100,000 ($200,000 in the case of a corporation), imprisoned not more than one year, or both. IRC § 7207 applies to both tax returns and other documents. This statute is rarely used; its use has been limited to prosecuting persons who alter canceled checks and invoices to support inflated deductions in circumstances in which felony prosecutions are not warranted.

Furnishing Fraudulent Statement or Failing to Provide a Withholding Statement to an Employee According to IRC § 7204, instead of any penalty other than the one provided by IRC § 6674 (pertaining to furnishing a fraudulent statement or failure to furnish a statement to an employee), any person convicted under IRC § 7204 can be fined—as modified by 18 USC § 3571—not more than $100,000 ($200,000 in the case of a corporation), be imprisoned not more than one year, or both.

IRC § 6674 stipulates the penalty for providing fraudulent statements to employees or the failure to furnish a statement to employees in accordance with IRC § 6051 (employers must provide a W-2 statement to their employees on which their wages, withholding amounts, and other information is to be reported). The civil penalty provided in IRC § 6674 is in addition to the criminal penalty specified in IRC § 7204 and is $50 for each failure to provide a W-2. IRC § 7207 is the exclusive criminal sanction for providing a false W-2 form to an employee and is the exclusive sanction when the employer provides a false **W-3 form** to the IRS.

Fraudulently Withholding Exemption Certificate and Failing to Supply Information IRC § 7205(a) states that any individual required to furnish an employer information about income tax withholding violates that law if the employee willfully supplies false or fraudulent information or willfully fails to supply the required information and the failure results in the withholding of less tax than had the true information been supplied. The penalty under this section, in addition to any other penalty provided by law, is—as modified by 18 USC § 3571—a maximum fine of up to $1,000, imprisonment of not more than one year, or both.

Invocation of this section can occur if the taxpayer employee signed a **W-4 form** that was false or fraudulent or failed to furnish a signed W-4 form and did so willfully.

The government proves the employee's failure to furnish a signed W-4 form by obtaining a subpoena for this information from the employer. As to whether the information was false or fraudulent, the government must prove that the employee knew the W-4 form was false or fraudulent when he signed and submitted it to the employer and acted willfully. The government need not prove that the defendant intended to deceive nor is reliance on the information required to prove the number of exemptions to which the defendant is entitled.

When an employee files a false W-4 form and fails to file returns while a significant **tax deficiency** exists, evasion charges may be filed under IRC § 7201, IRC § 7203, and IRC § 7205.

IRC § 7205(b) addresses a related matter. It provides that taxpayers must furnish taxpayer identification numbers to banks and other payers of interest and dividends. Failure to provide this information or providing false information can result in penalties as high as $1,000, imprisonment of not more than one year, or both.

Committing Fraud and Making False Statements   According to IRC § 7206(1), any person who willfully makes (i.e., prepares and files) and subscribes to (e.g., signs) any return, statement, or other document that contains or is verified by a written declaration that it is made under penalties of perjury and that the person does not believe to be true and correct as to every material matter, can be subject to penalties including a fine of not more than $100,000 (now $250,000 per 18 USC § 3571) in the case of individuals ($500,000 in the case of a corporation), imprisonment of not more than three years, or both, in addition to paying the costs of prosecution. This section applies to income tax returns of individuals, corporations, and partnerships, as well as amended returns, gift and estate tax returns, excise tax returns, extensions of time to file, and offers in compromise. It applies to a much broader array of offenses than does IRC § 7201. For example, IRC § 7206(1) applies if the taxpayer characterized illicit sales of drugs as sales of nutritional supplements on an income tax return.

Note that no tax deficiency is required for IRC § 7206(1). Usually, this provision is utilized when the government can prove that a material deficiency exists but has difficulty proving a precise amount (if it could prove a tax deficiency amount, it would indict under IRC § 7201). IRC § 7206(1) may be asserted when IRC § 7201 is also asserted in case the tax deficiency requirement of IRC § 7201 cannot be supported.

One of the requirements of IRC § 7206(1) is that the return (or other statement or document) be signed. A signature on a return is preliminary evidence that the person who signed it knew its contents. Although the government is required to prove beyond a reasonable doubt that the signature is that of the taxpayer, the fact that an individual's name is signed to the return, statement, or other document is **prima facie** evidence that the person actually signed the return. Therefore, if the taxpayer does not present evidence that suggests that the signature is not hers, the signature is assumed to be her signature.

One distinction between IRC § 7201 and IRC § 7206(1) is that under IRC § 7201, the government must prove that a substantial amount of tax is due—*substantial* meaning material in terms of *amount.* When charging under IRC § 7206(1), however, the government need not prove a tax deficiency; thus, the materiality element of IRC § 7206(1) can be one that refers to a matter such as the truthfulness of a statement made on a tax return. This means that the taxpayer could have avoided taking deductions to which he was entitled and, if he did so willingly, could be prosecuted under IRC § 7206(1). The definition of *material* for purposes of IRC § 7206(1) refers to whether the item has an inherent tendency to influence the ability of the IRS to ascertain the accuracy of the return, statement, or document. Note that the item must have only an "inherent tendency to influence"; therefore, the false statement need not have actually affected an IRS examination, nor must the IRS show that it relied on the false statement.

Examples of false statements of a material matter include overstating inventories, omitting gross receipts, falsely describing items of income and deductions, failing to include persons on payroll tax returns who were improperly characterized as contractors, and falsely claiming that estimated tax payments had been made.

A taxpayer can be charged with IRC § 7201 and IRC § 7206(1) offenses. If the government cannot support the IRC § 7201 charge, the taxpayer could still be convicted on the IRC § 7206(1) count as long as there is a factual basis for distinguishing between the two charges. For example, assume that a taxpayer is charged under IRC § 7201 and IRC § 7206(1). Even though the taxpayer reported all interest and dividends, he was charged with the IRC § 7206(1) offense because he indicated on the Schedule B of Form 1040 that he had no interest in foreign bank accounts. Also assume that the IRC § 7201 charge was unrelated to this false statement and arose because the taxpayer underreported his business income on Schedule C. In this example, a factual basis exists to distinguish between the IRC § 7201 and the IRC § 7206(1) charges.

If, however, no factual basis exists to distinguish between the IRC § 7201 and the IRC § 7206(1) charges, the IRC § 7201 count cannot be submitted to the jury because it would have no factual or legal basis for separating the two and thus the jury cannot acquit on the higher count of IRC § 7201 and find the taxpayer guilty of the IRC § 7206(1) count.

If the IRC § 7206(1) count is incidental to the tax evasion count of IRC § 7201, the IRC § 7206(1) charge is considered a lesser offense and merges with the IRC § 7201 charge of evasion. For example, assume that three owners of a hotel were convicted for filing a false partnership return that resulted in the underreporting of partnership income, an offense under IRC § 7206(1). Furthermore, the partners evaded the personal income tax, an offense under IRC § 7201. Filing a false partnership return would most likely be considered incidental to the evasion of personal income tax. Therefore, the conviction under IRC § 7206(1) would be merged with the convictions of the individuals under IRC § 7201.

According to IRC § 7206(2), any person who aids, assists, procures, counsels, or advises the preparation or presentation of any matter arising under the internal revenue laws related to a return, affidavit, claim, or other document that is fraudulent or false as to any material matter can be fined not more than $100,000 (now $250,000 per 18 USC § 3571) or $500,000 in the case of a corporation, imprisoned for not more than three years, or both in addition to paying the costs of prosecution.

Under IRC § 7206(2), the taxpayer is not required to have been aware of the falsity of the return or document for the tax preparer or adviser to be guilty. Furthermore, the tax preparer can be charged under IRC § 7206(1) for preparing a return or document that is false as to a material matter, particularly when the preparer signs the return as a representative of the taxpayer. The government could also charge the taxpayer and tax preparer with 18 USC § 371 (discussed later) if the taxpayer conspired with the tax preparer to make a false statement on a return or other document. Each partner who aided or assisted in the preparation of filing a false partnership return could be prosecuted under IRC § 7206(2).

Although IRC § 7206(2) has several names, such as *return preparer statute* and *aiding and abetting provision,* those names are misnomers; IRC § 7206(2) applies to a much broader array of potential defendants, not just tax preparers and advisers. One group of persons who has been the object of an IRC § 7206(2) indictment includes persons who cash winning tickets at racetracks for the actual winners. These persons furnish racetracks their name, address, and identifying number instead of the winners' information. The cashing individual is paid a percentage for this service and reimbursed by the winner for the tax paid on the winnings (usually, the tax rate of the cashing individual is lower than that of the winner). The IRS has prosecuted both parties (i.e., winner and cashing individual) under IRC § 7206(2). The basis for charging both persons is that the government is hindered in its ability to determine the correct amount of income the winner receives.

Other persons who have been prosecuted under IRC § 7206(2) include employers who pay their employees cash wages and provide their employees false W-2 forms; providers of false invoices purporting to evidence payment of goods who do not actually exchange merchandise but instead return payment to the "purchasers" (less a commission for their services); and appraisers who provide false appraisals so that the taxpayer can claim inflated charitable deductions.

Unlike IRC § 7206(1), IRC § 7206(2) does not require that the document contain a statement that it was made under penalties of perjury or explicitly require the filing of the return or document in which the false matter exists. Instead, it addresses the "preparation or presentation" of a return or document that contains a false statement that is material. Similar to IRC § 7206(1), a tax deficiency is not required under IRC § 7206(2), nor does the government have to show that evasion occurred; the false statement or item is the critical aspect of this section.

Interference with Tax Laws

IRC § 7212(a) specifies that anyone who attempts to interfere with the administration of internal revenue laws corruptly or by force or threats of force (including any threatening letter or communication) by trying to intimidate or impede the efforts of any officer or employee of the United States or in any way corruptly or by force or threats of force (including any threatening letter or communication) obstructs or impedes, or endeavors to obstruct or impede the administration of the Internal Revenue Code can be fined not more than $5,000, imprisoned not more than three years, or both. (If the person uses only threats of force, the person can be fined not more than $3,000, imprisoned not more than one year, or both.) For purposes of this section, the term *threat of force* means a threat of bodily harm to an officer or employee of the United States or a member of her family.

Notice that IRC § 7212(a) does not require the person to be successful in the endeavor to intimidate, obstruct, or impede; therefore, the actions of a violator do not have to affect an investigation; the government need only show that the person intended to intimidate or impede.

Force—or even the explicit threat of force—is not required for successful prosecution under this section. Implicit threats, such as a taxpayer displaying a firearm in view of an IRS agent or bragging about success in firearm target practice could, under certain circumstances, be sufficient to trigger the imposition of IRC § 7212(a). Furthermore, the person making the threat or otherwise obstructing an investigation does not have to be the taxpayer under investigation. For example, if John T. Obstructor impedes the investigation of another taxpayer, John can be prosecuted under IRC § 7212(a). In fact, the reach of IRC § 7212(a) is so broad that the offense does not have to be directed at a specific officer or employee of the government for a conviction to occur because of the section's wording: ". . . or in any way corruptly or by force or threats of force (including any threatening letter or communication) obstructs or impedes, or endeavors to obstruct or impede, the due administration of this title. . . ." IRC § 7212(a) then, applies to a broad range of offenses.

IRC § 7212(a) has become a versatile weapon against tax fraud. It does not require proof of a tax deficiency (as required by IRC § 7201), the existence of a return or document as required by IRC § 7206(1), or proof of a false or fraudulent return or document as required by IRC § 7206(2).

Forcible Rescue of Seized Property

According to IRC § 7212(b), any person who acts willfully to forcibly rescue or causes the rescue of any property after it has been seized legally or attempts to do so can be fined, for each offense, not more than $500 or not more than double the value of the property rescued or attempted to be rescued, whichever is higher, or be imprisoned not more than two years.

Two tests of "forcible" must be met before IRC § 7212(b) is invoked. These are (1) the use of any amount of force to successfully rescue the property and (2) any action that disrupts possession by the government. For example, if a taxpayer removes IRS warning stickers on the taxpayer's car after it has been legally seized, the taxpayer can be found guilty under IRC § 7212(b).

Termination and Jeopardy Assessments of Income Tax

If the IRS becomes aware that a taxpayer is likely either to depart quickly from the United States, to remove his property from the United States, in any way conceal himself or his property from the authorities or becomes aware that the taxpayer's financial status is in peril, it can act to make a jeopardy assessment according to IRC §§ 6861, 6862, and 6867.

A termination assessment can be made by the IRS when it believes the taxpayer might act to stop or interfere with the collection of taxes for the current or immediately preceding year. The tax becomes immediately due and the assessment includes the tax as well any applicable interest. For the current year, the tax year begins on the first day of the taxpayer's current tax year and ends on the date the IRS determines the tax due to be paid. The authority for termination assessments is found in IRC § 6851(a)(1).

The benefit of jeopardy and termination assessments is that they allow the IRS to act more quickly to collect tax debt, penalties, and interest than they normally could; that is, it can levy without prior notice. These sections are often used successfully against drug dealers and those who have a long history of not paying their taxes.

Related Title 18 Offenses

LO7 In addition to the Title 26 offenses of the Internal Revenue Code, certain offenses in Title 18 apply to persons who commit tax fraud. These include the false statement statute of 18 USC § 1001, the false claims statute of 18 USC § 287, and the aiding and abetting statute of 18 USC § 2, and the conspiracy statute of 18 USC (set section mark) 371.

The False Statement Statute of 18 USC § 1001

According to 18 USC § 1001, any person who willfully falsifies, conceals, or covers up information or who makes any materially false, fictitious, or fraudulent statement or representation or makes any document that contains any materially false, fictitious, or fraudulent statement or entry can be fined as much as $250,000 in the case of an individual ($500,000 in the case of a corporation), can be imprisoned not more than five years, or both.

Usually, in tax cases, the government charges that the offense described in 18 USC § 1001 occurs when a false statement or document is made or furnished to the IRS during an audit or investigation. These false statements or documents could include false affidavits provided to IRS agents, backdated documents, documents that had been altered, and even oral answers. Furthermore, the taxpayer *does not have to make the statement;* a defendant who knowingly and willfully caused the statement to be made can be found guilty.

The statement must be materially false, fictitious, or fraudulent. The word *material* here does not necessarily pertain to a monetary amount. A statement is considered material if it could affect or influence governmental decisions or functions. Note that the statement does not have to have an actual effect or influence but just the capability to affect or influence. Also, the false statement need not be submitted directly to a department or agency of the United States; this statute can apply to false statements submitted to federally funded organizations including private agencies. A taxpayer who seeks to avoid penalties as a result of relying on an adviser must show that all material facts were disclosed to the adviser and that the taxpayer relied on the adviser in good faith.

The False Claims Statute of 18 USC § 287

According to 18 USC § 287, any person who makes or presents a claim, such as a request for a tax refund, that the person knows is false, fictitious, or fraudulent to any department or agency of the United States is subject to a fine of not more than $250,000 in the case of an individual ($500,000 in the case of a corporation), imprisonment of not more than five years, or both. This section has been used to prosecute tax protesters, tax return preparers, tax shelter participants, and prisoners who file false refund claims. Proof that the claim was paid is not required for prosecution.

The Aiding and Abetting Statute of 18 USC § 2

According to 18 USC § 2, any person who commits an offense against the United States or aids, abets, counsels, commands, or otherwise solicits the commission of a crime against the United States will be punished as a principal. Furthermore, whoever causes the commission of an act that would be an offense against the United States is punishable as a principal.

The effect of this statute is to eliminate the distinction between principal and accessory developed under common law. Therefore, anyone who aids, abets, or assists a person in committing a violation of Title 26 (the Internal Revenue Code) is as guilty of the offenses as had he committed the offense himself. Mere association between a principal and a taxpayer charged with aiding and abetting is not sufficient grounds to convict, nor is even presence at the scene of the crime. Furthermore, the person charged with aiding and abetting must have committed some affirmative act and consciously assisted in the commission of a crime. The offense of aiding and abetting is not complete until the crime has been committed.

18 USC § 2 has been asserted in criminal tax cases against tax protesters, tax shelter promoters, and those who have assisted in the concealment of assets in tax evasion cases. The maximum fine is $250,000, imprisonment of not more than 10 years, or both.

The Conspiracy Statute of 18 USC § 371

18 USC § 371 addresses conspiracies to commit offenses against or defraud the U.S. government. If two or more persons conspire either to commit any offense against the United States or to defraud the United States or any agency of it and one or more of the conspirators perform any act to further the objective of the conspiracy, each can be fined, imprisoned not more than five years, or both. If the commission of the conspiracy's objective is a misdemeanor, the punishment for conspiring cannot exceed the maximum punishment provided for the misdemeanor. The act does not have to be illegal. It could be establishing a corporation or something as simple as mailing a letter. Any act directed at achieving the objective of the conspiracy can trigger the application of this section.

Note that 18 USC § 371 describes two separate offenses, either of which can be used as the basis for a conviction. These two offenses are called the *offense clause* and the *defraud clause*. The offense clause represents a conspiracy to violate a federal statute other than 18 USC § 371. The offense clause can be used to charge a conspirator who agrees to engage in conduct prohibited by any other federal statute. The government is not required to prove that the United States (or any agency of it, such as the Internal Revenue Service) was a target of the conspiracy.

The defraud clause represents a conspiracy to defraud the United States. It is used when a taxpayer or other person is charged with interfering with or obstructing governmental functions. Under either clause, the government need not sustain any loss to convict the

IRC § 6531 states that the rules of IRC § 6513 apply. Specifically, IRC § 6513(a) states that a return filed before the due date shall be considered filed on the due date for that return. If an amended return is filed to correct the filing of a false return, the statute begins with the filing of the amended return, not the original return. IRC § 6531 also provides that if a complaint is filed (in which the defendant is charged with a crime) before the end of the statute of limitations, the filing acts to extend the period by nine months so that an indictment can be brought.

If the defendant is "outside the United States or is a fugitive from justice" during any part of the statutory period of limitations, the time he is outside the United States or a fugitive does not count as a part of the statute (IRC § 6531).

Assessment and Collection of Tax

According to IRC § 6501, the statute of limitations on the assessment and collection of tax is generally three years. That is, any tax that arises under the Internal Revenue Code is to be assessed within three years after the return was filed (regardless of whether the return was filed on or after the due date, including extensions). If the return is filed before the due date, the statute of limitations on assessment begins on the due date. If, however, the taxpayer filed a false or fraudulent return with the intent to evade tax, willfully attempted to defeat or evade tax, or failed to file a return, the government can assess the tax or begin a proceeding in court for collection of the tax *at any time.* Note the difference between IRC § 6351 and IRC § 6501: IRC § 6351 applies to criminal prosecutions that can result in imprisonment whereas IRC § 6501 applies to assessment and collection of taxes and therefore can result only in a monetary penalty.

Liens and Seizures

When taxpayers owe taxes and do not have the means to pay the entire assessment (including interest and penalties), they can agree to an installment plan, negotiate an offer-in-compromise, or declare bankruptcy (but not all tax debts are dischargeable in bankruptcy). Installment plans merely allow a taxpayer a longer time to pay her taxes whereas offers-in-compromise may offer the taxpayer an opportunity to settle tax debt at an amount less than assessed by the IRS.

If, however, the taxpayer does not avail herself of these options or fails to make the proper payments under an installment plan or offer-in-compromise, the IRS has the option to file a lien on her property. Stronger steps the IRS can take include the use of levies, a legal seizure of property. Assets subject to levy include property, houses, automobiles, stocks and bonds and, most frequently, bank accounts. Equipment and accounts receivable of business taxpayers are also subject to levy. In addition to these actions, the wages of employees who owe back taxes can be garnished.

A taxpayer has 30 days after receiving a notice of levy to appeal it. Hearings are held by IRS appeals officers who issue determination letters. A taxpayer who does not agree with the determination letter can appeal the determination in court.

According to IRC § 7206(4), a taxpayer who attempts to place any assets beyond the reach of the IRS to evade or defeat the assessment or collection of any income tax and anyone who aids in this endeavor can be sentenced up to three years in prison and fined not more than $250,000 ($500,000 if a corporation). Similarly, in connection with an offer-in-compromise (or a closing agreement made with the IRS as to assessment of tax due), a taxpayer who conceals any property he owns or withholds, falsifies, or destroys records related to his financial condition can be imprisoned for up to three years and fined $250,000 ($500,000 if a corporation).

See Figure 16.1 for a summary of selected criminal and civil statutes.

FIGURE 16.1   **Summary of Selected Statutes**

Section Number	Description of Offense	Maximum Penalty per Each Occurrence
Part 1: Criminal Statutes		
26 USC 7201	Willfully attempting to evade or defeat any tax imposed by IRC or failure to pay such tax	$250,000 for individuals, imprisonment of 5 years; $500,000 for corporations
26 USC 7202	Willfully failing to collect or remit tax	$250,000 for individuals, imprisonment of 5 years; $500,000 for corporations
26 USC 7203	Willfully failing to file a return, supply information, maintain records, or pay tax	$100,000 for individuals, imprisonment of 1 year; $200,000 for corporations
26 USC 7204	Furnishing a fraudulent statement or failing to furnish a withholding statement to employee	$100,000 for individuals, imprisonment of 1 year; $200,000 for corporations
26 USC 7205(a)	An employee's furnishing false or fraudulent information related to income tax withholding	$1,000, imprisonment of 1 year
26 USC 7205(b)	Furnishing a false or fraudulent taxpayer identification number to banks or other payers of interest and dividends	$1,000, imprisonment of 1 year
26 USC 7206(1)	Making a false statement on any return or document that contains a declaration that the contents are correct when the signatory does not believe this to be true	$250,000 for individuals, imprisonment of 3 years; $500,000 for corporations
26 USC 7206(2)	Aiding or advising the preparation of a return, claim, or other document that is false as to a material matter	$250,000 for individuals, imprisonment of 3 years; $500,000 for corporations
26 USC 7206(4)	Attempting to place assets beyond the reach of the IRS with intent to evade or defeat the assessment or collection of any income tax	$250,000 for individuals, imprisonment of 3 years; $500,000 for corporations
26 USC 7206(5)	Concealing property or withholding, falsifying, or destroying records related to the financial position of the taxpayer in connection with an offer-in-compromise (or a closing agreement made with the IRS as to assessment of tax due)	$250,000 for individuals, imprisonment of 3 years; $500,000 for corporations
26 USC 7207	Delivering fraudulent returns, statements, or other documents	$100,000 for individuals, imprisonment of 1 year; $200,000 for corporations
26 USC 7212(a)	Attempting to interfere with internal revenue laws or threatening to intimidate or impede officers or employees of the United States	$5,000 and imprisonment of 3 years ($3,000 and 1 year if only threats were made)
26 USC 7212(b)	Willfully and forcefully rescuing (or attempting to rescue) property seized legally	$500 or double the value of property involved, whichever is greater and imprisonment of 2 years
26 USC 7215	Failing to collect, account for truthfully, or remit taxes held in trust or failing to make deposits, payments, or file returns relating to taxes held in trust	$100,000 for individuals, imprisonment of 1 year; $200,000 for corporations

(Continued)

FIGURE 16.1   *(Continued)*

Section Number	Description of Offense	Maximum Penalty per Each Occurrence
18 USC 2	Committing an offense against the United States or aiding or otherwise soliciting the commission of an offense against the United States	$250,000, imprisonment of 10 years
18 USC 287	Making a claim known by the maker to be false, fictitious, or fraudulent to any department or agency of the United States	$250,000 for individuals, imprisonment of 5 years; $500,000 for corporations
18 USC 371	Conspiring to commit an offense against or defraud the United States	$250,000, imprisonment of 5 years; if misdemeanor, maximum punishment for the particular charge
18 USC 1001	Willfully falsifying, concealing, or covering up information or making any materially false, fictitious, or fraudulent statement	$250,000 for individuals, imprisonment of 5 years; $500,000 for corporations
18 USC 1341	Committing mail fraud	$250,000, imprisonment of 20 years
18 USC 1343	Committing wire fraud	$250,000, imprisonment of 20 years
Part 2: Civil Statutes		
26 USC 6662	Underpaying tax due to negligence	20 percent of underpayment due to negligence
26 USC 6663	Underpaying tax due to fraud	75 percent of underpayment attributable to fraud
26 USC 6651(a)(1)	Fraudulently failing to file a return	75 percent of tax due
26 USC 6674	Providing fraudulent statement or failing to provide statement to employees	$50 per statement plus penalty under 26 USC 7204

METHODS OF PROOF

LO11   Much like the gathering of evidence for any crime that is committed, there are two basic methods of obtaining proof related to tax crimes: direct and indirect.

Direct Method

The **direct method** is called the *specific item method* by the IRS. An example of this proof method is the process performed by the IRS when it matches **Form 1099** with the tax return of the taxpayer to determine any failure to report gross income. It is a direct form of proof because it associates specific financial transactions with understatements. It is prosecutors' preferred technique because it produces the most straightforward evidence and the most difficult proof to dispute. Each transaction has two sides: payment and receipt. The "point-of-payment analysis" is an analysis that begins with the origin of the transaction whereas the "point-of-receipt analysis" begins with the destination of the payment.

Point-of-Payment Analysis

This analysis focuses on the payments made by the entity against which fraud is perpetrated. For example, assume that Sam Logan works for Victim, Inc. He was able to take a check written to Intended Corp. before it was mailed and, after altering the payee, cashed it at a bank located near his residence. Sam was caught when an investigator contacted Intended to determine whether it had received the check.

Point-of-Receipt Analysis

This analysis focuses on the expected receipt of cash by the entity against which fraud is suspected. For example, assume that Victim, Inc., collected $1,000 for a sale it had made to Source, Inc. An investigator requested confirmation from Source that the check for $1,000 had been cashed, thus matching Victim's copy of the sales receipt; it did. The investigator then identified the deposit slip on which the $1,000 was listed. She noted that $700 was deposited and $300 was given in cash to the depositor (who very likely did not intend to pay tax on the $300).

Indirect Methods

The other method of proof is a collection of methods called the **indirect methods.** There are three primary indirect methods: net worth, expenditures, and bank deposits. These methods can be used to show that the taxpayer's estimated income is higher than his reported income. These methods, however, cannot show the source of the understatement. The "proof" provided by these three methods is much like circumstantial evidence. In fraud cases, it must be combined with other evidence to support the assertion that the understatement of taxable income was due to fraud.

Whereas the direct method initially focuses on the details of specific transactions, the indirect methods begin with the generality of a transaction that gives little detail about the specifics of any income determined to be underreported. The indirect methods are based on this simple principle: Significant amounts of unreported income will eventually surface as assets or expenditures (e.g., a lavish lifestyle). All cash is either (1) spent for assets, personal living expenditures, or paying debt or (2) saved. Using these indirect methods, the forensic accountant can identify the proceeds of tax evasion at the point of receipt.

The indirect methods of proof are now known as *financial status audit techniques.* The IRS often begins its investigation by interviewing the taxpayer. For business returns, in addition to interviewing the taxpayer, the IRS tours the business facilities, evaluates internal controls, performs ratio analysis, and prepares a financial status analysis to estimate underreported income. It also may prepare a **cash T,** a list of sources and uses of cash, which allows the government to make a preliminary judgment as to whether the taxpayer has underreported income.

The starting point of any indirect method is the development of a financial profile, an overview of the taxpayer's financial condition. Four components of the financial profile are the taxpayer's assets, liabilities, earnings, and expenditures. Sources used to develop this financial picture of the taxpayer include the taxpayer (through interview), public information sources, business associates (including employers and employees), and records maintained by financial institutions.

The objective of indirect methods is not to identify specific transactions that could represent underpayments of tax although in some cases, these methods lead to specific items. Indirect methods allow inferences to be drawn about the appropriateness of the level of income reported by the taxpayer on her tax return. Regardless of the indirect method chosen, the method of accounting (e.g., cash or accrual) used is the same method the taxpayer used to report items of income and deductions on her originally filed income tax return.

Use of the direct method is not always possible, particularly when cash is not reflected on the taxpayer's books and records. In these situations, indirect or circumstantial methods are used. These include net worth analysis, the expenditures method, and the bank deposit method. (Besides these three, several other indirect methods such as the markup method and unit and volume method can be used. These methods are briefly discussed later.)

Net Worth Analysis

The net worth method compares the taxpayer's net worth at the beginning of the year with the net worth at the end of the year to arrive at a change in net worth during the year. The change in net worth is adjusted by various items (e.g., personal living expenses, inheritances) to arrive at a corrected taxable income amount. This corrected taxable income is then compared with the taxable income shown on the taxpayer's income tax return. Any difference is considered underreported or overreported income.

The beginning point for the net worth analysis is the financial profile previously mentioned. The financial profile is performed for the year preceding the one in which the taxpayer is suspected of understating his income. This preceding year is called the *base year* and is crucial to the correct performance of the net worth analysis. If the financial profile is not correctly determined, the credibility of the net worth analysis could be adversely affected.

The most important asset to be determined in the financial profile is cash on hand. This asset does not include currency in financial institution accounts or in investments but does include paper, silver, and checks that the taxpayer has not deposited. The most frequent allegation made by a taxpayer when faced with the results of a financial profile that suggests a material understatement of taxable income is that the taxpayer had additional cash on hand. This **cash hoard** argument can be compelling to a judge if the taxpayer can present evidence not uncovered by the forensic accountant during her examination.

Establishing the amount of cash in bank accounts—not a part of cash on hand—also requires careful analysis. Bank statements may not have a cut-off date that corresponds to the end of the taxpayer's year. Large transactions that occur at the end of the year should be analyzed to determine whether they should be included or excluded from the net worth analysis. A consistent treatment of similar transactions is extremely important in maintaining credibility. Other assets should be valued at cost, not market, value. Therefore, depreciation and appreciation of assets are ignored in net worth analyses.

The net worth formula is as follows:

	Assets
−	Liabilities
	Net worth of year being investigated
−	Prior year net worth (in first year, the "base year")
=	Increase in net worth
+	Identified expenses*
=	Total net worth increase
−	Funds from known sources†
=	Funds from unknown sources

*These are expenses that did not increase assets or decrease liabilities. They were used to pay for things such as personal expenses. Taxpayers should be given the benefit of the doubt when this item is estimated and only documented expenses should be used.

†These items include wages, interest, and other items that were not previously considered in the computation of net worth.

See Figure 16.2 for an example of the net worth method.

Expenditures Method

The expenditures method is also called the *sources and uses or applications of funds* method. It involves comparing the taxpayer's known sources of funds with known *uses or applications* (expenditures) of funds for the same period. The expenditures method is similar to the net worth analysis but examines items in a slightly different manner. The net worth analysis considers the difference between the assets and liabilities. Use of the expenditures method considers the difference between sources and uses of funds. In a sense, the

FIGURE 16.2
Example of Net Worth Method

	12/31/2008	12/31/2009	12/31/2010
Assets			
Cash on hand	$ 500	$ 1,000	$ 1,200
Cash in banks	12,000	16,000	18,000
Securities	15,000	20,000	14,000
Inventory	30,000	40,000	50,000
Accounts receivable	22,000	31,000	37,000
Furniture and fixtures	45,000	48,000	56,000
Real estate	125,000	125,000	190,000
Personal auto	30,000	30,000	42,000
Total assets	$279,500	$311,000	$408,200
Liabilities			
Accounts payable	$ 22,000	$ 17,000	$ 21,500
Notes payable	8,000	12,000	15,000
Mortgage payable	120,000	100,000	140,000
Accumulated depreciation	18,000	27,000	30,500
Total liabilities	$168,000	$156,000	$207,000
Net worth	$111,500	$155,000	$201,200
Less: Prior year net worth		111,500	155,000
Increase in net worth		$ 43,500	$ 46,200
Adjustments to Arrive at Adjusted Gross Income			
Adjustments to increase net worth (See Schedule 1 following)		56,800	65,200
Subtotal		$100,300	$111,400
Adjustments to decrease net worth (See Schedule 2 following)		2,300	36,100
Corrected AGI		$ 98,000	$ 75,300
Adjustments to Arrive at Corrected Taxable Income			
Adjustments to arrive at taxable income (See Schedule 3 following)		24,000	28,600
Corrected taxable income		$ 74,000	$ 46,700
Taxable income per return		42,900	25,700
Taxable income not reported		$ 31,100	$ 21,000

Schedule 1
Adjustments to Increase Net Worth (nondeductible items)

	12/31/2009	12/31/2010
Personal living expenses (following)	$ 47,600	$ 52,900
Federal income tax	5,000	6,300
Nondeductible hobby loss	1,700	2,300
Gifts made	2,500	3,700
Total adjustments	$ 56,800	$ 65,200
Personal Living Expenses		
Food & outside meals	$ 6,200	$ 6,700
Home repairs	2,700	1,400
Utilities	2,300	2,800

(Continued)

FIGURE 16.2
(Continued)

	12/31/2009	12/31/2010
Auto expense	2,700	1,000
Department store purchases	6,000	8,000
Recreation & entertainment	3,500	4,300
Vacation	4,600	5,200
Charitable contributions	1,700	2,800
Interest paid	9,800	13,000
Taxes	5,200	5,500
Medical	2,900	2,200
Total personal living expenses	$47,600	$52,900

Schedule 2
Adjustments to Decrease Net Worth (nontaxable items)

	12/31/2009	12/31/2010
Tax-exempt interest	$ 2,300	$ 3,100
Social security	–0–	–0–
Life insurance proceeds	–0–	25,000
Inheritance	–0–	8,000
Total adjustments	$ 2,300	$36,100

Schedule 3
Adjustments to Arrive at Taxable Income

	12/31/2009	12/31/2010
Itemized or standard deduction		
Medical (net of limitation)	$ –0–	$ –0–
Taxes	5,200	5,500
Interest	9,800	13,000
Casualty loss	–0–	–0–
Contributions	1,700	2,800
Total itemized deductions	$16,700	$21,300
Standard deduction (joint)	11,400	11,400
Higher of itemized or standard deduction	$16,700	$21,300
Add personal exemptions (2)	7,300	7,300
Total adjustments	$24,000	$28,600

net worth analysis is a modified balance sheet approach and the expenditures method is a modified income statement approach.

The formula for the expenditures method follows:

$$\begin{array}{rl} & \text{Total expenditures for year} \\ - & \underline{\text{Known sources of funds for year}} \\ = & \underline{\text{Funds from unknown sources}} \end{array}$$

Although the formula involves expenditures and sources of funds, information as to assets and liabilities is still collected because increases and decreases to these balance sheet items are either sources or uses of funds. See Figure 16.3 for a list of examples of applications and sources of funds.

The expenditures method, then, uses changes to assets, liabilities, as well as personal living expenses. See Figure 16.4 for an example (unrelated to the taxpayer depicted in Figure 16.2) of the expenditures method for an accrual basis taxpayer.

FIGURE 16.3
Examples of Expenditures (Applications and Sources of Funds) Method

Expenditure (Application/Uses of Funds)	Source (Source of Funds)
Cash on hand increases	Cash on hand decreases
Bank account increases	Bank accounts decrease
Any other assets increase	Assets decrease
Liabilities decrease	Liabilities increase
Personal living expenses	Earnings (salaries or business profit)
Purchases of assets	Sales of assets
Loans and gifts made to others	Loans, gifts, inheritances received

Bank Deposit Method

The bank deposit method is used to identify unknown sources of funds by reviewing bank records and other financial transactions. The formula used to conduct this method is:

$$
\begin{array}{rl}
 & \text{Total deposits to all accounts} \\
- & \text{Transfers and redeposits} \\
= & \text{Net deposits to all accounts} \\
+ & \text{Cash on hand increase} \\
+ & \text{Cash expenditures (see below)} \\
= & \text{Total receipts from all sources} \\
- & \text{Funds from known sources} \\
= & \text{Funds from unknown sources}
\end{array}
$$

Total deposits to all accounts refer to the gross deposits shown on the deposit slip less cash received (i.e., the net deposit). *Transfers* are funds deposited from another bank account of the taxpayer whereas *redeposits* are amounts withdrawn and deposited again (e.g., an NSF check). *Cash expenditures* are the total amounts paid out by the taxpayer during the period investigated less *net bank disbursements. Funds from known sources* include wages, gifts, inheritances, loans, and business receipts.

Net bank disbursements are calculated by using the following formula:

$$
\begin{array}{rl}
 & \text{Net deposits to all accounts} \\
+ & \text{Beginning balances} \\
= & \text{Net bank funds available} \\
- & \text{Ending balances} \\
= & \text{Net bank disbursements}
\end{array}
$$

The amount *net bank disbursements* is the maximum amount that the taxpayer could have paid by check. See Figure 16.5 for an example for an accrual basis taxpayer. (This example is unrelated to the examples shown in Figures 16.2 and 16.4.)

Other Indirect Methods

In addition to the net worth analysis, expenditures method, and bank deposit method, several other types of indirect methods are used to determine an approximation of business income. Two of these—the markup method and the unit and volume method—are discussed in this section.

Markup Method   The markup method is the preferred method when cash is not deposited and the total cash expenditures cannot be determined unless divulged by the taxpayer.

FIGURE 16.4
Example of
Expenditures Method

	For Year 2012
Funds Applied	
Increase in cash on hand	$ 3,000
Increase in cash in banks	6,000
Increase in accounts receivable	23,000
Increase in inventory	18,000
Increase in stocks and bonds	13,000
Increase in furniture and fixtures	9,800
Increase in real estate	150,000
Increase in personal automobile	26,000
Decrease in accounts payable	10,000
Decrease in mortgage payable	22,000
Personal living expenses	40,000
Federal income tax paid	8,000
Nondeductible personal loss	2,500
Gifts made	12,000
Total funds applied	$343,300
Sources of Funds	
Decrease in cash on hand	$ 2,200
Decrease in bank balance	2,500
Decrease in securities	12,500
Increase in accounts payable	12,000
Increase in notes payable	20,000
Increase in mortgage payable	125,000
Increase in accumulated depreciation	21,000
Tax-exempt interest	2,700
Inheritance	60,000
Total sources of funds	$257,900
Understatement (Overstatement) of Income	
Total application of funds	$343,300
Total sources of funds	257,900
Adjusted gross income as corrected	85,400
Less: Adjusted gross income as reported	49,050
Understatement of adjusted gross income	$ 36,350

The following example is an adaptation from IRM § 4.10.4.6.5.3. Assume that a taxpayer sells two products, P and T, and reports $190,000 of gross sales on his income tax return. The costs—verified with vendors—associated with the gross revenue are $70,000 for product P and $90,000 for product T. The forensic accountant ascertains—by means of taxpayer records and industry standards—that the gross profit margin for product P is 15 percent and for product T is 25 percent. Therefore, the cost of goods sold percentage for product P is 85 percent (100 percent − 15 percent) and for product T is 75 percent (100 percent − 25 percent).

Because the costs of goods sold (in dollars) and the gross profit percentages associated with the two products have been verified, this information can be used to determine the correct gross receipts and thus an estimate of underreported gross receipts as shown in Figure 16.6.

FIGURE 16.5
Bank Deposit Method

	For Year 2012
Total bank deposits	$170,000
Less: Nontaxable receipts deposited	(25,000)
Net deposits resulting from taxable receipts	$145,000
Add: Business expenses paid by cash	$78,350
Capital items paid by cash (personal and business)	26,250
Personal expenses paid by cash	9,350
Accumulated cash per receipts	3,000
Expenses paid and cash accumulated	$116,950
Subtotal (net deposits plus expenses paid and cash accumulated)	$261,950
Less: Nontaxable cash used to pay for expenses, capital items, and accumulate cash	(10,000)
Add: Accounts receivable ending balance	22,000
Less: Accounts receivable beginning balance	(18,000)
Gross receipts (as corrected)	$255,950

Unit and Volume Method Use of this method involves multiplying the number of units that were handled during the current period by the sales price. At times, the number of units can be determined from cost of goods sold if, historically, that account has been reliable. In other cases, the number of units can be determined by reference to major suppliers. This method is especially useful when the business being investigated produces (or sells) a large number of products that are not custom made.

The following example is an adaptation from IRM § 4.10.4.6.6.4. Assume that the taxpayer operates a coin laundry. The principal costs of washer loads are for the water and electricity consumed. According to the utility bills, the taxpayer consumed 4,000,000 gallons of water during the taxable year. Reducing the amount of water consumed by a reasonable amount of consumption pertaining to nonwasher functions, the amount believed to be directly associated with providing washer loads is 3,900,000 gallons.

Dividing the total number of gallons consumed (3,900,000) by the approximate average number of gallons used (30 gallons) during each washer load results in 130,000 washer loads. If the average price of a washer load is $2.25, the approximate receipts for washer loads is 130,000 × $2.25 = $292,500. Observation of a typical week reveals that customers' use of dryers equals 80 percent of their washer loads and that the average price customers pay to dry a load of laundry is $1.75. Therefore, gross receipts associated with dryer use is (130,000 × .80) × $1.75 = $182,000. Calculation of any understatement or overstatement of gross receipts is shown in Figure 16.7.

IRS agents and, in some cases, forensic accountants use these methods and others to determine any understatement or overstatement of taxable income not only in tax cases but also as an aid when investigating misstated financial statements or embezzlement schemes.

FIGURE 16.6
Markup Method

Calculation of correct gross receipts		
Product P	$ 70,000/.85 =	$ 82,353
Product T	$ 90,000/.75 =	120,000
Total corrected gross receipts		$202,353
Less: Sales per income tax return		190,000
Understatement (overstatement) of gross receipts		$ 12,353

FIGURE 16.7
Unit and Volume
Method Calculation
of Understatement
(Overstatement)

Gross estimated receipts from washers	$292,500
Gross estimated receipts from dryers	182,000
Other receipts (e.g., vending)	20,000
Total estimated receipts	494,500
Less: Sales per income tax return	422,500
Understatement (overstatement) of gross receipts	$ 72,000

TAX PROTESTERS

LO12   Tax protesters deserve mention because other taxpayers have believed some of the protesters' arguments justifying failure to pay taxes or have, at one time or another, been influenced to pay less than the amount required by law. The Internal Revenue Manual (Audit) § 4293.11 defines **tax protester** as any individual who advocates and/or uses a "tax protester" scheme. Furthermore, it defines *tax protester scheme* as a "scheme without basis in law or fact for the ostensible purpose of expressing dissatisfaction with the substance, form, or administration of the tax laws by either interfering with such administration or attempting to illegally avoid or reduce tax liabilities."

Tax protesters can be divided into two groups: (1) those who refuse to pay taxes because they do not agree with nontax policies of the federal government and (2) those who refuse to pay taxes because they believe the federal government has no right to impose an income tax. Those in the first group do not disagree with the government's right to assess and collect an income tax but with the manner in which the government uses the money it collects. For example, a number of persons who disagreed with the Vietnam War refused to pay taxes during that time because they believed that funding that war was unconscionable. Although this type of protest is interesting, it adds nothing to our understanding of the possible disagreements with the government over its authority to tax individuals and other entities. Therefore, our discussion is confined to the second type of protester—the type who has offered various arguments for refusal to comply with laws they believe do not apply to them. These protesters rely on several common arguments based on fallacies (see Figure 16.8).

Categories of Tax Protester Arguments

Some common fallacies underlie the arguments used by tax protesters to justify nonpayment of taxes. According to Daniel Evans (http://evans-legal.com/dan/tpfaq.html), the arguments themselves fall into one of three principal categories: constitutional arguments, statutory arguments, and procedural arguments.

Constitutional Arguments

Many arguments against the income tax are based on the Constitution. One of these is the argument that the federal income tax is a "direct tax" that must be apportioned among the states according to the census. This argument is not valid because of both a series of court decisions and the Sixteenth Amendment:

> The Congress shall have the power to lay and collect taxes on incomes, from whatever source derived, without apportionment among the several States, and without regard to any census or enumeration.

Another argument is that the Sixteenth Amendment was not properly ratified and is, therefore, not law. Tax protesters point out, for example, that only a few states approved the exact language of the Sixteenth Amendment proposed by the Congress and that errors of

FIGURE 16.8   Common Fallacies in Tax Protester Arguments

Action	Example
Taking quotations out of context	The quotation "Our tax system is based upon voluntary assessment and payment and not upon distraint" (*Flora v. United States,* 362 U.S. 145, 175) has been used by some tax protesters to indicate that the payment of income tax is not required.
Failing to understand the meaning of the word *includes*	IRC section 7701(a)(10) states that "The term 'State' shall be construed to include the District of Columbia. . . ." Some tax protesters claim that this definition *excludes* the states of the United States from the definition of "State" and that "State" means only the District of Columbia, thus failing to understand that the word "includes" is not a restrictive word but an illustrative word.
Failing to realize that generalities do not hold in every case	Certain tax protesters proceed from the generality that every person has a right to his own labor to the erroneous conclusion that the government cannot tax the results of that person's labor.
Assuming that the converse of the statement is true	Some tax protesters assert that if the IRC says "corporate profit is income," then the only income that exists is "corporate profit" and, therefore, the only entities that should be taxed are corporations.
Believing that labels determine the substance of what is being labeled	Some protesters believe they are not liable for the income tax because they are not "taxpayers" as defined by the IRC.
Inconsistently applying ad hoc arguments	Some tax protesters point out typographical errors in the various versions of the Sixteenth Amendment in an attempt to support the argument that the Sixteenth Amendment was not properly ratified while ignoring the fact that similar mistakes were present in the ratification of other amendments to the Constitution.

grammar were present in the language that other states approved. However, many court cases have upheld the validity of the Sixteenth Amendment, as mentioned in *Betz v. United States,* 40 Fed. Cl. 286, 295 (1998):

> Despite plaintiffs and numerous other tax protesters' contention that the Sixteenth Amendment was never ratified, courts have long recognized the Sixteenth Amendment's ratification and validity.

Statutory Arguments

Quite a few statutory arguments include the assertion that wages are not income. According to IRC § 61(a), "Except as otherwise provided in this subtitle, gross income means all income from whatever source derived, including (but not limited to) the following items: (1) Compensation for services, including fees, commissions, fringe benefits, and similar items. . . ." As far back as 1913, the courts have held that wages are income (see *Stratton's Independence Ltd. v. Howbert,* 231 US 399 [1913]). Typical of these cases is *Perkins v. Comm'r,* 746 F2d 1187, 1188 (6th Cir. 1984), in which the court said, "Wages are taxable income."

Another assertion is that the income tax does not apply to citizens who live in areas other than the District of Columbia and territories such as Puerto Rico. They base this assertion on the fact that the definition contained in the Internal Revenue Code does not include states; at times, this assertion is referred to as the *Section 861 argument* because tax protesters believe that wages paid within the United States are not a source of income as defined in IRC § 861 and thus are not a part of taxable income. However, the regulation that defines gross income, Reg. § 1.1-1(b), states

> In general, all citizens of the United States, wherever resident, and all resident alien individuals are liable to the income taxes imposed by the Code whether the income is received from sources within or without the United States.

In fact, IRC § 861 does not apply to U.S. citizens; it was created to specify the sources of income on which nonresident aliens and foreign corporations are to pay U.S. income tax because these taxpayers are taxed only on income earned from U.S. sources.

Procedural Arguments

These arguments include the assertion that the IRS is not an agency of the federal government but a private corporation incorporated in the State of Delaware or that it is a governmental agency of the Puerto Rican government. This argument is fallacious because the IRC established the IRS as an agency of the U.S. government. Specifically, IRC § 7801(a) indicates that the administration of and enforcement of the Code is to be performed by or under the supervision of the Secretary of the Treasury. Furthermore, IRC § 7802(a) established the Office of Commissioner of Internal Revenue in the Department of the Treasury and states that the officeholder shall have duties and powers as prescribed by the Secretary of the Treasury; IRC § 7803(a) indicates that the Secretary of the Treasury is authorized to employ persons to administer and enforce the Internal Revenue Code.

Pursuant to this law, the Department of the Treasury has adopted regulations in which the Internal Revenue Service was created. Reg. § 601.101(a) states that the IRS is a bureau of the Department of the Treasury and that the IRS is the agency by which the functions of assessment and collection of taxes occurs. The courts have subsequently upheld the authority of the IRS (e.g., *Young v. Internal Revenue Service,* 596 F.Supp. 141 (ND Ind. 1984) and *Crain v. Comm'r,* 737 F2d 1417 [5th Cir. 1984]).

Another procedural argument is that the tax laws apply to only "taxpayers" and anyone who is not a "taxpayer" is not required to file returns or pay taxes. This argument is rebutted by the court in *United States v. Bowers,* 920 F2d 220, 222 (4th Cir. 1990):

> The Code defines the term "person" to include "individual." 26 U.S.C. section 7701(a). The term "taxpayer," in turn, refers to "any person subject to any internal revenue tax." 26 U.S.C. section 7701(a)(14). The Code imposes a tax on all income, see *United States v. Sloan,* 939 F2d 499, 500 (7th Cir. 1991), and any person required to pay any tax must file a return, see 26 U.S.C. sections 6001, 6011, 7203.

These arguments, then, are often founded on misinformation and, at times, deliberate falsehoods. Most likely, the taxpayer desires to believe in the arguments to justify keeping more money for herself. However, the income tax and other taxes are here to stay. As long as the courts hold that the taxes and their collection are lawful, the government will continue to prosecute those who willfully attempt to pay less than the government believes should be paid.

Summary

Taxpayers are subject to various taxes, including income, payroll (FICA), estate, gift, excise, and sales. Failure to report and pay the appropriate amount of tax, as required by Title 26 (the Internal Revenue Code), can result in an offense described in any one of various fraud statutes such as tax evasion, willful failure to file returns and documents or pay tax, willful failure to collect and remit tax, making false statements, and aiding in the preparation of false returns or documents. Taxpayers can also be charged with crimes under Title 18 such as making false claims and conspiracy as well as mail and wire fraud. In addition to facing fines and imprisonment for criminal tax violations, taxpayers can also face civil tax penalties including the civil fraud penalty, the accuracy-related penalty, the penalty for failure to file, and the penalty for underpayment of tax.

The IRS uses various methods to determine an understatement of taxable income, including direct and indirect methods. The direct method specifically identifies unreported income or overstated deductions taken by the taxpayer. Indirect methods, while less precise, have been used to determine an estimate of the amount of understated taxable income. Indirect methods include the net worth analysis and the expenditures and bank deposit methods. Two other methods, used primarily to determine underreported business taxable income, are the markup method and the unit and volume method.

Taxpayers have used various arguments to rationalize the nonpayment of taxes (and, at times, the nonfiling) of income tax returns. These arguments are often based on constitutional, procedural, or statutory grounds and usually are based on either incomplete information or misinformation. If the taxpayer intentionally disregards the tax law and believes that it is either unconstitutional or that it does not apply to her, she is often labeled a "tax protester" and can be convicted of tax fraud.

Glossary

acquit Act of discharging a defendant (e.g., a taxpayer) from charges previously asserted by the plaintiff.

ad valorem tax Tax imposed by applying a rate to the value of the property taxed.

Bank Secrecy Act Act of Congress that authorizes the United States Treasury Department to require financial institutions to report any suspicious transaction that could indicate violations of laws or regulations.

cash hoard Accumulated amount of cash kept usually without the knowledge of others.

cash T Analysis of the cash received and spent by the taxpayer during a specified period; similar to the indirect method called *source and applications of funds,* but dissimilar to it because it is limited to an analysis of cash only.

compliance auditing Act of determining whether a person or entity has correctly complied with a law (e.g., the Internal Revenue Code) or procedure.

conspiracy Act in which two or more persons work (usually in secrecy) together to commit an illegal act or use illegal means to achieve an objective.

direct method Method of proof by which a specific item of income is identified as being unreported.

estimated tax Tax paid quarterly in advance of filing a return; the payment reduces the amount of tax due with the annual return.

felony A crime for which the potential punishment is either death or imprisonment of more than one year.

Form 1099 Informational form sent to taxpayers to indicate their earnings on certain types of gross income during the past tax year such as interest, dividends, and proceeds from the sale of stock.

good faith belief Belief formulated without intent to deceive or manipulate.

indirect methods   Methods of proof used to estimate understated income, such as taxable income, by reference to changes either in net worth or in the expenditures made by the person (or business) during the year.

joint return   Income tax return filed by two persons who were legally married on the last day of their taxable year.

Klein conspiracy   Tax conspiracy in which taxpayer is charged with conspiring with another person to obstruct the collection of income taxes.

lesser included offense doctrine   Doctrine invoked when a taxpayer is charged with two or more sections of the law and one of the sections is incidental to the offense described in one of the other sections; the lesser offense is merged with the section representing the more serious offense so that the taxpayer cannot be charged with both lesser and more serious offenses.

mail fraud   Use of the United States Postal Service or any commercial or private mail service to further a scheme or fraud.

misdemeanor   Crime for which the maximum penalty is imprisonment of less than one year.

money laundering   Process of obfuscating the source of illegally obtained income so that the income can be used for legitimate purposes.

net operating loss (NOL)   The excess of business deductions over business revenues; can be carried back two years to obtain an immediate refund and carried forward for 20 years to reduce the taxable income of those years until the loss is exhausted.

prima facie   Term that means "on the face"; refers to the appearance of what is being examined, not necessarily the true nature of the examined item.

standard of proof   Level of proof required in court; in criminal cases, is *beyond a reasonable doubt;* in civil fraud cases, is *clear and convincing* evidence. A lower standard, *preponderance of the evidence,* is often the burden of proof required of litigants to rebut the evidence presented by the plaintiff.

statute of limitations   Period of time within which charges against a potential defendant must be brought; if charges are not brought within this period and the taxpayer raises it as a defense, the charges ordinarily must be dropped.

tax deficiency   Excess of correct tax liability over the tax payments made by the taxpayer.

tax evasion   Legal term for tax fraud.

tax fraud   Act of deceiving or misrepresenting for the purpose of misstating a tax liability or to avoid the payment of tax.

tax protester   Person who refuses to file a return or pay tax (or both) as a result of the belief that the taxing authority is not using the tax collected in a morally just manner or that the person is not subject to the tax.

W-3 form   "Transmittal of Wage and Tax Statements" form on which the employer who pays wages and salaries reports to the Internal Revenue Service the amount of wages, federal income tax withheld, social security tax withheld, and other information filed; includes the number of W-2 forms transmitted.

W-4 form   "Employee's Withholding Allowance Certificate" to be completed by the employee for the purpose of indicating the number of allowances the employee wishes to claim for withholding tax purposes.

wire fraud   Use of electronic transmission to aid in the commission of a fraud.

Review Questions

1. Which of the following does *not* include tax fraud?

   a. A tax return in which the taxpayer deliberately underreports one income item but makes a mistake and overreports a second income item. The second income item more than offsets the first income item so that overall the taxpayer overpays taxes.

   b. A tax return that underreports income to correct for an error in overreported income in the previous year.

   c. Neither *a* nor *b* involves tax fraud.

   d. Both *a* and *b* involve tax fraud.

2. In identifying tax fraud, what do affirmative indications represent?

   a. Signs or symptoms indicating possible fraud intent.

   b. Evidence of intent to defraud.

   c. Signs or symptoms of evidence of intent to defraud.

   d. None of the above.

3. Which of the following is sufficient grounds to charge a taxpayer with tax fraud?

   a. The commission of an illegal act leading to underpayment of taxes.

   b. Underpayment of taxes.

   c. The commission of a negligent act that leads to underpayment of taxes.

   d. None of these.

4. Which of the following is a CPA *not* permitted to do in relation to federal taxation?

   a. Argue a client's case before an IRS office representative.

   b. Prepare complicated tax forms that involve complex legal issues.

   c. Act as a client's legal representative in a tax court.

   d. CPAs are permitted to perform all of the preceding functions.

5. Which of the following is *not* a division of the IRS?

   a. Wage and Investment Division.

   b. Small Business/Self-Employed Division.

   c. Large and Mid-Size Business Division.

   d. Estates and Trusts Division.

6. Special agents in the IRS Criminal Investigation Division are *not* involved in which of the following cases?

   a. Cases involving legal sources of income.

   b. Cases involving all violations of tax laws.

   c. Cases involving money laundering.

   d. Special agents in the IRS Criminal Investigation Division are involved in all of the preceding cases.

7. The income tax of most states is a flat rate tax; on what is it based?

   a. The net income from the federal income tax return.

   b. The AGI from the federal tax return.

   c. The taxable income from the federal tax return.

   d. None of these.

8. To what are use taxes somewhat similar?

   a. Intangible taxes.

   b. Franchise taxes.

   c. Sales taxes.

   d. None of these.

9. What is the most likely illegal scheme to evade estate taxes?

   a. Underreporting assets.

   b. Underreporting income.

   c. Undervaluing assets.

   d. Undervaluing income.

10. Ad valorem taxes may apply to which of the following?

   a. Real estate.

   b. Business inventories.

   c. Business automobiles.

   d. All of these.

11. A taxpayer who intentionally fails to report two items of income over a two-year period may be subject to possible maximum prison sentence of how many years?

   a. 5.

   b. 10.

   c. 15.

   d. None of these.

12. Which of the following applies to a taxpayer who files a fraudulent tax return and then, as a matter of conscience, immediately files a correct and honest amended return?

   a. Protected from prosecution after filing the amended return.

   b. Protected from prosecution if the IRS accepts the amended return.

   c. Protected from prosecution after a two-year waiting period.

   d. None of these.

13. When does the IRS normally bring actions for civil penalties?

   a. Before it brings actions for criminal penalties.

   b. During the time it brings actions for criminal penalties.

   c. After it brings actions for criminal penalties.

   d. After it brings actions for criminal penalties, but only in some districts.

14. A married couple files a joint federal return in which $10,000 in underpaid taxes is due. One spouse signs the return without understanding it. If the other spouse responsible for the tax preparation disappears without paying the $10,000, which of the following could be the fate of the spouse who does not disappear?

   a. Could avoid paying all or part of the taxes per IRC § 7201 as an innocent spouse.

   b. Could be held fully liable for the $10,000.

   c. Could be held liable for one-half of the $10,000.

   d. Could be held liable for 75 percent of the $10,000.

15. Which option is likely for a taxpayer with no knowledge of tax laws who files a personal federal tax return and claims depreciation on the big-screen television in his living room?

   a. Could be charged with fraud.

   b. Could be charged with fraud if a prosecutor could prove motive.

    c. Could be charged with fraud if a prosecutor could prove willful intent to make the depreciation deduction.

    d. Could not be charged with fraud.

16. An employer withholds federal taxes from employees' paychecks and periodically makes payments of the withheld taxes to the IRS. What happens if the employer files bankruptcy and is unable to remit the final payment of taxes withheld?

    a. The matter would be resolved in the bankruptcy court.

    b. The employer could be criminally charged regardless of what happens in the bankruptcy court.

    c. The employer could be criminally charged only if sufficient funds do not emerge from the bankruptcy to pay the taxes due.

    d. None of these.

17. Willful failure to file a federal tax return is which of the following?

    a. A criminal offense.

    b. A civil offense.

    c. Sometimes a criminal offense.

    d. None of these.

18. Failure to supply information associated with a federal tax return is a criminal offense defined by which of the following?

    a. IRC § 7201.

    b. IRC § 7202.

    c. IRC § 7203.

    d. None of these.

19. A taxpayer who alters an invoice to support an inflated deduction violates which statute that governs the delivery of fraudulent returns, statements, and other documents?

    a. IRC § 7201.

    b. IRC § 7202.

    c. IRC § 7203.

    d. None of these.

20. When a taxpayer files a false W-4 form and fails to file a return when a significant tax deficiency exists, evasion charges may be filed under which of the following in addition to charges under IRC § 7203 and IRC § 7205?

    a. IRC § 7201.

    b. IRC § 7202.

    c. IRC § 7212.

    d. None of these.

21. Which of the following applies to a taxpayer who, in an act of charity to the federal government, does not take material deductions that she is entitled to take on her federal income tax?

    a. Is acting as a good citizen.

    b. Is subject to a civil penalty that depends on the amount of taxes overpaid.

    c. Is subject to criminal prosecution.

    d. None of these.

22. Which of the following states that any person who aids, assists, procures, counsels, or advises the preparation or presentation of any matter arising under the internal revenue laws related to a return, affidavit, claim, or other document that is fraudulent or false as to any material matter can be fined not more than $100,000 (now $250,000 per 18 USC § 3571) in the case of individuals ($500,000 in the case of a corporation), imprisonment of not more than three years, or both, as well as the costs of prosecution?
    a. IRC § 7206(1).
    b. IRC § 7206(2).
    c. IRC § 7206(3).
    d. None of these.

23. What is the maximum penalty for a taxpayer and paid tax preparer who work together to falsely claim a refund on the taxpayer's federal tax return?
    a. Up to 1 year in prison for each person plus fines.
    b. Up to 5 years in prison for each person plus fines.
    c. At least 10 years in prison for each person plus fines.
    d. None of these.

24. Failure to file a return is prima facie evidence of which of the following?
    a. Negligence.
    b. Consciousness of guilt.
    c. Criminal intent when it happens two years in a row.
    d. None of these.

25. What is the statute of limitation applying to civil fraud and tax returns?
    a. 1 year.
    b. 3 years.
    c. 6 years.
    d. There is none.

Discussion Questions

26. What crimes are included in the term *tax evasion*?
27. What are some indicators of federal income tax fraud?
28. Who is permitted to practice before the IRS?
29. What is the basic formula for computing individual federal taxable income?
30. What is a use tax, and how can an individual incur a use tax liability?
31. What are the basic federal employment taxes, and who pays them?
32. What are other crimes associated with federal income tax fraud?
33. What is the relationship between the U.S. Code and the Internal Revenue Code?
34. What is the penalty for federal income tax evasion under IRC § 7201?
35. What three elements must be proved for successful prosecution under IRC § 7201?
36. When is ignorance of the law *not* an excuse in criminal tax fraud cases?
37. What does "in trust" mean in relation to payroll-related taxes?
38. What are the four punishable offenses under IRC § 7203?
39. What determines whether an individual has a legal duty to file a tax return?
40. How must a taxpayer go about asserting a Fifth Amendment privilege in relation to items on a federal tax return?

41. When is the inability to pay a valid defense against criminal liability for willfully not paying federal income taxes? When is it *not* a valid defense?

42. How could W-4 forms be linked to federal income tax evasion?

43. Can a taxpayer be charged with filing a false statement in the case of willfully filing a false statement that has no material impact on the taxpayer's tax liability?

44. How does the "lesser included offense doctrine" apply to false taxpayer statements and income tax evasion?

45. Can a taxpayer be subjected to civil and criminal fraud penalties if a paid tax preparer files a fraudulent return on her behalf but without her knowledge?

46. What are some ways that an individual could be guilty of violating IRC § 7212(a), which applies to interfering with the administration of internal revenue laws?

47. What are some crimes under USC Title 18 that are related to tax fraud?

48. What is the distinction as to when the IRS files civil tax fraud versus criminal tax fraud charges?

49. When could innocent errors result in civil fraud charges?

50. When could the IRS use an indirect method of proof in assessing additional taxes or in cases of suspected tax fraud?

51. How does the net worth analysis work?

52. On what basis have some tax protesters argued that the federal government has no right to collect income taxes?

53. What does the term *tax protester scheme* mean?

54. Are resident aliens treated differently in any way from U.S. citizens with respect to tax fraud?

55. What is the merit of the argument that tax laws apply only to "taxpayers" and anyone who is not a "taxpayer" is not required to file returns or pay taxes?

Cases

56. Tom Anderson is a CPA who is engaged to prepare the annual tax return for Mary West, the CEO of a company to which Tom provides regular consulting services. Each year Mary brings Tom several brown bags full of documents relating to her income and expenses. This year, when Tom is sorting through the documents, he finds something he hadn't seen in previous years: a deposit receipt from a foreign trust in the Cayman Islands. The receipt for $50,000 was written by a Cayman Islands attorney, with a notation that it was for deposit in a trust account for the benefit of Mary West. Tom asked Mary about the receipt. "What is this?" he asked.

    "Forget about it," she said. "I want you to act like you never saw this."

    Tom is concerned that Mary may be evading taxes by not reporting income from the trust, and he is also concerned about the need to disclose the existence of the foreign trust on her tax return.

    Should Tom immediately withdraw from the engagement without discussing it further, try to convince Mary to report the foreign trust and any related income, or report the incident to the IRS or other authorities and continue to do consulting for the company?

57. Sonya Fuentez, an IRS-enrolled agent, has been contacted by Carlito Alverez, who is interested in having her prepare his annual income tax return. Sonya is a little apprehensive about the engagement because she's heard rumors that he is a major drug trafficker with roots in Colombia.

At Carlito's request, Sonya visits his home to discuss the details of his return. When she arrives, she's shocked by the opulence she sees. The house is on 2 acres of land just west of the Intracoastal Waterway in Miami Beach. The land is completely surrounded by canals and connects to the rest of the city only via a narrow bridge that has a small guardhouse and security team protecting the entrance to the driveway. She sees other uniformed security guards walking around the perimeter of the property.

The three-story house appears to be as large as a small city block. Sonya is escorted by a housekeeper to a rear patio and garden where Carlito is sipping a martini and watching the large boats go by.

"Welcome to my humble abode," he says. "I hear you're really good. I hate paying taxes, so I need an accountant who can save me as much money as possible."

Sonya smiled and accepted a martini from a tray brought to her by a man wearing crisp black and white tuxedo-type clothes.

"I'll pay you $50,000 for your help," he said. "All in cash, if you want."

Sonya needed the money, so she said, "Okay, I'll accept your very generous offer."

"Great," he said. "Let's get started."

"One thing first," she said. "I must ask you before we start not to tell me about any illegal activities. I won't be able to help you if you do that. I must also tell you that you must be completely truthful in your tax return, and you must report all income."

"Okay," he said, "I get most of my money from commissions on my international import and export business." He grinned from ear to ear. "I don't mind paying my taxes on that. The U.S. has been good to me, and I'm happy to do my part in the tax system here."

"You're a Colombian citizen?" she asked.

"I'm a naturalized U.S. citizen," he replied.

He went on to show her detailed records of income and expenses. Most of the incoming funds had been deposited directly into foreign banks.

"I'll take these documents back to my office," she said.

She returned to her office and spoke to Julia Whitaker, her partner.

"Don't even think about doing this guy's tax return," said Julia.

"What do you mean?" asked Sonya. "He wants to pay his taxes. All I want to do is help him."

"Yes, but we both know what he imports and exports."

"You don't know anything for sure," snapped Sonya. "Just because he's rich and has a reputation doesn't make him guilty of anything."

"Forget that," said Julia. "Let's just assume he's a drug trafficker. Given that, can you accept this engagement?"

Can and should Sonya accept the engagement with Alverez? Why or why not?

Bankruptcy, Divorce, and Identity Theft

CHAPTER LEARNING OBJECTIVES

After reading Chapter 17, you should be able to:

- LO1: Define *bankruptcy fraud* and explain bankruptcy fraud penalties.
- LO2: Identify and explain the major types of bankruptcy fraud.
- LO3: Explain basic bankruptcy procedures.
- LO4: Explain how the forensic accountant can investigate bankruptcy fraud cases.
- LO5: Explain how the forensic accountant can investigate divorce fraud cases.
- LO6: Define *identity theft.*
- LO7: Explain federal laws relating to identity theft.
- LO8: Explain how to prevent identity theft.
- LO9: Explain how to investigate identity theft and recover.

This chapter discusses some of the major types of financial crimes in which forensic accountants could be called to investigate. The focus is on how the fraud is committed and methods used for prevention and investigation.

BANKRUPTCY FRAUD

LO1   According to estimates from the U.S. Department of Justice (DOJ), more than 10 percent of bankruptcy cases involve **bankruptcy fraud.** The official DOJ Bankruptcy Trustee Manual (http://www.usdoj.gov/ust/) lists the most commonly committed frauds in bankruptcy proceedings as defined in 18 U.S.C. § 152. These apply to anyone who "knowingly and fraudulently" does any of the following:

1. **Conceals property from the bankruptcy proceedings**   In many cases, debtors hide assets so they do not have to give them to the creditors.
2. **Makes a false oath or account in relation to a bankruptcy case**   Debtors who hide assets tend to file false bankruptcy petitions that omit and make false statements during discovery or when questioned at the meeting of the creditors.
3. **Makes a false declaration, certification, verification, or statement in relation to a bankruptcy case.**

4. **Makes a false proof of claim**   Creditors can submit fraudulent claims to the bankruptcy account in an attempt to gain assets to which they are not entitled. By submitting proofs of claims, creditors submit themselves to the jurisdiction of the bankruptcy court.

5. **Receives a material amount of property from the debtor with intent to defeat the bankruptcy code**   In some bankruptcy fraud schemes, the debtor could give assets to friends, family, or associates in an attempt to hide assets from bankruptcy proceedings. Simply accepting such assets from a debtor in furtherance of such a scheme is illegal.

6. **Gives, offers, receives, or attempts to obtain money, property, reward, or advantage for acting or forbearing to act in a bankruptcy case**   This pertains to using bribery or extortion to interfere with a bankruptcy case.

7. **Transfers or conceals property with the intent to defeat the bankruptcy code**   This involves the same scheme as discussed in Item 5.

8. **Conceals, destroys, mutilates, or falsifies documents relating to the debtor's property or affairs**   For example, the debtor could alter a brokerage statement to show fewer assets.

9. **Withholds documents related to the debtor's property or financial affairs from the standing trustee or other officer of the court**   Hiding documents could amount to fraud if the intention is to deceive the bankruptcy court. Simply failing to produce required documents or otherwise fully cooperate with the bankruptcy court can be grounds for the dismissal of the debtor's case.

Bankruptcy Fraud Penalties

The typical penalty for committing one of these crimes is a maximum of five years in prison or a maximum fine of $250,000, or both, per offense. Many cases could include more than one offense. For example, a typical bankruptcy case could involve false declarations, property concealment, conspiracy, mail fraud (use of the mail to send fraudulent information relating to the case), and money laundering, each carrying its own significant criminal penalty. The money-laundering crime typically occurs when a debtor launders the proceeds from concealed assets. That is, money laundering occurs when the debtor performs acts to make the proceeds appear to come from a legitimate source.

Section 802 of the Sarbanes-Oxley Act (SOX) of 2002 creates severe criminal penalties applicable to bankruptcy proceedings:

> Whoever knowingly alters, destroys, mutilates, conceals, covers up, falsifies, or makes a false entry in any record, document, or tangible object with the intent to impede, obstruct, or influence the investigation or proper administration of any matter within the jurisdiction of any department or agency of the United States or any case filed under title 11, or in relation to or contemplation of any such matter or case, shall be fined under this title, imprisoned not more than 20 years, or both.

Additional criminal penalties related to bankruptcy include those for bank fraud, tax fraud, mail fraud, and wire fraud. An individual committing a simple bankruptcy scheme can easily become criminally liable for several serious crimes. For example, a person who conceals a single asset could be liable for filing a false petition, falsely testifying under oath, concealing the asset, and committing tax fraud, mail fraud (because of using the mail to send false documents relating to the bankruptcy proceedings), money laundering, and, finally, crimes defined in SOX section 802.

Frequent Bankruptcy Frauds

LO2   **Concealment of assets** is the most common type of fraud (see Figure 17.1); it occurs in about 70 percent of bankruptcy fraud cases. It frequently occurs on a large scale in business bankruptcies when debtors move large amounts of cash or other assets out of the business in anticipation of filing for bankruptcy. The goal of the debtor-fraudster is to prevent assets from being included in the bankruptcy proceeding and being distributed to the creditors. Sometimes assets are concealed using **fraudulent conveyances,** that is, by secretly transferring (or selling below market value) assets to others, perhaps to family or friends, to keep the assets out of the bankruptcy estate and maintain control over them.

Petition mills and multiple filing schemes are the second and third most common bankruptcy frauds. A **petition mill** typically involves unqualified persons who offer fee-based financial advice, credit counseling, and bankruptcy filing services. In many cases, these bankruptcy filing documents are of low quality with serious errors and omissions. The petition mills give the substandard petitions to the debtor-victims with instruction to file them *pro se* (with no attorney). In some cases, the fraudsters even steal the debtors' assets by persuading them to give the fraudsters legal title to them. The problem of petition mills is so pervasive that a significant portion of the DOJ Bankruptcy Trustees Handbook is devoted to their identification.

In **multiple filing schemes,** fraudsters typically file bankruptcy petitions in a number of states using different identities. Such schemes can be related to lending fraud. For example, an individual could establish an identity in different states, take out loans under

FIGURE 17.1

Major Bankruptcy Fraud Schemes

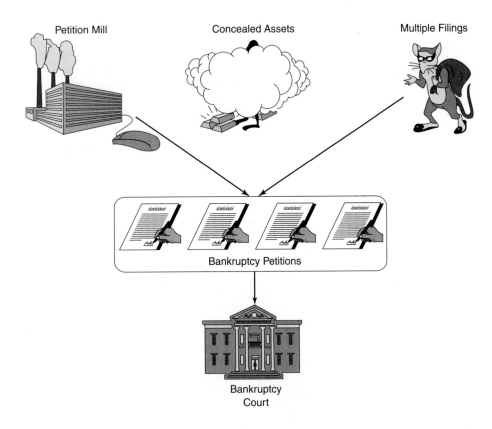

Petition Mill   Concealed Assets   Multiple Filings

Bankruptcy Petitions

Bankruptcy Court

each identity, and then file a separate bankruptcy for each identity in each state. In another multiple-filing scheme, fraudsters accumulate debts and assets under a false name and then file for bankruptcy while concealing some of the assets. This scheme could be repeated over and over using multiple identities in different states.

Additional forms of bankruptcy fraud include trustee fraud, attorney fraud, forged filings, embezzlement, credit card fraud, and **bust-outs,** which occur when fraudsters set up a business and order large amounts of merchandise with no intention to pay for it.

Bankruptcy Procedures

LO3 This section presents a highly abbreviated discussion of bankruptcy procedures and their relationship to fraud.

The bankruptcy code sets six types of bankruptcy proceedings:

- **Chapter 7**   Applies to both individuals and businesses; designed to completely liquidate the debtor's assets and discharge the debtor's liabilities as permitted by the bankruptcy code. Not all debts can be discharged in bankruptcy.
- **Chapter 9**   Applies to municipalities.
- **Chapter 11**   Applies to businesses (and sometimes wealthy individuals) and focuses on working out a creditor payment plan without liquidating the businesses.
- **Chapter 12**   Applies to farmers and those in the fishing business.
- **Chapter 13**   Applies to individuals whose means-tested income is too large to permit them to file under Chapter 7. The focus is on working out a payment plan to pay creditors at least partially. Some debts could be completely discharged.
- **Chapter 15**   Applies to cross-border cases and certain other ancillary cases.

Chapter 7 and Chapter 13 are used most frequently by individuals (see Figure 17.2), although the laws typically force individuals with substantial income to file under Chapter 13. Moreover, Chapter 13 is less desirable for the debtor because it requires debt repayment from the debtor's future income. Chapter 7, on the other hand, completely discharges the debtor from all debt with no obligation to make payments from future income.

Bankruptcy petitions are filed in federal bankruptcy courts, and the proceedings are administered by DOJ trustees. Trustees are appointed as part of the DOJ trustee program, which consists of a national Executive Office for U.S. Trustees (in Washington, D.C.), headed by the U.S. Trustee and with 21 regional U.S. Trustees and about 100 field offices.

Bankruptcy trustees are responsible for maintaining fair and orderly proceedings as well as ensuring compliance with all bankruptcy laws. Trustees have an affirmative obligation to collect and review the required documentation and refer any cases of suspected fraud to the U.S. Attorney's Office and sometimes to the FBI. They are also responsible for recommending to the U.S. Trustee the filing of a motion with the court for dismissal of the debtor's petition if the debtor does not cooperate as required or commits fraud, or if the petition is abusive (see Figure 17.3). Petitions are considered abusive if they involve any of the following elements:

- **Misclassification of nonconsumer debt as consumer debt**   In some cases, this type of abuse is subtle. For example, an individual could incur credit card debt to finance a business.
- **Ability to pay**   Chapter 7 filings may be dismissed if the debtor has the means to repay the debts. However, the debtor may convert the filing to Chapter 13.

FIGURE 17.2   **Chapter 7 versus Chapter 13 Bankruptcy for Individuals**

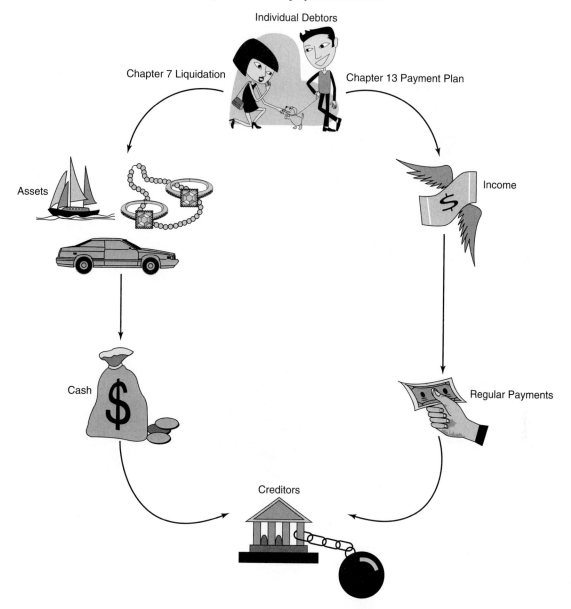

- **Debtor honesty**   This is not a well-defined concept and can vary from one jurisdiction to the next. However, the trustee may recommend dismissal in cases when she believes that the debtor is using bankruptcy in an abusive way. For example, the trustee could recommend a dismissal if the debtor ran up large amounts of debt for extravagant purchases shortly before filing.
- **Involuntary bankruptcy**   When there is sufficient delinquent debt and a sufficient number of creditors, any one creditor could force an individual or business into involuntary bankruptcy. However, petitions by creditors for involuntary bankruptcy may be dismissed if they are deemed abusive. A primary reason for them being declared abusive is the debtor's ability to pay.

FIGURE 17.3 **Judges May Dismiss Abusive Bankruptcy Filings**

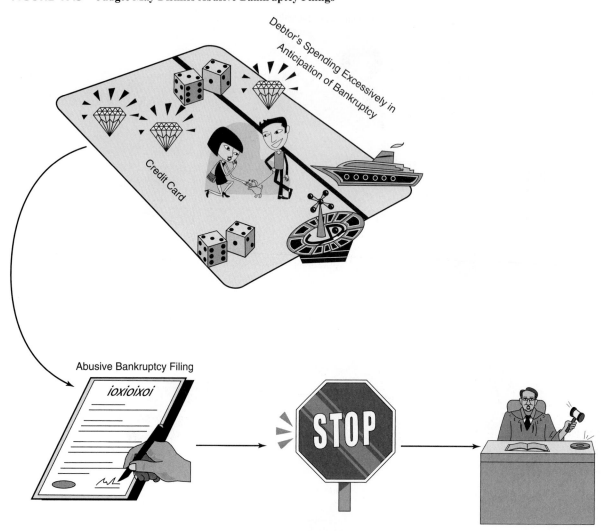

In cases of debtor fraud, the trustee will likely recommend that the court deny the debtor's petition.

Filing of Documents, Discovery, and the Meeting of the Creditors

The bankruptcy normally includes filing the following schedules and related statements:

- Schedule A—Real Property.
- Schedule B—Personal Property.
- Schedule C—Property Claimed as Exempt.
- Schedule D—Creditors Holding Secured Claims.
- Schedule E—Creditors Holding Unsecured Priority Claims.
- Schedule F—Creditors Holding Unsecured Nonpriority Claims.
- Schedule G—Executory Contracts and Unexpired Leases.
- Schedule H—Codebtor.

- Schedule I—Current Income of Individual Debtor(s).
- Schedule J—Current Expenditures of Individual Debtor(s) Statement of Financial Affairs.

Also required are the submission of federal tax returns and detailed accounting and financial records as well as financial statements for business debtors.

Additional information can be obtained through discovery, which is typically applicable to adversarial issues in bankruptcy proceedings. The Federal Rules of Bankruptcy Procedure list various adversarial proceedings. Examples follow:

- Proceedings to recover money or property other than proceedings to compel the debtor to deliver property to the trustee.
- Proceedings to determine the validity, priority, or extent of a lien or other interest in certain properties.
- Proceedings to object to or revoke a discharge.
- Proceedings to determine the dischargeability of a debt.

The Federal Rules of Bankruptcy Procedure generally follow the Federal Rules of Civil Procedure except for some specific rules that pertain to issues unique to bankruptcy such as those relating to the filing and the proofs of claims.

Bankruptcy discovery rules incorporate the federal discovery rules, but through Rule 2004 they specifically give any party in interest the right to obtain a court order to examine any entity involved with the case. For all practical purposes, this means that attorneys can obtain court orders to depose opposing parties in adversarial issues. One obvious case in which this applies is to creditors' deposing debtors to uncover concealed assets.

In addition to the discovery process, all bankruptcy proceedings, with few exceptions, require debtors to appear in person at the first meeting of the creditors. At that meeting, the debtor is placed under oath and must answer questions from the trustee and the creditors. Creditors are not required to appear at the meeting, and they frequently do not appear unless they suspect fraud.

Discovery of Fraud, Abuse, and Concealed Assets

LO4 The forensic accountant could be called on to investigate possible fraud not only in bankruptcy but also in various situations in which assets are distributed to interested parties. The various situations involve common investigatory methods; therefore they are discussed here together.

Bankruptcy Bankruptcies frequently involve various parties with an interest in discovering concealed assets. Examples include the following:

- A creditor who wants to make sure there is no fraud by the debtor.
- A creditor who suspects that another's credit claim is fraudulent or unjustified.
- A trustee who wants a particular issue investigated.
- An accounting firm that is auditing the bankruptcy estate.

Divorce Asset concealment is common in divorce cases.

Estates Heirs and others could seek to abscond with assets from an estate. This could be done to deprive other heirs, to avoid estate taxes, to deprive creditors, and so on.

Business Acquisitions In some cases, after reaching an agreement concerning the sale of a business, the seller conceals business assets to prevent the buyer from assuming ownership and control of them after the acquisition is complete.

FIGURE 17.4
**Likely Places to Look
for Hidden Assets**

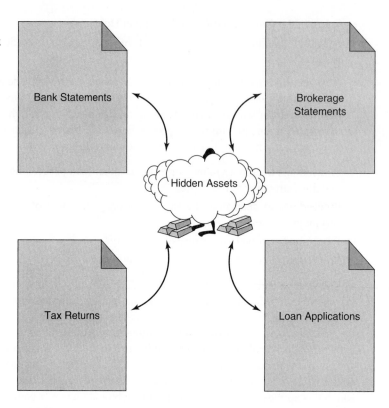

Partnership Dissolutions By concealing assets, it is sometimes possible for partners to obtain more than their fair share in a dissolution.

Regardless of the general situation, the methods for finding concealed assets are similar (see Figure 17.4). The forensic accountant examines available financial records, including tax returns, bank statements, brokerage statements, loan applications, business records, and so on. Various sources of useful investigatory information are discussed in the sections that follow.

Tax Returns

State, local, and federal tax returns often have signs that lead to hidden assets. For example, in bankruptcy or divorce, the involved party's recent federal tax returns should be carefully examined with respect to the following items:

- **W-2 forms** Research 401(k), 403(b), and other deferred compensation plans that could be marital assets.
- **Income distributions from deferred compensation plans** Verify the disposition of any distributed funds.
- **Form 6251 (tax preferences)** Research various tax preference items, such as accelerated depreciation, that could be related to concealed assets.
- **Interest and dividend income** Verify the disposition of any assets that generate interest or dividend income.
- **Investment interest expense deductions** Research the possible existence of a margin-based brokerage account.
- **Real estate tax deductions** Verify the disposition of the underlying properties.

- **Interest expense deductions**   Verify the proceeds of any loans.
- **Casualty loss deductions**   Research the possible existence of proceeds from insurance claims and verify the disposition of any such proceeds.
- **Miscellaneous deductions**   Look for safe deposit fees, which can point to hidden safe deposit boxes. Deductions for attorney's fees could point to a hidden estate plan.
- **Form 1040, Schedule B, Lines 11 and 12**   Research the possible existence of foreign (offshore) trusts often used to shield assets from others.
- **Form 1040, Schedule C (profit and loss from a business)**   Look for contributions to Keogh plans.
- **Form 1040, Schedule D (disposition of assets sales)**   Verify the disposition of the proceeds from assets sales.
- **Schedule E (income from rental properties, royalties, and estates and trusts, partnerships, and S corporations)**   Verify the dispositions of the underlying assets and that activity loss carryovers were treated as assets.

Related to Tax Returns

The following items are related to income tax returns:

- **Loss carryforwards**   Can be related to Schedules C, D, and E and should be treated as assets.
- **Overpaid taxes and accrued refunds**   Can be intentionally overpaid as a means of banking future refunds.
- **Payment of taxes on nonmarital assets**   Could have been paid from marital assets.

Bank, Brokerage, and Other Statements

The forensic accountant should review all bank and brokerage statements for sources of income and verify the disposition of all underlying assets.

Loan Applications

By studying tax returns, bank statements, and other records, the forensic accountant can determine whether the individual or entity under investigation has obtained one or more loans. He should obtain copies of any loan applications.

A loan application is an excellent source of information in uncovering concealed assets. Individuals tend to portray their financial condition in a favorable light when applying for loans. Therefore, the forensic accountant should carefully study the lists of assets included on loan applications. It is a federal crime to lie on loan applications made to FDIC-insured financial institutions.

Cash Flow Analyses

The forensic accountant can perform a complete cash flow analysis for the individual or entity under investigation. This should normally be done for the current year and at least several previous years. The analysis should involve several steps:

- Use tax records and statements from financial institutions to list all cash income month by month for the period studied.
- List all expenses, month by month, for the same period of study.

In a bankruptcy proceeding, substantial unaccounted-for assets could be grounds for the denial of the debtor's bankruptcy petition. In a divorce proceeding, a court might charge such assets to the responsible spouse.

Investigations of Businesses

Reviewing for concealed assets of businesses, especially large ones or those with complex structures, can be difficult. Furthermore, straightforward audits or business valuations could be of little help because they are designed primarily to detect overvaluations rather than undervaluations. For this reason, the forensic accountant should perform several special procedures:

- **Review all sales records for sources of income** Verify that all collections from sales have been deposited to the business's bank account.
- **Verify all vendors** Ensure that vendors exist and conduct detailed follow-ups on payments made to any vendors related to the debtor.
- **Review communications** Check all available e-mail, faxes, phone records, and mail for evidence of transactions relating to hidden assets.
- **Scrutinize payments** Check all payments to owners and officers, all loan payments that could disguise fraudulent conveyances, and all employee payments for unwarranted or excessive compensation.
- **Verify the existence of inventories, fixed assets, and all other assets** Prepare a schedule of fixed assets for recent years. Valuable assets could exist but not appear on the balance sheet because they could have been fully depreciated but are still valuable.
- **Study previous income tax returns and income statements for evidence of expenses for patents, R&D, and other intangible assets** Such assets could have been expensed in the year they occurred and not appear on balance sheets.
- **Work in progress and unbilled work** These items could be easily concealed, especially in service firms. For example, an architect could have completed a large portion of a design project and not yet billed the client.

Credit Reports

Credit reports could include information about debts used to finance concealed real estate or other property.

Public Records

Public records can be accessed online to find information about real estate, mortgages, liens, and so on.

Unusual Assets

Some types of assets could easily go unnoticed or be difficult to identify. These include executory contracts, interests in trusts, interests in limited partnerships, various types of options, pending interests in estates, and personal collections (e.g., coins and stamps).

Conveyances

All significant sales and transfers of assets to others should be examined, especially those relating to periods surrounding the filing of a divorce, bankruptcy, or other proceeding. Conveyances should be scrutinized to make sure that they were made at arm's length. Any conveyances made with the intent or effect of defeating creditors, spouses, or others, could be set aside by the court.

In general, the forensic accountant must verify that all incoming cash and assets are accounted for and that all payments are legitimate. However, this process can be difficult if the subject of investigation has systematically engaged in any "off-the-books" business. In such cases, auditing techniques are not particularly effective because they tend to deal with what is reported in the financial records.

The forensic accountant should pay special attention to the period leading up to and around the bankruptcy or divorce filing because fraud often occurs in the immediate period surrounding the decision to file. That said, however, it is not uncommon for owners of closely held businesses to siphon off business assets for personal use to avoid income taxes. If this is the case, the fraud could have taken place over a much longer period than that surrounding the filing of the bankruptcy.

A forensic accountant who suspects any siphoning off or embezzlement of assets in a bankruptcy could obtain an order from the bankruptcy court to subpoena financial records of nonbusiness owners or subject them to depositions. Evidence of such suspicions should be reported to the trustee, who is obligated under the rules to keep the case open as long as any reasonable suspicion of fraud exists. The trustee presents any evidence of fraud to the DOJ, which in turn may use its subpoena powers to investigate further.

One tactic is for the forensic accountant to take advantage of bankruptcy rules that require trustees to oppose Chapter 7 discharges when a debtor engages in fraud or does any of the following:

- Fails to preserve or conceals financial records.
- Fails to explain satisfactorily the loss or deficiency of assets.
- Refuses to obey an order of the court or to testify after being granted immunity.

Bankruptcy Fraud Cases

Some examples of bankruptcy fraud, abstracted from public IRS cases files (www.irs. gov/compliance/enforcement/), follow:

- **Taco Bell Franchise Owner**   The owner of a chain of more than 50 Taco Bell restaurant franchises pleaded guilty to bankruptcy fraud. He was charged with siphoning off more than $3 million (and fraudulently concealing more than $2 million from the bankruptcy court) in business income and assets by making false accounting entries. The details of the charge included accusations that he created fake, backdated loan documents from his father to the business. Fake loan documents are sometimes used to justify fraudulent transfers of money away from the business.
- **Jaweed Siddiqui**   Siddiqui was sentenced to 51 months in prison after pleading guilty to bankruptcy fraud and mail fraud, use of an unauthorized access device, and aiding and abetting an IRS revenue officer in the receipt of unauthorized compensation. Siddiqui admitted to applying for many loans, some under the names of others and using false income information and social security numbers. The scheme involved defaulting on the loans and filing for bankruptcy.
- **Two Texas Business Owners**   Jerry Lewis Poore and Lori Kay Spurlock were given prison sentences after being found guilty of one count of conspiracy to commit bankruptcy fraud. Spurlock was also convicted on two counts of concealing bankruptcy assets. According to the charges, the two concealed more than $427,000 by diverting receipts from Color Laser Institute (a business they owned) to a bank account opened by Poore. The prosecutor argued that the diverted receipts were used to purchase personal assets that included a home and a Mercedes-Benz.
- **Joseph James Russo**   Russo pled guilty to one count of bankruptcy fraud. According to court documents, he was accused of concealing money received from the sale of real estate by placing it in an account under his father's name.

Cases such as these are normally in the IRS case files because they involve charges of income tax fraud. As mentioned, it is common for bankruptcy fraud to be connected to other related crimes. Many individuals who commit bankruptcy fraud have no idea how many federal laws they are breaking.

DIVORCE FRAUD

Divorce fraud is similar to bankruptcy fraud. In both, a court may divide the assets of an estate. In bankruptcy, the estate is composed of the debtor's assets to be divided among creditors. In divorce, the estate is composed of the marital assets to be divided between the divorcing couple; considerations are given to the possible additional issues of child support, alimony, and custody and visitation rights.

As is in the case of bankruptcy, the most common area of fraud connected with divorce is asset concealment. The fraudster conceals assets from the divorce proceedings to prevent them from being divided during the divorce. In some cases, the concealment could be unintentional because many individuals are not good with finances and financial records. For this reason, the forensic accountant should know what to look for and where to look for it to ensure that all marital assets have been identified.

Discovery in Divorce Cases

LO5 In most states, people involved in divorce cases are required to supply each other and the court with complete financial statements. The level of scrutiny could be considerably less than that in bankruptcy cases for the following reasons:

- Divorce attorneys do not always have the financial expertise that many bankruptcy attorneys have.
- Bankruptcy cases tend to involve creditors who possess information-rich credit applications from debtors. Creditors tend to be very good at asking the right questions and looking in the right places when searching for concealed assets.
- Bankruptcy cases tend to involve fraudulent conveyances and hidden assets immediately prior to the filing. In divorce, however, one spouse could hide assets from the other for many years prior to the filing.
- While many bankruptcies genuinely have no assets to hide, divorcing couples are more likely to be solvent and have assets to hide.

Also, discovery is normally available in divorce cases through interrogatories, requests for documents, and depositions.

Identification of Concealed Assets in Divorce Cases

Finding concealed assets in divorces cases involves the same basic techniques used in bankruptcy cases.

IDENTITY THEFT

LO6 The fastest growing crime in the United States, **identity theft,** occurs when one person uses another's personal identifying information, such as driver's license or SSN, to obtain goods and/or services in the other person's name (see Figure 17.5). The largest part of identity theft is caused by organized crime groups. This problem is so pervasive that its annual cost to U.S. consumers and businesses is estimated to be around $50 billion. One indictment alone charged a single individual with using various identities to prepare and submit thousands of fraudulent student loan applications that totaled more than $40 million.

FIGURE 17.5   Identity Theft

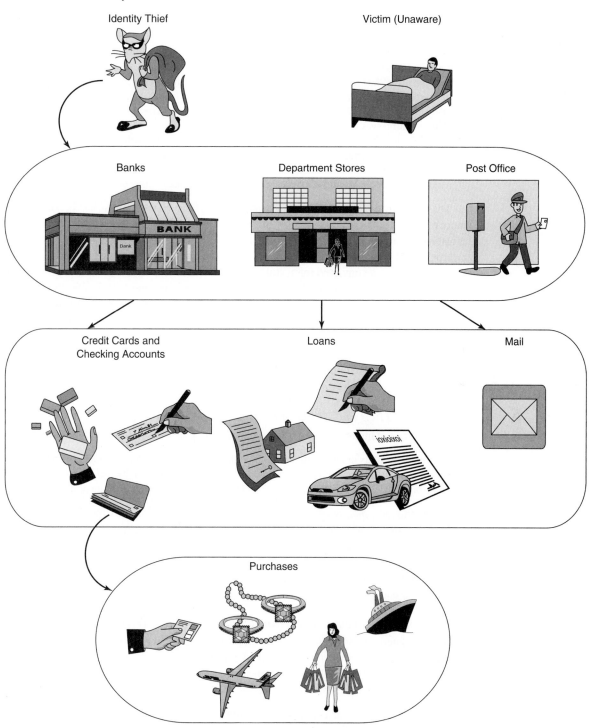

The damage caused by identity theft is not limited to financial ramifications. President George W. Bush expressed this view when he signed the Identity Theft Penalty Enhancement Act:

> The crime of identity theft undermines the basic trust on which our economy depends. When a person takes out an insurance policy, or makes an online purchase, or opens a savings account, he or she must have confidence that personal financial information will be protected and treated with care. Identity theft harms not only its direct victims, but also many businesses and customers whose confidence is shaken. Like other forms of stealing, identity theft leaves the victim poor and feeling terribly violated.
>
> But the losses are not measured only in dollars. An identity theft-thief can steal the victim's financial reputation. Running up bills on credit card accounts that the victim never knew existed, the criminal can quickly damage a person's lifelong efforts to build and maintain a good credit rating. Repairing the damage can take months or years.

The problem of identity theft has existed throughout history, but it has become much more prevalent with the advent of the Internet and our electronic society. Almost everyone's private personal information, such as that contained in medical and bank records, tax returns, credit files, and so on, is only a few clicks away from potential criminals. In one well-known case, a convicted felon stole one person's identity and then incurred more than $100,000 in credit card debt, obtained a federal home loan, and bought motorcycles and handguns, all in the victim's name, but that is not the end of the story: The fraudster also called and taunted the victim. It cost the victim more than $15,000 and four years of his time to restore his and his wife's credit and reputation.

Federal Laws Relating to Identity Theft

LO7 Congress has passed several laws to combat identity theft.

The Identity Theft and Assumption Deterrence Act of 1998

This was the first major act passed to combat identify theft. It punishes anyone who

> knowingly transfers or uses, without lawful authority, a means of identification of another person with the intent to commit, or to aid or abet, any unlawful activity that constitutes a violation of federal law, or that constitutes a felony under any applicable state or local law.

Under this act, *means of identification* is broadly interpreted to include any type of information that can identify a particular individual such as numbers for social security, credit cards, drivers' licenses, and the unique electronic serial ones associated with an individual's cell phone. Criminal penalties under this act include up to 15 years in prison plus the possibility of forfeiture of any assets either used or intended to be used in a crime covered under the act.

The Fair and Accurate Credit Transaction Act of 2003 (FACTA)

This act updated the Federal Fair Credit Reporting Act by adding laws to help consumers protect themselves against identity theft. A number of FACTA's provisions direct federal agencies such as the Federal Trade Commission to make regulations to implement it.
Some of the provisions of FACTA follow:

- **Free consumer credit reports** Consumers are entitled to obtain a free credit report each year from the three largest U.S. credit card bureaus. The reports can be obtained through www.annualcreditreport.com. Not surprisingly, however, large numbers of imposter Web sites, some with similar names, have been set up to steal individuals' identities or charge fees rather than provide free credit reports. The FTC devotes a Web page dedicated to the real free reports to prevent people from being steered to the wrong Web site. See www.ftc.gov/bcp/conline/edcams/freereports/index.html or visit www.ftc .gov and enter "free credit report" in to the site's search box.

- **Fraud and active duty alerts**   Victims of identity theft are entitled to ask reporting agencies to flag accounts for possible fraud for an initial 90-day period. This period can be extended for up to seven years by providing the agency a police report related to the suspected or actual theft. Active duty military persons can request that their accounts be flagged for up to 12 months.

  As part of the fraud alert request, the legitimate customer gives the credit-reporting agency a telephone number. Once the alert is in place, all businesses must contact the customer using that telephone number before extending any credit under her name. Also, credit-reporting agencies must provide some additional free copies of credit reports for accounts with active fraud alerts.

- **Truncation of identifying numbers**   This provision, subject to a phase-in period for older machines, prohibits merchants from including more that the last five digits of account numbers or expiration date on credit card and debit card receipts. The rule does not apply to handwritten receipts or receipts generated from manual imprints of cards.

- **Documents to victims**   Upon request, victims may obtain from businesses copies of credit applications and related documents made in their names. The same documents must be provided to law enforcement authorities.

- **Collection agencies**   The victim is entitled to receive copies of all documents (applications, account statements, late notices, demands for collection, and so on) in regard to any debts in his name in the hands of a collection agency. Furthermore, after being notified that a given debt is due to identity theft, the creditor is not permitted to sell the debt or place it in collections.

- **Business compliance**   Creditors and financial institutions are required to implement systems designed to detect identity theft, notify customers and credit bureaus, process customer disputes, and reconcile conflicting customer addresses. This provision of the law is the subject of ongoing regulation.

- **Disposal of consumer reports**   Businesses and individuals that use credit reports must have systems in place to ensure secure disposal of the reports. This requirement applies to broad groups of individuals and employers, landlords, automobile dealers, government agencies, and insurance companies.

- **Notice of consumer rights**   This provision requires credit-reporting agencies to notify victims of their right to fraud alerts, to block their reporting of information that has resulted from fraud, and to obtain copies of documents related to fraud on their accounts.

- **Credit scores**   Consumers are entitled to their credit scores and information about how they are computed.

- **Disputes of inaccurate information**   This provision requires any business or individual who reports information to credit agencies to investigate customer claims of identity theft. The business or individual is not permitted to report negative information while an investigation is pending.

- **Negative information in reports by financial institutions**   Businesses that regularly report to credit-reporting agencies must notify their customers within 30 days of reporting any negative information to these agencies. Negative information includes late, missed, or partial payments.

- **Medical information and consumer reports**   Credit-reporting agencies must use coded names for medical providers on credit reports and may not include their names, addresses, or phone numbers on the reports to protect debtors' medical privacy. Credit reports cannot contain any information that could identify medical conditions. Another provision of the law prevents creditors, subject to certain exceptions, from using medical information in making credit-granting decisions.

- **Nationwide specialty consumer reporting agencies**   Consumers have the right to obtain free annual reports from what the act calls *nationwide specialty consumer reporting agencies* (NSCRAs). These agencies provide specialized noncredit-type reports (that could contain some credit information) relating to areas such as medical records, medical payments, residential or tenant history, check-writing history, employment history, and insurance claims. With proper authorization, forensic accountants and law enforcement investigators can find NSCRA reports helpful in financial fraud investigations. Some of the main providers follow:

  - Medical Information Bureau (www.mib.com).
  - Insurance reports via CheckPoint's CLUE system (www.choicetrust.com).
  - Check-writing histories (www.chexsystems.com and www.telecheck.com).
  - Law enforcement databases discussed elsewhere in this text.
  - General background checks, including criminal records (www.intelius.com and similar information providers).
  - General Web-based public record searches available in many jurisdictions.

- **Workplace investigations**   Employers may use outside agencies to investigate employee misconduct without obtaining permission from the employee and without notifying the employee. When the investigation is complete, the employer is not required to disclose to the employee sources of information used to generate the investigation report. In general, the FACTA consumer report protections do not apply to workplace investigations and reports.

- **Marketing opt-out requirements**   Many times companies that do business with consumers share their information with affiliates for marketing purposes. Under the FACTA, consumers are allowed to opt out from this information sharing.

- **Risk-based pricing**   Lenders are required to notify customers when they send them offers with interest rate quotes but then later charge them higher rates because of something in their credit history.

Identity Theft Penalty Enhancement Act

This act of Congress created the crime of **aggravated identity theft,** defined as identity theft, or intended identity theft, committed in connection with certain other crimes (see the following list). The penalty for most crimes listed in it is an extra two years in prison. However, for crimes related to terrorism, the penalty is an extra five years in prison. The extra prison sentences are mandatory and must be served in addition to the normal prison sentences for identity theft; courts are prohibited from reducing the normal sentence for identity theft to compensate for the mandatory sentences.

The crimes listed in the act associated with aggravated identity theft not directly related to terrorism follow:

- Theft relating to employee benefit plans.
- False impersonation of citizenship.
- False statements made in the acquisition of a firearm.
- Crimes relating to mail, bank, and wire fraud.
- Crimes relating to nationality and citizenship, passports, and visas.

- Crimes relating to obtaining customer information by false pretenses.
- Crimes relating to failing to willfully leave the United States after a deportation order and use of counterfeit alien registration cards.
- Various other offenses relating to immigration and to the Social Security Act.

The Internet False Identification Prevention Act of 2000

This act makes selling counterfeit versions of certain official identification cards illegal. It was designed to quash those who had previously sold such cards on the Internet as "novelties," but it did not stop many, especially those in other countries, from selling such cards.

The law also makes it illegal to sell electronic templates for making counterfeit identification cards. There is a potential one-year prison sentence if one fake identification card is made from a given template, but the potential prison sentence increases to 20 years if the template is used to make five or more cards.

Many Web sites and message boards contain instructions on how to make false identification cards. The process is not terribly difficult with a computer, and there are even instructions on how to counterfeit the holograms that are used on driver's licenses.

Unfortunately, false identification cards are often very real looking. In one investigation, Government Accountability Office (GAO) investigators managed to use false identification cards to easily breach security at 21 of the most secure buildings in the United States, including the Central Intelligence Agency, the Federal Bureau of Investigation (FBI), and several airports. The investigators obtained their false identification cards from various fake-ID–related Web sites. The fake IDs worked so well that the investigators were routinely waved around metal detectors at security checkpoints.

Identity Theft and Other Federal Statutes

Many identity theft schemes involve violations of related federal statutes, some of which carry penalties of up to 30 years in prison. These statutes include crimes in the areas of computer fraud, credit card fraud, wire fraud, mail fraud, social security fraud, and financial institution fraud. In some cases, laws relating to conspiracy, racketeering, and obstruction of justice may also apply.

State Laws and Identity Theft and False Identification

Individual state laws also play an important role in the war against identity theft. The FBI cannot possibly prosecute many of the small cases that occur, especially those relating to single crimes committed by individuals not associated with organized crime groups. Even state governments may not have the resources to thoroughly investigate isolated cases of identity theft. As with all economic crimes, law enforcement agencies tend to focus their resources on relatively large crimes and those that affect many people.

Laws vary considerably from one state to the next, but identity theft is generally illegal in all states. Furthermore, many states add their own protections and penalties relative to federal laws.

- **Security freeze**   Customers in California can instruct credit-reporting agencies not to disclose their name, address, birth date, SSN, and credit information. The credit-reporting agencies give customers with frozen accounts a unique personal identification number (PIN) and password that they can use to temporarily unfreeze their accounts when they need to obtain credit.
- **Obtaining an Illinois driver's license under false pretenses**   In Illinois, the maximum penalty for obtaining a driver's license through a false affidavit is one to three years in prison and a $25,000 fine.

- **Fake ID in Illinois** One individual in Illinois was charged with forgery, making false application and affidavit for a driver's license, possession of a fraudulent and fictitious driver's license, possession of a fictitious driver's license ghost application, and multiple counts of possession of fraudulent social security cards. This is a good example of the state laws that can be brought to bear against those involved in identity-related crimes.

Terrorism, Identity Theft, and False Identification

Terrorists for years have used false documents to facilitate their travel around the world and conduct their operations. For example, the FBI alleged in federal court that as many of five of the 9/11 hijackers applied for official state identification cards based on false identification documents at the Virginia Department of Motor Vehicles about six weeks before the hijacking.

It is well known that worldwide terrorist organizations have members who specialize in making false passports and other documents. Some terrorists have been known to possess many fraudulent passports.

Identify Theft Prevention

LO8   People can prevent identity theft by protecting themselves in a number of ways. They should be aware of possible fraudsters (see Figure 17.6):

- **Dumpster divers and garbage pickers** These fraudsters go through discarded documents containing sensitive personal information from individuals and businesses.

- **Shoulder surfers** Some fraudsters look over people's shoulders while they fill out applications with sensitive information or when they enter personal identification numbers into ATM machines.

- **Hackers** Internet hackers break into databases containing credit card information, customer files, employment files, and so on. Many cases of such break-ins against major companies are on record. In some cases, thousands of social security numbers or credit card numbers have been compromised. Hackers also break into individual computers and steal personal information.

- **Company insiders** Many cases of identity theft are traced back to trusted company employees, temporary workers, or cleaning persons. In some cases, criminal organizations have infiltrated companies for the sole purpose of stealing identity information.

- **Impersonators** These fraudsters pretend to be their victims to obtain their personal information. For example, an imposter could call a local department store and trick someone in the billing department into disclosing a customer's account information. In some cases, thieves have ordered copies of individuals' credit reports by posing as employers, landlords, or loan officers.

- **Mail thieves** Mailboxes are relatively easy targets where thieves can find credit card statements, bank statements, newly issued credit cards, preapproved credit card offers, and even tax forms containing social security numbers.

- **Public records diggers** Genealogy, birth, and death records and publicly probated wills can supply thieves with mothers' maiden names, an often-used piece of identifying information. Some public records filed with courts have buried within them birth dates, social security numbers, and driver's license numbers.

- **Scammers** These thieves perform scams designed to trick victims into supplying personal information. **Phishing** is a billion-dollar-a-year Internet scam in this category. In one form, the fraudster sends the victim an e-mail message concerning some issue or problem associated with the victim's credit card account, bank account, or other type of

FIGURE 17.6
Types of Identity Thieves

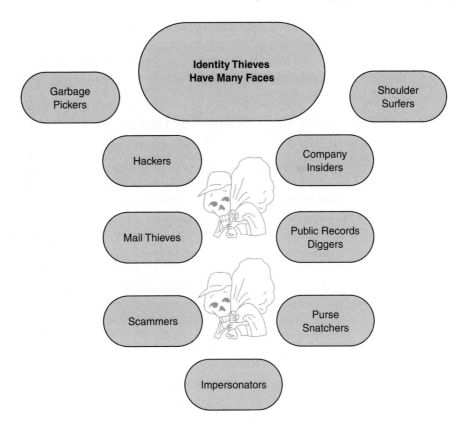

account. The e-mail message gives the victim a Web link to the fraudster's account and he is told to log in to deal with the issue. The link could appear genuine; for example, it could appear as www.wachovia.com (the Web address for Wachovia Bank), but what the victim sees is only the "anchor text"; the real link is hidden in the message's html code, so clicking on the link takes the victim to a site controlled by the fraudster. At this point, the victim is able to see the real Web address in the browser's address bar, but it will probably be cleverly designed to look very much like a legitimate address. For example, it could be www.service-wachovia.com, which is a completely different site. Finally, this fraudulent Web site is designed to look just like the real Web site, further encouraging the victim to fill out a log-in form and give away personal data.

- **Telephone Scams** Posing as employees from insurance companies, government agencies, credit bureaus, and so on, fraudsters phone their victims and trick them into supplying their personal information.
- **Fake ATM** One of the most notorious scams involved fraudsters who placed a fake ATM machine in a mall. The machine produced an error message when people tried to withdraw funds, but it also recorded the card number and PIN of each person who used it.
- **Purse snatchers and pickpockets** Some identity thieves get their information the old-fashioned way by picking a pocket or snatching a purse.

In general, identity thefts often can be prevented by giving personal information only on an absolute need-to-know basis, never clicking on e-mail links to access personal accounts, securing postal mail, never giving personal information to incoming callers without calling them back at an independently verified phone number, keeping computers up to date with security software and patches, and shredding all personal information before putting it in the garbage. Experts also strongly advise that people review their credit reports at least once a year. Finally, no credit card numbers or other personal data should be given to businesses that do not have good security controls.

Warning Signs of Identity Theft

People should be alert to certain signals that could be related to identity theft.

- **Unauthorized address changes** A serious warning sign is evidence of any type of unauthorized change in a mailing address. For example, bank or credit card statements could be missing as the result of being sent to a different, fraudulent address.
- **Unauthorized account transactions** All monthly statements should be carefully inspected for unauthorized activity. Improper transactions should be immediately reported.
- **Incorrect information on credit reports** Any significant incorrect information on a credit report could indicate identity fraud. Any unauthorized access to credit reports (as shown on credit reports) can indicate a problem.
- **Bill collectors** Unfortunately, one of the first symptoms of identity fraud victimization could be phone calls or letters from bill collectors for unknown credit transactions. Bill collectors normally show up after the fraudster is long gone.

Identity Theft Investigation

LO9 Identity thieves can be caught various ways.

- **Tracing** The true identities of fraudsters can be obtained by using video surveillance records, telephone records, and the Internet methods discussed in the earlier chapter on forensic science to trace them. However, sophisticated identity thieves are aware of such tracing methods and take countermeasures so that tracing methods alone are often not helpful.
- **Catching thieves in the act** In theory, identity thieves can be caught in the act of obtaining or using others' identity information. This approach is not generally helpful because immediate arrests do not normally take place unless a law enforcement officer happens to be at the scene of the crime. Furthermore, professional identity thieves are likely to avoid putting themselves in situations where they could be subject to immediate apprehension. However, some identity thieves have been caught in the act by presenting a stolen or false identification document to immigration officials or members of law enforcement.
- **Controlled delivery** Simply stated, **controlled delivery** means catching thieves in an act such as receiving mail obtained fraudulently or withdrawing bank funds using a stolen identity. This is the strongest and most reliable way to catch identity thieves. A common method used by identity thieves is to put through changes of addresses or use their own addresses to receive mail relating to credit accounts set up in the victim's name. This permits the fraudsters to secretly receive credit cards in the victim's name as well as statements and other account-related documents.

  In the case of mail, for example, controlled delivery involves arresting the suspect when she receives mail from the stolen account. In the case of a bank account, the arrest could be made when she attempts to withdraw funds from the bank account. Bank employees are trained to monitor certain accounts and notify the police when suspicious events occur.

Chapter **Eighteen**

Organized Crime, Counterterrorism, and Anti-Money Laundering

CHAPTER LEARNING OBJECTIVES

After reading Chapter 18, you should be able to:

- LO1: Explain what organized crime and terrorism have in common.
- LO2: Explain international efforts to curb organized crime.
- LO3: Explain the activities, organizational structure, and history of La Cosa Nostra.
- LO4: Explain the methods and laws used by the FBI to fight organized crime.
- LO5: Explain the activities and history of other major organized crime groups.
- LO6: Explain the history, development, and structure of modern terrorist organizations.
- LO7: Explain the development of the al Qaeda organization.
- LO8: Define *money laundering.*
- LO9: Explain the major money-laundering schemes.
- LO10: Explain anti-money laundering laws and processes.

LO1 This chapter discusses criminal and terrorist organizations and the one thing they have in common: money although their ultimate ends may differ, both criminal and terrorist organizations need money to prosper. This presents challenges to forensic accountants in several areas:

- Working with law enforcement in analyzing financial records relating to criminal and terrorist organizations.
- Working with law enforcement in tracing financial transactions through financial and banking systems.
- Working with law enforcement in developing and managing data-mining systems designed to help identify criminal and terrorist activities.
- Working with client compliance programs intended to help in identifying and avoiding money-laundering problems.

The remainder of the chapter is divided into three main sections: organized crime, terrorism, and money laundering.

ORGANIZED CRIME

International Crime-Fighting Efforts

LO2 Organized crime is a global problem that sucks more than a trillion dollars a year out of the legitimate world economy. The problem is so large that in the year 2000, the United Nations General Assembly passed the **United Nations Convention against Transnational Organized Crime and Its Protocols** (the Convention). Signed by nearly 150 countries including the United States, the Convention deals with the major issues relating to organized crime such as money laundering, corruption, and obstruction of justice. The Convention is also supplemented by The Protocol against the Smuggling of Migrants and The Protocol against Trafficking in Persons, which deal with the illegal transportation of individuals across borders, often for exploitation, and organized human slavery.

Countries adopting the Convention commit to passing laws and implementing controls that fight organized crime. For example, Article 3 of the Convention commits ratifying countries to criminalizing the participation in criminal organizations. Article 4 commits the countries to establishing anti-money laundering regulatory mechanisms. Additional articles relate to such topics as cooperation across countries, extradition, and corruption.

The **European Law Enforcement Organization (Europol)** fights organized crime across the European Union member states. Most major countries have their own enforcement divisions to counter organized crime. Within the United States, the Federal Bureau of Investigation (FBI) is the primary organization charged with fighting organized crime. The FBI's organized crime section contains three units (see Figure 18.1):

- **La Cosa Nostra/Italian organized crime/Labor Racketeering Unit** Focuses on three designated areas of organized crime: the American La Cosa Nostra (LCN), Italian organized crime (IOC), and labor racketeers. The FBI considers LCN to be the dominant crime organization in the United States. These groups include the so-called Italian and Sicilian mafias.

- **Eurasian organized crime (EOC) Unit** Focuses on crime groups whose members originate from, are linked to, or operate from within former Soviet-bloc countries and who operate within the United States, Africa, or Europe. These groups include the so-called Russian mafia, for example.

FIGURE 18.1
FBI Organized Crime Units

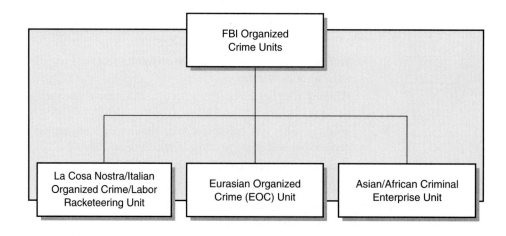

- **The Asian/African Criminal Enterprise Unit** Focuses on crime groups whose members originate predominantly from Eastern and Southeastern Asian and African nations.

Organized crime corresponding to each of the three FBI units is separately discussed.

La Cosa Nostra

LO3 **La Cosa Nostra (LCN)** (see Figure 18.2) has its roots in mid-19th century Sicily about the time that Italy became a sovereign state. The Sicilian mafia began in and around the city of Palermo, where a group of people who included important aristocrats and politicians lived.

The mafia originally served a useful function in Sicily in protecting the large lemon and orange estates that surrounded Palermo. Later, during the fascist period, the mafia fell out of favor with the local government, and under fear of jail, many of its members fled to the United States.

During its early years in the United States, which began around 1890, the mafia comprised various groups, gangs, and syndicates, including the Black Hand (around 1900), the Five Point Gang (1910s and 1920s), and Al Capone's notorious Chicago crime syndicate (1920s). Then, after an internal war in New York City around 1930, La Cosa Nostra emerged as a single organization under the leadership of Salvatore Maranzano.

Maranzano was murdered after only six months on the job, but during his brief tenure, he defined LCN's organizational structure (i.e., the "five families" in New York City) and its code of conduct.

He was murdered because of his high ambitions. He was not satisfied controlling only the New York mafia; he wanted to be boss of the entire United States and plotted to murder his main competitors for power, Al Capone in Chicago and Charles "Lucky" Luciano, his number 2 man in New York. Lucky Luciano and his associate Meyer Lansky learned of the plot, however, and they quickly dispatched five gunmen posing as government agents who shot and stabbed Maranzano to death in his office.

In time, Luciano was convicted on prostitution charges and sentenced from 30 to 50 years in prison. He continued to run his organization from within prison for 10 years, and during World War II, ingratiated himself with the U.S. government by providing helpful contacts in Italy and Sicily and providing security for the port in New York City. As a result, he was paroled in 1946 and deported to Italy.

FIGURE 18.2 **Chronology of LCN Bosses**

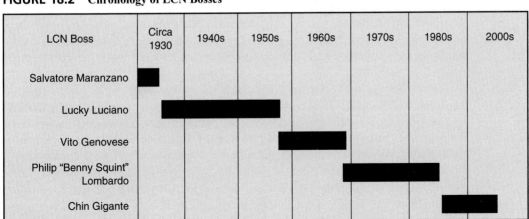

While in Italy, Luciano continued to hold strong influence over LCN, and in 1946, he quietly moved to Cuba where he continued to run the organization. While in Cuba, he ordered the hit on Bugsy Siegel for squandering the syndicate's money in constructing the Flamingo Hotel in Las Vegas.

Government officials soon learned of Luciano's operations from Cuba and forced him to return to Italy where he continued to exert control. In time, his health failed, causing his power to fade in the late 1950s. In 1962, he died of a heart attack, and his body was sent to New York City where he was buried in St. John's cemetery.

When Luciano entered prison, Frank Castello became acting boss and maintained operational control over the syndicate for 20 years until Vito Genovese ordered Vincent "the Chin" Gigante to assassinate Castello in 1957. The assassination failed, but Castello relinquished power, and, in keeping with the mafia code of secrecy, refused to testify against his would-be assassin.

Only two years later, Vito Genovese was convicted on narcotics charges and sentenced to 15 years in prison where he continued to run the syndicate until he died in 1969. His successor was Philip "Benny Squint" Lombardo, who quietly ran the Genovese family from behind the scenes through a series of bosses who served as fronts for his power. In 1985, his boss Anthony "Fat Tony" Salerno and the bosses of the four other New York LCN families were convicted of running a criminal enterprise, the La Cosa Nostra Commission. Needless to say, this was an earthshaking blow to LCN.

After the convictions of Salerno and the other family bosses, Lombardo was in failing health, so he appointed Gigante as his successor. Gigante tried to insulate himself from law enforcement by pretending that he was mentally incompetent. He would walk around the East Village in his bathrobe, earning him the nickname of "the Odd Father."

In 1997, Gigante was sentenced to 12 years in prison on racketeering charges although he was acquitted on other serious charges including an attempt to murder John Gotti, another well-known mobster from the Gambino family. In 2002, Gigante was indicted for running waterfront extortion rackets while in prison. A plea bargain added three more years to his sentence. In December 2005, while still in prison, he died.

Lucky Luciano, Frank Castello, Vito Genovese, Philip Lombardo, and Chin Gigante were members of the "ruling" Genovese family. The other four families in the **five-family LCN Commission** were the Bonanno, Colombo (also called Profaci), Gambino, and Lucchesse families.

Considerable attention in recent years has been given to John Gotti, the boss of the Gambino family. Gotti lived a very flamboyant lifestyle and loved to pose for news cameras. He was so well dressed that he earned the nickname "The Dapper Don." In 2002, he died in prison where he had continued to serve as the family boss. All of the five families are reported to be still active to this day, with some of the bosses allegedly serving current prison sentences. According to the FBI, the Gambino and Genovese families continue to be among the most powerful LCN families, not only in New York but also in the United States.

LCN Activities

According to FBI reports, LCN and its associates remain actively engaged in drug trafficking, murder, assault, gambling, extortion, loan-sharking, labor racketeering, money laundering, arson, gasoline bootlegging, infiltration of legitimate businesses, stock market manipulation, and various other illegal frauds and schemes. Some of these crimes are discussed in more detail.

Labor Racketeering The FBI defines **labor racketeering** as the domination, manipulation, and control of a labor movement that affects related businesses and industries. According to U.S. Senate and other investigations, the domination of labor unions has traditionally been one of LCN's fundamental sources of power and profit. For example, the 1986 President's Council on Organized Crime reported that LCN dominated the Independent Laborers Association (ILA), the Laborers International Union of North America (LIUNA), the International Brotherhood of Teamsters (Teamsters), and the Hotel Employees and Restaurant Employees International Union. Paul Castellano, the former boss of the Gambino family, is quoted as saying, "Our job is to run the unions."

Investigations have shown that a primary goal of labor racketeering has been to control labor health, welfare, and pension funds. In the 1980s, these funds for the Teamsters had total assets in excess of $9 billion; today, the value of the assets is about $100 billion.

The FBI focuses its labor racketeering investigations in the major industrialized U.S. cites that traditionally have had strong union bases: New York, Buffalo, Chicago, Cleveland, Detroit, and Philadelphia. The main legal tool used by the FBI has been the Racketeer Influenced and Corrupt Organization (RICO) statute, which provides for both criminal and civil sanctions against racketeering. The civil sanctions have been especially helpful because they have empowered the FBI to attack and change the racketeer-influenced organizations themselves rather than just a few individuals within them. Criminal sanctions, although helpful, are limited in their usefulness because they only remove corrupt individuals who can quickly be replaced by other corrupt individuals. For example, even after indicting four of eight consecutive Teamster presidents, LCN control over the Teamsters persisted. However, with the 1988 Teamster's civil case, LCN control over the organization was effectively removed.

Gambling **Gambling** has always been a mainstay of LCN. Before casino gambling was legalized in Nevada in 1931, LCN ran luxurious illegal casinos in various parts of the country, bribing and paying off officials to persuade them to look the other way. Later, LCN played a major role in creating and promoting Las Vegas. It not only built its own hotels and casinos but also financed many others through shady loans that included pension funds from the LCN-controlled Teamsters union. Eventually, however, the state of Nevada stepped in and created strict laws and rules that prevented any association between casino ownership and organized crime. Today, Las Vegas is considered to be relatively free from any LCN influence.

One type of illegal gambling traditionally controlled by LCN is the **numbers game.** In this lottery-type game, gamblers try to guess three or four numbers that are derived from an unpredictable financial figure that is published daily in the newspaper and cannot be manipulated. Bets are placed with **bookies,** who typically operate out of bars, taverns, and social clubs and on the street.

The advent of state lotteries did much to diminish the numbers game, but by some estimates, it is still a $5 billion-a-year industry in the United States. Many prefer the illegal numbers game to the lottery for several reasons: Bookies routinely accept bets on credit, they accept bets over the telephone, winnings are quickly and easily collected, and winnings are never reported to the IRS.

The most challenging part of a bookie's job is collecting from clients. Because their operations are illegal, they cannot sue their clients for bad debts. They instead resort to various types of force, including breaking arms and legs.

Loan-Sharking **Loan-sharking** is closely related to gambling because compulsive gamblers frequently overextend themselves and need to borrow money to cover their gambling debts. That is when they turn to mafia lenders known as **loan sharks,** who lend money at sky-high rates of interest. With loan shark loans, the interest (called the **"vig"**) is added to the loan every week at the rate of about three to five points with a point equaling 1 percent of the amount borrowed. For example, if a loan is for $10,000 with four points, the borrower must pay the loan shark $400 in interest every week. That adds up to a one-year payback totaling $30,000 including principal, or an annual percentage that is roughly in the 300 percent range.

To make things more difficult for the borrower, the loan sharks do not accept partial payments of principal. The borrower must therefore pay the entire principal balance at one time, which of course, is difficult for those who are already without the financial discipline and resources to borrow money in the legal financial system. The result is that borrowers typically end up continually paying large sums of interest, and so the whole business becomes lucrative for the loan shark.

Sometimes loan sharks offer **fast-money loans,** such as the nine-to-five loan. The terms of this loan are simple: you borrow $500 on Monday and pay back $900 on Friday. The harsh terms of this loan and the usual loan shark loan have been exemplified by the term *blood money,* which means that borrower either repays in cash or in blood.

Life in LCN and Its Organizational Structure

No one simply joins LCN. He must know an insider in the organization who will vouch for him by introducing him to others in the organization as "a friend," which means that the insider vouches for the newcomer. The newcomer might be introduced to either an **associate** or a full-fledged member called a *made man.* **Made men** are always 100 percent Italian on their father's side of the family and meet certain other criteria discussed later. In any case, the newcomer must first prove his loyalty, general capabilities, and ability to earn money before progressing in the organization.

In time, the newcomer can become an associate member, which makes him a somewhat trusted business associate in the organization, but he will not be privy to the inside secrets of the organization, such as its true organizational structure, the details of the various rackets, and so on.

Only a small percentage of associates ever become made men. The organization is extremely strict and careful in whom it invites to become a true insider. This is one of the reasons that LCN is nearly impossible to fully infiltrate with informers. In one case, an FBI agent infiltrated LCN as an associate under the assumed name Donnie Brasco, but there are no publicly known cases of any agents ever becoming made men.

When an associate accepts an invitation to become a made man, he enters the organization (see Figure 18.3) through a ritual ceremony that includes taking the **omerta** (oath of silence). He swears total loyalty above all, including family and country, to LCN. He must also prove his loyalty by carrying out a hit (murder) according to orders made by the family boss. Once the associate becomes a made man, the penalty for disloyalty or violating the oath is death.

The newly made man is called a **soldier.** There are two levels of soldiers: The first-level soldier, or **picciotto,** is very much like an associate except that he enjoys the protection of the organization. That means for one thing that no one in the organization can kill him without the boss's permission. The second-level soldier, a **sgarrista,** usually runs his own rackets but kicks up a high percentage of his profits to his immediate boss called a **capo.** The capo takes whatever percentage he likes, but his cut is generally in the 50 to 70 percent range unless he is especially greedy, in which case it might be as high as 90 percent. The money flows from the capo to the **boss,** who is the head of the family (see Figure 18.4). The capo normally gives the boss anywhere from 10 to 40 percent of the money he receives from soldiers. The underboss (the number 2 man, who reports directly to the boss) may receive a portion of what goes to the boss.

The boss has absolute authority in the family organization. This means that he approves all new members, all major illegal business dealings, and all internal and contract killings.

FIGURE 18.3
LCN Organizational
Structure

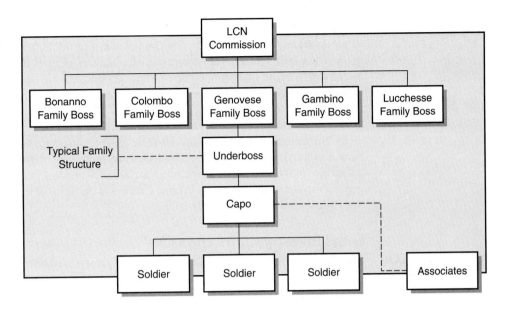

FIGURE 18.4
Money Flows Upward
in LCN

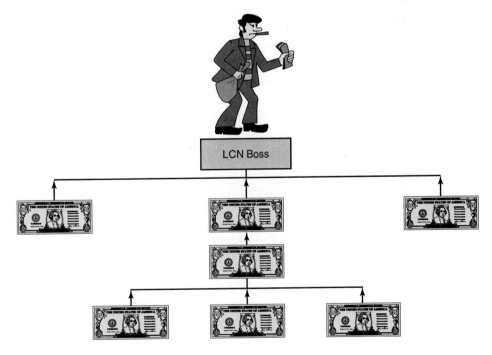

LCN bosses seldom authorize killings with those somehow not involved in LCN dealings, but one possible exception occurred when John Favara, one of John Gotti's neighbors, killed Gotti's 12-year-old son in a car accident. Shortly after the accident, John Favara disappeared under suspicious circumstances. Gotti was conveniently in Florida at the time, but when he was later interviewed by the police, he said, "I'm not sorry that the guy is missing. I would not be sorry if the guy turned up dead."

Money Flows in LCN

In corporations, money tends to flow from the top to the bottom. Corporate executives approve budgets, which in turn determine expenditures at lower levels. On the other hand, as just discussed, in LCN, money flows from the bottom to the top. A second characteristic of money in LCN is that the illegal money is cash. That means that soldiers, capos, and bosses are accustomed to hiding boxes and bags of cash. Unlike the average citizen, they avoid credit cards, debit cards, bank checks, and so on.

LCN members frequently place all their legal assets (e.g., automobiles, houses, and bank accounts) in others' names. The idea is to protect the assets from being seized by authorities in the event that the members are arrested and to hide them from the IRS. The general method of putting assets in others' names is one form of money laundering, a topic that is discussed more thoroughly later.

Legal Investigations and LCN

LO4
The FBI uses various legal statutes and investigatory methods in combating organized crime. The primary statutes used by the FBI are as follows:

- Title 18, United States Code, Section 1961 (Racketeer Influenced Corrupt Organizations).
- Title 18, United States Code, Section 1955 (Illegal Gambling Business).
- Title 18, United States Code, Section 1952 (Interstate Transportation in Aid of Racketeering).
- Title 18, United States Code, Section 1953 (Interstate Transportation of Wagering Paraphernalia).
- Title 18, United States Code, Section 1084 (Interstate Transmission of Wagering Information).
- Title 18, United States Code, Section 892 (Making Extortionate Credit Transactions).
- Title 18, United States Code, Section 224 (Bribery in Sporting Contests).

Of course, more general statutes relating to conspiracy, obstruction of justice, and mail fraud are also used.

A primary investigative tool that has met with great success has included covert monitoring, including the use of wiretaps, bugs, and other listening devices. John Gotti was finally brought down when federal officials placed bugs in an apartment over his regular meeting place. Mafia members attempt to counter covert listening by always speaking in vague or coded language. For example, a mafia member might say, "The thing we talked about last week needs to be done by the other guy we talked about, but I'm not comfortable with the problems we are having. . . ." The idea is to speak in such a way that any recording would be meaningless to a jury who might listen to it.

Eurasian Organized Crime

Russian Mafia

LO5
The Eurasian organized crime (EOC) groups, sometimes called the *Russian mafia,* the *Red mafia,* and **Russian organized crime (ROC),** trace their modern origins to the Soviet prison systems, where inmates elected their leaders and developed hierarchical structures. When the Soviet Union collapsed in 1991, these same individuals joined ex-KGB agents, displaced military officers, and corrupt officials in controlling newly privatized companies. The result was an enormous movement of money and power into the hands of organized crime. Many of these individuals migrated from the former Soviet and Warsaw Pact

states to the West. Therefore, the term *Russian mafia* refers to organized crime originating not only in Russia but also in the surrounding states.

The FBI lists the eight most prevalent crimes committed by the Russian mafia in the United States: health care fraud, auto insurance fraud, securities and investment fraud, money laundering, drug trafficking, extortion, auto theft, and interstate transportation of stolen property. Most recently, reports indicate the Russian mafia's desire to expand via the drug trafficking and illegal arms sales, and FBI investigations indicate the group's recent involvement in commercial alien smuggling. Some believe the Russian mafia is at the center of the large alien smuggling operation that is currently a problem in Europe.

The Russian mafia has not received the same degree of media attention given to LCN. All indications are that the Red mafia is now the FBI's most formidable adversary. According to Colonel Stanislav Lunev, the highest-ranking Cold War Soviet defector, hundreds of ROC syndicates operate internationally, and the total membership in these and other ROC syndicates exceeds 1 million "soldiers." Even worse, the ROC bosses tend to be highly educated, multilingual former KGB agents who work for Russian agencies and are still bent on destroying the United States.

The power of ROC syndicates is evidenced by intelligence estimates that the majority of all Russian business and banks, as well as dozens of stock exchanges and government enterprises, are controlled by the ROC syndicates. The extent of ROC control is so pervasive that many argue that Russia is now a mafia state.

Some believe that ROC syndicates are being used by the Russian government to secretly continue the Cold War polices of selling arms and nuclear technology to terrorists and enemies of the United States. The only difference now, according to those who take this position, is that Moscow claims that the mafia is responsible for these activities and is out of the government's control.

Evidence suggests that the ROC syndicates have established alliances with Colombian and Mexican drug cartels. For example, the largest cocaine seizure in maritime history involved the U.S. Coast Guard's seizure of a whopping 26,937 pounds of cocaine from a fishing boat, the *Svesda Maru,* about 1,500 miles south of San Diego. All of the boat's 10 crew members were Russian and Ukrainian nationals.

Military and other analysts suggest that the Colombian drug cartel is aligned with **Fuerzas Armadas Revolucionarias de Colombia (FARC),** a Colombian revolutionary, military organization that reportedly finances the majority of its operations through narcotics trafficking. The result is a de facto alliance between ROC, FARC, and the Colombian and Mexican drug cartels. The U.S. Department of Justice classifies FARC as a narco-terrorist organization.

Analysts suggest that ROC syndicates are more ruthless than their LCN counterparts. Traditionally, LCN has shied away from killing reporters, judges, and members of law enforcement. Some suggest, however, that ROC is not so restrained because it has been blamed for killing more than a dozen Russian journalists. Rumors even suggest that in some cases, ROC syndicates will kill not only internal traitors but also their entire families.

Although ROC has been involved in a wide array of criminal schemes, its activities in the area of computer crime have become especially well known. Some examples follow:

- **Windows WMF exploit**   The Windows WMF exploit was a piece of malicious software code that entered a computer through visited Web sites. A person needed only to visit an infected Web site for her computer to become infected by the exploit. The WMF exploit created an open door that permitted outside hackers the ability to easily take control of infected computers. News reports at the time indicated that Russian hackers were selling copies of the exploit for $4,000 weeks before it was discovered by the anti-virus companies.

- **Department of Defense attacks**   The U.S. Department of Defense has acknowledged a series of coordinated and organized cyber attacks on it coming from within Russia.
- **Superhacker 99**   This was a software program that sold widely on the streets in Russia. Its main functions included tools to create viruses and fake credit card numbers.
- **Grafix Softech F.A. raid**   A group of Russian hackers raided Grafix Softech F.A., one of the world's largest online gaming companies. Despite the latest and best security controls, the hackers seized control of the servers that supported Grafix's operations. The company paid the hackers an undisclosed ransom, but when it regained control of the servers, one key server appeared to have been stripped of its data. This key server contained operational data for 120 gaming sites. The loss of the data would have been a devastating blow to the company, but it was able to recover the data with the help of a professional data-recovery service.
- **Credit card thefts**   According to one FBI warning, ROC attackers stole more than 1 million credit card numbers. After hacking into companies' systems, the Eastern European criminals routinely asked for a ransom or extortion payment in exchange for helping the hacked companies fix their security problems.
- **Denial of service attacks**   Eastern European hackers have been blamed for a series of denial of service attacks against the Web sites of many businesses in Western Europe and the United States. In a typical case, the hackers demand money, and when the money is not paid, they attack and crash the victims' Web sites.
- **Citibank attack**   A Russian gang electronically attacked Citibank's money management system and managed to steal more than $10 million in a series of fraudulent transactions (see Figure 18.5). The alleged ringleader was a young mathematician running the operation from a small apartment in St. Petersburg, Russia.

The head of Division K, Russia's Internet crime division, claimed that Russian hackers are the best in the world. The only way to stop them, he stated, is to create laws that make it easier to prosecute those who live in one country and commit their crimes in another. In one case, the FBI used creative measures to prosecute two Eastern European hackers: It offered them jobs in the United States and then arrested them when they took the bait and arrived in the United States.

The art and science of hacking in Russia has been elevated to the formal level, as embodied by the Russian Civil Hackers School. This school ostensibly exists for legitimate security training, but some argue that its really a KGB-dominated organization that spews out the world's most sophisticated cyber-criminals.

ROC Bosses and Activities   Some individuals have allegedly been ROC bosses. Vyacheslav Ivankov was convicted of extortion in the United States with three codefendants. He served a 10-year prison sentence and then was deported to Russia. He was known by many as a "Russian godfather," if not *the* "Russian Godfather." Other major figures associated with the ROC have been implicated in a wide variety of schemes in at least 50 different countries. The schemes range from petty street crime to human trafficking, diamond smuggling, and arms sales to the Taliban and al Qaeda. Given their close associations with high-level Russian officials, ROC syndicates will remain a major world threat for many years to come.

Asian/African Organized Crime

Asian Criminal Enterprise Working Groups and Initiatives   The FBI participates in various working groups as part of its effort to combat **Asian organized crime (AOC).**

FIGURE 18.5
Russian Hackers
Penetrated a Major
New York Bank

Participation in these groups helps organizations identify and target criminal organizations for international investigation. The working groups are as follows:

- **The FBI/National Police Agency of Japan Working Group** Meets once a year and supports interagency cooperation and FBI extraterritorial operations on Japanese soil.
- **Australian Federal Police.**
- **Hong Kong Police.**
- **Royal Canadian Mounted Police in the Asian Organized Crime Operational Working Group.**
- **Project Bridge, an Interpol initiative** Focuses on Asian alien smuggling syndicates.
- **The Interagency Working Group on Alien Smuggling** Focuses on alien smuggling and the trafficking of women and children; sponsored by the National Security Council.
- **The International Asian Organized Crime Conference** Devoted to strategies and methods for combating AOC.
- **The Canadian/United States Cross-Border Crime Forum** Deals with issues relating to the U.S.–Canadian border.
- **The International Law Enforcement Academy in Bangkok, Thailand** Geared toward helping law enforcement agencies in various Southeast Asian countries.
- **Department of Justice Nigerian Crime Initiative** Organized initiative through which a wide range of U.S. federal agencies works together in joint task forces to coordinate investigations against Nigerian organized crime syndicates.
- **The Interpol West African Fraud Conference** Focuses on financial fraud perpetrated by Nigerian and West African organized criminal enterprises.

AOC includes criminal enterprises relating to a large number of countries in Eastern and Southeastern Asia including China, Korea, Japan, Thailand, the Philippines, Cambodia, Laos, Vietnam, South Pacific island nations and in Southwest Asia including Pakistan, India, Afghanistan, Nepal, and Iran. Within the United States, AOC concentrates mostly in certain large cities, including Boston, Chicago, Honolulu, Las Vegas, Los Angeles, New Orleans, New York, Newark, Philadelphia, Portland, San Francisco, Seattle, and Washington, D.C.

Some AOC enterprises are very sophisticated with multilingual members and those with advanced skills in banking and money laundering. The traditional AOC enterprises include the Japanese Yakuza or Boryokudan and the Chinese triads based in Hong Kong, Taiwan, and Macau. In the Chinese triads, a single member known as the "master" manages operations. Some of the Chinese triads have initiation ceremonies and internal structures that are somewhat similar to those of LCN. Sometimes the triads work with ROC groups, who, with extensive banking connections, help launder their profits. Nontraditional AOC enterprises mainly include the Chinese-influenced tongs (secret societies) and the Chinese triad affiliates.

Traditionally, few AOC groups have been hierarchically organized, but that has begun to change in recent years with competition and the globalization of the world economy. Furthermore, these groups have become proficient in not only local crimes (such as loan-sharking, gambling, and prostitution) but also international crimes (such as alien smuggling, drug trafficking, counterfeiting computer and clothing products, and international money laundering).

The largest percentage of the FBI's investigations of AOC has consistently been related to Chinese organized crime, which is composed of large numbers of loosely organized, independent enterprises spread throughout the United States.

Check Fraud and Asian Organized Crime   One example of Asian/African organized crime is in the area of check fraud, which has been one of the most prevalent problems affecting the banking industry. **Check fraud** and related crimes involve various forms of negotiable instruments, including traveler's checks, credit cards, certified bank checks, money orders, and currency.

In the United States, the main organized crime syndicates involved with check fraud have traditionally included individuals connected to Nigeria, Vietnam, Russia, Armenia, and Mexico. Some of the more prominent of these groups have tended to focus on the West Coast, especially in California in the Orange County, San Francisco, and Sacramento areas, although they also have significant networked operations in Chicago, Houston, and Washington, D.C. The Nigerian and Russian groups tend to move around all parts of the United States.

Although the organizations are loosely organized, Asian check fraud schemes typically have these members (see Figure 18.6):

- **Leader**   This person is typically well educated, frequently with a college degree in business. Some even have law degrees.
- **Procurer**   This member is in charge of stealing legitimate checks. In many cases, procurers work in financial institutions.
- **Counterfeiter**   This individual is an expert in producing fake or duplicate payroll checks, money orders, credit cards, bank checks, currency, and identification cards.
- **Information broker**   This member specializes in collecting personal information on possible targets of impersonation. The ultimate goal can be anything from passing checks in the victim's name to complete identity theft.

FIGURE 18.6 **Asian Organized Crime Check-Passing Scheme**

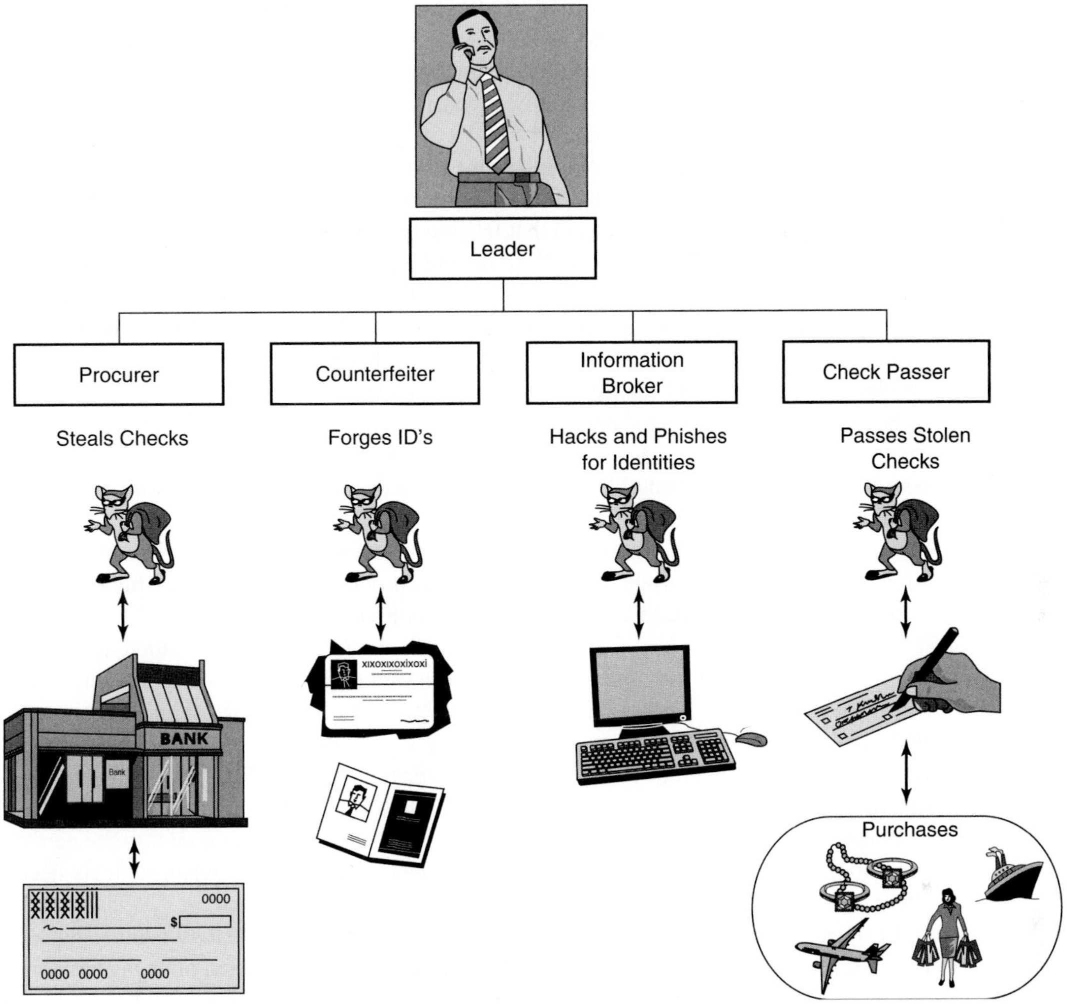

- **Check passer** This person specializes in negotiating stolen or counterfeit checks. The groups often negotiate only a small percentage of the checks they steal and sell the rest on the black market.

TERRORISM

Islamic Background and Influence

LO6 Much of today's worldwide terrorism has its roots in a radical interpretation of the Islamic religion. The pernicious tenet of this radicalism is simple: Allah directly commands a violent **jihad** (struggle) against all non-Muslims. This in turn means death for anyone anywhere in the world who stands for anything but an Islamic theocratic government ruled very strictly by the **Sharia** (Islamic law).

Many who teach **Islamic radicalism** (or fundamentalism, as it is sometimes called) further amplify the need for violent jihad by declaring that all of Islam is under attack by the non-Muslims, so true believers must defend the faith by destroying secular governments, including that of the United States, wherever they exist. This burning belief in attacking and destroying applies not only to the democracies of the United States and Europe but also to the predominantly Muslim countries of the Middle East. Any type of government other than an "Islamic state" is considered evil and needs to be destroyed.

The teaching that Islam is under attack is of great theological significance. This is because the **Qur'an** (the holy book of Islam) teaches that Muslim nations should defend themselves against enemy attacks. It does not teach the indiscriminate killing of people around the world. It is for this reason that Islamic terrorists so strongly preach that Islam is under attack. The call for jihad is a call to defend Islam against the infidels (nonbelievers) and apostates, those who have left the religion of Islam. Muslims who do not share the extremist beliefs are commonly labeled as apostates. Under Islamic theology, apostasy is a crime similar to treason, punishable by death. This explains why Islamic terrorists have no problem killing innocent Muslims to further their jihad.

Because Islamic terrorists' beliefs are deeply rooted in their religion, there is no room for compromise. They will accept nothing less than Islamic theocracy for the entire world. For this reason, the problem of Islamic terrorism is a de facto world war that is not likely to end until the terrorists are defeated.

The rise of the radical jihad in recent decades traces back to the Afghan War of the 1980s when the Soviets invaded Afghanistan. This produced a situation in which Muslims were truly defending their land against secular, Communist nonbelievers.

Because of Cold War anti-Communist sympathies, the United States sided against the Soviets by providing substantial amounts of covert aid to the Afghans. The Western Europeans did their part by granting political asylum to large numbers of Islamic radicals who fled persecution from the Soviets. Then, after the war, large numbers of displaced Afghan fighters and refugees migrated to Western European countries. The Europeans assumed that the radical beliefs of the new immigrants would somehow dissipate within the context of European society and that the Afghans would integrate and be absorbed into the general population. However, this did not happen as expected, and many Afghan radicals began using their new homeland as a base of operations to continue the jihad.

In time, the Western European countries became a magnet that drew Islamic radicals from a wide variety of countries where they had been either persecuted or engaged in their own wars against secular governments. For example, not far south of Spain was North Africa, which was experiencing several conflicts, especially the civil war in Algeria. Many Islamic radicals in Algeria had gone to Afghanistan to fight the jihad there and later returned more radical then ever, starting Islamic wars in their own countries.

In Algeria, the **Groupes Islamiques Armes (GIA)** became the dominant Islamic militant group. More important, the group established strong roots in Europe, especially in France, where members joined the ranks of hundreds of thousands who already lived in and around the major cities. They established Europe as a safe haven, a base of operations, from which they could plan and fund attacks back in Algeria. They also found Europe to be fertile ground for recruiting new jihadists to send to join in the distant war.

The Europeans were mostly indifferent to the fact that foreign nationals living on their soil were supporting terrorist organizations in other parts of the world. There were no laws against supporting terrorist jihads as long as they were conducted someplace else. The French government did little or nothing to the local jihadists who supported the GIA, whose acts of terror rose to wiping out entire villages, including men, women, and children.

Eventually, however, the GIA attacked French interests in Algeria, and this led to a crackdown on the Algerian network in Paris. This caused many of the radicals to flee to London, which had a great tolerance for all kinds of refugees, including radical ones.

In time, the GIA decided to retaliate against the French, and soon the terrorist organization engaged in a Paris metro bombing that killed 12 people. The jihad had expanded into war against the European continent, and some of the bombers fled to London for protection.

The tolerance in Britain was so great that it took nearly a decade for the French government to extradite Rachid Ramda from Britain for his alleged participation (through financing) of the Paris metro bombings. Ramda was active in the publication of *Al Ansar,* a GIA-affiliated radical newsletter. This newsletter became a beacon for terrorists across Europe, and two of its editors became some of al Qaedas' most influential "spiritual leaders" in Europe. One of them, Mustafa Setmariam Nasar, became a trainer in an al Qaeda military cell in Afghanistan and was an alleged mastermind of the Madrid train bombings as well as a chief ideologue for al Zarqawi's Iraq campaign.

The European Legal System and Terrorists

This chapter discusses Europe in regard to terrorism because it is the one area of the world that has permitted terrorists to operate the most freely. Hundreds of years of laws and traditions have built a European legal system that has greatly protected civil rights but has also made it nearly impossible to prosecute terrorists not actually caught in the final planning stages of an attack. Although the laws vary from one country to the next, some of the legal hurdles to prosecuting terrorism in Europe follow.

Evidence Gathering

For legal and security reasons, information gathered from intelligence sources can be difficult to share with prosecutors. The problem is that the intelligence agencies are best at collecting evidence on terrorism. In one Dutch case, 12 accused terrorists were released after a Dutch court ruled that the evidence was not admissible because it had been gathered by intelligence services rather than police.

Terrorism Not Clearly Defined

Because laws do not clearly define terrorism as a crime, accomplices who assist in terrorist plots may be charged only with lesser offenses. For example, an individual who supplies false passports to terrorists who bomb a train could be charged only for supplying false passports, not for the murder of those killed in the bombing.

Inability to Stop Plots in Progress

In many cases, authorities can observe a plot in progress but not be able to make any arrests. It is not uncommon for European groups of individuals with terrorist ties to publicly preach jihad and openly commit themselves to suicide attacks while the authorities can only stand by and watch.

Transnational Investigation Bureaucracy

Terrorists routinely move from one country to the next in Europe, and coordinating investigations across borders can sometimes be overly complicated.

Inability to Deport Terrorists

As mentioned, it took nearly a decade for France to extradite Rachid Ramda from Britain for his alleged role in financing Paris metro bombings. One argument to block the extradition made by his supporters was that if he were returned to France, he would then be illegally sent back to Algeria, where he faced a death sentence for his conviction in an Algerian airport bombing. Middle East countries typically apply the death penalty for acts of terrorism, so European countries will not deport them to these countries.

The European Terrorist Profile
Muslims Converted to Jihad

Estimates suggest that more than 30 million Muslims presently live in Europe with especially high concentrations in France, Germany, Austria, and the Scandinavian Peninsula. France alone, for example, has several million Muslims. The problem is that a large number of them on the Continent have not become integrated into European society. The large Muslim ghettos in and around major cities in France are evidence of this problem.

Most Muslims in Europe do not subscribe to radical Islamic fundamentalism, and many of those who do support the idea of the Islamic state do not subscribe to violence. However, given their large population in Europe, Muslims have provided a fertile recruiting ground by Islamic terrorists.

Much of the recruiting takes place in prisons. In France, more than half of the prison population is Muslim, and many inmates have ready-made criminal skills that can be put to use in terrorist cells. In fact, the French prisons have been such desirable recruiting grounds that terrorist recruiters have been known to commit a crime just to be "admitted" to prison.

Recruiting often takes place in **mosques,** places of worship for Muslims. While they are normally filled with peace-loving people, some mosques have been led by imams who preach fiery radicalism. Even in mosques with nonradical leaders, factions or groups of radicals may exist and recruit for jihad.

The recruiting process usually begins in small groups that meet within the mosques, often with an experienced recruiter playing a lead role. The recruits are slowly indoctrinated until they begin to reach a point of radicalization. Then the groups are moved to locations outside the mosques, typically to private apartments, where the indoctrination becomes stronger.

Once the recruits have begun to believe strongly in jihad, they are repeatedly shown videos of jihadists fighting in foreign wars and of terrorist executions of civilians. Eventually, the recruits become fully radicalized, at which time the recruiter is likely to spend much time alone with each individual recruit for days at a time, learning all about the recruit's strengths and weaknesses.

After recruits are fully developed in jihadism, the recruiter may assign them to a terrorist cell or send them to one of the foreign wars where Islamists are fighting secular states, such as Bosnia, Afghanistan, Chechnya, and Iraq. Fighting in foreign wars is considered not only a way to help the jihad cause but also a way to develop character and serves as informal proof of initiation. Consequently, many who return from fighting in foreign wars achieve high positions in the European terrorist networks.

Non-Muslims Converted to Jihad

Current estimates suggest that hundreds of thousands of non-Muslim Europeans have converted to Islam, including more than 100,000 Christians in France. Most converts embrace Islam in its peaceful form, but a small percentage embraces radical fundamentalism. This small percentage includes highly desirable targets for terrorist recruiters.

Recruits of non-Middle Eastern descent are especially desirable because, being Europeans, they can travel freely to the United States without visas and without so easily becoming terrorist suspects. This increases the likelihood of terrorist attacks against the United States by individuals with names like Smith or Jones.

Proof of terrorist successes in recruiting non-Muslims can be seen from the various accounts of native citizens from Germany, France, and England who were captured on the battlefields in Afghanistan, Chechnya, and Iraq, for example. Undoubtedly, other converts who are captured return to their home countries even more radicalized and ready to carry out terrorist activities.

The Integration Issue

As discussed, many Muslim immigrants have not integrated well into European society. As is well known from experiences in the United States, poor social conditions lead to gangs, crime, and a myriad of social problems. Youths are often eager to join an organization, whether it be a gang or a jihad, when it gives them a sense of belonging and stability. Without doubt, this **integration issue** accounts for a substantial portion of the spread of radical jihadism in Europe.

However, a substantial portion of European terrorists have come from well-adjusted middle-class and upper-middle-class families. Mohammed Atta, the leader in the 9/11 attack on the World Trade Center, became radicalized in Europe when studying in Hamburg, Germany. After becoming radicalized, he went to Chechnya to join in the fighting there, but on the way, through a coincidental meeting, he was diverted to the Afghanistan area and ended up being the personal choice of Usama bin Laden to lead the attack on the World Trade Center.

Lone Wolves and Families   Traditionally, individuals have become involved in terrorism after being recruited. However, an increasing number of "lone wolves" take it upon themselves to develop terrorist cells without being recruited. There has also been a trend toward entire families becoming involved in terrorist cells and plots.

Operation of Terrorist Cells

Various specializations exist with respect to terrorists cells (see Figure 18.7). These include the following:

- **Spiritual leadership**   Most terrorist cells are guided by spiritual leaders who sometimes issue *fatwas* (religious pronouncements) giving the cell members the green light to kill innocent Muslims and non-Muslims.
- **Logistics support**   This includes making false documents, providing transportation across borders, making contacts, and identifying safe houses.
- **Weapons experts**   Some cell members are sent to specialized training camps where they acquire bomb-making and other military-type skills.
- **Financial support**   Some cells, especially those with dedicated terror missions, are financed by handlers who receive money from a wide variety of sources, including charities, wealthy financiers, nongovernmental organizations, and organized crime—including groups engaged in narcotics and human trafficking, robbery, petty theft, and other street crimes. In some cases, cell members are instructed to support themselves with legitimate jobs or criminal activities.

Terrorist Training Camps

Terrorist training camps have been central in toughening terrorists. Before 9/11, Afghanistan, under the Taliban government, hosted large training camps run by Usama bin Laden. After the United States expelled the Taliban and crushed bin Laden's training camps in Afghanistan, other training camps sprang up in Northern Iraq. Jihadists from all over the world traveled to these camps before going into war or on terrorist operations. Other countries that openly ran training camps included Iran, Pakistan, Lebanon, and Syria. Still other countries including Palestinian-controlled Gaza, the Philippines, Malaysia, and Indonesia ran more clandestine training camps. Reports also suggest clandestine training campus in remote mountain areas in Western Europe.

FIGURE 18.7 **Structure of a Terrorist Cell**

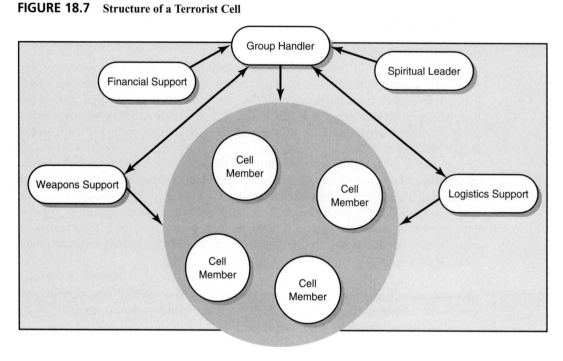

However, training can take place almost anywhere: The terrorists who carried out the bombing of the World Trade Center in 1993 trained in the woods in Connecticut. These clandestine training camps are not as effective as the others because they draw attention if they try to train recruits to use live machine guns, bombs, and rocket-propelled grenades.

The Central Mosques

Several **central mosques** in Europe have served as international hubs for terrorists. These include mosques in London, Milan, and Hamburg. Almost all major terrorists had some connection to these mosques, and terrorists connected to them had some type of hand in virtually all major terrorist attacks in the world.

Using wiretaps and other types of covert surveillance against many key individuals associated with these mosques, authorities have managed to unravel many details relating to most major terror attacks in Europe. However, this has led many high-ranking terrorists to plan their operations away from the umbrella of the mosques.

Usama bin Laden and the Globalization of Jihad

LO7   **Usama bin Laden (UBL)** built a substantial military operation and related financial backing during the Soviet occupation of Afghanistan. After the war, he continued to operate his international training camps in support of jihad groups from various parts of the world. In 1988, he helped create the **al Qaeda** terrorist group and soon thereafter became its undisputed leader.

UBL's training camps and connections to central mosques facilitated the collaboration and cooperation of diverse terrorist groups. Each group had its own goal in fighting against its secular government, but UBL, being in a central position, began to take on a worldview in which he foresaw the diverse groups uniting to participate in a single global struggle. At the core of his worldview was the belief that the United States was the primary enemy of his global jihad, a primary reason for ordering the 9/11 attacks against the World Trade Center and other targets.

In 1998 he formed an international terrorist group, the **International Islamic Front for Jihad against the Jews and Crusaders.** It included terrorist groups from Egypt, Pakistan, and Bangladesh. In February 1998, five members of the group, including UBL, signed the **world Islamic front statement,** which included the following call for Muslims everywhere to kill Americans:

> We—with Allah's help—call on every Muslim who believes in Allah and wishes to be rewarded to comply with Allah's order to kill the Americans and plunder their money wherever and whenever they find it. We also call on Muslim ulema [scholars], leaders, youths, and soldiers to launch the raid on Satan's U.S. troops and the devil's supporters allying with them, and to displace those who are behind them so that they may learn a lesson.

Despite UBL's central position in training jihadists and his alliances with other terrorist organizations, he became a figurehead in the larger scope of al Qaeda. Although he called for all Muslims to unite against Americans, the focus of many jihad organizations remained local. After all, terrorist organizations that had actively been engaged in war against their own governments were not about to forget about their local struggles and focus on the United States. Furthermore, terrorist groups everywhere had seen what happened to al Qaeda and the Taliban in Afghanistan. Al Qaeda continued to have a hand in post-9/11 attacks in different parts of the world, supplying financial and logistical support.

al Qaeda Funding

Although much of what is known about al Qaeda's finances is probably classified, a reasonable amount is known about them pre-9/11. In particular, it is well known that UBL financed the war against the Soviets in Afghanistan through what was widely referred to as the **golden chain,** a fund-raising operation that obtained some $30 million a year from Muslim charitable organizations and businesses around the world controlled and influenced by sympathizers.

Money in the golden chain was funneled through a core group of financial facilitators with good international contacts, especially in Saudi Arabia. Some of the money raised by the financial facilitators was diverted from donations collected in mosques and elsewhere known as *zakat.* One of the five pillars of the Sunni sect of Islam, it is an obligation for the faithful to give a certain amount each year.

After 9/11, the United States and other countries placed great pressure on al Qaeda financial networks by arresting and capturing key financial facilitators, freezing funds, and prosecuting members of some charitable organizations. These pressures, plus the defeat of the Taliban and al Qaeda's expulsion from Afghanistan, have caused the organization to splinter into smaller groups and cells. This, in turn, has increased its reliance on petty crime and, according to some experts, drug trafficking. Still, it is believed that al Qaeda continues to receive funds through the golden chain.

MONEY LAUNDERING

LO8   In the broadest sense, **money laundering** involves practices that hide the connection between the sources of funds and their ultimate use. In the case of organized crime, it means disguising the source of ill-gotten money and making it appear to have come from legitimate sources. In other words, the laundering process washes dirty money and makes it appear clean.

Some reports suggest the term *money laundering* has its roots in the mafia's use of coin-operated laundries to introduce illegal slot-machine profits into the legitimate economy. Supposedly, coins from slot machines were mixed in with coins from the laundries and then deposited into legitimate bank accounts. Regardless of the truth of this story, it is certainly a good example of how money is laundered.

Whereas the money-laundering process in organized crime begins with dirty money and ends with clean money, the reverse is often true with terrorism. In many cases, terrorist organizations begin with clean money and end with dirty money. That is, they raise money from apparently legitimate sources and then put it to use in terrorist activities while disguising its origin. As with organized crime, the objective is to hide the connection between the source and the use of money.

Terrorist organizations are increasingly becoming criminal syndicates that raise money through the broad spectrum of illegal activities that include everything from petty street crime to extortion, human smuggling, and drug trafficking. These activities generate large amounts of money that cannot simply be deposited into bank accounts without drawing the attention of the authorities. So, like the mafia, terrorist organizations need to find ways to channel illegally obtained monies into apparently legitimate bank accounts. Of course, not all of this money needs to flow through bank accounts, but it is much more convenient to move large amounts of cash around the world by wire transfer than it is to smuggle bulk quantities of cash across international borders.

The Three-Step Money-Laundering Process

LO9   Money laundering involves basic phases: placement, layering, and integration.

In the **placement phase,** the money launderer introduces illegally obtained profits into the financial system. The main objective of this phase is to get the money into the financial system in a way that cannot be traced to its illegal source.

In the **layering phase,** the money launderer uses complicated sets of transactions to move the money around the financial system and further distance it from its original illegal source. The main objective is to thoroughly destroy any audit trail that could trace the money back to its original placement in the financial system.

In the **integration phase,** the launderer moves the money a final time into accounts under his legal control to make it appear to come from a legitimate source.

As an example of the three-phase process (see Figure 18.8), consider a small-time drug smuggler who needs to launder $50,000. The process might proceed as follows:

- **Placement**   A U.S.-based drug smuggler deposits the money in equal amounts into 10 different bank accounts.
- **Layering**   *Step 1:* The smuggler wires the money to a single offshore bank account that belongs to the XYZ Company, an offshore company that he controls. The privacy laws of the offshore country would not allow a U.S. investigation to establish that he controls the XYZ Company or subpoena its bank records. *Step 2:* The ABC Company, a U.S. company that the smuggler controls, sells a piece of real estate that it owns in a third country. The buyer of the real estate is the XYZ Company, which wires payment to ABC Company's U.S. bank account.
- **Integration**   The smuggler is paid a $50,000 consulting fee for work that he supposedly does for the ABC Company.

As an extra layer of protection, the drug smuggler might set things up so that the XYZ and ABC companies are legally owned by trusted friends or associates in his criminal organization.

FIGURE 18.8 **Typical Money-Laundering Scheme**

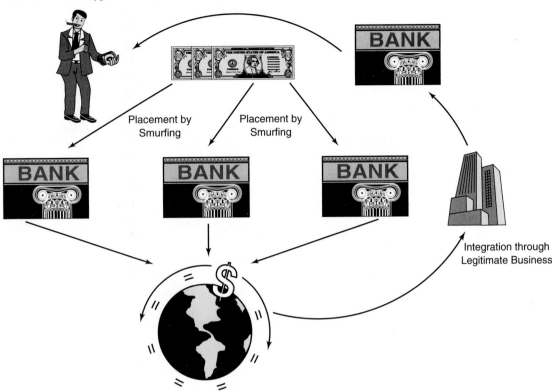

Layering by Moving Money Around

Placement Methods

The placement process involves a number of different methods, such as the following:

- **Smurfing** A form of "currency structuring," **smurfing** circumvents the requirement that U.S. banks file currency transaction reports (CTRs) for cash transactions of $10,000 or more. This method involves placing large amounts of money in many random deposits, each less than $10,000, with many banks. Smurfing is probably the most common form of money laundering.

- **Cash smuggling** The **cash smuggling method** involves smuggling cash across international borders to accomplish two objectives. First, it can relocate the cash in a second country where it is easier (through regulatory or for other reasons) to deposit large sums without alerting authorities. Second, the very act of moving money far away from its source can have a layering effect.

- **Negotiable instruments** Another form of currency structuring involves the **negotiable instruments method;** this method involves using cash to purchase negotiable financial instruments such as money orders, cashier's checks, and so on. The individual instruments can then be bundled together and sold to a money-laundering specialist or can be used to purchase things like drugs or guns.

- **Cash exchange for negotiable goods** The **cash exchange for negotiable goods method** involves exchanging cash for goods, such as diamonds, that can be more easily stored and transported across international borders. The goods themselves can be used as a payment medium, or they can be converted back into cash for placement in the financial system.

- **ATM deposits**   The **ATM deposits method** involves sprinkling cash deposits through the system of ATM machines that accept bank deposits. One drug dealer was caught having his wholesalers deposit money directly into his account using this approach.

- **Cash-value insurance policies**   Insurance policies, such as a single-premium life policy that has cash value, are purchased in the **cash-value insurance policies method.** Money launderers can either borrow against the policies or cash them in. This scheme can be amplified by purchasing multiple policies from various insurers.

- **Corporate bank accounts**   This method involves placing money in legitimate businesses (or charities or other legal entities) that normally collect large amounts of cash. The illegal cash is mixed in with legal cash. In some cases, the legitimate businesses are only shell companies set up in foreign countries with offshore bank accounts.

- **Buy a bank**   The **buy a bank method** involves either establishing a new bank or purchasing an existing one. Ownership permits the money launderer to deposit large sums of money without needing to worry about currency transaction reports. It also facilitates the improper use of *pass-through accounts,* which are accounts that banks open in other, remotely located banks. This permits the bank holding these accounts to quickly provide funds to their clients in the remote locations. In some parts of the world, it is possible to set up instant banks, which exist primarily electronically and on paper.

- **Buy a banker**   The **buy a banker method** involves bribing a banker. It is the next best thing to owning a bank.

Layering Methods

As indicated, the object of layering is to destroy any audit trail that connects the funds with their original point of placement into the financial system.

Informal Value Transfer System (IVTS)   Also known as an *alternative remittance system,* an **informal value transfer system (IVTS)** is any type of money transfer system that operates outside the normal financial system. Such systems date back thousands of years and go by many names. For example, they are called the *hawala* in Afghanistan, Pakistan, and the Middle East; the *hundi* in India; *he fe ch'ien* in China; the *phoe kuan* in Thailand; and the black market peso exchange in South America.

IVTSs are used for both legitimate and illegitimate reasons. In many parts of the world, especially in remote places, the local payment systems are inadequate because they are inaccessible, unreliable, too expensive, or too slow. IVTSs are generally simple, efficient, and cost effective (frequently offering the best currency exchange rates), and they provide anonymity to both the sender and receiver.

The typical IVTS requires only a phone call, fax, or e-mail message between two participating IVTS providers in different locations. The sender of the money merely gives cash to a local IVTS provider with a fee for the service and the details as to where to send the money. The IVTS provider then calls an affiliated IVTS provider with the payment instructions, which typically include a secret code number and the amount to be paid. The affiliate provider then gives the money to anyone who knows the secret code number and the amount of money sent.

In some countries, IVTS providers comprise networks of family-related tribal individuals who have run the system for hundreds or even thousands of years. They normally maintain credit accounts with each other and only occasionally settle balances between each other. Its believed that a considerable amount of terrorist-related money has passed through the *hawala* system.

Tax Havens and Offshore Banks   Money launderers often use **tax havens and offshore banks** to move their money in and out of countries that have weak antilaundering controls. This includes countries whose controls are good on paper but whose banking officials are easily corrupted with bribes and extortion. Also, the more countries through which money is moved, the more difficult it is to trace. Many U.S. money launderers have sent large amounts of money in and out of the Bahamas and the Cayman Islands. Although the Cayman Islands comprises only a tiny group of small islands, it is considered the fifth largest financial center in the world behind major cities such as New York and Tokyo.

Bank Secrecy Laws   Some countries have protected money launderers with **bank secrecy laws** that make it difficult or impossible for foreign governments to investigate their account holders. In some cases, banks have permitted their customers to open "numbered accounts" associated only with numbers and code words, not customer names.

In the post 9/11 world, international pressures have encouraged more and more countries to become "compliant" with international anti-money laundering standards, leaving fewer places for money launderers to hide behind bank secrecy laws. Furthermore, many money launderers prefer to avoid countries that do maintain secrecy because simply transferring funds to or from such countries can create suspicion in the United States.

Offshore   This layering scheme works by transferring ownership of a company to an **offshore trust** controlled by the money launderer. In some jurisdictions, such trusts (and international business corporations) are administered by unregulated trust companies that can obscure the financial ownership audit trail by changing the company's name or merging it with other companies. Sometimes offshore trusts contain "flee provisions" that instruct the trustees to move the trusts to other locations in the event of investigations by law enforcement.

Shell Corporations   Most large-scale money launderers are likely to use shell corporations to help layer ill-gotten money. The ideal **shell corporation** exists in an offshore haven that has strong bank secrecy laws that do not require companies to maintain corporate records and permit bearer stock certificates. Bearer stock certificates permit ownership to be passed from one person to the next with complete secrecy.

Walking Accounts   A **walking account** is a layering tool in which the money launderer sets up a bank account with instructions to immediately transfer all deposits to an account in a second jurisdiction. The money launderer might also give instructions for the bank in the second jurisdiction to automatically transfer all incoming funds to a third jurisdiction. Using this tool, the money launderer can transfer money around the globe, making it very difficult to trace. As an extra layer of protection, the money launderer might make sure the money passes thorough at least one bank that will tip off the money launderer if any inquiries about the account are made by any law enforcement agency.

Buy a Bank   Money launderers may pass funds through banks that they own or control (see Figure 18.9). The sophisticated money launderer might create an "instant" bank in an offshore banking haven, pass large sums of money through the bank, and then close it. New banks can be open and closed as needed. Also, banks owned by the money launderer can destroy records as needed to break the audit trail.

FIGURE 18.9
Purchasing Banks Can Be a Tactic for Money Launderers

Financial Intermediaries Money launderers sometimes use powerful, influential persons who are trusted in the local economy, such as accountants, lawyers, brokers, and other financial intermediaries, as **financial intermediaries** to handle their transactions for them. Although laws may require the intermediaries to use due diligence in accepting clients and business, corrupt intermediaries who are adept in looking the other way exist. Some corrupt intermediaries specialize in creating false documents representing sham transactions to satisfy authorities. Attorneys make especially useful intermediaries because their clients are generally protected by the attorney/client privilege.

Integration Method

In the third and final stage of the money-laundering process, the money launderer puts the money to personal use.

Offshore Debit and Credit Cards Using the **offshore debit and credit cards method,** the money launderer obtains a credit or debit card linked to an account in an offshore bank and uses it to make cash withdrawals and pay bills. In recent years, the U.S. Internal Revenue Service managed to obtain a federal John Doe summons that directed MasterCard and Visa to produce credit card account records relating to cards issued in various Caribbean banks.

Offshore Consulting and Directors Fees Using **offshore consulting and directors fees,** money launderers pay themselves generous consulting or directors fees from offshore companies that they control.

Corporate Loans In the **corporate loan method,** money launderers borrow funds (disbursed in the form of checks) from offshore companies that they control. This approach even permits the money launderer to deduct interest paid on the loan; by paying interest, the money launderer is able to place even more money offshore.

Gambling In this scheme, money launderers purchase large amount of casino chips, gamble some, and then collect the cash value of their chips in the form of a bank check, money order, or wire transfer from the casinos.

Real Estate Flips In a **real estate flip** scheme, money launderers sell real estate for inflated prices to offshore companies they secretly own or control.

Under-the-Table Cash Deals In this scheme using **under-the-table cash deals,** money launderers purchase real estate or other valuable assets, including entire companies, at below market value. The money launderer makes up in cash the difference between the amount paid and the market value. For example, a money launderer might, on paper, purchase an office building that is worth $3 million for $2 million. He might then pay the seller the extra $1 million in cash plus an extra $100,000 as compensation for dealing under the table. Of course, the seller is then left with a money-laundering problem but might be in a better position to launder or spend the cash.

Stock Purchases In the **stock purchase method,** the money launderer works with a dishonest stock broker and both buys long and sells short in the same volatile stock, thus ensuring a capital gain in one transaction and a capital loss in the other, regardless of whether the stock price goes up or down. When the money launderer takes the capital gain, the dishonest broker tears up the record of the opposing capital loss. The same game can be played in the commodities and derivatives markets.

Legitimate Businesses Money launderers use the **legitimate business method** to place cash in legitimate businesses that they control. They then report the cash as part of regular earnings. This amounts to placement, layering, and integration all rolled up into one.

Sham Import Transactions In this scheme, **sham import transaction** money launderers engage in trade between domestic and offshore companies they control. The offshore company pays inflated prices for goods it purchases from the domestic company.

In another import scheme, money launderers use cash or offshore money to purchase goods in a foreign country. Next, to conceal the source of the payment, the goods are shipped to a free trade zone, where they are shipped to the home country of the money launderer. The goods are then sold in an apparently legitimate sales transaction.

Anti-Money Laundering Organizations and Laws

The Financial Action Task Force

LO10 In 1989, what is now the G8 (then the G7), a group of eight major countries that includes Canada, France, Germany, Italy, Japan, the United Kingdom, the United States, and the Russian Federation set up the **Financial Action Task Force (FATF) on Money Laundering.** The FATF produced 40 recommendations to combat money laundering and 9 recommendations to combat terrorist financing.

Some of the key 40 recommendations follow:

- Creating and implementing international anti-money laundering conventions.
- Criminalizing the act of money laundering.
- Setting policies and procedures for seizing money-laundering proceeds.
- Requiring financial (and certain nonfinancial) institutions to implement due diligence anti-money laundering programs.
- Increasing international cooperation in anti-money laundering investigations and prosecutions.

The 9 recommendations relating to terrorist financing expanded the 40 recommendations to cover issues especially related to financing terrorism. These additional recommendations are as follows:

1. **Ratification and implementation of U.N. instruments** Calls for all countries to implement the U.N. International Convention for the Suppression of the Financing of Terrorism and other U.N. acts relating to antiterrorism.
2. **Criminalizing the financing of terrorism and associated money laundering** Calls for all countries to criminalize the financing of terrorism, terrorist acts, and terrorist organizations.
3. **Freezing and confiscating terrorist assets** Calls for all countries to freeze and confiscate assets belonging to terrorists, terrorist organizations, and terrorist financiers.
4. **Reporting suspicious transactions related to terrorism** Calls for all countries to implement systems that require financial (and certain nonfinancial) institutions to report suspicious transactions to law enforcement.

5. **International cooperation** Calls for all countries to cooperate with other countries in investigations, prosecutions, and extraditions relating to terrorist-related financing and activities.

6. **Alternative remittance system** Calls for all countries to license and regulate alternative remittance systems and subject them to anti-money laundering and antiterrorism laws.

7. **Wire transfers** Calls for all countries to pass laws that require financial institutions to maintain a complete audit trail for all wire transfers.

8. **Nonprofit organization** Calls for all countries to pass laws and regulations that prevent nonprofit organizations from being used for terrorist financing.

9. **Cash courier** Calls for all countries to control the flow of cash across their borders through the use of regulations, inspections, and confiscation of illegally transported cash.

Collectively, the 49 recommendations are consistent with the official U.S. government's money-laundering strategy.

FATF Publications Through its Web site (www.fatf-gafi.org), the FATF regularly issues some very important publications relevant to anti-money laundering:

- **FATF standards** The **FATF standards** set forth general standards for anti-money laundering laws, regulations, and policies.

- **FATF reports on noncooperating countries and territories** The **FATF reports on noncooperating countries and territories** include details on which countries and territories do not fully comply with its criteria. Noncomplying countries are obvious weak points for money laundering. However, even if a country is compliant, its financial industry and government officials might be relatively more subject to corruption. Anti-money laundering laws are only as good as the people who apply them.

- **FATF money-laundering trends and techniques** The **FATF money-laundering trends and techniques** publications include in-depth looks at the latest money-laundering schemes.

A thorough knowledge of these publications is essential for any forensic accountant specializing in anti-money laundering.

Financial Crimes Enforcement Network

The **Financial Crimes Enforcement Network (FinCEN)** is organized under the U.S. Department of the Treasury to oversee and implement policies to prevent and detect money laundering. FinCEN's primary enforcement tool is its application of the **Bank Secrecy Act (BSA)**—also known as the *Currency and Foreign Transactions Reporting Act*—to require recordkeeping and reporting by banks and other financial institutions. FinCEN also provides intelligence reports to law enforcement agencies.

FinCEN requires banks and other financial institutions to file currency transaction reports (CTRs) for cash transactions of more than $10,000 and suspicious activity reports (SARs) for transactions that could be related to money laundering. These reports, along with other data, are then made available to authorized organizations through the FinCEN data warehousing system, **BSA Direct,** which permits law enforcement officials to access all BSA data through a single Web portal.

BSA is one of a group of U.S. anti-money laundering acts. Other important acts include the 1986 Money Laundering Control Act (MLCA) as part of the Anti-Drug Abuse Act of 1986, and the Money Laundering Suppression Act of 1994 as part of the Riegle-Neal Community Development and Regulatory Improvement Act of 1994. Collectively, these acts name more than 170 crimes relating to money laundering.

Money-Laundering Penalties

In the United States, penalties for money laundering are harsh. The statutes permit prison sentences of up to 20 years per money-laundering transaction. Fines may be as large as $500,000 per money-laundering transaction or twice the amount of the transaction, and any funds linked to such transactions may be subject to seizure and forfeiture.

CFR Regulations

As implemented by the Code of Federal Regulations (CFR), U.S. banks and certain financial institutions are subject to various anti-money laundering regulations. Some of these regulations follow:

- **Required internal BSA compliance programs**   Applicable financial intuitions are required to set up internal programs that maintain compliance with anti-money laundering laws and regulations. Such programs must be properly approved by the board of directors, include an adequate system of internal controls and independent tests of compliance, have a designated person to coordinate and monitor compliance daily, and provide proper employee training.
- **Reporting requirements**   All BSA-regulated institutions are required to submit the following five reports to the government:
  - **IRS Form 4789, Currency Transaction Report (CTR)**   CTRs apply to any type of deposit, withdrawal, payment, or transfer connected with a regulated financial institution. Financial institutions must treat multiple currency transactions as related when there is reason to believe they are.
  - **U.S. Customs Form 4790, Report of International Transportation of Currency or Monetary Instruments (CMIR)**   CMIRs are required to be filed by both individuals and banks that physically mail, ship, or otherwise move currency or various monetary instruments in excess of $10,000 into and out of the United States.
  - **Department of the Treasury Form 90-22.1, Report of Foreign Bank and Financial Accounts (FBAR)**   FBARs must be filed by anyone having an interest or signatory power in a banking, securities, or other financial account in a foreign country if the aggregate value of such foreign accounts exceeds $10,000 at any time during the year.
  - **Treasury Department Form 90-22.47 and OCC Form 8010-9, 8010-1, Suspicious Activity Report (SAR)**   SARs must be filed anytime activities may indicate money laundering.
  - **"Designation of Exempt Person" Form TDF 90-22.53**   This form is filed to indicate certain customers who are exempt from CTR filing.
- **Recordkeeping requirements**   Regulated institutions are required to maintain a wide variety of records relating to the sale of monetary instruments (such as money orders, cashier's checks, and traveler's checks) whose amounts are in the aggregate between $3,000 and $10,000. Detailed records of many fund transfers that are $3,000 or more must also be kept.

Suspicious Activity Reporting Requirements

Suspicious activity reports must be filed for the following:

- Insider abuse involving any amount.
- Violations of federal law related to aggregating $5,000 or more when a suspect can be identified.

- Violations of federal law related to aggregating $25,000 or more regardless of a potential suspect.

- Transactions aggregating $5,000 or more that involve potential money laundering or violations of the BSA if the bank knows, suspects, or has reason to suspect that the transaction involves funds from illegal activities or is intended or conducted to hide or disguise illicit funds or assets as part of a plan to violate or evade any law or regulation or to avoid any transaction reporting requirement under federal law or is designed to evade any of the BSA regulations.

- Any transaction that has no business or apparent lawful purpose or is not the type of transaction in which the particular customer would normally be expected to engage and the bank knows of no reasonable explanation for the transaction after examining the available facts, including the background and possible purpose of the transaction.

Related regulations require banks to know their customers in order to understand the types of transactions that may appear suspicious and to obtain and record proper documentation regarding the customer's identity. Accounts are not permitted to be opened for customers who do not provide proper documentation and identification, and such documentation and identification must be verified by the financial institution. For example, financial institutions routinely verify customer telephone numbers.

Red Flags That Trigger SARs

- Activity inconsistent with the customer's business.
- Acts that appear oriented to avoid reporting or recordkeeping requirements.
- Fund (wire) transfers without apparent good reasons.
- Insufficient or suspicious information provided by customer.
- Bank employee activities, such as lavish lifestyles.
- Unusual bank-to-bank transactions.
- Other suspicious customer activity such as depositing an unusual number of large bills, deposits of musty or dirty bills, deposits by couriers rather than in person, and so on.

Certain types of customers and transactions in high-risk areas should be given special scrutiny. Such high-risk areas include international correspondent banking relationships, Fedwire and Clearing House Interbank Payments System (CHIPS), wire transfers (especially those to and from high-risk countries), courier deliveries to and from banks in other countries, pass-through accounts (special accounts that permit people to write U.S. checks with the money being drawn from a single foreign bank account in a U.S. bank), special use accounts, banks' internal special use accounts, private banking accounts (those with high net worth clients), foreign branches and offices of national banks, and high-risk clients (such as casinos, check-cashing stores, used car dealers, and so on).

This chapter discusses organized crime, terrorist organizations, and money laundering. Organized crime is a global problem, and various governments cooperate in fighting it through the U.N. Convention against Transnational Organized Crime and its Protocols. Europol fights organized crime across the European Union member states. In the United States, the FBI is the primary organization charged with fighting organized crime. Its organized crime section contains separate units relating to La Cosa Nostra (LCN) and Italian organized crime, Eurasian organized crime, and Asian/African organized crime.

LCN originally comprised various groups but emerged as a single organization around 1930 under the leadership of Salvatore Maranzano. Since that time, it has been run though five New York families (Bonanno, Colombo, Gambino, Lucchesse, and Genovese), primarily under the leadership of the Genovese family.

The overall LCN syndicate has generally been ruled by a single boss. Over the years, the succession of bosses has included Lucky Luciano, Frank Castello, Vito Genovese, and Chin Gigante. According to FBI reports, LCN and its associates remain actively engaged in drug trafficking, murder, assault, gambling, extortion, loan-sharking, labor racketeering, money laundering, arson, gasoline bootlegging, infiltration of legitimate businesses, stock market manipulation, and various other illegal frauds and schemes.

LCN membership includes associates and made men. Only a small number of associates become made men. The organization is extremely strict and careful in whom it invites to become a true insider. This is one of the reasons that the organization is nearly impossible to fully infiltrate with informers.

Money flows upward in LCN. The first-level soldiers typically give 50 to 70 percent of their illegal earnings to the capo (their immediate boss). The capo in turn gives 10 to 40 percent of his share to the family boss, the man who has absolute authority in the family organization.

The family boss approves all new members, all major illegal business dealings, and all internal and contract killings. LCN bosses seldom authorize killings of those not involved somehow with LCN dealings.

LCN members manage their illegal business using cash, and soldiers, capos, and bosses are accustomed to hiding boxes and bags of cash. They also tend to protect their personal assets (e.g., automobiles, houses, and bank accounts) by placing them in others' names.

The FBI has used various legal statutes and investigatory methods in combating organized crime. The primary statutes include RICO and statutes against conspiracy, money laundering, and income tax evasion in addition to those relating to specific crimes. A primary investigative tool that has met with great success has included covert monitoring, including wiretaps, bugs, and other listening devices.

EOC groups are sometimes called the *Russian mafia,* the *Red mafia,* and *Russian organized crime (ROC).* According to the FBI, the eight most prevalent crimes committed by this group include health care fraud, auto insurance fraud, securities and investment fraud, money laundering, drug trafficking, extortion, auto theft, and interstate transportation of stolen property. Most recently, reports indicate their desire to expand via drug trafficking and illegal arms sales, and FBI investigations indicate their recent involvement in commercial alien smuggling.

ROC bosses tend to be highly educated, multilingual former KGB agents who still work for Russian agencies and are dedicated to destroying the United States. According to intelligence estimates, ROC controls the majority of all Russian businesses and banks as well as dozens of stock exchanges and government enterprises. The extent of ROC control is so pervasive that many argue that Russia is now a mafia state.

Evidence suggests that ROC syndicates have established alliances with Colombian and Mexican drug cartels. Military and other analysts suggest that the Colombian drug cartel is aligned with Fuerzas Armadas Revolucionarias de Colombia (FARC), a Colombian revolutionary, military organization that reportedly finances the majority of its operations through narcotics trafficking. The result is a de facto alliance between ROC, FARC, and the Colombian and Mexican drug cartels.

ROC has been especially good at implementing Internet-based criminal schemes. The art and science of hacking in Russia has been elevated to the formal level, as embodied by the Russian Civil Hackers School, which ostensibly exists for legitimate security training, but some argue that it is really a KGB-dominated organization that spews out the world's most sophisticated cyber criminals.

Asian organized crime (AOC) includes criminal enterprises relating to a large number of countries in East and Southeastern Asia, including China, Korea, Japan, Thailand, the Philippines, Cambodia, Laos, and Vietnam. It also includes criminal enterprises relating to the South Pacific island nations and to Southwest Asia, including Pakistan, India, Afghanistan, Nepal, and Iran. Within the United States, AOC concentrates in certain large cities.

The largest percentage of FBI AOC investigations has consistently been related to Chinese organized crime, which is composed of large numbers of loosely organized, independent enterprises spread throughout the United States. Some of the Chinese triads have initiation ceremonies and internal structures that are somewhat similar to those of LCN.

Much of today's worldwide terrorism has its roots in a radical interpretation of the Islamic religion. Many who teach Islamic radicalism (or fundamentalism) further call for violent jihad by declaring that all of Islam is under attack by non-Muslims and that true believers must defend the faith by destroying secular governments, including the United States, wherever they exist.

Because the Islamic terrorists' beliefs are deeply rooted in their religion, there is no room for compromise. They will accept nothing less than Islamic theocracy for the entire world. For this reason, Islamic terrorism is a de facto world war that is not likely to end until the terrorists are defeated.

The beginning of the radical jihad as it is known today is traced back to the Afghan War of the 1980s in which the Soviets invaded Afghanistan. That produced a situation in which Muslims were truly defending their land against secular, Communist nonbelievers. After the war, however, many of the jihadists migrated to Western Europe, where it was believed they would integrate into society. However, after migrating, many jihadists simply continued their struggle, and the Western European countries became a magnet that drew Islamic radicals from a wide variety of countries where they had either been persecuted or engaged in their own wars against secular governments.

The European legal system is not equipped to deal with terrorism, and its laws permitted jihadists to freely operate on the Continent and plan and support terrorist operations against their original home countries. In time, the terrorist operations shifted from their original home countries to the jihadists' new home countries.

Much of the jihad recruiting occurs in mosques and prisons. The fully developed jihadist is often sent to a foreign jihadist war or is assigned to a local terrorist cell. Fighting in foreign wars strengthens the terrorists' ability to kill and serves as proof of loyalty.

The typical terrorist cell includes support from a spiritual leader, logistics support (including false documents), weapons training, and financial support. Terrorist training camps and central mosques serve as nerve centers where diverse terrorist groups congregate and form alliances.

Usama bin Laden's organization (al Qaeda) began in the jihad against the Soviet occupation of Afghanistan. In 1998, he formed an international terrorist group, the International Islamic Front for Jihad against the Jews and Crusaders, which included terrorist groups from Egypt, Pakistan, and Bangladesh. Despite bin Laden's internationalization of terrorism, most terrorist struggles remain local.

Usama bin Laden was financed through the golden chain, a fund-raising operation that obtained some $30 million a year from Muslim charitable organizations and businesses around the world controlled and influenced by sympathizers. After 9/11, the United States and other countries placed great pressure on al Qaeda financial networks by arresting and capturing key financial facilitators, freezing funds, and prosecuting members of some charitable organizations.

Money laundering is related to organized crime and terrorism. Both need money, and both need to hide the connection between its sources and uses. The money-laundering process has three basic phases: placement, layering, and integration. Money launderers use a variety of methods to implement these phases.

Various organizations exist to fight money laundering. The U.S. Financial Crimes Enforcement Network (FinCEN) enforces the anti-money laundering provisions of the Bank Secrecy Act (BSA). FinCEN requires banks and other financial institutions to file currency transaction reports for cash transactions of more than $10,000 and suspicious activity reports for transactions that could be related to money laundering. These reports, along with other data, are then made available to authorized organizations through BSA Direct, FinCEN's data warehousing system; it permits law enforcement officials to access all BSA data through a single Web portal.

Glossary

al Qaeda   Terrorist organization responsible for the 9/11 attacks in the United States and partially responsible for subsequent attacks against the West.

Asian organized crime (AOC)   Assortment of criminal enterprises relating to a large number of countries in East and Southeastern Asia, the South Pacific Island nations, and Southwest Asia, including Pakistan, India, Afghanistan, Nepal, and Iran.

associate   Position of person in LCN who is not a full member.

ATM deposit method   Deposit through the system of ATM machines used as a money-laundering placement method; involves collecting payments.

Bank Secrecy Act (BSA)   Congressional act, also known as the *Currency and Foreign Transactions Reporting Act,* that requires recordkeeping and reporting by banks and other financial institutions; enforced by FinCEN.

bank secrecy law   Law that may protect information relating to one's bank account. Money launderers prefer to layer funds by moving them through countries that protect them with bank secrecy laws.

bookie   Individual who takes illegal bets from players of the numbers game.

boss   Person in LCN family organization who has absolute authority.

BSA Direct   Online FinCEN database that contains currency transaction reports (CTRs), suspicious activity reports (SARs), and other data.

buy a bank method   Money-laundering placement method that involves either setting up a new bank or purchasing an existing one, allowing the money launderer to deposit large sums of money without needing to worry about currency transaction reports.

buy a banker method   Money-laundering placement method that involves bribing a banker.

capo   Person (captain) who overseas La Cosa Nostra soldiers.

cash exchange for negotiable goods method   Money-laundering placement method that involves exchanging cash for goods, such as diamonds, that can be more easily stored and transported across international borders; can be used as a payment medium or converted into cash for placement in the financial system.

cash smuggling method   Money-laundering placement method that involves smuggling cash across international borders.

cash-value insurance policy method   Money-laundering placement method that involves purchasing insurance policies, such as single-premium life insurance policies with cash value that money launderers can either borrow against or cash in; can be amplified by purchasing multiple policies from various insurers.

central mosque   Large mosques in Europe such as those in London, Milan, and Hamburg that served as an international hub for terrorists.

check fraud   Criminal scheme perpetrated by some organized crime groups.

corporate bank account method   Money-laundering placement method that involves placing money in legitimate businesses (shell companies set up in foreign countries), charities, or other legal entities that normally collect large amounts of cash.

corporate loan method   Integration scheme in which money launderers borrow money from offshore companies that they control.

Department of the Treasury Form 90-22.1, Report of Foreign Bank and Financial Accounts (FBAR)   Report that must be filed by anyone having an interest or signatory power in a banking, securities, or other financial account in a foreign country if the aggregate value of such foreign accounts exceeds $10,000 at any time during the year.

European Law Enforcement Organization (Europol)   European Union organization that fights organized crime across its member states.

fast-money loan   Loan-sharking loan that must be paid back rapidly, typically within a week.

FATF money-laundering trends and techniques   In-depth FATF reports that include the latest money-laundering schemes.

FATF reports on noncooperating countries and territories   Detailed FATF reports about which countries and territories do not fully comply with its criteria.

FATF standard   FATF document that sets international standards for anti-money laundering laws, regulations, and policies.

Financial Action Task Force (FATF) on Money Laundering   International G7/G8 organization that produced recommendations to combat money laundering and terrorist financing.

Financial Crimes Enforcement Network (FinCEN)   Organization under the U.S. Department of the Treasury charged with overseeing and implementing policies to prevent and detect money laundering.

financial intermediary   Person (typically powerful, influential person trusted in the local economy, often an accountant, lawyer, broker, and other financial expert) with whom money launderers place their money.

five-family LCN commission   Representatives from five families (Bonanno, Colombo/Profaci, Gambino, Lucchesse, and Genovese) believed to dominate LCN family.

Fuerzas Armadas Revolucionarias de Colombia (FARC)   Colombian revolutionary military organization that reportedly finances the majority of its operations through narcotics trafficking; classified by the DOJ as a narco-terrorist organization.

gambling   A favorite source of revenue for some organized crime groups. Also, a money-laundering scheme involving purchase of large amount of casino chips, some gambling, and then collecting the cash value of their chips in the form of a bank check, money order, or wire transfer from the casinos.

golden chain   Fund-raising operation that supplied funds to al Qaeda.

Groupes Islamiques Armes (GIA)   Algerian terrorist network that established strong roots in Europe, especially in France, where they joined the ranks of hundreds of thousands who already lived in and around the major cities.

informal value transfer system (IVTS) Money-laundering layering channel; alternative money transfer system that operates outside the normal financial system.

integration issue Problem related to the failure of many Muslim immigrants to assimilate into European society, which made them targets for terrorist recruiters.

integration phase Third and final phase of the money-laundering process that moves money made to appear to come from a legitimate source a final time into an account under the money launderer's legal control.

International Islamic Front for Jihad against the Jews and Crusaders International terrorist organization whose members from Egypt, Pakistan, and Bangladesh signed the world Islamic front statement, which for the first time called for internationalization of terrorism against the United States and the West.

IRS Form 4789, Currency Transaction Report (CTR) Report required for a cash transaction of more than $10,000 or multiple currency transactions treated as related when there is reason to believe they are connected.

Islamic radicalism Radical interpretation of Islam that calls for using violent means to ensure that all governments in the world operate under strict Islamic law.

jihad Literally means *to struggle;* violent struggle that radical Muslims have called for in keeping with the tenets of Islamic radicalism.

labor racketeering Domination, manipulation, and control of a labor movement that affects related businesses and industries.

La Cosa Nostra (LCN) Crime syndicate often called the *mafia* that began around Palermo, Sicily, where it consisted of people who included important aristocrats and politicians; later moved to the United States and became especially dominant in the New York area.

layering phase Second phase of the money-laundering process that uses complicated transactions to move the money around the financial system to further distance it from its original illegal source and thoroughly destroy any audit trail that could trace the money back to its original placement in the financial system.

legitimate business method Money-laundering scheme in which money launderers place cash in businesses that they control. They then report the cash as part of regular earnings. This amounts to placement, layering, and integration all rolled into one.

loan shark Person who illegally lends money at sky-high rates of interest; noted for carrying out violent acts against late payers.

loan-sharking Business of illegal sky-high interest rate lending; a favorite mafia business, typically related to illegal gambling.

made man Full-fledged LCN member.

money laundering Process that involves disguising the source of ill-gotten money and making it appear to come from legitimate sources.

mosque Muslim place of worship that also serves as a social and cultural center and that terrorists have used as recruiting grounds.

negotiable instrument method Money-laundering method and form of currency structuring that involves using cash to purchase negotiable financial instruments such as money orders, cashier's checks, and so on.

numbers game Type of illegal lottery often run by the mafia.

offshore consulting and directors fee   Payment that money launderers pay themselves from offshore companies that they control.

offshore debit and credit cards method   Scheme by which a money launderer obtains a credit or debit card linked to an account in an offshore bank that is then used to make cash withdrawals and pay bills.

offshore trust   Property (as money or securities) settled or held in trust that is part of a layering scheme that works by transferring ownership of a company to a offshore trust controlled by the money launderer.

omerta   Oath of silence that all LCN members take as part of their swearing-in ceremony.

picciotto   First-level soldier in LCN.

placement phase   First phase of the money-laundering process that introduces illegally obtained profits into the financial system in a way that cannot be traced back to its illegal source.

Qur'an   Holy Book of Islam.

real estate flip   Integration scheme in which money launderers sell real estate for inflated prices to offshore companies they secretly own or control.

Russian organized crime (ROC)   Also called the *Red mafia* and the *Russian mafia;* organized crime group closely linked to corrupt government officials in Russia; has many loosely organized groups that collectively could control a majority of Russian banks and businesses.

sgarrista   Second-level soldier in LCN.

sham import transaction   Business action that is part of a money-launderer scheme in which an offshore company pays inflated prices for goods it purchases from a related domestic company.

Sharia   Islamic law.

shell corporation   Corporation in an offshore haven with strong bank secrecy laws that helps layer ill-gotten money.

smurfing   Money-laundering method and a form of "currency structuring" designed to circumvent the requirement that U.S. banks file currency transaction reports for cash transactions of $10,000 or more.

soldier   Synonym for *made man,* or full member of LCN.

stock purchase method   Scheme in which a money launderer works with a dishonest stockbroker to both buy long and sell short in the same volatile stock, thus ensuring a capital gain in one transaction and a capital loss in the other, regardless of whether the stock price goes up or down.

tax haven and offshore bank   Money-laundering placement channel through which money launderers move their money in and out of countries that have weak antilaundering controls.

terrorist training camp   Place to which many terrorist recruits are sent for training; before 9/11, hosted by Afghanistan, Iran, Pakistan, Lebanon, and Syria.

Treasury Department Form 90-22.47 and OCC Form 8010-9, 8010-1, Suspicious Activity Report (SAR)   Report that must be filed for any activity that could indicate money laundering.

under-the-table cash deal   Scheme in which a money launderer purchases real estate or other valuable assets, including entire companies, at below-market value and makes up in cash the difference between the amount paid and the market value.

United Nations Convention against Transnational Organized Crime and Its Protocols   Agreement signed by nearly 150 countries, including the United States, that deals with the major issues relating to organized crime, including money laundering, corruption, and obstruction; supplemented by The Protocol against the Smuggling of Migrants and The Protocol against Trafficking in Persons, which deal with the illegal transportation of individuals across borders often for exploitation.

Usama bin Laden (UBL)   Terrorist leader who built a substantial military operation to support jihad groups and related financial backing during the Soviet occupation of Afghanistan; helped create al Qaeda and soon became its undisputed leader.

U.S. Customs Form 4790, Report of International Transportation of Currency or Monetary Instruments (CMIR)   Report required to be filed by both individuals and banks that physically mail, ship, or otherwise move currency or various monetary instruments in excess of $10,000 in and out of the United States.

vig   Interest on loans made by loan shark that is added every week at the rate of about 3 to 5 points (about 1 percent) of the amount borrowed.

walking account   Bank account a money launderer sets up with instructions to immediately transfer all deposits to an account in a second jurisdiction.

world Islamic front statement   Statement published by five terrorist groups calling for Muslims everywhere to kill Americans.

zakat   One of the five pillars of the Sunni sect of Islam, an obligation of the faithful to give a certain amount each year.

Review Questions

1. Which of the following issues is *not* dealt with in the United Nations Convention against Transnational Organized Crime and its Protocols?
   a. Money laundering.
   b. Organized crime.
   c. Obstruction of justice.
   d. The Convention deals with all of these.

2. Within the United States, which is the primary organization charged with fighting organized crime?
   a. The Executive Office Organized Crime Division.
   b. The Federal Bureau of Investigation.
   c. The Department of Justice.
   d. None of these.

3. Which of these is considered the dominant crime organization in the United States?
   a. La Cosa Nostra (LCN).
   b. Russian organized crime (ROC).
   c. Italian organized crime (IOC).
   d. None of these.

4. Organized crime groups tied to Northern Africa would be the focus of which of the following?
   a. European Organized Crime Unit.
   b. Eurasian Organized Crime Unit.
   c. The Trans-African and Southern European Organized Crime Unit.
   d. None of these.

5. Around 1930, who was the leader of a single organization called La Cosa Nostra?
   a. Al Capone.
   b. Salvatore Maranzano.
   c. Lucky Luciano.
   d. None of these.

6. Which LCN boss assisted the U.S. government in World War II?
   a. Al Capone.
   b. Salvatore Maranzano.
   c. Lucky Luciano.
   d. None of these.

7. Who became acting boss of LCN when Luciano entered prison and maintained operational control of the syndicate for 20 years until 1957, when Vito Genovese ordered Vincent "the Chin" Gigante to assassinate him?
   a. Al Capone.
   b. Salvatore Maranzano.
   c. Lucky Luciano.
   d. None of these.

8. Which mobster was known as the "Odd Father" because he wandered around the East Village in his bathrobe?
   a. Vito Genovese.
   b. Benny Lombardo.
   c. Vincent Gigante.
   d. None of the above.

9. According to the FBI, which family remains the most powerful LCN family?
   a. Gambino.
   b. Genovese.
   c. Colombo.
   d. Lucchesse.

10. Of which family was John Gotti a member?
    a. Gambino.
    b. Genovese.
    c. Colombo.
    d. Lucchesse.

11. Which of these has traditionally been one of LCNs most fundamental sources of power?
    a. Narcotics.
    b. Loan-sharking.
    c. Labor racketeering.
    d. None of these.

12. What is the numbers game?
    a. An illegal type of lottery.
    b. An extinct game that was run by bookies.
    c. A game now confined to states that do not permit casino gambling.
    d. All of these.

13. In loan-sharking, the "vig" is typically expressed as the interest rate for which period of time?
    a. Day.
    b. Week.
    c. Month.
    d. Year.

14. An LCN "associate" is the same as which of these?
    a. A made man.
    b. A friend of the organization.
    c. A soldier.
    d. None of these.

15. What is LCN code of silence called?
    a. Picciotto.
    b. Sgarrista.
    c. *Omerta*.
    d. None of these.

16. In LCN, which way does money flow?
    a. Upward.
    b. Downward.
    c. Laterally.
    d. All of these.

17. Which of the following crimes is *not* normally associated with Russian organized crime?
    a. Health care fraud.
    b. Auto insurance fraud.
    c. Drug trafficking.
    d. All of these are normally associated with Russian organized crime.

18. Which of these is another name for Islamic law?
    a. Qur'an.
    b. Jihad.
    c. Sharia.
    d. None of these.

19. To which of these can the rise of Islamic terrorism in recent decades be traced?
    a. The war in Chechnya.
    b. The war in Afghanistan.
    c. The war in Algeria.
    d. None of these.

20. How do radical jihadists normally begin recruiting new terrorists?
    a. In small groups.
    b. One on one.
    c. In large groups.
    d. In the streets.

21. Which of the following is *not* a source of funding for terrorist cells?
    a. Charities.
    b. Wealthy financiers.
    c. Human trafficking.
    d. All of these are sources of financing for terrorist cells.

22. A money launderer who breaks up a large amount of cash and deposits it in small amounts into many banks is engaging in which of these?
    a. Currency layering.
    b. Currency structuring.
    c. Currency fracturing.
    d. None of these.

23. Smurfing is a type of which of these?
    a. Money-laundering placement.
    b. Money-laundering layering.
    c. Money-laundering integration.
    d. None of these.

24. Which of these is an example of transferring money through an *hawala*?
    a. Money-laundering placement.
    b. Money-laundering layering.
    c. Money-laundering integration.
    d. None of these.

25. In the United States, the penalty for money laundering is a prison sentence of up to how many years per money-laundering transaction?
    a. 5.
    b. 10.
    c. 15.
    d. 20.

Discussion Questions

26. Describe the FBI's organized crime section.
27. What is the main thrust of the United Nations Convention against Transnational Organized Crime and its Protocols?
28. How and where did La Cosa Nostra begin?
29. Why has law enforcement not been able to completely eliminate La Cosa Nostra?
30. How is La Cosa Nostra different from Russian organized crime?
31. How does money flow through La Cosa Nostra?
32. Why has labor racketeering traditionally been so important to La Cosa Nostra?
33. Discuss the organizational structure of La Cosa Nostra.
34. Why does the illegal numbers game remain popular even in states with public lotteries?
35. How does someone become a member of La Cosa Nostra?
36. What are some of the major characteristics of Russian organized crime?
37. Who are the major players in a typical organized crime check fraud scheme?
38. Why has Europe been a central terrorist base?

39. Why do terrorists frequently claim that Islam is under attack by the West?

40. What role have mosques played in the spread of terrorism?

41. What is meant by the *integration issue*?

42. Describe the typical terrorist cell.

43. In 1998 when Usama bin Laden called for international jihad against the United States, why did terrorist organizations in many countries not respond to his call?

44. What have been the primary funding sources for al Qaeda?

45. What does money laundering by terrorists have in common with money laundering by organized crime?

46. What are the three phases of money laundering?

47. How is money laundering prevented?

48. What is an informal value transfer system (IVTS), and what role has it played in money laundering?

49. How might money launderers use credit cards to integrate laundered funds?

50. What factors are important in triggering a suspicious activity report in financial institutions?

Cases

51. Stewart Burger is a forensic accountant who works for a large Houston CPA firm. His specialty is the investigation of financial crimes and money laundering. He has extensive experience working with the FBI in the areas of narcotics interdiction, bank fraud schemes, organized crime, and international terrorism. Stewart was recently contacted by Maria Fuerte in the FBI's counterterrorism unit in Houston. She told him that she was in the middle of an ongoing terrorist investigation and that she needed his immediate help.

    "What kind of help do you need?" asked Stewart.

    She smiled. "You know the drill. I can't tell you anything unless you first join the team. If you do, we'll have to reinstate your security clearance."

    Stewart knew the case would take a lot of time, and the FBI would pay him more with gratitude than with money. "I'm pretty busy these days. Can it wait a couple of weeks?"

    Maria leaned over and whispered in his ear, "I understand that you have a daughter working inside the Loop?"

    Stewart was a trained interrogator. Her body language and her eyes were warning him of something.

    "That bad?" he asked.

    She nodded imperceptibly. He immediately agreed to let her drive him to her office.

    In the office, the paperwork had already been done, and within a few minutes Stewart was wearing a counterterrorism field agent badge. Maria's supervisor called his office and told the partner in charge that he was assisting a "routine investigation" as a matter of national security.

    "Okay, here's what we have," said Maria as she displayed photos of four men on her computer monitor. "These four men are loose in the city, and we know they are planning a bomb attack within the next 48 hours. I need you to help me find them."

    All four men appeared to be of U.S. descent and were wearing expensive business suits.

"We identified them through an informant," she said. "They're all executives in the Westwood Construction Development Company in Clear Lake."

Stewart recognized the company's name. It was one of the largest commercial developers in the area.

Maria continued. "We managed to get a sneak and peek warrant, and last night our agents went in and made copies of all their computer files and paper records. Our guys were out before daylight, and no one but us even knows we were there."

She led him to a room in which there was a large conference table on which piles of documents and six computers were sitting. She explained that the computers were exact copies of the six computers in Westwood's offices. "We also imaged and printed all of their paper documents too."

"You're fast," said Stewart.

Maria laughed. "We sent in 14 of our best agents. They knew exactly what to do. Now you've got to hurry. We don't have much time. We believe that Westwood has been funding the terrorist cell with bomb plans. We need some kind of evidence—any kind of evidence—to arrest these guys. We think we can stop the plot if we can."

Stewart asked for 10 field auditors. She told them that she had anticipated his request and already had them checked in. They were waiting in another part of the building.

   a. How should Stewart proceed with his investigation? How should he use the 10 field auditors? What areas should he focus on the most?

   b. What types of leads might Stewart develop for follow-up by Maria?

52. Joey Nariz is a narcotics trafficker who has made a career of smuggling cocaine into the United States. Over the years, he has bought most of his supply from Colombia but more recently had begun to obtain it in Peru.

His base of operations in the United States is San Lauro, a small California town northwest of San Diego. He controls his southern operations through encrypted satellite phones and fax machines.

Working in a small town provides the perfect cover, but he enhances his secrecy by operating out of a large farm supply store that he had purchased when he first came to San Lauro. He deals with his distributors in other small towns in California, Nevada, and Arizona. He prefers small towns because the people are trusting, and small towns never possess any serious antinarcotics capabilities.

Joey never personally transports or handles any drugs. He reserves those tasks for a network of undocumented Mexicans who can earn more working for him in a single day than they can earn back home in several years. Most of them are otherwise honest people willing to break the law so they can send money home to their families.

His largest problem is managing the cash. He has learned the hard way that he must handle the cash himself. Despite having more than $90 million in cash stashed away in warehouses, he lives a very frugal life. He spends whenever he can, but he's afraid to try to buy real estate or other large-ticket items with cash for fear of drawing attention to himself.

He decides, however, to travel to Miami and purchase a large house and boat. He packs the trunk of his car with cash and heads east. Once in Miami, he uses his contacts with local distributors to find a real estate agent who would be willing to work for cash. He instructs the agent to find him a large waterfront house for which the seller would accept an all-cash deal. He ends up paying $14 million for an $8 million house, but he's very happy with the property. The seller had no mortgage, so they were able to make the deal quietly in an attorney's office. They told the attorney that they were relatives and that the payment had already been made "out of closing," which meant the closing involved only some paperwork and no money.

Joey used the same method to purchase a $3 million yacht for which he paid $4 million. He then sold it for $2.5 million. The sale yielded a check net of commissions from the yacht broker. He deposited it into a bank account that he had opened with only $500 in cash and a check for $5,000 from his San Lauro bank account. When he opened the bank account, he told the bank representative that he was from San Lauro, California, and in the farm supply business. He even provided the bank a letter of introduction from his San Lauro bank.

a. Is Joey's money-laundering scheme likely to work?

b. Is the bank likely to report the deposit of the payment for the yacht by filing a currency transaction report or a suspicious activity report?

c. Is law enforcement likely to discover his purchase of the house or boat for cash?

d. How would a forensic accountant go about investigating Joey for drug trafficking and money laundering if given subpoena power? Would the investigation discover the under-the-table house and yacht purchases?

Part V

Other Forensic
Accounting Services

Chapter **Nineteen**

Business Valuation

CHAPTER LEARNING OBJECTIVES

After reading Chapter 19, you should be able to:

- LO1: Explain the objectives of business valuation.
- LO2: Explain the role of international, governmental, and professional organizations with respect to standards, practices, and certifications relating to business valuation.
- LO3: Explain the major concepts underlying basic business valuation theory.
- LO4: Explain the approaches and methods of business valuation.

FINANCIAL ASSET VALUATION

LO1   **Business valuation** in the most general sense deals with the appraisal of various financial assets. Virtually any type of financial asset is subject to appraisal. Some examples follow:

- Business entities (proprietorships, partnerships, corporations, LLCs).
- Government entities (municipalities).
- Real estate (raw land, office buildings, leaseholds).
- Securities (common stock, bonds, options).
- Intangible assets (patents, royalties, copyrights, trademarks).
- Trusts (all types).
- Individual tangible assets (plant and equipment).
- Estates (marital, testimonial, bankruptcy).
- Contractual rights (buy-sell agreements).
- Economic damages and insurance losses (business interruption).
- Individual or partial interests in any of the preceding items.

There is no one right way to value an asset, and in many cases, the process of assigning a single dollar value to a complex asset is as much art as it is a science, although this is not something that many valuation specialists are likely to tell all their clients. For example, consider the possible challenge of determining the fair market value of a closely held biotech startup company whose major asset is a single secret product that is years away from final development and uncertain government approval. In this case, the market value of the company obviously depends on the value of the secret product, but it is likely that any effort to value such a highly uncertain product will require a tremendous amount of judgment. Of course, a valuation specialist can search for comparable products if they exist, estimate future costs and income streams, estimate the likelihood that the future product will be accepted by the market, estimate the likelihood it will receive FDA approval, and so on. The analyst can further apply rigorous mathematical formulas to calculate the various estimates, but in the end, the final value number will be no better than the many uncertain estimates it is based on. Of course, the skilled valuation analyst will formally incorporate the uncertainty into the process, but in doing so is simply adding another layer of estimation and uncertainty. In the end, the final estimate is basically a wild guess.

Despite the many difficulties that exist in valuing assets, business appraisers strive to achieve results that meet certain general requirements (see Figure 19.1):

- **Consistency**   Ideally, different skilled appraisers should produce a similar valuation for a given asset.
- **Defensibility**   Business valuations are made with respect to assets, and assets are always the property of some entity or individual. Because they are property, they are always subject to possible taxation issues or legal disputes. Thus, there is always the general possibility that any valuation could be subjected to legal challenges. Therefore, valuation analysts must be concerned about the legal defensibility of their work products.

FIGURE 19.1
Valuation Objectives

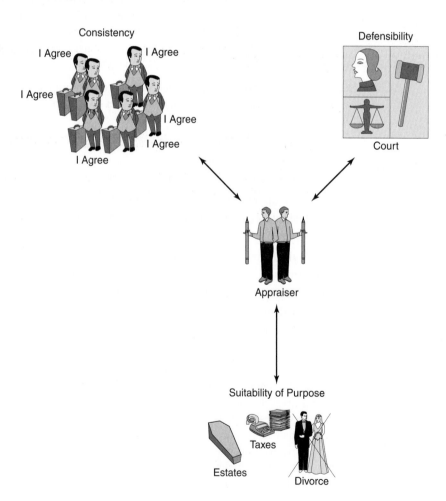

- **Suitability for purpose** Valuations must be suitable to the purposes and circumstances of the individuals needing the information. For an example, a taxpayer who donates noncash property may need an IRS "qualified appraisal" to substantiate the fair market value of the donated property.

RELEVANT PROFESSIONAL ORGANIZATIONS

LO2 To help ensure that the preceding requirements are met, various organizations have promulgated standards of professional appraisal practice.

Standards Promulgators

Various individual organizations promulgate professional appraisal standards. Some of these organizations are discussed individually.

The Appraisal Foundation

A private, nonprofit umbrella organization, **The Appraisal Foundation** (www.appraisal-foundation.org) comprises two independent boards. The Appraiser Qualifications Board (AQB) promulgates qualification standards for appraisers. The Appraisal Standards Board promulgates the widely recognized uniform standards of professional appraisal practice (USPAP).

The USPAP are mandatory for all federally related transactions, and many federal, state, and local agencies have adopted them. Many professional appraisal organizations in the United States and other countries require their members to comply with the USPAP.

The general components of the USPAP include the following:

- **Standards and standards rules** For example, Standard 10 deals with business appraisal reporting.
- **Statements on appraisal standards** For example, Statement on Appraisal Standard 2 deals with discounted cash flow analysis.
- **Advisory opinions** These opinions relate to specific subjects. For example, Advisory Opinion 10 deals with the appraiser-client relationship.

Overall, the USPAP are widely recognized as the generally recognized practice standards for virtually all appraisers.

The International Valuation Standards Committee

The **International Valuation Standards Committee (IVSC)** (www.ivsc.org/) is a nongovernment member of the United Nations (UN) that works with various national and international organizations and UN member states to internationally harmonize valuation standards. Participating international organizations include the World Bank, the Organisation for Economic Cooperation and Development, the International Federation of Accountants, and the national organizations that participate in the development of international accounting standards including professional appraisal-related societies in more than 50 countries, including the United States, the United Kingdom, Germany, Japan, Russia, Spain, South Africa, Latvia, and China.

The IVSC publishes the international valuation standards (IVS), which consist of the following components:

- Valuation concepts and principles.
- Code of conduct.

- Individual valuation standards.
- Applications (of standards).
- Guidance notes.
- Information papers.

The IVSC focuses on developing valuation standards relevant to developing international accounting standards. However, IVSs are also relevant to other areas, including international standards for bank capital requirements as set forth under the Basel Accord. The Basel Accord was developed by the Basel Committee on Banking Supervision, a group that comprises the Central Bank Governors whose members include representatives from Belgium, Canada, France, Germany, Italy, Japan, the Netherlands, Sweden, Switzerland, the United Kingdom, and the United States.

Professional Organizations and Designations

A number of organizations award professional designations (such as certification and accreditation).

American Society of Appraisers

The **American Society of Appraisers (ASA)** (www.appraisers.org) is one of the oldest appraisal-related organizations and one of eight appraisal organizations that joined together to form The Appraisal Foundation discussed earlier.

The ASA accepts individual members, unlike The Appraisal Foundation, which accepts only affiliate organizations. ASA recognizes various levels of individual membership such as candidate members and accredited members. To become candidate members, individuals must first interview with and be approved by a local ASA chapter. To receive the accredited member designation, individuals must pass an ethics examination and an examination on the USPAP and meet certain education and practice requirements. Additional designations may be obtained through experience and specialization. All members must meet continuing education standards to maintain accreditation.

Institute of Business Appraisers

A nonprofit organization that focuses on appraising closely held businesses, the **Institute of Business Appraisers (IBA)** (www.go-iba.org) offers professional certification programs including these:

- Certified Business Appraiser Accreditation (CBA).
- Master Certified Business Appraiser Accreditation (MCBA).
- Accredited by IBA (AIBA).
- Business Valuator Accredited for Litigation (BVAL).

Each certification has its own educational, experience, and examination requirements.

National Association of Certified Valuation Analysts

Identifying itself as a "global, professional association that supports the business valuation, litigation consulting, and fraud deterrence disciplines within the CPA and professional business advisory communities," the **National Association of Certified Valuation Analysts (NACVA)** (www.nacva.com) issues several certifications.

Certified Valuation Analyst (CVA)   A primary requirement for the CVA certificate is that the candidate must hold a valid certified public accountant (CPA) license. The CVA designation demonstrates that the certificate holder is qualified to provide "capable and

premises because two of them (the going concern and assemblage of assets premises) normally take place only in orderly sales.

Another dimension that can be added to the valuation premise is the distinction between entry and exit prices. *Entry* (or *input*) *prices* represent the prices that a business pays to purchase assets, whereas *exit* (or *output*) *prices* represent the prices at which a business sells assets. For example, the entry price for the inventory of a business is the price the business pays to purchase it, and the exit price is the price at which the business sells it.

The orderly sale premise is consistent with exit prices. On the other hand, the forced liquidation premise is consistent with any price up to and equal to the exit price, depending on the markets available to liquidate assets.

Estimating Market Value

The concept of a value hierarchy is closely related to the value premise. The **fair value hierarchy** represents a continuum of possibilities, defined along the lines of relative certainty, used to estimate market value from historical data. For example, one such fair value hierarchy for estimated market value (adapted from the Financial Accounting Standards Board's Fair Value Project) follows:

- **Level 0**   Based on a sale or exchange of the asset being appraised. For example, if a business (or other asset) was recently purchased at a given price, there is a likely presumption that such a purchase price represents fair market value for that same business.

- **Level 1**   Based on quoted prices for an identical asset that is traded in a currently active market. This level frequently involves more uncertainty than Level 0, depending on how identical the comparable asset really is and how active the comparative market is.

- **Level 2**   Based on quoted prices for a similar asset with adjustments made for differences between the subject asset and the similar asset.

- **Level 3**   Based on mathematical models that use directly related market variables as indicators of market value. Examples of directly related market variables include interest rates, foreign exchange rates, and stock market indices.

- **Level 4**   Based on mathematical models that use indirectly related market variables as indicators of market value.

- **Level 5**   Based on mathematical models that use internal business inputs as indicators of market value. For example, the market value of finished goods could be estimated by adding a markup percentage to input costs (labor, materials, and overhead).

In theory, Level 5 includes valuations based on historical cost and current replacement cost.

- **Historical cost**   This cost primarily involves the traditional balance sheet valuations using generally accepted accounting principles, which list assets at their cost less accumulated depreciation and amortization. This valuation premise is seldom used to estimate market value because historical cost valuations generally do not reflect economic value. As an aside, historical cost numbers are very certain in the sense that they can be calculated with exact precision, but they are extremely uncertain estimators of market value unless applied to assets very recently purchased, in which case they constitute Level 0 indicators.

- **Replacement cost**   This cost is sometimes used in real estate valuations to value build-ings and other structures. In using this method, it is common to adjust the replacement cost downward to account for the age of the building.

This hierarchy was originally developed primarily to value individual assets and liabili-ties in financial reports, but it is also relevant to valuing an entire business using one of the valuation approaches to be discussed. The important thing is that the value hierarchy repre-sents various ways to estimate the market value of an asset based on historical data.

It is also possible to form estimates of the market value of income-earning assets based on projections of future economic income. Depending on the circumstances, such esti-mates may be more or less certain than those in the value hierarchy. Still, for asset (and liability) valuations on balance sheets, the accounting profession prefers to use historical data rather than projections; hence, the value hierarchy focuses on historical numbers.

Unlike Levels 0–2, Levels 3–5 estimate market value using nonmarket transaction information. Thus, Levels 3–5 estimates are only loosely linked to the usual notion of a value premise, which is based on a hypothetical sales transaction.

Using the Valuation Premise and Value Hierarchy in Financial Reporting

Financial reporting as defined by both U.S. and international standards is moving away from historical cost reporting and toward fair value reporting on the balance sheet. With respect to financial reporting, the normal value premise is that the business is a going con-cern and that its assets would be sold in an orderly manner. Some additional assumptions also apply.

Marketplace Participants   The hypothetical market transaction used to value assets and liabilities generally assumes that market participants act independently and are fully informed, able, and motivated but not forced to transact.

Most Advantageous Reference Markets   The hypothetical market transaction used to value assets is presumed to take place in whatever reference market is the most advanta-geous for the business. If no market exists, the market value is estimated as per Levels 3–5 in the value hierarchy. The most advantageous reference market will vary from one asset (or liability) to another and on the asset's (or liability's) unit of account, which defines whether the asset is sold as an individual item or in a group of related items.

Transaction Costs   In general, no adjustment is made to the value for the direct transac-tion costs relating to exchanging the particular asset in the most advantageous reference market. In some cases, however, an adjustment may be made for transportation costs asso-ciated with a hypothetical sale.

Highest and Best Use   In valuing the asset, it is assumed that the asset is put to the **highest and best use** that results in the maximum value, subject to the use being physi-cally possible, legally permissible, appropriately justified, and financially feasible. Two general possibilities for a given asset exist for highest and best use: *in use* (retained for use as part of the business) and *in exchange* (sold rather than retained for use in the business). Given the going concern assumption, the highest and best use for nonfinancial assets is generally in use. However, in some cases, the best use for a nonfinancial asset could be in exchange. For financial assets, the presumption is always in exchange.

Liabilities   The valuation of a liability is the amount that would be paid to transfer it to a willing party of comparable credit standing. Liabilities are assumed to be settled at the most advantageous price in the most advantageous market.

Valuation Approaches

LO4 Three broad **valuation approaches** are used to value businesses or other assets: the income approach, the market approach, and the asset approach (see Figure 19.4).

The Income Approach

Under the **income approach,** an asset's value is the present value of the future economic income associated with the asset. This is the approach most commonly used to value businesses. The main problems in applying the income approach are estimating the future economic income and deciding what discount rate to use in the present value calculation. Neither of these problems is simple. Future income can be highly speculative, and even slight differences of opinion regarding discount rates can lead to substantially different valuations.

In terms of basic economic theory, future economic income should normally be measured in terms of cash flows of the assets being valued to the owners. This could lead to the supposition that cash flows from operations (or some similar or related number) could be the best measure of income to use when valuing a business. However, this is not always the case, and accounting income is sometimes the preferred measure.

It is not commonly understood, especially among nonaccountants, that in theory, the usual accrual-based accounting income and cash flows are identical over the life of a company that begins with cash and ends with liquidation after allowing for dividends and capital contributions. If a company begins with cash, operates for a number of years, and then liquidates, the accounting income over the life of the company will be the cash on hand after liquidation minus the cash on hand at the beginning, plus any dividends paid in the interim. In other words, accrual income and cash flows are the same over the life of the company. Therefore, the main difference between cash flows and accrual income is one of timing, not one of fundamental economic substance.

With respect to timing, the primary objective of accrual accounting is to produce an income measure that is more immediately relevant than cash flow. Specifically, this is exactly the effect of the matching principle, one of the basic concepts underlying accrual accounting, which requires including related income and expenses in the same reporting period regardless of the timing of the actual cash collections and disbursements. Consider the following example for the XYZ Bicycle Retail Company:

XYZ buys a bicycle on 12/18/20X1 from its supplier for $300 on account.

XYZ sells the bicycle for cash on 12/19/20X1 for $500.

XYZ pays its supplier for the bicycle sometimes in 20X2.

XYZ engages in no other transactions in 20X1 or 20X2.

Under this scenario, the profit is as follows:

Cash Accounting

20X1: $500
20X2: −$300

Accrual Accounting

20X1: $0
20X2: $200

Notice that the total income for the two years under both methods is the same. However, the timing of the accrual income makes much more sense when viewed as an indicator of

FIGURE 19.4
Valuation
Approaches and
Their Characteristics

	Characteristics			
Valuation Approach	**Discounted Economic Income**	**Focuses on the Business Entity as a Whole**	**Focuses on Comparable Assets**	**Balance Sheet Orientation**
Income	Yes	Yes	No	No
Market	No	Yes	Yes	No
Asset	Sometimes	No	Sometimes	Yes

the future. For this reason, accounting income is sometimes the preferred measure of economic income. In practice, the income approach may be applied to either measure of cash flows or accounting income. Also, the valuation analyst typically uses reported accounting cash flows or earnings only as a starting point in estimating future economic income. For example, an analyst could wish to estimate the value of a business based on "sustainable" income, which will likely differ from reported accounting income that includes substantial sources of nonrecurring income.

The Market Approach

Under the **market approach,** the value of the asset is what the asset can be sold for in an open market within some reasonable time period. This approach has the advantage of being fairly objective, especially when there is a busy market for the asset being valued.

Market value is frequently established with reference to recent sales of a comparable asset (i.e., by applying Level 2 in the fair value hierarchy). For example, in valuing an office building, the valuation analyst could refer to three recent sales of nearly identical office buildings. The market value estimates based on the recent sales would then be adjusted for differences between the comparison and subject properties.

When applied to valuing a business, the market approach involves valuing the business as a whole. This differs from the asset approach, discussed next, which focuses on valuing the individual assets of the business.

The Asset Approach

Under the **asset approach,** the value of an asset, especially a business, is the sum of the individual assets that it comprises. For a business, this means that its value is determined by the value of each of its individual assets less the value of any offsetting liabilities.

The valuation under the asset approach corresponds to the notion of owner's equity on a balance sheet, which is simply "assets minus liabilities." However, under the asset approach, all assets are valued at their fair market value. Historical cost valuation (as applicable to generally accepted accounting principles [GAAP]) is not used. Furthermore, the asset approach may include assets on its balance sheet that are not included on a balance sheet prepared under GAAP. For example, under GAAP, a fully depreciated asset will not appear on the balance sheet, but if such an asset still has market exchange value, it will be included on the balance sheet under the asset approach.

The asset approach can be applied with any of the valuation premises. For example, assets can be valued as a group or individually, and they can be valued under either the premise of an orderly sale or a forced liquidation. They can also be valued from any level within the value hierarchy.

When applied to single assets, the asset approach and the market approach are essentially the same thing. Because the two approaches are essentially the same with respect to single assets, the term *cost approach* is sometimes used instead of the asset approach, especially in real estate and with respect to financial accounting standards and financial statements. The **cost approach** is an asset or market approach applied to a single asset and based on a Level 5 premise that uses replacement cost to estimate market value. This is typically applied in a real estate context by adjusting the replacement cost downward via depreciation. At the same time, the value of the land portion of the real estate asset is estimated from comparative land sales.

Valuation Adjustments

Valuations determined under each approach may require upward or downward adjustments to reflect certain special factors that can have a significant effect on value. These special factors follow.

Extent of Ownership Control over Income-Producing Assets

This factor applies especially to the valuation of businesses or ownership securities of a business when *control* means not only the ability to affect the business's future through management and governance but also the ability to control dividends, determine compensation for related-party employees, and even liquidate the business.

When the asset being valued is a partial interest in a business, the value of the partial interest is likely to be less than a pro rata value of the total business. For example, assume that a closely held business is valued at $1,000 and is capitalized with 10 shares of common stock. This works out to $100 per share. Further assume that a single person sells only two shares to another individual. The issue arises as to the value of the two shares in the hands of the one individual verses the value of the eight shares in the hands of the other.

In this example, the two shares would be valued at a discount below the $100 per share because they provide their owner with a noncontrolling minority interest. The eight shares, on the other hand, would be valued at a premium above the $100 per share because they provide their owner a controlling interest.

Marketability and Liquidity

The concept of *marketability* relates to the availability of a market in which an asset can be sold within some reasonable time at some reasonably predictable price. A closely related concept is **liquidity,** which relates to the amount of time it takes to convert an asset into cash.

Publicly traded securities make a good example of highly marketable and liquid assets. Furthermore, securities that trade in the large, highly organized securities exchanges (such as the NYSE or NASDAQ) are likely to trade constantly and be very liquid. However, some securities on the smaller exchanges may trade only occasionally and be relatively illiquid.

The general rule is that the valuation analyst applies a downward adjustment to the extent that poor marketability or liquidity impairs the value of the asset under valuation.

Restrictions on Transferability   In general, three types of **restrictions on transferability**—contractual, legal, and economic—can impair the value of an asset. An example of each type of restriction follows:

- **Contractual restriction**   Securities may be given to employees as part of a compensation package. In such cases, a restriction could exist to prevent the employees from publicly selling the securities.

- **Legal restriction** Securities that are not registered with the Securities and Exchange Commission cannot be sold on the public security exchanges.
- **Economic restriction** A block of securities in a given company may be so large that the block's sale will significantly depress the stock's underlying market price. For example, a single share of a given medium-size company could sell for $100. But if a source were to try to sell tens of thousands of shares in the same company, the price could fall so that the shares sold last garner an amount significantly less than $100.

Business-Specific Risks

Businesses frequently have **business-specific risks** (various idiosyncratic risk factors), and discounts are typically applied to account for them. Examples of business-specific risks (also called *nonsystematic risks*) follow:

- The business depends entirely on a single employee.
- The business depends entirely on a single supplier.
- The business depends entirely on a single customer.
- All of the business's products are at the end of their marketing life cycle, and new products are only speculative.
- The business depends on high-margin products but is facing new, strong low-margin competitors.

Valuation Estimates

In general, the valuation analyst chooses the approach or combination of approaches that are most relevant to the valuation objective. The end result is the final valuation estimate, which can take two basic forms:

- **A single dollar figure** For example, the analyst could determine that the final value estimate for a given business is $2,235,000.
- **A range of dollar values** For example, the analyst could determine that the final value estimate is between $1,000,000 and $2,000,000.

THE PROCESS OF VALUING A BUSINESS

A number of steps primarily relate to valuing a business, but they are generally applicable to all types of valuation assignments.

- Define the valuation assignment.
- Collect and analyze information about the business.
- Research the industry in which the business operates.
- Study and analyze the business's financial statements.
- Select and apply a valuation method (with related assumptions given the standard of value, the valuation premise, and the valuation approach) to produce a valuation estimate.
- Make any appropriate adjustments (as previously discussed) to the valuation estimate to produce a final valuation estimate.
- Produce the valuation report.

Each step is discussed individually.

Define the Valuation Assignment

As with all accounting engagements, it is important to carefully define the assignment. Basic elements of the **valuation assignment** include identifying the following:

- **The client**   The client may be the owner of the business or an interested third party such as a lender, potential buyer, estate, or taxing authority.

  The specific legal property interests   The legal interests represent rights or legal claims relative to some asset(s) or entity. Legal interest serves as the underlying asset to be evaluated. For example, common stock shares represent a legal ownership interest in a company. In turn, the value of the common stock depends not only on the value of the company but also the specific legal rights associated with the common stock shares. Legal interests can take many forms. Some examples are given here:

  - *Full ownership* represents simple, direct, and unencumbered ownership rights. However, even full ownership rights can implicitly be encumbered. For example, a person can have full ownership over a piece of land, but the right to use it may be subject to zoning restrictions.
  - *Partial ownership* represents direct, unencumbered, ownership rights shared with others. For example, one person can have a 20 percent ownership in a partnership.
  - *Option rights* are generally rights to buy or sell some property under specified conditions. For example, a person could have a first-right-of-refusal option to purchase a business.
  - Regarding general ownership characteristics and business characteristics, the primary ownership characteristics relate to the extent of ownership control, marketability, and liquidity. Business characteristics include unique, value-influencing aspects of the business, such as reliance on key persons, products, markets, technologies, and general legal, industry, and market factors that affect the business.

- **The standard of value to be used**   The choice of the standard of value depends on the objectives of the individual or entity seeking an appraisal. Fair market value is by far the most common standard of value. However, other standards may be required for individual, taxation, contractual, or other legal reasons.
- **The valuation premise to be used**   For a business, the general premise is either going concern or liquidation, and a liquidation premise can be either orderly or forced.
- **The form and scope of the valuation report, including any special requirements**   The typical valuation report includes a final valuation estimate supported by the methods, reasoning, and data underlying the conclusions; the justification for using the chosen methods, reasons, and data; and applicable limitations. The report also includes the appraiser's certification and credential details.

Collect and Analyze Information About the Business

This step involves becoming familiar with all major aspects of the business and its history. Special attention should be given to anything that affects the adjustment factors described earlier. The analysis process includes document reviews, on-site visits, and interviews with key officers, employees, and third parties. The following elements are reviewed for the business:

- **All legal documents**   Includes reviewing items such as corporate charters or partnership agreements, partnership withdrawal schedules, dividend records, minutes of the board of directors, ownership records, employee stock ownership plans, equity-based and other employee compensation plans, incomplete agreements, documents in public records, general contracts, and lawsuits.

- **History** Determined reviewing the company's Web sites, brochures, catalogs, and so on.
- **Financial review** Reviews current and previous financial statements, budgets, forecasts, internal reports, tax returns, credit reports, a fixed-asset schedule, and a schedule of any off-balance-sheet assets, liabilities, or contingent liabilities.
- **Key employees** Focuses on the history of key employees and their respective roles in the ongoing business.
- **Products, plans, and strategies** Determines the business's key success factors and evaluates the reasonableness of its strategies and plans; also studies the business's current products and services, their position in the marketing life cycle, their competitive position, and any planned and emerging products and services.
- **Supply chain** Assesses vendors' relationships and the supply chain logistics.
- **Human resource infrastructures and information system** Includes a qualitative assessment of the extent that synergistic or intangible value exists in the business's information systems and human resources, the extent to which they are properly maintained, and the extent to which they require future capital expenditures.
- **Internal control processes** To gain some understanding regarding the reliability of the financial reports, the internal control process must be studied. Ideally, it is best to begin with audited financial statements and rely on the auditor's assessment of internal control and the financial statements. However, an audit report is not always available, making it necessary for the valuation analyst to do at least some very basic due diligence audit-type work. The valuation report can indicate that the final value is based on unaudited financial reports.

Much of the preceding data must be obtained by on-site interviews of employees and officers. Additional insight can be gained by interviewing suppliers, customers, bankers, and industry analysts.

Research the Industry in Which the Business Operates

It is not possible to properly value a business without understanding the environment in which it operates and how it relates to that environment. The valuation analyst should collect economywide, regional, local, and industry data that affect the business's outlook. Such information is published in the form of reports, articles, and databases by government and other nonprofit agencies including trade associations. Detailed financial analyst reports for some industries are available and especially helpful, sometimes providing great detail about individual firms.

Study and Analyze the Business's Financial Statements

Three major objectives in studying and analyzing the financial reports are to ensure that the account balances are reasonably stated, to adjust the business's financial statements to make them comparable to the financial statements of other businesses, and to compare the business's financial statements with those of other businesses.

Ensure That Certain Account Balances Are Reasonably Stated

This is a task that is best done as part of a formal audit, but some due diligence is necessary even with audited financial statements. Therefore, assuming that there is overall compliance with generally accepted accounting principles, certain accounts and transactions that correspond to the most common types of financial statement fraud deserve special attention. These accounts and transactions are discussed in more detail in Chapter 14.

- **Revenue problems** This single largest area of financial statement fraud includes sham sales, premature revenue recognition, recognition of conditional sales, improper cutoff of sales, misstatement of the percentage of completion, unauthorized shipments and channel stuffing, and improperly reported consignment sales.

- **Asset problems** Asset overstatements represent the second largest area of fraud, and inventories represent the most common fraud involving overstatement of assets. This fraud is so simple that it requires only miscounting ending inventories; no fancy manipulation of the accounting books is needed. The result is not only higher inventories but also lower cost of goods sold and higher profits. A similar problem occurs when obsolete inventory is permitted to remain on the books.

- **Accounts receivable problems** Understating allowances for bad debts or simply falsifying accounts balances can affect accounts receivable.

- **Fixed assets** These can be overstated by not taking depreciation when it should be taken or overstating property, plant, and equipment with a corresponding misstatement of revenues.

Adjust the Financial Statements to Make Them Comparable to Those of Other Businesses

Many closely held businesses do not follow generally accepted accounting principles, rendering their financial statements not comparable to those of other businesses. Even if a given business does follow generally acceptable accounting methods, its particular choices of permissible accounting methods can prevent its financial statements from being comparable to those of other businesses. Therefore, the analyst could need to make adjustments to financial statements before making them comparable to others. Some of the adjustments that may be needed when the company follows generally accepted accounting principles follow:

- **Different inventory methods** In times of changing prices, the FIFO and LIFO inventory methods can produce very different income and balance sheet numbers.

- **Different depreciation and depletion methods** Assumptions relating to useful lives of plant and equipment and the depreciation methods can vary (e.g., straight line versus declining balance) and produce radically different balance sheet and income numbers. The same is also true for differences in accounting for depletion.

- **Different treatments of intangible assets** It is possible that one company expenses the costs associated with developing an internally developed intangible asset while another capitalizes the same asset when purchased rather than internally developed.

- **Differences in revenue timing** Accounting standards permit various permissible treatments for contract sales, installment sales, and sales involving actual or contingent liabilities.

- **Nonrecurring and extraordinary items** Comparability is often enhanced by adjusting for the effects of nonrecurring items such as discontinued operations, gains and losses from the sale of fixed assets and some investment assets, the sale of business segments, and losses due to strikes.

- **Differences in accounting for subsidiaries or affiliates** One business may account for an owned interest in another company using the cost method (treating it as an investment) while another business may consolidate its financial statements in a similar situation.

- **Market value**   If the analyst is to rely on the asset approach, it is be necessary to adjust all balance sheet accounts to market value.

Analyze the Financial Statements

The analyses of the financial statements should assess at least the following:

- **Leverage**   The extent to which the capital structure includes debt.
- **Liquidity**   The ability of the business to meet current obligations as they become due.
- **Operational efficiency**   The efficiency with which a company uses its assets.
- **Profitability**   The amount of profit relative to the business's assets and capital base.
- **Solvency**   The ability of the business to remain a going concern in the foreseeable future.

These analyses are typically carried out using financial ratios. Ratios can be compared to those of reference firms, usually in the same industry, and to the subject business's ratios in previous years.

Select and Apply Valuation Methods and Approaches to Produce a Valuation Estimate

This step involves applying one or more of the valuation approaches (with their related assumptions given the standard of value and the valuation premise) to produce a value estimate. Legal, regulatory, contractual, and assignment-related constraints as well as available data may dictate the approaches. In the absence of any such constraints, the analyst generally uses all possible approaches and then bases the final value estimate on either the most appropriate approach or some combination of the approaches used.

Each of the three valuation approaches can be applied in various ways. These approaches are called *valuation methods*. More specifically, a **valuation method** applies a valuation approach to produce a valuation estimate. Therefore, each valuation approach can be applied using more than one valuation method (see Figure 19.5). Individual valuation methods are discussed shortly.

Produce a Final Valuation Estimate

Finally, the analyst combines the results of the valuation methods into a single value estimate or range of estimates. The analyst could make the combination by taking a judgmentally based weighted average of the individual estimates or selecting a single estimate based on its being the most relevant. The analyst then applies the adjustment factors discussed (i.e., the extent of ownership control over income-producing assets, marketability and liquidity, restrictions on transferability, business-specific risk) to adjust the value estimate up or down to produce the final value estimate.

Issue the Valuation Report

As discussed, the typical valuation report includes a final valuation estimate supported by the methods, reasoning, and data underlying the conclusions and the justification for using the chosen methods, reasons, and data; and the applicable limitations. The report also includes the appraiser's certification along with details on the appraiser's credentials.

FIGURE 19.5 **Valuation Approaches and Related Methods**

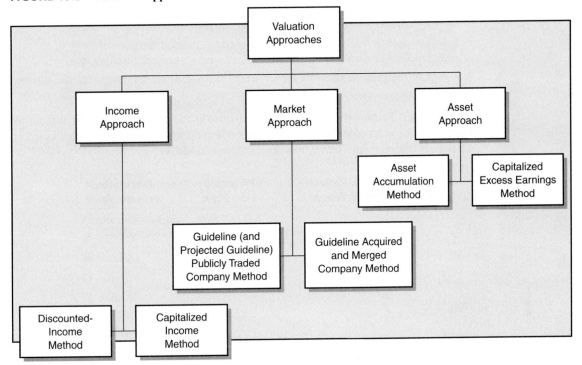

VALUATION METHODS

As discussed, the analyst must use one or more valuation methods to implement a given valuation approach. The following sections discuss the major valuation methods associated with each of the three valuation approaches.

Valuation Methods Associated with the Income Approach

It is a widely accepted principle among economists that competitive financial markets value assets based on the discounted value of their future economic income to their owners. This is how income-based valuation methods work. They reduce future income to a single valuation number based on the application of an appropriate discounting method. The choice of the discounting method and the measure of future economic income determine valuation methods that are based on the income approach. The two primary income-approach valuation methods are the discounted-income approach and the capitalized-income approach.

The Discounted-Income Method

The theory behind the **discounted-income method** is very simple. The analyst follows a four-step process:

1. Select a measure of future economic income. As stated, this normally is some version of accounting income or cash flow from operations.
2. Make a schedule of projected future income or cash flows using the selected measure. The schedule typically includes the future income or cash flows for Year 1, Year 2,

Year 3, and so on. All future years are included through some assumed final terminal year. For example, a firm could be assumed to produce cash flows of $1 million per year for 10 years and then a liquidation value of $50 million at the end of Year 10.

3. Select an appropriate discount rate to be used to compute the present value of the projected income or cash flows. For example, assume a 5 percent discount rate.

4. Compute the present value of the projected income or cash flows using the selected discount rate.

Continuing the example, the estimated valuation is the present value of $1 million for 10 consecutive years plus the present value of $50 million 10 years in the future based on a 5 percent discount rate. This works out as follows to $38,417,397.61.

Cash Flow Projected for End of Year N	Projected Cash Flow	Discounted Present Value
1	$ 1,000,000	$ 952,380.95
2	1,000,000	907,029.48
3	1,000,000	863,837.60
4	1,000,000	822,702.47
5	1,000,000	783,526.17
6	1,000,000	746,215.40
7	1,000,000	710,681.33
8	1,000,000	676,839.36
9	1,000,000	644,608.92
10	1,000,000	613,913.25
10	50,000,000	30,695,662.68
Net Present Value		$38,417,397.61

Each year, the discounted present value is computed by multiplying the projected cash flow by $1/(1 + .05)^N$; N is the year from the first column.

Present value simply converts money in the future into money in present dollars while accounting for the time value of money. This can easily be seen assuming that the numbers in the last column are invested for the number of years in the first column at a 5 percent rate of return. For example, if $952,380.95 is invested for one year at a 5 percent rate of return, at the end of Year 1, the accumulated investment value will be $1,000,000. Specifically, in Year 1, the $952,380.95 would earn $47,619.05 ($952,380.95 × 5 percent) interest. At the end of the year, the investment would have an accumulated value of the $952,380.95 investment plus the $47,619.05 in interest, or $1,000,000.

The Discounted-Income Method and Estimation of Future Income or Cash Flows
Various measures of income and cash flows are used as surrogates for projected economic income. Some of these measures follow:

• Projected accounting income after taxes.

• Projected dividends.

• Projected **free cash flow available to equity (FCFE),** defined as the amount of cash available to shareholders after all expenses, reinvestment, debt, and preferred dividend payments. This number can be computed from the financial statements according to the following formula:

FCFE = Net Income + Depreciation and Amortization
$\qquad$ − Changes in Working Capital − Principal Repayment of Debt
$\qquad$ + Proceeds from New Debt and Preferred Stock
$\qquad$ − Preferred Dividends − Capital Expenditures

- Projected free cash flow to equity before debt payment, sometimes called **debt-free cash flow available to equity (DFCFE)** defined according to the following formula:

DFCFE = FCFE + Interest Expense × (1 − Tax Rate)
$\qquad$ + Principal Repayment of Debt
$\qquad$ − Proceeds from New Debt and Preferred Stock + Preferred Dividends

This is the amount of cash available to shareholders assuming no debt or preferred stock obligations. The debt-free cash flow to equity is most applicable to situations in which the valuation objective assumes the purchase of the business assets without assuming any debt.

The Discounted Income Method and the Selection of a Discount Rate In theory, the discount rate should be the rate of return that could be earned on an alternative investment with the same risk and investment characteristics. Several methods are used to estimate the discount rate.

- **The business's weighted average cost of capital (WACC)** This involves the before-tax averaging of the cost of equity capital (CEC) and debt capital (CDC) based on the relative proportions of total equity capital (TEC) to total debt capital (TDC). This works out to

WACC = [TEC/(TEC + TDC) × CEC] + [TDC/(TEC + TDC) × CDC]

- **The implied discount rate for similar businesses** The technique involves using the income or cash flows of similar businesses whose market values are known. Because the income or cash flows and market value are known, it is possible to solve the present value formulas for the implied rate of return.
- **The CAPM expected market return from similar businesses** Various models exist for estimating the expected market return for a given firm. These include various versions of the **capital asset pricing model (CAPM).** Roughly speaking, the CAPM states that a firm's rate of return contains three components: (1) the risk-free rate of return, (2) the rate of return associated with marketwide risk, and (3) the rate of return associated with firm-specific factors. More specifically, a formula for the firm's return is as follows:

Firm Return = (Risk-Free Rate of Return) + B × (Market Return)
$\qquad$ + Firm-Specific Return

where B is a market risk factor that varies from one firm to the next.

This relationship is commonly estimated using regression analysis based on the following formula:

$$R(it) = a(i) + B(i) \times RM(t) + e(it)$$

where $R(it)$ represents the market return for firm i in period t, $B(i)$ represents the "beta" (or market risk factor) for firm i, $RM(t)$ represents the market index of returns in period t, and $e(it)$ represents a random error for firm i in period t.

In this model, a(i) is estimated with B(i) and roughly depends on the risk-free rate of return.

In any case, because e(it) is assumed to be a random error, the expected return, E[R(i)], for any given firm is simply E[R(i)] = a(i) + B(i) × RM(t), or a constant plus beta times the market index of returns. For example, if a(i) = .02, beta = 1, and the market return = .03, then the expected return is .02 + .03, which equals .05.

Regression analysis can be used to estimate a(i) and B(i), or firm betas can be obtained from one of many published sources. Some sources publish both a(i) and B(i); others publish B(i) to be used with the risk-free rate of return as follows:

$$E[R(i)] = RF(t) + B(i) \times RM(t)$$

where RF(t) is the risk-free rate of return for period t.

In some cases it may be helpful to estimate beta based on market data for a comparable firm. The comparable firm used to compute beta must have the same proportion of leverage (i.e., the proportion of debt capital to total capital) as the subject firm to be valued. If this is not the case, the beta of the comparable firm must be adjusted to account for the difference in leverage. This is done by first removing the effect of leverage on beta on the comparable firm and then recomputing the resulting unlevered beta based on the degree of leverage in the firm to be valued. The formula to compute the unlevered beta is as follows:

$$B(U) = B(L)/[1 + (1 - t)(W(d)/W(e))]$$

where B(U) and B(L) are the unlevered and levered betas respectively, and W(d) and W(e) are the proportions of debt and equity in the capital structure.

Once B(U), the unlevered beta, is computed, it can be relevered based on the capital structure of the firm being valued (or any other desired capital structure), using the following formula:

$$B(L) = B(U) \times [1 + (1 - t)(W(d)/W(e))]$$

where W(d) and W(e) represent the debt and equity proportions for the firm being valued or for some other hypothetical firm of interest.

CAPM models tend to underestimate returns for relatively small firms and overestimate returns for relatively large firms. For this reason, it is common to adjust upwards the discount factor for small firms and sometimes to decrease it for large firms. The adjustment can be incorporated by directly including a size measure (such as total assets or total income) into the regression model. Alternatively, size premiums can be obtained from published sources.

Finally, adjustments may be made for firm-specific factors (such as new product ideas, high-quality management, and so on.). To avoid double counting, it is important that any adjustments made to the discount rate are not also made to the projected income or cash flows.

• **Expected returns from other pricing models**   Models in addition to the CAPM can be used to compute expected returns. One such class of models includes those based on the **arbitrage pricing theory (APT).** APT models are more general than those based on the CAPM. Whereas the CAPM estimates returns based only on a single factor—a market index—APT models estimate returns based on many possible factors.

The APT itself does not specify exactly what factors should be used to estimate returns, but it has been commonly implemented with models that use factors such as inflation rates, overall business default rates, and interest rates. In using any pricing model, whether based on the CAPM or the APT, the analyst should consult with the most recent accounting and finance literature regarding evidence to support her choice of a model. This is especially true if it is likely that the model will require defending in court.

The Capitalized Income Method

The **capitalized income method** is a variation on the discounted income method. The main difference with the capitalized income method is that the income or cash flows are assumed to exist for an indefinite period in the future. When this happens, the present value formula reduces to very simple terms:

Present Value = Economic Income/Discount Rate

In other words, the present value is simply the annual income or cash flow divided by the discount rate. This is the formula for discounting a perpetuity, which involves repeatedly receiving the same amount of economic income in each period forever. For example, a cash flow of $1,000 per year forever would amount to perpetuity. Discounting this perpetuity at 10 percent, for example, yields a present value of $1,000 / .10, or $10,000. More formally, the present value of a perpetuity is as follows:

$$PV = EI/k$$

where EI is the periodic economic income and k is the discount rate.

It could be tempting to think that a cash flow of $1,000 a year forever could be worth much more money than $10,000. After all, at $1,000 per year, one would receive $100,000 in payments over 100 years. The simple proof of the $10,000 value, however, is that if someone places $10,000 in the bank with a 10 percent annual rate of return, he will receive exactly $1,000 per year in interest payments forever. So anyone with $10,000 can get $1,000 a year if the return is 10 percent.

The basic perpetuity model can be expanded to accommodate growth in the periodic economic income. If the annual growth rate is represented by the symbol g, then the perpetuity model becomes

$$PV = EI/(k - g)$$

which is widely known as the *Gordon Growth Model*. Notice that subtracting g makes the denominator smaller, which in turn makes the present value larger. Continuing with the example, the present value would be higher if the annual cash flows were assumed to grow at a rate of 1 percent per year:

$$PV = \$1,000/(.10 - .01) = \$11,111.11$$

Notice that a 1 percent growth rate relative to a 10 percent rate of return has a disproportionate effect on the present value. This is generally the case, and if the basic rate of return and the growth rate are close to each other, even a small error in estimating either rate can have a very large percentage effect on the present value.

The model can also account for the effects of inflation. No adjustment may be necessary if the discount rate (k) and growth rate (g) are both in nominal terms so that they already incorporate anticipated inflation. If the discount rate does not already do so (as is the case with CAPM-based rates), however, an inflation premium may be added to the discount rate. The important point is that the discount rate and the growth rate must both be expressed in the same terms, either nominal or real.

- **The income capitalization method: Estimating the capitalization rate**   The capitalization rate is simply the net rate used in the denominator after factoring in growth and inflation. For example, if the nominal discount and growth rates are 5 percent and 3 percent, respectively, the capitalization rate is 2 percent (i.e., 5 percent minus 3 percent, as per the Gordon Growth Model).

- **The income capitalization method: Estimating the economic income Economic income** can be estimated by using any of the income or cash flow measures discussed previously in relation to the discounted income method. The normal goal with the capitalization method is to use a measure of economic income that is sustainable and represents the future. This is frequently done by basing the estimate of future income on either the most recent year's income, cash flow, or some average of the income or cash flows for recent years. In many cases, it could be necessary to adjust the recent income or cash flow up or down to remove the effect of nonrecurring items. Additional adjustments may be necessary to incorporate any known or likely future events such as anticipated strategic alliances, new products, and so on.

Valuation Methods Associated with the Market Value Approach

Market value methods estimate a company's market value based on the market values of comparable companies that have been established. One commonly used market-based method is the guideline publicly traded company method.

The Guideline Publicly Traded Company Method

Four basic steps are involved in the **guideline publicly traded company method:** (1) Select guideline companies, (2) adjust the financial statements of the guideline companies to make them comparable to the subject company, (3) compute various price-based financial ratios for the guideline companies, and (4) apply the price-based financial ratios to the subject company.

The guideline method is frequently used by security analysts who value companies using price-earnings multiples of comparable companies. For example, if a comparable company has a price-earnings multiple of 10 (i.e., Price/Earnings = 10) and the subject company has earnings of $5 per share, the securities analyst could value the subject company at $50 per share (10 × $5). The assumption is that the price-earnings multiple of the subject company is the same as that of the comparable company.

In mathematical terms, this can be expressed as follows:

$$P(G)/E(G) = P(S)/E(S)$$

where

$P(G)$ = the price per share of the guideline company

$E(G)$ = the earnings per share of the guideline company

$P(S)$ = the price per share of the subject company

$E(S)$ = the earnings per share of the subject company

This equation can be rewritten as follows:

$$P(S) = [P(G)/E(G)] \times E(S)$$

In other words, the price of the subject company equals the price-earnings ratio of the guideline company times the earnings of the subject company. In the preceding example, this works out as

$$\$50 = 10 \times \$5$$

This method can be applied by substituting any accounting number (such as sales, cash flows, or assets) in place of earnings. For example, if a comparable (guideline) company has a sales-price multiple of 25 and the subject company has sales of $3 per share, the subject company would be valued at $75 per share.

Details on applying the guideline method follow.

Select Comparable Companies   Normally, at least three comparable (guideline) companies are selected, possibly many more. The selection is made based on matching characteristics of the comparable companies with those of the subject company. Some characteristics commonly used for matching include capital structure, credit status, products, markets, quality of management, nature of competition, earnings, sales, growth rates, earnings volatility, and the company's position in its industry. These are only examples of possible matching characteristics; the idea is to find the best matches possible, and the analyst should always be prepared to defend them in court.

The matching process may be facilitated by the use of comparative financial ratio analysis. For example, firms within the same industry could be matched based on ratios such as debt/equity, sales/earnings, and sales/assets. Various public databases (e.g., Compustat and CRSP) that contain accounting and market-price information for publicly traded companies are available.

Adjust the Financial Statements   The financial statements of the comparable companies must be adjusted based on the same considerations already discussed in relation to the income approach.

Compute Price-Based Ratios   Various price-based ratios (sometimes called *value measures* or *multiples*) are computed for the comparable companies using price in the numerator and an accounting number in the denominator. Some of the most commonly used accounting numbers include earnings, sales, total assets, owner's equity, and cash flows. It is common to base the calculations on the data for the most recent five years.

Apply the Price-Based Ratios to the Subject Company   When more than just several comparative companies are involved, the analyst may use the mean, harmonic mean, or median value for each price-based ratio as the standard to apply to the subject company. In some cases, there may be excessive dispersion across firms for one or more of the ratios. This could lead the analyst to drop one or more comparative companies or ratios from further consideration.

The Projected Guideline Publicly Traded Company Method

This method works the same way as the guideline publicly traded company method except that the price-based ratios are based on projected rather than historical accounting data.

The Guideline Acquired and Merged Company Method

The **guideline acquired and merged company method** works the same way as the guideline publicly traded company method except that the comparative data are based on acquired and merged companies. This method is applicable to situations in which a controlling interest is being valued. As discussed, a controlling interest can be much more valuable than a minority interest.

Various special issues apply to the guideline acquired and merged company method. First, obtaining comparable data could be difficult because the number of merged and acquired companies is small relative to the total population of firms. Second, because of limited data availability, the analyst could be forced to base comparatives on data from earlier years and then perform a difficult adjustment for time differences. Third, many acquisitions involve both cash and other consideration that may be difficult to value, such as shares of the acquiring company or of *junk bonds*. Finally, many acquisitions may reflect the investment value of the acquirer (because of unique synergies between the acquirer and the acquired company) rather than the general fair market value.

Valuation Methods Associated with the Asset-Based Approach

The Asset Accumulation Method

The primary asset-approach method is the **asset accumulation method.** It involves restating, as needed, all individual assets and liabilities on the balance sheet to market value (or other value, such as liquidation value, as required by the appraisal objectives). Next, any off-balance-sheet assets and liabilities are added to the balance sheet. Finally, the business is valued as the difference between the resulting assets and liabilities.

Needless to say, valuing each asset for anything but a very small company can be a difficult task. In many cases, the analyst needs to consult specialized appraisers to estimate individual asset values. Consequently, this method can sometimes be time consuming and expensive.

On the other hand, the asset accumulation method has some advantages:

- The results are presented in balance sheet format and are easy to understand.
- The results are likely to be appreciated by lenders, who prefer to see loans backed by marketable assets rather than intangibles such as earnings power.
- The results can be useful in a negotiation to buy or sell a business and in litigation. The value of the assets sets a floor on the value of the business.

As an aside, the asset accumulation method often uses income or market methods to value individual assets.

The Capitalized Excess Earnings Method

The **capitalized excess earnings method** combines the asset-based and market approaches. Under this method, the value of the firm equals the value of the net assets using the asset accumulation method *plus* an estimate of the value of goodwill. The steps proceed as follows:

1. Apply the asset-accumulation method to estimate the value of the firm. This is sometimes done excluding intangible assets (such as patents, trademarks, and so on) from the asset base.

2. Estimate the value of goodwill (and other intangibles if they are excluded from the asset base). This is done by estimating and capitalizing excess income using a three-step process:

    a. Estimate a "normal" income for the net assets determined by the asset-accumulation method. This is done by multiplying the value of the net assets by a rate of return that is determined using factors similar to those used to determine the capitalization rate in applying the income approach.

    b. Subtract the normal income from the actual income. The difference represents the income associated with goodwill (and any assets excluded from the asset base). This is the excess earnings. In computing actual income, it is important to adjust the compensation of owners upward or downward to a reasonable level.

    c. Capitalize the excess earnings.

3. Add the accumulated net assets to the capitalized earnings.

In applying the capitalized excess earnings method, it is sometimes desirable to exclude nonoperating assets, liabilities, and income if the goal is to establish a value for the operating portion of the business.

Summary

Business valuation involves the appraisal of various types of financial assets while seeking consistency, defensibility, and suitability for purpose. To help achieve these goals, organizations such as The Appraisal Foundation have set valuation standards that serve as guides for professional valuation analysts. The Appraisal Foundation promulgates the uniform standards of professional appraisal practice, which form the mostly widely recognized body of professional appraisal standards. On a similar level, the International Valuation Standards Committee publishes international valuation standards especially applicable to valuing assets and liabilities in the context of financial reports.

Also important in the valuation arena are professional organizations that award professional designations and certificates. Such organizations include the American Society of Appraisers, the Institute of Business Appraisers, the National Association of Certified Valuation Analysts, and the American Institute of Certified Public Accountants.

Basic valuation theory depends on several key concepts: standards of value, valuation premises, valuation approaches, valuation methods, and valuation adjustments. Standards of value focus on the needs of the individual or entity receiving the appraisal. The main standards of value are fair market value, intrinsic (or fundamental) value, investment value, and fair value. Fair market value and fair value sometimes mean the same thing, especially in the context of financial reporting, but fair value sometimes has its own special meaning in certain legal contexts. Intrinsic value is sometimes used in investment contexts to represent the theoretical value of an asset based on assumed economic considerations. Finally, the investment value is normally used to represent the value of an asset to a particular investor.

Valuation premises define the circumstances surrounding a hypothetical disposition (i.e., sale) of an asset or group of assets on some valuation date. The two major factors influencing these circumstances are the extent to which synergistic value is derived from the sale of the group of assets and the speed and effort devoted to their sale. Regarding synergy, assets may be sold as an entire business (the going concern premise), as a synergistic assemblage of assets, or individually with no synergy. Regarding the speed of the sale, either an orderly sale or a forced liquidation can be assumed to take place.

Closely related to the value premise is the fair value hierarchy, which roughly defines a continuum, arranged along the lines of uncertainty, of possibilities that may be used to estimate market value from historical data. The highest level of certainty exists when the market value is estimated from a recent sale of the asset being appraised. The lowest level of uncertainty exists when the market value is estimated using a mathematical model based on internal business inputs. Between the highest and lowest levels of uncertainty, assets are valued based on reference to the market prices of comparable assets. For income-earning assets, it is also possible to form estimates of the market value based on projections of future economic income.

Regarding financial reporting, both U.S. and international standards are moving away from historical cost reporting and toward fair value reporting on the balance sheet. Financial reporting normally assumes going concern status and orderly sale premises with various assumptions regarding the market participants, the assets being sold in the most advantageous markets, the noninclusion of most transaction costs, and the assumed highest and best use of the assets. Liabilities are valued at the amount that would be paid to transfer them to a willing party of comparable credit standing when the transfer takes place in the most advantageous markets.

The three broad approaches to valuing businesses or other assets are the income approach, the market approach, and the asset approach. Under the income approach, the asset's value is the present value of the future economic income associated with the asset. Under the market approach, the asset's value is what the asset can be sold for in an open market within some reasonable time period. Under the asset approach, the value of an asset, especially a business, is the sum of the individual assets that it comprises. Regardless of which approach is used, it could be necessary to adjust the estimated value for the extent of ownership control, for marketability and liquidity, for restrictions on transferability, and for business-specific risk. The valuation analyst chooses the approach or combination of approaches that are most relevant to the valuation objectives.

The process of valuing a business includes the following steps: define the valuation assignment; collect and analyze information about the business; research the industry in which the business operates; study and analyze the business's financial statements; select and apply a valuation method (with related assumptions given the standard of value, the valuation premise, and the valuation approach) to produce a valuation estimate; make any appropriate adjustments to the valuation estimate to produce a final valuation estimate; and produce the valuation report. The final report includes justifications for the particular standards of value, premises, approaches, and methods used.

Each valuation approach is implemented by applying one or more specific valuation methods. The primary valuation methods associated with the income approach are the discounted income method and the capitalized income method. Both methods discount future income or cash flows; the discounted income method assumes some terminal date for the asset, after which it is liquidated into cash. On the other hand, the capitalized method assumes that income from the asset continues in perpetuity.

The primary valuation method associated with the market approach is the guideline publicly traded company method. This method computes price-based multiples (such as the price-earnings ratio) for comparable companies and then applies them to the subject company. If the accounting numbers used to compute the multiples are based on projected numbers, the method is instead called the *projected guideline publicly traded company method*.

The primary method associated with the asset approach is the asset accumulation method. This method involves restating, as needed, all individual assets and liabilities on the balance sheet to market value (or other value, such as liquidation value, as required by the appraisal objectives). Next, any off-balance-sheet assets and liabilities are added to the balance sheet. Finally, the business is valued as the difference between the resulting assets and liabilities.

The capitalized excess earnings method combines the asset-based and market approaches. Under this method, the value of the firm equals the value of the net assets using the asset accumulation method *plus* an estimate of the value of goodwill. Goodwill is estimated by capitalizing excess earnings, the difference between actual earnings and estimated normal earnings. Normal earnings are computed by applying a normal rate of return to the net assets computed from the asset accumulation approach.

Glossary

American Institute of Certified Public Accountants (AICPA)   Organization that offers the accredited in business valuation (ABV) designation to its CPA members who pass a specialized valuation examination, provide evidence of professional experience (10 valuation engagements), and offer evidence of 75 hours of lifelong learning related to business valuation.

American Society of Appraisers (ASA)   Appraisal-oriented organization that accredits its members who pass an examination on ethics and on the USPAP as well as meet certain education and practice requirements.

The Appraisal Foundation   Private, nonprofit umbrella organization that promulgates the widely recognized uniform standards of professional appraisal practice (USPAP); also promulgates qualification standards for appraisers.

arbitrage pricing theory (APT)   Theory that leads to various models that can be used to estimate the expected rate of return for individual firms.

assemblage of assets value premise   Business assets are sold as a group but not as part of an assumed going concern.

asset accumulation method   Primary valuation method used in the asset approach to business valuation that involves restating, as needed, all individual assets and liabilities on the balance sheet to market value (or other value, such as liquidation value, as required by the appraisal objectives).

asset approach   Valuation approach in which the value of an asset, especially a business, is considered the sum of the individual assets that it comprises.

business-specific risk   Idiosyncratic factors that uniquely affect the risk of a single business.

business valuation   Discipline that deals with the appraisal of various types of financial assets.

capital asset pricing model (CAPM)   Model that can be used to estimate the expected rate of return for individual firms; roughly states that a firm's rate of return contains three components: (1) the risk-free rate of return, (2) the rate of return associated with marketwide risk, and (3) the rate of return associated with firm-specific factors, commonly estimated using regression analysis based on the formula $R(it) = a(i) + B(i) \times RM(t) + e(it)$, where $R(it)$ represents the market return for firm i in period t, $B(i)$ represents the "beta" (or market risk factor) for firm i, $RM(t)$ represents the market index of returns in period t, and $e(it)$ represents a random error for firm i in period t.

capitalized excess earnings method   Valuation method that combines the asset-based and market approaches by calculating the firm's value as the value of the net assets using the asset accumulation method *plus* an estimate of the value of goodwill.

capitalized income method   Income-approach valuation method in which the value of an income-producing asset is estimated based on the discounted present value of an assumed perpetuity of economic income; implemented by dividing the assumed periodic economic income by a capitalization rate.

cost approach   Asset- or market-based approach applied to a single asset and based on a replacement cost premise; frequently used in real estate valuations.

debt-free cash flow available to equity (DFCFE)   Amount of cash available to shareholders assuming no debt or preferred stock obligations: DFCFE = FCFE + Interest Expense $\times$ (1 − Tax Rate) + Principal Repayment of Debt − Proceeds from New Debt and Preferred Stock + Preferred Dividends.

discounted-income method   Income-approach valuation method in which the value of an income-producing asset is based on the present value of future economic income generated by the asset; normally discounts economic income over some finite period in the future.

economic income   Abstract economic concept normally measured in terms of cash flow or accounting income.

fair market value   A amount that an asset will sell for (1) within a reasonable time, (2) in an open market, (3) to a willing buyer, (4) with normal means of consideration, and (5) when seller and buyer are both fully informed and motivated.

fair value   Standard of value that has special meaning in some legal contexts; also used by the Financial Accounting Standards Board and the International Accounting Standards

Board in the context of setting generally accepted accounting principles when fair value represents a carefully defined version of fair market value.

fair value hierarchy　Continuum, defined along the lines of relative certainty, of possibilities that may be used to estimate market value from historical data.

forced liquidation premise　Concept that assets are quickly sold in appropriate markets with less than normal market exposure.

free cash flow available to equity (FCFE)　Amount of cash available to shareholders after all expenses, reinvestment, debt, and preferred dividend payments: FCFE = Net Income + Depreciation and Amortization − Changes in Working Capital − Principal Repayment of Debt + Proceeds from New Debt and Preferred Stock − Preferred Dividends − Capital Expenditures.

going concern value premise　Concept that a firm's assets are sold as part of the sale of the entire ongoing business, a sale that extracts the maximum possible synergistic value from the assets.

guideline acquired and merged company method　Valuation method that works in the same way as the guideline publicly traded company method except that it bases comparative data on acquired and merged companies.

guideline publicly traded company method　Market-approach valuation method in which the value of an income-producing asset is estimated based on the relationship between price and accounting measures in comparable companies.

highest and best use　Assumption in valuing an asset that it is put to the use that results in the maximum value, subject to the use being physically possible, legally permissible, appropriately justified, and financially feasible.

income approach　Business valuation approach that values an asset based on the present value of the future economic income associated with the asset; most commonly used to value businesses.

individual asset disposition value premise　Concept that the assets of a business will be sold individually.

Institute of Business Appraisers (IBA)　Nonprofit organization that focuses on appraising closely held businesses and offers professional certification programs including certified business appraiser (CBA) accreditation, master certified business appraiser accreditation (MCBA), accredited by IBA (AIBA), and business valuator accredited for litigation (BVAL).

International Valuation Standards Committee (IVSC)　Nongovernmental organization member of the United Nations (UN) that works with various national and international organizations and UN member states to harmonize valuation standards internationally with an emphasis on financial reporting; publishes the international valuation standards (IVS).

intrinsic or fundamental value　Standard of value determined by analytical methods that seek to find the "true value" or the "underlying value" of an asset—in other words, what the asset is "really worth."

investment value　Standard of value that defines *value* in terms of what is relevant to a particular investor.

liquidity　Amount of time it takes to convert an asset into cash.

market approach　Business valuation approach that an asset's value is what the asset can be sold for in an open market within some reasonable time period.

National Association of Certified Valuation Analysts (NACVA)　Self-described "global, professional association that supports the business valuation, litigation consulting, and fraud deterrence disciplines within the CPA and professional business advisory communities"; issues certifications for certified valuation analyst (CVA), accredited valuation analyst (AVA), certified forensic financial analyst (CFFA), and certified fraud deterrence analyst (CFD).

orderly sale premise   Assumption that assets are to be sold in their normal markets and with normal market exposure.

restrictions on transferability   Legal, contractual, and economic restrictions that can impair the value of an asset.

standard of value   Definition of value relevant to a particular entity or individual including fair market value (also called *market value* in reference to some types of assets such as real estate), intrinsic or fundamental value, investment value, and fair value.

valuation approach   A method or combination of methods used to value businesses or other assets. Three broad valuation approaches are used in practice: the income approach, the market approach, and the asset approach.

valuation assignment   Appointment in which the basic elements include identifying the client, specific legal property interests to be evaluated, general ownership and business characteristics, standard of value to be used, valuation premise to be used, and form and scope of the valuation report including any special requirements.

valuation method   Application of valuation techniques to produce a valuation estimate.

valuation premise   Assumptions regarding the circumstances surrounding a hypothetical disposition (i.e., sale) of an asset or group of assets on some valuation date including going concern, assemblage of assets, or individual assets.

weighted average cost of capital (WACC)   Before-tax averaging of the cost of equity capital (CEC) and debt capital (CDC) based on the relative proportions of total equity capital (TEC) to total debt capital (TDC):

$$WACC = [TEC/(TEC + TDC) \times CEC] + [TDC/(TEC + TDC) \times CDC]$$

Review Questions

1. Which of the following would not be the subject of business valuation?
   a. Corporations.
   b. Trusts.
   c. Plant and equipment.
   d. All of the above are the subjects of business valuation.

2. Which of the following is *not* among the desired characteristics of business valuations?
   a. Source and use.
   b. Consistency.
   c. Defensibility.
   d. All of these are desired characteristics of business valuations.

3. The uniform standards of professional appraisal practice are promulgated by which organization?
   a. American Society of Appraisers.
   b. NACVA.
   c. The Appraisal Foundation.
   d. International Valuation Standards Committee.

4. CVA is a designation of which of these?

a. American Society of Appraisers.

b. NACVA.

c. The Appraisal Foundation.

d. International Valuation Standards Committee.

5. How many standards of value are generally recognized?

a. 1.

b. 2.

c. 3.

d. 4.

6. Which standard of value is most applicable to investors seeking undervalued securities?

a. Fair market value.

b. Intrinsic value.

c. Investment value.

d. None of these.

7. In business valuation, the going concern assumption helps define which of the following?

a. Valuation premise.

b. Valuation standard.

c. Valuation approach.

d. None of these.

8. With respect to inventory, exit prices most closely represent which of these?

a. Replacement cost prices.

b. Wholesale prices.

c. Retail prices.

d. Inflation-adjusted wholesale prices.

9. The value hierarchy is relevant to valuing which of these?

a. Individual assets of a business.

b. An entire business.

c. Both *a* and *b*.

d. Neither *a* nor *b*.

10. Financial reporting as defined by both U.S. and international standards is moving away from and toward which of these?

a. From fair value reporting and toward replacement cost reporting.

b. From historical cost reporting and toward replacement cost reporting.

c. From historical cost reporting and toward fair value reporting.

d. None of these.

11. In ongoing businesses, what is normally the highest and best use for nonfinancial assets?

a. In use.

b. In exchange.

c. Both *a* and *b*.

d. None of these.

12. Which is the approach most commonly used to value businesses?
    a. The income approach.
    b. The market approach.
    c. The asset approach.
    d. All approaches are used equally often.

13. When the asset being valued is a partial, noncontrolling interest in a business, what value is likely to be assigned to it?
    a. Less than a pro rata value of the total business.
    b. Close to a pro rata value of the total business.
    c. More than a pro rata value of the total business.
    d. The answer depends on the valuation approach.

14. The single largest area for financial statement fraud involves which of these?
    a. Revenues.
    b. Inventories.
    c. Securities.
    d. None of these.

15. Which of the following is *not* a major objective in studying and analyzing financial reports when valuing a business?
    a. Ensuring that all account balances are reasonably stated.
    b. Adjusting the business's financial statements to make them comparable to the financial statements of other businesses.
    c. Comparing the business's financial statements with those of other businesses.
    d. All of these are major objectives.

16. What area does the most common type of financial statement fraud by overstating assets involve?
    a. Accounts receivable.
    b. Inventories.
    c. Securities.
    d. Plant and equipment.

17. Which of these is the basis for the discounted income method estimate of the value of a business?
    a. Accounting income.
    b. Cash flows.
    c. Both *a* and *b.*
    d. Neither *a* nor *b.*

18. In applying the discounted income method, which of the following would *not* normally be used as a surrogate for economic income?
    a. Dividends.
    b. Free cash flow available to debt service.
    c. Debt-free cash flow available to equity.
    d. All of these could be normally used as a surrogate for economic income.

19. The capital asset pricing model would likely be most applicable to which of the following general valuation approaches?
    a. Income.
    b. Asset.

c. Market.

d. None of these.

20. In applying the capitalized income method, it is common to estimate discount rates and growth rates. Which of the following is true regarding the impact of errors in estimating these two numbers?

a. The impact of the estimation error will be the largest when the two numbers are farther from each other.

b. The impact of the estimation error will be the largest when the two numbers are closest to each other.

c. The impact of the estimation error will be the largest when both numbers are relatively large.

d. The impact of the estimation error will be the largest when both numbers are relatively small.

21. In applying the guideline publicly traded company method, comparable companies are selected based on which of these?

a. Capital structure.

b. Credit status.

c. Products.

d. All of these.

22. In which general valuation approach is a price-based ratio most likely to be used by the analyst?

a. Income.

b. Asset.

c. Market.

d. All of these.

23. Which general valuation approach is especially appealing to lenders?

a. Income.

b. Asset.

c. Market.

d. All of these.

24. Which of the following is *not* true regarding the capitalized excess earnings method?

a. It combines asset-based and market approaches.

b. Its computations involve estimating normal income based on net assets as determined by the asset accumulation method.

c. Its computation involves capitalizing the normal income.

d. All of these are true.

25. In applying the excess earnings method, it is sometimes desirable to exclude which of the following if the goal is to establish a value for the operating portion of the business?

a. Nonoperating assets, liabilities, and income.

b. Nonoperating assets and liabilities.

c. Nonoperating assets and income.

d. Nonoperating liabilities and income.

Discussion Questions

26. What are some general objectives of appraisals?

27. Describe one major membership-related difference between The Appraisal Foundation and the American Society of Appraisers.

28. What valuation-related designation is available to CPAs through the American Institute of Certified Public Accountants?

29. What is the importance of defining a standard of value as part of a valuation engagement?

30. If a building for sale has an estimated market value of $800,000, could it at the same time have an investment value of $10,000,000? Why or why not?

31. What does the term *highest and best use* concept mean? When is this concept applicable?

32. Why is historical cost seldom used as a valuation premise?

33. Give an example of the use of replacement cost as a valuation premise.

34. What are the three basic valuation approaches?

35. What does the asset approach have in common with the market approach?

36. The market approach bases its estimates on *comparable assets.* Explain.

37. In many cases, bank lenders prefer the asset approach. Explain why.

38. Explain the difference between marketability and liquidity.

39. Give two examples of business-specific risks that could have a negative effect on a valuation estimate.

40. Give a valuation example in which the legal interest in an asset differs from the underlying asset itself.

41. What type of general due diligence must a valuation analyst do when valuing a small business?

42. Why is the balance sheet insufficient when applying the asset approach?

43. What is the difference between a valuation approach and a valuation method?

44. What is meant by *economic income* in relation to the discounted income method?

45. What is the possible advantage of using APT rather than CAPM in estimating discount rates?

46. What is the impact on present value caused by adding a growth rate to a model that discounts future cash flows?

47. Describe two or three price-based financial ratios that could be used as part of the guideline publicly traded company method, and explain when one ratio could be preferable over another.

48. Why is the asset accumulation method relatively easy for many to understand?

49. What is meant by *excess earnings* with respect to the capitalized earnings method?

50. What is meant by *normal income* with respect to the capitalized earnings method?

Cases

51. Cermco produces and sells specialty customer relationship management (CRM) solutions to small and medium-size businesses in the United States and Canada. The company is more than 20 years old and has a steady, loyal customer base.

    A major reason for Cermco's success lies in the ability of its product to easily integrate with various accounting and ERP systems. As a result, even when clients upgrade their entire accounting systems to expensive ERP solutions, they continue to use Cermco's CRM because of its superior features.

Annual revenues for Cermco's three most recent years are about $11 million (20X3), $7 million (20X4), and $3 million (20X5), respectively. Overall interest expenses and operating margins have remained a relatively constant percentage of revenues.

Cermco attributes the decline in revenues to declines in market share as a result of natural client turnover and the entrance of many other small competing software companies into the market. Nevertheless, Cermco's CRM product continues to enjoy the highest industry ratings and a loyal customer base.

Cermco's balance sheets for the most recent three years follow:

CERMCO
BALANCE SHEET
DECEMBER 31

Thousands	20X5	20X4	20X3
Assets			
Current assets			
Cash and cash equivalents	$ 390	$1,386	$ 2,603
Short-term investments	—	—	—
Net receivables	720	664	1,225
Inventory	—	—	—
Other current assets	412	469	892
Total current assets	**$1,522**	**$2,519**	**$ 4,720**
Long-term investments	1,215	—	—
Property, plant, and equipment	76	258	454
Goodwill	545	1,757	2,194
Intangible assets	999	1,844	3,644
Accumulated amortization	—	—	—
Other assets	—	—	—
Deferred long-term asset charges	—	—	—
Total assets	**$4,357**	**$6,378**	**$11,012**
Liabilities			
Current liabilities			
Accounts payable	$ 469	$1,174	$ 1,436
Short/Current long-term debt	—	—	600
Other current liabilities	1,227	1,358	1,496
Total current liabilities	**$1,696**	**$2,532**	**$ 3,532**
Long-term debt	—	—	—
Other liabilities	—	—	—
Deferred long-term liability charges	—	—	—
Minority interest	—	—	—
Negative goodwill	—	—	—
Total liabilities	**$1,696**	**$2,532**	**$ 3,532**

Stockholders' equity

Misc. stock option warrants	—	—	—
Redeemable preferred stock	—	—	—
Preferred stock	3,014	3,211	2,333
Common stock	16	16	13
Retained earnings	−25,513	−23,814	−19,165
Treasury stock	—	—	—
Capital surplus	25,168	25,564	25,862
Other stockholders' equity	−24	−1,131	−1,563
Total stockholders' equity	**$ 2,661**	**$ 3,846**	**$ 7,480**

Produce a valuation estimate for Cermco for December 31, 20X5. Use whatever valuation method you think best but justify your choice. Note that you can estimate the annual income from year-to-year changes in the balance sheet.

52. Bob Mark is the executor of his parents' estate that is being divided equally among his two brothers, Tom and Mike, and himself. The estate consists of cash and marketable securities worth $4.2 million and a duplex apartment building located in the Fort Lauderdale beach area.

The terms of the will gives Mike, the younger brother, the option of keeping the apartment building as part of his equal share of the estate. Thus, Bob must value the apartment building in order to determine how much to "charge" Mike's total share of the estate.

The apartment building is rather unusual because it is located on a deepwater lot with only 50 feet of waterfront exposure rather than the usual 100 feet. In fact, Bob's search of the entire area did not reveal any other waterfront properties with less than 100 feet of dock space.

Bob located three recently sold somewhat comparable buildings, each on a 100-foot deepwater lot. They were similar to the subject property except that each has four apartments instead of two apartments in the subject property. They were also considerably newer. The subject property was 60 years old, whereas the comparable properties were only 25 years old.

The average selling price of the comparable properties was $1.6 million with net annual rental values averaging $64,000 per year per building after property taxes and expenses. The subject property produces net annual rentals of $43,000 after property taxes and expenses.

Bob estimates that the replacement cost of the subject building is $500,000. The average replacement cost of the comparable buildings is $800,000.

To complicate the situation, the owner of the property adjacent to the subject property is willing to pay $1.7 million for it because annexing the subject property would give the owner a large enough lot on which to construct a 50-story condominium complex.

Mike argues that he has no desire to sell the property to the adjacent owner but that he wants to live on the property, and it should therefore be valued accordingly. He backs up his argument by reminding his brothers that their deceased parents hated the next-door neighbor and would never have sold to him under any conditions. In fact, the next-door neighbor had made repeated offers to buy from the parents while they were still alive.

How should Bob value the duplex apartment building? The other two brothers have agreed that they will accept whatever decision he makes.

Chapter **Twenty**

Dispute Resolution Services

CHAPTER LEARNING OBJECTIVES

After reading Chapter 20, you should be able to:

- LO1: Define *alternative dispute resolution* and explain its benefits.
- LO2: Contrast and compare mediation and arbitration.
- LO3: Explain the accounting practice of litigation support services.
- LO4: Explain nontraditional alternative dispute resolution techniques.
- LO5: Discuss various applications of alternative dispute resolution techniques.
- LO6: Describe the steps in setting up an in-house alternative dispute resolution program.

INTRODUCTION

LO1 Disputes are inevitable in the business world. They can occur between individuals and groups in every area imaginable including, for example, between companies and their suppliers, companies and their customers, companies and their employees, and even companies and government entities. Disputes can also arise between one individual and another (e.g., in divorce cases), between individuals and government entities (e.g., with income taxes), and between government entities.

The traditional means for resolving disputes range from all-out wars (between countries) to friendly negotiations. In many cases, however, disputes end up in the court system with all of the financial and emotional costs frequently associated with litigation. In fact, almost every large organization contains a legal department that is constantly engaged in legal disputes and litigation.

LO2 In recent years, there has been a major trend toward using **alternative dispute resolution (ADR)** approaches to resolve disputes outside the court system. The traditional methods for ADR include mediation and arbitration (see Figure 20.1). **Mediation** involves a neutral third party who helps those involved in a dispute to resolve their differences through structured negotiations. Similarly, **arbitration** also involves a neutral third party, but the neutral third party is empowered to issue findings that can be binding on the disputants in cases of binding arbitration. In cases of nonbinding arbitration, the neutral person's findings serve as recommendations.

FIGURE 20.1
Mediation versus
Arbitration

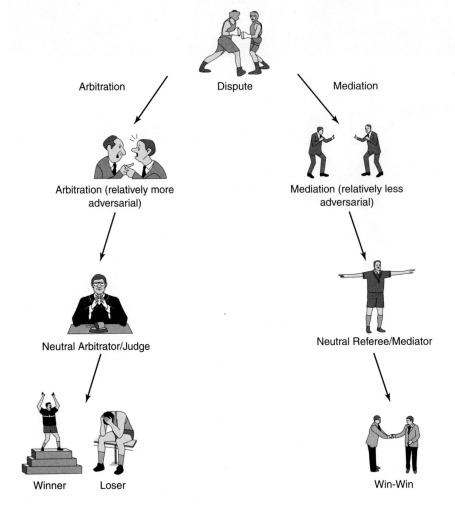

Forensic accountants can play various roles in dispute resolutions. Some of these roles follow:

- **ADR neutral mediator or arbitrator** Most states have no special licensing requirements for mediators and arbitrators.

- **Dispute participant** Accounting firms can become involved in disputes with their clients and employees. Also, sometimes partnership-agreement disputes arise between the firm's partners.

- **Expert consultant** Forensic accountants can serve as **expert consultants** performing expert investigations, analyzing facts, and offering what-if analyses that can be used by one or more parties to a dispute.

- **Expert witness** Forensic accountants can be **expert witnesses** and give expert opinions in both ADR processes and in formal litigation.

LO3 Collectively, these four roles comprise an area of forensic accounting practice commonly called **litigation services** or **litigation support services,** which provide support not only for disputes but also any issue that involves or potentially involves multiple parties in a legal context. After all, any matter that exists in a legal context is always subject to a possible dispute. Therefore, in the present chapter, the term *dispute* is used to include possible disputes as well as actual ones.

Some areas of disputes that commonly involve forensic accountants follow:

- Bankruptcy disputes.
- Insurance claims.
- Fraud investigations.
- Financial and economic damages.
- Government grants and contracts.
- Intellectual property and technology assets.
- Antitrust and anticompetition issues.
- Merger, acquisition, and divestiture problems.
- General contract disputes.

The first major section of this chapter discusses ADR. The second section discusses applications of ADR for forensic accountants (including forensic accountants as participants in disputes); the third section discusses corporate ADR programs; the fourth section discusses expert consulting and testimony; and the final section discusses forensic accountants as expert witnesses.

ALTERNATIVE DISPUTE RESOLUTION

Alternative dispute resolution has some distinct advantages over litigation:

- **ADR costs less than litigation**   Court battles can be very expensive. Lawyers love to battle with each other, and cases can drag on for years. Moreover, litigation can be a significant distraction that prevents management from focusing on its core business activities.
- **ADR is private but litigation is public**   Many companies would prefer not to air their problems in public courtrooms. Doing so can tarnish a company's image even in cases of successful litigation, and court testimony can disclose proprietary information.
- **ADR mediation tends to preserve relationships but litigation tends to destroy them**   Litigation often embitters the participants, but in many cases, ADR mediation can actually help build business relationships.
- **ADR tends to bring quicker resolution**   Courts that try both civil and criminal cases must give precedence to criminal cases due to a defendant's right to a speedy trial. For this and other reasons, civil courts are often clogged, and it sometimes takes years for civil cases to work their way through the court system. ADR, on the other hand, tends to resolve cases relatively quickly.
- **ADR permits the choice of decision maker**   In many cases, ADR permits the parties involved to select the mediator or arbitrator. This contrasts with civil cases in which the parties cannot select judges. Furthermore, by choosing the mediator or arbitrator, the parties are able to ensure that their case will be resolved by someone with proper expertise. In many civil cases, jury members are forced to try to understand highly technical matters that are beyond their grasp.
- **Flexible remedies**   ADR permits the parties involved to form their own remedies. This contrasts with uncertain and runaway awards made by juries in the civil court systems.
- **Fairness and expertise**   ADR resolutions are sometimes fairer than court-based resolutions. One reason is that in mediation and sometimes in arbitration, the involved parties have control over the possible outcomes.

Despite its many advantages, ADR is not always the preferable means to resolve disputes. There are certain advantages to litigation:

- **Litigation can establish legal precedents** Legal precedents can prevent future disputes or set legal standards for resolving future disputes. ADR, on the other hand, resolves only one dispute at a time, and the ADR resolution of one dispute sets no precedent for resolving future disputes.
- **Litigation is better at establishing clear winners** In civil lawsuits, the jury finds either for or against the plaintiff. In ADR cases, on the other hand, mediation or arbitration is much more likely to lead to some compromise solution, so litigation could be preferred when one side or the other is not willing to compromise at all.

Arbitration

Binding (nonbinding) arbitration is a nonjudicial adversarial process in which one or more neutral persons (arbitrators) render a binding (nonbinding) decision to resolve a dispute among opposing parties. The arbitration process is normally governed by a set of rules that are agreed to in advance by the disputing parties.

In almost all cases, arbitration is triggered by contractual provisions that require contract disputes to be resolved through arbitration. The contracts themselves sometimes spell out the rules to govern the arbitration process. Alternatively, the contracts may require the involved parties to submit to **administered arbitration,** which is administered by one of the organizations, such as the American Arbitration Association (www.adr.org), that facilitates administered arbitration. The American Arbitration Association does not actually arbitrate disputes but provides administrative support of the arbitration process, including the selection of arbitrators. It also provides sets of arbitration rules for general use and for specific industries. For example, it has developed industry-specific dispute resolution rules for professional accounting and related services.

In cases of **nonadministered arbitration,** each of the two disputing parties typically selects one arbitrator, and these two selected arbitrators in turn select a third arbitrator. The arbitrators may need to agree on the rules of arbitration if they have not been clearly spelled out in the contract that triggers the arbitration.

In some cases, courts may order **court-annexed arbitration,** in which case the court may appoint arbitrators as part of the litigation process. Court-annexed arbitration programs (CAAPS) are usually mandatory but nonbinding. In federal courts, CAAPS are governed by the federal ADR Act. Each state may have its own laws governing CAAPS in state courts.

International disputes, including disputes between countries, are sometimes arbitrated in the **Permanent Court of Arbitration (PCA)** (www.pca-cpa.org), also known as the *Hague Tribunal,* or under the rules of the **International Chamber of Commerce Court of Arbitration** (www.iccwbo.org). Submitting to the arbitration rules of these organizations is generally voluntary, and their decisions are generally final and not subject to appeal.

The typical arbitration clause in a contract reads somewhat like this: "Any controversies, claims, or disputes arising under this contract will be settled by arbitration under the administration and applicable rules of the American Arbitration Association. Any decision or award made by the arbitrator may be submitted to any relevant court of jurisdiction for enforcement and/or summary judgment."

In general, decisions of arbitrators are legally binding and enforceable in court. However, exceptions exist. For example, a decision by an arbitrator that clearly ignores public law would likely not be enforceable. Similarly, decisions by an arbitrator that are arbitrary, capricious, or biased may not be enforceable. Still, courts generally uphold arbitrator decisions even when arbitrators make mistakes in determining, interpreting, or applying facts. In other words, arbitration awards are generally final and not subject to appeal.

Arbitration clauses in contracts are generally enforceable. In other word, parties who sign contracts containing arbitration clauses generally waive their right to take disputes to court. The main exception to this rule is the **adhesion contract,** whereby one party with superior bargaining power forces another party to accept an arbitration clause on a take-it-or-leave-it basis.

Arbitrator decisions are enforceable not only within a given country but also commonly from one country to the next. More than 130 countries have signed the New York Agreement by which countries agree to enforce commercial arbitration awards from other countries.

The Arbitration Process

The arbitration process is in many ways like the process followed in traditional court litigation. Depending on the rules, the arbitration sessions may proceed like a trial, with discovery, testimony, cross-examination, and so on. The main difference is that arbitration is likely to be somewhat less formal and lawyers are more likely to take a back seat, although it is common for lawyers experienced in arbitration to represent clients in arbitration proceedings. On the other hand, many jurisdictions have no requirement that any of the participants, including the arbitrators, be attorneys. Finally, the rules of evidence in arbitration tend to be more liberal and more likely to admit evidence not admissible in a court trial, because some courts have rejected arbitration decisions when evidence was not admitted.

Mediation

Mediation is an ADR technique in which a neutral mediator provides a structured process that helps those engaged in disputes to work out their differences among themselves. The mediator's style can be either facilitative or evaluative. The mediator using the **facilitative mediation** style does not express opinions with respect to the facts of the case or the reasonableness of the participants' negotiating positions. Instead, the mediator focuses on helping and prodding the participants toward a mutually satisfactory compromise.

With **evaluative mediation,** the mediator actively expresses opinions about the facts of the case and the reasonableness of the participants' negotiating positions. For example, the mediator could give one party the opinion that an offer from the other party is very generous and should be accepted.

Mediation works best when both sides desire in advance to reach a negotiated solution. It is not the best ADR approach, however, when any of the participants rules out all compromise. However, it is frequently the best approach when both sides are willing to negotiate. This is so because the resulting resolution is not in any way imposed on the participants, so they are much more likely to take ownership of what they themselves produce. This ownership often bodes well not only for the participants' desire to carry out the terms of the resolution but also for the future of their ongoing relationship.

Because mediation involves a negotiated resolution, there is no mediator's award or finding that can be enforced in a court. Instead, the disputing parties typically memorialize their negotiated settlement in a written agreement, which then becomes enforceable in a court.

As with the case with arbitration, mediation can be either administered or nonadministered. With administered mediation, the disputing parties use the services of an organization such as the American Arbitration Association, which provides the mediator and the rules of mediation. Ideally, the mediator should have considerable expertise in the area relating to the dispute, and an attorney-mediator is generally best if the dispute involves complicated legal issues. With nonadministered mediation, the participants select their own mediator and rules of mediation. The choice of a mediation administration service, the mediator, or the rules of mediation can be governed by a clause in a contract that triggers the mediation or by mutual agreement between the disputing parties.

Mediation sessions are quite different from arbitration sessions. In mediation, the process is not like a trial. Rather, the mediator often separates the disputing parties after some initial opening statements and then shuttles between the parties, carrying messages and offers. The rules may permit the parties to present evidence and argue their cases to the mediator and/or each other. Once an agreement is reached, the parties may come together again and reestablish their predispute relationship.

Because mediation is simply a structured form of negotiation, it does not always result in a resolution of the dispute. As a result, sometimes parties may agree to participate in mediation, but it could fail.

Nontraditional ADR Techniques

LO4 Various combinations and variations of arbitration and mediation are sometimes called *nontraditional ADR techniques* (see Figure 20.2). Some nontraditional ADR techniques follow:

- **Med-arb**   The **med-arb** technique is a combination of mediation and arbitration. The parties first engage in mediation, and if that does not produce a resolution, the proceedings switch to arbitration. In theory, this approach is the best of both worlds because the parties are first given a chance to reach a negotiated settlement before one is forced on them. Furthermore, the fact that a settlement will be forced on both parties sometimes provides the pressure needed to get them to work out their differences themselves. The downside is that the side with the stronger hand could resist mediated compromise, preferring to play the stronger hand in arbitration when a win is likely. If this happens, the mediation is likely to be perfunctory, and the chances for a mediated settlement could even be less than they would be without the specter of a forced settlement.

- **Rent-a-judge**   The participating parties in a **rent-a-judge** process can hire a retired judge who conducts a formal trial, perhaps even with a rented jury that renders a decision. An important advantage of this approach over real litigation is speed: There is no long wait for the case to work though the court system. Furthermore, the judge's decision is final and not subject to appeal as it is in the court system. Finally, the parties and the rented judge can agree to the rules, procedures, and possible outcomes ahead of time.

- **Early neutral evaluation**   The **early neutral evaluation** technique involves hiring a **neutral,** usually a judge or an attorney, to review the entire case before it goes to court. The neutral writes an advisory opinion that helps the litigants see more clearly how likely their cases are to succeed in a trial. The neutral's advisory opinion can then be used as a prelude for pretrial settlement talks, mediation, or arbitration.

- **Mini-trials, summary-jury trials, and mock-jury trials**   The techniques in **mini-trials, summary-jury trials, and mock-jury trials** are an extension of the rent-a-judge technique, but the trial is held in front of a jury that is possibly composed of neutral experts and corporate officers and decision makers from the disputing companies. Jury-based ADR trials typically use procedures that are simpler than those used in formal courts, and they normally proceed much more rapidly. The opinions from the ADR juries are normally nonbinding, and the goal is to facilitate negotiations and mediation. Jury-type ADR techniques can be helpful in resolving complex cases because the jury members can be selected from multiple areas of expertise.

FIGURE 20.2
**Traditional and
Nontraditional ADR
Techniques**

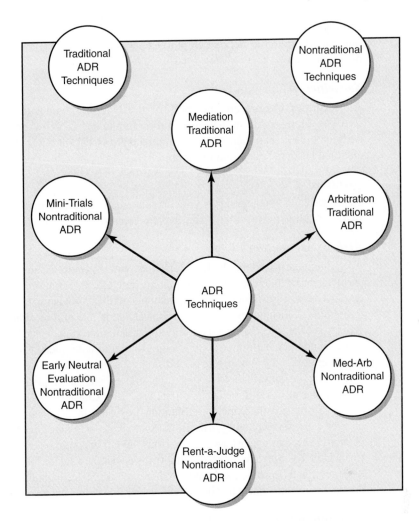

APPLICATIONS OF ALTERNATIVE DISPUTE RESOLUTION

LO5   ADR is routinely applied in various industries. Some examples follow.

Labor Interest Arbitration

Interest arbitration or **labor interest arbitration** involves resolving conflicting demands, typically in labor contract negotiations. Major-league baseball has historically used this type of arbitration to resolve salary disputes between a player and his team's management. When a player and management cannot reach a salary accord, the player files for arbitration. The arbitrator listens to both the player and management and then renders a decision. For the most part, this arrangement tends to favor the players because the arbitrators do not normally award the players less than the team would be willing to pay without arbitration. Players also like the privacy provided by the process.

Union Contract Arbitration

Union contracts frequently contain mandatory arbitration provisions. **Union contract arbitration** can be triggered by complaints about a wide array of issues, including employee compensation, working conditions, employer evaluations, work assignments, and discrimination. In some cases, it could not be legally permissible to use mandatory, binding arbitration to deprive employees access to the courts on certain matters such as discrimination.

Securities Arbitration

All securities brokers are members of the National Association of Security Dealers (NASD). Membership in that organization requires **securities arbitration** for disputes between brokers and their clients. Complaints to NASD are normally handled through its National Dispute Resolution Program.

Divorce Mediation

To reduce bad feelings and to save court time, many divorce judges order **divorce mediation** or nonbinding arbitration for divorce disputes.

ADR in Accounting Practice

Accounting firms routinely have disputes with employees and ex-employees, among partners, and with clients. For example, in some cases, accounting firms may require their employees to sign noncompete agreements with a provision to settle related disputes through ADR techniques. Such provisions are generally enforceable in court, although the standards of enforceability vary from one jurisdiction to the next. In general, noncompete agreements must be limited to protecting the legitimate interests of the accounting firm. For example, an accounting firm that practices in only one city on the U.S. East Coast would not be permitted to use a noncompete clause to prevent ex-employees from practicing, say, in a different state on the U.S. West Coast.

CPA firms sometimes include arbitration provisions in their audit engagement letters. This practice can save accounting firms from runaway jury verdicts, large legal bills, and very bad publicity. Lawsuits against accounting firms are not uncommon, especially when clients fail financially. The problem for accounting firms is that they are the "deep pockets," so there is a tendency for them to be sued anytime there is a problem. Including ADR clauses will not protect them from nonclients, but it may be possible to persuade nonclients to use ADR.

Accounting Services in ADR Cases

Accounting firms often specialize in ADR and litigation support services in the areas of evidence analysis, summarization, and interpretation. Accountants are skilled in the analyses of complex financial data, and they provide expert opinions relating to financial transactions, financial condition, and financial reports.

Accounting firms can also provide comprehensive ADR services. Such services can include anything from administering dispute resolution cases to actually mediating or arbitrating them. Of course, an accounting firm needs licensed attorneys to draw up legal documents and give legal advice, so it is best for the firm to maintain licensed attorneys on staff when doing ADR work.

Some examples of specific services that accountants can provide in ADR cases follow:

- In corporate acquisitions, preparing for the buyer a notice of objection to the seller's closing balance sheet according to the provisions set forth in the acquisition agreement.
- In corporate acquisitions, evaluating for the seller the buyer's notice of objection to the closing balance sheet.
- Suggesting mediation or arbitration procedures or ADR administrators to clients.
- Identifying, locating, and evaluating documents and information relevant to evaluating disputed issues.

- Analyzing the issues and planning and drafting positions.
- Preparing documents and exhibits for submission to an arbitrator or for use in hearings.
- Analyzing proposals made by the opposing side in mediation or arbitration.
- Serving as an expert witness.

Online Dispute Resolution

Sometimes disputes are completely resolved using **online dispute resolution (ODR)** services. Some examples follow:

- OnlineResolution.Com (www.onlineresolution.com) provides online mediation services to assist in disputes related to eBay (www.ebay.com) transactions. Typical disputes include nonpaying bidders, shipping problems, dissatisfied buyers, and disagreements on terms.
- CyberSettle (www.cybersettle.com) offers a fully automated online service that focuses on resolving disputes through negotiating financial settlements. Those involved in a dispute exchange offers and counteroffers through the system, subject to time limits.

The main advantages of ODR include very low costs, time saving (no need for the parties to meet anyone in person), and asynchronicity. The asynchronous aspect permits disputing parties to take their time and think more carefully between offers and counteroffers that take place in live mediation sessions. Furthermore, the parties to disputes can easily participate even though they are in different time zones or parts of the world.

The main disadvantage of ODR is that it is impersonal. It is universally agreed that mediation works best when the disputing parties work face to face.

CORPORATE ADR PROGRAMS

Some companies seek to include ADR in all their business dealings whether with clients, customers, suppliers, employees, or business partners. Many companies publish an ADR pledge signed by the CEO that commits the company to using ADR techniques to resolve disputes.

The **CPR International Institute for Conflict Prevention & Resolution** (www.cpradr.org) publishes one model corporate pledge that is used by many companies. The copyrighted pledge reads in part:

> We recognize that for many disputes there is a less expensive, more effective method of resolution than the traditional lawsuit . . . .
>
> In the event of a business dispute between our company and another company which has made or will then make a similar statement, we are prepared to explore . . . resolution of the dispute through negotiation or ADR techniques before pursuing full-scale litigation. . . .

The CPR Institute also publishes a separate model pledge for law firms.

Steps in Setting up a Corporate ADR Program

LO6   Setting up a corporate ADR program begins with a commitment at the top of the organization. The following steps are needed to set up the ADR program (see Figure 20.3).

Step 1. Appoint Someone to Be in Charge

Someone must be in charge of the ADR program. Possibilities include the head of the legal staff, the head of risk management, or the chief compliance officer, depending on the organizational structure. In small companies, almost anyone in top management could take on the job.

FIGURE 20.3 **Establishment of a Corporate Dispute Resolution System**

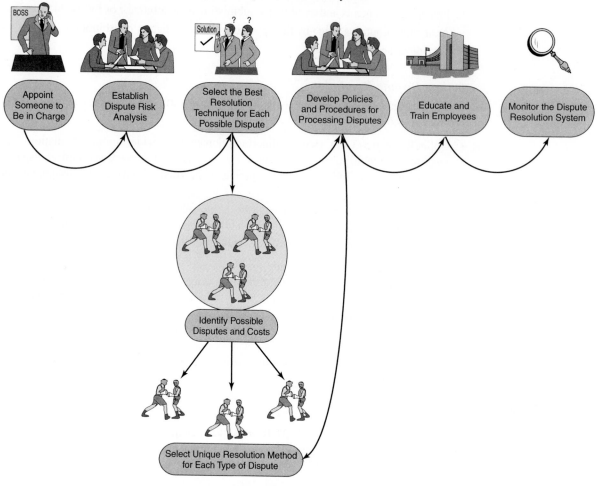

Step 2. Establish Dispute Risk Analysis

Dispute risk analysis should be established. If the company already has an organized risk-management program, it likely already has documentation identifying many possible disputes because they tend to pose risks to the company. If such documentation does not already exist, the company should undertake a comprehensive internal risk audit/review to identify all possible disputes. For each possible dispute, the following information would be documented:

- The possible disputing party and the relationship to the company.
- The nature of the possible dispute.
- A range of dollar values applicable to liability in the dispute, likely litigation costs, and costs to the company in employee time.
- The likelihood of winning the possible dispute.
- The current status and importance of the relationship of the company to the possible disputing party.
- The company's history of similar disputes including how they were settled.

- The resources required to resolve the possible dispute.
- An assessment of possible damages from bad publicity.
- The need to establish a precedent if the possible dispute arises.

For each possible dispute, various factors that define the extent of the risk should be identified. The required information can be collected by questionnaires and interviews as appropriate.

ADR techniques may not apply to some disputes. For example, a company generally cannot ask the Internal Revenue Service to use ADR to solve a tax bill that the company disputes. Disputes that can be settled by ADR techniques should be included in the company's enterprise risk management program.

Step 3. Select the Best Resolution Technique for Each Possible Dispute

For each possible dispute, a resolution technique should be selected whether it be mediation, mediation and arbitration combined, arbitration, or even litigation. Litigation may be preferred for issues in which the company wants to establish a precedent or is unwilling to compromise. Some types of disputes can effectively be handled by a company ombudsperson and/or internal dispute panels.

Step 4. Develop Policies and Procedures for Processing Disputes

Each functional unit of the company must know who has the authority to resolve disputes in which it is involved, the desired resolution methods, and the procedures to be followed. Internal procedures can require, for example, that employees first try to resolve employment-related disputes with their immediate superior and then with the company ombudsperson before requesting mediation or arbitration. Similarly, customers can be required by contract to follow certain steps before demanding mediation or arbitration.

Step 5. Educate and Train Employees

Employees must be trained to identify and process disputes according to the established dispute resolution policies.

Step 6. Monitor the Dispute Resolution Program

The person in charge of the dispute resolution program should receive periodic reports regarding disputes and their resolutions. The reports should contain the information necessary for the person in charge to monitor the effectiveness and efficiency of the program. Changes to the program should be made as required.

Summary

Alternative dispute resolution (ADR) involves resolving disputes outside the court system. The primary ADR methods are mediation and arbitration. Mediation involves having a neutral third party help those involved in a dispute to resolve their differences through structured negotiations. Arbitration also involves a neutral third party, but in this case, that person is empowered to issue findings that can be binding on the disputants.

Forensic accountants can play various roles in dispute resolutions, including as neutrals, dispute participants, expert consultants, and expert witnesses. Collectively, these four roles compose the litigation services practice area of accounting.

ADR has various advantages over litigation: it costs less, is private, preserves relationships (with mediation), is faster, permits the choice of the decision maker, has flexible remedies, and is often fairer. However, in cases in which a clear win is needed or a precedent needs to be set, litigation may be preferred.

Binding (nonbinding) arbitration is a nonjudicial, adversarial process in which one or more neutral arbitrators render a binding (nonbinding) decision to resolve a dispute among opposing parties. Arbitration is frequently triggered by contractual provisions that require arbitration in the event of disputes. Arbitration can be either administered or nonadministered. Administered arbitration usually takes place under the rules of an organization such as the American Arbitration Association, which not only supplies the rules but also provides the arbitrators from its referral lists.

In nonadministered arbitration, each disputing party typically selects one arbitrator, and these two selected arbitrators in turn choose a third arbitrator. The arbitrators may need to agree on the rules of arbitration if they are not clearly spelled out in the contract that triggers the arbitration. In some cases, courts appoint arbitrators as part of the litigation process. Court-annexed arbitration programs (CAAPS) are usually mandatory but nonbinding.

The decisions of arbitrators are normally legally binding, enforceable in court, and not subject to appeal. However, decisions by arbitrators that clearly ignore public law or are arbitrary or capricious could not be enforceable. Arbitrator errors in fact or opinion generally do not render their decisions unenforceable.

Arbitration processes work very much like traditional court litigation. They frequently include a trial with discovery, testimony, cross-examination, and so on. In many jurisdictions, there is no requirement that any of the participants, including the arbitrators, be attorneys.

Mediation involves a neutral mediator who helps those involved in a dispute to work out their differences among themselves. The mediator's style can be either facilitative or evaluative. Mediation works best when both sides desire in advance to reach a negotiated solution. It is not the best approach if any of the participants rules out all compromise. When it does work, it has the advantage of the participants' taking ownership for their own solution, which helps preserve relationships. As with arbitration, mediation can be either administered or nonadministered.

Various combinations and variations of arbitration and mediation are sometimes called *nontraditional ADR techniques.* These include med-arb, rent-a-judge, early neutral evaluation, and mini-trials. Each involves some combination or variation of arbitration and mediation.

ADR is routinely applied in many types of disputes, such as in labor interest arbitration, union contract arbitration, securities arbitration, divorce mediation, and accounting practices. In the latter, accountants can use ADR for their own disputes and provide dispute-related services to clients. Some of the client services are in the areas of evaluating negotiation offers, drafting dispute positions, and serving as expert witnesses.

Some types of disputes are resolved through online dispute resolution (ODR). It has the advantage of being inexpensive, and it accommodates individuals in different geographical locations. It is also somewhat impersonal, which can inhibit the effectiveness of mediation.

Many companies set up corporate ADR programs. Such programs seek to include ADR in all of their business dealings whether with clients, customers, suppliers, employees, or business partners. Companies frequently begin by publishing an ADR pledge signed by the CEO that commits the company to using ADR techniques to resolve disputes. The complete set of steps in setting up a corporate ADR program includes appointing someone to be in charge of the program, performing a dispute risk analysis, selecting the best resolution technique for each possible dispute, developing policies and procedures for processing disputes, educating and training employees, and monitoring the program.

Glossary

adhesion contract   A contract in alternative dispute resolution in which one party with superior bargaining party forces another party to accept an arbitration clause on a take-it-or-leave-it basis but that courts may disregard.

administered arbitration   Arbitration administered by an organization such as the American Arbitration Association that advises concerning the selection of arbitrators and the rules of arbitration.

alternative dispute resolution (ADR)   Approach including mediation and arbitration to resolve disputes outside the court system.

arbitration   Dispute resolution method in which a neutral third party is empowered to issue findings that can be binding on the disputants in cases of binding arbitration or recommendations in nonbinding arbitration.

court-annexed arbitration   Programs (CAAPS) that are usually mandatory but nonbinding; governed in federal courts by the federal ADR Act but by state laws in state courts.

CPR International Institute for Conflict Prevention & Resolution   Organization that publishes a model corporate pledge used by many companies to commit to using ADR techniques to solve disputes.

dispute risk analysis   Part of an organization's overall dispute resolution system that focuses on identifying possible disputes and their possible impact on the company.

divorce mediation   Application of arbitration that involves resolving conflicting demands in divorce cases.

early neutral evaluation   Nontraditional ADR technique that involves hiring a neutral, usually a judge or attorney, to review a case before it goes to court and to write an advisory opinion that helps the litigants see more clearly how likely their cases are to succeed in a trial.

evaluative mediation   Mediation in which the mediator actively expresses opinions about the facts of the case and the reasonableness of the participants' negotiating positions.

facilitative mediation   Mediation in which the mediator does not express opinions with respect to the facts of the case or the reasonableness of the participants' negotiating positions but focuses on helping and prodding the participants to reach a mutually satisfactory compromise.

interest arbitration (or labor interest arbitration)   Application of arbitration that involves resolving conflicting demands, typically in labor contract negotiations.

International Chamber of Commerce Court of Arbitration   Organization that helps resolve international disputes, including disputes between/among countries.

litigation services (litigation support services)   The forensic accounting work of providing support for disputes and any issue that involves or potentially involves multiple parties in a legal context.

med-arb   Nontraditional ADR technique that is a combination of mediation and arbitration; parties first engage in mediation, and if that does not produce a resolution, switch to arbitration.

mediation   Dispute resolution method that involves a neutral third party who helps those involved in a dispute to resolve their differences through structured negotiations.

mini-trial, summary-jury trial, and mock-jury trial   Nontraditional ADR techniques that are extensions of the rent-a-judge technique, but the trial is held in front of a jury that is possibly composed of neutral experts, corporate officers, and decision makers from the disputing companies.

neutral   Another name for a mediator or arbitrator who facilitates resolution of disputes in mediation and arbitration.

nonadministered arbitration   Arbitration in which the participants make up (or adopt) their own rules and select the arbitrators themselves.

online dispute resolution (ODR)   Dispute resolution service that completely resolves disputes online; tends to focus on processing offers and counteroffers between disputing parties.

Permanent Court of Arbitration (PCA)   Also known as the *Hague Tribunal,* an organization that helps resolve international disputes, including disputes between countries.

rent-a-judge   Nontraditional ADR technique in which the participating parties hire a retired judge who conducts a formal trial, perhaps even with a rented jury, and renders a decision.

securities arbitration   Arbitration that involves resolving conflicting demands, typically in disputes between securities brokers and their clients; required of members of the National Association of Security Dealers (NASD) in disputes with clients through the NASD National Dispute Resolution Program.

union contract arbitration   Application of arbitration that involves resolving conflicting demands, typically in disputes relating to union contracts.

Review Questions

1. Which of the following is *not* an advantage of ADR over litigation?
   a. ADR is private whereas litigation is public.
   b. ADR tends to preserve relationships whereas litigation tends to destroy them.
   c. ADR sets helpful precedents to avoid future problems.
   d. All of these are advantages of ADR over litigation.

2. Which of the following is *not* a characteristic of administered arbitration?
   a. The administrator supplies the arbitration rules.
   b. The administrator helps to select the arbitrators.
   c. The administrator is a third-party organization.
   d. All of these are characteristics of administered arbitration.

3. Which of the following usually applies to court-annexed arbitration programs?
   a. Mandatory but not binding.
   b. Both mandatory and binding.
   c. Binding but not mandatory.
   d. Neither mandatory nor binding.

4. Which of these generally is true of decisions of arbitrators?
   a. Legally binding and enforceable in court.
   b. Occasionally binding and enforceable in court.
   c. Legally binding but not generally enforceable in court.
   d. Binding in cases of med-arb.

5. Arbitrator decisions in one country may be enforceable in other countries when which of the following applies to them?
   a. Have signed the New York Agreement.
   b. Are members of the Hague Tribunal.
   c. Subscribe to the International Fair Arbitration Treaty.
   d. None of these.

6. Which of the following statements is correct?

   a. Mediation more closely resembles court litigation than does arbitration.

   b. Arbitration more closely resembles court litigation than does mediation.

   c. Mediation and arbitration both closely resemble court litigation.

   d. Neither mediation nor arbitration resembles court litigation.

7. As compared to court litigation, the rules of evidence in mediation or arbitration are likely to be which of the following?

   a. More strict.

   b. More liberal.

   c. About the same.

   d. It depends on whether the ADR method is mediation or arbitration.

8. Mediation works best in which of the following?

   a. Evaluative mediation.

   b. Facilitative mediation.

   c. When the opposing parties are prepared to compromise.

   d. When both parties have a cordial relationship before the dispute arises.

9. Advantages of mediation include which of these?

   a. Mediation is a sure way to resolve a dispute.

   b. Mediation costs less that litigation.

   c. In mediation, the disputing parties tend to take ownership of the resolution.

   d. All of these are advantages of mediation.

10. In labor dispute arbitration, the arbitration process tends to favor which of these?

    a. Labor.

    b. Management.

    c. Neither.

    d. The answer is entirely situation specific.

11. Which of the following areas would *not* be applicable to ADR?

    a. Union contract disputes.

    b. Divorce.

    c. Accounting practice.

    d. All of these areas are applicable to ADR.

Discussion Questions

12. What is alternative dispute resolution?

13. What disadvantages exist, if any, for alternative dispute resolution?

14. What roles do forensic accountants serve in dispute resolution cases?

15. What credentials are required to serve as an ADR neutral?

16. What are some advantages of alternative dispute resolution over formal litigation?

17. What does *administered arbitration* mean?

18. How could international disputes be resolved?

19. What is an adhesion contract?

20. When could facilitative administration be preferred to evaluative mediation?

21. When could mediation be preferred to arbitration?

22. What is the advantage of a mini-trial?

23. Why does labor interest arbitration tend to favor labor over management?

24. Give an example of how ADR could be used within an accounting practice.

25. What is the primary disadvantage of online dispute resolution?

26. What must be done first in setting up an in-house ADR program?

27. What is the relationship between enterprise risk management and ADR?

Case

28. Margaret Willis is the owner of Willis Concrete Company. Her company supplies poured concrete to residential and commercial construction sites throughout the San Diego area. She recently ran into a major problem with Telweda Construction Company, one of her oldest and largest customers. Telweda is a residential construction company that specializes in upscale new housing developments. Willis Concrete routinely pours concrete for hundreds of Telweda's job sites every month.

A recent problem occurred when it was discovered that because of improper concrete mixing, the concrete foundations and slabs for 23 of Telweda's new homes did not meet minimum materials standards. A local homeowner, a retired engineer, had discovered the problem only after he had moved into his new home. The bottom line was that none of the 23 homes was safe to live in. All had to be evacuated immediately, and the very expensive process of retrofitting foundations and slabs had to begin. The work would take months to complete, and Telweda's reputation has been severely damaged. Several homeowner lawsuits had already been filed, and more were on the way.

Margaret had always known of the possibility that mixing problems could occur. That is the reason that her contracts with all vendors included clauses that made it the responsibility of the vendor to perform tests on the quality of the concrete before relying on it.

Telweda argued that despite this clause in its contract with Willis, there was still a reasonable expectation that Willis would provide quality materials and assume responsibility for any problems. Therefore, the CEO of Telweda demanded that Willis pay $20 million to cover the damages.

a. From Willis's point of view, is litigation or ADR preferred? Why?

b. From Telweda's point of view, is litigation or ADR preferred? Why?

c. Which form of ADR could be preferred by the two companies?

Index

A

Accelerated revenues, 424
Acceptable audit risk (AAR), 89–90
Acceptable detection risk (ADR), 89–90, 119
Acceptable risk of assessing control risk too low (ARACR), 104, 119
Acceptable risk of incorrect acceptance (ARIA), 106, 119
Access controls, 47, 152–153
  abuse of access privileges, 398–399
  defined, 152, 157
  layered approach to data protection, 152–153, 159
  passwords, 153, 399
  super-user privileges, 399
  unauthorized access, 399
Accident, fraud discovery by, 169
Accountability, independent, 57
Accounting
  accrual, 424–425
  aggressive techniques in, 425–428, 431
  alternative dispute resolution (ADR) in, 630–631
  areas of, 4
  big-bath, 427–428, 429, 431
  cookie jar, 427, 432
  defined, 82, 119
  forensic. See Forensic accounting
  fundamental law of conservation, 426–427, 431
  indications of fraud, 422
  tax practitioners, 470–471
  traditional versus forensic accounting, 4, 5–6
  types of, 4
Accounting and Auditing Enforcement Releases (AAERs), 414–415, 431
Accounting equation, 263
Accounting information system (AIS), 47–71
  employee fraud and, 398–400
  enterprise resource planning (ERP) systems, 49–50, 69, 183
  internal control process, 50–58, 72
  of small public companies, 457
  systems development, 50, 69, 73
  transaction cycles, 48, 73
  transaction processing controls, 48, 58–68, 73
Accounting knowledge, of forensic accountants, 7
Accounts receivable
  accounts receivables fraud, 392–393
  in business valuation, 601
  factoring, 113, 119
  lapping of, 392, 403
  number of days in, 276–277
  overstating, 413
Accounts receivable turnover, 276

Accredited Business Valuation (ABV) credential, 10, 589–590, 612
Accredited Valuation Analyst (AVA), 589
Accrual accounting, 424–425
Accrued refunds, 519
Accuracy. See also Errors
  in application controls, 58–59
  defined, 58, 71
ACL Services Ltd., 183
Acquaintances, as source of document evidence, 251
Acquit, 479, 502
Actimize Employee Fraud Solution, 182
Active surveillance, 268
Active threats
  defined, 134, 157
  types of, 137–138
Act phase, of plan-do-check-act (PDCA) methodology, 133–134, 140–141
Address changes, unauthorized, 530
Adelphia, 81
Adhesion contracts, 627, 635
Administered arbitration, 626, 635
Administrative law, 18, 38
Admission-seeking questions, 297–299, 312
Ad valorem tax, 474, 502
Advanced sales skimming, 390, 402
Adverse audit report, 95, 119
Affidavits, 21–22, 38
Affiliates, in business evaluation, 601–602
Affirmative acts of fraud, 470
Affirmative indications of fraud, 470
African organized crime, 551–552
Aggravated identity theft, 526–527, 533
Aggressive accounting techniques, 425–428, 431
Agreed-upon procedures engagements, 113
AICPA. See American Institute of Certified Public Accountants (AICPA)
Aiding and abetting, 33
  provision of IRC, 481
  statute of USC, 484
AIM@Fraud Intelligent Fraud Detection, 183
Alibis, 288, 298, 312
Allocation assertion, 97
Al Qaeda, 8, 550, 554, 555, 558–559, 571
Altered documents, 266
Alternative dispute resolution (ADR), 210, 623–634
  in accounting practice, 630–631
  applications of, 629–631
  arbitration. See Arbitration
  corporate programs, 631–633
  defined, 623, 635
  litigation versus, 625–626
  mediation. See Mediation
  nontraditional techniques, 628–629
Altman Z-Score, 179

American Arbitration Association (AAA), 626–628
American College of Forensic Examiners, 9
American Institute of Certified Public Accountants (AICPA), 9, 83, 84, 442
  Accredited Business Valuation (ABV) credential, 10, 589–590, 612
  antifraud initiative, 112
  Business Valuation and Forensic and Litigation Services section, 10
  classification of forensic accounting, 5
  specialty assurance services, 112, 114–115
American Society of Appraisers (ASA), 588, 612
American Society of Crime Laboratory Directors, 327
Analytical procedures
  Benford analysis, 186, 257, 274
  comparison of expected financial results with nonfinancial data, 258–259
  comparison of financial data with industry data, 257–258
  comparison of financial data with prior period data, 257
  comparison of financial data with results expected by entity itself, 259
  content analysis, 186, 188
  defined, 99, 102, 119, 256, 274
  as evidence-gathering procedure, 99–100, 256–265, 275–277
  for financial statement fraud, 256–265, 275–277
  horizontal analysis, 257, 258, 274
  nature of, 102–103
  performance of, 108
  reconciliations, 64–66, 180, 261–262
  surprise counts, 260, 274
  symptoms of financial statement fraud, 265–267, 421–423, 422–423
  text analysis, 186, 188
  types of, 256–265
  vertical analysis, 257, 258, 275
Anonymity
  confidentiality versus, 168
  of tips, 168–169
ANSI-ASQ National Accreditation Board, 142
Anti-Drug Abuse Act of 1986, 566
Antiforensic software, 337, 347
Antisocial personality disorder, 388, 402
Antiterrorism, 36
Apparent errors, in data-driven fraud detection, 180
Appellate courts, 18
Application controls, 58–59, 71
Application layer, of access controls, 153, 157
Application service provider (ASP), 457
Applied security, 151–154
The Appraisal Foundation, 587, 588, 613

T